Environmental Law in Cyprus

Environmental Law in Cyprus

Natalia Charalampidou

This book was originally published as a monograph in the International Encyclopaedia of Laws/Environmental Law.

Founding Editor: Roger Blanpain
General Editor: Frank Hendrickx
Volume Editor: Kurt Deketelaere

Wolters Kluwer

Published by:
Kluwer Law International B.V.
PO Box 316
2400 AH Alphen aan den Rijn
The Netherlands
E-mail: lrs-sales@wolterskluwer.com
Website: www.wolterskluwer.com/en/solutions/kluwerlawinternational

Sold and distributed by:
Wolters Kluwer Legal & Regulatory U.S.
920 Links Avenue
Landisville, PA 17538
United States of America
E-mail: customer.service@wolterskluwer.com

Printed on acid-free paper

ISBN 978-94-035-2836-6

e-Book: ISBN 978-94-035-2946-2
web-PDF: ISBN 978-94-035-2956-1

This title is available on www.kluwerlawonline.com

Printed in the United Kingdom.

The Author

Natalia Charalampidou, a native of Thessaloniki (Greece), teaches International Environmental and Energy Law in the Faculty of Law at the Democritus University of Thrace in Greece.

Natalia's areas of expertise include the Energy Charter Treaty, contaminated site investigation and remediation, environmental liability, solid and hazardous waste, environmental due diligence, energy compliance, prospection, research and exploitation of hydrocarbons, renewable electricity, unconventional energy sources and smart grids and cities. She is the author of the *International Encyclopaedia of Laws* contributing to the Monographs on Energy, Environment and Contract Law in Cyprus.

Prior to focusing on academic research and teaching in 2012, Natalia had joined the corporate and dispute resolution teams of high-profile law firms in Cyprus and overseas and acquired treasured experience in stock-exchange regulations, the European company (Societas Europaea), due diligence, fraud, anti-money laundering and investment arbitration in the energy sector. For these compelling and captivating times, she is much grateful to the heads of the departments and all her colleagues.

Natalia is pursuing her PhD at the University of Heidelberg, Germany. She has an LLM from the University of Heidelberg, 2004, an LLB from Democritus University of Thrace (Greece), 2003, Diploma in Turkish Language from the Institute for Balkan Studies (Greece), 2002. She was admitted to the Bar Association of Thessaloniki (Greece) in 2014 and to Cyprus in 2006

She has contributed to various publications, and the indicative list includes monographs on *Environmental Law: The Implementation of Directives of the European Union in Cyprus* (in Greek) (Sakkoulas Publications, Athens, 2013), contributions in collective volumes of 'The Energy Charter Treaty' (in Greek) 23–48 in: K. Antonopoulos & H. Aroni (eds) *Introduction to International Energy Law* (Athens: Nomiki Bibliothiki, 2020); 'Renewable Energy' (in Greek) 173–188 in: K. Antonopoulos & H. Aroni (eds) *Introduction to International Energy Law* (Athens: Nomiki Bibliothiki, 2020); she is the co-author of 'Cyprus', in: C. Esplugues (ed.)

Civil and Commercial Mediation in Europe (Intersentia 2014) 103–124. Her journal publications include 'Pressing Measures in Perilous Times: The Investment Perspective', 18 (2) *TDM* (2021); 'Energy Corporations and Their Information Duties Towards State Authorities', 30 (2) *EEELR* 62–71 (2021); 'Smart Buildings – From Flat-Rates to Smart Metering' (in Greek), 23 (4) *Periballon & Dikaio* (*Greek Legal Journal*) 540–559 (2019); 'Supply of Fuels and Diesel Generators' *Lighthouse v. Timor-Leste* (in Greek), 23 (3) *Periballon & Dikaio* 511–520 (2019); 'International Energy Disputes That Arose from the Financial Crisis in Argentina (1999–2002)' *Pan American & BP v. Argentina* and *Total v. Argentina* (in Greek), 23 (2) *Periballon & Dikaio* 350–360 (2019); 'International Energy Disputes That Arose from the Financial Crisis in Argentina (1999–2002)' *CMS v. Argentina* and *El Paso v. Argentina* (in Greek), 23 (1) *Periballon & Dikaio* 142–168 (2019); 'Investment on Oil Refinery and Electricity Production Unit' *Plama v. Bulgaria* (in Greek), 22 (4) *Periballon & Dikaio* 673–678 (2018); 'The Applicability of the Energy Charter Treaty' *Yukos Universal v. Russia* (in Greek), 22 (3) *Periballon & Dikaio* 544–552 (2018); 'Issues of Environmental Damage from Oil Activities' *Chevron and Texaco v. Ecuador* (in Greek), 22 (3) *Periballon & Dikaio* 536–544 (2018); 'Range of Disputes under the Energy Charter Treaty', 15 (7) *TDM* (OGEL/TDM Special Issue with ArbitralWomen 'Strategic Considerations in Energy Disputes') No. 10 (2018); 'The Notion of Waste: An Overview of the Legislation on Waste' (in Greek), 22 (2) *Periballon & Dikaio* 246–258 (2018); 'Greek Soil Law', 2 *International Yearbook of Soil Law and Policy* 245–276 (2017); 'Annulment of Adoption Orders Due to Fraud and Perjury Before the Supreme Court of Cyprus' (in Greek), *Epitheorisi Politikis Dikonomias* (*Greek Legal Journal*) 177–186 (2013); 'European Protection of the Soil: The Struggle for Uniform Regulation' (in German), 8 (4) *Europarecht* 593–611 (2011); 'The Protection of Land in Greece', 19 (4) *EEELR* 160–174 (2010).

Table of Contents

List of Abbreviations

BAT	Best Available Techniques
BB	Betriebsberater
BimSchG	Bundes-Immissionsschutzgesetz (of the Federal Republic of Germany)
Cap. 31	Antiquities Law
Cap. 60	Law on Forests (in force until 1967)
Cap. 83	Public Roads Law
Cap. 96	Streets and Buildings Regulation Law
Cap. 270	Law on Mines and Quarries
CG	Cyprus Gazette (issued until 1960)
CJEU	Court of Justice of the European Union (previously named European Court of Justice)
CLR	Cyprus Law Reports
CML Rev	Common Market Law Review
DA	Droit Administrative
DVBl.	Deutsches Verwaltungsblatt
EC	European Commission
ECR	European Court Reports
EEEurD	Elliniki Epitheorisi Europaikou Dikaiou ('Ελληνική Επιθεώρηση Ευρωπαϊκού Δικαίου')
EIA	Environmental Impact Assessment
EMAS	Eco-Management and Audit Scheme
EnvLRev	Environmental Law Review
EuR	Europarecht
EuLR	European Law Reporter
EurUP	Zeitschrift für europäisches Umwelt- und Planungsrecht
EuZW	Europäische Zeitschrift für Wirtschaftsrecht
FS	Festschrift
GewArch	Gewerbearchiv
IMF	International Monetary Fund

List of Abbreviations

JEL	Journal of Environmental Law
JEEPL	Journal for European Environmental & Planning Law
JSC	Judgments of the Supreme Court (of Cyprus)
KDP 118/2006	Regulations on Fertilizers
KDP 170/2004	Regulations on the Control of Air Pollution (Plants Not Requiring a Permit)
KDP 515/2002	Regulations on Water Pollution Control (Prevention and Reduction of Water Pollution from Asbestos)
KDP 528/2002	Regulations on Air Pollution Control (Prevention and Reduction of Air Pollution by Asbestos) No. 528 of 2002
KrWG	Kreislaufwirtschaftsgesetz (of the Federal Republic of Germany)
Law No. 25(I)/2012	Law on Forests
Law No. 32(I)/2002	Law on Packing and Packaging Waste
Law No. 32(I)/2006	Law on Fertilizers
Law No. 34(I)/2014	Law on Biocidal Products
Law No. 82(I)/2009	Law on Management of Extractive Waste
Law No. 90/1972	Law on Urban and Land Planning
Law No. 102(I)/2005	Law on Assessment of the Effects of Certain Plans and Programmes
Law No. 106(I)/2002	Law on Water and Soil Pollution Control
Law No. 110(I)/2011	Law on Greenhouse Gas Emission Trading
Law No. 119(I)/2004	Law on Public Access to Environmental Information
Law No. 125(I)/2000	Law on Free Access of the Public to Environmental Information
Law No. 127(I)/2018	Law on Assessment of the Effects of Certain Projects on the Environment
Law No. 141(I)/2011	Law on Plant Production Products
Law No. 152(I)/2003	Law on Protection and Management of Wild Birds and Games
Law No. 153(I)/2003	Law on Protection and Management of Nature and Wildlife
Law No. 158(I)/1999	Law on General Principles of Administrative Law
Law No. 164(I)/2018	Law on Protection from Ionizing Radiation and Nuclear and Radiological Safety
Law No. 184(I)/2013	Law on Industrial Emissions
Law No. 185(I)/2011	Law on Waste
Law No. 187(I)/2002	Law on Air Pollution Control
M en R	Milieu en recht

NJB	Nederlands juristenblad
NoB	Nomiko Bima ('Νομικό Βήμα')
NuR	Natur und Recht
NTER	Nederlands tijdschrift voor Europees recht
NVwZ	Neue Zeitschrift für Verwaltungsrecht
OG	Official Gazette of the Republic of Cyprus (issued since 1960)
OJ	Official Journal of the European Union
RDR	Revue de droit rural
RECIEL	Review of European Community and International Environmental Law
REDE	Revue européenne de droit de l'environnement
RJE	Revue juridique de l'environnement
RMC	Revue du marché commun
RTD Com.	Revue trimestrielle de droit commercial et de droit économique
UN	United Nations
UPR	Umwelt- und Planungsrecht
WEEE	Waste Electrical and Electronic Equipment
ZfU	Zeitschrift für Umweltpolitik
ZfV	Zeitschrift für Verwaltung
ZUR	Zeitschrift für Umweltrecht

List of Abbreviations

Preface to Second Edition

Updating this monograph in 2018 was preordained due to the new Law on Environmental Impact Assessment (EIA) for Specific Projects issued on 31 July 2018, which in view of its supreme importance for practitioners could not be left unnoticed, especially in light of the Euroasia Interconnector. This aside, all amending laws have been considered and included, as of November 2018. I would like to cordially communicate my gratitude to Prof. Kurt Deketelaere, Mr Joeri Lauwers and Prof. Konstantinos Antonopoulos for their generous support and kind understanding. I am equally grateful for the brilliant cooperation of Mrs Suzanne Leppen, Mrs Pradhiba Shiva and Mrs Pritha. I am perpetually grateful to Utku for being my role model. Finally, let me express my deepest appreciation to Aydın Hocam and Ayhan Hocam for gently facilitating a sublime, kind-hearted and benevolent solitude that empowered brisk penning. Thank you all!

Komotini, December 2018

Preface to First Edition

This monograph examines the most important aspects of Environmental Law of Cyprus, which in its majority consists of national laws implementing directives of the European Union (EU). The implemented directives have been cited under each legislation and, where possible, each national provision has been collated into the implemented European one. In addition, case law of the Court of Justice of the EU has been mentioned next to European provisions. These are intended to enable further research on specific matters, should this be wished. With a view to providing a prompt and effective overview of pollution control and nature conservation and management, two outlines have been prepared. A further systematic approach and analysis of Cypriot Environmental Law encounter some difficulties. The most important is the enduring search for the principles that govern Cypriot Administrative Law. It has been ruled that Cypriot Administrative Law follows the tradition of continental Administrative Law. Nevertheless, the influence of common law is nothing but weak, as demonstrated throughout this monograph. Further, the inconsistency of legal terms, i.e., *negative effects* and *adverse effects* in Law No. 140(I)/2005, may not contribute to any systematic analysis. They rather cause confusion and stress regarding accurate and effective application of environmental laws.

The Cyprus question will not be addressed therein, despite the fact of it being an important feature of Cypriot reality that has affected the legal system, as this already been roughly analysed and does not directly affect national environmental legislation.

I would like to extend warm thanks to Prof. Dr Kurt Deketelaere for his kind invitation and valuable advice as well as to Joeri Lauwers. To my *Doktormutter*, Prof. Dr iur. Ute Mager, Professor of Public Law at the University of Heidelberg, Prof. Dr iur. Dr h.c. Burkhard Hess, Executive Director of Max Planck Institute Luxembourg for International, European and Regulatory Procedural Law, and assistant professor Konstantinos Antonopoulos, LLM (Cantab), PhD (Nottingham) at the Democritus University of Thrace, I am deeply grateful at all times for their most valuable teachings and guidance. Warmest thanks are lastly expressed for their kind hospitality to the libraries of the Institute for Balkan Studies in Thessaloniki, the Supreme Court of Cyprus in Nicosia, the Law Faculty at Aristotle University of Thessaloniki and the Centre of International and European Economic Law in Thessaloniki.

Comments, remarks or suggestions are most welcome at natalia.charalampidou@alumni.uni-heidelberg.de.

Thessaloniki, December 2015

General Introduction

§1. General Background

I. Geography and Population

1. Cyprus is an island, lying in the eastern Mediterranean, south of Turkey and west of Syria. The country's capital is Nicosia. In 2018, its estimated population amounted to 1,237,088.[1] Since 1974, more than a third of the island is not under governmental control.[2]

II. Legal and Political Structure

2. Cyprus, which joined the EU on 1 May 2004, is a common law country, as a former Colony of Great Britain (1914–1960). However, specific areas of law follow the continental law tradition. One of those areas is administrative law. Judicial review of administrative actions is established in the Constitution (Article 146), and general principles of administrative law are set out in legislation (Law No. 158(I)/ 1999).[3] Further, due to the fact that *the process of judicial review of administrative acts existing in continental countries such as Greece, France or Germany has been introduced in Cyprus, it is reasonable to hold that principles of administrative law can be adopted and applied by this Court as Cyprus law laid down by the Courts of Cyprus.*[4]

3. Common law has, however, expanded its influence into administrative law, as the following demonstrates. First, judgments are considered in Cyprus to be binding in the sense of case law. Second, judgments of the Greek Council of State on proportionality, which has significant elements in common with the German notion

1. Central Intelligence Agency, *The World Factbook*, Europe: Cyprus – Geography / People and Society, https://www.cia.gov/library/publications/the-world-factbook/geos/cy.html (accessed 21 Jan. 2020).
2. Central Intelligence Agency, *The World Factbook*, Europe: Cyprus – Introduction, https://www.cia.gov/library/publications/the-world-factbook/geos/cy.html (accessed 21 Jan. 2020).
3. N. Charalambous, ***Η Δράση και ο Έλεγχος της Δημόσιας Διοίκησης*** (in Greek) (Nicosia 2004); A. Aggelides, ***ο περί Γενικών Αρχών του Διοικητικού Δικαίου Νόμος (Ν. 158(Ι)/1999) και η μεταγενέστερη νομολογία του Ανωτάτου Δικαστηρίου της Κυπριακής Δημοκρατίας*** (in Greek) (Research, Studies and Publications Service of the House of Representatives 2008).
4. *Stelios Morsis v. The Republic of Cyprus* (1965) 1 JSC 12 (16).

of 'Verhaltensmäßigkeit', are cited by the Supreme Court of Cyprus in administrative matters, along with case law on Wednesbury unreasonableness, a much-celebrated institution of English law, without any apparent distinction to be made between the two. Third, no law on administrative procedure, such as Verwaltungsverfahrensgesetz (of the Federal Republic of Germany) or 'Κώδικας Διοικητικής Διαδικασίας', has been enacted in Cyprus. Rather, each law sets out the powers and duties of competent authorities in a very detailed manner, possibly in view of avoiding activity being ultra vires, which is also a common law institute. Fourth, the dominant common law tradition is evident from the absence of a state mechanism for the enforcement of administrative decisions and judgments, including the recovery of public expenses from citizens. Instead of law on enforcement of administrative acts, such as the German 'Verwaltungs-Vollstreckungsgesetz' or the Greek 'Κώδικας Είσπραξης Δημοσίων Εσόδων', compliance is ensured through establishing that noncompliance constitutes a penal offence, and recovery of expenses takes place through filing civil lawsuits before civil courts requesting payment of such expenses as civil debts owed to the state. Hence, enforcement of administrative matters is delegated to civil and criminal courts. Lastly, the authority of penal courts to amend and revoke administrative actions, such as authorizations and permits, during a penal procedure is strange to the continental tradition of administrative law.

III. Economic Characteristics

4. Cyprus has been a member of the Eurozone since January 2008, and therefore the national currency is euro, which replaced the Cyprus pound. The economy is being dominated by the service sector, such as banking and legal services. The island's industry relates to tourism, food and beverage processing, cement and gypsum, ship repair, refurbishment, textiles, light chemicals, metal products, wood, paper, stone and clay products. The commodities exported are citrus, potatoes, pharmaceuticals, cement and clothing, whereas the commodities imported include consumer goods, petroleum, lubricants, machinery and transport equipment.[5]

5. In March 2013, an economic adjustment programme for Cyprus, which aims to address financial, fiscal and structural challenges facing the economy and to allow Cyprus to return to a sustainable growth path, was agreed between Cyprus, the European Commission (EC), the European Central Bank and the International Monetary Fund (IMF).[6] In a statement of November 2015, it was set out that economic activity has continued on a positive trend since early 2015, while the banking system continues to heal. Currently, the number one priority is reducing the excessive level of non-performing loans. Further, continued sound public finances are needed

5. Central Intelligence Agency, *The World Factbook*, Europe: Cyprus – Economy, https://www.cia.gov/library/publications/the-world-factbook/geos/cy.html (accessed 29 Jun. 2017).
6. *See* in detail the programme: http://ec.europa.eu/economy_finance/publications/occasional_paper/2013/pdf/ocp149_en.pdf (accessed 5 Dec. 2015). More information on the Economic Adjustment Programme for Cyprus is available in: http://ec.europa.eu/economy_finance/assistance_eu_ms/cyprus/index_en.htm (accessed 5 Dec. 2015).

to ensure that the public debt ratio returns to an acceptable level while steering public spending towards growth-enhancing activities.[7] Cyprus exited its three-year economic adjustment programme in March 2016.[8] The outstanding stock of non-performing loans, however, still remains at a very high level.[9] Developing offshore hydrocarbon resources, although only one commercially exploitable reserve was discovered in 2013, remains a critical component of the government's economic recovery efforts.[10] The forecasts for Cyprus are: gross domestic product growth – 5.8% for 2020, 3.2% for 2021 and 3.1% for 2022; inflation – 1.1% for 2020, 0.7% for 2021 and 1.1% for 2022; unemployment 8.2% for 2020, 7.8% for 2021 and 7.2% for 2022.[11]

IV. Social and Cultural Characteristics

6. The official languages of Cyprus are Greek and Turkish (Article 3(1) of the Constitution), but English is widely spoken. The ethnic groups residing in the government-controlled area are Greek (98.8%), Maronite, Armenian and Turkish-Cypriot (1%) and unspecified (0.2%).[12] Apart from EU nationals residing on the island as a result of the free movement of individuals within the common market, female migrants from the Philippines and Sri Lanka, who are entrusted with housekeeping, childcare and elderly care, also reside in Cyprus. Until recently, 'artiste' or 'entertainment' visas were granted to female artists mainly from Eastern Europe.[13] These visas have been abolished within the efforts of the government to combat trafficking of human beings.[14]

---

7. Statement by the European Commission, the ECB and the IMF on Cyprus, 16 Nov. 2015, http://ec.europa.eu/economy_finance/articles/eu_economic_situation/2015-11-16-statement-cyprus_en.htm (accessed 5 Dec. 2015).
8. Eurogroup Statement on Cyprus, 7 Mar. 2016, http://www.consilium.europa.eu/press-releases-pdf/2016/3/40802209631_en.pdf (accessed 29 Jun. 2017).
9. European Commission, Post-programme Surveillance Report, Autumn 2016, https://ec.europa.eu/info/sites/info/files/file_import/ip042_en_2.pdf (accessed 29 Jun. 2017).
10. Central Intelligence Agency, *The World Factbook*, Europe: Cyprus – Economy, https://www.cia.gov/library/publications/the-world-factbook/geos/cy.html (accessed 29 Jun. 2017).
11. European Commission, Economic and Social Affairs, Cyprus – Economic Outlook, Spring 2017, http://ec.europa.eu/economy_finance/eu/countries/cyprus_en.htm (accessed 7 Apr. 2021).
12. Central Intelligence Agency, *The World Factbook*, Europe: Cyprus – People and Society, https://www.cia.gov/library/publications/the-world-factbook/geos/cy.html (accessed 21 Jan. 2020).
13. *See* in this respect a straightforward analysis: R. Lenz, *Migrantische Dienstleisterinnen in der Republik Zypern – zuständig für Sex- und Sorgearbeit, unfähig zur Reproduktion der Nation*, 46 Südeuropa Mitteilungen 70 (2006). On 'artiste' visas issued by Cyprus *see*: *Rantsev v. Cyprus and Russia*, no. 25965/04, ECHR 2010-I.
14. Group of Experts on Action Against Trafficking in Human Beings, *Report Concerning the Implementation of the Council of Europe Convention on Action Against Trafficking in Human Beings by Cyprus, First Evaluation Round*, 12 Sep. 2011, paras 17 et seq., http://www.coe.int/t/dghl/monitoring/trafficking/Docs/Reports/GRETA_2011_8_FGR_CYP_en_final.pdf (accessed 5 Dec. 2015). *See* country profile and evaluations in: https://www.coe.int/t/dghl/monitoring/trafficking/Docs/Profiles/CYPRUSProfile_en.asp (accessed 5 Dec. 2015).

7. Byzantine architecture and painting dating back to the fourth century AD[15] co-exist with Ottoman,[16] Frankish, Venetian[17] and British Colonial architecture in Cyprus, in a similar way that Catholic, Orthodox and Armenian churches and mosques do. Most of these have been declared ancient monuments (*see* in this respect paragraphs 452 et seq. below). An exquisite example of colonial architecture is Ledra Palace Hotel, which was constructed of yellow sandstone and made distinct by the pointed arches of the window frames, a reminiscent of the arches of the Latin Abbey of Bellapais in the Kyrenia Mountains. The architect, Benzion Guinsberg (or Ginsberg), commuted frequently from Israel to oversee the construction of this and other important buildings on the island. While in operation Ledra Palace Hotel was hosting the grandeur of Middle East colonial cosmopolitanism. Now, it is situated in the Cypriot United Nations (UN)-controlled Buffer Zone, housing the UN Force in Cyprus,[18] whose role is to create and maintain a climate of intercommunal calm conducive to the political search for a peaceful settlement of problems since 1964.[19]

8. Education became an institutionalized affair last century, as during the Ottoman era, education of the civil masses was considered a charitable act and not a state affair. More specifically, when Cyprus was a part of the Ottoman Empire and was administrated by the ottomans (1571–1878), vakfs, which in essence are religious trusts or pious foundations in Muslim societies, were used for establishing and running schools, such as *sibyan*, providing elementary education, and *medrese*, providing religious and legal knowledge. The first *sibyan* school, which was established immediately upon the conquest of the island in 1571, was the Saint Sophia Sibyan School.[20] The archbishop of the Greek Orthodox community, who was an important political personality due to the title *ethnarque* that was appointed to him by the Sultan in 1754,[21] and due to him administrating justice among Orthodox Christian subjects in all areas of private law,[22] established various schools, the success of which depended on the competence of the individual cleric and on political conditions. One of those, the Greek School of Holy Trinity established in 1812, reconstituted in

15. N. Gkioles, *Byzantine Art in Cyprus* (in Greek), (11–12) Parousia 511 et seq. (1997).
16. H.M. Atun, *The Influence of Ottoman Architecture in Cyprus*, in *Milletarası Birinci Kıbrıs Tetkikleri Kongresi* 261 (Ankara 1971).
17. A. Langdale, *At the Edge of Empire: Venetian Architecture in Famagusta, Cyprus*, 41 Viator 155 (2010).
18. O. Demetriou, *Grand Ruins: Ledra Palace Hotel and the Rendering of 'Conflict' as Heritage in Cyprus*, in *War and Cultural Heritage: Biographies of Place* 185 (M.L. Stig Sørensen & D. Viejo-Rose ed., War and Cultural Heritage: Biographies of Place, Cambridge University Press 2015).
19. F. Henn, *The Nicosia Airport Incident of 1974: A Peacekeeping Gamble*, in 124 (R.C. Sharma & S.A. Epaminondas ed., Cyprus: In Search of Peace and Justice, Somali Publications New Delhi 1997).
20. A. Suha, *Turkish Education in Cyprus*, in *Milletarası Birinci Kıbrıs Tetkikleri Kongresi* 236 (Ankara 1971).
21. H. Nowacki, *Der Zypernkrieg 1974 – Eine Analyse seiner Ursachen* 21 (Hamburg 1982). It was also noted that the priests became the real administrators of the Community. H Özdemir, *Ottoman Administration in Cyprus*, 20 Osmanlı Araşmtırmalari 123 (2000).
22. D.G. Seremetis, *Η απονομή δικαιοσύνης εν Κύπρῳ* in *Minutes of the First International Cyprus Congress* Vol. 3 A, 312 (Th. Papadopoulos & M. Christodoulou ed., Nicosia 1973).

1893 as the Pancyprian Gymnasium operates until today.[23] Upon arrival of the British in 1878, seventy schools were operating in Cyprus, which were funded by the Evqaf, the then supervisory body for all vakfs, the Ottoman government and residents of villages.[24] The British enacted education laws as early as 1895, in order to place education under state supervision and control.[25] Today the archbishop continues the tradition of supporting education and research, and education is given high regard, as seven universities, most of them privately funded, operate in Cyprus.[26] Similar is the situation in the area not under government control.

V. Main Environmental Problems

9. On Yale University's Environmental Performance Index, Cyprus came twenty-fourth in 2018.[27] The UN's Human Development Index ranks it as thirty-third best place to live in the world.[28] The main environmental problem of the island relates to water, as no natural reservoir catchments are available. At the same time, water pollution from sewage and industrial wastes[29] endangers the water available. The northern part of the island, which is not under governmental control, has been supplied with water from Turkey since October 2015, when the water pipeline project ('Asrın Projesi') was successfully completed.[30]

10. A further matter of concern was Amiantos Asbestos Mine, which forms a part of the Troodos National Forest Park, an area of the Natura 2000 network, as the asbestos mine was abandoned in 1988 due to financial problems of the operator without any restoration works. As a result, asbestos fibres were released into the air and in all probability reached water supply. No specific information on this is

23. T. Tollefson, *American Missionary Schools for Cyprus (1834–1842): A Case Study in Cultural Differences*, 10/11 Modern Greek Stud. YB 44 (1994/1995).
24. *Ibid.*, p. 240.
25. A. Suha, *Turkish Education in Cyprus*, in *Milletarası Birinci Kıbrıs Tetkikleri Kongresi* 241 (Ankara 1971).
26. These are: the University of Cyprus, https://www.ucy.ac.cy/en/ (accessed 5 Dec. 2015); the Open University of Cyprus, http://www.ouc.ac.cy/web/guest/home (accessed 5 Dec. 2015); the Cyprus University of Technology, http://www.cut.ac.cy/?languageId=2 (accessed 5 Dec. 2015); the University of Nicosia, http://www.unic.ac.cy/ (accessed 5 Dec. 2015); the European University Cyprus, http://www.euc.ac.cy/ (accessed 5 Dec. 2015); the Frederick University Cyprus, http://www.frederick.ac.cy/ (accessed 5 Dec. 2015); the Neapolis University Cyprus, http://www.nup.ac.cy/gr/ (accessed 5 Dec. 2015).
27. *See* in detail: http://epi.yale.edu/downloads (accessed 21 Jan. 2020).
28. *See* in detail: http://hdr.undp.org/en/countries/profiles/CYP (accessed 8 Jun. 2021).
29. Central Intelligence Agency, *The World Factbook*, Europe: Cyprus – Geography, https://www.cia.gov/library/publications/the-world-factbook/geos/cy.html (accessed 21 Jan. 2020).
30. Euronews, *Turkish Water Begins to Flow to Northern Cyprus as Vast Pipeline Project Goes Onstream*, http://www.euronews.com/2015/10/17/turkish-water-begins-to-flow-to-northen-cyprus-as-vast-pipeline-project-goes/ (accessed 1 Dec. 2015); Deutschlandfunk, *Herrscher über den Wasserhahn*, http://www.deutschlandfunk.de/tuerkei-herrscher-ueber-den-wasserhahn.799.de.html?dram:article_id=278863 (accessed 1 Dec. 2015); Habertürk, *Asrın Projesi'nde açılış gerçekleşiyor*, http://www.haberturk.com/ekonomi/ekonomi/haber/1141214-asrin-projesinde-acilis-gerceklesiyor (accessed 1 Dec. 2015).

provided on the governmental webpage on air quality of Cyprus (http://www.airquality.dli.mlsi.gov.cy/) and on the webpage of the competent ministry. The project of restoration and management of Amiantos Asbestos Mine took place from 2013 to 2015 and was funded by the government and the European Economic Area grants of Iceland, Liechtenstein and Norway.[31] The project included wildlife conservation actions, creation of water pond, mine restoration, realization of training events, publication of guides and improved visitor access and information. Reducing the release of asbestos fibres in the air, which was the aim of most of its activities,[32] has been achieved through revegetation of a significant part of asbestos wastes[33] and through paving of existing roads and construction of small bridges, edges and trenches.[34] The restoration works are expected to last up to 2025.[35]

§2. Basic Principles of Environmental Law

I. Definitions and Notions

11. The basic principles of national environmental law derive from the European environmental law and in particular from Article 191(2) TFEU, as no national legislation sets out such principles and European law is superior thereto, including the constitution (Article 1A of the Constitution).

12. The preventive and precautionary principles, which are always used together[36] and not distinguished by the Court of Justice of the EU,[37] were pivotal to European environmental law, due to potentially very serious consequences of a lack of foresight.[38] They formed the basis of the (then) Community waste policy,[39] as well as today's Union waste policy,[40] and were implemented in environmental

31. Project title: Biodiversity Conservation in Restoration and Management of the Amiantos Asbestos Mine in Troodos National Forest Park, Project number: CY02-0001. *See* detailed information in http://www.amiandos.eu/en (accessed 1 Dec. 2015).
32. *Biodiversity Conservation in Restoration and Management of the Amiantos Asbestos Mine in Troodos National Forest Park*, Project application, p. 18. http://www.amiandos.eu/images/docs/1._%CE%A4%CE%97%CE%95_PROPOSAL.pdf (accessed 1 Dec. 2015).
33. *Ibid.*, p. 19.
34. *Ibid.*, p. 9.
35. T. Tsintides, *Biodiversity Conservation in Restoration and Management of the Amiantos Asbestos Mine in Troodos National Forest Park*, http://www.amiandos.eu/en/articles-presentations-en.html (accessed 1 Dec. 2015).
36. L. Krämer, *EU Environmental Law* 24 (Sweet & Maxwell 2012).
37. W. Kahl, in *EUV/AEUV* 1841 (R.Streinz ed., C.H. Beck 2012).
38. Commission of the EC, *Communication Implementing Community Environmental Law*, COM(96) 500 final, para. 7, www.eur-lex.europa.eu (accessed 1 Dec. 2015).
39. Commission of the EC, *Communication on the Review of the Community Strategy for Waste Management*, COM(96) 399 final, para. 18, www.eur-lex.europa.eu (accessed 1 Dec. 2015).
40. Preamble no. 30 to Directive 2008/98/EC of the European Parliament and of the Council of 19 Nov. 2008 on waste and repealing certain Directives, OJ L 312, 22 Nov. 2008, p. 3.

liability.[41] In addition, they have recognized principles of international environmental law[42] and are laid down in Principle 15 of the Rio Declaration on Environment and Development.[43]

13. The precautionary principle (in French 'principe de précaution', in German 'Vorsorgeprinzip' and in Dutch 'voorzorgsbeginsel'), which arose from the German *Vorsorgeprinzip*,[44] is not defined in the treaties.[45] It aims to minimize risks and sustain natural resources for the future and therefore widens environmental protection, taking it further from merely avoiding immediate dangers and remediation of materialized damage.[46] This principle justifies the adoption of restrictive measures, where it proves impossible to determine with certainty the existence or extent of the risk envisaged because of the insufficiency, inconclusiveness or imprecision of the results of the studies conducted, but the likelihood of real harm to human or animal health or to the environment persists, should the risk materialize.[47] Some authors are of the opinion that this principle is best expressed with the phrase in *dubio pro natura*.[48] Examples of its application are taking measures to ban or restrict the circulation of substances or products such as best cadmium and phthalates[49] and the Environmental Impact Assessment (EIA) Directive.[50]

14. The preventive principle (in French 'principe de préventive', in German 'Vorbeugungsprinzip' and in Dutch 'preventiebeginsel') requires that, when measures are taken, they should be aimed at preventing, rather than mitigating or repairing, environmental damage.[51] The Third Environment Action Programme was

---

41. Commission of the EC, *White Paper on Environmental Liability*, COM(2000) 66 final, para. 3.1, www.eur-lex.europa.eu (accessed 1 Dec. 2015).
42. N. de Sadeler, *Environmental Principles*, S. Leubuscher (translation), 64, 94 et seq. (OUP 2005); L. Krämer, *EU Environmental Law* 22 (Sweet & Maxwell 2012).
43. L. Bergkamp, *Liability and Environment* 13 (Kluwer Law International 2001).
44. N. de Sadeler, *Environmental Principles*, S. Leubuscher (translation), 93 (OUP 2005); W. Kahl, in *EUV/AEUV* 1846 (R. Streinz ed., C.H. Beck 2012).
45. The definition given in the Convention on the Protection of the Marine Environment in the North Atlantic (OSPAR) is proposed to be taken. L. Krämer, *EU Environmental Law* 22 (Sweet & Maxwell 2012).
46. K. Meßerschmidt, *Europäisches Umweltrecht* 286 (C.H. Beck 2011); J.H. Jans & H.H.B. Vedder, *European Environmental Law* 37 (Europa Law Publishing 2008).
47. Case C-192/01, *Commission v. Denmark* [2003] ECR I-9693, para. 52; Case C-219/07, *Nationale Raad van Dierenkwekers en Liefhebbers und Andibel* [2008] ECR I-4475, para. 38; judgment of 10 Sep. 2009 in Case C-100/08, *Commission v. Belgium, digital* ECR, para. 102; and judgment of 28 Jan. 2010 in Case C-333/08, *Commission v. France, digital* ECR, para. 93. On the applicability of the precautionary principle *see* Commission, *Communication on the Precautionary Principle*, COM(2000) 1 final, www.eur-lex.europa.eu (accessed 1 Dec. 2015).
48. C.W. Backes & J.M. Verschuuren, *The Precautionary Principle in International, European and Dutch Wildlife Law*, 9 Colo. J. Int'l Envtl. L. & Pol'y 43(1998).
49. L. Krämer, *EU Environmental Law* 23 (Sweet & Maxwell 2012).
50. M. Nettesheim, in *Das Recht der EU – Kommentar*, Art. 191 Abs. 2, p. 28 (E. Grabitz, M. Hilf & M. Nettesheim ed., C.H. Beck 2011).
51. L. Bergkamp, *Liability and Environment* 14 (Kluwer Law International 2001); J.H. Jans & H.H.B. Vedder, *European Environmental Law* 41 (Europa Law Publishing 2008).

focused strongly on this principle, which has been the pillar of mainly the EIA Directive,[52] the Directive on Groundwater[53] and the REACH Regulation.[54]

15. Environmental damage should as a priority be rectified at source (in French 'principe de correction par priorité à la source ou prévention à la source', in German 'Ursprungsprinzip' and in Dutch 'beginsel van bestrijding bij de bron'), without excluding the option to act at a later point.[55] This principle, which was introduced in the Third Environment Action Programme,[56] suggests a strong preference for emission standards rather than environmental quality standards, especially when dealing with air and water pollution.[57] It further gives a geographic reference to environmental protection.[58] It is being materialized in the legislation on waste, where it is specified as the proximity principle (in French 'principe de proximité', in German 'Näheprinzip' and in Dutch 'beginselen van nabijheid').[59]

16. The costs of remediating environmental pollution are to be borne by the polluter according to the polluter pays principle (in French 'principe du pollueur-payeur', in German 'Verursacherprinzip' and in Dutch 'beginsel dat de vervuiler betaalt'). This principle dominated the First Environment Action Programme and has been the cornerstone of European environmental policy even before it was incorporated into the treaty.[60] The legality or illegality of the relevant action is indifferent.[61] Unlike the German principle of imposing an obligation to act, along with the obligation to settle the costs, it refers solely to the costs resulting from prevention of environmental pollution and removal of pollutants.[62] It has been expressed in the Environmental Liability Directive.[63]

52. Preamble to Council Directive 85/337/EEC of 27 Jun. 1985 on the assessment of the effects of certain public and private projects on the environment, OJ L 175, 5 Jul. 1985, p. 40; Preamble to Directive 2011/92/EU of the European Parliament and of the Council of 13 Dec. 2011 on the assessment of the effects of certain public and private projects on the environment, OJ L 26, 28 Jan. 2012, p. 1.
53. Preamble to Council Directive 80/68/EEC of 17 Dec. 1979 on the protection of groundwater against pollution caused by certain dangerous substances, OJ L 20, 26 Jan. 1980, p. 43; Preamble nos 11, 40 to Directive 2000/60/EC of the European Parliament and of the Council of 23 Oct. 2000 establishing a framework for Community action in the field of water policy, OJ L 327, 22 Dec. 2000, p. 1.
54. Preamble nos 17 and 70 to Regulation (EC) No. 1907/2006 of the European Parliament and of the Council of 18 Dec. 2006 concerning the Registration, Evaluation, Authorisation and Restriction of Chemicals (REACH), OJ L 396, 30 Dec. 2006, p. 1.
55. K. Meßerschmidt, *Europäisches Umweltrecht* 305 (C.H. Beck 2011).
56. M. Nettesheim, in *Das Recht der EU – Kommentar*, Art. 191 Abs. 2, p. 30 (E. Grabitz, M. Hilf & M. Nettesheim ed., C.H. Beck 2011).
57. J.H. Jans & H.H.B. Vedder, *European Environmental Law* 42 (Europa Law Publishing 2008).
58. A. Epiney, *Umweltrecht in der EU* 105 (Carl Heymanns 2005); M. Kloepfer, *Umweltrecht* 686 (C.H. Beck 2004).
59. K. Meßerschmidt, *Europäisches Umweltrecht* 305 et seq. (C.H. Beck 2011); M. Nettesheim, in *Das Recht der EU – Kommentar*, Art. 191 Abs. 2, p. 31 (E. Grabitz, M. Hilf & M. Nettesheim ed., C.H. Beck 2011); W. Kahl, in *EUV/AEUV* 1844 (R.Streinz ed., C.H. Beck 2012).
60. J.H. Jans & H.H.B. Vedder, *European Environmental Law* 43 (Europa Law Publishing 2008).
61. W. Kahl, in *EUV/AEUV* 1846 (R.Streinz ed., C.H. Beck 2012).
62. A. Epiney, *Umweltrecht in der EU* 106 (Carl Heymanns 2005); M. Kloepfer, *Umweltrecht* 686 (C.H. Beck 2004); M. Nettesheim, in *Das Recht der EU – Kommentar*, Art. 191 Abs. 2, p. 31 (E. Grabitz,

II. Constitutional Provisions

17. No constitutional provision relates directly to environment or environmental protection. It has been ruled, however, that the natural environment is contained in the right to life (Article 7(1) of the Constitution). The Supreme Court of Cyprus has been reluctant to accept that the prerequisite of legal interest ('έννομο συμφέρον') of the appellant was fulfilled, and dismissed the appeal of a non-governmental organization against an administrative act, which allegedly affected the environment negatively, without addressing the merits of the case.[64] Still, this ruling was decided before the implementation of Directive 2003/35/EC and therefore, it would be highly unlikely for such a judgment to be reached today under the new legislation.

§3. Historical Background

18. Cyprus has not experienced environmental tragedies such as the Love Canal in the United States of America,[65] the Bielefeld-Braker and the Dortmund-Dorstfeld in Germany[66] or the Chemie-Pack fire at Moerdijk in the Netherlands.[67] Health hazards related to asbestos mining were regulated by law.[68] More specifically, health hazards, those being death or total impotence due to asbestosis or asbestosis accompanied with tuberculosis or the illness of asbestosis or asbestosis accompanied with tuberculosis, caused to employees of certain mining and quarry industries were compensated.[69] Compensation was paid to the person suffering such hazard or its close relatives in the event of death, as long as no other statutory or contractual compensation was due and a period of twenty-five years since last employment at those industries had not lapsed.[70]

M. Hilf & M. Nettesheim ed., C.H. Beck 2011); L. Krämer, *EU Environmental Law* 26 (Sweet & Maxwell 2012). The opposite is also supported: W. Kahl, in *EUV/AEUV* 1846 (R. Streinz ed., C.H. Beck 2012).

63. M. Nettesheim, in *Das Recht der EU – Kommentar*, Art. 191 Abs. 2, p. 32 (E. Grabitz, M. Hilf & M. Nettesheim ed., C.H. Beck 2011); W. Kahl in *EUV/AEUV* 1846 (R.Streinz ed., C.H. Beck 2012).
64. *The Republic v. Koinotitas Pyrgon* (1996) 3 CLR 503, *Somateio Filoi tou Akama v. the Republic* (1998) 4 CLR 767. The Supreme Court of Cyprus refused the binding effect of judgments of the Council of State of Greece Nos 4576/77, 2233/79, 89/81, 366/93 and 4665/96, on the grounds of statutory differences in the two countries, as in Greece environmental protection rests on constitutional provisions.
65. *See* in this respect, E.C. Beck, *The Love Canal Tragedy*, http://www2.epa.gov/aboutepa/love-canal-tragedy (accessed 5 Dec. 2015).
66. J. Hofmann-Hoeppel, J. Schumacher & J. Wagner, *Bodenschutzrecht – Praxis* 36 (Springer 1999).
67. N. Bouman, *Fire at Chemie Pack* (Ministry of Infrastructure and the Environment of the Kingdom of the Netherlands 2012), http://ec.europa.eu/environment/legal/liability/pdf/eld_meetings/Fire_Chemiepack.pdf (accessed 5 Dec. 2015).
68. Law on Asbestosis (Compensation) ('ο περί Πνευμοκονιάσεως (Αποζημιώσεως) Νόμος') No. 11 of 1960, OG I(I) No. 23 of 15 Dec. 1960, p. 59. This law has been repealed in 1972.
69. Section 3(i), (ii) and (iii) Law No. 11/1960.
70. Sections 3(a), (b) and (c), 6 and 7 *ibid.*

§4. Role of Government Institutions in the Shaping and Administration of Environmental Law and Policy

I. The Governmental Institutions and Their Competencies

19. Ministers competent for environmental matters are the Minister of Agriculture, Rural Development and Environment; the Minister of Interior; and the Minister of Labour and Social Security, as each environmental law specifies. These Ministers, who normally issue permits and authorizations under environmental laws, as well as the Council of Ministers, play an important role in the environmental legislation, due to their competence to issue secondary legislation such as decrees and regulations for fully and effectively carrying out and giving effect to, all or any of the purposes, provisions and effectively carrying out and giving effect to, all or any of the purposes, provisions and powers contained in environmental laws.

20. The Council of Ministers has further the authority to act as a dispute resolution institution concerning administrative disputes and reaches a final and conclusive decision. Whether this prevents such disputes to be brought before the administrative court is a matter to be decided by the latter. The clear wording of the provisions of the laws is possible to prevail, as the right to a fair trial is borne by humans and not by governmental institutions, who are in some cases parties to such disputes. In other cases, it is easier to comprehend such provisions within their historical frame. This was the power exercised by the governor of the island when Cyprus was a British Colony, and judicial control of the administration in common law was *terra incognito*. After the establishment of the Republic of Cyprus and the enactment of the Constitution that prescribes the judicial control of administration via an appeal under Article 146 of the Constitution, these powers were taken over by the Council of Ministers. Hence, in such cases, bringing an administrative dispute before the administrative court should be admissible.

21. Application and enforcement of environmental law are usually entrusted with inspectors-in-chief and inspectors, who are appointed by Ministers under environmental laws that also describe in great detail their duties and powers. In view of the strong similarity of duties and powers of the inspectors under these laws, as well as of the administrative sanctions that may be imposed by them, it would not be irrational to suggest the enactment of a single legislation addressing these matters. The same could be suggested regarding the advisory committees established under environmental laws.

II. The Actual Role of the Governmental Institutions

22. The actual role of governmental institutions is elaborated under each piece of environmental legislation.

§5. SOURCES OF ENVIRONMENTAL LAW

23. The source of Cypriot Environmental Law is in its majority the legislation of the EU, as national laws have been enacted for the purpose of implementing directives thereof, with the exception of some Colony laws that though amended are still in force today. In view of the scarcity of relevant national case law and the simplicity of the explanatory reports accompanying the government bills, mention is made to the directive(s) that each national law implements. The aim is to enable further research in the preparatory documents of the European institutions, as well as taking into consideration judgments of the Court of Justice of the EU, if this is wished for the purpose of interpreting the national provisions. Such interpretation may be further assisted by other material, such as judgments and academia concerning national provisions of Greece, France or Germany implementing same directives, in view of the Cypriot case law allowing for adoption and application of administrative principles from these countries. Hence, a judgment of the *Bundes-Verwaltungsgericht* or the Council of State of Greece addressing a matter under consideration before courts of Cyprus is regarded binding, despite the fact that in continental law judgments are binding under specific circumstances only between the parties of the dispute ('Rechtskraft' §121 Verwaltungsgerichtsordnung (of the Federal Republic of Germany); 'δεδικασμένο' §197 Greek Code of Administrative Court Procedure).

Part I. Pollution Control

24. An overview of matters examined under this part is set out in Table 1.

Table 1 Pollution Control: Overview

	Air *Law No. 187(I)/2002*	*Water and Soil* *Law No. 106(I)/2002*	*Waste* *Law No. 185(I)/2011*	*Noise* *Law No. 224(I)/2004*	*Radiation and Vibrations* *Law No. 164(I)/2018*	*Industrial Emissions* *Law No. 184(I)/2013*
Implemented Directive(s) and Decisions according to the statutory preambles	94/63/EC; 87/217/EEC; 2000/76/EC;[71] 2001/80/EC;[72] 2006/21/EC; 2008/1/EC;[73] 2009/126/EC	75/440/EEC;[74] 79/869/EEC;[75] 76/160/EEC;[76] 76/464/EEC;[77] 78/659/EEC;[78] 79/923/EEC;[79] 80/68/EEC;[80] 82/176/EEC;[81] 84/156/EEC;[82] 83/513/EEC;[83] 84/491/EEC;[84] 86/280/EEC;[85] 91/271/EEC; 91/676/EEC; 96/61/EC[86]	96/59/EC; 1999/31/EC; 2002/96/EC;[87] 2006/66/EC; 2011/65/EU; 2012/19/EU	2002/49/EC	2006/117/Euratom; 2009/71/Euratom; 2014/87/Euratom; 2013/59/Euratom	2010/75/EU

71. This directive has been repealed by Directive 2010/75/EU of the European Parliament and of the Council of 24 Nov. 2010 on industrial emissions (integrated pollution prevention and control), OJ L 334, 17 Dec. 2010, p. 17.
72. This directive has been repealed by the aforementioned Directive 2010/75/EU.
73. Also this directive has been repealed by the aforementioned Directive 2010/75/EU.
74. This Directive has been repealed by Directive 2000/60/EC of the European Parliament and of the Council of 23 Oct. 2000 establishing a framework for Community action in the field of water policy, *OJ L 327, 22* Dec. *2000*, p. 1.
75. Also this directive has been repealed by Directive 2000/60/EC.
76. This directive has been repealed by Directive 2006/7/EC of the European Parliament and of the Council of 15 Feb. 2006 concerning the management of bathing water quality and repealing Directive 76/160/EEC, OJ L 64, 4 Mar. 2006, p. 37.
77. Also this directive has been repealed by Directive 2000/60/EC.
78. Similarly this directive has been repealed by Directive 2000/60/EC.
79. Equally, this directive has been repealed by Directive 2000/60/EC.
80. Also this directive has been repealed by Directive 2000/60/EC.
81. This directive has been repealed by Directive 2008/105/EC of the European Parliament and of the Council of 16 Dec. 2008 on environmental quality standards in the field of water policy, amending and subsequently repealing Council Directives 82/176/EEC, 83/513/EEC, 84/156/EEC, 84/491/EEC, 86/280/EEC and amending Directive 2000/60/EC of the European Parliament and of the Council, OJ L 348, 24 Dec. 2008, p. 84.
82. This directive has been repealed by Directive 2008/105/EC.
83. Also this directive has been repealed by Directive 2008/105/EC.
84. This directive has been repealed by Directive 2008/105/EC.
85. Similarly this directive has been repealed by Directive 2008/105/EC.
86. This directive has been repealed by Directive 2008/1/EC of the European Parliament and of the Council of 15 Jan. 2008 concerning integrated pollution prevention and control (Codified version), OJ L 24, 29 Jan.2008, p. 8, which has been also repealed by Directive 2010/75/EU.

Competent Ministry	Ministry of Agriculture, Rural Development and the Environment Security	Ministry of Agriculture, Rural Development and the Environment	Ministry of Agriculture, Rural Development and the Environment and Ministry of Interior	Ministry of Agriculture, Rural Development and the Environment	Ministry of Labour and Social Security	Ministry of Agriculture, Rural Development and the Environment
Administrative Act	Air-waste permit (section 8(1))	Disposal permit (section 8(1))	Waste treatment permit (section 49)	Strategic noise mapping (section 8), action plan (section 9) [quality of administrative act to be determined]	Notification (section 13), registration or authorization (section 14), authorization (section 15)	Industrial emissions permit (section 8)
Public Participation in issuing this act	Opportunity to submit views and suggestions (section 8(8))	Opportunity to submit opinions and suggestions (section 9(4)(c))	No – participation only to waste management plans and waste prevention programmes (sections 37–41)	reaction plant: consultations (section 9 (5, 6))		Submission of views and representations (section 37(1)(g))/re activities of Annex IV: early and effective opportunity to participate (section 36(1)(a))
Legal Remedy against this act	Administrative appeal with the Council of Ministers (section 17) and appeal (Article 146 Constitution)	Appeal (Article 146 Constitution)	Appeal (Article 146 Constitution)	Appeal (Article 146 Constitution), under the conditions that: (i) it is an administrative act, (ii) the appellant has a legal interest to filing such an appeal[88]	Objection with the Minister (section 29) and appeal (Article 146 Constitution)	Appeal (Article 146 Constitution)

87. This directive has been repealed by Directive 2012/19/EU of the European Parliament and of the Council of 4 Jul. 2012 on waste electrical and electronic equipment (WEEE) Text with EEA relevance, OJ L 197, 24 Jul. 2012, p. 38.
88. Direct, present and personal legal interest ('άμεσο, ενεστώς και προσωπικό έννομο συμφέρον') is necessary for filing an appeal. *Loukis Kritiotis v. The Municipality of Paphos a.a.* (1986) 3 C.L.R. 322.

	Air *Law No. 187(I)/2002*	*Water and Soil* *Law No. 106(I)/2002*	*Waste* *Law No. 185(I)/2011*	*Noise* *Law No. 224(I)/2004*	*Radiation and Vibrations* *Law No. 164(I)/2018*	*Industrial Emissions* *Law No. 184(I)/2013*
Revocation of this act	For the protection of public health, public safety and environment (section 16)	For the protection of public health, public safety and environment (section 12)	For prevention of risk to water, soil, plants, animals, nuisance through noise or odours, negative effect to protected species and natural habitats and adverse effect to the countryside or places of special interest (section 31)	N/A	At any time –grounds to be set by the Radiation Control and Inspection Service (section 25)	For the protection of public health, public safety and environment (section 19(1))/re activities of Annex IV: were appropriate – no grounds specified (section 32(1)(b))
Sanctions	Administrative (section 22), penal (sections 15, 20, 22, 26, 30), other (sections 27, 28)	Administrative (sections 24, 31A), penal (sections 6, 29), other (section 30)	Administrative (sections 45, 46 51), penal (sections 49, 46(4), 45(8)), other (section 49(2)–(5))	N/A	Administrative (sections 37–42), penal (section 43), other (section 43(4)(a)	Administrative (sections 86, 91), penal (sections 87, 20, 18), other (sections 88, 90)
Archive	Yes (sections 18 and 19)	Yes (section 28)	Yes (sections 33, 42)	Strategic noise maps are made public (section 9)	Yes (section 28)	Yes (section 95)
Public or NGO Initiative	Local authority may initiate penal procedure (section 29)	N/A	N/A	N/A	N/A	N/A

Chapter 1. General Law

25. No general legislation on pollution control has been enacted in Cyprus. Rather, pollution control is regulated through special provisions for each environmental medium.

Chapter 2. Air Pollution

26. Air pollution control is regulated by Law on Air Pollution Control[89] (hereinafter 'Law No. 187(I)/2002'), as amended, that implements a number of directives of the EU.[90] Law No. 187(I)/2002 has upheld the Law on Air Pollution Control of 1991.[91]

§1. Objective

27. The objective of this law is prevention, elimination and control of air pollution originating from plants aiming to improve public health and prosperity along with protecting and improving the environment, fauna and flora.[92] Air pollution ('ατμοσφαιρική ρύπανση') stands for the introduction by man, directly or indirectly, of substances or energy into the air resulting in deleterious effects of such a nature as to endanger human health, harm living resources and ecosystems and material property, and impair or interfere with amenities and other legitimate uses of the environment.[93] Plant ('εγκατάσταση') is any establishment or other stationary plant, where activities that could cause air pollution are carried out and includes any other directly associated activities which have a technical connection with said activities.[94]

89. Law on Air Pollution Control ('ο περί Ελέγχου της Ρύπανσης της Ατμόσφαιρας Νόμος') No. 187 of 2002, OG I(I) No. 3649 of 1 Nov. 2002.
90. According to the preamble of Law No. 187(I)/2002, this law implements the following directives: Directive 94/63/EC; Directive 87/217/EEC; Decision of 21 Apr. 1997 on harmonized measurement methods to determine the mass concentration of dioxins and furans in atmospheric emissions in accordance with Art. 7(2) of Directive 94/67/EC; Directive 2000/76/EC; Directive 2001/80/EC; Directive 2006/21/EC; Directive 2008/1/EC; and Directive 2009/126/EC. However, it should be noted that Directive 2001/80/EC has been repealed by Directive 2010/75/EU of the European Parliament and of the Council of 24 Nov. 2010 on industrial emissions (integrated pollution prevention and control), OJ L 334, 17 Dec. 2010, p. 17, since 1 Jan. 2016. Similarly, Directives 2008/1/EC and 2000/76/EC are repealed by Directive 2010/75/EU from 7 Jan. 2014. Interestingly, Directive 2010/75/EC is equally implemented in national legislation via Law No. 184(I)/2013, according to the preamble of the latter.
91. Law on Air Pollution Control ('ο περί Ελέγχου της Ρύπανσης της Ατμόσφαιρας Νόμος') No. 70 of 1991, OG I(I) No. 2585 of 29 Mar. 1991, p. 1109.
92. Section 3 Law No. 187(I)/2002.
93. Section 2 *ibid.*, which has a wording very close to Art. 2(1) Directive 84/360/EEC. The French version of this directive makes mention to 'pollution atmosphérique', the German to 'Luftverunreinigung' and the Dutch to 'Luchtverontreiniging'.
94. Section 2 Law No. 187(I)/2002. This provision has mixed elements from both Art. 2(2) Directive 84/360/EEC and Art. 2(3) Directive 2008/1/EC. As it includes movable and immovable things, it has been preferred to translate the word 'εγκατάσταση' into plant, which was used in Directive 84/360/EEC, and not installation, which was used in Directive 2008/1/EC. The French version of the directives makes mention to 'installation', the German to 'Anlage' and the Dutch to 'inrichting'.

§2. AREA OF APPLICATION

28. This law applies to all plants, safe for a different explicit provision therein.[95] It equally applies to plants that belong to or are occupied by the state and plants operating by or on behalf of the state.[96] More specifically, all plants mentioned in Annexes II and III of Law No. 187(I)/2002 are considered to be *plants requiring a permit* ('αδειοδοτούμενες εγκαταστάσεις') and must, therefore, obtain a permit from the Minister under this law.[97] Other plants called *plants not requiring a permit* ('μη αδειοδοτούμενες εγκαταστάσεις') are equally regulated by this law, however, in a different way, as elaborated below.

29. This law is not applicable to operations, in which members of the armed forces of Cyprus participate and have military nature, including any operations in the sea or air.[98] This law also does not authorize any authority to control pollution arising from ionizing radiation.[99]

§3. COMPETENT AUTHORITIES

I. The Minister of Agriculture, Rural Development and the Environment

30. The Minister of Agriculture, Rural Development and the Environment (hereinafter 'the Minister') mainly decides on the applications for air-waste permits[100] as well as on the revocation, annulment and amendment thereof.[101] The Minister is also authorized to issue a decree establishing general operating conditions for certain categories of plants requiring a permit.[102] He further has the powers given to him under this law with the aim of ensuring that the operators comply with the terms of operation set out in air-waste permits of the plants requiring a permit or with the terms of operation of plants not requiring a permit. Similarly, he determines measurement and monitoring methods regarding emissions originating from plants.[103] The Minister also has the power to request the application of standards approved by Cyprus Organization for the Promotion of Quality,[104] regardless of those being international, European or Cypriot and to determine duties imposed in relation to the air-waste permit (*see* in this regard paragraphs 38 et seq. below).[105] Save for the provisions of this law on confidentiality, the Minister further exchanges information

95. Section 7 Law No. 187(I)/2002.
96. Section 5(1) *ibid.*
97. Section 8(1) *ibid.*
98. Section 5(2) *ibid.*
99. Section 6 *ibid.*
100. Section 8 *ibid.*
101. Section 16 *ibid.*
102. Section 8(15) *ibid.*
103. Section 4(1) *ibid.*
104. Established by the Standardisation, Accreditation and Technical Notification Law ('ο περί Τυποποίησης, Διαπίστευσης και Τεχνικής Πληροφόρησης Νόμος') No. 156 of 2002, OG I(I) No. 3627 of 2 Aug. 2002.
105. Section 9(5) Law No. 187(I)/2002.

with other Member States and the EC in experience and knowledge acquired with reference to preventive measures and measures for reducing air pollution as well as the methods, technical equipment and emission limit values.[106] The Minister also provides to any Member State any information registered with the Registry on Emissions and Air-Waste Permits.[107] Finally, the Minister may delegate any of his powers and competence regarding the proper application of this law and relevant decrees to any department or service of a ministry, any public servant or any person with the proper know-how and training, or public institution established for the public interest or local authority. The relevant procedure involves deliberating with this other public servant, person, authority or organization to which the authority shall be delegated and a written agreement between the Minister and this other person. Such agreement must contain explicitly the specific authority that is being delegated, its range and the time frame within which it may be exercised and may contain any instructions of the Minister in relation to exercising this power. Lastly, a notice of this agreed delegation must be published in the Official Gazette. This delegation may be recalled or amended as the Minister sees fit.[108]

II. The Council of Ministers

31. The Council of Ministers is a competent authority to the extent that it issues regulations as per the explicit provisions in this law, as well as when regulating any specific matter that is considered to be necessary, and generally for the best application of this law.[109] In particular, regulations may qualify further plants' categories as plants requiring a permit[110] as well as set out new operating conditions, emission limit values, technical requirements, additional obligations for certain categories of plants requiring a permit, which are binding for the holder of the permit.[111] They may also refer to regulation of certain categories of air waste,[112] imposing financial burdens on specific categories of plants requiring a permit in accordance with the polluter pays principle[113] and providing motivation for reduction of air waste on the source, as well as for the use of best available techniques (BAT).[114] Regulations may also define areas, for which emission limit values more stringent than those applicable to the rest of the authorized plants are fixed,[115] and decide the categories of plants that may operate within said areas as well as the conditions that need to be

106. Section 4(3) *ibid.*
107. Sections 4(4) and 18(2) *ibid.*
108. Section 4A(1), (2), (3) and (5) *ibid.*
109. Section 9(1) *ibid.*
110. Section 9(2)(a) *ibid.*
111. Section 9(2)(b) *ibid.*
112. Section 9(2)(c) *ibid.*
113. Section 9(2)(d) *ibid.*
114. Section 9(2)(e) *ibid.*
115. Section 9(2)(f) *ibid.*, which corresponds to Art. 5 Directive 84/360/EC.

met.[116] These regulations may also set out penalties for breach thereof[117] and empower the Minister to issue decrees for their best implementation.[118]

III. Technical Committee for the Protection of Air

32. The Technical Committee for the Protection of Air ('Τεχνική Επιτροπή για την Προστασία της Ατμόσφαιρας') has been established via this law. The persons participating in this are the following: a representative of the Ministry of Labour and Social Security,[119] a representative of the Ministry of Agriculture, Rural Development and Environment,[120] a representative of the Ministry of Health,[121] a representative of the Ministry of Interior,[122] a representative of the Ministry of Energy, Commerce, Industry and Tourism,[123] a representative of the Ministry of Communications and Works,[124] a representative of the Technical Chamber of Cyprus[125] and a representative of the Federation of Environmental Organizations of Cyprus.[126] Each representative may be accompanied at the sessions of the committee by a couple of scientific or technical advisors.[127] The main competence of the committee is to advise the Minister prior to reaching any decision on terms of operation for any plant,[128] on determination of emission limit values[129] and on revocation and amendment of an air-waste permit.[130]

33. The chairman of the committee is the representative of the Ministry of Labour and Social Security whereas in his absence another person is being elected by the present members.[131] The chairman has the power to send notices of meetings[132] and the duty to inform about any subject that shall be discussed at least seven days prior to the meeting.[133] Any such information needs to be detailed especially with reference to particulars relating to emission limit values,[134] the general terms

116. Section 9(2)(g) Law No. 187(I)/2002, which corresponds to Art. 5 Directive 84/360/EC.
117. Section 9(3) Law No. 187(I)/2002.
118. Section 9(4) *ibid.*
119. Annex I Part I(1)(a) *ibid.*
120. Annex I Part I(1)(b) *ibid.*
121. Annex I, Part I(1)(c) *ibid.*
122. Annex I, Part I(1)(d) *ibid.*
123. Annex I, Part I(1)(e) *ibid.*
124. Annex I, Part I(1)(f) *ibid.*
125. Annex I, Part I(1)(g) *ibid.*
126. Annex I, Part I(1)(h) *ibid.*
127. Annex I, Part I(3) *ibid.*
128. Annex I, Part II(4)(1)(a) and Part II(4)(2) *ibid.*
129. Annex I, Part II(4)(1)(b) and Part II(4)(2) *ibid.*
130. Annex I, Part II(4)(1)(c) and Part II(4)(2) *ibid.*
131. Annex I, Part I(4) *ibid.*
132. Any member of the committee may request in writing an extraordinary meeting, while setting out the reasons that support such a meeting and the subject to be discussed. These extraordinary meetings are to be convened within fourteen days from the day that they are requested. Annex I, Part I(6) *ibid.*
133. Annex I, Part I(8) *ibid.*
134. Annex I, Part I(9)(a) *ibid.*

of operation that are or must be adopted and any additional terms, if related to plants requiring a permit under this law,[135] the air-waste permit under discussion and any terms that have been imposed or are to be imposed,[136] annulment, revocation or amendment of an air-waste permit under discussion or its terms[137] and any other discussed matter.[138] The notice for the meeting of the committee along with the agenda and copies of the relevant documentation are also forwarded to the local authorities, when the matters under discussion relate directly or indirectly to their territorial competence,[139] and the operator, whose application for an air-waste permit is to be evaluated by the committee.[140]

IV. Inspector-in-Chief and Inspectors

34. An inspector-in-chief and inspectors are appointed by the Minister for the purpose of implementing this law.[141] Their powers are related to entering plants, performing inspections at any part of those in safe conditions, requesting information and transferring samples outside the plants. In particular, these public officers may enter freely and without previous notice to any plant, in which they reasonably think that an activity takes place or is about to take place, which may lead to violation of any provision of this law[142] or of any operation condition attached to an air-waste permit or foreseen in the regulations,[143] and more importantly, they may demand safe access to any part of the plant as well as reasonable means for performing any tests, measurements inspections or examinations.[144]

35. A police officer may accompany them in case of reasonable suspicion that performance of their duties is going to face serious obstruction.[145] Also, an expert or any other auxiliary persons may accompany them having all equipment and material needed for the performance of their duties.[146] They are free to perform tests, measurements and sampling,[147] as well as inspect, examine and check the operation of any machines and equipment in the plant or measurements and take photographs, as long as these actions are deemed necessary for the proper exercise of their duties.[148] Inspectors may also give instructions on stable operation conditions of any plant, any part thereof, any equipment or machine for a reasonable period and for the purpose of performing the above-mentioned tests, measurements

135. Annex I, Part I(9)(b) *ibid.*
136. Annex I, Part I(9)(c) *ibid.*
137. Annex I, Part I(9)(d) *ibid.*
138. Annex I, Part I(9)(e) and (f) *ibid.*
139. Annex I, Part I(10) *ibid.*
140. Annex I, Part I(11) *ibid.*
141. Section 24 *ibid.*
142. Section 25(1)(a) *ibid.*
143. Sections 25(1)(b) and 4(1) *ibid.*
144. Section 25(1)(l) *ibid.*
145. Section 25(1)(c) *ibid.*
146. Sections 25(1)(d) and (e) and 24(2) *ibid.*
147. Section 25(1)(f) *ibid.*
148. Section 25(1)(g) *ibid.*

and operation controls. However, this instruction may not lead to termination of any vital part of the production process or have any negative effect on the same process.[149]

36. Inspectors have further the authority to request the presentation of any books or documents, under the condition that they reasonably believe that these contain information related to the scope of their inquisition.[150] Similarly they may require any information, which is relevant to the scope of the investigation, from the operator of the plant, any person in the plant or any person, for whom it is reasonably believed that he was employed in the plant or had any connection to the plant in the last three months, as long as such person is believed to have access thereto.[151] Inspectors are also authorized to transfer any object or sample of any substance that is necessary for the purpose of further inquisition or penal procedure, according to this law.[152]

37. Lastly, the law specifies, in relation to burden of proof, that the results of the measurements and analysis of the samples taken within the application of this law are legally presumed to be correct.[153] Hence, any person wishing to challenge them must prove them to be wrong.

§4. Air-Waste Permit

38. Despite the widely stated application area of this law, only specific plants, called *plants requiring a permit* ('αδειοδοτούμενες εγκαταστάσεις'), need to obtain an air-waste permit ('άδεια αέριων αποβλήτων') for their lawful operation. These are listed in detail in Annex II and Annex III[154] of this law.

39. In particular, Annex II of this law reads as follows:

(1) Energy Industry: 1.1 Installations for the production of lubricants from crude oil; 1.2 Installations for the production, treatment and storage of oil products, natural or synthetic gas and carbons; 1.3 Coal production installations; and 1.4 Combustion installations using light and/or heavy fuel oil with sulphur content of more than 1%.

(2) Production and Treatment of Metals: 2.1 Integrated installations for the production of rough pig iron or rough steel with a capacity not exceeding 2.5 tonnes per hour; 2.2 Ferrous metal foundries with a production capacity not exceeding 20 tonnes per day; 2.3 Installations for the production

149. Section 25(1)(h) *ibid.*
150. Section 25(1)(i) *ibid.*
151. Section 25(1)(j) *ibid.*
152. Section 25(1)(k) *ibid.*
153. Section 25(3) *ibid.*
154. Great part of this annex has been repealed in 2016, and today it only includes combustion installations with a rated thermal input exceeding 50MW (Annex III(1.1) *ibid.*).

and the smelting of nonferrous metals and alloys including recovered products, (refining, foundry casting, etc.) with a melting capacity not exceeding 4 tonnes per day for lead and cadmium or 20 tonnes per day for all other metals; and 2.4 Installations for surface treatment of metals and plastic materials using an electrolytic or chemical process or galvanization where the volume of the treatment vats does not exceed 30 m^3.

(3) Mineral Industry: 3.1 Installations for the production of cement clinker in rotary kilns with a production capacity not exceeding 500 tonnes per day or lime in rotary kilns with a production capacity not exceeding 50 tonnes per day or in other furnaces with a production capacity not exceeding 50 tonnes per day; 3.2 Installations for the manufacture of glass including glass fibre with a melting capacity not exceeding 20 tonnes per day; 3.3 Installations for melting mineral substances including the production of mineral fibres with a melting capacity not exceeding 20 tonnes per day; and 3.4 Installations for the manufacture of ceramic products by firing, in particular roofing tiles, bricks, refractory bricks, tiles, stoneware or porcelain, with a production capacity not exceeding 75 tonnes per day, and/or with a kiln capacity not exceeding 4 m^3 and with a setting density per kiln not exceeding 300 kg/m^3.

(4) Chemical Industry: 4.1 Chemical installations for the production of olefins, its derivatives, monomeric and polymeric; 4.2 Chemical installations for the production of other organic intermediates; 4.3 Installations using amines for the production of other products; 4.4 Installations using ammonia for the production of other products; 4.5 Installations using calcium carbide for the production of other products; 4.6 Installations using acetylene for the production of other products; 4.7 Installations using for production purposes chlorine (Cl), bromine (Br), fluorine (F), iodine (I), sulfane ($H2_S$), sulphur-containing organic compounds, carbon monoxide (CO) and dioxide (CO_2), nitrogen oxide (NO_x), nitrous oxide and sulphur oxide; 4.8 Installations for the production of medical and veterinary drugs; 4.9 Installations for the production and/or packaging of pesticides in general; 4.10 Installations for the production and/or packaging of surface-active agents and surfactants; and 4.11 Installations for the production and/or packaging of organic and non-organic fertilizers.

(5) Waste Management: 5.1 Installations for the incineration of hazardous waste, including clinical waste, with a capacity not exceeding 10 tonnes per day; 5.2 Installations for the treatment of other solid and liquid waste; 5.3 Installations for the disposal or recovery of hazardous waste (as defined in Annex I of Law No. 127(I)/2018) and waste oils (meaning any semi-liquid or liquid used product totally or partially consisting of mineral or synthetic oil, including the oily residues from tanks, oil-water mixtures and emulsions) and actions that may lead to disposal of waste without endangering human health and without using processes or methods which could harm the environment and involve solvent reclamation/regeneration, regeneration of acids or bases, recovery of components used for pollution abatement, oil re-refining or other reuses of oil and use principally as a fuel or other means to generate energy with a capacity not exceeding 10 tonnes

per day; 5.4 Municipal waste incineration plant (meaning any technical equipment used for the treatment of municipal waste by incineration, with or without recovery of the combustion heat generated, but excluding plants used specifically for the incineration of sewage sludge, chemical, toxic and dangerous waste, medical waste from hospitals or other types of special waste, on land or at sea, even if these plants may burn municipal waste as well. This definition covers the site and the entire installation comprising the incinerator, its waste, fuel and air-supply systems and the devices and systems for checking incineration operations and continuously recording and monitoring incineration conditions) with a capacity not exceeding 3 tonnes per day; 5.5 Installations for the disposal of non-hazardous waste (Annex I(10) Law No. 127(I)/2018), with a capacity not exceeding 50 tonnes per day; 5.6 Landfills receiving no more than 10 tonnes per day or with a total capacity not exceeding 25 000 tonnes, excluding landfills of inert waste; 5.7 Incineration plants for animal carcases or remains; 5.8 Central stations for the treatment of municipal or industrial liquid waste; and 5.9 Mining waste installations.

(6) Other activities: 6.1 Plants for the production of pulp from timber or other fibrous materials with a capacity not exceeding 20 tonnes; 6.2 Slaughterhouses with a carcase production capacity less than 50 tonnes per day; 6.3 Installations for the disposal or recycling of animal carcases and animal waste with a treatment capacity not exceeding 10 tonnes per day; 6.4 Plants for the production of smoked meat with a final product capacity not exceeding 75 tonnes per day; 6.5 Refineries of edible oils, olive-pomace oils or seed oils with a final product capacity not exceeding 300 tonnes per day; 6.6 Plants for the production of particle board or other wood products with chemical or thermal methods; 6.7 Plants for the production of furniture or wood and wood products processing with a capacity exceeding 100 m^3 per year; 6.8 Plants for the production or use of dyes, inks, varnishes or other glazing material with production or consumption exceeding 5 tonnes per year; 6.9 Plants for the printing on paper with a total consumption of printing material exceeding 5 tonnes per year; 6.10 Plants for the production or use of organic solvents; 6.11 Plants for the production or assembling of solar collectors; 6.12 Plants for the pre-treatment (operations such as washing, bleaching, mercerization) or dyeing of textiles fibres or textiles where the treatment capacity does not exceed 10 tonnes per day; 6.13 Plants for the tanning of hides and skins where the treatment capacity does not exceed 12 tonnes of finished products per day; 6.14 Plants for the electrostatic dyeing of objects; and 6.15 Plants for cremation.

I. Application for an Air-Waste Permit

40. Every plant must submit to the Minister an application for an air-waste permit prior to the commencement of its operation.[155] This application is to be filed in a specific form and contain a description of the following: the plant and the nature

155. Section 8(4) *ibid.*, which implements the obligation set out in Art. 4 Directive 2008/1/EC.

and extent of its activities;[156] the main alternative technical solutions that have been studied by the operator in outline;[157] the products produced by the plant;[158] the raw and auxiliary materials, other substances and the energy used in or generated by the plant;[159] the sources of emissions from the plant;[160] the conditions of the site of the plant;[161] the nature and quantities of foreseeable emissions from the plant into atmosphere and identification of significant effects of the emissions on the environment;[162] the proposed technology and other techniques for preventing or, where this not possible, reducing emissions from the plant;[163] where necessary, measures for the prevention and recovery of emissions generated by the plant;[164] the projected measures to monitor emissions into the environment;[165] where necessary, the projected measures to monitor the air quality in the area of the plant;[166] any other measures foreseen in the provisions of this law;[167] and a non-technical summary of the details referred to above.[168] The Minister may further order the submission of any additional information, item or study that he considers necessary for the thorough evaluation of the submitted application. However, such additional requests must be excused in view of the category, the kind, the size or other qualities of the plant requiring a permit.[169] Lastly, a fee for submitting an application may be imposed, which has to be adequate to cover the expenses related to evaluating the application.[170]

II. Evaluation of an Application for an Air-Waste Permit

41. All applications are forwarded to the Minister,[171] who is the competent authority for issuing an air-waste permit,[172] imposing operating conditions in said

156. Section 8(5)(a) Law No. 187(I)/2002, which corresponds to Art. 6(1)(a) Directive 2008/1/EC.
157. Section 8(5)(b) Law No. 187(I)/2002, which corresponds to Art. 6(1)(j) Directive 2008/1/EC. Operator ('φορέας εκμετάλλευσης' in Greek, 'exploitant' in French, 'Betreiber' in German, 'exploitant' in Dutch) means any natural or legal person who operates or controls the installation or to whom decisive economic power over the technical functioning of the installation has been delegated (s. 2 Law No. 187(I)/2002, which corresponds to Art. 2(13) Directive 2008/1/EC).
158. Section 8(5)(c) Law No. 187(I)/2002.
159. Section 8(5)(d) *ibid.*, which corresponds to Art. 6(1)(b) Directive 2008/1/EC.
160. Section 8(5)(e) Law No. 187(I)/2002, which corresponds to Art. 6(1)(c) Directive 2008/1/EC.
161. Section 8(5)(f) Law No. 187(I)/2002, which corresponds to Art. 6(1)(d) Directive 2008/1/EC.
162. Section 8(5)(g) Law No. 187(I)/2002, which corresponds to Art. 6(1)(e) Directive 2008/1/EC.
163. Section 8(5)(h) Law No. 187(I)/2002, which corresponds to Art. 6(1)(f) Directive 2008/1/EC.
164. Section 8(5)(i) Law No. 187(I)/2002, which corresponds to Art. 6(1)(g) Directive 2008/1/EC.
165. Section 8(5)(j) Law No. 187(I)/2002, which corresponds to Art. 6(1)(i) Directive 2008/1/EC.
166. Section 8(5)(k) Law No. 187(I)/2002.
167. Section 8(5)(l) *ibid.*
168. Section 8(6) *ibid.*, which corresponds to Art. 6(1) Directive 2008/1/EC.
169. Section 6(7) Law No. 187(I)/2002.
170. Section 23(1)(a) *ibid.*
171. Section 8(13) and Annex I, Part II(3) *ibid.*
172. Section 8(11) *ibid.*

permit[173] and defining emission limit values.[174] However, before reaching a decision, he must consult the Technical Committee.[175] The consultation takes place in a session of the Technical Committee. In case of disagreement, any member of the said committee may ask the chairman to bring the matter to the Council of Ministers[176] that shall reach a final decision on it.[177]

42. During the evaluation of the application, the following factors must be taken into consideration. First, it will be assessed, whether the applicant has the machines and equipment required in order to comply with all demands of this law, any issued regulations and any terms that will be imposed on the permit.[178] Further, it will be examined, whether all adequate measures for air pollution prevention, including the use of BAT not exceeding excessive cost, have been taken.[179] The term 'BAT' ('βέλτιστες διαθέσιμες τεχνικές') is not defined in this law. However, taking into consideration that this law implements Directive 2008/1/EC, it is safe to assume that the therein-contained definition may be adopted. Pursuant to that, BAT ('meilleures techniques disponibles' in French, 'beste verfügbare Techniken' in German, 'beste beschikbare technieken' in Dutch) means the most effective and advanced stage in the development of activities and their methods of operation which indicate the practical suitability of particular techniques for providing in principle the basis for emission limit values designed to prevent and, where that is not practicable, generally to reduce emissions and the impact on the environment as a whole: (a) 'techniques' shall include both the technology used and the way in which the installation is designed, built, maintained, operated and decommissioned; (b) 'available techniques' means those developed on a scale which allows implementation in the relevant industrial sector, under economically and technically viable conditions, taking into consideration the costs and advantages, whether or not the techniques are used or produced inside the Member State in question, as long as they are reasonably accessible to the operator; (c) 'best' means most effective in achieving a high general level of protection of the environment as a whole. In determining the BAT, special consideration should be given to the items listed in Annex IV (Article 2(12) Directive 2008/1/EC).[180] Equally, any important air pollution during the operation

---

173. Section 8(13) and Annex I, Part II(4)(1)(a) *ibid.*
174. Section 8(13) and Annex I, Part II(4)(1)(b) *ibid.*
175. Section 8(13) and Annex I, Part II(4)(2) *ibid.*
176. Section 8(13) and Annex I, Part II(5)(1) *ibid.*
177. Section 8(13) and Annex I, Part II(5)(2) *ibid.*
178. Section 8(9) *ibid.*
179. Section 8(11) (a) *ibid.*
180. Annex IV Directive 2008/1/EC specifies that considerations to be considered are: (1) the use of low-waste technology; (2) the use of less hazardous substances; (3) the furthering of recovery and recycling of substances generated and used in the process and of waste, where appropriate; (4) comparable processes, facilities or methods of operation which have been tried with success on an industrial scale; (5) technological advances and changes in scientific knowledge and understanding; (6) the nature, effects and volume of the emissions concerned; (7) the commissioning dates for new or existing installations; (8) the length of time needed to introduce the best available technique; (9) the consumption and nature of raw materials used in the process and energy efficiency;

of the plant, especially through the emission of substances stated in Annex IV,[181] will be estimated,[182] along with any exceeding of existing emission limit values ('οριακή τιμή εκπομπής').[183] The term 'emission limit value' ('valeur limite d'émission' in French, 'Emissionsgrenzwert' in German, 'emissiegrenswaarde' in Dutch) means the concentration and/or mass of polluting substances in emissions from plants during a specified period which is not to be exceeded.[184] The definition of the same in the implemented directives is different. More specifically, in the directive on limitation of emissions of certain pollutants into the air from large combustion plants, it means the permissible quantity of a substance contained in the waste gases from the combustion plant which may be discharged into the air during a given period; it shall be calculated in terms of mass per volume of the waste gases expressed in mg/nm^3, assuming an oxygen content by volume in the waste gas of 3% in the case of liquid and gaseous fuels, 6% in the case of solid fuels and 15% in the case of gas turbines (Article 2(3) Directive 2001/80/EC). In the directive for incineration of waste, emission limit value is the mass, expressed in terms of certain specific parameters, concentration and/or level of an emission, which may not be exceeded during one or more periods of time (Article 3(9) Directive 2000/76/EC). In the directive on integrated pollution prevention and control, it means the mass, expressed in terms of certain specific parameters, concentration and/or level of an emission, which may not be exceeded during one or more periods of time; emission limit values may also be laid down for certain groups, families or categories of substances, in particular for those listed in Annex III. The emission limit values for substances normally apply at the point where the emissions leave the installation, any dilution being disregarded when determining them; with regard to indirect releases into the water, the effect of a water treatment plant may be taken into account when determining the emission limit values of the installation involved, provided that an equivalent level is guaranteed for the protection of the environment as a whole and provided this does not lead to higher levels of pollution in the environment, without prejudice to Directive 2006/11/EC or the Directives implementing it (Article 2(6) Directive 2008/1/EC). In the directive on the management of waste from extractive industries (Directive 2006/21/EC) and the one on Stage II petrol vapour recovery during refuelling of motor vehicles at service stations (Directive 2009/126/EC) no definition are foreseen. Similarly, air quality limit

(10) the need to prevent or reduce to a minimum the overall impact of the emissions on the environment and the risks to it; (11) the need to prevent accidents and to minimize the consequences for the environment; (12) the information published by the European Commission or by international organizations.

181. This reads: (1) Sulphur dioxide and other sulphur compounds; (2) Oxides of nitrogen and other nitrogen compounds; (3) Carbon monoxide; (4) Volatile organic compounds; (5) Metals and their compounds; (6) Dust; (7) Asbestos (suspended particulates, fibres); (8) Chlorine and its compounds; (9) Fluorine and its compounds; (10) Arsenic and its compounds; (11) Cyanides; (12) Substances and preparations which have been proved to possess carcinogenic or mutagenic properties or properties which may affect reproduction via the air; (13) Polychlorinated dibenzodioxins and polychlorinated dibenzofurans.

182. Section 8(11)(b) Law No. 187(I)/2002.

183. Section 8(11)(c) *ibid.*

184. Section 2 *ibid.*, which corresponds to Art. 2(5) Directive 84/360/EEC that has been upheld by Directive 2008/1/EC.

values ('οριακές τιμές ποιότητας του αέρα') shall be evaluated.[185] Lastly, in an application regarding an existing plant, it will be examined whether it has an urban planning permission ('πολεοδομική άδεια') in accordance with section 2 of Law on Urban and Land Planning,[186] a building permit ('άδεια οικοδομής') in accordance with section 3 of Streets and Buildings Regulation Law[187] or a certification of approval ('πιστοποιητικό έγκρισης') in accordance with section 10 of Streets and Buildings Regulation Law.[188] Should the application involve a new plant, that being a plant submitting the application on or after 27 December 2013, it shall be examined whether it has a certification of approval.[189]

III. Granting an Air-Waste Permit

43. Operating conditions may be attached to an air-waste permit, as per the discretion of the competent authority. Adherence to those constitutes a necessity for the lawful operation of the plant. Nonrestrictively, this law sets out three groups of operating conditions: the ones related to equipment, the ones related to emission limit values and the ones being positive actions imposed on the operator. The operating conditions related to equipment relate to technical requirements for any machines or equipment used in the plant,[190] to equipment that has to be installed and used for prevention of emission of substances into the air or for making them hazard-free before their emission into the air,[191] to equipment or organs that have to be installed at proper spots and be used for measuring concentrations, emission pace or total amount of any substance emitted into the air during a specific period of time or any other operational parameter,[192] to installation of instruments for measurement or other equipment by the operator and on his own expense at spots that the Minister approves, for the purpose of measuring air quality,[193] to specific conditions or technical requirements, including height, regarding construction of stacks through which

185. Section 8(11)(d) Law No. 187(I)/2002. This law does not specify the meaning of air quality limit values. Taking into consideration that same law was initially issued for the purpose of implementing the directive on the combating of air pollution from industrial plants (Council Directive 84/360/EEC), which was later upheld by Directive 2008/1/EC, it may be concluded that air quality limit is defined as per the relevant provision of said directive. Hence, air quality limit value ('valeur limite de qualité de l'air' in French, 'Luftqualitätsgrenzwert' in German, 'grenswaarde van de luchtkwaliteit' in Dutch) means the concentration of polluting substances in the air during a specified period which is not to be exceeded (Art. 2(4) Directive 84/360/EEC).
186. Law on Urban and Land Planning ('ο περί Πολεοδομίας και Χωροταξίας Νόμος') No. 90 of 1972, OG No. 977 of 8 Dec. 1972, p. 929.
187. Streets and Buildings Regulation Law No. 12 of 1946 ('Cap. 96'), CG No. 3253 of 18 Jul. 1946, p. 227.
188. Section 8(11)(e)(i) Law No. 187(I)/2002.
189. Section 8(11)(e)(ii) *ibid.*
190. Section 8(12)(a) *ibid.*
191. Section 8(12)(c) *ibid.*
192. Section 8(12)(e) *ibid.*
193. Section 8(12)(f) *ibid.*

emissions shall go into the air[194] and to organs, equipment or systems for the storage of measurements and their transmission to the authority appointed by the Minister.[195] Operating conditions may further relate to emission limit values for any specific substance or group of substances emitted into the air by the plant[196] or to quality standards of any material, including fuel, used in the plant.[197] Lastly, operating conditions imposing positive action involve providing any reasonable help to inspectors for conducting measurements and collecting samples of any substances used in the plant or emitted into the air,[198] conducting scheduled measurements by the operator, as well as preparing technical reports and collecting other environmental data, along with the frequency of their submission to the Minister[199] and preparation of reports on environmental management on matters of air pollution control.[200] The discretion of the Minister is so wide, that he may impose specifications on the exact location of the plant.[201]

44. Necessarily, air-waste permits state the exact time period, within which generally no revocation may take place.[202] Equally, they specify a time period for each operating condition, which may not be altered within this period,[203] and a time period, during which addition of any new condition is prohibited.[204]

45. Annual fee may be imposed on operators in order to cover the expenses of usual monitoring and performing of air-waste measurement.[205] These are not necessarily fixed and may vary as the case may be,[206] safe for not discriminating among operators.[207] In the event that the operator installs equipment for measurement or monitoring of any substance or parameter, the Minister may decide to repay partly or fully the annual fee, according to its discretion.[208]

46. The operator bears a certain set of responsibilities upon acquiring an air-waste permit. These include compliance with operating conditions attached to the said permit,[209] informing the Minister of results of emissions of the plant, to the extent that this is required by the permit,[210] informing the Minister without any delay of any incident or accident significantly affecting the environment[211] and

194. Section 8(12)(g) *ibid.*
195. Section 8(12)(j) *ibid.*
196. Section 8(12)(b) *ibid.*
197. Section 8(12)(d) *ibid.*
198. Section 8(12)(h) *ibid.*
199. Section 8(12)(i) *ibid.*
200. Section 8(12)(k) *ibid.*
201. Section 8(12)(l) *ibid.*
202. Section 14(1)(a) *ibid.*
203. Section 14(1)(b) *ibid.*
204. Section 14(1)(c) *ibid.*
205. Section 23(1)(b) *ibid.*
206. Section 23(1)(c) *ibid.*
207. Section 38(1), (2) and (3) Law No. 158(I)/1999.
208. Section 23(1)(c) Law No. 187(I)/2002.
209. Section 11(a) *ibid.*, which corresponds to Art. 14 Directive 96/61/EC.
210. Section 11(b) Law No. 187(I)/2002, which corresponds to Art. 14 Directive 96/61/EC.
211. Section 11(c) Law No. 187(I)/2002.

affording the chief inspector and inspectors all necessary assistance for carrying out any inspections within the plant, taking samples and gathering any information necessary for the performance of their duties for the purposes of this law.[212]

47. Especially with reference to existing plants, the Minister may issue an air-waste permit, even if machines and equipment necessary for compliance with all demands of this law, any issued regulations and any operating conditions that will be imposed on the permit, as required by section 8(9) Law No. 187(I)/2002 are not in place. However, the Minister must specify a time period, within which such machines and equipment need to be installed[213] and a time period, within which the operator shall not comply with any specified operating conditions.[214] During the latter, the Minister may impose new operating conditions or alter the existing ones that shall be binding only after this time period has lapsed.[215]

IV. Rejection of an Application for an Air-Waste Permit

48. In the event of rejection of an application for an air-waste permit, the applicant may lodge an administrative appeal ('ιεραρχική προσφυγή') against this decision. The ground on which such an appeal may be filed is restricted to the applicant having possession of all necessary machines and equipment for issuing an air-waste permit.[216] The competent authority is the Council of Ministers.[217]

49. Self-evidently, the applicant may submit an appeal with the Supreme Court of Cyprus under Article 146 of the Constitution on the grounds of violation of this law, as well as of Law No. 158(I)/1999 or any case law.

V. Revocation and Alteration of an Air-Waste Permit

50. For the purpose of protection of public health, public safety or the environment, the Minister may revoke an air-waste permit,[218] annul or amend any condition thereof,[219] add a new operating condition thereto[220] or shorten the validity period thereof.[221] The procedure for granting an air-waste permit is applied *mutatis mutandis.*[222] Especially in the case of amendment, a new time period, within which

212. Section 11(d) *ibid.*
213. Section 13(1)(a) *ibid.*
214. Section 13(1)(b) *ibid.*
215. Section 13(2) *ibid.*
216. Section 17(1) *ibid.*
217. Section 17(4) *ibid.*
218. Section 16(1)(a) *ibid.*
219. Section 16(1)(b) *ibid.*
220. Section 16(1)(c) *ibid.*
221. Section 16(1)(d) *ibid.*
222. Section 16(2), Annex I, Part II *ibid.*

no amendment may take place without a compensation, will be set out.[223] Also, a reasonable period for compliance with the amended or new conditions must be determined.[224]

51. Should the amendment, either in the form of amending a condition or introducing a new one, take place within the time period that was specified in the permit to be immune to amendments, compensation is paid to the permit holder. The same applies in case of permit revocation. However, under the following circumstances, no compensation is paid. First, this applies when the revocation or amendment was due to a change in circumstances that could not have been reasonably foreseen at the time of attaching the conditions on the permit. As a change of circumstances is also understood, any new information on air-waste emissions of the plant being at the disposal of the Minister.[225] Further, no compensation is paid, when the change of conditions is due to a new legislation enacted for the purpose of implementing an EU directive or to the development of BAT.[226]

52. The air-waste permit holder may lodge an administrative appeal ('ιεραρχική προσφυγή') with the Council of Ministers[227] against the imposed amendments within twenty-one days. Ground for such an appeal may be unreasonableness of the imposed amendment, taking into consideration the location, the plant and any other circumstances.[228] Generally, unreasonableness is understood as the Wednesbury unreasonableness[229] of common law,[230] although Cypriot administrative law is said to follow the tradition of continental law.

53. The Minister may further modify issued air-waste permits, depending on any developments in BAT, which are monitored by the Technical Committee.[231] In particular, he may at his discretion impose any appropriate operating conditions, as long as these do not impose an excessive cost on the plants.[232] He may further issue a decree on applicable policies and strategies that include appropriate measures for gradual adaptation of existing plants to BAT, taking into consideration mainly the characteristics of plants,[233] their use and expected working life,[234] the nature and amount of emissions[235] and the object of not generating excessive cost.[236]

223. Section 16(5) *ibid.*
224. Section 16(6) *ibid.*
225. Section 16(3) *ibid.*
226. Section 16(4) *ibid.*
227. Section 17(4) *ibid.*
228. Section 17(3) *ibid.*
229. *Associated Provincial Picture Houses Ltd v. Wednesbury Corporation* [1948] 1 KB 223.
230. *Cytechno Ltd v. the Republic* (1979) 3 CLR 513; *Stylianou v. Stylianou* (1988) 1 CLR 520; *Achilleos v. the Republic* (1988) 3 CLR 930; *O. Ghalanos & Son Ltd v. the Republic* (1989) 3 CLR 2004; *Nicolaides v. the Republic a.a.* (1990) 3 CLR 1766; *Re Apak Agro Industries Ltd* (2000) 1 CLR 287; *Re General Attorney* (2003) 1 CLR 108; *Re Kitalides and City Project Financiers Ltd*, judgment of 2 Nov. 2000 in appeal no. 99/2000, not published in CLR.
231. Section 10(1) Law No. 187(I)/2002, which corresponds to Art. 11 Directive 96/61/EC.
232. Section 10(1) Law No. 187(I)/2002.
233. Section 10(2)(a) *ibid.*
234. Section 10(2)(b) *ibid.*
235. Section 10(2)(c) *ibid.*
236. Section 10(2)(d) *ibid.*

54. Any extension, amendment or other change of the plant that the operator wishes to undertake, prerequisite a new application for an air-waste permit before their commencement, under the condition that they may have significant negative effects on the air.[237] A decree providing guidance on significant negative effects on the air may be issued by the Minister.[238] Especially operators of a plant that falls under Annex II may apply to the Minister for a written confirmation that the intended extension, amendment or change of the plant shall not demand the granting of a new permit. If such a written confirmation is provided, no application for a new air-waste permit is needed.[239]

VI. Especially Plants Using Asbestos

55. Preventing and reducing pollution by asbestos is regulated in secondary legislation, that being KDP 528/2002,[240] which has been issued for the purpose of harmonizing with EU law.[241] Pursuant to that, plants, where activities involving the use of asbestos or working of products containing asbestos takes place, are considered plants requiring a permit.[242] For the purpose of this law, asbestos ('αμίαντος') means the following fibrous silicates: crocidolite (blue asbestos), actinolite, anthophyllite, chrysotile (white asbestos), amosite (brown asbestos), tremolite.[243] Use of asbestos ('χρησιμοποίηση αμιάντου') stands for activities which involve the handling of a quantity of more than 100 kg of raw asbestos per year and which concern the production of raw asbestos ore excluding any process directly associated with the mining of the ore and/or the manufacturing and industrial finishing of the following products using raw asbestos: asbestos cement or asbestos-cement products, asbestos friction products, asbestos filters, asbestos textiles, asbestos paper and card, asbestos jointing, packaging and reinforcement materials, asbestos floor coverings, asbestos fillers.[244] Working on products containing asbestos ('κατεργασία

237. Section 20(1) *ibid.*
238. Section 20(3) *ibid.*
239. Section 20(2) *ibid.*
240. Regulations on Air Pollution Control (Prevention and Reduction of Air Pollution by Asbestos) ('οι περί Ελέγχου της Ρύπανσης της Ατμόσφαιρας (Πρόληψη και Μείωση της Ατμοσφαιρικής Ρύπανσης από Αμίαντο) Κανονισμοί') No. 528 of 2002, OG III(I) No. 3650 of 1 Nov. 2002, p. 5655, as last amended by Regulations on Air Pollution Control (Prevention and Reduction of Air Pollution by Asbestos) ('οι περί Ελέγχου της Ρύπανσης της Ατμόσφαιρας (Πρόληψη και Μείωση της Ατμοσφαιρικής Ρύπανσης από Αμίαντο) Κανονισμοί') No. 412 of 2021, OG III(I) No. 5607 of 4.10.2010, p. 3047.
241. Council Directive 87/217/EEC of 19 Mar. 1987 on the prevention and reduction of environmental pollution by asbestos, OJ L 085, 28 Mar. 1987, p. 40.
242. Regulation 4 KDP 528/2002.
243. Regulation 2 *ibid.*, which corresponds to Art. 2(1) Directive 87/217/EEC. The French term mentioned in the directive is 'amiante', the German one 'Asbest' and the Dutch one 'asbest'.
244. Regulation 2 KDP 528/2002, which corresponds to Art. 2(3) Directive 87/217/EEC. The French term stated in the directive is 'utilisation de l'amiante', the German one 'Verwendung von Asbest' and the Dutch one 'gebruik van asbest'.

προϊόντων που περιέχουν αμίαντο') means activities other than the use of asbestos, which are liable to release asbestos into the environment.[245]

56. The relevant application and necessary documentation that must be filed along with the evaluation procedure and criteria are regulated by Law No. 187(I)/2002, as per the above stated. In addition, it is prescribed that for issuing such a permit, it must be ensured that the concentration of asbestos emitted through the discharge ducts into the air during the use of asbestos does not exceed a limit value of 0.1 mg/m^3 (milligrams of asbestos per m^3 of air discharged).[246] This obligation may not be imposed on plants emitting less than 5,000 m^3/hour total gaseous discharges, where the discharge of asbestos into the air is not more than 0.5 g per hour at any time under normal operating conditions. When this exemption applies, the Minister takes appropriate measures in order to ensure that the thresholds referred to above are not exceeded.[247] Compliance with the limit values is ensured through regular measurements performed by the operator or the Minister.[248] The measurements are performed with certain methods specified in this law.[249] In case that another procedure, which gives equivalent results, is used, special mention needs to be made in the operating conditions of the permit.[250] Should this method involve a system of continuous measurement or monitoring of dust emissions, it should be accompanied by a proper alarm system that is activated upon excess of limit values.[251]

57. The operator of any plant, where activities involving the use of asbestos or working of products containing asbestos takes place, has the following duties apart from the statutory one of obtaining an air-waste permit. He must take all necessary measures to ensure that asbestos emissions into the air are, as far as reasonably practicable, reduced at source and prevented using the best available technology and not entailing excessive cost.[252] Further, he has to comply with the limit values set out in KDP 528/2002[253] and keep a record of measurements, in which performed measurements are to be documented along with reasons for any excess thereof. This record must be available for inspection at any time.[254] The last obligation is performing yearly measures of asbestos emissions into plant's air waste and forwarding the results of those to the Minister.[255]

245. Regulation 2 KDP 528/2002, which corresponds to Art. 2(4) Directive 87/217/EEC. The French term stated in the directive is 'travail des produits contenant de l'amiante', the German one 'Bearbeitung asbesthaltiger Erzeugnisse' and the Dutch one 'werken met asbesthoudende produkten'.
246. Regulation 5(1) KDP 528/2002, which corresponds to Art. 4(1) Directive 87/217/EEC.
247. Regulation 5(2) KDP 528/2002, which corresponds to Art. 4(2) and (3) Directive 87/217/EEC.
248. Regulation 9(1) KDP 528/2002, which corresponds to Art. 6(2) Directive 87/217/EEC.
249. These are specified in Annex KDP 528/2002, which corresponds to Annex B Directive 87/217/EEC.
250. Regulation 9(1) KDP 528/2002.
251. Regulation 9(2) *ibid.*
252. Regulation 6(a) *ibid.*, which corresponds to Art. 3(1) Directive 87/217/EEC.
253. Regulation 6(b) KDP 528/2002.
254. Regulation 6(c) *ibid.*
255. Regulation 6(d) *ibid.*

58. On his part, the Minister takes the measures necessary to ensure that activities involving the working of products containing asbestos do not cause significant air pollution by asbestos fibres or dust,[256] and the demolition of buildings, structures and installations containing asbestos and the removal therefrom of asbestos or materials containing asbestos involving the release of asbestos fibres or dust do not cause significant asbestos air pollution.[257] Equally, the Minister takes the measures necessary to ensure that in the course of the transport and deposition of waste containing asbestos fibres or dust, no such fibres or dust is released into the air and no liquids which may contain asbestos fibres are spilled[258] and where waste containing asbestos fibres or dust is landfilled at sites authorized for the purpose, such waste is so treated, packaged or covered, with account being taken of local conditions, that the release of asbestos particles into the environment is prevented.[259] Lastly, the Minister ensures that the EC is notified of the procedures and methods being used together with the information relevant to assess the pertinence of such procedures and methods.[260] He also informs the EC about the results from the application of these regulations regarding prevention and reduction of air pollution by asbestos.[261]

59. Any person violating these regulations is committing an offence. If found guilty by a court of law, he may be imprisoned for up to one year or convicted to pay a fine of up to EUR 34,200.[262]

VII. Ensuring Compliance of Plants Requiring a Permit

60. Acting contrary to or failing to comply with provisions of this law is an administrative as well as a criminal offence, as elaborated below. Cyprus has no special legal system for enforcement and mandatory carrying out of administrative acts.

A. Administrative Sanctions Related to Plants Requiring a Permit

61. If an inspector finds violation of any condition of an air-waste permit, he may at his discretion serve the operator with an improvement notification ('ειδοποίηση βελτίωσης') that has a statutory-specified content. In particular, it contains the fact of violation finding,[263] the specific operating condition(s) that were violated[264] and a time period of no less than twenty-one days, within which this violation has to cease.[265] Should the violation continue after this time period has

256. Regulation 7(a) *ibid.*, which corresponds to Art. 7 Directive 87/217/EEC.
257. Regulation 7(b) KDP 528/2002, which corresponds to Art. 7 Directive 87/217/EEC.
258. Regulation 8(a) KDP 528/2002, which corresponds to Art. 8 Directive 87/217/EEC.
259. Regulation 8(b) *ibid.*
260. Regulation 12(a) *ibid.*, which corresponds to Art. 6(3) Directive 87/217/EEC.
261. Regulation 12(b) KDP 528/2002.
262. Regulation 11 *ibid.*, s. 26(2) Law No. 187(I)/2002.
263. Section 22(1)(a) *ibid.*
264. Section 22(1)(b) *ibid.*
265. Section 22(1)(c) *ibid.*

lapsed, the inspector may serve the operator with a notification of prohibition ('απαγορευτική ειδοποίηση'), which sets out the particular measures specified in the improvement notification that the operator failed to implement,[266] the direct measures concerning the plant's cessation of activities[267] and that the plant's reoperation prerequisites full compliance with the measures stated in the improvement notification.[268]

62. A notification of prohibition may also be issued even prior to its operation, if it is estimated that a danger of serious damage to any person or the environment is anticipated either through the manner of its operation, which shall lead to fire, explosion, emission of any toxic substance, or through serious violation of the air-waste permit conditions.[269] This notification specifies the reasons leading to such danger be anticipated,[270] instructions for specific measures that must be taken for elimination or mitigation of such danger[271] and a time period, after which the plant shall cease operating, if the reasons leading to such danger still exist and the specific measures are not taken.[272] In the event that the danger is imminent, the prohibited notification shall also set out the direct steps for the plant's cessation of activities. It shall be further stated that the plant shall not operate until the reasons leading to such danger lapse and specific measures are taken.[273]

63. It is lastly foreseen that the state and the public officers do not bear any responsibility for any negative effects caused by compliance of any person with a notification of prohibition or an improvement notification. This shall not apply if action upon bad faith is proven.[274] Acting upon good faith is a fundamental principle of Cypriot administrative law. According to that, the administration must avoid acting in a non-consistent, contradictory and bad-faith manner that results in deceiving or troubling the citizen without just cause and interfering with his justified confidence towards the administration.[275] Good faith is understood as a part of natural justice, according to common law.[276] With reference to the burden of proof, it is settled that the presumption of the administration acting in good faith remains valid until the opposite is proven.[277] The obligation of the administration to act in good faith is not new in Cyprus. It can be traced back to 1859, when Cyprus was a part of the Ottoman Empire. It had been prescribed that all state officers, aside from

266. Section 22(2)(a) *ibid.*
267. Section 22(2)(b) *ibid.*
268. Section 22(2)(c) *ibid.*
269. Section 22(3) *ibid.*
270. Section 22(4)(a) *ibid.*
271. Section 22(4)(b) *ibid.*
272. Section 22(4)(c) *ibid.*
273. Section 22(4) *ibid.*
274. Section 22(6) *ibid.*
275. Section 51(1) Law No. 158(I)/1999.
276. *Byrne v. Kinematograph Renters Society Ltd* [1958] 2 All ER 579 and *University of Ceylon v. Fernando* [1960] 1 All ER 631 cited in: *The Republic v. Georghiades* (1972) 3 CLR 594 (672).
277. *Suleiman v. the Republic* (1987) 3 CLR 224 (225).

being willing to apply for laws, regulations, decrees and orders, preserving the dignity of their service and respecting human rights, were expected by law to protect subjects from any injustice and damage and apply the principles of justice and equity.[278]

B. Criminal Sanctions Related to Plants Requiring a Permit

64. Generally, any person violating or failing to comply with the provisions of this law or the regulations issued thereunder is guilty of an offence and may be imprisoned for up to one year or convicted to a fine of up to EUR 34,200 unless a different penalty is set out.[279] Further, more specific offences are related to operating without an air-waste permit, violation of operating conditions, not complying with a notification, inspections and commercial secrets.

65. Operating or knowingly allowing the operation of a plant requiring a permit without an air-waste permit,[280] or in a manner incompatible with any operating condition attached thereto,[281] is an offence. If the accused is found guilty, he may be imprisoned for up to one year or convicted to a fine of up to EUR 34,200.[282] Act or omission of a third party may be considered as a defence, under the condition that the accused provides the prosecution office with information helping to identify and locate this third party at least seven days prior to the hearing,[283] or alternatively, a leave is given by the court.[284] The third party may be found guilty, regardless of whether the initially accused person is convicted or not.[285] Especially if the offence relates to violating any operating condition of the air-waste permit, the accused may put forward the defence that such violation was due to action or omission of a third party, an accident or any other cause beyond his control. However, he must prove that all reasonable protection measures for avoiding such violation were taken and upon realizing that such violation has taken place, all practicable remedial steps without any undue delay were taken.[286] Further defence concerning the same offence, in cases that an employee is accused, is that his actions or omissions constituting the relevant offence were mere instructions given by the employer, whereas the accused had no reason to believe that complying with such instructions would lead him to commit such crime. This defence may also be put forward in cases of violating instructions of the Minister regarding the location of the plant.[287]

278. Article 5 Orders on Duties of General Administrators, Administrators, Sub-Administrators and Mayors of 13 Safar 1275, in *Nicolaides*, Ottoman Codes (in Greek), Istanbul, 1869, Vol. I, p. 792.
279. Sections 15(1) and 26(2) Law No. 187(I)/2002.
280. Section 15(1)(a) *ibid.*
281. Section 15(1)(b) and (c) *ibid.*
282. Sections 15(1) and 26(2) *ibid.*
283. Section 15(3)(a)(i) *ibid.*
284. Section 15(3)(a)(ii) *ibid.*
285. Section 15(3)(b) *ibid.*
286. Section 15(2) *ibid.*
287. Section 15(4) *ibid.*

66. Operating a plant, while it has been extended, amended or otherwise changed, without a new permission or a written confirmation by the Minister, is also an offence,[288] which may lead to imprisonment for up to three years or conviction to a fine of up to EUR 500,000.[289] The same penalties may be enforced for refusal or failure to comply with a notification of prohibition as well as failure to comply within the set time period or any reasonable time period.[290]

67. The set of criminal offences related to the inspections are the following. Any person obstructing an inspector during the performance of his duties or exercise of his powers commits an offence.[291] The same applies to anyone obstructing any police officer or other person, who provides an inspector with lawful assistance, from entering the premises together with an inspector,[292] or fails to comply with an order of an inspector,[293] or fails to provide any book or document within reasonable time to an inspector, when this is required pursuant to section 25(1)(i) Law No. 187(I)/2002, unless he is unaware that this is requested by an inspector,[294] had no access to it[295] or had no authority to do so.[296] Providing an inspector with no information or alternatively with information that is not true, accurate or complete, equally constitutes an offence, when performed by the operator, any person in the plant or any person, who according to reasonable belief of the inspector was employed or had any connection to the plant during the last three months.[297] Lastly, an operator, its representatives or its employees, who do not provide safe access to an inspector and any accompanying party of his to any part of the plant[298] or do not provide said persons with reasonable means for tests, measurements, inspections or examinations, under the condition that they are authorized to do so.[299] If said persons are found guilty, they may be imprisoned for up to three years or convicted to a fine of up to EUR 500,000.[300] In the event that said offences are committed by a public officer with the consent of or in cooperation with any other public officer, the latter shall also be prosecuted.[301]

68. Information obtained directly or indirectly by a person during the exercise of their duties pursuant to this law is confidential. Especially, when this information relates to commercial secrets ('εμπορικά μυστικά'), its disclosure is an offence.[302] Special mention on commercial secrecy ('εμπορικό απόρρητο' in

288. Section 20(4) *ibid.*
289. Section 26(2) *ibid.*
290. Sections 22(5), 15(1) and 26(2) *ibid.*
291. Section 26(1)(a) *ibid.*
292. Section 26(1)(b) *ibid.*
293. Section 26(1)(c) *ibid.*
294. Section 26(1)(d)(i) *ibid.*
295. Section 26(1)(d)(ii) *ibid.*
296. Section 26(1)(d)(iii) *ibid.*
297. Section 26(1)(e) *ibid.*
298. Section 26(1)(f)(i) *ibid.*
299. Section 26(1)(f)(ii) *ibid.*
300. Sections 15(1) and 26(2) *ibid.*
301. Section 26(3) *ibid.*
302. Section 30 *ibid.*

Greek, 'secret commercial' in French, 'Firmen- und Geschäftsgeheimnis' in German, 'handelsgeheim' in Dutch) and its exclusion from information available to the public or provided to other European authorities has been made in the implemented directives.[303] Disclosing such secrets is, however, no offence, when it takes place with the consent of the operator or the person entitled to use or keep this secret.[304] Equally no offence is committed, when disclosure is necessary for the discloser's statutory duty to apply any law,[305] during criminal procedure[306] or any investigation performed on behalf of the Minister or the Council of Ministers.[307]

69. Special mention is made of legal persons. If any of the above-stated offences is performed by such with the consent of or in agreement with any chief executive officer, chairman, director, secretary or another officer of this legal person, both of them, that being the legal person and the natural person, shall be prosecuted and convicted, if found guilty.[308]

70. Generally, the competent authority to initiate all criminal procedures is the Attorney General. Especially criminal procedures for criminal offences under this law may be initiated by local authorities as well, under the condition that these offences are committed within their boundaries.[309] However, the afore-state offences related to operation of a plant without a permit or not in conformity with the issued permit and with regard to inspections may be settled out-of-court.[310] This process is initiated with the competent authority, that being the inspector-in-chief or an inspector, as the case may be, issuing a notice specifying the offence, the time that it was done and the amount due.[311] The competent authority may withdraw or amend the notice, if new indications satisfying such withdrawal or amendment arise and a duly reasoned decision in writing is notified to the affected person.[312] If the amount due, which can vary up to EUR 20,000 depending on the severity of the offence, is paid within fourteen days no criminal proceedings shall be initiated.[313] Upon settlement, the competent authority issues a receipt stating the name of the person believed to have performed the offence, a brief statement of the offence, the place and the date that it was done and the amount paid.[314] Furthermore, the notice may include a request to perform or abide an activity. Should the affected person not comply with

303. Article 7 Directive 84/360/EEC, Art. 9 Directive 89/369/EEC, Art. 8 Directive 89/429/EEC, Art. 12(3) Directive 1999/13/EC, Art. 7(5) Directive 2006/21/EC.
304. Section 30(a) Law No. 187(I)/2002.
305. Section 30(b) *ibid.*
306. Section 30(c) *ibid.*
307. Section 30(d) *ibid.*
308. Section 31 *ibid.*
309. Section 29 *ibid.*
310. Sections 26A(1)(a) & (b) and 15, 20(4) & 26(1) and (2) *ibid.*
311. Section 26A(2) *ibid.*
312. Section 26A(8) *ibid.*
313. Section 26A(5) *ibid.*
314. Section 26A(4) *ibid.*

this request within forty-eight hours, the competent authorities may issue an out-of-court fine double the initial amount. Further, it is deemed that a new offence is being committed and the competent authorities shall initiate criminal proceedings.[315]

C. Other Sanctions Related to Plants Requiring a Permit

71. During a criminal procedure regarding penal offences, those being: violation of the operator's obligations; operation without an air-waste permit or in violation thereof; operation of an extended, amended or significantly changed plant without an air-waste permit; and for failing to comply with a notification of prohibition, an application for an interim order prohibiting the continuation of the alleged illegal act may be filed.[316] It may be filed ex parte with the President of the District Court by the Attorney General or by an interested local authority.[317] If granted, this interim order expires upon the final decision on the initiated penal procedure.[318]

72. Following conviction of an accused operator for offences related to his statutory obligations (section 11), plants requiring a permit (section 15), operating an amended, expanded or significantly changed plant requiring a permit, without authorization of such a change (section 20(4)), comply with notification or prohibition (section 22(5)), the court may in addition to those order the immediate termination of the specific plant's operation for as long and under the conditions that it deems fit.[319] Failure to comply with such order is a new penal offence that may lead to imprisonment of up to two years and/or a monetary fine of up to EUR 34,200.[320]

§5. Plants Not Requiring a Permit

73. Plants not listed in Annexes II and III of this law are *plants not requiring a permit* ('μη αδειοδοτούμενες εγκαταστάσεις'), as no air-waste permit is needed. However, their operation is not unregulated.

I. Provisions in Law No. 187(I)/2002

74. The operating conditions of plants not requiring a permit are set out in regulations issued by the Council of Ministers and may address the same issues as operating conditions of an air-waste permit do, apart from specifying the location of the plant. In particular, these are technical standards for any machines or equipment

315. Section 26A(3)(a)&(b) ibid.
316. Section 27(1) *ibid.*
317. Section 27(2) and (4) *ibid.*
318. Section 27(1) *ibid.*
319. Section 28(1) *ibid.*
320. Section 28(2) *ibid.*

used in the plant,[321] emission limit values of any particular substance or group of substances emitted by the plant into the air,[322] equipment that must be installed and used to prohibit emission of substances into the air or to make them hazard-free before their emission,[323] quality standards of any material, including fuel, used in the plant,[324] equipment or organs that must be installed and used to measure concentrations, rate of emission or total amount of any substance emitted into the air in a particular time period or any other parameter of plant operation,[325] equipment for measuring that the operator must install on its own expenses, at spots approved by the Director of the Department of Labor Inspection for measuring air quality, conditions or quality standards regarding erection of stacks for emissions into the air,[326] reasonable help for measurements and collecting samples of any substances used in the plant or emitted in the air,[327] measurement schedule of the operator, technical reports that may include measurement reports and other environmental data and the frequency of their submission to the Minister,[328] organs, equipment and systems for data storage and transmission,[329] and reports of the operator on environmental management of matters regarding air pollution control.[330]

75. These regulations may include provisions on transition periods for specific categories of plants not requiring a permit. During those, reasonable restrictions may be imposed.[331] In addition, the regulations may be retroactively binding, as long as no obligation is retroactively imposed.[332]

76. An inspector finding that the plant or the equipment of the operator does not meet the operating standards set out for emissions into the air may be authorized by such regulations to serve notification of improvement.[333] Similarly, it may be foreseen that a prohibition notification is served, if serious danger to the health of any person or the environment is likely to be caused through the operation of a plant in violation of such regulations.[334] Operators, importers, constructors, suppliers or anyone maintaining the equipment used in the plant not requiring a permit may be requested to provide information via such regulations.[335] Regulations may further set out criminal offences for violation of their provisions or of prohibition imposed according to the same[336] and relevant penalties that may be imprisonment of no

321. Section 21(1)(a) *ibid.*
322. Section 21(1)(b) *ibid.*
323. Section 21(1)(c) *ibid.*
324. Section 21(1)(d) *ibid.*
325. Section 21(1)(e) *ibid.*
326. Section 21(1)(f & g) *ibid.*
327. Section 21(1)(h) *ibid.*
328. Section 21(1)(i) *ibid.*
329. Section 21(1)(j) *ibid.*
330. Section 21(1)(k) *ibid.*
331. Section 21(2) *ibid.*
332. Section 21(2A) *ibid.*
333. Section 21(3)(b) *ibid.*
334. Section 21(3)(c) *ibid.*
335. Section 21(3)(f) *ibid.*
336. Section 21(3)(a) *ibid.*

more than one year or a monetary fine of no more than EUR 5,130.[337] Any defence of general nature or limited to specific circumstances may also be articulated.[338]

II. Operating Conditions of Plants Not Requiring a Permit

77. Regulations have been issued by the Council of Ministers.[339] Air wastes of plants not requiring a permit are to be emitted into the air via stacks in a regulated manner aiming at effective environmental protection.[340] These plants and their equipment must be constructed and operated according to conditions set out therein and comply with the emission limit values equally specified therein.[341] Said conditions and values vary depending on the nature of the plants involved and are demonstrated in Table 2.[342]

Table 2 Operating Conditions of Plants Not Requiring a Permit

Type of Plant	*Smoke Scale*	*Emission of Dust*	*CO Emission*
Furnace of up to 5 MW burning liquid fuel	Up to three of Bacharach scale, CO_2 level more than 10% and oxygen level less than 7.5%	n/a	n/a
Furnace of up to 5 MW burning coal/wood/paper/dry olive stones/nuts remains	n/a	150 mg/nm^3 on an oxygen volume ratio of 7% for coal, 11% for wood, dry olive stones or nuts remains and 12% for paper	200 mg/nm^3 on an oxygen volume ratio of 7% for coal and 11% for wood, dry olive stones or nuts remains and 12% for paper

337. Section 21(3)(e) *ibid.*
338. Section 21(3)(d) *ibid.*
339. Regulations on the Control of Air Pollution (Plants Not Requiring a Permit) No. 170 of 2004, OG III(I) No. 3827 of 26 Mar. 2004, p. 1193 (hereinafter 'KDP 170/2004'). They have been amended through: Regulations on the Control of Air Pollution (Non-Authorised Plants) (Amendment) No. 198 of 2008, OG III(I) No. 4280 of 30 May 2008, p. 1691; Regulations on the Control of Air Pollution (Non-Authorised Plants) (Amendment) No. 219 of 2013, OG III(I) No. 4688 of 28 Jun. 2013, p. 1361; Regulations on the Control of Air Pollution (Non-Authorised Plants) (Amendment) No. 184 of 2015, OG III(I) No. 4875 of 29 May 2015, p. 1231; Regulations on the Control of Air Pollution (Non-Authorised Plants) (Amendment) No. 228 of 2018, OG III(I) No. 5103 of 27 Jul. 2018, p. 1438; and Regulations on the Control of Air Pollution (Non-Authorised Plants) (Amendment) No. 108 of 2021, OG III(I) No. 5479 of 12 Mar. 2021.
340. Regulation 4(1) KDP 170/2004.
341. Regulation 5(1) *ibid.*
342. Annex I *ibid.*

Type of Plant	*Smoke Scale*	*Emission of Dust*	*CO Emission*
Furnace of 5–50 MW burning liquid fuel	Up to three of Bacharach scale, CO_2 level more than 10% and oxygen level less than 7.5%	100 mg/nm^3 on an oxygen volume ratio of 3%	200 mg/nm^3 on an oxygen volume ratio of 3%
Furnace of 5–50 MW burning coal/ wood/paper/dry olive stones/nuts remains	n/a	100 mg/nm^3 on an oxygen volume ratio of 7% for coal and 11% for wood, dry olive stones or nuts remains	200 mg/nm^3 on an oxygen volume ratio of 7% for coal and 11% for wood, dry olive stones or nuts remains
Production of ready-mixed concrete	n/a	100 mg/nm^3	n/a
Grinding, sifting, transporting, mixture, storage, packing, dehydrating or other natural processing	n/a	Reasonably best methods for limiting the emission of dust into the environment	n/a

78. In case of plants not requiring a permit that emit smoke from a furnace burning liquid or solid fuel, additional requirements are foreseen. In particular, black smoke, which means smoke causing tarnishing ('αμαύρωση') of more than No. 4 on the Bacharach scale,[343] may be emitted from a stack of such a plant for no longer than ten minutes in aggregate in any period of eight hours.[344] This is extended to eighteen minutes, if the stack is connected to two furnaces, to twenty-four minutes, if the stack is connected to three furnaces, and to twenty-nine minutes, if the stack is connected to four or five furnaces.[345] Lastly, upon starting the operation of such a furnace, which is additionally at ambient temperature, black smoke may be emitted for a period of less than fifteen minutes.[346]

79. Further obligations are foreseen for operators. These include reasonably affording the performance of measurements and taking samples of any substances used in the plant or emitted into the air. Such help includes building proper furnace platforms and glory holes for securing free and safe access.[347] Equipment and organs for measurement of drop of pressure, in cases that bag filters are used for

343. Annex II(2) *ibid.*
344. Annex II(1)(a) *ibid.*
345. Annex II(1)(b) *ibid.*
346. Annex II(1)(c) *ibid.*
347. Regulation 6(1)(a) *ibid.*

limiting the emission of dust in the air, must be installed. In addition, documentation of the data related to the drop in pressure in a special book is to be performed daily.[348] Stock of spare and replacement parts of the equipment installed and used for limiting the emission of substances in the air must also be available.[349] An annual report on environmental management of matters related to control of air pollution, the specific content of which is being specified by a Decree of the Minister, is to be prepared and submitted to the Minister until 31 March. However, plants using furnace of up to 5 MW do not have to submit such a report,[350] but are obliged to keep data and information on the maintenance of furnace and emission of air waste.[351]

80. Burning fuel coal ('άνθρακα'), natural or synthetic gas ('φυσικό ή σύνθετο αέριο'), light fuel oil, diesel oil, kerosene, wood not impregnated with or covered by any chemical substance, dry olive stones, nuts remains, paper not impregnated with or covered by any chemical substances may be used by plants not requiring a permit. Burning of other substances, as well as their possession for the purpose of burning, is prohibited.[352]

III. Ensuring Compliance Regarding Plants Not Requiring a Permit

A. Administrative Sanctions Regarding Plants Not Requiring a Permit

81. In a manner similar to the aforementioned on plants not requiring a permit, if an inspector finds that the plant does not operate in accordance with the operating standards or within the limit values set out in the regulations, he may at his discretion serve the operator with an improvement notification ('ειδοποίηση βελτίωσης'). In this, the inspector's findings shall be stated,[353] along with the necessary measures for lifting the violation[354] and a time period of no less than twenty-one days, within which this violation must cease.[355] Should the violation continue after the lapse of set time period, the inspector may serve the operator with a notification of prohibition ('απαγορευτική ειδοποίηση'). This shall set out the particular measures specified in the improvement notification that the operator failed to implement,[356] direct measures for the plant's closing down[357] and that the plant's operation shall only recommence upon full compliance with the measures specified in the improvement notification.[358]

348. Regulation 6(1)(b) *ibid.*
349. Regulation 6(1)(c) *ibid.*
350. Regulation 6(1)(d) *ibid.*
351. Regulation 6(2) *ibid.*
352. Regulation 7 *ibid.*
353. Regulation 10(1)(a) *ibid.*
354. Regulation 10(1)(b) *ibid.*
355. Regulation 10(1)(c) *ibid.*
356. Regulation 10(2)(a) *ibid.*
357. Regulation 10(2)(b) *ibid.*
358. Regulation 10(2)(c) *ibid.*

82. A notification of prohibition may also be issued even prior to its operation, if it is estimated that a danger of serious damage to any person or the environment is anticipated either through the manner of its operation, which shall lead to fire, explosion, emission of any toxic substance, or through serious violation of the air-waste permit conditions.[359] This notification shall specify the reasons leading to such danger be anticipated,[360] instructions for specific measures that must be taken for elimination or mitigation of such danger[361] and a time period, after which the plant shall stop operating, if the reasons leading to such danger still exist and the specific measures are not taken.[362] In the event that the danger is imminent, the notification of prohibition shall also set out the direct steps for the plant's closing down. It shall be further stated that the plant shall not operate until the reasons leading to such danger lapse and the specific measures materialize.[363]

B. Penal Sanctions Regarding Plants Not Requiring a Permit

83. Any person violating or failing to comply with said regulations is committing a penal offence.[364] Refusing or failing to comply with a notification of prohibition, as well as failing to timely comply with the content of an improvement notification is also a penal offence.[365] The accused may put forward as a defence that he was ensured of the plant fulfilling the demands set out in these regulations, due to the terms of the contract with the supplier of the equipment.[366] Additionally, he may purport that he took all reasonable measures and acted with due attention for avoiding to commit this crime,[367] whereas upon realizing that the plant was not complying with said demands, he terminated its operation.[368] This defence may be put forward, only under the condition that the accused informed the chief inspector of the plant not complying with said demands without any delay and gave to him the name of his supplier,[369] or alternatively a leave was granted by the court.[370] If found guilty by a court of law, he may be imprisoned for up to one year and/or convicted to a fine of no more than EUR 5,130.[371]

84. Especially for violating the provisions on allowed fuels, the defence is foreseen that the accused was an employee and acted according to instruction or order given to him by or on behalf of his employee. In addition, the accused must prove

359. Regulation 10(3) *ibid.*
360. Regulation 10(3)(a) *ibid.*
361. Regulation 10(3)(b) *ibid.*
362. Regulation 10(3)(c) *ibid.*
363. Regulation 10(3) *ibid.*
364. Regulation 8 *ibid.*
365. Regulation 10(4) *ibid.*
366. Regulation 9(1)(a) *ibid.*
367. Regulation 9(1)(b) *ibid.*
368. Regulation 9(1)(c) *ibid.*
369. Regulation 9(2)(a) *ibid.*
370. Regulation 9(2)(b) *ibid.*
371. Regulation 8 *ibid.*

that he had no reason to believe that complying with such instruction or order could have led to committing the crime, for which he is accused.[372]

§6. ARCHIVE

85. An archive on applications submitted for obtaining or renewing an air-waste permit is established.[373] This also includes information on air-waste permits granted, the operation conditions attached to them and any later amendments to them[374] and the results of measurements of emissions into the air.[375] Keeping and maintaining this archive is entrusted to the Minister.[376] An operator may apply to the Minister for exempting any operation condition from publication. The Minister shall decide on this according to its discretionary power, but he shall take into consideration the private interest of the applicant regarding commercial secrets, his harm from exposing those as well as public interest.[377]

86. Without prejudice to the general provisions of Law on Access to Environmental Information, any person may apply for a copy of any entry into the archive and receive such following payment of a fee, which is determined by the Minister.[378] Up to this date, the website of the Ministry contained no information on the archive or on instructions as to providing access to same, despite the fact that promoting electronic access to environmental information has been one of the scopes of Law No. 119(I)/2004.

372. Regulation 9(3) *ibid.*
373. Section 18(1)(a) Law No. 187(I)/2002.
374. Section 18(1)(b) *ibid.*
375. Section 18(1)(c) *ibid.*
376. Section 18(1) *ibid.*
377. Section 19 *ibid.*
378. Section 18(2) *ibid.*

Chapter 3. Water Pollution

87. Water pollution control is regulated by Law on Water and Soil Pollution Control,[379] (hereinafter 'Law No. 106(I)/2002') as amended, that implements a number of directives of the EU,[380] the majority of which has been since repealed.[381] Law No. 106(I)/2002 has itself repealed the Law on Water Pollution Control of 1991.[382]

§1. Objective

88. This law does not set out explicitly its object. However, in view of the fact that European law has been implemented, it is safe to conclude that the purposes of the implemented directives have been adopted. Hence, it concerns:

- the quality requirements which surface freshwater used or intended for use in the abstraction of drinking water must meet after application of appropriate treatment;[383]
- reference methods of measurement and frequencies of sampling and analysis;[384]
- the quality of bathing water, with the exception of water intended for therapeutic purposes and water used in swimming pools;[385]
- taking appropriate steps to eliminate pollution of inland surface water, territorial waters, internal coastal waters and groundwater;[386]
- the protection or improvement of the quality of those running or standing freshwaters which support or which, if pollution were reduced or eliminated, would become capable of supporting fish belonging to indigenous species offering a natural diversity, or species the presence of which is judged desirable for water management purposes;[387]

379. Law on Water and Soil Pollution Control ('ο περί Ελέγχου της Ρύπανσης των Νερών και του Εδάφους Νόμος') No. 106 of 2002, OG I(I) No. 3621 of 12 Jul. 2002, p. 2121.
380. According to the preamble of Law No. 106(I)/2002, these are: Directive 75/440/EEC; Directive 79/869/EEC; Directive 76/160/EEC; Directive 76/464/EEC; Directive 78/659/EEC; Directive 79/923/EEC; Directive 80/68/EEC; Directive 82/176/EEC; Directive 84/156/EEC; Directive 83/513/EEC; Directive 84/491/EEC; Directive 86/280/EEC; Directive 91/271/EEC; Directive 91/676/EEC; Directive 96/61/EC; and Council Decision 77/795/EEC.
381. In particular Directives 75/440/EEC, 76/464/EEC, 78/659/EEC, 79/869/EEC, 79/923/EEC, 80/68/EEC and Council Decision 77/795/EEC have been repealed by Directive 2000/60/EC; Directive 76/160/EEC has been repealed by Directive 2006/7/EC; Directives 82/176/EEC, 83/513/EEC, 84/156/EEC, 84/491/EEC and 86/280/EEC have been repealed by Directive 2008/105/EC; Directive 96/61/EC has been repealed by Directive 2008/1/EC, which in turn has been repealed by Directive 2010/75/EU of the European Parliament and of the Council of 24 Nov. 2010 on industrial emissions (integrated pollution prevention and control), OJ L 334, 17 Dec. 2010, p. 17.
382. Law on Water Pollution Control ('ο περί Ελέγχου Ρύπανσης των Νερών Νόμος') No. 69 of 1991, OG I(I) No. 2585 of 29 Mar. 1991, p. 1089.
383. Article 1 Directive 75/440/EEC.
384. Article 1 Directive 79/869/EEC.
385. Article 1 Directive 76/160/EEC.
386. Articles 1 and 2 Directive 76/464/EEC.
387. Article 1(3) Directive 78/659/EEC.

- the quality of shellfish waters and contributes to the high quality of shellfish products directly edible by man;[388]
- the prevention of pollution of groundwater by substances belonging to certain families and groups of substances and as far as possible checking or eliminating the consequences of pollution which has already occurred;[389]
- laying down limit values for emission standards for mercury, meaning the chemical element mercury and the mercury contained in any of its compounds, in discharges from industrial plants, quality objectives for mercury in the aquatic environment, the time limits for compliance with the conditions of granted authorizations in the case of existing discharges, the reference methods of measurement enabling the mercury content in discharges and in the aquatic environment to be determined, and establishing a monitoring procedure;[390]
- laying down limit values for emission standards for cadmium, meaning the chemical element cadmium and the cadmium contained in any of its compounds, in discharges from industrial plants, quality objectives for cadmium in the aquatic environment, the time limits for compliance with the conditions of granted authorizations in the case of existing discharges, the reference methods of measurement enabling the cadmium content in discharges and in the aquatic environment to be determined, and establishing a monitoring procedure;[391]
- laying down limit values for emission standards for hexachlorocyclohexane (HCH), meaning the isomers of 1, 2, 3, 4, 5, 6-HCH, in discharges from industrial plants, quality objectives for HCH in the aquatic environment, the time limits for compliance with the conditions of granted authorizations in the case of existing discharges, the reference methods of measurement enabling the concentration of HCH in discharges and in the aquatic environment to be determined, and establishing a monitoring procedure;[392]
- laying down limit values for emission standards for dangerous substances, belonging to certain families and groups of substances,[393] in discharges from industrial plants, quality objectives for same substances in the aquatic environment, the time limits for compliance with the conditions of granted authorizations in the case of existing discharges, the reference methods of measurement enabling the content of such substances in discharges and in the aquatic environment to be determined, and establishing a monitoring procedure;[394]
- the protection of the environment from the adverse effects of waste water discharges from certain industrial sectors;[395]
- reducing water pollution caused or induced by nitrates from agricultural sources and preventing further such pollution;[396]

---

388. Article 1 Directive 79/923/EEC.
389. Article 1(1) Directive 80/68/EEC.
390. Articles 1(1) and 2(a) Directive 82/176/EEC and Arts 1(2) and 2(a) Directive 84/156/EEC.
391. Articles 1(1) and 2(a) Directive 83/513/EEC.
392. Articles 1(1) and 2(a) Directive 84/491/EEC.
393. Such dangerous substances are related to carbon tetrachloride, DDT and pentachlorophenol. *See* Annex II Directive 86/280/EEC.
394. Articles 1(1) and 2(a) *ibid.*
395. Article 1 Directive 91/271/EEC.
396. Article 1 Directive 91/676/EEC.

- achieving integrated prevention and control of pollution arising from certain activities[397] and laying down measures designed to prevent or, where that is not practicable, to reduce emissions in the air, water and land from the above-mentioned activities, including measures concerning waste, in order to achieve a high level of protection of the environment taken as a whole;[398] and
- the establishment of a common procedure for the exchange of information on the quality of surface freshwater in the Union.[399]

§2. Area of Application

89. The area of application is defined solely in a negative manner. More specifically, it is foreseen that no provision of this law provides any authorization regarding pollution control from ionizing radiation.[400] Further, this law is not applicable to plants underlying the provisions of the Law on Industrial Emissions.[401] However, a positive definition of the same could be deduced from the relevant provisions of the implemented directives, which in their majority apply to water, that being surface water,[402] bathing water,[403] inland surface water, territorial waters, internal coastal waters, groundwater,[404] waters designated as needing protection or improvement,[405] coastal and brackish waters designated as needing protection[406] and waters.[407] In view of this, Law No. 106(I)/2002 specifies that the term 'waters of Cyprus' ('νερά της Κύπρου') includes the territorial sea and all inland surface water and groundwater of Cyprus as well as all water of any sluice or public tank, but does not include waters of private culverts, drainage, municipal waste treatment plants and waters of private water tanks, reservoirs or other vessel or private tanks.[408] *Inland surface water* ('επιφανειακά χερσαία νερά') stands for surface water, except groundwater, and includes any river, creek or other streams, lake, conservation reservoir, or any part of those, natural or man-made of fresh, brackish or saltwater. Any reference to surface waters includes reference to canal or bed of such waters that are dry from time to time.[409] *Groundwater* ('υπόγεια νερά') means all water which is below the surface of the ground in the saturation zone and in direct

397. These are specified in detail in Annex I Directive 96/61/EC.
398. Article 1 *ibid.*
399. Article 1 77/795/EEC: Council Decision.
400. Section 4 Law No. 106(I)/2002.
401. Section 8(3) *ibid.*
402. Article 1(1) Directive 75/440/EEC.
403. Article 1(1) Directive 76/160/EEC.
404. Article 1(1) Directive 76/464/EEC.
405. Article 1(1) Directive 78/659/EEC.
406. Article 1 Directive 79/923/EEC.
407. Article 1(2) Directives 82/176/EEC, 83/513/EEC, 84/156/EEC, 84/491/EEC, 86/280/EEC.
408. Section 2 Law No. 106(I)/2002.
409. Section 2, *ibid.* This definition, by being very detailed, differs from the European one, according to which inland surface water ('εσωτερικά ύδατα επιφανείας' in Greek, 'eaux intérieures de surface' in French, 'oberirdische Binnengewässer' in German, 'oppervlaktewateren in het binnenland' in Dutch) means all static or flowing fresh surface water situated in the territory of a Member State (Art. 1(2)(a) Directive 76/464/EEC).

contact with the ground or subsoil.[410] Creek ('ρυάκι') is any flow of water on the surface of the land, either natural or man-made, but does not include any drainage belonging to local administration authority.[411]

§3. Competent Authorities

I. The Minister of Agriculture, Rural Development and the Environment

90. The Minister of Agriculture, Rural Development and the Environment (hereinafter 'the Minister') is a major player in this law, as this law's implementation is entrusted upon him. It is expected that he properly acts and takes all necessary measures, within his powers, so that all provisions of this law along with the conditions attached to permits are properly and sufficiently applied.[412] He ensures that effective control of quality of the waters of Cyprus is constantly performed and to this effect regular inspections are performed on the waters, soil and subsoil in areas, where groundwater exist or are likely to exist.[413] He further ensures that the quality of water according to quality standards set out in this law is preserved.[414]

91. For the purpose of protecting the waters of Cyprus, the Minister may issue decrees defining environmental quality standards regarding any category of the waters of Cyprus,[415] the categories of the waters of Cyprus and soils that due to special circumstances need special protection from pollution,[416] the methods to be used for sampling and definition of quality of any category of waters or soil[417] or of waste or any other objects or substances discharged with or without permit.[418] Said decrees may also define the areas or spots that for special reasons or due to circumstances prevailing there or due to being areas of special interest, no permit for discharging any waste or other substances shall be authorized. Alternatively, special conditions may be applicable with reference to waste discharge.[419] These decrees may further set out general conditions applicable to all permit holders or to permit holders of specific categories of plants,[420] and in particular, providing details on any substance or group of substances and any natural, chemical and microbiological

410. Section 2 Law No. 106(I)/2002, which corresponds to Art. 1(2)(a) Directive 80/68/EEC. In the Greek version of this directive mention to 'υπόγεια ύδατα' is made, in the French one to 'eaux souterraines' is made, in the German one to 'Grundwasser' and in the Dutch one to 'grondwater'.
411. Section 2 Law No. 106(I)/2002.
412. Section 3(1) *ibid.*
413. Section 3(2)(a) *ibid.*
414. Section 3(2)(b) *ibid.*
415. Section 5(1)(a) *ibid.*
416. Section 5(1)(b) *ibid.*
417. Section 5(1)(c)(i) *ibid.*
418. Section 5(1)(c)(ii) *ibid.*
419. Section 5(1)(d) *ibid.*
420. Section 5(1)(e) *ibid.*

parameters of discharged waste,[421] conditions and parameters of plant's operation,[422] technical requirements for any machines or equipment or organs for measurement used in the plant,[423] quality requirements of any material, including fuels used in the plant,[424] methods and procedures for the collection, transport, storage, process and disposal of waste resulting from the operation of the plant, including the authorized disposal sites[425] and any additional demands that the Minister may deem necessary for reducing pollution in the water or the soil for the purpose of effective protection of the water, the soil and public health.[426] Lastly, said decrees may specify the technology, technical standards of any equipment or construction, quality standards of any material as well as techniques and operation parameters that must be applied by certain categories of plants for the purpose of preventing water and soil pollution.[427]

II. The Council of Ministers

92. The Council of Ministers may issue regulations aiming at the effectiveness of the protection of the waters of Cyprus and its soil from pollution, under the condition that the Minister is not empowered to issue decrees pursuant to section 5(1) Law No. 106(I)/2002.[428] More practically, the Council of Ministers has the power to issue regulations on setting discharge limit values and regulating any other matter on discharge of certain substances,[429] those being Carbon tetrachloride (CCl_4), DDT, Pentachlorophenol (PCP), Aldrin, Dieldrin, Endrin, Isodrin, Hexachlorobenzene (HCB – C_6Cl_6), Hexachlorobutadiene (HCBD – C_4Cl_6), Trichloromethane ($CHCl_3$), 1,2-Dichloroethane (EDC), Trichloromethane (TRI), Tetrachloroethylene (PER), Trichlorobenzenes (TCB), Cadmium (Cd) and its compounds, Mercury (Hg) and its compounds and Hexachlorocyclohexane (HCH).[430] It should be noted that environmental quality standards ('norme de qualité environnementale' in French, 'Umweltqualitätsnorm' in German, 'milieukwaliteitsnorm' in Dutch), meaning the concentration of a particular pollutant or group of pollutants in water, sediment or biota which should not be exceeded in order to protect human health and the environment, have been set on a European level for all above-mentioned substances, apart from cyclodiene pesticides (Aldrin, Dieldrin, Endrin, Isodrin), in Annex I Part A to Directive 2008/105/EU, as amended.

421. Section 5(1A)(a) *ibid.*
422. Section 5(1A)(b) *ibid.*
423. Section 5(1A)(c) *ibid.*
424. Section 5(1A)(d) *ibid.*
425. Section 5(1A)(e) *ibid.*
426. Section 5(1A)(f) *ibid.*
427. Section 5(1)(f) *ibid.*
428. Section 5(2) *ibid.*
429. Section 34(1)(a) *ibid.*
430. Annex, Table 3, *ibid.* Cadmium, mercury, hexachlorobenzene and hexachlorobutadiene have been identified as priority hazardous substances (Annex X Directive 2000/60/EC).

93. Further, the Council of Ministers has the power to issue regulations on any matter regarding discharge of any other substance or waste or any measures for the protection of the waters of Cyprus,[431] on waste discharge into open sea through pipelines,[432] on the protection of groundwater,[433] on taking special measures for the protection of water and soil from areas of management and storage of hydrocarbons[434] and on taking special measures for the protection of inland surface water from hazardous substances and priority substances.[435] The terms 'hazardous substances' and 'priority substances' are not defined in this law. Thus the mandate of the Council of Ministers is extremely vague, allowing for wide discretion. However, it is fortunate that the intention to use these terms in the meaning of Directive 2000/60/EC can be attributed to the legislator. Hence, *hazardous substances* mean substances or groups of substances that are toxic, persistent and liable to bioaccumulate, and other substances or groups of substances which give rise to an equivalent level of concern,[436] and *priority substances* are substances listed in Annex X thereof.[437]

94. This law further empowers the Council of Ministers to issue regulations on numerous matters, those being: the spots on land or water, at which discharge may take place, and construction of exhaust ports for discharging;[438] the nature, origin, composition, temperature, volume and frequency of discharges and the time periods, during which discharges may take place;[439] necessary measures before or after discharging, the process of any substance that may affect the description of the substance being discharged or any other process for the purpose of eliminating pollution from discharging in controlled waters;[440] control of sludge originating from

431. Section 34(1)(b) Law No. 106(I)/2002.
432. Section 36A(2) *ibid.*
433. Section 34(1)(c) and (e) *ibid.*
434. Section 34(1)(d) *ibid.*
435. Section 34(1)(f) *ibid.*
436. Article 2(29) Directive 2000/60/EC. The French term is 'substances dangereuses', the German one 'gefährliche Stoffe' and the Dutch one 'gevaarlijke stoffen'.
437. These are: Alachlor, Anthracene, Atrazine, Benzene, Brominated diphenylethers, Cadmium and its compounds, Chloroalkanes (C10-13), Chlorfenvinphos, Chlorpyrifos (Chlorpyrifos-ethyl),1,2-dichloroethane, Dichloromethane, Di(2-ethylhexyl)phthalate (DEHP), Diuron, Endosulfan, Fluoranthene, Hexachlorobenzene, Hexachlorobutadiene, Hexachlorocyclohexane, Isoproturon, Lead and its compounds, Mercury and its compounds, Naphthalene, Nickel and its compounds, Nonylphenols, Octylphenols, Pentachlorobenzene, Pentachlorophenol, Polyaromatic hydrocarbons (PAH), Simazine, Tributyltin compounds, Trichlorobenzenes, Trichloromethane (chloroform), Trifluralin, Dicofol, Perfluorooctane sulfonic acid and its derivatives (PFOS), Quinoxyfen, Dioxins and dioxin-like compounds, Aclonifen, Bifenox, Cybutryne, Cypermethrin, Dichlorvos, Hexabromocyclododecanes (HBCDD), Heptachlor and heptachlor epoxide, Terbutryn. Art. 2(30) and Annex X *ibid.* The French term is 'substances prioritaires', the German one 'prioritäre Stoffe' and the Dutch one 'prioritaire stoffen'.
438. Section 34(2)(a) Law No. 106(I)/2002.
439. Section 34(2)(b) *ibid.*
440. Section 34(2)(c) *ibid.*

effluent treatment plants and being used in farming;[441] providing facilitation for collecting samples of discharged substances;[442] keeping archives or data regarding origin, composition, temperature, volume and frequency of discharges;[443] preparing statistics and providing other information to the Minister regarding nature, origin, composition, temperature, volume and frequency of discharges;[444] defining minimum criteria for inspections;[445] and penalties for violating the regulations.[446]

95. Another area that the Council of Ministers may regulate is that of sampling. In particular, it may define the manner of sampling, the amount of samples, the sample spots, the substances or matters to be collected, the frequency of collection and the relevant day and time.[447] Also, the Council of Ministers regulates matters relating to the archive that must be kept according to this law. More specifically, it sets out details regarding registration of applications for disposal permits,[448] issued permits,[449] any reports on monitoring and results of measurements according to conditions attached to permits,[450] environmental quality standards for any parts of the waters of Cyprus,[451] frequency of sampling and results of measurements for waters of any area,[452] any measures taken for the purpose of water rehabilitation,[453] dates of any rehabilitation of the quality of any parts of the waters of Cyprus[454] and any crimes committed in violation of this law.[455]

III. Technical Committee for the Protection of Waters and Soil

96. The Technical Committee for the Protection of Waters and Soil ('Τεχνική Επιτροπή για την Προστασία των Νερών και του Εδάφους') has been established via this law. It is composed of a representative from each of the following bodies: the Ministry of Labour and Social Security,[456] the Ministry of Agriculture, Rural Development and Environment,[457] the Ministry of Health,[458] the Ministry of

441. Section 34(2)(d) *ibid.*
442. Section 34(2)(e) *ibid.*
443. Section 34(2)(f) *ibid.*
444. Section 34(2)(g) *ibid.*
445. Section 34(2)(h) *ibid.*
446. Section 34(2)(i) *ibid.*
447. Section 26(2) *ibid.*
448. Section 28(1)(a) *ibid.*
449. Section 28(1)(b) *ibid.*
450. Section 28(1)(c) *ibid.*
451. Section 28(1)(d) *ibid.*
452. Section 28(1)(e) *ibid.*
453. Section 28(1)(f) *ibid.*
454. Section 28(1)(g) *ibid.*
455. Section 28(1)(h) *ibid.*
456. Table A, Part I(1)(a) *ibid.*
457. Table A, Part I(1)(b) *ibid.*
458. Table A, Part I(1)(c) *ibid.*

Interior,[459] the Ministry of Energy, Commerce, Industry and Tourism,[460] the Ministry of Communications and Works,[461] the Technical Chamber of Cyprus[462] and the Federation of Environmental Organizations of Cyprus.[463] Each representative may be accompanied at the sessions of the committee by a couple of scientific or technical advisors.[464] The main competence of the committee is to advise the Minister prior to issuing any regulations,[465] issuing a decree on determination of environmental quality standards,[466] granting a disposal permit[467] or deciding on termination, revocation or amendment of a disposal permit or the conditions attached to the same.[468]

97. The chairman of the committee is the representative of the Ministry of Agriculture, Rural Development and Environment whereas in his absence another person is being elected by the members present.[469] The chairman has the power to call meetings[470] and the duty to inform about any subject that shall be discussed at least seven days prior to the meeting.[471] Any such information needs to be detailed especially with reference to particulars relating to environmental quality standards,[472] the general terms of operation that are in force or must be adopted by specific categories of plants,[473] the disposal permit and the conditions, which are attached or should be attached to same,[474] the annulment, revocation or amendment of the permit under discussion or conditions of such[475] and the application form of a disposal permit.[476] The notice for the meeting of the committee along with the agenda and copies of the relevant documentation are also forwarded to the local authorities, when the matters under discussion relate directly or indirectly to their territorial competence.[477]

98. Extraordinary meetings may be requested by any member of the committee, provided that he states the reasons for such necessity and the matter, which should be discussed. Such a meeting is called by the chairman within fourteen days of the request thereof.[478]

---

459. Table A, Part I(1)(d) *ibid.*
460. Table A, Part I(1)(e) *ibid.*
461. Table A, Part I(1)(f) *ibid.*
462. Table A, Part I(1)(g) *ibid.*
463. Table A, Part I(1)(h) *ibid.*
464. Table A, Part I(3) *ibid.*
465. Section 5(1) *ibid.*
466. Table A, Part II(1)(a) *ibid.*
467. Table A, Part II(1)(b) *ibid.*
468. Table A, Part II(1)(c) *ibid.*
469. Table A, Part I(4) *ibid.*
470. Table A, Part I(6) *ibid.*
471. Table A, Part I(8) *ibid.*
472. Table A, Part I(9)(a) *ibid.*
473. Table A, Part I(9)(b) *ibid.*
474. Table A, Part I(9)(c) *ibid.*
475. Table A, Part I(9)(d) *ibid.*
476. Table A, Part I(9)(e) *ibid.*
477. Table A, Part I(10) *ibid.*
478. Table A, Part I(6) *ibid.*

IV. Inspector-in-Chief and Inspectors

99. For the purpose of effective application of the provisions of this law and the regulations or decrees issued, the Minister appoints a public employee of the Ministry as inspector-in-chief as well as other public employees of the Ministry as inspectors. The inspector-in-chief is under the supervision and the orders of the Minister, whereas the inspectors are under the supervision and the orders of the inspector-in-chief.[479] The Minister may also appoint other persons, who are not employed in the public sector and are properly qualified according to the Minister's discretion, to exercise such powers as it will be specified in their written appointment.[480] This shall also contain the conditions for the termination of their appointment. They underlie the instructions and the control of the inspector-in-chief,[481] whereas their fees are relevant to the services provided and are specified by the Minister after consultation with the Minister of Finance.[482]

100. The powers of the inspector-in-chief and the inspectors are related to entering plants, performing inspections at any part of those in safe conditions, requesting information and transferring samples outside the plants. In particular, these persons may enter any plant, in which they reasonably think that an activity takes place or is about to take place, which may lead to violation of any provision of this law. Such entry may take place during the activity or at any time if there is reasonable suspicion that any imminent danger of serious personal damage to any person exists.[483] They may be accompanied by a police officer or any other person, whose presence is necessary for the purpose of properly performing his duties.[484] More importantly, they may demand safe access to any part of the plant as well as reasonable means for performing any tests, measurements, inspections or examinations.[485]

101. They are free to perform tests and measurements,[486] as well as inspect, examine and check the operation of any machines and equipment in the plant or measurements and take photographs, as long as these actions are deemed necessary for the proper exercise of their duties.[487] Inspectors may also give instructions on stable operation conditions of any plant, any part thereof, any equipment or machine for a reasonable period and for the purpose of performing the above-mentioned tests, measurements and operation controls. However, this instruction may not lead to termination of any vital part of the production process or have any negative effect on the same process.[488]

---

479. Section 23(1) *ibid.*
480. Section 23(2) *ibid.*
481. Section 23(4) *ibid.*
482. Section 23(5) *ibid.*
483. Section 24(1)(a) *ibid.*
484. Section 24(4) *ibid.*
485. Section 24(1)(f) (i) and (ii) *ibid.*
486. Section 24(1)(b) *ibid.*
487. Section 24(1)(c) *ibid.*
488. Section 24(1)(g) *ibid.*

102. Inspectors have the authority to request any books or documents to be presented, under the condition that they reasonably believe that they contain information related to the scope of their inquisition.[489] Similarly they may require any information, which is relevant to the scope of the investigation, from the operator of the plant, any person in possession of the plant or any person, their representatives or their employees being present.[490] Information may also be requested from any person, for whom it is reasonably believed that he was employed in the plant or had any connection to the plant in the last three months, as long as such person is believed to have access thereto.[491] Lastly, any object or sample of any substance that is necessary for the purpose of further inquisition of an offence or of evidence before a court may be removed from the plant.[492]

V. Environmental Authority

103. The Environmental Service of the Ministry of Agriculture, Rural Development and Environment is the Environmental Authority ('Περιβαλλοντική Αρχή')[493] for the purpose of this law. Its duties concern the receiving of opinions and representations by the public, publishing announcements on suggestions and views and keeping archives, as will be elaborated below.

§4. Disposal Permit

104. A disposal permit ('άδεια απόρριψης αποβλήτων') is necessary for the lawful operation of any plant ('εγκατάσταση'),[494] that being any establishment or other stationary plant, including installations of mining waste, where one or more industrial activities as well as other directly associated activities standing in technical connection with the first one are carried out and may affect disposal and pollution.[495,496] Pollution ('ρύπανση') means the direct or indirect introduction, as a result of human activity, of substances, vibrations, heat or noise into water or land which may be harmful to human health or the quality of the environment, result in

489. Section 24(1)(d) *ibid.*
490. Section 24(1)(f)(iii) *ibid.*
491. Section 24(1)(h) *ibid.*
492. Section 24(1)(e) *ibid.*
493. Section 2 *ibid.*
494. Section 8(1) *ibid.*
495. Section 2 *ibid.*
496. The term 'plant' instead of 'installation' has been used here for the same reasons as in the control of air pollution (*see* above at footnote 74). The definition has been changed via Amending Law No. 181(I)/2013, whose purpose is to implement Directive 2010/75/EU. However, the definition set out is difference to that of the implemented directive, which reads: 'installation' ('installation' in the French version, 'Anlage' in the German one, 'installatie' in the Dutch one) means a stationary technical unit within which one or more activities listed in Annex I or in Part 1 of Annex VII are carried out, and any other directly associated activities on the same site which have a technical connection with the activities listed in those Annexes and which could have an effect on emissions and pollution (Art. 3(3) Directive 2010/75/EU).

damage to material property, or impair or interfere with amenities and other legitimate uses of the environment, to cause damage to living organisms living in water or land, to harm the water or land ecosystem or to destroy biological resources.[497]

I. Application for a Disposal Permit

105. The application for a disposal permit is to be submitted in a specific form, as this shall be defined by a decree of the Minister.[498] The requested information includes a description of the plant and its activities,[499] the first and auxiliary materials, substances, products and energy used in or produced in the plant,[500] the sources of emissions of solid and liquid waste from the plant,[501] the conditions of the site of the plant,[502] the nature and quantities of foreseeable solid and liquid waste disposed from the plant into waters and land as well as identification of significant effects of the disposals on the environment,[503] the proposed technology and other techniques for preventing or, where this is not possible, reducing disposal of solid and liquid waste from the plant,[504] measures for the prevention and recovery of solid and liquid waste generated by the plant,[505] measures planned to monitor disposals in water and land[506] and the main alternatives studied by the operator.[507] An application for a permit shall also include a non-technical summary of the aforementioned details[508] and a copy of the urban planning permission, building permission or certification of approval, whichever is applicable.[509] In the event that the application relates to a plant that underlies the provisions of Law No. 187(I)/2002, Law No. 185(I)/2011, or any other legislation regulating management issues of waste,

497. Section 2 Law No. 106(I)/2002, which is wider than the definition of *pollution* ('pollution' in French, 'Umweltverschmutzung' in German, 'verontreiniging' in Dutch) according to Art. 3(2) Directive 2010/75/EU, as well as Art. 1(2)(e) Directive 76/464/EEC, Art. 2(2) Directive 96/61/EEC, which were initially implemented via this law.
498. Section 9(1) Law No. 106(I)/2002.
499. Section 9(1)(a) *ibid.*, which corresponds to Art. 6(1) Directive 96/61/EEC, Art. 6(1)(a) Directive 2008/1/EC and Art. 12(1)(a) Directive 2010/75/EU.
500. Section 9(1)(b) Law No. 106(I)/2002, which corresponds to Art. 6(1) Directive 96/61/EEC, Art. 6(1)(b) Directive 2008/1/EC and Art. 12(1)(b) Directive 2010/75/EU.
501. Section 9(1)(c) Law No. 106(I)/2002, which corresponds to Art. 6(1) Directive 96/61/EEC, Art. 6(1)(c) Directive 2008/1/EC and Art. 12(1)(c) Directive 2010/75/EU.
502. Section 9(1)(d) Law No. 106(I)/2002, which corresponds to Art. 6(1) Directive 96/61/EEC, Art. 6(1)(d) Directive 2008/1/EC and Art. 12(1)(d) Directive 2010/75/EU.
503. Section 9(1)(e) Law No. 106(I)/2002, which corresponds to Art. 6(1) Directive 96/61/EEC, Art. 6(1)(e) Directive 2008/1/EC and Art. 12(1)(f) Directive 2010/75/EU.
504. Section 9(1)(f) Law No. 106(I)/2002, which corresponds to Art. 6(1) Directive 96/61/EEC, Art. 6(1)(f) Directive 2008/1/EC and Art. 12(1)(g) Directive 2010/75/EU.
505. Section 9(1)(g) Law No. 106(I)/2002, which corresponds to Art. 6(1) Directive 96/61/EEC, Art. 6(1)(g) Directive 2008/1/EC and is similar to Art. 12(1)(h) Directive 2010/75/EU.
506. Section 9(1)(i) Law No. 106(I)/2002, which corresponds to Art. 6(1) Directive 96/61/EEC, Art. 6(1)(i) Directive 2008/1/EC and Art. 12(1)(j) Directive 2010/75/EU.
507. Section 9(1)(j) Law No. 106(I)/2002, which is similar to Art. 6(1)(j) Directive 2008/1/EC and Art. 12(1)(k) Directive 2010/75/EU.
508. Section 9(3) Law No. 106(I)/2002, which corresponds to Art. 6(1) Directive 96/61/EEC, Art. 6(1) Directive 2008/1/EC and Art. 12(1) Directive 2010/75/EU.
509. Section 9(3) Law No. 106(I)/2002.

pollution or facing dangers emanating from storage, keeping or use of any substances, this shall be mentioned in the application. In addition, mention shall be made to technology or other techniques and measures that shall be applied to the plant and cause emissions to the air.[510] The application shall be submitted to the Minister.[511]

106. The content of the application set out in this law mainly transposes the European provisions of Article 6(1) Directive 96/61/EEC, the corresponding ones in the legislation that repealed it, that being Article 6(1) Directive 2008/1/EC, as well as the corresponding ones that repealed the later one and are now in force, that being Article 12(1) Directive 2010/75/EU, under national law. However, national law does not require them to submit measures planned to comply with the general principles of the basic obligations of the operator,[512] those being taking appropriate preventive measures against pollution, in particular through application of the BAT,[513] causing no significant pollution,[514] avoidance of waste production and where such is produced, recovered or, where that is technically and economically impossible, disposal while avoiding or reducing any impact on the environment,[515] efficient use of energy,[516] taking necessary measures to prevent accidents and limit their consequences[517] and taking necessary measures upon definitive cessation of activities for avoidance of any pollution risk and returning the site of operation to a satisfactory state.[518] Another differentiation lies in the usage of the word *emissions*[519] in the implemented European provisions, whereas the national law makes mention of *emission of solid and liquid waste* and *disposal of solid and air waste*. This could lead to confusion due to their different meaning, as *waste* in national law has the meaning defined in Law No. 185(I)/2011[520] whereas the meaning of *emission* is not set out.

---

510. Section 9(2) *ibid.*
511. Section 9(1) *ibid.*
512. Article 6(1) Directive 96/61/EEC, Art. 6(1)(h) Directive 2008/1/EC and Art. 12(1)(i) Directive 2010/75/EC.
513. Article 3(1)(a) Directive 96/61/EEC, Art. 3(1)(a) Directive 2008/1/EC and Art. 11(a) and (b) Directive 2010/75/EU.
514. Article 3(1)(b) Directive 96/61/EEC, Art. 3(1)(b) Directive 2008/1/EC and Art. 11(c) Directive 2010/75/EU.
515. Article 3(1)(c) Directive 96/61/EEC, Art. 3(1)(c) Directive 2008/1/EC and, with some differentiations, Art. 11(d) and (e) Directive 2010/75/EU.
516. Article 3(1)(d) Directive 96/61/EEC, Art. 3(1)(d) Directive 2008/1/EC and Art. 11(f) Directive 2010/75/EU.
517. Article 3(1)(e) Directive 96/61/EEC, Art. 3(1)(e) Directive 2008/1/EC and Art. 11(g) Directive 2010/75/EU.
518. Article 3(1)(f) Directive 96/61/EEC, Art. 3(1)(f) Directive 2008/1/EC and Art. 11(h) Directive 2010/75/EU.
519. *Emission* ('émission' in the French version, 'Emission' in the German one, 'emissie' in the Dutch one) means the direct or indirect release of substances, vibrations, heat or noise from individual or diffuse sources in the installation into the air, water or land. Art. 2(5) Directive 96/61/EEC, Art. 2(5) Directive 2008/1/EC and Art. 3(4) Directive 2010/75/EU.
520. Section 2 Law No. 106(I)/2002. *Waste* ('déchets' in French, 'Abfall' in German, 'afvalstof' in Dutch) means any substance or object which the holder discards or intends or is required to discard. Section 2 Law No. 185(I)/2011, which corresponds to Art. 3(1) Directive 2008/98/EC.

II. Examination of an Application for a Disposal Permit

107. Upon receiving an application for a disposal permit, the Minister ensures the publication of a notification in the Official Gazette of the Republic. This notification specifies the date, on which the application was received,[521] the place, where the same application is available for inspection by the public,[522] and the fact that any interested party may submit to the Minister opinion or suggestions regarding the requested permission or the content of the application.[523]

108. The first step for the evaluation of the application for a disposal permit is a recommendation of the Technical Committee for the Protection of Waters and Soil, which is issued following the examination of the application and then provided to the Minister.[524] However, this may be skipped, in the event that the conditions, which shall be attached to the requested permit, fall within the general conditions that the committee has already approved and are valid via a decree of the Minister.[525] The wide discretion powers of the Minister are constrained by the provision stating that no disposal permit may be granted, when it is found that the operator may not adhere to disposal limit values and/or quality standards[526] and when the existing plant does not have a valid urban planning permission, building permission or certification of approval, as the case may be,[527] or in case of a new plant a certification of approval.[528] Lastly, mandatory prerequisite to be established prior to granting a disposal permit is a written statement of the operator committing himself that he can and shall comply with all operating conditions of the permit.[529]

III. Granting a Disposal Permit

109. The Minister may grant a disposal permit and attach any conditions on waste disposal thereto. In doing so, he must consider the nature, composition and

521. Section 9(4)(a) Law No. 106(I)/2002.
522. Section 9(4)(b) *ibid.*
523. Section 9(4)(c) *ibid.*
524. Section 9(6) and Table A Part II(1) *ibid.*
525. Section 9(6) and Table A Part II(4) *ibid.* The following have been issued: Pollution Control of Waters (General Conditions for Waste of Cattle Breeding Units) Decree No. 433 of 2006, OG III(I) No. 4148 of 17 Nov. 2006, p. 3701; Pollution Control of Waters (General Conditions for Waste of Oil Mils) Decree No. 270 of 2005, OG III(I) No. 4000 of 3 Jun. 2005, p. 2345; Pollution Control of Waters (General Conditions for Waste of Piggery) Decree No. 737 of 2003, OG III(I) No. 3755 of 3 Oct. 2003, p. 3989; Pollution Control of Waters (General Conditions for Waste of Winery) Decree No. 38 of 2007, OG III(I) No. 4167 of 19 Jan. 2007, p. 292; Pollution Control of Waters (General Conditions for Waste of Bird Slaughterhouses) Decree No. 271 of 2005, OG III(I) No. 4000 of 3 Jun. 2005, p. 2349; Pollution Control of Waters (General Conditions for Waste of Urban Waste Water Treatment Plants) Decree No. 269 of 2005, OGIII(I) No. 4000 of 3 Jun. 2005, p. 2338.
526. Section 9(6) and Table A Part II(8) Law No. 106(I)/2002.
527. Section 8(2)(a) *ibid.*
528. For the purpose of this provision, a *new plant* means a plant submitting an application for a disposal permit on or after 27 Dec. 2013. Section 8(2)(b) *ibid.*
529. Section 9(6) and Table A Part II(7) *ibid.*

amount of disposed substances or waste,[530] the nature and quality of the soil and subsoil at which disposal shall take place,[531] the proximity of any surface water or groundwater to the disposal site and their use or possible use[532] and any other elements regarding public health, public security and the protection of the environment.[533] Especially with reference to groundwater,[534] and particularly the assessment of the chemical status of a body or a group of bodies of groundwater, the competent authority uses groundwater quality standards ('ποιοτικά πρότυπα υπόγειων υδάτων')[535] as set out in the law[536] and threshold values ('ανώτερες αποδεκτές τιμές') that are established by the competent authority for the pollutants, groups of pollutants and indicators of pollution which, within the territory of Cyprus, have been identified as contributing to the characterization of bodies or groups of bodies of groundwater as being at risk,[537] taking into account at least the list contained in the law.[538]

110. More specifically, such additional conditions may specify the place and manner of waste disposal or disposition of the plant,[539] the disposal frequency, the total amount of disposals at any time period,[540] the total amount of any substance or microorganisms being disposed,[541] the nature, composition and any natural or chemical characteristics of the disposed substances,[542] the maximum concentration of any composition, substance or microorganism in the disposed waste[543] and temperature, acidity (pH value) and conductivity of any disposed waste.[544] Additional conditions may further relate to sampling. In particular, they may set out means of access to disposal site for sampling control of the disposed waste and measurement

---

530. Section 10(2)(a) *ibid.*
531. Section 10(2)(b) *ibid.*
532. Section 10(2)(c) *ibid.*
533. Section 10(2)(d) *ibid.*
534. Section 10(2)(e) *ibid.*
535. Regulation 3(1)(a) KDP 272/2009, which corresponds to Art. 3(1)(a) Directive 2006/118/EC.
536. These are set out in Annex I KDP 272/2009, which corresponds to Annex I Directive 2006/118/EC.
537. Regulation 3(1)(b) KDP 272/2009, which corresponds to Art. 3(1)(b) Directive 2006/118/EC.
538. Annex II Part B KDP 272/2009, which corresponds to Annex II Part B Directive 2006/118/EC. This reads:

> Minimum list of pollutants and their indicators for which the competent authority have to consider establishing threshold values in accordance with Regulation 3:
> 1. Substances or ions or indicators which may occur both naturally and/or as a result of human activities: Arsenic, Cadmium, Lead, Mercury, Ammonium, Chloride, Sulphate
> 2. Man-made synthetic substances: Trichloroethylene, Tetrachloroethylene
> 3. Parameters indicative of saline or other intrusions: Conductivity.
>
> Asbestos was not included in this list of pollutants. This is puzzling taking into consideration the fact that Cyprus' soil is rich in asbestos as well as the abandoned asbestos' mine.

539. Section 10(1)(a) Law No. 106(I)/2002.
540. Section 10(1)(b) *ibid.*
541. Section 10(1)(c) *ibid.*
542. Section 10(1)(d) *ibid.*
543. Section 10(1)(e) *ibid.*
544. Section 10(1)(f) *ibid.*

of the flow rate[545] and the frequency of sampling and analysis of any substance of plant's waste by the operator.[546] Information-related obligations may also be imposed on the operation, including submission of an annual report on complying with the conditions regarding waste disposal,[547] the obligation of immediate information of the Minister in case of leaking of waste due to accident or negligence[548] and compilation of and compliance with a monitoring programme of the quality of waters and soil at disposal sites and submission of a relevant annual report to the Minister.[549] Lastly, additional conditions may refer to taking any measures and specifying any necessary practical detail for the protection of the waters and soil.[550]

111. The disposal permit may comprise of one or more written decisions of the Minister. It may further refer to a plant in whole or in part or regard one or more of a plant's parts operating at the same place by the same operator.[551] Apart from the additional conditions, it further includes the time period, during which compliance with those is to be achieved,[552] the time frame, during which the Minister may not revoke this permit or add new conditions or amend any of the existing conditions, without paying satisfactory compensation to the operator, unless the operator is at fault[553] and its validity period, which may not be more than four years.[554]

112. Granting a disposal permit is followed by the imposition of certain obligations to its holder. He has to comply at all times consistently and accurately with the conditions of the permit[555] and to immediately inform the Minister of any incident or accident that takes place at or near the plant, for which the permit was granted, and that affects or is likely to affect surface water, groundwater, soil or subsoil, the air or any person at the area of the plant or the disposal. The same information obligation applies in cases of unforeseeable danger of affecting same goods.[556] The operator also has to regularly monitor the quality of the plant's waste and inform the Minister of the results in time periods specified in the permit.[557] Lastly, he has to afford the representatives of the competent authority all necessary assistance to enable them to carry out any inspections within the installation, to take samples and to gather any information necessary for the performance of their duties for the purposes of this law.[558]

---

545. Section 10(1)(g) *ibid.*
546. Section 10(1)(h) *ibid.*
547. Section 10(1)(i) *ibid.*
548. Section 10(1)(j) *ibid.*
549. Section 10(1)(k) *ibid.*
550. Section 10(1)(l) *ibid.*
551. Section 11(1) *ibid.*
552. Section 11(2)(a) *ibid.*
553. Section 11(2)(b) *ibid.*
554. Section 11(2)(c) *ibid.*
555. Section 14(1)(a) *ibid.*, which is similar to Art. 14 Directive 96/61/EEC and Art. 14(a) Directive 2008/1/EC.
556. Section 14(1)(b) Law No. 106(I)/2002, which is similar to Art. 14 Directive 96/61/EEC and Art. 14(b) Directive 2008/1/EC.
557. Section 14(1)(c) Law No. 106(I)/2002.
558. Section 14(1)(d) *ibid.*, which corresponds to Art. 14 Directive 96/61/EEC and Art. 14(c) Directive 2008/1/EC.

113. Regarding renewal of the disposal permit, the holder has to submit a relevant application to the Minister at least six months prior to its expiration.[559] If the permit expires and is not yet renewed, the operator has to comply at all times consistently and accurately with all conditions of the expired permit, unless the inspector requests the operator to act in a different manner for the purpose of protecting water and soil.[560]

IV. Rejecting an Application for a Disposal Permit

114. No provision refers to the rejection of an application for a disposal permit. However, it is undisputable that in such a case, the applicant may lodge an appeal according to Article 146 Constitution based on violation of the provisions of this law or of Law No. 158(I)/1999, which binds all actions and inactions of public authorities and marks the limits of their discretion powers. It is true that since the *Ibrahim* case[561] and the law of necessity, the rule of law has lost its supremacy. However, the law of necessity may not allow for the absence of judicial control of administration.

V. Revocation and Alteration of a Disposal Permit

115. For the purpose of protection of public health, public safety or the environment, the Minister may revoke a disposal permit,[562] shorten the validity period thereof,[563] add any new conditions thereto, as long as such conditions may be attached to a disposal permit,[564] or amend any imposed condition.[565] The Minister may also revoke the permit or order the cessation of disposals, if the operator fails to comply with any condition thereof.[566] Such revocation or amendment takes place in a procedure similar to the one for granting a permit, safe for necessary adjustments.[567]

116. In the event of cessation of a plant's activities, which may be ordered upon failing to comply with an inspector's notification issued due to suspicion of danger of environmental damage[568] or upon immediate danger of environmental damage,[569] the disposal permit is considered as automatically being annulled from the

559. Section 14(1)(e) Law No. 106(I)/2002.
560. Section 14(2) *ibid.*
561. *Attorney-General of the Republic v. Ibrahim* (1964) CLR 195.
562. Section 12(1)(a) Law No. 106(I)/2002.
563. Section 12(1)(b) *ibid.*
564. Section 12(1)(c) *ibid.*
565. Section 12(1)(d) *ibid.*
566. Section 12(2) *ibid.*
567. Section 12(3) and Table 1 Part II *ibid.*
568. Section 24(2)(d) *ibid.*
569. Section 24(3) *ibid.*

date of said cessation.[570] For the operation of such a plant, an application for a disposal permit, as per the above stated, must be filed.[571]

117. An operator wishing for any change in the nature or functioning or any expansion of the plant, which may have consequences on the water and soil, has to inform the Minister accordingly in advance.[572] Change in the nature or functioning of a plant ('αλλαγή στη φύση ή την λειτουργία της εγκατάστασης') means a change in the nature or functioning, or an extension, of the plant which may have consequences for the environment.[573] In such a case, the Minister may amend the conditions of the permit, if he deems this necessary for the purpose of reducing or eliminating such effects.[574]

118. An operator wishing any substantial change in the operation of a plant, which may have significant negative effects on human beings or waters and soil, has to obtain a prior written approval from the Minister. Substantial change in the operation of a plant ('ουσιαστική αλλαγή στην λειτουργία της εγκατάστασης') stands for a change in operation which, in the opinion of the Minister, may have significant negative effects on human beings or the environment.[575] For the purpose of effecting this change, the operator is called to submit a relevant application mentioning the parts of the plant, which may be changed,[576] and any of the aspects described in his application for the permit, which may be effected by the proposed changes.[577] The provisions on assessment of an application for a discharge permit apply *mutatis mutandis*.[578]

VI. Change of the Operator

119. In case the operator of a plant, for which a disposal permit has been granted, changes for any reason whatsoever, the new operator is obliged to notify

570. Section 12(4)(a) *ibid.*
571. Section 12(4)(b) *ibid.*
572. Section 17(1) *ibid.*, which corresponds to Art. 12(1) Directive 96/61/EEC, Art. 12(1) Directive 2008/1/EC and Art. 20(1) Directive 2010/75/EU.
573. Section 17(4) Law No. 106(I)/2002, which corresponds to Art. 2(10)(a) Directive 96/61/EEC and Art. 2(10) Directive 2008/1/EC. However, the term used in the national law is different than the one in the European legislation, that being 'μεταβολή της λειτουργίας' in Greek, 'change in operation' in English, 'modification de l'exploitation' in French, 'Änderung des Betriebs' in German, 'wijziging van de exploitatie' in Dutch.
574. Section 17(1) Law No. 106(I)/2002, which corresponds to Art. 12(1) Directive 96/61/EEC, Art. 12(1) Directive 2008/1/EC and Art. 20(1) Directive 2010/75/EU.
575. Section 17(4) Law No. 106(I)/2002, which corresponds to Art. 2(10)(b) Directive 96/61/EEC and Art. 2(11) Directive 2008/1/EC. The term used in national law differs than the European terms, those being 'ουσιαστική μεταβολή' in Greek, 'substantial change' in English, 'modification substantielle' in French, 'wesentliche Änderung' in German and 'belangrijke wijziging' in Dutch.
576. Section 17(2)(a) Law No. 106(I)/2002, which corresponds to Art. 12(2) Directive 96/61/EEC, Art. 12(2) Directive 2008/1/EC and Art. 20(2) Directive 2010/75/EU.
577. Section 17(2)(b) *ibid.*
578. Section 17(3) *ibid.*, which corresponds to Art. 12(2) Directive 96/61/EEC and Art. 12(2) Directive 2008/1/EC.

the Minister of this change.[579] He further has to comply with the conditions of the granted permit.[580] The new operator also takes over all rights and obligations of the previous operator set out in this law upon taking control of the operation of the plant.[581]

VII. Ensuring Compliance

A. Administrative Sanctions

120. When an inspector has reasonable cause to believe that any plant operates or is going to operate in a manner causing danger of environmental pollution due to possible fire, explosion or disposal of any substance or waste, he has the authority to serve the operator a notification.[582] This notification shall mention the reasons causing the existence of the danger, according to the assessment of the inspector,[583] instructions for taking specific measures of reducing or eliminating the danger,[584] the time period, within which these measures have to be taken,[585] and state that the operation of the plant shall be ceased if these measures are not taken within the specified time period.[586] If the danger believed to exist is considered imminent, and therefore, an immediate response is necessary, the notification may include the order of immediate cessation of the plant's operation or any activity in this. It may be further instructed that its operation shall not begin again unless the measures stated are taken and the danger ceases to exist.[587]

121. If committing any offence foreseen in this law results in pollution of water or soil, the Minister may order the convicted person to proceed with reducing or eliminating the pollution by taking the measures specified by the Minister within a reasonable time.[588] If this person refuses or fails to comply with this, then these measures are taken by the Minister and the relevant expenses are claimed as a civil debt to the state.[589]

B. Penal Sanctions

122. The penal offences of this law are quite extensive. Roughly, they may be put into three groups: the ones related to pollution of the water and soil, the ones for violating provisions of this law and the ones regarding violation of disposal permit's conditions.

579. Section 14A(1)(a) Law No. 106(I)/2002.
580. Section 14A(1)(b) *ibid.*
581. Section 14A(2) *ibid.*
582. Section 24(2) *ibid.*
583. Section 24(2)(a) *ibid.*
584. Section 24(2)(b) *ibid.*
585. Section 24(2)(c) *ibid.*
586. Section 24(2)(d) *ibid.*
587. Section 24(3) *ibid.*
588. Section 31A(1) *ibid.*
589. Section 31A(2) *ibid.*

123. Anyone polluting water and soil may be sentenced to imprisonment of up to three years and/or a penal fine of up to EUR 500,000. The act of pollution of water and soil is specified in the law and may be best elaborated in Table 3.

Table 3 Penal Offences Regarding Water Pollution Control

Section	*Subject*	*Action*	*Place*	*Object*
6(1)(a)	Person	Discharging, depositing, disposing, causing or allowing discharge, deposit or disposal	Creek, dry bed of a creek, coastal water, lake or sluice	Any object, substance or matter that pollutes or may pollute such water
6(1)(b)	Person	Discharging, depositing, disposing, causing or allowing discharge, deposit or disposal	Soil or subsoil	Any object, substance or matter that pollutes or may pollute coastal water, groundwater, water of creek or water of sluice
6(1)(c)	Person	Depositing, causing or allowing discharge or deposit	Any place, where transport to creek, dry bed of a creek, coastal water, lake or sluice is possible	any object, substance or matter that pollutes or may pollute such water
6(1)(d)	Person	Discharging, depositing, causing or allowing discharge or deposit	Soil or subsoil	Any object, substance or matter, liquid waste, sludge or other semi-liquid or solid waste
6(1)(e)	Person	Discharging, depositing, causing, allowing or tolerating discharge or deposit from any plant	Surface inland water or coastal water	Any liquid or solid waste or any other liquid containing suspended matter
6(1)(f)	Person	Discharging, depositing, causing, allowing or tolerating discharge or deposit	Sea	Sludge or any other substance or matter deriving from waste treatment

124. A person performing the above is committing no offence if he holds a disposal permit, issued in accordance with this law.[590] Defence to the offences under section 6(1)(b) and (c) is proving that such actions were performed in accordance with good agricultural practice.[591] Defence to the offences under section 6(1)(a) and (b) is proving that this action was due to a cause beyond his control, that he further

590. Section 6(2) *ibid.*
591. Section 6(3) *ibid.*

demonstrated due care for preventing or obstructing this offence and that, as soon as he understood this being not possible, he took all possible measures for rehabilitation, without undue delay.[592]

125. Any person failing to comply with the mandatory provisions of this law is committing an offence. If found guilty by a court of law, he may be sentenced to imprisonment for up to three years and/or a penal fine of up to EUR 500,000.[593] The court may additionally order the sale or in any other way disposal of the movable or immovable assets of the plant.[594] Any person obstructing an inspector from performing his duties[595] or any police officer or other person accompanying the inspector from entering into the plant or assisting the inspector[596] commits an offence. Equally, it is an offence, when anyone refuses to provide safe access to a plant to an inspector or anyone accompanying him,[597] refuses or fails to provide him with information, as per the relevant inspector's authorities of this law, or fails to comply with instructions on stable operation conditions of any plant,[598] and refuses to collect an out-of-court notification.[599] If the accused is convicted by a court of law, he may be imprisoned for up to six months and/or a monetary fine of up to EUR 10,000 may be imposed on him.[600]

126. Noncompliance with the conditions of a disposal permit is also an offence and may lead to imprisonment of up to three years and/or a penal fine of up to EUR 500,000.[601] The court may additionally order the sale or in any other way disposal of the movable or immovable assets of the plant.[602]

127. If offences of section 29 are committed by a legal person to its profit and with the consensus or due to failed supervision or control or other omission of a person, who holds a managing position and acts on representative powers,[603] decision-reaching powers[604] or controlling powers of this legal person,[605] then this natural person along with the legal one is committing the offence and may be convicted to the aforementioned sentences.[606]

592. Section 6(4) *ibid.*
593. Section 29(1) *ibid.*
594. Section 29(5) *ibid.*
595. Section 29(3)(a) *ibid.*
596. Section 29(3)(b) *ibid.*
597. Section 29(3)(c) *ibid.*
598. Section 29(3)(d) *ibid.*
599. Section 29(3)(e) *ibid.*
600. Section 29(3) *ibid.*
601. Section 29(2) *ibid.*
602. Section 29(5) *ibid.*
603. Section 29A(1)(a) *ibid.*
604. Section 29A(1)(b) *ibid.*
605. Section 29A(1)(c) *ibid.*
606. Section 29A(1) *ibid.*

C. Other Sanctions

128. During the criminal procedure initiated for all above-mentioned offences, a request for an interim order for the prohibition of the purported illegal act or omission causing pollution until the final judgment may be filed[607] ex parte[608] by the General Attorney or the interested local authority. It will be decided by the President of the District Court.[609] If anyone does not comply with such an interim order, he commits an offence facing imprisonment of up to two years and/or a penal fine of up to EUR 500,000.[610]

§5. Especially Plants Involving Asbestos-Related Activities

129. Specific provisions are foreseen for plants related to asbestos in secondary legislation.[611] Asbestos stands for the following fibrous silicates: crocidolite (blue asbestos), actinolite, anthophyllite, chrysotile (white asbestos), amosite (brown asbestos), tremolite.[612] Generally, the Minister takes the measures necessary to ensure that activities involving the working of products containing asbestos do not cause significant environmental pollution by asbestos fibres or dust.[613] In addition, he takes the measures necessary where waste containing asbestos fibres or dust is landfilled at landfill sites, that such waste is so treated, packaged or covered, with account being taken of local conditions, that the release of asbestos particles into the air and soil is prevented.[614] The Minister notifies the EC of the procedures and methods he is using together with the information relevant to assess the pertinence of such procedures and methods[615] as well as the results from the implementation of these regulations as to prevention and reduction of water and soil pollution from asbestos.[616]

130. Plants, where disposal of asbestos or products containing asbestos takes place, are granted disposal permits, only if the Minister is ensured that all aqueous effluent arising in the manufacture of asbestos cement, asbestos paper or board is recycled.[617] In addition to the conditions that may be attached to the permit as per

607. Section 30(1) *ibid.*
608. Section 30(4) *ibid.*
609. Section 30(2) *ibid.*
610. Section 30(5) *ibid.*
611. Regulations on Water Pollution Control (Prevention and Reduction of Water Pollution from Asbestos) ('οι περί Ελέγχου της Ρύπανσης των Νερών (Πρόληψη και Μείωση της Ρύπανσης των Νερών από Αμίαντο) Κανονισμοί') No. 515 of 2002, OG III(I) No. 3647 of 25 Oct. 2002, p. 5603.
612. Regulation 2(1) KDP 515/2002, which corresponds to Art. 2(1) Directive 87/217/EEC.
613. Regulation 7 KDP 515/2002, which corresponds to Art. 7 Directive 87/217/EEC.
614. Regulation 8 KDP 515/2002, which corresponds to Art. 8 Directive 87/217/EEC. However, the directive refers to sites licensed for the specific purpose of asbestos disposal, whereas the national law mentions generally a landfill site.
615. Regulation 12(a) KDP 515/2002, which corresponds to Art. 6(3) Directive 87/217/EEC.
616. Regulation 12(b) KDP 515/2002.
617. Regulation 4 *ibid.*, which corresponds to Art. 5(a) and (b) Directive 87/217/EEC.

the provisions of Law No. 106(I)/2002, it may be further ordered for each plant concerned, specific volume of discharges into water or specific total quantity of suspended matter discharged per tonne of product taking account of the specific situation of the plant.[618] Also, it may be allowed during routine cleaning or maintenance of the plant to discharge aqueous effluent containing not more than 30 g of suspended matter per m^3 of water.[619]

131. The permit holder and operator of such a plant is obliged to take the measures necessary to ensure that asbestos discharges into the aquatic environment and solid asbestos waste are, as far as reasonably practicable, reduced at source and prevented using best available technology not entailing excessive costs.[620] He further ensures to comply with the set limit values[621] and perform measurements of asbestos discharge in liquid waste[622] of the plant at least once every three months and notify within a month the results of those measurements to the Minister.[623] Lastly, he has to keep a measurements' register, in which these are recorded and any non-compliance with the limit values is well-founded. This register has to be available for inspection at any time.[624]

132. Any person violating these regulations is committing an offence. If found guilty by a court of law, he may be imprisoned for up to three years or convicted to a fine of up to EUR 500,000.[625]

§6. Especially Pollution Caused by Nitrates from Agricultural Sources

133. Pollution caused by nitrates ('νιτρορύπανση'), that being pollution caused by deposit, application or discharge of livestock effluents or by excessive use of fertilizers, is regulated in this law. The Minister takes all measures necessary for the protection of water from such pollution. In particular, he may issue

618. Regulation 5(a) KDP 515/2002, which corresponds to Art. 5(a) Directive 87/217/EEC.
619. Regulation 5(b) KDP 515/2002, which corresponds to Art. 5(b) Directive 87/217/EEC.
620. Regulation 6(a) KDP 515/2002, which corresponds to Art. 3(1) and (2) Directive 97/217/EEC. However, the European provision refers also to *asbestos emissions into the air*.
621. Regulation 6(b) KDP 515/2002, which corresponds to Art. 4 Directive 87/217/EEC.
622. Methods of sampling and analyses are specified in Annex KDP 515/2002, which corresponds to Annex Part A Directive 87/217/EEC. This reads:

> 1. The reference method of analysis to determine total suspended matter (filterable matter from the non precipitated sample) as expressed in mg/l shall be filtering through a 0.45 mm filter membrane, drying at 105 °C and weighing. 2. Samples must be taken in such a way as to be representative of the discharge over a 24-hour period. 3. This determination must be conducted to a precision of ± 5% and an accuracy of ± 10%.

623. Regulation 6(d) KDP 515/2002, which corresponds to Art. 6(1) Directive 87/217/EEC.
624. Regulation 6(c) KDP 515/2002.
625. Regulation 11 *ibid.*, s. 29 Law No. 106(I)/2002.

decrees designating any areas of land as vulnerable zones due to pollution caused by nitrates,[626] identifying waters affected by pollution and waters which could be affected by pollution,[627] establishing and approving action programmes in respect of designated vulnerable zones,[628] drawing up and approving suitable monitoring programmes to assess the effectiveness of action programmes,[629] and defining measures and procedures regarding any matters related to pollution caused by nitrates of waters of any other Member State of the EU.[630] The Minister may further issue a decree approving a code of good agricultural practice and setting up a programme promoting the application of the code(s) of good agricultural practice.[631] He also ensures that the application of such code(s) does not cause any negative effects to the environment, property or ease of any persons by giving instructions and taking proper measures.[632] The Council of Ministers is also authorized to issue regulations for the best materialization of the above scopes.[633]

134. Regarding action programmes in respect of designated vulnerable zones specific provisions on public participation apply. These provisions have been set out for the purpose of partial implementation of directive on public access to environmental information.[634] The Minister ensures that the public is given a timely and effective opportunity to participate in the preparation, amendment or revision thereof.[635] The applicability of this provision is challenged by the term 'public' ('κοινό'). It is stated that public is one or more natural or legal persons as well as unions, organizations or groups.[636] It is further stated that public with whom the Minister consults is the public being or is possibly affected by or whose interests are in danger due to the decision-taking process on such action programmes and non-governmental organizations, such as organizations promoting environmental protection.[637] As no specific provision on consultations between the Minister and the public is foreseen, it could be assumed that this definition is not applicable. Additionally, it could be supported that the first definition prevails, as this definition is also used in Article 2(6) Directive 2003/4/EC. In any case, for the purpose of giving a timely and effective opportunity the Minister notifies the public about any

626. Section 7(2)(a) *ibid.*, which corresponds to Art. 3(2) Directive 91/676/EEC.
627. Section 7(2)(b) Law No. 106(I)/2002, which corresponds to Art. 3(1) Directive 91/676/EEC.
628. Section 7(2)(c) Law No. 106(I)/2002, which corresponds to Art. 5(1) Directive 91/676/EEC.
629. Section 7(2)(d) Law No. 106(I)/2002, which corresponds to Art. 5(6) Directive 91/676/EEC.
630. Section 7(2)(f) Law No. 106(I)/2002. Art. 3(3) Directive 91/767/EEC foresees that in such cases the Member State whose waters are affected may notify the other Member States and the Commission of the relevant facts.
631. Section 7(2)(e) Law No. 106(I)/2002, which corresponds to Art. 4(1)(a) and (b) Directive 91/676/EEC. A code of good agricultural practice has been issued by Decree No. 263 of 2007, OG III(I) No. 4202 of 22 Jun. 2007, p. 1597.
632. Section 7(3) Law No. 106(I)/2002.
633. Section 7(4) *ibid.*
634. Preamble to Law on Water Pollution Control (Amendment) ('ο περί Ελέγχου της Ρύπανσης των Νερών (Τροποποιητικός) Νόμος') No. 160 of 2005, OG I(I) No. 4064 of 30 Dec. 2005, p. 1173.
635. Section 7B(1) Law No. 106(I)/2002.
636. Section 7A(1) *ibid.*
637. Section 7B(4)(a) and(b) *ibid.*

proposal regarding adoption, amendment or revision of such programmes in the Official Gazette, in two daily newspapers and on the Internet.[638] In this notification, he also mentions that information regarding such proposal is available to the public during working days and hours at the office of Environmental Agency,[639] and that any person may submit to the Environmental Agency opinions or representations regarding their content within thirty-five days from the publication of the notification.[640] Notification of said proposals and opinions or representations is published by the Environmental Agency on the Internet.[641]

135. In cases of important action programmes in respect of designated vulnerable zones, which are not specified in the law, the Council of Ministers may decide on a public hearing following a reasoned proposal of the Environmental Agency, which is submitted after consultations with the Minister and the Technical Committee.[642] Its scope, procedure, interested public and other matters are set out in regulations issued by the Council of Ministers.[643]

136. The Minister reaches a decision on action programmes and important action programmes, after taking into consideration opinions and representations expressed by the public or the results of the public hearing.[644] The public is informed of him taking such a decision through a notification, which is published in the Official Gazette, in two daily newspapers and on the Internet. This notification also mentions that certain information is available at a certain time and place, and same information is also filed in the archive.[645] This information is a description of the action programme or the important action programme,[646] a short statement on the manner that opinions and representations of the public or the results of the public hearing were taken into consideration[647] and the grounds and estimations, on which the decision was based.[648]

137. The Environmental Agency is obliged to keep an archive. This archive includes the aforementioned information,[649] the proposals of preparation, amendment or revision of action programmes[650] and submitted opinions or representations

638. Section 7B(2)(a) *ibid.*
639. Section 7B(2)(b) *ibid.*
640. Section 7B(2)(c) *ibid.*
641. Section 7B(3) (a) and (b) *ibid.*
642. Section 7C(1) *ibid.*
643. Section 7C(2) *ibid.*
644. Section 7D *ibid.*
645. Section 7E *ibid.*
646. Section 7E(a) *ibid.*
647. Section 7E(b)(i) *ibid.*
648. Section 7E(b)(ii) *ibid.*
649. Section 7F(c) *ibid.*
650. Section 7F(a) *ibid.*

of any person.[651] Access of the public to the archive is regulated by Law No. 119(I)/ 2004,[652] which implements the directive on public access to environmental information.[653]

§7. ARCHIVE

138. The Minister keeps an archive, according to the regulations issued by the Council of Ministers.[654] These regulations clarify details relating to the filling of applications for disposal permit,[655] permits issued along with their amendments,[656] any monitoring reports and measurements results,[657] environmental quality standards for any waters of Cyprus,[658] frequency of sampling and analysis results of waters of any area,[659] any measures taken for water restoration[660] and their dates[661] and any offences committed along with the imposed penalties.[662]

139. Certain information may not be disclosed in the archive, as per the content of section 4(1)(b) of Law on Free Access to Environmental Information of 2000,[663] which mentions that confidential information, in particular related to the confidentiality of the proceedings of public authorities,[664] international relations,[665] national defence and public security,[666] matters which are, or have been, in course of justice, or under enquiry (including disciplinary enquiries), or which are the subject of preliminary investigation proceedings,[667] commercial and industrial confidentiality, including intellectual property,[668] the confidentiality of personal data and/or files,[669] material supplied by a third party without that party being under a legal obligation

651. Section 7F(b) *ibid.*
652. Law on Public Access to Environmental Information ('ο περί Πρόσβασης του Κοινού σε Πληροφορίες που είναι σχετικές με το Περιβάλλον Νόμος') No. 119, OGI(I) No. 3850 of 30 Apr. 2004, p. 2366.
653. Directive 2003/4/EC of the European Parliament and of the Council of 28 Jan. 2003 on public access to environmental information and repealing Council Directive 90/313/EEC, OJ L 41, 14 Feb. 2003, p. 26.
654. Section 28(1) Law No. 106(I)/2002.
655. Section 28(1)(a) *ibid.*
656. Section 28(1)(b) *ibid.*
657. Section 28(1)(c) *ibid.*
658. Section 28(1)(d) *ibid.*
659. Section 28(1)(e) *ibid.*
660. Section 28(1)(f) *ibid.*
661. Section 28(1)(g) *ibid.*
662. Section 28(1)(h) *ibid.*
663. Law on Free Access of the Public to Environmental Information ('ο περί Ελεύθερης Πρόσβασης του Κοινού σε Πληροφορίες που σχετίζονται με Θέματα Περιβάλλοντος') No. 125 of 2000, OGI(I) No. 3420 of 21 Jul. 2000.
664. Section 4(1)(b)(i) Law No. 125(I)/2000, which corresponds to Art. 3(2) Directive 90/313/EEC.
665. Section 4(1)(b)(ii) Law No. 125(I)/2000.
666. Section 4(1)(b)(iii) *ibid.*
667. Section 4(1)(b)(iv) *ibid.*
668. Section 4(1)(b)(v) *ibid.*
669. Section 4(1)(b)(vi) *ibid.*

to do so[670] and material, the disclosure of which would make it more likely that the environment to which such material related would be damaged.[671] However, this law has been repealed by Law No. 119(I)/2004. Hence, public authorities may decline access to environmental information only on the following grounds: the confidentiality of the proceedings of public authorities, where such confidentiality is provided for by law;[672] international relations, public security or national defence;[673] the course of justice, the ability of any person to receive a fair trial or the ability of a public authority to conduct an enquiry of a criminal or disciplinary nature;[674] the confidentiality of commercial or industrial information where such confidentiality is provided for by national or Union law to protect a legitimate economic interest, including the public interest in maintaining statistical confidentiality and tax secrecy;[675] intellectual property rights;[676] the confidentiality of personal data and/or files relating to a natural person where that person has not consented to the disclosure of the information to the public, where such confidentiality is provided for by national law;[677] the interests or protection of any person who supplied the information requested on a voluntary basis without being under, or capable of being put under, a legal obligation to do so, unless that person has consented to the release of the information concerned[678] and the protection of the environment to which such information relates, such as the location of rare species.[679]

140. The Minister publishes a catalogue of information and data on granted permissions on the Internet. These include the name of the plant,[680] the nature and its category,[681] the area of operation,[682] the date of issuing the permit[683] and the date of its expiration.[684] The author was not successful in finding this.

670. Section 4(1)(b)(vii) *ibid.*
671. Section 4(1)(b)(viii) *ibid.*
672. Section 8(3)(a) Law No. 119(I)/2004, which corresponds to Art. 4(2)(a) Directive 2003/4/EC.
673. Section 8(3)(b) Law No. 119(I)/2004, which corresponds to Art. 4(2)(b) Directive 2003/4/EC.
674. Section 8(3)(c) Law No. 119(I)/2004, which corresponds to Art. 4(2)(c) Directive 2003/4/EC.
675. Section 8(3)(d) Law No. 119(I)/2004, which corresponds to Art. 4(2)(d) Directive 2003/4/EC.
676. Section 8(3)(e) Law No. 119(I)/2004, which corresponds to Art. 4(2)(e) Directive 2003/4/EC.
677. Section 8(3)(f) Law No. 119(I)/2004, which corresponds to Art. 4(2)(f) Directive 2003/4/EC.
678. Section 8(3)(g) Law No. 119(I)/2004, which corresponds to Art. 4(2)(g) Directive 2003/4/EC.
679. Section 8(3)(h) Law No. 119(I)/2004, which corresponds to Art. 4(2)(h) Directive 2003/4/EC.
680. Section 28(3)(a) Law No. 106(I)/2002.
681. Section 28(3)(b) *ibid.*
682. Section 28(3)(c) *ibid.*
683. Section 28(3)(d) *ibid.*
684. Section 28(3)(e) *ibid.*

Chapter 4. Waste

141. Waste management is regulated by Law on Waste[685] (hereinafter 'Law No. 185(I)/2011'), which implements Directive 2008/98/EC,[686] among others,[687] according to its preamble. Law No. 185(I)/2011 repealed Law on Solid and Hazardous Waste of 2002.[688]

§1. Object

142. Law No. 185(I)/2011 lays down measures to protect the environment and human health by preventing or reducing the generation of waste, the adverse impacts of the generation and management of waste and by reducing overall impacts of resource use and improving the efficiency of such use, which are crucial for the transition to a circular economy and for guaranteeing the Union's long-term competitiveness.[689] Waste ('απόβλητα') is defined as any substance or object which the holder discards or intends or is required to discard.[690] A substance or object, resulting from a production process, the primary aim of which is not the production of that item, is regarded as not being waste but as being a by-product ('υποπροϊόντα') when the following conditions are met: further use of the substance or object is certain; the substance or object can be used directly without any further processing other than normal industrial practice; the substance or object is produced as an integral part of a production process; and further use is lawful, i.e., the substance or object fulfils all relevant product, environmental and health protection requirements for the specific use and will not lead to overall adverse environmental

685. Law on Waste ('ο περί Αποβλήτων Νόμος') No. 185 of 2011, OG I(I) No. 4313 of 23 Dec. 2011, p. 1531, as last amended by Law on Waste (Amendment) ('ο περί Αποβλήτων (Τροποποιητικός) Νόμος') No. 48 of 2022, OG I(I) No. 4885 of 8 Apr. 2022.
686. Directive 2008/98/EC of the European Parliament and of the Council of 19 Nov. 2008 on waste and repealing certain Directives, OJ L 312, 11 Nov. 2008, p. 3, as amended.
687. These are: Council Directive 96/59/EC of 16 Sep. 1996 on the disposal of polychlorinated biphenyls and polychlorinated terphenyls (PCB/PCT), OJ L 243, 24 Sep. 1996, p. 31; Council Directive 1999/31/EC of 26 Apr. 1999 on the landfill of waste, OJ L 182, 16 Jul. 1999, p. 1; Directive 2002/96/EC of the European Parliament and of the Council of 27 Jan. 2003 on waste electrical and electronic equipment (WEEE), OJ L 37, 13 Feb. 2003, p. 24; Directive 2006/66/EC of the European Parliament and of the Council of 6 Sep. 2006 on batteries and accumulators and waste batteries and accumulators and repealing Directive 91/157/EEC, OJ L 266, 26 Sep. 2006, p. 1; Directive 2011/65/EU of the European Parliament and of the Council of 8 Jun. 2011 on the restriction of the use of certain hazardous substances in electrical and electronic equipment, OJ L 174, 1 Jul. 2011, p. 88; Regulation (EC) No. 1013/2006 of the European Parliament and of the Council of 14 Jun. 2006 on shipments of waste, OJ L 190, 12 Jul. 2006, p. 1; and Directive 2012/19/EU of the European Parliament and of the Council of 4 Jul. 2012 on waste electrical and electronic equipment (WEEE), OJ L 197, 24 Jul. 2012, p. 38. However, Directive 2002/96/EC has been repealed by Directive 2012/19/EU.
688. Law on Solid and Hazardous Waste ('ο περί Στερεών και Επικίνδυνων Αποβλήτων Νόμος') No. 215 of 2002, OG I(I) No. 3666 of 27 Dec. 2002, p. 3375.
689. Section 3 Law No. 185(I)/2011, which corresponds to Art. 1 Directive 2008/98/EC. *See also* §1 KrWG.
690. Section 2 Law No. 185(I)/2011, which corresponds to Art. 3(1) Directive 2008/98/EC. The French term is 'déchets', the German one 'Abfall' and the Dutch one 'afvalstof'.

or human health impacts. The Minister is entrusted with the duty of taking the appropriate measures.[691] The Commission has been given the authority to adopt implementing acts in order to establish detailed criteria on the uniform application of afore-stated conditions for specific substances or objects. Those detailed criteria shall ensure a high level of environmental protection and protection of human health; they shall further facilitate prudent and rational utilization of natural resources.[692] Where criteria have not been set at Union level, the Minister may establish detailed criteria on the application of said conditions to specific substances or objects. If he chooses to do so, he shall communicate the established criteria to the Commission.[693]

143. Waste management ('διαχείριση αποβλήτων') means the collection ('συλλογή'),[694] transport ('μεταφορά'), recovery ('ανάκτηση')[695] (including sorting) and disposal ('διάθεση')[696] of waste, including the supervision of such operations and the after-care of disposal sites, and including actions taken as a dealer or broker.[697] It is further set out that waste management is carried out without endangering human health, without harming the environment and, in particular: without risk to water, air, soil, plants or animals;[698] without causing a nuisance through noise or odours;[699] without negatively affecting protected species and

691. Section 6(1) Law No. 185(I)/2011, which corresponds to Art. 5(1) Directive 2008/98/EC. The French term is 'sous-produits', the German one 'Nebenprodukte' and the Dutch one 'bijproducten'.
692. Section 6(2) Law No. 185(I)/2011, which corresponds to Art. 5(2) Directive 2008/98/EC.
693. Section 6(3) Law No. 185(I)/2011, which corresponds to Art. 5(3) Directive 2008/98/EC.
694. *Collection* ('collecte' in French, 'Sammlung' in German, 'inzameling' in Dutch) means the gathering of waste, including the preliminary sorting and preliminary storage of waste for the purposes of transport to a waste treatment facility. Section 2 Law No. 185(I)/2011, which corresponds to Art. 3(10) Directive 2008/98/EC.
695. *Recovery* ('valorization' in French, 'Verwertung' in German, 'nuttige toepassing' in Dutch) means any operation the principal result of which is waste serving a useful purpose by replacing other materials which would otherwise have been used to fulfil a particular function, or waste being prepared to fulfil that function, in the plant or in the wider economy. Annex I sets out a non-exhaustive list of recovery operations. Section 2 Law No. 185(I)/2011, which corresponds to Art. 3(15) Directive 2008/98/EC.
696. *Disposal* ('elimination' in French, 'Beseitigung' in German, 'verwijdering' in Dutch) is any operation which is not recovery even where the operation has as a secondary consequence the reclamation of substances or energy and includes the disposal operations set out in Annex II. Section 2 Law No. 185(I)/2011, which corresponds to Art. 3(19) Directive 2008/98/EC.
697. Section 2 Law No. 185(I)/2011, which corresponds to Art. 3(9) Directive 2008/98/EC. The French term is 'gestion des déchets', the German one 'Abfallbewirtschaftung' and the Dutch one 'afvalstoffenbeheer'.
698. Section 10(1)(a) Law No. 185(I)/2011, which corresponds to Art. 13(a) Directive 2008/98/EC. *See* in this respect *European Commission v. Hellenic Republic*, judgment of 17 Jul. 2014 in Case C-600/12, *digital* ECR [I. Koufaki, ***Διαχείριση αποβλήτων και προστασία περιοχών δικτύου*** *Natura 2000*, 62 NoB 1988 (2014)]; *European Commission v. Italian Republic*, judgment of 15 Oct. 2014 in Case C-323/13, *digital* ECR; *Società Edilizia Turistica Alberghiera Residenziale (SETAR) SpA v. Comune di Quartu S. Elena*, judgment of 18 Dec. 2014 in Case C-551/13, *digital* ECR; *European Commission v. Hellenic Republic*, judgment of 11 Dec. 2014 in Case C-677/13, *digital* ECR.
699. Section 10(1)(b) Law No. 185(I)/2011, which corresponds to Art. 13(b) Directive 2008/98/EC.

natural habitats;[700,701] and without adversely affecting the countryside or places of special interest.[702]

144. Properties of waste which render it hazardous (in original 'επικίνδυνα απόβλητα', in French 'déchets dangereux', in German 'gefährlicher Abfall', in Dutch 'gevaarlijke afvalstof') are explosive, oxidizing, flammable, irritant – skin irritation and eye damage, Specific Target Organ Toxicity (STOT)/aspiration toxicity, acute toxicity, carcinogenic, corrosive, infectious, toxic for reproduction, mutagenic, release of an acute toxic gas, sensitizing, ecotoxic and waste capable of exhibiting a hazardous property listed above not directly displayed by the original waste. These notions, which are set out in detail in the law,[703] are explained below (Tables 4–12).

145. HP 1 *Explosive* (in original 'εκρηκτικό', in French 'explosif', in German 'explosiv', in Dutch 'ontplofbaar') is waste which is capable by chemical reaction of producing gas at such a temperature and pressure and at such a speed as to cause damage to the surroundings. Pyrotechnic waste, explosive organic peroxide waste and explosive self-reactive waste is included. When a waste contains one or more substances classified by one of the hazard class and category codes and hazard statement codes shown in Table 4, the waste shall be assessed for HP 1, where appropriate and proportionate, according to test methods. If the presence of a substance, a mixture or an article indicates that the waste is explosive, it shall be classified as hazardous by HP 1.

Table 4 Hazard Class and Category Code(s) and Hazard Statement Code(s) for Waste Constituents for the Classification of Wastes as Hazardous by HP 1

Hazard Class and Category Code(s)	*Hazard Statement Code(s)*
Unst. Expl.	H 200
Expl. 1.1	H 201
Expl. 1.2	H 202
Expl. 1.3	H 203

700. Protected species and natural habitats mean the following as long as they are within suggested special protection areas as defined in the respective law and in state forests according to Cap. 31: the species listed in Annexes II and III Law No. 153(I)/2003; the species listed in Annexes I, II, IV, VI and IX Law No. 152(I)/2003; the habitats that are included in Annex II Law No. 153(I)/2003; the habitats that are included in Annexes I and V Law No. 152(I)/2003; allium marathasicum, crypsis hadjikyriakou, limonium mucronulatum, malcolmia nana var. glabra, astragalus suberosus var. hartmannii, peucedanum kyriakae and solenopsis antiphonitis; protected areas, coasts and areas of protection, and certain zones according to the policy statement, which are prepared pursuant to s. 34A Law No. 90/1972, and certain zone according to local plans, that are prepared according ss 10 et seq. Law No. 90/1972. Section 10(2) Law No. 185(I)/2011 and s. 2 Law No. 189(I)/2007.
701. Section 10(1)(c) Law No. 185(I)/2011.
702. Section 10(1)(d) *ibid.*, which corresponds to Art. 13(c) Directive 2008/98/EC.
703. Annex III Law No. 185(I)/2011, which corresponds to Annex III Directive 2008/98/EC.

Hazard Class and Category Code(s)	*Hazard Statement Code(s)*
Expl. 1.4	H 204
Self-react. A	H 240
Org. Perox. A	
Self-react. B	H 241
Org. Perox. B	

HP 2 *Oxidizing* (in original 'οξειδωτικό', in French 'comburant', in German 'brandfördernd', in Dutch 'oxiderend') is waste which may, generally by providing oxygen, cause or contribute to the combustion of other materials. When a waste contains one or more substances classified by one of the hazard class and category codes and hazard statement codes shown in Table 5, the waste shall be assessed for HP 2, where appropriate and proportionate, according to test methods. If the presence of a substance indicates that the waste is oxidizing, it shall be classified as hazardous by HP 2.

Table 5 Hazard Class and Category Code(s) and Hazard Statement Code(s) for the Classification of Wastes as Hazardous by HP 2

Hazard Class and Category Code(s)	*Hazard Statement Code(s)*
Ox. Gas	H 270
Ox. Liq. 1	H 271
Ox. Sol. 1	
Ox. Liq. 2, Ox. Liq. 3	H 272
Ox. Sol. 2, Ox. Sol. 3	

HP 3 *Flammable* (in original 'εύφλεκτο', in French 'inflammable', in German 'entzündbar', in Dutch 'ontvlambaar') includes the following waste:

- flammable liquid waste, which is a liquid waste having a flash point below 60 °C or waste gas oil, diesel and light heating oils having a flash point > 55 °C and ≤ 75 °C;
- flammable pyrophoric liquid and solid waste that is solid or liquid waste which, even in small quantities, is liable to ignite within five minutes after coming into contact with air;
- flammable solid waste that is solid waste which is readily combustible or may cause or contribute to fire through friction;
- flammable gaseous waste that is gaseous waste which is flammable in air at 20 °C and a standard pressure of 101.3 kPa;
- water reactive waste that is waste which, in contact with water, emits flammable gases in dangerous quantities;
- other flammable waste, which are flammable aerosols, flammable self-heating waste, flammable organic peroxides and flammable self-reactive waste.

When a waste contains one or more substances classified by one of the following hazard class and category codes and hazard statement codes shown in Table 6, the waste shall be assessed, where appropriate and proportionate, according to test methods. If the presence of a substance indicates that the waste is flammable, it shall be classified as hazardous by HP 3.

Table 6 Hazard Class and Category Code(s) and Hazard Statement Code(s) for Waste Constituents for the Classification of Wastes as Hazardous by HP 3

Hazard Class and Category Code(s)	*Hazard Statement Code(s)*
Flam. Gas 1	H 220
Flam. Gas 2	H 221
Aerosol 1	H 222
Aerosol 2	H 223
Flam. Liq. 1	H 224
Flam. Liq. 2	H 225
Flam. Liq. 3	H 226
Flam. Sol. 1	H 228
Flam. Sol. 2	
Self-react. CD	H 242
Self-react. EF	
Org. Perox. CD	
Org. Perox. EF	
Pyr. Liq. 1	H 250
Pyr. Sol. 1	
Self-heat. 1	H 251
Self-heat. 2	H 252
Water-react. 1	H 260
Water-react. 2	H 261
Water-react. 3	

HP 4 *Irritant – skin irritation and eye damage (*in original 'ερεθιστικό – ερεθισμός του δέρματος και οφθαλμική βλάβη', in French 'irritant – irritation cutanée et lésions oculaires', in German 'reizend – Hautreizung und Augenschädigung', in Dutch 'irriterend – huidirritatie en oogletsel') is waste which on application can cause skin irritation or damage to the eye. When a waste contains one or more substances in concentrations above the cut-off value that are classified by one of the following hazard class and category codes and hazard statement codes and one or more of the following concentration limits is exceeded or equalled, the waste shall be classified as hazardous by HP 4. The cut-off value for consideration in an assessment for Skin corr. 1A (H 314), Skin irrit. 2 (H 315), Eye dam. 1 (H 318) and

Eye irrit. 2 (H 319) is 1%. If the sum of the concentrations of all substances classified as Skin corr. 1A (H 314) exceeds or equals 1%, the waste shall be classified as hazardous according to HP 4. If the sum of the concentrations of all substances classified as H 318 exceeds or equals 10%, the waste shall be classified as hazardous according to HP 4. If the sum of the concentrations of all substances classified H 315 and H 319 exceeds or equals 20%, the waste shall be classified as hazardous according to HP 4. Note that wastes containing substances classified as H314 (Skin corr.1A, 1B or 1C) in amounts greater than or equal to 5% will be classified as hazardous by HP 8. HP 4 will not apply if the waste is classified as HP 8.

HP 5 *STOT/Aspiration Toxicity* (in original: 'Ειδική τοξικότητα στα όργανα-στόχους (ΕΤΟΣ)/τοξικότητα από αναρρόφηση', in French: 'Toxicité spécifique pour un organe cible (STOT)/toxicité par aspiration', in German: 'Spezifische Zielorgan-Toxizität (STOT)/Aspirationsgefahr', in Dutch: 'Specifieke doelorgaan-toxiciteit (STOT)/aspiratietoxiciteit') is waste which can cause STOT from either a single or repeated exposure, or which cause acute toxic effects following aspiration. When a waste contains one or more substances classified by one or more of the following hazard class and category codes and hazard statement codes as shown in Table 7, and one or more of the concentration limits in Table 4 is exceeded or equalled, the waste shall be classified as hazardous according to HP 5. When substances classified as STOT are present in a waste, an individual substance has to be present at or above the concentration limit for the waste to be classified as hazardous by HP 5. When a waste contains one or more substances classified as Asp. Tox. 1 and the sum of those substances exceeds or equals the concentration limit, the waste shall be classified as hazardous by HP 5 only where the overall kinematic viscosity (at 40 °C) does not exceed 20.5 mm^2/s.

Table 7 Hazard Class and Category Code(s) and Hazard Statement Code(s) for Waste Constituents and the Corresponding Concentration Limits for the Classification of Wastes as Hazardous by HP 5

Hazard Class and Category Code(s)	*Hazard Statement Code(s)*	*Concentration Limit (%)*
STOT SE 1	H 370	1
STOT SE 2	H 373	10
STOT SE 3	H 335	20
STOT RE 1	H 372	1
STOT RE 2	H 373	10
Asp. Tox. 1	H 304	10

HP 6 *Acute Toxicity* (in original 'οξεία τοξικότητα', in French 'toxicité aiguë', in German 'akute Toxizität', in Dutch 'acute toxiciteit') is which can cause acute toxic effects following oral or dermal administration, or inhalation exposure. If the sum of the concentrations of all substances contained in a waste, classified with an acute toxic hazard class and category code and hazard statement codes given in

Table 8, exceeds or equals the threshold given in that table, the waste shall be classified as hazardous by HP 6. When more than one substance classified as acute toxic is present in a waste, the sum of the concentrations is required only for substances within the same hazard category.

The following cut-off values shall apply for consideration in an assessment:

- For Acute Tox. 1, 2 or 3 (H 300, H 310, H 330, H 301, H 311, H 331): 0.1%.
- For Acute Tox. 4 (H 302, H 312, H 332): 1%.

Table 8 Hazard Class and Category Code(s) and Hazard Statement Code(s) for Waste Constituents and the Corresponding Concentration Limits for the Classification of Wastes as Hazardous by HP 6

Hazard Class and Category Code(s)	*Hazard Statement Code(s)*	*Concentration Limit (%)*
Acute Tox. 1 (Oral)	H 300	0.1
Acute Tox. 2 (Oral)	H 300	0.25
Acute Tox. 3 (Oral)	H 301	5
Acute Tox. 4 (Oral)	H 302	25
Acute Tox. 1 (Dermal)	H 310	0.25
Acute Tox. 2 (Dermal)	H 310	2.5
Acute Tox. 3 (Dermal)	H 311	15
Acute Tox. 4 (Dermal)	H 312	55
Acute Tox. 1 (Inhal.)	H 330	0.1
Acute Tox. 2 (Inhal.)	H 330	0.5
Acute Tox. 3 (Inhal.)	H 331	3.5
Acute Tox. 4 (Inhal.)	H 332	22.5

HP 7 *Carcinogenic* (in original 'καρκινογόνο', in French 'cancérogène', in German 'karzinogen', in Dutch 'kankerverwekkend') is waste which induces cancer or increases its incidence. When a waste contains a substance classified by one of the following hazard class and category codes and hazard statement codes and exceeds or equals one of the following concentration limits shown in Table 9, the waste shall be classified as hazardous by HP 7. When more than one substance classified as carcinogenic is present in a waste, an individual substance has to be present at or above the concentration limit for the waste to be classified as hazardous by HP 7.

Table 9 Hazard Class and Category Code(s) and Hazard Statement Code(s) for Waste Constituents and the Corresponding Concentration Limits for the Classification of Wastes as Hazardous by HP 7

Hazard Class and Category Code(s)	*Hazard Statement Code(s)*	*Concentration Limit (%)*
Carc. 1A	H 350	0.1
Carc. 1B		
Carc. 2	H 351	1.0

HP 8 *Corrosive* (in original 'διαβρωτικό', in French 'corrosif', in German 'ätzend', in Dutch 'corrosief') is waste which on application can cause skin corrosion. When a waste contains one or more substances classified as Skin corr. 1A, 1B or 1C (H 314) and the sum of their concentrations exceeds or equals 5%, the waste shall be classified as hazardous by HP 8. The cut-off value for consideration in an assessment for Skin corr. 1A, 1B, 1C (H 314) is 1.0%.

HP 9 *Infectious* (in original 'μολυσματικό', in French 'infectieux', in German 'infektiös', in Dutch 'infectueus') is waste containing viable microorganisms or their toxins which are known or reliably believed to cause disease in man or other living organisms. The attribution of HP 9 shall be assessed by the rules laid down in reference documents or legislation.

HP 10 *Toxic for reproduction* (in original 'τοξικό για την αναπαραγωγή', in French 'toxique pour la reproduction', in German 'reproduktionstoxisch', in Dutch 'vergiftig voor de voortplanting') is waste which has adverse effects on sexual function and fertility in adult males and females, as well as developmental toxicity in the offspring. When a waste contains a substance classified by one of the following hazard class and category codes and hazard statement codes and exceeds or equals one of the following concentration limits shown in Table 10, the waste shall be classified as hazardous according to HP 10. When more than one substance classified as toxic for reproduction is present in a waste, an individual substance has to be present at or above the concentration limit for the waste to be classified as hazardous by HP 10.

Table 10 Hazard Class and Category Code(s) and Hazard Statement Code(s) for Waste Constituents and the Corresponding Concentration Limits for the Classification of Wastes as Hazardous by HP 10

Hazard Class and Category Code(s)	*Hazard Statement Code(s)*	*Concentration Limit (%)*
Repr. 1A	H 360	0.3
Repr. 1B		
Repr. 2	H 361	3.0

HP 11 *Mutagenic* (in original 'μεταλλαξιογόνο', in French 'mutagène', in German 'mutagen', in Dutch 'mutageen') is waste which may cause a mutation, that is a permanent change in the amount or structure of the genetic material in a cell. When a waste contains a substance classified by one of the following hazard class and category codes and hazard statement codes and exceeds or equals one of the following concentration limits shown in Table 11, the waste shall be classified as hazardous according to HP 11. When more than one substance classified as mutagenic is present in a waste, an individual substance has to be present at or above the concentration limit for the waste to be classified as hazardous by HP 11.

Table 11 Hazard Class and Category Code(s) and Hazard Statement Code(s) for Waste Constituents and the Corresponding Concentration Limits for the Classification of Wastes as Hazardous by HP 11

Hazard Class and Category Code(s)	*Hazard Statement Code(s)*	*Concentration Limit (%)*
Muta. 1A	H 340	0.1
Muta. 1B		
Muta. 2	H 341	1.0

HP 12 *Release of an acute toxic gas (*in original 'έκλυση αερίου οξείας τοξικότητας', in French 'dégagement d'un gaz à toxicité aiguë', in German 'Freisetzung eines akut toxischen Gases', in Dutch 'afgifte van een acuut toxisch gas') is waste which releases acute toxic gases (Acute Tox. 1, 2 or 3) in contact with water or an acid. When a waste contains a substance assigned to one of the following supplemental hazards EUH 029, EUH 031 and EUH 032, it shall be classified as hazardous by HP 12 according to test methods or guidelines.

HP 13 *Sensitizing* (in original 'ευαισθητοποιητικό', in French 'sensibilisant', in German 'sensibilisierend', in Dutch 'sensibiliserend') is waste which contains one or more substances known to cause sensitizing effects to the skin or the respiratory organs. When a waste contains a substance classified as sensitizing and is assigned to one of the hazard statement codes H 317 or H 334 and one individual substance equals or exceeds the concentration limit of 10%, the waste shall be classified as hazardous by HP 13.

HP 14 *Ecotoxic* (in original 'οικοτοξικό', in French 'écotoxique', in German 'ökotoxisch', in Dutch 'ecotoxisch') is waste which presents or may present immediate or delayed risks for one or more sectors of the environment.

HP 15 *Waste capable of exhibiting a hazardous property listed above not directly displayed by the original waste* (in original 'απόβλητο ικανό να επιδείξει μια επικίνδυνη ιδιότητα που αναφέρεται ανωτέρω, που δεν είναι άμεσα εμφανής στο αρχικό απόβλητο', in French 'déchet capable de présenter une des propriétés dangereuses susmentionnées que ne présente pas directement le déchet d'origine', in German 'Abfall, der eine der oben genannten gefahrenrelevanten

Eigenschaften entwickeln kann, die der ursprüngliche Abfall nicht unmittelbar aufweist', in Dutch 'afvalstoffen die een van de hierboven genoemde gevaarlijke eigenschappen doen ontstaan die de oorspronkelijke afvalstof niet bezat') is waste which presents or may present immediate or delayed risks for one or more sectors of the environment. When a waste contains one or more substances assigned to one of the hazard statements or supplemental hazards shown in Table 12, the waste shall be classified as hazardous by HP 15, unless the waste is in such a form that it will not under any circumstance exhibit explosive or potentially explosive properties.

Table 12 Hazard Statements and Supplemental Hazards for Waste Constituents for the Classification of Wastes as Hazardous by HP 15

Hazard Statement(s)/Supplemental Hazard(s)	
May mass explode in fire	H 205
Explosive when dry	EUH 001
May form explosive peroxides	EUH 019
Risk of explosion if heated under confinement	EUH 044

Lastly, the competent authority may characterize a waste as hazardous by HP 15 based on other applicable criteria, such as an assessment of the leachate.

146. List of waste, including hazardous waste, may be specified in a decree of the Minister.[704] This list is binding as regards the determination of the waste which is to be considered as hazardous waste.[705] However, the inclusion of a substance or object in the list shall not mean that it is a waste in all circumstances. A substance or object shall be considered to be waste only where the definition in this law is met.[706] The competent authority may consider waste as hazardous waste where, even though it does not appear as such on the list of waste, it displays one or more of the properties listed in Annex III of this law. The competent authority publishes a relevant notification in the Official Gazette and notifies the EC of any such cases along with all necessary evidence without any undue delay.[707] Also the opposite is possible. More specifically, the competent authority may consider specific waste that appears on the said list as hazardous waste as non-hazardous waste, as long as this does not display any of the properties listed in the said annex. Similarly, the EC is notified without delay and all necessary evidence. Such adaption, however, is only effective following a review of the list by the EC.[708] Lastly, it is explicitly provided that the reclassification of hazardous waste as non-hazardous waste may not be

704. Section 8(1) Law No. 185(I)/2011.
705. Section 8(2) *ibid.*, which partially corresponds to Art. 7(1) Directive 2008/98/EC.
706. Section 8(3) Law No. 185(I)/2011, which partially corresponds to Art. 7(1) Directive 2008/98/EC.
707. Section 8(4) Law No. 185(I)/2011, which partially corresponds to Art. 7(2) Directive 2008/98/EC.
708. Section 8(5) Law No. 185(I)/2011, which corresponds to Art. 7(3) Directive 2008/98/EC.

achieved by diluting or mixing the waste with the aim of lowering the initial concentrations of hazardous substances to a level below the thresholds for defining waste as hazardous.[709]

147. Certain waste ceases to be waste, when it has undergone a recovery, including recycling, operation and complies with specific criteria to be developed in accordance with the following conditions: the substance or object is commonly used for specific purposes; a market or demand exists for such a substance or object; the substance or object fulfils the technical requirements for the specific purposes and meets the existing legislation and standards applicable to products; and the use of the substance or object will not lead to overall adverse environmental or human health impacts.[710] Waste, which ceases to be waste, as per the aforementioned, also ceases to be waste for the purpose of the recovery and recycling targets set out in other legislation,[711] when the recycling or recovery requirements of that legislation are satisfied.[712]

§2. Area of Application

148. The area of application of this law is negatively specified. In particular, it is set out that the following are excluded from the application of this law: gaseous effluents emitted into the atmosphere;[713] land (in situ) including unexcavated contaminated soil and buildings permanently connected with land;[714] uncontaminated

709. Section 8(6) Law No. 185(I)/2011, which corresponds to Art. 7(4) Directive 2008/98/EC.

710. Section 7(1) Law No. 185(I)/2011, which corresponds to Art. 6(1) Directive 2008/98/EC. *See* in this respect *Lapin elinkeino-, liikenne- ja ympäristökeskuksen liikenne ja infrastruktuuri -vastuualue v. Lapin luonnonsuojelupiiri ry*, Case C-358/11, *digital* ECR [relevant review: S. Roset, *Déchets. Entre le règlement REACH et la directive déchet: le statut juridique d'anciens poteaux de télécommunication traités avec des solutions à base d'arsenic conduit la Cour à préciser la fin du statut du déchet*, Europe 34 (2013); F. Le Bot, *Les déchets dangereux peuvent perdre leur statu de déchet. A propos de l'articulation entre la directive Déchets et le règlement REACH*, RAE 161 (2013)].

711. These are: Law on Packaging and Packaging Waste ('ο περί Συσκευασιών και Αποβλήτων Συσκευασιών Νόμος') No. 32 of 2002, OG I(I) No. 3594 of 12 Apr. 2002, p. 1355, which implements Directive 94/62/EC of 20 Dec. 1994 on packaging and packaging waste, OJ L 365, 31 Dec. 1994, p. 10, as amended; Law on End-of Life Vehicles ('ο περί Οχημάτων στο Τέλος του Κύκλου Ζωής τους Νόμος') No. 157 of 2003, OGI(I) No. 3758 of 3 Oct. 2003, p. 1376, which implements Directive 2000/53/EC of the European Parliament and of the Council of 18 Sep. 2000 on end-of life vehicles, OJ L 269, 21 Oct. 2000, p. 34, as amended; Regulations on Solid and Hazardous Waste (Waste Electrical and Electronic Equipment) ('Στερεών και Επικίνδυνων Αποβλήτων (Απόβλητα Ηλεκτρικού και Ηλεκτρονικού Εξοπλισμού) Κανονισμοί') No. 668 of 2004, OG III(I) No. 3888 of 30 Jul. 2004, p. 6629, as amended, which implement, among others, Directive 2002/96/EC (*see* n 687 above); Regulations on Solid and Hazardous Waste (Batteries and Accumulators) ('Στερεών και Επικίνδυνων Αποβλήτων (Ηλεκτρικές Στήλες ή Συσσωρευτές) Κανονισμοί') No. 82 of 2003, OG III(I) No. 3679 of 31 Jan. 2003, p. 313, as amended, which implement Directive 2006/66/EC (*see* n 687 above); and any other relevant legislation.

712. Section 7(4) Law No. 185(I)/2011, which corresponds to Art. 6(3) Directive 2008/98/EC.

713. Section 4(1)(a) Law No. 185(I)/2011, which corresponds to Art. 2(1)(a) Directive 2008/98/EC.

714. Section 4(1)(b) Law No. 185(I)/2011, which corresponds to Art. 2(1)(b) Directive 2008/98/EC.

soil and other naturally occurring material excavated in the course of construction activities where it is certain that the material will be used for the purposes of construction in its natural state on the site from which it was excavated;[715] radioactive waste;[716] decommissioned explosives;[717] faecal matter, straw and other natural non-hazardous agricultural or forestry material used in farming, forestry or for the production of energy from such biomass through processes or methods which do not harm the environment or endanger human health;[718] and incineration of carcasses of humans.[719] Further, the following are excluded from the scope of this law to the extent that they are covered by other legislation: save for section 24(2) of this law, waste waters;[720] animal by-products including processed products covered by Regulation (EC) No. 1774/2002,[721] except those which are destined for incineration, landfilling or use in a biogas or composting plant;[722] carcasses of animals that have died other than by being slaughtered, including animals killed to eradicate epizootic diseases, and that are disposed of in accordance with Regulation (EC) No. 1774/2002;[723] waste resulting from prospecting, extraction, treatment and storage of mineral resources and the working of quarries covered by Law on Management of Extractive Waste;[724],[725] and substances that are destined for use as feed materials as defined in Article 3(2)(g) of Regulation (EC) No. 767/2009[726] and that do not consist of or contain animal by-products.[727] Lastly and without prejudice to obligations under other relevant legislation, sediments relocated inside surface waters for the purpose of managing waters and waterways or of preventing floods or mitigating the effects of floods and droughts or land reclamation shall be excluded from the scope of this law, if it is proved that the sediments are non-hazardous.[728]

715. Section 4(1)(c) Law No. 185(I)/2011, which corresponds to Art. 2(1)(c) Directive 2008/98/EC.
716. Section 4(1)(d) Law No. 185(I)/2011, which corresponds to Art. 2(1)(d) Directive 2008/98/EC.
717. Section 4(1)(e) Law No. 185(I)/2011, which corresponds to Art. 2(1)(e) Directive 2008/98/EC.
718. Section 4(1)(f) Law No. 185(I)/2011, which corresponds to Art. 2(1)(f) Directive 2008/98/EC.
719. Section 4(1)(g) Law No. 185(I)/2011.
720. Section 4(2)(a) *ibid.*, which corresponds to Art. 2(2)(a) Directive 2008/98/EC.
721. Regulation (EC) No. 1774/2002 of the European Parliament and of the Council of 3 Oct. 2002 laying down health rules concerning animal by-products not intended for human consumption, OJ L 273, 10 Oct. 2002, p. 1.
722. Section 4(2)(b) Law No. 185(I)/2011, which corresponds to Art. 2(2)(b) Directive 2008/98/EC.
723. Section 4(2)(c) Law No. 185(I)/2011, which corresponds to Art. 2(2)(c) Directive 2008/98/EC.
724. Law on Management of Extractive Waste ('ο περί Διαχείρισης των Αποβλήτων της Εξορυκτικής Βιομηχανίας Νόμος') No. 82 of 2009, OG I(I) No. 4213 of 17 Jul. 2009, p. 621. This law implements Directive 2006/21/EC of the European Parliament and of the Council of 15 Mar. 2006 on the management of waste from extractive industries, OJ L 102, 11 Apr. 2006, p. 15.
725. Section 4(2)(d) Law No. 185(I)/2011, which corresponds to Art. 2(2)(d) Directive 2008/98/EC.
726. Regulation (EC) No 767/2009 of the European Parliament and of the Council of 13 Jul. 2009 on the placing on the market and use of feed, amending European Parliament and Council Regulation (EC) No 1831/2003 and repealing Council Directive 79/373/EEC, Commission Directive 80/511/EEC, Council Directives 82/471/EEC, 83/228/EEC, 93/74/EEC, 93/113/EC and 96/25/EC and Commission Decision 2004/217/EC, OJ L 229, 1.9.2009, p. 1–28.
727. Section 4(2)(e) Law No. 185(I)/2011, which corresponds to Art. 2(2)(e) Directive 2008/98/EC.
728. Section 4(3) Law No. 185(I)/2011, which corresponds to Art. 2(3) Directive 2008/98/EC.

§3. COMPETENT AUTHORITIES

I. The Minister of Agriculture, Rural Development and the Environment

149. The Minister of Agriculture Rural Development and the Environment (hereinafter 'the Minister') is the competent authority for the application of this law. As per the explicit statutory provision, he is also the competent authority for the application of Regulation (EC) No. 1013/ 2006[729] and Regulation (EC) No. 1102/ 2008.[730,731] This law applies without prejudice to the competence of local authorities *on management*t of certain waste according to this law, as set out in the Law on Municipalities and Communities.[732,733] Finally, the Minister may delegate any of his powers and competence regarding the proper application of this law and relevant decrees,[734] in the fashion already discussed under Law No. 187(I)/2002 (*see* in this regard paragraph 31 above).

150. The Minister may issue decrees for the regulation of any matters of technical and administrative nature.[735] These decrees may also determine any of the following matters: determining general terms and/or special measures for management of certain categories of waste or specific waste management activities, which shall be the base for granting waste treatment permits;[736] determining measures and general terms that are obligatory for waste holders, plants' managers or producers;[737] determining controls and inspections at sites of waste disposal or production;[738] drafting management plants for specific categories of waste, including public information and participation;[739] drafting waste prevention programmes;[740] public information and participation related to rehabilitation of existing plants managing waste;[741] defining the type, content and procedure of submitting applications or other forms or the waste record;[742] categorizing persons managing waste and/or

729. Regulation (EC) No. 1013/2006 of the European Parliament and of the Council of 14 Jun. 2006 on shipments of waste, OJ L 190, 12 Jul. 2006, p. 1.
730. Regulation (EC) No. 1102/2008 of the European Parliament and of the Council of 22 Oct. 2008 on the banning of exports of metallic mercury and certain mercury compounds and mixtures and the safe storage of metallic mercury, OJ L 304, 14 Nov. 2008, p. 75. Still, this regulation has been repealed since 1 Jan. 2018 by Regulation (EU) 2017/852 of the European Parliament and of the Council of 17 May 2017 on mercury, and repealing Regulation (EC) No 1102/2008, OJ L 137, 24 May 2017, p. 1.
731. Section 5(1) Law No. 185(I)/2011.
732. Law on Municipalities ('ο περί Δήμων Νόμος') No. 111 of 1985, OG I(I) No. 2082 of 18 Oct. 1985, p. 2257, as amended; Law on Communities ('ο περί Κοινοτήτων Νόμος') No. 86 of 1999, OG I(I) No. 3337 of 9 Jul. 1999, p. 235, as amended.
733. Section 5(2) Law No. 185(I)/2011.
734. Section 5A *ibid.*
735. Section 54(4) *ibid.*
736. Section 54(5)(a) *ibid.*
737. Section 54(5)(b) *ibid.*
738. Section 54(5)(c) *ibid.*
739. Section 54(5)(d) *ibid.*
740. Section 54(5)(e) *ibid.*
741. Section 54(5)(f) *ibid.*
742. Section 54(5)(g) *ibid.*

such plants;[743] specifying technical details and standards for waste management plants;[744] determining criteria for reception of certain categories of waste to specific plants or persons managing waste;[745] determining measurement methods and technical standards;[746] and determining special measurements for the encouragement of establishing legal persons for management of specific categories of waste.[747]

II. The Council of Ministers

151. The Council of Ministers has the power to issue regulations. These regulations may state measures ensuring extended producer responsibility[748] and other matters related to producer's responsibility,[749] any measure necessary for the disposal of waste,[750] additional measures for separate collection and proper treatment of waste oil.[751] Regulations may further set out waste management plants,[752] waste prevention programmes[753] and matters related to public participation.[754]

152. It is further broadly stated that the Council of Ministers may issue regulations deemed necessary for any other matter that need to be determined and generally for the best application of this law.[755] Without prejudice to this general provision, regulations may also determine matters related to batteries and accumulators, waste electrical and electronic equipment (WEEE), landfill sites, polychlorinated biphenyls and polychlorinated terphenyls (PCB/PCT), permit for atomic or collective waste management systems, waste oils.[756]

153. Under exceptional circumstances, the Council of Ministers may impose administrative sanctions.[757] It is further the competent authority to hear administrative appeals ('ιεραρχική προσφυγή').[758]

III. Consultation Committee for Waste Management

154. The Consultation Committee for Waste Management ('Συμβουλευτική Επιτροπή Διαχείρισης Αποβλήτων') is established via this law.[759] As already

743. Section 54(5)(h) *ibid.*
744. Section 54(5)(i) *ibid.*
745. Section 54(5)(j) *ibid.*
746. Section 54(5)(k) *ibid.*
747. Section 54(5)(l) *ibid.*
748. Section 11(1) *ibid.*
749. Sections 15(5) and 23(4) *ibid.*
750. Section 14(2) *ibid.*
751. Section 21(2) *ibid.*
752. Section 35(1) *ibid.*
753. Section 36(1) *ibid.*
754. Section 39(2) *ibid.*
755. Section 54(1) *ibid.*
756. Section 54(2) *ibid.*
757. Section 51(3) *ibid.*
758. Section 52 *ibid.*
759. Section 43(1) *ibid.*

seen in the Technical Committee for the Protection of Air under Law No. 187(I)/2002 (*see* in this respect paragraphs 32 et seq. above), representatives from various Ministries participate in this committee.[760] In addition to those, further members of the Technical Committee for Waste Management are the Union of Cyprus Municipalities[761] and the Union of Cyprus Communities.[762] The competence of this committee is to advise the competent authority on any matter related to issuing regulations, decrees or notifications,[763] approving atomic or collective waste management systems[764] and any measures to be imposed for reduction of waste management, proper management and disposal of waste, including waste management plants of section 35 of this law and waste prevention programmes of section 36 of this law.[765]

155. The particulars of meetings of the committee, its chairman, notices and agendas are similar to the ones elaborated under the Technical Committee for the Protection of Air under Law No. 187(I)/2002 (*see* in this respect paragraphs 32 et seq. above).[766]

IV. Local Authorities

156. Local authorities ('αρχές τοπικής αυτοδιοίκησης') are the competent authorities for a number of issues related to municipal waste ('δημοτικά απόβλητα').[767] More specifically, these consist of preparing local action plans for the prevention of littering and the management of municipal waste, estabishing a system of sorting at the source and separate collection for municipal waste, as well as applying 'pay-as-you-throw' schemes on municipal waste.[768] Local authorities may also have any power allocated to them by the Minister.[769]

760. Section 43(1)(a)–(f), (i) and (j) *ibid.*
761. Section 43(1)(g) *ibid.*
762. Section 43(1)(h) *ibid.*
763. Section 43(7)(b) *ibid.*
764. Section 43(7)(c) *ibid.*
765. Section 43(7)(d) *ibid.*
766. Section 43(2)–(6), (8) and (9) *ibid.*
767. *Municipal waste* ('déchets municipaux' in French, 'Siedlungsabfall' in German, 'stedelijk afval' in Dutch) means (a) mixed waste and separately collected waste from households, including paper and cardboard, glass, metals, plastics, bio-waste, wood, textiles, packaging, waste electrical and electronic equipment, waste batteries and accumulators, and bulky waste, including mattresses and furniture; (b) mixed waste and separately collected waste from other sources, where such waste is similar in nature and composition to waste from households; Municipal waste does not include waste from production, agriculture, forestry, fishing, septic tanks and sewage network and treatment, including sewage sludge, end-of-life vehicles or construction and demolition waste. Section 2 Law No. 185(I)/2011, which corresponds to Art. 3(2b) Directive 2008/98.
768. Section 5(1A)(a), (b) & (c) Law No. 185(I)/2011.
769. Section 5A(1)(d) *ibid.*

V. Inspector-in-Chief and Inspectors

157. For the purpose of effective application of this law, the competent authority may appoint public officers of his Ministry as inspector-in-chief and inspectors.[770] It may also appoint any private persons deemed to have appropriate qualifications to exercise certain powers of the inspectors and underlie certain conditions, as specified in the appointment that is also published in the Official Gazette.[771] The fees of such a person are decided by the competent authority and the Minister of Finance.[772] Such private persons further declare their financial interests in order to ensure that they have no financial or other interest in the field of waste, which could affect their impartiality.[773]

158. Inspectors undertake regular and irregular inspections on every person that performs treatment ('επεξεργασία')[774] of waste or professionally collects or transports waste, on brokers ('μεσίτες')[775] and dealers ('έμποροι'),[776] on every waste producer ('παραγωγός αποβλήτων')[777] and their plants, in order to ensure whether the activities, including rehabilitation works following cessation of activities, are executed according to operating conditions of waste treatment permits and the provisions of this law.[778] During those inspections, the inspectors may enter any plant and transport means, in which they reasonably think that an activity takes place or is about to take place, which may lead to violation of any provision of this law. When there is reasonable suspicion of imminent danger of serious pollution or danger to public health, inspections may take place at any time.[779] Apart from that, inspections may also be performed, when the plant is active.[780] Moreover, inspectors conduct inspections regarding the obligation of producers and processors of municipal waste to separate them properly at the source and to place them for separate collection. Further, the inspectors have the same powers as under Law No.

---

770. Section 44(1) *ibid.*
771. Section 44(2)(a) *ibid.*
772. Section 44(4) *ibid.*
773. Section 44(2)(b) *ibid.*
774. *Treatment* ('traitement' in French, 'Behandlung' in German, 'verwerking' in Dutch) means recovery or disposal operations, including preparation prior to recovery or disposal. Section 2 Law No. 185(I)/2011, which corresponds to Art. 3(14) Directive 2008/98/EC.
775. *Broker* ('courtier' in French, 'Makler' in German, 'makelaar' in Dutch) means any undertaking arranging the recovery or disposal of waste on behalf of others, including such brokers who do not take physical possession of the waste. Section 2 Law No. 185(I)/2011, which corresponds to Art. 3(8) Directive 2008/98/EC.
776. *Dealer* ('négociant' in French, 'Händler' in German, 'handelaar' in Dutch) means any undertaking which acts in the role of principal to purchase and subsequently sell waste, including such dealers who do not take physical possession of the waste. Section 2 Law No. 185(I)/2011, which corresponds to Art. 3(7) Directive 2008/98/EC.
777. *Waste producer* ('producteur de déchets' in French, 'Abfallerzeuger' in German, 'afvalstoffenproducent' in Dutch) means anyone whose activities produce waste (original waste producer) or anyone who carries out pre-processing, mixing or other operations resulting in a change in the nature or composition of this waste. Section 2 Law No. 185(I)/2011, which corresponds to Art. 3(5) Directive 2008/98/EC.
778. Section 45(1) Law No. 185(I)/2011.
779. Section 45(3A) *ibid.*
780. Section 45(2)(a) *ibid.*

106(I)/2002 (*see* in this respect paragraphs 99 et seq. above).[781] Finally, inspectors have the power to control, under the Union and national provisions for the protection of personal data, the contains of containers and bags in order to trace and verify the producers and/or processors of urban waste, who do not comply with the provisions of this law.[782]

159. Inspections concerning collection and transport operations cover the origin, nature, quantity and destination of the waste collected and transported.[783] The inspector-in-chief may take account of registrations obtained under the Community Eco-Management and Audit Scheme (EMAS), in particular regarding the frequency and intensity of inspections.[784]

§4. Waste Treatment Permit

160. Generally, no person may place, abandon, dispose or store waste at a public or private place or authorize or tolerate any of these actions, unless he holds a waste treatment permit or placing, abandoning, disposal or storage is performed at a place controlled by a person holding such permit and with the consent of this person.[785] More specifically, save for section 28 of this law, any person performing the operations listed in Annexes I[786] and II[787] must have a waste treatment permit from the Director of the Department for the Environment of the Ministry prior to commencing his operations.[788] Further, a waste treatment permit is also required for ship recycling facilities, along with the apposite provisions of EU law[789].[790]

781. Section 45(2)(b)–(h) *ibid.*
782. Section 45(2)(i) *ibid.*
783. Section 45(3) *ibid.*, which corresponds to Art. 34(2) Directive 2008/98/EC.
784. Section 45(4) Law No. 185(I)/2011, which corresponds to Art. 34(3) Directive 2008/98/EC.
785. Section 49(1)(b)(i) and (ii) Law No. 185(I)/2011.
786. Annex I *ibid.*, which corresponds to Annex II Directive 2008/98/EC. *See also* Annex II KrWG.
787. Annex II Law No. 185(I)/2011, which corresponds to Annex I Directive 2008/98/EC. *See also* Annex I KrWG.
788. Section 24 Law No. 185(I)/2011, which corresponds to Art. 23(1) Directive 2008/98/EC. *See* in this respect: *European Commission v. Hellenic Republic*, judgment of 11 Dec. 2014 in Case C-677/13, *digital* ECR. As Art. 23 corresponds to Art. 6 of the repealed Directive 75/439/EEC, *see*: *Groupement d'Intérêt Economique 'Rhône-Alpes Huiles' a.o. v. Syndicat National des Fabricants Raffineurs d'Huile de Graissage a.o.*, Case 295/85, [1984] ECR 00575; *Procureur de la République v. Association de défense des brûleurs d'huiles usages*, Case 240/83, [1985] ECR 00531 [relevant review: R. Kreutzberger, *Der Umweltschutz als Aufgabe der europäischen Gemeinschaften – gleichzeitig eine Besprechung der Urteile des EuGH vom 7. Februar 1985 in den Rs 173 und 240/83*, ZfU 169 (1986); A. Riesenkampff, *Die private Abfallentsorgung und das Kartellrecht*, 50 BB 833 (1995); W. Frenz, *Die Europäische Unternehmerfreiheit*, GewArch 427 (2009)]; *Commission of the European Communities v. Italian Republic*, Case C-366/89, [1993] ECR I-04201 [relevant review: A. Huteau-Mouglasis, *Une condamnation opportune pour l'effectivité du droit des déchets en Italie et en Europe*, REDE 431 (2007)]; *Commission of the European Communities v. Portuguese Republic*, Case C-392/99, [2003] ECR I-03373.
789. Regulation (EU) No 1257/2013 of the European Parliament and of the Council of 20 Nov. 2013 on ship recycling and amending Regulation (EC) No 1013/2006 and Directive 2009/16/EC Text with EEA relevance, OJ L 330, 10 Dec. 2013, p. 1, as amended.
790. Section 25(12) Law No. 185(I)/2011.

161. However, the competent authority may issue a decree exempting establishments or undertakings from the obligation to have a waste treatment permit for certain waste recovery operations, hazardous waste recovery operations and disposal of their own non-hazardous waste at the place of production.[791] This decree must include mandatory general operating conditions and/or special measures and define the types and quantities of waste covered by this exemption. Also the necessary treatment method must be specified. Especially for hazardous waste, the following must additionally be laid down: any further demands deemed necessary for recovery methods, any other necessary requirement for carrying out different forms of recovery and, where relevant, the limit values for the content of hazardous substances in the waste as well as the emission limit values. These general operating conditions and/or special measures are designed to ensure that waste is treated in accordance with section 10 of this law. Especially for exemptions for disposal of their own non-hazardous waste at the place of production, general operating conditions and/or special measures BAT must be considered.[792] The competent authority informs the EC of these decrees.[793]

162. It is explicitly stated that the costs of waste treatment, including the necessary infrastructure and its operation, are borne by the original waste producer or by the current or previous waste holders, in accordance with the polluter pays principle.[794] Product producers bear the responsibility of waste treatment of their products as well as of financing collection, reuse, preparation for reuse, treatment, recycling, recovery and disposal of same according to waste hierarchy and protection of human health and the environment.[795] Depending on the case, the competent authority may decide that the costs of waste treatment are to be borne partly or wholly by the producer of the product, from which the waste came, and that the distributors of such product may share these costs.[796] Regulations of the Council of Ministers may set out the responsibility of producers of products in relation to produced waste for certain waste streams and the shaping of collective or private management system.[797]

I. Application for a Waste Treatment Permit

163. The application for a waste treatment permit is submitted to the Director of the Department for the Environment of the Ministry and is accompanied by: (a) an

791. Section 28(1) *ibid.*, which corresponds to Art. 24 Directive 2008/98/EC.
792. Section 28(1) and (2) Law No. 185(I)/2011, which corresponds to Art. 25(1) and (2) Directive 2008/98/EC.
793. Section 28(3) Law No. 185(I)/2011, which corresponds to Art. 25(3) Directive 2008/98/EC.
794. Section 23(1) Law No. 185(I)/2011, which corresponds to Art. 14(1) Directive 2008/98/EC. As Art. 14 corresponds to Art. 15 of repealed Directive 2006/12/EC, *see Futura Immobiliare srl Hotel Futura a.o. v. Comune di Casoria*, Case C-254/08, [2009] ECR I-06995.
795. Section 23(2) Law No. 185(I)/2011.
796. Section 23(3) *ibid.*, which corresponds to Art. 14(2) Directive 2008/98/EC.
797. Section 23(4) Law No. 185(I)/2011.

urban planning permission ('πολεοδομική άδεια'), if Law No. 90/1972 is applicable, the positive view of the Director of Planning and Housing Department in cases of governmental departments or services or a building permission ('άδεια οικοδομής'); (b) a clear criminal record certificate; (c) a certificate by the fire department regarding the applicant complying with his obligations related to fire safety and fire safety on the premises; and (d) the security measures and measures of precaution that must be taken under the evaluation of the risks accompanied by an affidavit of the applicant reassuring that these are followed.[798] Following receipt of an application, the Director ensures that on the webpage of the Ministry a notification is posted stating the date that the application was received, the place where the public can review it during working days and hours and informing that any interested person may submit his views and recommendations on the content of the application.[799] Incomplete applications are not evaluated. They are returned to the applicant with a note specifying the missing items.[800]

II. Evaluation of an Application for Waste Treatment Permit

164. The Consultation Committee on Waste Management, along with the local authorities, prepare a consulting opinion for the Director, who shall decide on the application for a waste treatment permit. The Director has the power to ask for the views and opinions of any Ministry, Service or Organization.[801] If the permit is related to using waste as fuel or other means of producing energy, the Minister consolidates with the Minister for Energy, Commerce and Industry and the Minister of Labour, Welfare and Social Insurance.[802] Prior to reaching such a decision, the Director performs an on-site inspection in order to ensure that the operating conditions, which shall be attached to the waste treatment permit, are complied with and that the personnel is properly trained.[803] Lastly, for the purpose of obviating the unnecessary duplication of information and the repetition of work by the operator or the competent authority, every permit to be issued on the grounds of other legislation may be combined with a waste treatment permit under section 24 of this law so that a *comprehensive permit* ('ενιαία άδεια') is issued.[804] In the event that a permit that has been issued under other environmental legislation includes a specific and explicit provision for compliance with this law and sets out the apposite conditions, then such permit is approved as *comprehensive* permit by the Director, who declares that due to said, previously issued, permit no waste treatment permit under section 24 of this law is required, while making explicit reference to the relevant conditions.[805] Especially undertakings that hold a permit under the Law on Industrial Emissions (*see* in this respect paragraphs 280 et seq below), are exempt

798. Section 25(1)(a) *ibid.*
799. Section 25(10)(a), (b) & (c) *ibid.*
800. Section 25(1)(b) *ibid.*
801. Section 25(2)(a) & (b) *ibid.*
802. Section 25(6) *ibid.*
803. Section 25(7) *ibid.*
804. Section 25(9)(a) *ibid.*
805. Section 25(9)(b) *ibid.*

from the obligation of holding a waste treatment permit, as long as the industrial emissions permit includes an explicit and specific condition for compliance with this law. The Director shall declare that due to said industrial emissions permit, the need for a waste treatment permit has lapsed.[806]

III. Granting a Waste Treatment Permit

165. The Director may grant a waste treatment permit and attach operating conditions thereto. Such conditions may specify: the types and quantities of waste that may be treated;[807] the technical and any other requirements relevant to the site concerned;[808] the safety and precautionary measures to be taken;[809] the method to be used for each type of operation;[810] such monitoring and control operations as may be necessary;[811] and such closure and after-care provisions as may be necessary.[812] The permit is granted for a specified period, which may not be longer than ten years.[813] Further, it shall be a condition of any waste treatment permit covering incineration or co-incineration with energy recovery that the recovery of energy takes place with a high level of energy efficiency.[814]

166. Prior to issuing a waste treatment permit under section 24 of this law, the applicant of same deposits with the Director of the Department for Environment a guarantee or sufficient insurance for the cost of expenses related to any incident of pollution that may be caused by his operations as well as for events of non-rational utilization of waste in violation of the general rule of protection of human health and the environment.[815] Should the applicant have already deposited a guarantee or sufficient insurance to the competent authority for another permit according to other statutory provision, this is duly taken into consideration for calculating the guarantee or sufficient insurance in question.[816] Nevertheless, this factor, which directly relates to the financial obligations of the applicant, is strange to the purpose served by the guarantee and insurance necessary under this law. The aim here served is the one of safeguarding remediation of environmental damage caused by activities regulated under this law, to the environment, where a plant – equally regulated

806. Section 25(9)(c) *ibid.*
807. Section 25(3)(b)(i) *ibid.*, which corresponds to Art. 23(1)(a) Directive 2008/98/EC.
808. Section 25(3)(b)(ii) Law No. 185(I)/2011, which corresponds to Art. 23(1)(b) Directive 2008/98/EC.
809. Section 25(3)(b)(iii) Law No. 185(I)/2011, which corresponds to Art. 23(1)(c) Directive 2008/98/EC.
810. Section 25(3)(b)(iv) Law No. 185(I)/2011, which corresponds to Art. 23(1)(d) Directive 2008/98/EC.
811. Section 25(3)(b)(v) Law No. 185(I)/2011, which corresponds to Art. 23(1)(e) Directive 2008/98/EC.
812. Section 25(3)(b)(vi) Law No. 185(I)/2011, which corresponds to Art. 23(1)(f) Directive 2008/98/EC.
813. Section 25(4) Law No. 185(I)/2011, which corresponds to Art. 23(4) Directive 2008/98/EC.
814. Section 25(3)(c) Law No. 185(I)/2011, which corresponds to Art. 23(4) Directive 2008/98/EC.
815. Sections 26(1) & 10 Law No. 185(I)/2011.
816. Section 26(3) *ibid.*

under this law – operates. Hence, taking into account the financial obligations of the plant operator, as per the statutory provision, contradicts the scope of this provision along with the 'polluter pays' principle enshrined in Article 191(2) TFEU.

167. General operating conditions and special measures for specific waste categories or part of their management may be specified by the competent authority in a decree, which is issued in the Official Gazette. These shall be a vital part of every relevant waste treatment permit.[817]

168. Holders of waste treatment permit underlie the following statutory obligations. They must adhere to all operating conditions attached to the permit.[818] They further have to monitor the operations of the plant and inform the competent authority of the results of this monitoring accordingly.[819] Also, they are obliged to assist every inspector in any way deemed necessary in order to perform plant's inspections, sampling and collection of data that are necessary for exercising their statutory duties.[820] Lastly, record-keeping obligations are imposed on them. In particular, they shall keep a chronological record of the quantity, nature and origin of the waste, and the quantity of products and materials resulting from preparing for reuse, recycling or other recovery operations, and, where relevant, the destination, frequency of collection, mode of transport and treatment method foreseen in respect of the waste. This information is made available via the electronic registers to the competent authority every March as well as every time that this is requested.[821] They further provide the competent authority or previous holder of hazardous waste documentary evidence regarding performance of hazardous waste treatment, when these are requested.[822] Record-keeping obligations also extend to persons exempt from the obligation to hold a waste treatment permit, to every producer of hazardous waste and persons collecting or transporting hazardous waste on a professional basis, or act as dealers and brokers of hazardous waste.[823] Record-keeping obligations with reference to hazardous waste apply to producers and holders of such waste, holders of waste treatment permit, dealers and brokers. These obligations generally have the above-stated content, albeit their precise content and the procedure of proper keeping are specified in a Ministerial Decree.[824] Record is kept for at least five years, with the exception of hazardous waste plants that keep this record for as long as they operate.[825] Upon cessation of waste production and management operations, said person hand over this record of hazardous waste to the competent authority.[826]

---

817. Section 27 *ibid.*
818. Section 29(a) *ibid.*
819. Section 29(b) *ibid.*
820. Section 29(c) *ibid.*
821. Section 32(1)(a)(i) and (ii) *ibid.*, which corresponds to Art. 35(1)(a)and (b) Directive 2008/98/EC.
822. Section 32(1)(a)(iii) Law No. 185(I)/2011.
823. Section 32(1)(a) *ibid.*
824. Section 32(2)(a) and (3) *ibid.*
825. Section 32(2)(a) *ibid.*
826. Section 32(2)(b) *ibid.*

IV. Rejection of an Application for Waste Treatment Permit

169. The Director rejects an application for a waste treatment permit, when the intended method of treatment is deemed unacceptable from the point of view of environmental protection. He equally rejects applications suggesting treatment methods not in accordance with the object of this law, that being without risk to water, air, soil, plants or animals, without causing a nuisance through noise or odours, without negatively affecting protected species and natural habitats and without adversely affecting the countryside or places of special interest.[827]

170. Against rejection of application for waste treatment permit, an appeal ('προσφυγή') may be filed with the Supreme Court of Cyprus according to Article 146 of the Constitution.

V. Alteration, Revocation and Renewal of Waste Treatment Permit

171. When the holder of a waste treatment permit intends to make any change to the nature or operation of the plant, he must previously inform in writing to the Director. It is specified that change to the nature or operation of a plant ('αλλαγή στην φύση ή τη λειτουργία της') means a change in the characteristics, manner of operation or extension of the plant. Said authority may then amend the operating conditions of the waste treatment permit, if he deems those to be necessary for the purpose of environment protection.[828] Especially for change to the nature or operation of a plant, which may cause significant negative effects ('σημαντικές αρνητικές επιπτώσεις') on public health and the environment, the holder of the permit has to report to the Director the parts of the plant that may be amended and the operating duration of the plant, which may be effected by suggested changes.[829]

172. The Director may amend the operating conditions of a waste treatment permit, if he deems this proper for the purpose of preventing risk to water, air, soil, plants or animals, nuisance through noise or odours, negative effect to protected species and natural habitats and adverse effect to the countryside or places of special interest.[830] For the same purpose, same authority may also impose any new operating conditions,[831] shorten its validity period[832] or revoke the waste treatment

827. Sections 25(5) and 10 *ibid.* that correspond to Art. 23(3) and 13 Directive 2008/98/EC.
828. Section 30(1) and (4) Law No. 185(I)/2011.
829. Sections 30(2)(a) and (b) and 25(4) *ibid.* Still, it is highly probable that the mention to section 25(4) was intended to be towards its old version, and not the current one that refers to operating duration of a plant. The old version refers to the type and amount of waste that may be treated, the technical and other demands related to any permitted activity, the safety and precautionary measures, the methods that must be used, the measures for emergency and serious danger, the required technical and scientific personel and the provisions related to closure and care following the ceasure of operations, if this is necessary.
830. Section 31(1)(d) *ibid.*
831. Section 31(1)(c) *ibid.*
832. Section 31(1)(b) *ibid.*

permit.[833] In cases of emergency ('έκτακτη ανάγκη') and when risk to water, air, soil, plants or animals, nuisance through noise or odours negatively affect protected species and natural habitats and adverse effect to the countryside or places of special interest have materialized, the Director may issue a notice of temporary staying of plant's operation.[834]

173. Following the expiration of a waste treatment permit, any person managing waste is obliged to rehabilitate any damage caused to the environment from their operation and the natural environment through setup and integration of the plant's site.[835] Responsibility and cost of rehabilitation measures lie exclusively to such person.[836] When these measures are taken, according to explicit provision of this law, the procedure for cessation of activities set out in Law on Integrated Pollution Prevention and Control of 2003 is followed.[837] However, that law has been repealed by Law No. 184(I)/2013 (*see* in this regard paragraphs 280 et seq. below). Hence, the latter is to be applied.

§5. Statutory Obligations

174. This law foresees important obligations related to waste for both the competent authority, which concern waste hierarchy, network of waste disposal plants, duties related to hazardous waste, waste oils and bio-waste, waste management plans and waste prevention programmes, and the operators involved, which include extended producer responsibility, responsibility of original waste producers and waste holders and obligations related to hazardous waste.

I. Statutory Obligations of the Competent Authority

A. *Waste Hierarchy*

175. In waste prevention and management legislation and policy, the following waste hierarchy applies:

(a) *prevention* ('prévention' in French, 'Vermeidung' in German, 'preventie' in Dutch);
(b) *preparation for reuse* ('préparation en vue du réemploi' in French, 'Vorbereitung zur Wiederverwendung' in German, 'voorbereiding voor hergebruik' in Dutch);
(c) *recycling* ('recyclage' in French, 'Recycling' in German, 'recycling' in Dutch);

833. Section 31(1)(a) *ibid.*
834. Sections 31(2) and 10 *ibid.*
835. Section 31(1)(a) *ibid.*
836. Section 34(1)(b) *ibid.*
837. Section 34(2) *ibid.*

(d) *other recovery*, e.g., energy recovery, ('autre valorisation, notamment valorisation énergétique' in French, 'sonstige Verwertung, z.B. energetische Verwertung' in German, 'andere nuttige toepassing, bv. energieterugwinning' in Dutch); and
(e) *disposal* ('élimination' in French, 'Beseitigung' in German, 'verwijdering' in Dutch).[838]

176. When applying this hierarchy, the competent authority takes all necessary measures to encourage the options that deliver the best overall environmental outcome. This may require specific waste streams departing from the hierarchy where this is justified by life cycle thinking on the overall impacts of the generation and management of such waste. The competent authority further takes into account the general environmental protection principles of precaution and sustainability, technical feasibility and economic viability, protection of resources as well as the overall environmental, human health, economic and social impacts.[839] The Minister makes use of economic instruments and other measures to provide incentives for the application of the waste hierarchy, such as those indicated in an annex of this law[840] or other appropriate instruments and measures.[841]

177. The competent authority takes the necessary measures to ensure that waste undergoes recovery operations, in accordance with the protection of human health and the environment, as these are specified in this law.[842]

178. Equally, it takes all necessary measures to promote the reuse of products and preparing for reuse activities, notably by encouraging the establishment and support of reuse and repair networks, the use of economic instruments, procurement criteria, quantitative objectives or other measures. It also promotes high-quality recycling and, to this end, sets up separate collections of waste at least for paper, metals, plastic and glass and, by 1 January 2025, for textiles.[843]

179. He also promotes selective demolition in order to enable removal and safe handling of hazardous substances and facilitate reuse and high-quality recycling by selective removal of materials, and ensure the establishment of sorting systems for construction and demolition waste at least for wood, mineral fractions (concrete, bricks, tiles and ceramics, stones), metal, glass, plastic and plaster.[844] Furthermore,

838. Section 9(1) *ibid.*, which corresponds to Art. 4(1) Directive 2008/98/EC. *See* in this respect also §6 Abs. 1 KrWG.
839. Section 9(2) and (3) Law No. 185(I)/2011, which corresponds to Art. 4(2) Directive 2008/98/EC.
840. Annex IV Law No. 185(I)/2011, which corresponds to Annex IVa Directive 2008/98/EC.
841. Section 9(4) Law No. 185(I)/2011, which corresponds to Art. 4(3) Directive 2008/98/EC.
842. Sections 12 and 10 Law No. 185(I)/2011, which correspond to Arts 10 and 13 Directive 2008/98/EC.
843. Section 13(1), (2) and (3) Law No. 185(I)/2011, which corresponds to Art. 11(1) Directive 2008/98/EC.
844. Section 13(3A) Law No. 185(I)/2011, which corresponds to Art. 11(1) Directive 2008/98/EC.

the Minister prevents waste generation by taking the following measures at a minimum; promoting sustainable production and consumption modes, encouraging reparable and reusable products, preventing critical raw materials from becoming waste, reducing food waste and encouraging food donation, reducing waste generation in industrial production and in particular waste that is not suitable for reuse or recycling, promoting the reduction of the content of hazardous substances in materials and products, identifying products that are the main sources of littering and preventing and reducing litter therefrom, halting the generation of marine litter and organizing and supporting information campaigns on waste prevention.[845] The Minister is obliged to monitor and assess the implementation of the waste prevention measures, the measures on reuse and the food waste prevention measures applying specific methodology and indicators.[846] It is further foreseen that for achieving the aims of this law and moving to a European circular economy with a high level of resource efficiency, the Minister takes all necessary measures for: (a) preparing for reuse and the recycling of waste materials such as at least paper, metal, plastic and glass from households and possibly from other origins as far as these waste streams are similar to waste from households, to be increased to a minimum of overall 50%;[847] (b) preparing for reuse, recycling and other material recovery, including backfilling operations using waste to substitute other materials, of non-hazardous construction and demolition waste excluding naturally occurring material defined in category 17 05 04 in the list of waste to be increased to a minimum of 70% by weight;[848] and (c) gradually increasing the preparing for reuse and recycling of municipal waste up to 65% by 2035.[849]Specific rules on the calculation of the attainment of said targets have been set out in the law.[850] The Council of Ministers has the power to issue regulations setting out all necessary measures for the best achievement of said targets and obligations.[851]

180. Lastly, waste undergoes safe disposal operations which meet the provisions for the protection of human health and the environment, where recovery is not undertaken.[852]

845. Section 11B(1)(a)–(m) Law No. 185(I)/2011, which corresponds to Art. 9(1)(a)–(m) Directive 2008/98/EC.
846. Section 11B(2), (3) & (4) Law No. 185(I)/2011, which corresponds to Art. 9(3), (4) & (5) Directive 2008/98/EC.
847. Section 13(4)(a) Law No. 185(I)/2011, which corresponds to Art. 11(2)(a) Directive 2008/98/EC.
848. Section 13(4)(b) Law No. 185(I)/2011, which corresponds to Art. 11(2)(b) Directive 2008/98/EC.
849. Section 13(4)(c), (d) and (e) Law No. 185(I)/2011, which corresponds to Art. 11(2)(c), (d) and (e) Directive 2008/98/EC.
850. In this respect *see* section 13A Law No. 185(I)/2011, which corresponds to Art. 11A Directive 2008/98/EC.
851. Section 13(6) Law No. 185(I)/2011.
852. Section 14(1) *ibid.*, which corresponds to Art. 12 Directive 2008/98/EC. *See* in this respect *European Commission v. Republic of Slovenia*, judgment of 16 Jul. 2015 in Case C-140/14, *digital* ECR.

B. Network of Waste Disposal Plants

181. An integrated and adequate network of waste disposal plants and of plants for the recovery of mixed municipal waste collected from private households, including where such collection also covers such waste from other producers, taking into account BAT, is established by the competent authority, in cooperation with other Member States, where this is necessary or advisable.[853] The competent authority may limit incoming shipments ('μεταφορά')[854] of waste destined to incinerators that are classified as recovery, where it has been established that such shipments would result in national waste having to be disposed of or waste having to be treated in a way that is not consistent with the waste management plans. This shall be done in order to protect the national network and by way of derogation from Regulation (EC) No. 1013/2006. The EC is informed of such decision. Limitation of incoming shipments may also be decided on environmental grounds as set out in Regulation (EC) No. 1013/2006.[855] This network is designed to enable the Union as a whole to become self-sufficient in waste disposal as well as in the recovery of waste and to enable Cyprus, as well as other Member States, to move towards that aim individually, taking into account geographical circumstances or the need for specialized installations for certain types of waste.[856] It shall further enable waste to be disposed of or waste to be recovered in one of the nearest appropriate installations, by means of the most appropriate methods and technologies, in order to ensure a high level of protection for the environment and public health.[857] However, the principles of proximity and self-sufficiency do not mean that Cyprus has to possess the full range of final recovery facilities within its jurisdiction.[858]

---

853. Section 16(1) Law No. 185(I)/2011, which corresponds to Art. 16(1) Directive 2008/98/EC. As Art. 16 corresponds to Art. 5 of repealed Directive 2006/12/EC, *see European Commission v. Italian Republic*, Case C-297/08, ECR 2010 I-01749 [relevant review: J. Dupont-Lassalle, *La crise des déchets en Italie aux prises avec le droit de l'Union européenne*, Europe 34 (2010); C. Feliziani, *The Duty of Member States to Guarantee the Right to a Healthy Environment: A Consideration of European Commission v. Italy* (C-297/08), 24 JEL 535 (2012)].
854. For the purpose of these limitations, *shipment* ('transfert' in French, 'Verbringung' in German, 'overbrenging' in Dutch) means the transport of waste destined for recovery or disposal which is planned or takes place: (a) between a country and another country; or (b) between a country and overseas countries and territories or other areas, under that country's protection; or (c) between a country and any land area which is not part of any country under international law; or (d) between a country and the Antarctic; or (e) from one country through any of the areas referred to above; or (f) within a country through any of the areas referred to above and which originates in and ends in the same country; or (g) from a geographic area not under the jurisdiction of any country, to a country. Section 16(2)(d) Law No. 185(I)/2011, Art. 2(34) Regulation 1013/2006.
855. Section 16(2) Law No. 185(I)/2011, which corresponds to Art. 16(1) Directive 2008/98/EC.
856. Section 16(3) Law No. 185(I)/2011, which corresponds to Art. 16(2) Directive 2008/98/EC.
857. Section 16(4) Law No. 185(I)/2011, which corresponds to Art. 16(3) Directive 2008/98/EC. *See* in this respect *Ragn-Sells AS v. Sillamäe Linnavalitsus*, Case C-292/12, *digital* ECR [relevant review: R. Conzelmann, *Dienstleistungskonzession für Sammlung und Transport von Abfällen*, 33 NVwZ 287 (2014); I. Koufaki, ***Επιχειρήσεις διάθεσης και αξιοποίησης αποβλήτων***, 62 NoB 448 (2014)].
858. Section 16(5) Law No. 185(I)/2011, which corresponds to Art. 16(4) Directive 2008/98/EC.

C. Obligations for Hazardous Waste, Waste Oils and Bio-waste

182. Especially for hazardous waste, it is specified that the competent authority takes the necessary action to ensure that the production, collection and transportation of hazardous waste, as well as its storage and treatment, are carried out in conditions providing protection for the environment and human health in order to meet the provisions on protection of human health and the environment. This includes action to ensure traceability from production to final destination and control of hazardous waste.[859]

183. Specific obligations are further set out with reference to waste oils. It must be ensured that: waste oils are collected separately, unless separate collection is not technically feasible taking into account good practices;[860] waste oils are treated giving priority to regeneration or alternatively to other recycling operations delivering an equivalent or a better overall environmental outcome than regeneration in accordance with provisions on protection of human health and the environment and waste hierarchy;[861] waste oils of different characteristics are not mixed, and waste oils are not mixed with other kinds of waste or substances, if such mixing impedes their regeneration or another recycling operation delivering an equivalent or a better overall environmental outcome than regeneration.[862] Additional measures such as technical requirements, producer responsibility, economic instruments or voluntary agreements are set out in Regulations of the Council of Ministers for the purposes of separate collection of waste oils and their proper treatment.[863]

184. Bio-waste is either separated and recycled at source, or is collected separately and is not mixed with other types of waste by 31 December 2023. The Minister may allow waste with similar biodegradability and compostability properties which complies with relevant European standards or any equivalent national standards for packaging recoverable through composting and biodegradation, to be collected together with bio-waste. At the same time, he takes all appropriate measures for: (a) encouraging the recycling, including composting and digestion, of bio-waste in a way that fulfils a high level of environmental protection and results in output which meets relevant high-quality standards; (b) encouraging home composting; and (c) promoting the use of materials produced from bio-waste.[864]

D. Waste Management Plans

185. Waste Management Plans are established by the Council of Ministers following a proposal of the Minister and a consulting opinion of the Consulting

859. Section 17(1) and (2) Law No. 185(I)/2011, which corresponds to Art. 17 Directive 2008/98/EC.
860. Section 21(1)(a) Law No. 185(I)/2011, which corresponds to Art. 21(1)(a) Directive 2008/98/EC.
861. Section 21(1)(b) Law No. 185(I)/2011, which corresponds to Art. 21(1)(b) Directive 2008/98/EC.
862. Section 21(1)(c) Law No. 185(I)/2011, which corresponds to Art. 21(1)(c) Directive 2008/98/EC.
863. Section 21(2) Law No. 185(I)/2011, which corresponds to Art. 21(2) Directive 2008/98/EC.
864. Section 22 Law No. 185(I)/2011, which corresponds to Art. 22 Directive 2008/98/EC.

Committee on Waste Management in accordance with the scope of this law, waste hierarchy and the principles of proximity and self-sufficiency, even if the waste streams fall within the competence of the local authorities. They are issued in the form of regulations and published in the Official Gazette. Those plans may be drafted for each waste stream or all of them and may, alone or in combination, cover the entire geographical territory of Cyprus.[865] For their drafting, the competent authority also cooperates with other interested parties and the Commission, depending on the case.[866]

186. It is further ensured that the public is given a timely and effective opportunity to participate in the preparation of waste management plans,[867] with the exception of cases of national defence or emergency ('καταστάσεις έκτακτης ανάγκης').[868] It is explained that the public,[869] which the Minister consults ('το κοινό με το οποίο ο Υπουργός διαβουλεύεται'), means the public being effected or possibly being effected or whose interests are effected from the decision-making process and non-governmental organizations, such as organizations for the protection of the environment.[870] For the aforementioned purpose of public participation, the Minister informs the public of every proposal regarding such plans[871] as well as of the fact that relevant information is available to the public during working days and hours at the office of Environmental Authority ('Περιβαλλοντική Αρχή').[872] The public is also informed that it may submit its opinion and representations regarding the proposal's content within thirty-six days.[873] These are stated in a notification, which is published in the Official Gazette, in two daily newspapers and on the Internet. In addition, the Environmental Authority publishes on the Internet an announcement, when proposals for a waste management plan are submitted to the Minister[874] and when opinions of any person regarding such proposals are submitted.[875] A public hearing ('δημόσια ακρόαση') may be held in cases of important waste management plans. The relevant decision is reached by the Minister, following the submission of a reasoned proposal by the Environment Authority, which prerequisites consultation with the Technical Committee for Waste Management.[876] The characteristics of the procedure, the procedure itself and any other relevant matter are regulated in Regulations of the Council of Ministers.[877]

865. Section 35(1), (1A) and (2) Law No. 185(I)/2011, which corresponds to Art. 28(1) Directive 2008/98/EC.
866. Section 35(8) Law No. 185(I)/2011.
867. Section 38(1) *ibid.* On participation of the public in Germany *see* §32 KrWG.
868. Section 37(2) Law No. 185(I)/2011.
869. Public means one or more natural or legal persons, as well as associations, organizations or groups thereof. Section 37(1) *ibid.*
870. Section 38(4)(a) and (b) *ibid.*
871. Section 38(2)(a) *ibid.*
872. Section 38(2)(b) *ibid.*
873. Section 38(2)(c) *ibid.*
874. Section 38(3)(a) *ibid.*
875. Section 38(3)(b) *ibid.*
876. Section 39(1) *ibid.*
877. Section 39(2) *ibid.*

Submitted opinions and representations of the public and the results of public hearings are to be duly taken into consideration by the Council of Ministers before deciding on waste management plans.[878]

187. The EC is informed of final decisions on waste management plans by the competent authority.[879] The latter also informs the public via a notification published in the Official Gazette, two newspapers and on the Internet, stating that the following information is available in the archive: description of the plant as approved;[880] short notice related to the manner that opinions and representations of the public, or the results of public hearing were taken into consideration;[881] and the reasons and evaluations, on which final decision was based.[882] Also, the place and time, during which the public has access to this information, is stated.[883]

188. Waste management plans set out an analysis of the current waste management situation in the geographical entity concerned, as well as the measures to be taken to improve environmentally sound preparation for reuse, recycling, recovery and disposal of waste and an evaluation of how the plan will support the implementation of the objectives and provisions of this law.[884]

189. Information, which needs to be contained in waste management plans, as appropriate and taking into account the geographical level and coverage of the planning area, is the following: the type, quantity and source of waste generated within the territory of Cyprus, the waste likely to be shipped from or to Cyprus, and an evaluation of the development of waste streams in the future;[885] existing major disposal and recovery installations, including any special arrangements for waste oils, hazardous waste, waste containing significant amounts of critical raw materials, or waste streams addressed by specific Union legislation;[886] an assessment of the need for closure of existing waste installations and additional waste installation infrastructure in accordance with the principles of proximity and self-sufficiency, and the investments and other financial means related thereto;[887] sufficient information on the location criteria for site identification and on the capacity of future disposal or major recovery installations, if necessary;[888] and general waste management policies, including planned waste management technologies and methods, or policies for waste posing specific management problems.[889] In addition waste management plans *may* contain, taking into account the geographical level and coverage of the

878. Section 40 *ibid.* Views of the public in Germany are taken into consideration in a proportional manner ('angemessen'). *See* §32 Abs. 2 Satz 4 KrWG.
879. Section 35(9) Law No. 185(I)/2011, which corresponds to Art. 33(1) Directive 2008/98/EC.
880. Section 41(a) Law No. 185(I)/2011.
881. Section 41(b)(i) *ibid.*
882. Section 41(b)(ii) *ibid.*
883. Section 41 *ibid.*
884. Section 35(3) *ibid.*, which corresponds to Art. 28(2) Directive 2008/98/EC.
885. Section 35(4)(a) Law No. 185(I)/2011, which corresponds to Art. 28(3)(a) Directive 2008/98/EC.
886. Section 35(4)(b) Law No. 185(I)/2011, which corresponds to Art. 28(3)(b) Directive 2008/98/EC.
887. Section 35(4)(c) Law No. 185(I)/2011, which corresponds to Art. 28(3)(c) Directive 2008/98/EC.
888. Section 35(4)(d) Law No. 185(I)/2011, which corresponds to Art. 28(3)(d) Directive 2008/98/EC.
889. Section 35(4)(e) Law No. 185(I)/2011, which corresponds to Art. 28(3)(e) Directive 2008/98/EC.

planning area, the following: organizational aspects related to waste management including a description of the allocation of responsibilities between public and private actors carrying out the waste management;[890] an evaluation of the usefulness and suitability of the use of economic and other instruments in tackling various waste problems, taking into account the need to maintain the smooth functioning of the internal market;[891] the use of awareness campaigns and information provision directed at the general public or at a specific set of consumers;[892] information on the measures to attain the objective that all waste suitable for recycling or other recovery shall not be accepted in a landfill or objectives in other strategic documents;[893] an assessment of existing waste collection schemes, including the material and territorial coverage of separate collection and measures to improve its operation, of any derogations granted and of the need for new collection schemes;[894] historical contaminated waste disposal sites and measures for their rehabilitation with Law No. 187(I)/2002;[895] cost evaluation of waste recovery and disposal operations;[896] measures to combat and prevent all forms of littering and to clean up all types of litter;[897] and appropriate qualitative or quantitative indicators and targets, including on the quantity of generated waste and its treatment and on municipal waste that is disposed of or subject to energy recovery.[898] It is noteworthy that the last two items, along with information on measures for attaining objectives and the assessment of waste collection schemes belong to the mandatory information of a waste management plan, under EU law; thus the competent authority does not enjoy discretion in including these in said plans.

190. Waste management plans conform to the waste planning requirements laid down in the legislation on packaging and packaging waste,[899] Law No. 32(I)/2002.[900] Their scope is prevention of waste packaging and especially reuse of package, recovery of material, recycle of waste package and energy recovery without polluting the environment with a view to reducing final waste disposal.[901] They further aim to apply the polluter pays principle and the principle of shared responsibility of all financial partners involved, regardless of those being public or

---

890. Section 35(5)(a) Law No. 185(I)/2011, which corresponds to Art. 28(4)(a) Directive 2008/98/EC.
891. Section 35(5)(b) Law No. 185(I)/2011, which corresponds to Art. 28(4)(b) Directive 2008/98/EC.
892. Section 35(5)(c) Law No. 185(I)/2011, which corresponds to Art. 28(4)(c) Directive 2008/98/EC.
893. Section 35(5)(ca) Law No. 185(I)/2011, which corresponds to Art. 28(3)(ca) Directive 2008/98/EC.
894. Section 35(5)(cb) Law No. 185(I)/2011, which corresponds to Art. 28(3)(cb) Directive 2008/98/EC.
895. Section 35(5)(d) Law No. 185(I)/2011, which partially corresponds to Art. 28(4)(d) Directive 2008/98/EC. The European directive does not specify any legal provision for rehabilitation measures.
896. Section 35(5)(e) Law No. 185(I)/2011.
897. Section 35(5)(f) Law No. 185(I)/2011, which corresponds to Art. 28(3)(f) Directive 2008/98/EC.
898. Section 35(5)(g) Law No. 185(I)/2011, which corresponds to Art. 28(3)(g) Directive 2008/98/EC.
899. Law on Packaging and Packaging Waste ('ο περί Συσκευασιών και Αποβλήτων Συσκευασιών Νόμος') No. 32 of 2002, OG I(I) No. 3594 of 12 Apr. 2002, which implements European Parliament and Council Directive 94/62/EC of 20 Dec. 1994 on packaging and packaging waste, OJ L 365, 31 Dec. 1994, p. 10, as amended.
900. Section 35(6) *ibid.*
901. Section 5(2)(a) Law No. 32(I)/2002.

private.[902] Also, public information and participation in management programmes are encouraged.[903] In addition, it is ensured that additional precautionary measures are taken, such as national programmes, plans for producer's responsibility, for the purpose of minimizing environmental effects of packaging, analogous actions that are approved, if necessary, after consultation with financial actors and are planned for the purposes of concentrating and processing initiatives taken by the state regarding prevention.[904]

191. Waste management plans also comply with the strategy for the implementation of the reduction of biodegradable waste going to landfills in accordance with Regulations on Solid and Hazardous Waste (Landfill of Waste).[905,906] In particular, it is foreseen that not later than 15 June 2010, biodegradable municipal waste going to landfills must be reduced to 75% of the total amount (by weight) of biodegradable municipal waste produced in 1995 or the latest year before 1995 for which standardized Eurostat data are available.[907] A further reduction to 50% of the total amount is to be achieved no later than 15 June 2012.[908] In the following four years, that being no later than 15 June 2016, a reduction to 35% of the total amount has to materialize.[909]

192. Waste management plans equally comply with the aim of moving towards a European circular economy with a high level of resource efficiency and the relevant measures designed to achieve the relevant targets (*see* in this respect paragraphs 177 et seq above). Finally, for the purposes of litter prevention, they shall conform to the statutory duty of achieving and maintaining good environmental status in respect of marine regions[910] and achieving the established environmental objectives with regard to river basin districts, both local and international[911].[912]

193. Waste management plans are evaluated at least every sixth year and revised as appropriate and, where relevant, in accordance with the provisions on the

902. Section 5(2)(b) and (c) *ibid.*
903. Section 5(2)(d) *ibid.*
904. Section 5(2)(e) *ibid.*
905. Regulations on Solid and Hazardous Waste (Landfill of Waste) ('οι Περί Στερεών και Επικινδύνων Αποβλήτων (Χώροι Υγειονομικής Ταφής)') No. 562 of 2003, OG III(I) No. 3735 of 11 Jul. 2003, p. 3177, which implement Council Directive 1999/31/EC of 26 Apr. 1999 on the landfill of waste, OJ L 182, 16 Jul. 1999, p. 1, as amended.
906. Section 35(6) Law No. 185(I)/2011.
907. Regulation 5(1) Regulations No. 562/2003, which corresponds to Art. 5(2)(a) Directive 1999/31/EC.
908. Regulation 5(2) Regulations No. 562/2003, which corresponds to Art. 5(2)(b) Directive 1999/31/EC.
909. Regulation 5(3) Regulations No. 562/2003, which corresponds to Art. 5(2)(c) Directive 1999/31/EC.
910. Section 13 Law on Marine Strategy, Law No. 18(I)/2011, which corresponds to Art. 13 Directive 2008/56/EC.
911. Section 19 Law on Water Protection and Management, Law No. 13(I)/2004, which corresponds to Art. 11 Directive 2000/60/EC.
912. Section 35(6) Law No. 185(I)/2011, which corresponds to Art. 28(5) Directive 2008/98/EC.

protection of human health and the environment.[913] The public is given a timely and effective opportunity to participate in amendment and revision of waste management plans.[914] The EC is informed of such amendments by the competent authority in the appropriate format established by the Commission.[915]

E. Waste Prevention Programmes

194. Waste prevention programmes are established by the Council of Ministers following a proposal of the Minister and a consulting opinion of the Consulting Committee on Waste Management in accordance with waste hierarchy and the scope of this law, that being protection of the environment and human health by waste prevention or reduction of waste generation, by preventing or reducing adverse impacts of waste generation and management and by reduction of overall impacts of resource use and improvement of the efficiency of such use. At a minimum it includes the aforementioned measures for the prevention of creation of waste (*see* in this respect paragraph 177 above).[916] The aforementioned regarding public participation in waste management plans applies *mutatis mutandis*.[917]

195. Such programmes are integrated either into the waste management plans or into other environmental policy programmes, as appropriate, or function as separate programmes. If any such programme is integrated into the waste management plan or into other programmes, the waste prevention measures are clearly identified.[918] When establishing such programmes, the competent authorities describe the contribution of certain instruments and measures[919] to waste prevention. They also evaluate the usefulness of some examples of measures.[920] Same programmes further describe existing waste prevention measures and their contribution to waste prevention. The aim of such measures is to break the link between economic growth and the environmental impacts associated with the generation of waste.[921] Finally, the Minister adopts specific food waste prevention programmes within the waste prevention programmes.[922]

---

913. Section 35(7) Law No. 185(I)/2011, which corresponds to Art. 30(1) Directive 2008/98/EC.
914. Section 38(1) Law No. 185(I)/2011.
915. Section 35(9) *ibid.*, which corresponds to Art. 33(1) and (2) Directive 2008/98/EC.
916. Section 36(1) Law No. 185(I)/2011, which corresponds to Art. 29(1) Directive 2008/98/EC.
917. Sections 37, 38, 39, 40 and 41 Law No. 185(I)/2011.
918. Section 36(2) *ibid.*, which corresponds to Art. 29(1) Directive 2008/98/EC.
919. These include measures such as charges and restrictions for landfilling and incineration of waste, 'pay-as-you-throw' schemes, fiscal incentives. They are set out analytically in Annex IV Law No. 185(I)/2011, which corresponds to Annex IVa Directive 2008/98/EC.
920. These measures are measures that can affect the framework conditions related to the generation of waste, measures that van affect the design and production and distribution phase and measures that can affect the consumption and use phase. They are set out in detail, albeit indicatively, in Annex VI Law No. 185(I)/2011, which corresponds to Annex IV Directive 2008/98/EC.
921. Section 36(3) Law No. 185(I)/2011, which corresponds to Art. 29(2) Directive 2008/98/EC.
922. Section 36(4) Law No. 185(I)/2011, which corresponds to Art. 29(2a) Directive 2008/98/EC.

196. These programmes are evaluated at least every sixth year and revised as appropriate and, where relevant, in accordance with the provisions on the protection of human health and the environment.[923] The EC is informed of waste prevention programmes once adopted and of any substantial changes thereto.[924]

II. Statutory Obligations of Operators

A. *Extended Producer Responsibility*

197. In order to strengthen reuse, prevention, recycling and other recovery of waste, the Council of Ministers issues regulations, which ensure that producers of products ('παραγωγός προϊόντος')[925] have extended producer responsibility. Such measures may include acceptance of returned products and of the waste that remains after those products have been used, as well as the subsequent management of the waste and financial responsibility for such activities. They may further consist of the obligation to provide publicly available information as to the extent to which the product is reusable and recyclable.[926]

198. Extended producer responsibility schemes are established via Regulations and define in a clear way the roles and responsibilities of all relevant actors involved, including producers of products placing products on the market organizations implementing extended producer responsibility obligations on their behalf, private or public waste operators, local authorities and, where appropriate, reuse and preparing for reuse operators and social economy enterprises.[927] They further set waste management targets, in line with the waste hierarchy, aiming to attain at least the quantitative targets relevant for the extended producer responsibility scheme as laid down in this law and certain other laws,[928] and set other quantitative targets and/or qualitative objectives considered relevant.[929] In addition, they ensure that a reporting system is in place to gather data on the products placed on the market by the producers of products subject to extended producer responsibility and data on the collection and treatment of waste resulting from those products specifying, where appropriate, the waste material flows, as well as other data relevant for the aforementioned purposes.[930] Moreover, they ensure equal treatment of producers of

---

923. Section 36(5) Law No. 185(I)/2011, which corresponds to Art. 30(1) Directive 2008/98/EC.
924. Section 33(1) Law No. 185(I)/2011, which corresponds to Art. 33(1) Directive 2008/98/EC.
925. *Producer of the product* ('le producteur du prodoit' in French, 'Hersteller des Erzeugnisses' in German, 'producent van het product' in Dutch) is any natural or legal person who professionally develops, manufactures, processes, treats, sells or imports products. Section 2 Law No. 185(I)/2011, which corresponds to Art. 8(1) Directive 2008/98/EC.
926. Section 11(1) and (2) Law No. 185(I)/2011, which corresponds to Art. 8(1) Directive 2008/98/EC.
927. Section 11A(1)(b) Law No. 185(I)/2011, which corresponds to Art. 8a(1)(a) Directive 2008/98/EC.
928. These are Law No. 32(I)/2002, Law No. 157(I)/2003, Regulations 668/2004 and Regulations 82/2003 (*see* n 715 above). Section 11A(1)(c)(i), (ii), (iii), (iv) & (v) Law No. 185(I)/2011, which corresponds to Art. 8a(1)(b) Directive 2008/98/EC.
929. Section 11A(1)(c) Law No. 185(I)/2011, which corresponds to Art. 8a(1)(b) Directive 2008/98/EC.
930. Section 11A(1)(d) Law No. 185(I)/2011, which corresponds to Art. 8a(1)(c) Directive 2008/98/EC.

products regardless of their origin or size, without placing a disproportionate regulatory burden on producers, including small and medium-sized enterprises, of small quantities of products.[931] Furthermore, they establish an adequate monitoring and enforcement framework with a view to ensuring that producers of products and organizations implementing extended producer responsibility obligations on their behalf implement their extended producer responsibility obligations, including in the case of distance sales, that the financial means are properly used and that all actors involved in the implementation of the extended producer responsibility schemes report reliable data.[932] Finally, for the purposes of monitoring and verifying compliance with the obligations of the producer of the product in relation to extended producer responsibility schemes, they lay down requirements to be recorded in the producers' register, information and submission of reports that both the extended producer responsibility schemes and the producers must fulfil, as well as registration, information and reporting requirements, to be met by a legal or natural person to be appointed as an authorized representative in Cyprus.[933]

199. A decree of the Minister set out measures to encourage the design of products and components of products in order to reduce their environmental impacts and the generation of waste in the course of the production and subsequent use of products, and in order to ensure that the recovery and disposal of products that have become waste takes place in accordance with provisions on waste hierarchy and protection of human health and the environment. Such measures may encourage, *inter alia*, the development, production and marketing of products that are suitable for multiple use, that contain recycled materials, that are technically durable and easily reparable and that are, after having become waste, suitable for preparing for reuse and recycling in order to facilitate proper implementation of the waste hierarchy. The measures shall take into account the impact of products throughout their life cycle, the waste hierarchy and, where appropriate, the potential for multiple recycling.[934]

200. When applying extended producer responsibility, the competent authority takes into account the technical feasibility and economic viability and the overall environmental, human health and social impacts, respecting the need to ensure the proper functioning of the internal market.[935] It is further applied without prejudice to the responsibility for waste management and without prejudice to existing waste stream-specific and product-specific legislation.[936]

---

931. Section 11A(1)(e) Law No. 185(I)/2011, which corresponds to Art. 8a(1)(d) Directive 2008/98/EC.
932. Section 11A(1)(f) Law No. 185(I)/2011, which corresponds to Art. 8a(5) Directive 2008/98/EC.
933. Section 11A(1)(g) Law No. 185(I)/2011, which corresponds to Art.8a(5) Directive 2008/98/EC.
934. Section 11(3) and (4) Law No. 185(I)/2011, which corresponds to Art. 8(2) Directive 2008/98/EC.
935. Section 11(5) Law No. 185(I)/2011, which corresponds to Art. 8(3) Directive 2008/98/EC.
936. Section 11(6) Law No. 185(I)/2011, which corresponds to Art. 8(4) Directive 2008/98/EC.

B. Responsibility of Original Waste Producers and Waste Holders

201. Original waste producers and other waste holders bear other set of statutory duties. They have to carry out the treatment of waste themselves or have the treatment handled by a dealer or an establishment or undertaking, which carries out waste treatment operations, or arranged by a private or public waste collector in accordance with provisions on waste hierarchy and protection of human health and the environment.[937] Dealers and brokers have to cooperate with authorized undertakings, who collect and transport waste and deliver similar to authorized undertakings for treatment.[938] When the waste is transferred from the original producer or holder to one of the aforementioned natural or legal persons for preliminary treatment, the responsibility for carrying out a complete recovery or disposal operation is not to be discharged as a general rule. Without prejudice to Regulation (EC) No. 1013/2006, the conditions under which the original producer retains responsibility for the whole treatment chain are specified in Regulations of the Council of Ministers. Further, the conditions under which the responsibility of the producer and the holder can be shared or delegated among the actors of the treatment chain may be set out therein.[939] In these regulations, it is also decided that the responsibility for arranging waste management is to be borne partly or wholly by the producer of the product from which the waste came and that distributors of such product may share this responsibility.[940] In any case, every waste holder and original waste producer not having a waste treatment permit is obliged, during this possession, to ensure that it shall not cause any danger to public health and the environment or any nuisance to any person.[941]

C. Obligations Concerning Hazardous Waste

202. At the outset, it is provided that all holders of hazardous waste and all original producers of same waste have to ensure their recovery and disposal via an arrangement with an establishment or an undertaking that bears a waste treatment permit.[942]

203. The pertinent obligation consists of the prohibition of mixing hazardous waste with other categories of hazardous waste or with other waste, substances or materials and it includes the dilution of hazardous substances. This obligation is

937. Section 15(1) Law No. 185(I)/2011, which corresponds to Art. 15(1) Directive 2008/98/EC. As Art. 15 corresponds to Art. 8 of the repealed Directive 2006/12/EC, *see*: *Commission of the European Communities v. Hellenic Republic*, Case C-286/08, [2009] ECR I-00142; *European Commission v. Portuguese Republic*, Case C-37/09, [2010] ECR I-00076.
938. Section 15(2) and (3) Law No. 185(I)/2011.
939. Section 15(4) and (5)(a) *ibid.*, which corresponds to Art. 15(2) Directive 2008/98/EC.
940. Section 15(5)(b) Law No. 185(I)/2011, which corresponds to Art. 15(3) Directive 2008/98/EC.
941. Section 15(6) Law No. 185(I)/2011, which partially corresponds to Art. 15(4) Directive 2008/98/EC.
942. Section 15(7) Law No. 185(I)/2011.

borne by producers, collectors, transporters and managers of waste.[943] However, mixing may take place, provided that: the mixing operation is carried out by an establishment or undertaking which has obtained a waste treatment permit; provisions on the protection of public health and the environment are complied with and the adverse impact of the waste management on human health and the environment is not increased; and the mixing operation conforms to BAT.[944] Where hazardous waste has been mixed in a manner contrary to the aforementioned, separation is carried out where technically feasible and necessary in order to comply with provisions on the protection of public health and the environment, without prejudice to the prohibition of abandonment, dumping or uncontrolled management of waste, including littering.[945] Should separation not be required, the persons producing, collecting, transporting or managing hazardous waste ensure that the mixed waste is treated in a facility that has obtained a relevant permit.[946]

204. In the course of collection, transport and temporary storage, hazardous waste is packaged and labelled in accordance with the international and Union standards in force.[947] Whenever hazardous waste is transferred within a Member State, it shall be accompanied by an identification document, which may be in electronic format, containing the appropriate data specified in Annex IB to Regulation (EC) No. 1013/2006.[948] This document is filled in by the hazardous waste producer or holder, by the person transporting hazardous waste and by the person recovering or disposing hazardous waste.[949] It must be further possessed by said persons during the necessary time period for the purpose of keeping the hazardous waste record.[950] Copies of this documentation are submitted annually every March to the competent authority by same persons, as well as when this is requested by the competent authority.[951] These obligations are not imposed on mixed waste produced by households,[952] whereas only some of those[953] are not applicable to separate fractions of hazardous waste produced by households until they are accepted for collection, disposal or recovery by an establishment or an undertaking which has obtained a waste treatment permit.[954]

943. Section 18(1) *ibid.*, which corresponds to Art. 18(1) Directive 2008/98/EC.
944. Section 18(2) Law No. 185(I)/2011, which corresponds to Art. 18(2) Directive 2008/98/EC.
945. Sections 18(3)(a), 10, 49, 50 & 51 Law No. 185(I)/2011, which correspond to Arts 18(3), 13 & 36 Directive 2008/98/EC.
946. Sections 18(3)(b), 24 & 25 Law No. 185(I)/2011, which correspond to Arts 18(3) & 23 Directive 2008/98/EC.
947. Section 19(1) Law No. 185(I)/2011, which corresponds to Art. 19(1) Directive 2008/98/EC.
948. Section 19(2) Law No. 185(I)/2011, which corresponds to Art. 19(2) Directive 2008/98/EC.
949. Section 19(3) Law No. 185(I)/2011.
950. Section 19(4) *ibid.*
951. Section 19(5) *ibid.*
952. Section 20(2) *ibid.*, which corresponds to Art. 20 Directive 2008/98/EC.
953. That being the ones set out in ss 19 and 32 Law No. 185(I)/2011.
954. Section 20(3) *ibid.*, which corresponds to Art. 20 Directive 2008/98/EC.

§6. ENSURING COMPLIANCE

I. Administrative Sanctions

205. Administrative sanctions may be imposed by the competent authority or inspectors upon danger of environmental pollution, actual environmental pollution or violation of the operating conditions attached to a waste treatment permit, as explained below. Plants operating in a manner causing danger of environmental pollution or danger of damaging public health due to possible fire, explosion or disposal of any substance or waste, may be served with a notification ('ειδοποίηση') by an inspector. The notification states the reasons for which this danger is deemed to exist,[955] instructions for taking specific measures for rehabilitation or minimization of same danger[956] and the time period, within which these measures are to be taken.[957] It further sets out that the operation shall be ceased, if these measures are not timely materialized and danger still exists.[958] Lastly, it may demand that the operator transfers waste to an authorized treatment facility within a reasonable time.[959] If said danger is deemed to be imminent, the notification may order the immediate cessation of activities of the plant and state that operation shall not be initiated before the described measures are taken and the grounds of the danger are eliminated.[960] Under exceptional circumstances and especially when due to nature, extent and importance of environmental degradation a danger of serious environmental damage exists, the Council of Ministers, following the order of temporary or final cessation of activities, may impose a daily fine of no more than EUR 40,000 for every day of violation of this order.[961] Prior to imposing this administrative fine, a relevant report is served to the operator of the alleged polluting plant by the competent authority and he is asked to submit his views.[962]

206. When environmental pollution or degradation is a fact, an administrative fine of up to EUR 500,000 may be imposed by the competent authority.[963] It may also impose temporary suspension and cessation of its operation, until the appropriate measures are taken for the purpose of rehabilitating pollution, damage and degradation of the environment. This suspension of activities may also be imposed upon danger to human health. When these measures are not taken or may not be taken, the competent authority may order final cessation of activities.[964] In case of serious environmental pollution, the fine may be up to EUR 4,000,000, as long as the Council of Ministers approves this.[965] Prior to imposing these administrative

955. Section 45(5)(a) Law No. 185(I)/2011.
956. Section 45(5)(b) *ibid.*
957. Section 45(5)(c) *ibid.*
958. Section 45(5)(d) *ibid.*
959. Section 45(5)(e) *ibid.*
960. Section 45(6) *ibid.*
961. Section 51(3) *ibid.*
962. Section 51(4) *ibid.*
963. Section 51(1)(a) *ibid.*
964. Section 51(2) *ibid.*
965. Section 51(1)(b) *ibid.*

fines, a relevant report is being served to the operator of the alleged polluting plant by the competent authority and he is asked to submit his views.[966]

207. When, according to the aforementioned, administrative sanctions are imposed due to violation of this law or Regulations and Decrees issued on the basis of same law, the competent authority may collect the provided guarantee or insurance. The same applies in cases, when the competent authority takes measures for removing or reducing pollution, for confiscating, removing or managing any waste or equipment, as well as for remediating any environmental damage. Thereafter, the competent authority has the power to ask for the renewal of the guarantee or insurance within thirty days. Failure to comply with such request, may lead to suspension of the issued waste management permit or revocation of the exception from same permit.[967]

208. The addressee of administrative fines may challenge those before the Council of Ministers and the Supreme Court of Cyprus. In particular, an administrative appeal ('ιεραρχική προσφυγή') may be filed within twenty-one days to the Council of Ministers, which examines it.[968] The Council of Ministers may hear in person the appellant or give him the opportunity to submit in writing further argumentation on the grounds, on which the administrative appeal was based.[969] This Council, which must reach a decision as soon as possible, has the authority to dismiss or grant the administrative appeal. In the latter case, it defines itself as the amount of the administrative fine providing sufficient reasoning.[970] Also an appeal ('προσφυγή') may be filed with the Supreme Court of Cyprus according to Article 146 of the Constitution.

209. Administrative fines are due after the expiration of the limitation period for an appeal with the Supreme Court of Cyprus or, if an appeal was filed, after the final decision of the court.[971] When the fine is not paid, the competent authority initiates a court procedure to recover it as a civil debt owed to the state.[972]

210. When operating conditions are violated, an improvement notification ('ειδοποίηση βελτίωσης') and a notification of prohibition ('απαγορευτική ειδοποίηση') may be issued by an inspector under the conditions and with the content and effect explained in Law No. 187(I)/2002 (*see* in this respect paragraphs 61 et seq. above).[973]

966. Section 51(4) *ibid.*
967. Section 26(4)(a) & (b) *ibid.*
968. Section 52(1) *ibid.*
969. Section 52(2)(a) *ibid.*
970. Section 52(2)(b) and (3) *ibid.*
971. Section 52(5) *ibid.*
972. Section 52(6) *ibid.*
973. Section 46(1), (2) and (3) *ibid.*

II. Penal Sanctions

211. When a person violates certain provisions of this law, those being sections 10, 11B(1)(k) and (l), 15(1), (2), (3) and (6), 18, 19, 22A, 24, 29, 30, 32(1) and (2), 33(1), (3) and (7), 34(1) and 49(1)(b), regulations and decrees issued on the basis of this law as well as Regulations (EC) No. 1013/2006, 1102/2008, 852/2017, 1257/2013 and 2020/2151 are committing a penal offence. The same applies upon failure to comply with the operating conditions of a waste treatment permit. If found guilty by a court of law, he may be convicted to imprisonment for a maximum period of up to three years and/or a monetary fine of up to EUR 500,000.[974] Any person obstructing an inspector from performing his statutory duties and powers set out in this law, or obstructs any police officer or other person accompanying the inspector to enter a facility or assist the inspector, is guilty of a crime and may be imprisoned for no more than six months and/or a monetary fine not exceeding EUR 10,000.[975] Failure to comply with a notification of prohibition or failure to timely comply with an improvement notification is equally a penal offence. This may lead to same penalties, those being imprisonment for a maximum period of up to three years and/or a fine of up to EUR 500,000.[976] Similarly, these penalties may be imposed following conviction for failure to comply with a notification upon danger of environmental pollution, or danger of damaging public health or imminent danger thereof.[977]

212. Violations of some provisions of this law, those being sections 10, 15, 18, 22A, 24, 29 and 33, as well as violations of regulations and decrees may be settled out-of-court with an inspector issuing a penalty of EUR 4,000 or EUR 20,000, as the case may be.[978] To this end, the inspector issues a notice that specifies the offence committed, the penalty fee and the request to terminate the violation within fourty-eight hours.[979] Repeating the offence leads to criminal prosecution before the court.[980]

III. Other Sanctions

213. During the penal procedure before a court for the aforementioned penal offences regarding violation of provisions of this law, the court may issue an interim order prohibiting continuance or repeat of the activity, on the grounds of environmental pollution, danger thereof or danger to public health. The court may further order transfer of waste placed, abandoned, dumped or stored in public or private

974. Section 49(1)(a) *ibid.*
975. Section 49(1)(c) *ibid.*
976. Section 46(4) *ibid.*
977. Section 45(8) *ibid.*
978. Section 50(1)(a), (b), (c) and (d) *ibid.*
979. Section 50(2), (3) & (5) *ibid.*
980. Section 50(3) & (4) *ibid.*

area.[981] Such an order may be issued by the President of the District Court following petition of the Attorney General or of the local authority.[982] Civil procedural rules, as well as the particulars of an ex parte procedure, are applied.[983]

§7. Archive

214. Special provisions on the Archive of Waste Managers ('Αρχείο Διαχειριστών Αποβλήτων', hereinafter 'the Archive') are set out in this law. Any person professionally collecting and transporting waste, or dealing and brokering waste or treating itself its own non-hazardous waste, including recovery or disposal operations on the site of waste production, ensures that it is registered with the Archive prior to initiating its operations.[984] The Minister may issue a catalogue of the persons falling under this obligation in the Official Gazette.[985] Persons bearing said obligation submit a relevant application to the Director of the Environmental Department.[986] This application is accepted, as long as the statutory provisions are fulfilled. However, the Director of the Environmental Department has the authority to deny registration, if he deems that environmental protection is not sufficiently safeguarded.[987] The registration is deemed to be indefinitely in force, under the condition that annually the following are submitted: (i) registration fees; (ii) information regarding waste management during the previous year including information on the producers, receivers and the total amount of waste and waste streams, (iii) identification and monitoring forms of waste transport issued during the previous year. In case of failing to submit this information, the registration is deleted and a new application for registration is required.[988] Any intended change to the registered information has to be communicated in writing prior to coming into effect.[989] Further technical obligations may be set out in regulations issued by the Minister.[990] Registration with the Archive does not free such a person from the obligation to obtain any other permits or authorizations required under applicable laws.[991] Should the Director of the Environmental Department decide that a registered person acts in violation of said technical obligations or the statutory obligations set out in section 10 of this law, he may recall, temporary suspend or delete the registration from the Archive.[992]

981. Section 49(2) *ibid.*
982. Section 49(3) *ibid.*
983. Section 49(4) and (5) *ibid.*
984. Section 33(1)(a), (b) and (c) *ibid.*
985. Section 33(2) *ibid.*
986. Section 33(3)(a) and (b) *ibid.*
987. Section 33(4) and (8) *ibid.*
988. Section 33(5) *ibid.*
989. Section 33(7) *ibid.*
990. Section 33(10) *ibid.*
991. Section 33(6) *ibid.*
992. Section 33(9) *ibid.*

215. The Director of Environmental Protection further has the obligation to keep an archive of the persons holding a waste treatment permit according to section 24 of this law and of the producers of hazardous waste.[993]

216. The Environmental Authority equally has to keep an archive, where proposals for waste management plans and waste prevention programmes including their amendment or renewal are recorded.[994] Opinions and representations of the public,[995] description of the approved plan and programme, notice of the manner that these were taken into consideration by the Council of Ministers and the reasons on which the final decision was based are also to be included in the archive.[996] This archive is at the disposal of the public and may be inspected during working days and hours.[997] Retrieving information from said archive is regulated by Law No. 119(I)/2004 (*see* in this respect paragraph 136 above).[998]

993. Section 33(11)(a) and (b) *ibid.*
994. Section 42(1)(a) *ibid.*
995. Section 42(1)(b) *ibid.*
996. Sections 42(1)(c) and 41 *ibid.*
997. Section 42(2) *ibid.*
998. Section 42(3) *ibid.*

Chapter 5. Soil Pollution

217. Soil pollution is controlled along with water pollution under Law No. 106(I)/2002 (*see* in this respect paragraphs 87 et seq. above), as well as especially in relation to pollution caused by nitrates (*see* in this respect paragraphs 132 et seq. above). Soil is further protected along with industrial emissions control under Law No. 184(I)/2013 (*see* in this respect paragraphs 339 et seq. below). Law No. 189(I)/2007 is in addition applicable to soil pollution under specific conditions, as specified therein (*see* in this respect paragraphs 749 et seq. below).

Chapter 6. Noise Pollution

218. Noise pollution is being regulated by Law on Assessment and Management of Environmental Noise[999] (hereinafter 'Law No. 224(I)/2004'), which implements Directive 2002/49/EC.[1000] Prior to this enactment noise pollution was treated solely as (private) nuisance according to section 46 Law on Civil Wrongs,[1001] which reproduced the English common law[1002] and settled case law.[1003]

§1. Objective

219. The aim of Law No. 224(I)/2004 is to define a common approach intended to avoid, prevent or reduce on a prioritized basis the harmful effects, including annoyance, due to exposure to environmental noise.[1004] The components of this aim are specified in this law. Environmental noise ('περιβαλλοντικός θόρυβος') means unwanted or harmful outdoor sound created by human activities, including noise emitted by means of transport, road traffic, rail traffic, air traffic and from sites of industrial activity such as those defined in Annex I.[1005], [1006] Harmful effects

999. Law on Assessment and Management of Environmental Noise ('ο περί Αξιολόγησης και Διαχείρισης του Περιβαλλοντικού Θορύβου Νόμος') No. 224 of 2004, OG I(I) No. 3888 of 30 Jul. 2004, p. 5275, last amended by Law on Assessment and Management of Environmental Noise (Amending) ('ο περί Αξιολόγησης και Διαχείρισης του Περιβαλλοντικού Θορύβου (Τροποποιητικός) Νόμος') No. 125 of 2019, OG I(I) No. 4724 of 31 Jul. 2019, p. 651.

1000. Directive 2002/49/EC of the European Parliament and of the Council of 25 Jun. 2002 relating to the assessment and management of environmental noise, OJ L 189, 18 Jul. 2002, p. 12, as amended.

1001. This reads:

> A private nuisance consists of any person so conducting himself or his business or so using any immovable property of which he is the owner or occupier as habitually to interfere with the reasonable use and enjoyment, having regard to the situation and nature thereof, of the immovable property of any other person. Provided that no plaintiff shall recover compensation in respect of any private nuisance unless he shall have suffered damage thereby. Provided also that the provisions of this section shall not apply to any interference with daylight.

1002. *Palantzi v. Agrotis* (1968) 1 CLR 448. *See* in this respect cited common law: *Crump v. Lambert* [1867] L.R. 3 Eq. 409; *Vanderpant v. Mayfair Hotel Co.* [1930] 1 Ch. 138 (166); *Leeman v. Montagu* [1936] 2 All E.R. 1677; *Metropolitan Properties Ltd v. Jones* [1939] 2 All E.R. 202; *Halsey v. ESSO Petroleum Co. Ltd* [1961] 2 All E.R. 145 (151).

1003. *Araouzos v. Ioannou* (1980) 1 CLR 591; *Palantzi v. Agrotis* (1968) 1 CLR 448; *Pafitis v. Stavrou* (1970) 1 CLR 140; *Ioannides v. Savvas* (1984) JSC 186; *Charalambous v. Antoniades* (1998) 1 CLR 2167; *Christos Agathocleous Ltd v. Sofocleous* (2000) 1 CLR 1953.

1004. Section 4(1) Law No. 224(I)/2004, which corresponds to Art. 1(1) Directive 2002/49/EC.

1005. *See* in this respect Annex I Law No. 224(I)/2004, which corresponds to Annex I Directive 96/61/EC.

1006. Section 2 Law No. 224(I)/2004, which corresponds to Art. 3(a) Directive 2002/49/EC. The French term is 'bruit dans l'environnement', the German one 'Umgebungslärm' and the Dutch one 'omgevingslawaai'.

('επιβλαβείς επιδράσεις') stands for negative effects on human health,[1007] whereas annoyance ('ενόχληση') means the degree of community noise annoyance as determined by means of field surveys.[1008]

220. To that end, the following actions are implemented progressively: the determination of exposure to environmental noise, through noise mapping;[1009] collecting information on environmental noise and its effects;[1010] preparation of action plans, based upon noise-mapping results, with a view to preventing and reducing environmental noise where necessary and particularly where exposure levels can induce harmful effects on human health and to preserving environmental noise quality where it is good.[1011] This law also aims at providing a basis for developing Union measures to reduce noise emitted by the major sources, in particular road and rail vehicles and infrastructure, aircraft, outdoor and industrial equipment and mobile machinery.[1012]

§2. Area of Application

221. This law applies to environmental noise to which humans are exposed in particular in built-up areas, in public parks or other quiet areas in an agglomeration, in quiet areas in open country, near schools, hospitals and other noise-sensitive buildings and areas.[1013] Quiet area in an agglomeration ('ήσυχη περιοχή πολεοδομικού συγκροτήματος') means an area, delimited by the competent authority, for instance, which is not exposed to a value of Lden or of another appropriate noise indicator greater than a certain value set by the Member State, from any noise source.[1014] A quiet area in open country ('ήσυχη περιοχή στην ύπαιθρο') is an area, delimited by the competent authority, that is undisturbed by noise from traffic, industry or recreational activities.[1015] However, this law is not applicable to noise that is caused by the exposed person himself, noise from domestic activities, noise created by neighbours, noise at work places or noise inside means of transport or due to military activities in military areas.[1016]

1007. Section 2 Law No. 224(I)/2004, which corresponds to Art. 3(b) Directive 2002/49/EC. The French term is 'effets nuisibles', the German one 'gesundheitsschädliche Auswirkungen' and the Dutch one 'schadelijke effecte'.
1008. Section 2 Law No. 224(I)/2004, which corresponds to Art. 3(c) Directive 2002/49/EC. The French term is 'gêne', the German one 'Belästigung' and the Dutch one 'hinder'.
1009. Section 4(2)(a) Law No. 224(I)/2004, which corresponds to Art. 1(1)(a) Directive 2002/49/EC.
1010. Section 4(2)(b) Law No. 224(I)/2004. The Directive provides in Art. 1(1)(b) for ensuring that information on environmental noise and its effects is made available to the public.
1011. Section 4(2)(c) Law No. 224(I)/2004, which corresponds to Art. 1(1)(c) Directive 2002/49/EC.
1012. Section 4(3) Law No. 224(I)/2004, which corresponds to Art. 1(2) Directive 2002/49/EC.
1013. Section 3(1) Law No. 224(I)/2004, which corresponds to Art. 2(1) Directive 2002/49/EC. *See also* the scope of the German national legislation §47a BImSchG.H. Schulze-Fielitz, in *Gemeinschaftskommentar zum Bundes-Immissionsschutzgesetz*, § 47c paras 1 et seq. (H.-J. Koch, E. Pache & D. H. Scheuing ed., Heymanns Verlag 2014).
1014. Section 2 Law No. 224(I)/2004, which corresponds to Art. 3(l) Directive 2002/49/EC.
1015. Section 2 Law No. 224(I)/2004, which corresponds to Art. 3(m) Directive 2002/49/EC.
1016. Section 3(2) Law No. 224(I)/2004, which corresponds to Art. 2(2) Directive 2002/49/EC.

§3. Competent Authorities

222. The competent authority ('αρμόδια αρχή') in this law is the Director of the Environmental Service of the Ministry of Agriculture, Rural Development and Environment. When mention to the Minister ('Υπουργός') is made, the Minister of Agriculture, Rural Development and Environment is meant.[1017] The Council of Ministers also plays an important role, as it issues regulations on limit values, participation of the public to action plans, notice indicators and limit values of specific activities or use causing annoyance and harmful effects, as well as the best application of this law and regulation of every matter needed to be specified in regulations.[1018]

§4. Limit Values

223. The Council of Ministers specifies in regulations limit values expressed in terms of Lden and Lnight and where appropriate, Lday and Levening, for road-traffic noise, rail traffic noise, aircraft noise around airports and noise on industrial activity sites.[1019] These values may be different for different types of noise, such as road-, rail-, air-traffic noise, industrial noise, for different surroundings and for different noise sensitiveness of the populations; they may also be different for existing situations and for new situations, where there is a change in the situation regarding the noise source or the use of the surrounding.[1020]

224. The values of Lden and Lnight are determined by means of certain assessment methods,[1021] until the EC establishes common assessment methods.[1022] Harmful effects may be assessed by certain means of the dose-effect relations.[1023] According to those, dose-effect relations should be used to assess the effect of noise on populations. The dose-effect relations introduced by future revisions of these means will concern in particular: the relation between annoyance and Lden for road-, rail- and air-traffic noise, and for industrial noise; and the relation between sleep disturbance and Lnight for road-, rail- and air-traffic noise, and for industrial noise. If necessary, specific dose-effect relations could be presented for dwellings with special insulation against noise, dwellings with a quiet façade, different climates/different cultures, vulnerable groups of the population, tonal industrial noise and impulsive industrial noise and other special cases.[1024]

1017. Section 2 Law No. 224(I)/2004.
1018. Sections 6(1), 9(7) and 12 *ibid.*
1019. Section 6(1) *ibid.*, which corresponds to Art. 5(4) Directive 2002/49/EC.
1020. Section 6(2) Law No. 224(I)/2004, which corresponds to Art. 3(s) Directive 2002/49/EC.
1021. These are specified in Annex III Law No. 224(I)/2004, which corresponds to Annex II Directive 2002/49/EC.
1022. Section 7(2) Law No. 224(I)/2004, which corresponds to Art. 6(2) Directive 2002/49/EC.
1023. Section 7(3) Law No. 224(I)/2004, which corresponds to Art. 6(3) Directive 2002/49/EC.
1024. These means are set out in Annex IV Law No. 224(I)/2004, which corresponds to Annex III Directive 2002/49/EC. The terms dwellings with special insulation and dwellings with a quiet façade are defined in Annex VII Law No. 224(I)/2004.

§5. Strategic Noise Mapping

225. Strategic noise map ('στρατηγική χαρτογράφηση θορύβου') is a map designed for the global assessment of noise exposure in a given area due to different noise sources or for overall predictions for such an area.[1025] Strategic noise maps showing the situation in the preceding calendar year for all agglomerations with more than 250,000 inhabitants and for all major roads, major railways and airports had to be made no later than 30 June 2007. These were approved by the Minister and were issued in a decree, which was published in the Official Gazette.[1026] The components of those maps are specified in this law. More specifically, major roads ('μεγάλος οδικός άξονας') are defined as means of a regional or national road, which has more than 6,000,000 vehicle passages a year.[1027] This differentiates from the European provision, which provides for 3,000,000 vehicle passages.[1028] Although in Cyprus no railways operate, the legal term of major railways ('μεγάλος σιδηροδρομικός άξονας') is defined as a railway, which has more than 60,000 train passages per year,[1029] and differentiates from the European provision that sets out 30,000 train passages per year.[1030] Further, airport ('αεροδρόμιο') means a civil airport, which has more than 50,000 movements per year (a movement being a take-off or a landing), excluding those purely for training purposes on light aircraft.[1031] Lastly, no later than 30 June 2012, more strategic noise maps had to be made, which demonstrated the situation in the preceding calendar year for all agglomerations and for all major roads and major railways.[1032]

226. Before drafting any strategic noise map, major roads, major railways, airports, quiet areas in agglomerations and quiet areas in open country are set out in a ministerial decree, which is published in the Official Gazette.[1033] Major agglomerations and agglomerations that were built before 30 June 2008 are also specified in a decree issued by the Minister of Interior.[1034]

227. For the preparation of strategic noise mapping, noise indicators Lden and Lnight, as referred to in this law,[1035] are applied by the competent authority.[1036] The

1025. Section 2 *ibid.*, which corresponds to Art. 3(r) Directive 2002/49/EC.
1026. Section 8(4)(a) Law No. 224(I)/2004. *See* in relation to strategic noise mapping in Germany ('Larmkärten') §47c BImSchG. H. Schulze-Fielitz, in *Gemeinschaftskommentar zum Bundes-Immissionsschutzgesetz*, § 47c paras 1 et seq. (H.-J. Koch, E. Pache & D. H. Scheuing ed., Heymanns Verlag 2014).
1027. Section 2 Law No. 224(I)/2004.
1028. Article 3(n) Directive 2002/49/EC. The term in French is 'grand axe routier', in German 'Hauptverkehrsstraße' and in Dutch 'belangrijke weg'.
1029. Section 2 Law No. 224(I)/2004.
1030. Article 3(o) Directive 2002/49/EC. The term in French is 'grand axe ferroviaire', in German 'Haupteisenbahnstrecke' and in Dutch 'belangrijke spoorweg'.
1031. Section 2 Law No. 224(I)/2004, which corresponds to Art. 3(p) Directive 2002/49/EC. However, the legal term in the directive is *major airport*, 'μεγάλο αεροδρόμιο' in Greek, 'grand aéroport' in French, 'Großflughafen' in German and 'belangrijke luchthaven' in Dutch.
1032. Section 8(4)(b) Law No. 224(I)/2004.
1033. Section 8(2) *ibid.*
1034. Section 8(3)(a) and (b) *ibid.*
1035. Annex II *ibid.*, which corresponds to Annex I Directive 2002/49/EC.

competent authority may additionally use supplementary noise indicators for special cases,[1037] as well as other noise indicators than Lden and Lnight for acoustical planning and noise zoning.[1038]

228. The minimum requirements that strategic noise maps must fulfil are data layout regarding one of the following aspects: an existing, a previous or a predicted noise situation in terms of a noise indicator; the exceeding of a limit value; the estimated number of dwellings, schools and hospitals in a certain area that are exposed to specific values of a noise indicator; and the estimated number of people located in an area exposed to noise.[1039] Such maps may be presented to the public as graphical plots, numerical data in tables or numerical data in electronic form.[1040] Especially said maps for agglomerations put a special emphasis on the noise emitted by road traffic, rail traffic, airports and industrial activity sites, including ports.[1041]

229. Strategic noise maps are used as a basis for the data to be sent to the EC, as a source of information for citizens and as a basis for action plans.[1042] Minimum requirements for the strategic noise maps concerning the data to be sent to the EC include particulars for the estimated number of people living in dwellings that are exposed to certain bands of values of Lden and the total area (in km^2) exposed to certain values of Lden.[1043] For the purposes of informing the citizens after the adoption of the strategic noise maps as well as the development of action plans, additional and more detailed information must be given in strategic noise maps, such as: a graphical presentation; maps disclosing the exceeding of a limit value; difference maps, in which the existing situation is compared with various possible future situations; maps showing the value of a noise indicator at a height other than 4 m where appropriate. The competent authority may lay down rules on the types and formats of these noise maps.[1044]

230. No later than 30 June 2005, and thereafter every five years, the competent authority informs the EC of the major roads, major railways, airports and the

1036. Section 5(1) Law No. 224(I)/2004, which corresponds to Art. 5(1) Directive 2002/49/EC.
1037. It is specified that in some cases, in addition to Lden and Lnight, and where appropriate Lday and Levening, it may be advantageous to use special noise indicators and related limit values. Some examples are given below: the noise source under consideration operates only for a small proportion of the time; the average number of noise events in one or more of the periods is very low; the low-frequency content of the noise is strong; LAmax, or SEL (sound exposure level) for night period protection in the case of noise peaks; extra protection at the weekend or a specific part of the year; extra protection of the day period; extra protection of the evening period; a combination of noises from different sources; quiet areas in open country; the noise contains strong tonal components; and the noise has an impulsive character. Annex II(3) Law No. 224(I)/2004, which corresponds to Annex I(3) Directive 2002/49/EC.
1038. Section 5(3) Law No. 224(I)/2004, which corresponds to Art. 5(3) Directive 2002/49/EC.
1039. Annex V(1) Law No. 224(I)/2004, which corresponds to Annex IV(1) Directive 2002/49/EC.
1040. Annex V(2) Law No. 224(I)/2004, which corresponds to Annex IV(2) Directive 2002/49/EC.
1041. Annex V(3) Law No. 224(I)/2004, which corresponds to Annex IV(3) Directive 2002/49/EC.
1042. Annex V(4) Law No. 224(I)/2004, which corresponds to Annex IV(4) Directive 2002/49/EC.
1043. Annexes V(5) and VII(1.5), (1.6), (2.5), (2.6.) and (2.7) Law No. 224(I)/2004, which correspond to Annexes IV(5) and VI(1.5), (1.6), (2.5), (2.6.) and (2.7) Directive 2002/49/EC.
1044. Annex V(6) Law No. 224(I)/2004, which corresponds to Annex IV(6) Directive 2002/49/EC.

agglomerations with more than 250,000 inhabitants within their territories.[1045] By 31 December 2008, the competent authority has informed the EC of all the agglomerations, and of all the major roads and major railways within its territory.[1046] Further, the competent authority ensures that the adopted strategic noise maps are made available and disseminated to the public in accordance with Law No. 119(I)/2004 (*see* in this respect paragraph 136 above) and in conformity with this law, including by means of available information technologies.[1047] This information must be clear, comprehensible and accessible. A summary setting out the most important points is also provided.[1048] The competent authority also forwards certain data[1049] to the EC within six months of the aforementioned dates.[1050]

231. Strategic noise maps are reviewed, and revised if necessary, at least every five years after the date of their preparation.[1051]

§6. Action Plans

232. Action plans are plans designed to manage noise issues and effects, including noise reduction.[1052] The competent authority has drawn up by 18 July 2008 action plans designed to manage, within its territory, noise issues and effects, including quiet areas against an increase in noise and noise reduction if necessary for places near the major roads, major railways and airports and major agglomerations.[1053] Also, by 18 July 2013, the competent authority had drawn up action plans notably to address priorities which may be identified by exceeding any relevant limit value.[1054] It is ensured that the public is consulted about proposals for action plans, that the public is also given early and effective opportunities to participate in the preparation and to review the action plans and that the results of that participation are taken into account. Also, reasonable time frames are provided allowing sufficient time for each stage of public participation.[1055]

1045. Section 8(5)(a) Law No. 224(I)/2004, which corresponds to Art. 7(1) Directive 2002/49/EC.
1046. Section 8(5)(b) Law No. 224(I)/2004, which corresponds to Art. 7(2) Directive 2002/49/EC.
1047. Section 10(1) Law No. 224(I)/2004, which corresponds to Art. 9(1) Directive 2002/49/EC.
1048. Section 10(2) Law No. 224(I)/2004, which corresponds to Art. 9(2) Directive 2002/49/EC.
1049. These are listed in Annex VII Law No. 224(I)/2004, which corresponds to Annex VI Directive 2002/49/EC.
1050. Section 11(1) Law No. 224(I)/2004, which corresponds to Art. 10(2) Directive 2002/49/EC.
1051. Section 8(6)(b) Law No. 224(I)/2004, which corresponds to Art. 7(5) Directive 2002/49/EC.
1052. Section 2 Law No. 224(I)/2004, which corresponds to Art. 3(t) Directive 2002/49/EC.
1053. Section 9(1) Law No. 224(I)/2004, which corresponds to Art. 8(1) Directive 2002/49/EC. *See* in relation to action plans in Germany ('Lärmaktionspläne') §47d BImSchG. H. Schulze-Fielitz, in *Gemeinschaftskommentar zum Bundes-Immissionsschutzgesetz*, § 47d paras 1 et seq. (H.-J. Koch, E. Pache & D.H. Scheuing ed., Heymanns Verlag 2014).
1054. Section 9(2) Law No. 224(I)/2004, which corresponds to Art. 8(2) Directive 2002/49/EC.
1055. Section 9(5) and (6) Law No. 224(I)/2004, which corresponds to Art. 8(7) Directive 2002/49/EC.

233. Minimum requirements for action plans are the following.[1056] An action plan must at least include the following elements: a description of the agglomeration, the major roads, the major railways or major airports and other noise sources taken into account; the authority responsible; the legal context; any limit values in place; a summary of the results of the noise mapping; an evaluation of the estimated number of people exposed to noise, identification of problems and situations that need to be improved; a record of the public consultations; any noise-reduction measures already in force and any projects in preparation; actions which the competent authorities intend to take in the next five years, including any measures to preserve quiet areas; long-term strategy; financial information (if available): budgets, cost-effectiveness assessment, cost-benefit assessment; and provisions envisaged for evaluating the implementation and the results of the action plan.[1057] The actions which the competent authorities intend to take in the fields within their competence may, for example, include: traffic planning, land-use planning, technical measures at noise sources, selection of quieter sources, reduction of sound transmission and regulatory or economic measures or incentives.[1058] Also, each action plan should contain estimates in terms of the reduction of the number of people affected (annoyed, sleep disturbed, or other).[1059]

234. The competent authority ensures that the adopted strategic noise maps are made available and disseminated to the public in accordance with Law No. 119(I)/2004 (*see* in this respect paragraph 136 above) and in conformity with this law, including by means of available information technologies.[1060] This information must be clear, comprehensible and accessible. A summary setting out the most important points is also provided.[1061] The competent authority also forwards certain aforementioned data in relation to action plans to the EC within six months of the aforementioned dates.[1062]

235. The action plans are reviewed and revised if necessary, when a major development occurs affecting the existing noise situation, and at least every five years after the date of their approval.[1063]

§7. Ensuring Compliance

236. No provision on ensuring compliance is foreseen in this law.

1056. Section 9(3) Law No. 224(I)/2004, which corresponds to Art. 8(4) Directive 2002/49/EC.
1057. Annex VI(1) Law No. 224(I)/2004, which corresponds to Annex V(1) Directive 2002/49/EC.
1058. Annex VI(2) Law No. 224(I)/2004, which corresponds to Annex V(2) Directive 2002/49/EC.
1059. Annex VI(3) Law No. 224(I)/2004, which corresponds to Annex V(3) Directive 2002/49/EC.
1060. Section 10(1) Law No. 224(I)/2004, which corresponds to Art. 9(1) Directive 2002/49/EC.
1061. Section 10(2) Law No. 224(I)/2004, which corresponds to Art. 9(2) Directive 2002/49/EC.
1062. Section 11(1) Law No. 224(I)/2004, which corresponds to Art. 10(2) Directive 2002/49/EC.
1063. Section 9(4) Law No. 224(I)/2004, which corresponds to Art. 8(5) Directive 2002/49/EC.

Chapter 7. Radiation and Vibrations (Nuclear and Non-nuclear)

237. Radiation is regulated by Law on Protection from Ionizing Radiation and Nuclear and Radiological Safety[1064] (hereinafter 'Law No. 164(I)/2018'), which implements Directives 2006/117/Euratom,[1065] 2009/71/Euratom[1066] as amended[1067] and 2013/59/Euratom,[1068] as well as the General Safety Requirements on Governmental, Legal and Regulatory Framework for Safety of IAEA[1069] (hereinafter 'IAEA GRS Part 1, Rev. 1') and the General Safety Requirements on 'Radiation, Protection and Safety of Radiation Sources of the IAEA[1070] (hereinafter 'IAEA GRS Part 3').

238. Law on Protection from Ionizing Radiation of 2002[1071] is hereby repealed.[1072] Still, any Regulations, Orders, Notifications or other regulatory or individual administrative acts that have been done or issued on the basis of said repealed law prior to Law No. 164(I)/2018 entering into force are deemed to have been done or issued on the basis of Law No. 164(I)/2018 and shall continue to be in force, but to the extent that they contradict Law No. 164(I)/2018, until their amendment or replacement.[1073] Moreover, any license or approval, including the terms or conditions that accompany those, which have been issued on the basis of the repealed law, shall be deemed to have been issued on the basis of the relevant provisions of Law No. 164(I)/2018, under the condition that they were lawful and in force prior Law No. 164(I)/2018 entering into force. They shall continue to be lawful and in force, unless and until they expire or are repealed, suspended or renewed under Law No. 164(I)/2018.[1074] The same applies to any register established according to the

1064. Law on Protection from Ionizing Radiation and Nuclear and Radioligical Safety ('ο περί Προστασίας από Ιονίζουσες Ακτινοβολίες και Πυρηνικής και Ραδιολογικής Ασφάλειας και Προστασίας Νόμος') No. 164 of 2018, OG I(I) No. 4680 of 21 Dec. 2018, p. 1075, which implemented Council Directive 96/29/Euratom of 13 May 1996 laying down basic safety standards for the protection of the health of workers and the general public against the dangers arising from ionizing radiation, OJ L 159, 29 Jun. 1996, p. 1.

1065. Council Directive 2006/117/Euratom of 20 Nov. 2006 on the supervision and control of shipments of radioactive waste and spent fuel, OJ L 337 of 5 Dec. 2006, p. 21.

1066. Council Directive 2009/71/Euratom of 25 Jun. 2009 establishing a Community framework for the nuclear safety of nuclear installations, OJ L 172 of 2 Jul. 2009, p. 18.

1067. Council Directive 2014/87/Euratom of 8 Jul. 2014 amending Directive 2009/71/Euratom establishing a Community framework for the nuclear safety of nuclear installations, OJ L 219 of 25 Jul. 2014, p. 42.

1068. Council Directive 2013/59/Euratom of 5 Dec. 2013 laying down basic safety standards for protection against the dangers arising from exposure to ionizing radiation, and repealing Directives 89/618/Euratom, 90/641/Euratom, 96/29/Euratom, 97/43/Euratom and 2003/122/Euratom, OJ L 13 of 17 Jan. 2014, p. 1.

1069. IAEA, IAEA Safety Standards, Governmental, Legal and Regulatory Framework for Safety, General Safety Requirements No. GSR Part 1 (Rev. 1), Vienna 2016.

1070. IAEA, IAEA Safety Standards, Radiation Protection and Safety of Radiation Sources: International Basic Safety Standards, General Safety Requirements Part 3 No. GRS Part 3, Vienna 2014.

1071. Law on Protection from Ionizing Radiation ('ο περί Προστασίας από Ιονίζουσες Ακτινοβολίες Νόμος') No. 115 of 2002, OG I(I) No. 3621 of 12 Jul. 2002, p. 2173, as amended.

1072. Section 64 Law No. 164(I)/2018.

1073. Section 65(a) *ibid.*

1074. Section 65(b) *ibid.*

repealed law, which shall continue to be kept under Law No. 164(I)/2018 with the apposite amendments.[1075] Similarly, any document, plan or report issued under the repealed law and referring to sections of the same shall continue to be in force and shall be deemed to refer to the relevant provisions of Law No. 164(I)/2018.[1076] Duties ordered under the repealed law, shall be deemed to have been imposed under Law No. 164(I)/2018 and shall continue to be in force until they are repealed or amended.[1077] Following the same pattern, any applications to the competent authority under the repealed law shall be treated and decided under Law No. 164(I)/2018, as long as their evaluation is pending upon Law No. 164(I)/2018 coming into force.[1078] Finally, the Council of Radiological Protection and Nuclear Safety established under section 42 of the repealed law shall continue to operate and perform the duties and powers of the Council of Radiological Protection and Nuclear Safety now being established under section 61 Law No. 164(I)/2018.[1079] The Inspector-in-Chief and Inspectors appointed under the repealed law are deemed to have been appointed under Law No. 164(I)/2018.[1080]

§1. Objective

239. The objective of this law is not explicitly stated therein.

§2. Area of Application

240. This law applies to any planned, existing exposure ('έκθεση')[1081] and any emergency exposure situation ('κατάσταση έκθεσης έκτακτης ανάγκης')[1082]

1075. Section 65(d) *ibid.*
1076. Section 65(e) *ibid.*
1077. Section 65(f) *ibid.*
1078. Section 65(h) *ibid.*
1079. Section 65(c) *ibid.*
1080. Section 65(g) *ibid.*
1081. *Exposure* ('exposition' in French, 'Exposition' in German, 'blootstelling' in Dutch) means the act of exposing or condition of being exposed to ionizing radiation emitted outside the body (external exposure) or within the body (internal exposure). Section 2 Law No. 164(I)/2018, which corresponds to Art. 4(37) Directive 2013/59/Euratom. *Existing exposure situation* ('situation d'exposition existante' in French, 'bestehende Expositionssituation' in German, 'bestaande blootstellingssituatie' in Dutch) means an exposure situation that already exists when a decision on its control has to be taken and which does not call or no longer calls for urgent measures to be taken. Section 2 Law No. 164(I)/2018, which corresponds to Art. 4(35) Directive 2013/59/Euratom. *Planned exposure situation* ('situation d'exposition planifiée' in French, 'geplante Expositionssituation' in German, 'geplande blootstellingssituatie' in Dutch) means an exposure situation that arises from the planned operation of a radiation source or from a human activity which alters exposure pathways, so as to cause the exposure or potential exposure of people or the environment. Planned exposure situations may include both normal exposures and potential exposures. Section 2 Law No. 164(I)/2018, which corresponds to Art. 4(62) Directive 2013/59/Euratom.
1082. E*mergency exposure situation* ('situation d'exposition d'urgence' in French, 'Notfall-Expositionssituation' in German, 'blootstelling in een noodsituatie' in Dutch) means a situation of exposure due to an emergency. Section 2 Law No. 164(I)/2018, which corresponds to Art. 4(27) Directive 2013/59/Euratom. Emergency ('urgence' in French, 'Notfall' in German, 'noodsituatie'

which involves or may involve a risk to human health from exposure to ionizing radiation ('ιονίζουσα ακτινοβολία')[1083] or radioactive contamination ('ραδιενεργός μίανση' or 'ραδιομίανση')[1084] or release of radioactive substances ('ραδιενεργός ουσία'),[1085] which cannot be disregarded from a point of view of safety, security or radiation security or with regard to the environment in view of long-term human health security.[1086] It equally applies to non-military nuclear installations or installations, where activities with ionizing radiation are performed, that operate under registration or authorization[1087] (*see* in this regard paragraphs 279 et seq. below).

241. More specifically, this law applies to:

- activities or practices, such as manufacture, production, processing, handling, disposal, use, storage, holding, transport, import, export, shipment, recycling, reuse, discharge and disposal of radioactive substances or radioactive material or radioactive waste or radiation generators or accelerators;[1088]
- at all stages in the lifetime of installations, such as drafting, planning, erection, construction, commence of operation, operation, maintenance, termination of operation, closing down, decommissioning or demolition;[1089]
- manufacture and operation of electrical equipment emitting ionizing radiation and containing components operating at a potential difference of more than 5 kV;[1090]

---

in Dutch) stands for a non-routine situation or event involving a radiation source that necessitates prompt action to mitigate serious adverse consequences for human health and safety, quality of life, property or the environment, or a hazard that could give rise to such serious adverse consequences. Section 2 Law No. 164(I)/2018, which corresponds to Art. 4(26) Directive 2013/59/Euratom.

1083. *Ionizing radiation* ('rayonnement ionisant' in French, 'ionisierende Strahlung' in German, 'ioniserende straling' in Dutch) means energy transferred in the form of particles or electromagnetic waves of a wavelength of 100 nm or less (a frequency of 3 × 1015 Hz or more) capable of producing ions directly or indirectly. Section 2 Law No. 164(I)/2018, which corresponds to Art. 4(46) Directive 2013/59/Euratom.

1084. *Radioactive contamination* ('contamination' in French, 'Kontamination' in German, 'besmetting' in Dutch) means the unintended or undesirable presence of radioactive substances on surfaces or within solids, liquids or gases or on the human body. Especially with regard to the human body, it includes external contamination of the skin, as well as internal contamination regardless of the intake path. Section 2 Law No. 164(I)/2018, which corresponds to Art. 4(18) Directive 2013/59/Euratom.

1085. *Radioactive substance* ('substance radioactive' in French, 'radioaktiver Stoff' in German, 'radioactieve stof' in Dutch) means any substance that contains one or more radionuclides the activity or activity concentration of which cannot be disregarded from a radiation protection point of view. Section 2 Law No. 164(I)/2018, which corresponds to Art. 4(78) Directive 2013/59/Euratom.

1086. Section 3(1)(a) Law No. 164(I)/2018, which corresponds to Art. 2(1) Directive 2013/59/Euratom.

1087. Section 3(1)(b) Law No. 164(I)/2018, which corresponds to Art. 2(1) Directive 2009/71/Euratom. The European provision, however, makes mention of *civilian* nuclear installations.

1088. Section 3(2)(a) Law No. 164(I)/2018, which corresponds to Art. 2(2)(a) Directive 2013/59/Euratom.

1089. Section 3(2)(b) Law No. 164(I)/2018. On safety standards covering all stages in the lifetime of facilities *see* point 1.7 IAEA GRS Part 1, Rev. 1.

1090. Section 3(2)(c) Law No. 164(I)/2018, which corresponds to Art. 2(2)(b) Directive 2013/59/Euratom.

– human activities which involve the presence of natural radiation sources that lead to a significant increase in the exposure of workers or members of the public, which cannot be overlooked from the perspective of radiological security, in particular: (i) the operation of aircraft and spacecraft, in relation to the exposure of crews; and (ii) the processing of materials with naturally occurring radionuclides;[1091]
– the exposure of workers or members of the public to indoor radon, the external exposure from building materials and cases of lasting exposure resulting from the after-effects of an emergency or a past human activity. The building materials, which are of interest from the perspective of radiological security are defined in regulations;[1092] and
– the preparedness for the planning of response to and the management of emergency exposure situations that are deemed to warrant measures to protect the health of members of the public or workers.[1093]

242. This law does not apply to exposure to the natural level of radiation, i.e., to radionuclides contained in the human body, to cosmic radiation prevailing at ground level or to above-ground exposure to radionuclides present in the undisturbed earth's crust. It equally does not apply to exposure of members of the public or workers other than air or spacecrew to cosmic radiation in flight or in space. Military nuclear installations are also excluded from the application thereof.[1094]

§3. COMPETENT AUTHORITIES

I. The Minister of Labour and Social Security

243. The Minister of Labour and Social Security is the competent authority for this law.[1095]

244. The Minister ensures the establishment and maintenance of a national legislative, regulatory and organizational framework for all issues falling within the scope of this law, including safety and security of facilities and radiation sources and security from ionizing radiation.[1096] This framework provides in particular for:

1091. Section 3(2)(d) Law No. 164(I)/2018, which corresponds to Art. 2(2)(c) Directive 2013/59/Euratom.
1092. Section 3(2)(e) Law No. 164(I)/2018, which partially corresponds to Art. 2(2)(d) Directive 2013/59/Euratom.
1093. Section 3(2)(f) Law No. 164(I)/2018, which corresponds to Art. 2(2)(e) Directive 2013/59/Euratom.
1094. Section 4 Law No. 164(I)/2018, which corresponds to Art. 3 Directive 2013/59/Euratom. *See* in this respect Case C-61/03, *Commission v. United Kingdom* [2005] ECR 1-2477; Case C-65/04, *Commission v. United Kingdom* [2006] ECR I-2239.
1095. Section 5 Law No. 164(I)/2018.
1096. Section 6(1) *ibid.*

- the safety principle for protecting people, individually and collectively, society and the environment from radiation risks, both at present and in the future;[1097]
- maintaining and promoting the continuous improvement of nuclear or radiological safety and its regulation, including appropriate national arrangements for a high level of nuclear or radiological safety to protect workers and the general public interest against the dangers arising from ionizing radiations;[1098]
- allocating duties between the relevant state authorities or organizations and coordinating those;[1099]
- national safety requirements for ionizing radiation and installation safety, including nuclear safety of nuclear installations covering all stages of the life cycle of sources of ionizing radiation and nuclear installations and the specification of the manner these requirements are settled and the means of enforcement;[1100]
- a system of authorizations and prohibition of operation of nuclear installations without authorization;[1101]
- assigning primal legal responsibility for safety, security and security from ionizing radiation to the undertaking or employer responsible for the facilities and activities (*see* in this respect paragraph 295 below), and for ensuring the continuity of this responsibility where activities are carried out by several undertakings successively;[1102]
- reviewing and assessing facilities and activities in accordance with a graded approach;[1103]
- a system of regulatory control of security from ionizing radiation, safety, including nuclear safety, and security performed by the competent authority;[1104]
- effective and proportionate enforcement actions, including, where appropriate, corrective action or suspension of operation and modification or revocation of an authorization;[1105]
- an interface with the system of accounting for, and control of, nuclear material;[1106]

1097. Section 6(1)(a) *ibid.*, which corresponds to point 2.5(1) IAEA GRS Part 1, Rev. 1.
1098. Section 6(1)(b) Law No. 164(I)/2018. *See* in this regard Art. 1 Directive 2009/71/Euratom.
1099. Section 6(1)(c) Law No. 164(I)/2018, which corresponds to Art. 4(1) Directive 2009/71/Euratom.
1100. Section 6(1)(d) Law No. 164(I)/2018. On the obligation to adopt national nuclear safety requirements *see* Art. 4(1)(a) Directive 2009/71/Euratom.
1101. Section 6(1)(e) Law No. 164(I)/2018, which corresponds to Art. 4(1)(b) Directive 2009/71/Euratom.
1102. Section 6(1)(f) Law No. 164(I)/2018, which corresponds to point 2.5(6) IAEA GRS Part 1, Rev. 1.
1103. Section 6(1)(g) Law No. 164(I)/2018, which corresponds to point 2.5(8) IAEA GRS Part 1, Rev. 1.
1104. Section 6(1(h) Law No. 164(I)/2018. The obligation to provide a system of nuclear safety supervision is stated in Art. 4(1)(c) Directive 2009/71/Euratom.
1105. Section 6(1)(i) Law No. 164(I)/2018, which corresponds to Art. 4(1)(d) Directive 2009/71/Euratom.
1106. Section 6(1)(j) Law No. 164(I)/2018, which corresponds to point 2.5(14) IAEA GRS Part 1, Rev. 1.

– responsibilities and obligations in respect of financial provisions for the management of radioactive waste and of spent fuel, and for decommissioning of facilities and termination of activities;[1107]
– criteria for release from regulatory control;[1108] and
– controls on the import and export of nuclear material and radioactive material, as well as for their tracking within, and to the extent possible outside, national boundaries.[1109]

245. The aforementioned framework ensures the effective independence of the competent authority from undue influence in its regulatory operation and during its regulatory decision-making.[1110] More specifically, it ensures that the Minister:

– is functionally separate from any other body or organization concerned with the promotion or utilization of nuclear energy or ionizing radiation or performance of any activities falling under the scope of this law and its staff shall not have direct or indirect interest in facilities and activities or authorized parties beyond the interest necessary for regulatory purpose;[1111]
– shall not ask or receive directions from any authority or organization during the performance of his duties; to this end, he is free from any pressures associated with political circumstances or economic conditions, or pressures from government departments, authorized parties or other organizations;[1112]
– takes regulatory decisions that are based on solid and transparent demands related to the security from ionizing radiation, safety and security of sources of ionizing radiation and nuclear or other facilities, which fall within the scope of this law;[1113]
– has access to exclusive and sufficient financial resources and has the necessary facilities and equipment, in order to exercise his regulatory duties, as defined in the national frame, and is responsible for the use of available resources;[1114]
– employs sufficient staff with the necessary qualifications, experience and expertise for fulfilling his duties;[1115]

1107. Section 6(1)(k) Law No. 164(I)/2018, which corresponds to point 2.5(16) IAEA GRS Part 1, Rev. 1.

1108. Section 6(1)(l) Law No. 164(I)/2018, which corresponds to point 2.5(17) IAEA GRS Part 1, Rev. 1.

1109. Section 6(1)(m) Law No. 164(I)/2018, which corresponds to point 2.5(18) IAEA GRS Part 1, Rev. 1.

1110. Section 6(2) Law No. 164(I)/2018, which corresponds to Art. 5(2) Directive 2009/71/Euratom.

1111. Section 6(2)(a) Law No. 164(I)/2018, which corresponds to Art. 5(2) Directive 2009/71/Euratom and point 2.10 IAEA GRS Part 1, Rev. 1.

1112. Section 6(2)(b) Law No. 164(I)/2018, which corresponds to point 2.8(d) IAEA GRS Part 1, Rev. 1.

1113. Section 6(2)(c) Law No. 164(I)/2018, which corresponds to Art. 5(2)(b) Directive 2009/71/Euratom. On open and transparent processes *see* point 4.14 IAEA GRS Part 1, Rev. 1.

1114. Section 6(2)(d) Law No. 164(I)/2018, which corresponds to Art. 5(2)(c) Directive 2009/71/Euratom. On financial resources *see* Art. 5(3) Directive 2009/71/Euratom and point 2.8(b) IAEA GRS Part 1, Rev. 1.

1115. Section 6(2)(e) Law No. 164(I)/2018, which corresponds to Art. 5(2)(d) Directive 2009/71/Euratom. On employment of competent staff *see* Art. 5(3) Directive 2009/71/Euratom and point 2.8(a) IAEA GRS Part 1, Rev. 1.

- enacts procedures for prevention and resolution of conflicts of interest;[1116]
- shall consistently and steadily perform regulatory control and take necessary measures so that the regulatory decisions are taken in an objective manner;[1117]
- gives independent advice and provides reports on matters relating to security from ionizing radiation, safety and security, including access to the highest levels of government, without the need for approval from other authority or organization, under the condition that this does not endanger supreme interests, such as national security, which are recognized as such by legislation or international acts;[1118]
- apply, evaluate and improve, where necessary, an appropriate management plan that is in compliance with, and contributes to achieving the purpose of security from ionizing radiation, safety and security that the Minister himself has set;[1119] and
- may auxiliary use the services of external technical advisors or any other professional expert service without affecting his responsibility to perform his regulatory duties.[1120]

246. The competent authority is given legal powers necessary to fulfil its obligations in connection with the national framework, on the basis of which it is entrusted with the following basic regulatory tasks:[1121]

- enact national policy and strategy for safety and security from ionizing radiation;[1122]
- propose, define or participate in the definition of national safety requirements for ionizing radiation, safety, including nuclear safety, and security;[1123]
- propose bills and/or participate in the preparation of bills, ensuring compliance with international and European standards of safety, security and security from ionizing radiation, and promote guidelines for its effective implementation;[1124]
- issue Decrees, Notifications, Codes of Practices, Standards and Specifications for the optimal application of this law;[1125]
- require that undertakings or employers comply and demonstrate compliance with national safety requirements for security from ionizing radiation, safety, including nuclear safety, and security, as well as the terms and conditions of the relevant authorization;[1126]

1116. Section 6(2)(f) Law No. 164(I)/2018, which corresponds to Art. 5(2)(e) Directive 2009/71/ Euratom. *See* also point 4.7 IAEA GRS Part 1, Rev. 1.
1117. Section 6(2)(g) Law No. 164(I)/2018.
1118. Section 6(2)(h) *ibid.*, which corresponds to Art. 5(2)(f) Directive 2009/71/Euratom. *See* also point 2.8(e) IAEA GRS Part 1, Rev. 1. The latter however does not set out any reservation whether on grounds of national security or other.
1119. Section 6(2)(i) Law No. 164(I)/2018.
1120. Section 6(2)(j) *ibid.*
1121. Section 6(3) *ibid.*, which corresponds to Art. 5(3) Directive 2009/71/Euratom.
1122. Section 6(3)(a) Law No. 164(I)/2018.
1123. Section 6(3)(b) *ibid.*, which corresponds to Art. 5(3)(a) Directive 2009/71/Euratom.
1124. Section 6(3)(c) Law No. 164(I)/2018.
1125. Section 6(3)(d) *ibid.*
1126. Section 6(3)(e) *ibid.*, which corresponds to Art. 5(3)(b) Directive 2009/71/Euratom.

– have access, either independently or together with the undertaking or the employer, to the facilities of any designer, supplier, manufacturer, contractor or organization related to the undertaking or the employer, so that he can perform the necessary controls and demand from those to provide to the undertaking or the employer the necessary technical information for safe management and efficient safety and security of radiation sources with which they supply the undertaking or the employer;[1127]
– verify the compliance of the undertaking or the employer through regulatory assessments and inspections;[1128] and
– propose and carry out effective and proportionate enforcement actions.[1129]

247. Finally, the competent authority functions as a national contact point for fostering cooperation and exchange of regulatory experience and information and communication with the competent authorities of other Member States of Euratom, the European Commission and other international organizations.[1130]

II. The Council of Ministers

248. The Council of Ministers following the recommendation of the Minister may issue regulations on every matter that needs to be regulated for the best application of this law and the accomplishment of its objective.[1131] Regulations may aim at regulating declarations, authorizations or exceptions of practices or sources as well as requirements for radiological or nuclear safety and security,[1132] along with regulating import, export, shipment, storage or disposal of radiological sources in Cyprus.[1133] These may also define exposure to ionizing radiation that are excluded from the area of application of this law, and specify obligations, including financial terms and terms of financial security that may be imposed on everyone possessing sources of radiation or apply practices that use radiation.[1134] Further, these may regulate: inspection of sources, practices and establishments and taking measures for the purpose of applying the terms and conditions of an authorization or of the legislation in force;[1135] fees of authorizations or for providing any other service under this law;[1136] prevention and remediation of emergencies and radioactive accidents from radiation;[1137] interventions in cases of long-term exposure;[1138] public

1127. Section 6(3)(g) Law No. 164(I)/2018.
1128. Section 6(3)(h) *ibid.*, which corresponds to Art. 5(3) Directive 2009/71/Euratom.
1129. Section 6(3)(i) Law No. 164(I)/2018, which corresponds to Art. 5(3)(d) Directive 2009/71/ Euratom.
1130. Section 6(4) Law No. 164(I)/2018.
1131. Section 62(1) *ibid.*
1132. Section 62(2) and Annex XI(a) *ibid.*
1133. Section 62(2) and Annex XI(b) *ibid.*
1134. Section 62(2) and Annex XI(c) and (d) *ibid.*
1135. Section 62(2) and Annex XI(e) *ibid.*
1136. Section 62(2) and Annex XI(f) *ibid.*
1137. Section 62(2) and Annex XI(g) *ibid.*
1138. Section 62(2) and Annex XI(h) *ibid.*

information or performing investigations related to radiation;[1139] medical supervision of persons exposed to ionizing radiation;[1140] professional and public exposure as well as exposure for medical purposes;[1141] investigation of accidents and hazardous events;[1142] investigation of matters related to the use of ionizing radiation or application of nuclear techniques;[1143] matters related to monitoring activity levels to environmental receivers and products or other goods;[1144] matters related to nuclear or radiological security and/or management of nuclear waste;[1145] matters related to supervision and control of shipments of nuclear waste and spent nuclear fuel;[1146] matters related to the protection of the public from radioactive substances contained in goods for human consumption;[1147] matters related to the control of closed radiological sources of high temperature;[1148] ensuring nuclear fuel ('πυρηνικό υλικό') as well as protecting such along with radiological material;[1149] and setting the basic safety standards and standards for radiological security.[1150]

III. Technical Committee for Authorizations

249. The Technical Committee for Authorizations ('Τεχνική Επιτροπή Αδειοδότησης') is established for the purpose of advising the Radiation Control and Inspection Service (*see* in this regard paragraphs 246 et seq. below) in matters of providing authorization (*see* in this regard paragraphs 286 et seq. below). As already seen in the Technical Committee for the Protection of Air under Law No. 187(I)/2002 (*see* in this respect paragraphs 32 et seq. above), this committee participate representatives from various Ministries, with the exception of representatives of the technical chamber and of the federation of environmental organizations.[1151]

250. The Chairman of the Technical Committee for Authorizations, who has the power to call meetings and regulate anything related to the operation of the committee that is not foreseen in this law, is the representative of the Ministry of Labour and Social Security.[1152] Should a representative of any of the Ministries involved, or a Ministry itself, have any direct or indirect involvement, including a personal,

1139. Section 62(2) and Annex XI(i) *ibid.*
1140. Section 62(2) and Annex XI(j) *ibid.*
1141. Section 62(2) and Annex XI(k) *ibid.*
1142. Section 62(2) and Annex XI(l) *ibid.*
1143. Section 62(2) and Annex XI(m) *ibid.*
1144. Section 62(2) and Annex XI(n) *ibid.*
1145. Section 62(2) and Annex XI(o) *ibid.*
1146. Section 62(2) and Annex XI(p) *ibid.*
1147. Section 62(2) and Annex XI(q) *ibid.*
1148. Section 62(2) and Annex XI(r) *ibid.*
1149. Section 62(2) and Annex XI(s) and (t) *ibid.*
1150. Section 62(2) and Annex XI(u) *ibid.*
1151. Annex II Part I, 1(a)(i)–(vi) *ibid.*
1152. Annex II, Part I, 3(a), (e) and (h) *ibid.*

financial or other interest to an issue discussed within the committee, then the Chairman shall decide on the apposite course of action. Under the law, the Chairman may decide that the representative in question shall not vote and shall not participate in the meeting or at the relevant part of the meeting, as the case may be.[1153] Regrettably, the law is silent on two points. First, it does not impose a duty of disclosure of conflict of interest. Second, it does not provide an appropriate procedure for the instances that the Chairman himself or the Ministry of Labour and Social Security may have a conflict of interest; unless, it is implied that the chairman himself shall decide on the conflict of interest involving his person or the Ministry that he represents.

251. The Radiation Control and Inspection Service (*see* in this regard paragraphs 246 et seq. below) invites to the meetings of the Technical Committee for Permits any local authority or municipality, which said service deems to have interest in matters to be discussed in the relevant meeting. The representative of the local authority has the statutory power to express an opinion during such a meeting; in the event that it is not possible for a representative to attend, the local authority may send its opinion in writing to the chairman of the committee.[1154]

IV. Council of Radiological Security and Nuclear Safety

252. The Minister has the power to establish the Council of Radiological Security and Nuclear Safety ('Συμβούλιο Ακτινοπροστασίας και Πυρηνικής Ασφάλειας').[1155] The chairman of this council is the inspector-in-chief (*see* in this regard paragraphs 249 et seq. below), whereas the other members are specified by the Minister.[1156] Should a member resign prior to the expiration of his office, the Minister has the power to appoint a new member. Moreover, the Minister has the power to replace any member of the Council of Radiological Security and Nuclear Safety, prior to the expiration of his office, if the Minister deems this fit and proper.[1157] This council has the duty to advise the Minister in shaping national politics in matters of radiation, including nuclear techniques, nuclear and radiological safety and matters of security and security of public health and safety from hazards of ionizing radiation.[1158] It also provides advice on all matters related to radiations or nuclear energy, including matters of possible exposure to radiation hazards from sources situated abroad,[1159] and any other matter within its authority that it deems proper.[1160]

1153. Annex II, Part I, 3(c) *ibid.*
1154. Annex II, Part I, 3(d) *ibid.*
1155. Section 61(1) *ibid.*
1156. Section 61(2)(a) *ibid.*
1157. Section 61(2)(b) *ibid.*
1158. Section 61(3)(a) *ibid.*
1159. Section 61(3)(b) *ibid.*
1160. Section 61(3)(c) *ibid.*

V. Radiation Control and Inspection Service

253. The Radiation Control and Inspection Service ('Υπηρεσία Ελέγχου και Επιθεώρησης για Ακτινοβολίες') are being established under the Minister of Labour and Social Security.[1161] The Radiation Control and Inspection Service are being coordinated and controlled by the inspector-in-chief (*see* in this regard paragraphs 249 et seq. below), who is also its director.[1162]

254. The aim of the Radiation Control and Inspection Service is to protect the public and workers from hazards during the usage of ionizing radiation or exposure to them, from hazards of release or dispersion of radioactive substances, of radioactive contamination, including protection from hazards due to ionizing radiation from nuclear facilities, which may not be ignored from the perspective of radiological security, or regarding the protection of the environment, as long as it aims for long-term protection of human health, in any event of exposure falling within the scope of this law.[1163] In addition, the Radiation Control and Inspection Service serves the purpose of maintaining and fostering continuous improvement of nuclear and radiological safety and security, as well as their regulation with the purpose of achieving a high level of nuclear and radiological safety and security.[1164]

255. The duties and powers of the Radiation Control and Inspection Service include the following, among others:

- suggest health and safety levels for practices that are likely to cause damage to human health due to exposure to ionizing radiation, environmental damage, loss of property use due to release or dispersion of radioactive substance or radioactive contamination;[1165]
- examine and evaluate information related to safety and security of facilities and radiation sources and the relevant practices and activities, and the protection of humans, property and the environment from ionizing radiation, for the purpose of compliance with the regulatory provisions and the terms and conditions set out in an authorization;[1166]
- inspect, for the purpose of application of this law, any practices or facilities, where activities take place that may cause health damage, environmental damage, loss of use of property due to release or dispersion of radioactive substance or radioactive contamination;[1167]
- receive notifications and issue authorizations;[1168]

1161. Section 7(a) *ibid.*
1162. Section 7(b) *ibid.*
1163. Section 8(a) *ibid.*
1164. Section 8(b) *ibid.*
1165. Section 9(a) *ibid.*
1166. Section 9(b) *ibid.*
1167. Section 9(c) *ibid.*
1168. Section 9(d) *ibid.*

- implement material and proportionate enforcement actions, including, to the extent that it is purposeful, amending actions or suspending the operation of a facility or terminating a practice and the amendment or of an authorization;[1169]
- ensure the coordination of educational, scientific or organisms of other forms, who are responsible for providing advice, education, training or other services in matters of radiological security;[1170]
- recognize the ability of experts and services set out in this law, as well as persons who may participate in practical aspects of medical reports, to act according to their expertise in issues falling under this law, as well as the qualifications of employees and other persons in issues of safety and radiological security;[1171]
- coordinate, in cooperation with other services, when this is necessary, the organization of a national system and planning for prevention or remediation of emergencies from nuclear or radioactive accidents or incidents;[1172]
- keep proper archives, including archives of sources of ionizing radiation, of buildings, of practices and of exposed workers as well as the dose that they receive;[1173]
- suggest the adoption of national nuclear safety requirements and their renewal taking into consideration experience acquired during operation and from safety studies of the operating nuclear facilities, technological developments and research results related to safety, when they are available;[1174]
- monitor activity levels in air, soil, waters, sea, food, animal feed, construction material and other products and goods and ensures the application of proper security measures, when deemed fit;[1175]
- produce documents for notification, submission and approval and the information to be provided with those;[1176] and
- where necessary, cooperate with external persons for technical support and advise in the matters within its authority.[1177]

VI. Inspector-in-Chief and Inspectors

256. The Minister appoints the inspector-in-chief and inspectors, as well as any other persons, for the purpose of effective application of this law. He equally has the power to terminate their appointments.[1178]

1169. Section 9(e) *ibid.* On competent authorities having the power to withdraw authorizations when the exposure situation is not in compliance with EU law, *see* Art. 105 Directive 2013/59/Euratom.
1170. Section 9(f) Law No. 164(I)/2018. On the obligation to provide appropriate radiation protection education *see* Art. 14(1) Directive 2013/59/Euratom.
1171. Section 9(g) Law No. 164(I)/2018.
1172. Section 9(h) *ibid.*
1173. Section 9(i) *ibid.*
1174. Section 9(j) *ibid.* The adoption of national nuclear safety requirements is set out in Art. 4(1)(a) Directive 2009/71/Euratom.
1175. Section 9(k) Law No. 164(I)/2018.
1176. Section 9(l) *ibid.*
1177. Section 9(k) *ibid.*
1178. Section 30(1) *ibid.*

257. Generally, the inspector-in-chief and inspectors have the authority to investigate operations conducted in the ordinary course of events, in order to establish compliance with the provisions of this law,[1179] as well as accidents ('ατύχημα')[1180] or severe incidents ('σοβαρό συμβάν')[1181] falling under the scope of this law.[1182]

258. Their duties and powers involve entering plants, document and information discovery, asking persons within plants to facilitate their investigation, taking photos and samples, ordering the plant to maintain its *status quo*, confiscating and issuing reports and notices, as discussed below. Inspector-in-chief and inspectors have the power to enter freely and without prior notice any area, as long as they reasonably believe that such entry is necessary for them at a reasonable time or at any time they believe that a situation exists, which is likely to cause direct danger of serious damage to public health or to the environment or serious loss of property.[1183] They equally have the power to enter into areas used as residence, as long as the possessor consents to it or, in the alternative, a court order has been issued. Said areas include, among others: (a) areas or facilities for which an application for authorization has been submitted or authorization has been issued or authorization has been or amended;[1184] (b) areas for which there is a reasonable suspicion that radioactive substances, radiation generators, accelerators or other electrical equipment that falls under the scope of this law are present;[1185] (c) areas that contain equipment related to the use of radioactive substances, radiation generators, accelerators or other electrical equipment that falls under the scope of this law, or where such equipment is manufactured;[1186] or (d) facilities, including nuclear facilities.[1187]

259. Investigations in the ordinary course of events include examinations, tests, controls and supervision that might be necessary, either by the investigators or by other persons authorized by them.[1188] More specifically, such actions may be conducting measurements or taking photos that are deemed necessary,[1189] taking

1179. Section 30(2)(a) *ibid.*
1180. Accident ('accident' in French, 'Unfall' in German, 'ongeval' in Dutch) means any unintended event, the consequences or potential consequences of which are significant from the point of view of radiation protection or nuclear safety. Section 2 *ibid.*, which corresponds to Art. 4(6) Directive 2013/59/Euratom.
1181. The notion *severe incident* is not defined in this law. However, incident ('incident' in French, 'Vorkommnis' in German, 'incident' in Dutch) means any unintended event, the consequences or potential consequences of which are not negligible from the point of view of radiation protection or nuclear safety. Section 2 Law No. 164(I)/2018, which corresponds to Art. 4(7) Directive 2013/59/Euratom.
1182. Section 30(2)(j) Law No. 164(I)/2018.
1183. Section 31(1)(a) *ibid.*
1184. Section 31(1)(b)(i) *ibid.*
1185. Section 31(1)(b)(ii) *ibid.*
1186. Section 31(1)(b)(iii) *ibid.*
1187. Section 31(1)(b)(iv) *ibid.*
1188. Section 31(2)(a) *ibid.*
1189. Section 31(2)(e) *ibid.*

samples of any objects or substances available in or around any building or facility.[1190] Upon investigation of accidents or serious incidents, such actions may involve confiscation of relevant exhibits,[1191] a term undefined under this law, which, however, could indicate anything deemed useful to support documentation for action plans and reports or evidence in criminal proceedings.

260. The document and information discovery authority vested in the inspectors is wide. They can order any archive, certificate, notification or document kept for the purposes of this law to be disclosed to them either through presentation or to be forwarded to them. The same applies to any other book, document or digital archive that they deem necessary for the purpose of any investigation. Finally, they have the power to examine and copy any of them.[1192] Inspectors equally have the power to demand from any person, who they reasonably believe that they might provide information related to any investigation, to answer relevant questions either alone or in the presence of any other person, whom they might allow to be present. Importantly, they have the authority to demand from said person to sign a statement declaring the truthfulness of his answers.[1193]

261. Further, inspectors have the power to issue preservation orders regarding any building or facility, in whole or in part, or any equipment, source or substance within buildings or facilities. In particular, it may be ordered that these remain as they are for as long as it is deemed reasonably necessary for the purpose of any testing, measurement, investigation or control.[1194]

262. Should inspectors find any object, source or substance in any building or facility, which they reasonably think that it might have caused or may cause danger from radiation, they have the power to order its dismantling or being processed, restricted, or tested, but not in a manner causing damage or its destruction, unless this is necessary under the circumstances for the purpose of application of this law.[1195] Such objects or substances may be confiscated and withheld for as long as deemed reasonably necessary for any of the following purposes: (a) examine, dismantle, process, restrict or test it; (b) ensure that it shall not be falsified until the completion of their examination; and (c) ensure that it shall be available as an exhibit to any criminal proceedings under this law.[1196]

263. Importantly, inspectors have the power to demand from any person within a building, facility or working area to provide them with assistance regarding the issues under such a person's control or responsibility. The requested assistance has to be necessary for the performance of the inspectors' duties and may in particular

1190. Section 31(2)(f) *ibid.*
1191. Section 31(2)(j) *ibid.*
1192. Section 31(2)(b) *ibid.*
1193. Section 31(2)(c) *ibid.*
1194. Section 31(2)(g) *ibid.*
1195. Section 31(2)(h) *ibid.*
1196. Section 31(2)(i) *ibid.*

involve safe passage to any part of a building, facility or source, as well as any reasonably available means to conduct any testing, measurements, controls, clarifications, inspections or examinations that are deemed reasonably necessary for the performance of their duties.[1197]

264. Finally, as the case may be, inspectors have the authority to prepare and issue letters, reports, announcements, certificates and notes, as well as improvement notifications, prohibition notifications (*see* in this regard paragraphs 325–326 below) and any other notification set out in this law.[1198]

265. During the performance of their duties, inspectors may be accompanied by a police officer, if they have reasonable cause to think that they shall be obstructed during said performance. They may further be accompanied by any other person and bring with them any equipment or material necessary to any purpose for which they enter the building or facility, as the case may be.[1199]

266. As long as inspectors perform their duties in good faith and within the scope of this law or the regulations issued under this law (*see* in this regard paragraph 241 above), no civil or criminal proceedings may be initiated against them.[1200]

§4. General Principles for Radiation Protection

267. For any exposure situation, a system of radiation protection is enacted on the basis of the principles of justification, optimization and dose limitation. Justification ('αιτιολόγηση')[1201] means that decisions introducing a practice shall be justified in the sense that such decisions shall be taken with the intent to ensure that the individual or societal benefit resulting from the practice outweighs the health detriment that it may cause. Decisions introducing or altering an exposure pathway for existing and emergency exposure situations shall be justified in the sense that they should do more good than harm. The principle of justification regarding practices or group of practices and medical exposure is further described in regulations[1202] (*see* in this regard paragraph 241 above). Optimization ('βελτιστοποίηση')[1203] indicates that radiation protection of individuals subject to public or occupational exposure shall be optimized with the aim of keeping the magnitude of individual doses, the likelihood of exposure and the number of individuals exposed as low as reasonably achievable taking into account the current

1197. Section 31(2)(d)(i) and (ii) *ibid.*
1198. Section 31(2)(k)(i), (ii) and (iii) *ibid.*
1199. Section 31(5)(a) and (b) *ibid.*
1200. Section 32 *ibid.*
1201. The French term is 'justification', the German one 'Rechtfertigung' and the Dutch one 'rechtvaardiging'.
1202. Section 10(a) Law No. 164(I)/2018, which corresponds to Art. 5(a) Directive 2013/59/Euratom.
1203. The French term is 'optimization', the German one 'Optimierung' and the Dutch one 'optimalisatie'.

state of technical knowledge and economic and societal factors. The optimization of the protection of individuals subject to medical exposure shall apply to the magnitude of individual doses and be consistent with the medical purpose of the exposure. This principle shall be applied not only in terms of effective dose but also, where appropriate, in terms of equivalent doses, as a precautionary measure to allow for uncertainties as to health detriment below the threshold for tissue reactions. The principle of optimization regarding professional and medical exposure and the exposure of the public is further described with regulations.[1204] Dose limitation ('όρια δόσεων')[1205] suggests that in planned exposure situations, the sum of doses to an individual shall not exceed the dose limits laid down for occupational exposure or public exposure. Dose limits shall not apply to medical exposures. Dose limits regarding occupational exposure, exposure of trainees and students and the exposure of the public are further regulated in regulations.[1206]

268. At this point, it is salient to elaborate on the term 'radiation protection' ('ακτινοπροστασία' in Greek, 'radioprotection' in French, 'Strahlenschutz' in German, 'stralingsbescherming' in Dutch). Aside from it being based on the aforementioned principles, Directive 2013/59/Euratom is silent as to its content and notion. However, Law No. 164(I)/2018 that has implemented said directive, among others, as already discussed above, is not. It offers a definition for *nuclear or radiological security* ('πυρηνική ή ραδιολογική προστασία'). This stands for the prevention of, detection of, and response to criminal or intentional unauthorized acts involving nuclear or radioactive material, as well as associated facilities, practices or activities; the term includes theft ('κλοπή'), corruption ('δολιοφθορά'), unauthorized access, illegal transport or other malicious act ('κακόβουλη πράξη') involving nuclear or radiological material and the associated facilities, practices or activities.[1207] This statutory definition, apart from the non-exclusive list of malicious acts, is identical to the one for the term 'nuclear security' followed by IAEA safety standards.[1208] IAEA further makes a distinction between nuclear security, already described above, and protection (against radiation); it clarifies that *radiation protection (also radiological protection)* is the protection of people from harmful effects of exposure to ionizing radiation, and the means for achieving this.[1209] IAEA also clarifies that *protection and safety* stands for the protection of people against exposure to ionizing radiation or exposure due to radioactive material and the safety of sources, including the means for achieving this and the means for preventing accidents and for mitigating the consequences of accidents if they do occur.[1210] Thus, *protection and safety* denotes preventive and remediation measures against exposure.

1204. Section 10(b) Law No. 164(I)/2018, which corresponds to Art. 5(b) Directive 2013/59/Euratom.
1205. The French term is 'limitation des doses', the German one 'Dosisbegrenzung' and the Dutch one 'Dosislimieten'.
1206. Section 10(c) Law No. 164(I)/2018, which corresponds to Art. 5(c) Directive 2013/59/Euratom.
1207. Section 2 Law No. 164(I)/2018.
1208. *See* IAEA GRS Part 3, p. 405.
1209. *Ibid.*, p. 408.
1210. *Ibid.*, p. 408.

269. Having said that, the difference between protection and security is straightforward and the discussion above seems to be superfluous. In truth that would have been the case, save for the term ***Προστασία*** being used for both notions in Law No. 164(I)/2018. Using a single term for two distinct notions could lead to complications in the applicability and effectiveness of the law. However, whether such complications do in fact arise remains to be seen in practice, in view of this legislation being a new, shiny, most recent addition to the arsenal of Cyprus law in the fight for the protection of the environment.

270. For the sake of completeness, some remarks on the term 'safety' ('ασφάλεια') are offered here. Nuclear or radiological safety ('πυρηνική ή ραδιολογική ασφάλεια') means the achievement of proper operating conditions or prevention of accidents and mitigation of accident consequences, resulting in protection of the health of workers and of the general public and protection of property and the environment from dangers arising from ionizing radiations from nuclear or non-nuclear installations.[1211] This definition, although broader, follows the one of *nuclear safety* set out in Directive 2009/71/Euratom[1212] and at the same time, is in alignment with one of (nuclear) the safety measures used by IAEA safety standards, which reads 'the achievement of proper operating conditions, prevention of accidents or mitigation of accident consequences, resulting in protection of workers, the public and the environment from undue radiation hazards'.[1213] Conclusively, IAEA provides that there is not an exact distinction between the general terms 'safety' and 'security'. In general, *security* is concerned with criminal acts or intentional unauthorized acts by humans that could cause or threaten harm to other humans; *safety* is concerned with the broader issue of harm to humans (or to the environment) from radiation, whatever the cause. The precise interaction between *security* and *safety* depends on the context.[1214]

§5. Prohibition of Practices

271. The deliberate addition of radioactive substances in the production of foodstuffs, animal feeding stuffs, toys, personal ornaments and cosmetics, as well as the import and export of such products is prohibited.[1215] Practices involving the activation of material resulting in an increase in activity in a consumer product, which at the time of placing on the market cannot be disregarded from a radiation protection point of view, as well as evaluation of such practices is further regulated with regulations.[1216]

1211. Section 2 Law No. 164(I)/2018.
1212. Article 3(2) Directive 2009/71/Euratom.
1213. *See* IAEA GRS Part 3, p. 405.
1214. *Ibid.*, p. 406.
1215. Section 11(1) Law No. 164(I)/2018, which corresponds to Art. 21(1), (3) and (4) Directive 2013/59/Euratom. However, the European provision sets as a thumb rule that these practices are deemed not to be justified.
1216. Section 11(2) Law No. 164(I)/2018, which corresponds to Art. 21(2) Directive 2013/59/Euratom.

§6. Graded Approach to Regulatory Control: Notification, Registration and Authorization

272. Practices, sources and installations falling within the scope of this law are subject to regulatory control for the purpose of radiation protection and radiological or nuclear safety and security by way of notification or authorization and appropriate inspections and, where necessary enforcement acts, commensurate with the magnitude and likelihood of exposures resulting from the practice, and commensurate with the impact that regulatory control may have in reducing such exposures or improving radiological or nuclear safety and security of the facilities and sources of radiation.[1217] This is the essence of the grated approach to regulatory control.

I. Notification

273. Regulatory control may be limited to notification ('γνωστοποίηση')[1218] and an appropriate frequency of inspections, where this is appropriate and in accordance with the general exemption criteria.[1219] The general exemption criteria, as set out in Annex III to Law No. 164(I)/2018, implementing Annex VII to Directive 2013/59/Euratom, are the following.

274. The general exemption rule prescribes that practices may be exempted from notification either directly, on the basis of compliance with specific exemption levels (activity values (in Bq) or activity concentration values (in kBq kg^{-1})) (*see* in this regard paragraph 268 below), or on the basis of higher values that, for specific applications, are established by the competent authority, satisfying the general exemption and clearance criteria (*see* in this regard paragraph 269 below). Practices subject to notification may be exempted from authorization by law or general administrative act, or through an ad hoc regulatory decision, on the basis of the information provided in conjunction with the notification of the practice and in line with general exemption criteria[1220] (*see* in this regard paragraph 269 below).

275. The exemption and clearance levels are set out as follows. The total activity values (in Bq) for exemption apply to the total activity involved in a practice and are laid down in column 3 of Table 16 for artificial radionuclides and for some naturally occurring radionuclides used in consumer products. For other practices involving naturally occurring radionuclides, such values are, in general, not applicable.[1221] The exempt activity concentration values (in kBq kg^{-1}) for the materials involved in the practice are laid down in Table 13, for artificial radionuclides, and

1217. Section 12(1) Law No. 164(I)/2018, which corresponds to Art. 24(1) Directive 2013/59/Euratom.
1218. The French term is 'notification', the German one is 'Anmeldung' and the Dutch one 'kennisgeving'.
1219. Section 12(2) Law No. 164(I)/2018, which corresponds to Art. 24(2) Directive 2013/59/Euratom.
1220. Annex III, Part I(1) Law No. 164(I)/2018, which corresponds to Annex VII Part I(1) Directive 2013/59/Euratom.
1221. Annex III, Part I(2)(a) Law No. 164(I)/2018, which corresponds to Annex VII Part I(2)(a) Directive 2013/59/Euratom.

in Table 15, for naturally occurring radionuclides. The values in Table 13, are given for individual radionuclides, where applicable, including short-lived radionuclides in equilibrium with the parent nuclide, as indicated. The values in Table 15, apply to all radionuclides in the decay chain of U-238 or Th-232, but for segments of the decay chain, which are not in equilibrium with the parent radionuclide, higher values may be applied.[1222] The concentration values in Table 13, or Table 15, also apply to the clearance of solid materials for reuse, recycling, conventional disposal or incineration. Higher values may be defined for specific materials or specific pathways, taking Community guidance into account, including, where appropriate, additional requirements, in terms of surface activity or monitoring requirements.[1223] For mixtures of artificial radionuclides, the weighted sum of nuclide-specific activities or concentrations (for various radionuclides contained in the same matrix) divided by the corresponding exemption value shall be less than unity. Where appropriate, this condition can be verified on the basis of best estimates of the composition of the radionuclide mix. The values in Table 15 apply individually to each parent nuclide. Some elements in the decay chain, e.g., Po-210 or Pb-210, may warrant the use of higher values taking Community guidance into account.[1224] The values in Table 15 may not be used to exempt the incorporation into building materials of residues from industries processing naturally occurring radioactive material. For this purpose, compliance with the relevant provisions set out in regulations shall be verified. The values laid down in Table 16, column 3, apply to the total inventory of radioactive substances held by a person or undertaking as part of a specific practice at any point in time. However, the competent authority may apply these values to smaller entities or packages, for instance, to exempt the transport or storage of exempted consumer products, if the general exemption criteria are satisfied (*see* in this regard paragraph 269 below).[1225]

276. The general criteria for the exemption of practices from notification or authorization or for the clearance of materials from authorized practices are as follows:

(i) the radiological risks to individuals caused by the practice are sufficiently low, as to be of no regulatory concern; and
(ii) the type of practice has been determined to be justified; and
(iii) the practice is inherently safe.[1226]

1222. Annex III, Part I(2)(b) Law No. 164(I)/2018, which corresponds to Annex VII Part I(2)(b) Directive 2013/59/Euratom.
1223. Annex III, Part I(2)(c) Law No. 164(I)/2018, which corresponds to Annex VII Part I(2)(c) Directive 2013/59/Euratom.
1224. Annex III, Part I(2)(d) Law No. 164(I)/2018, which corresponds to Annex VII Part I(2)(d) Directive 2013/59/Euratom.
1225. Annex III, Part I(2)(e) Law No. 164(I)/2018, which corresponds to Annex VII Part I(2)(e) Directive 2013/59/Euratom.
1226. Annex III, Part I(3)(a) Law No. 164(I)/2018, which corresponds to Annex VII Part I(3)(a) Directive 2013/59/Euratom.

277. Practices involving small amounts of radioactive substances or low activity concentrations, comparable to the exemption values laid down in Tables 13, 15 or 16 are deemed to fulfil criterion (iii).[1227] Practices involving amounts of radioactive substances or activity concentrations below the exemption values laid down in Table 13, or Table 16, are deemed to comply with criterion (i) without further consideration. This is also the case for the values in Table 15, with the exception of the recycling of residues in building materials or the case of specific exposure pathways, for instance, drinking water.[1228] In the case of moderate amounts of material, as specified by the competent authority for specific types of practice, the activity concentration values laid down in Table 16, column 2, may be used instead of the values laid down in Table 13, for the purpose of exemption from authorization.[1229]

278. For the purpose of exemption from notification or for the purpose of clearance, where amounts of radioactive substances or activity concentrations do not comply with the values laid down in Tables 13, 15 or 16, an assessment shall be made in the light of the general criteria (i) to (iii) above. For compliance with the general criterion (i), it shall be demonstrated that workers should not be classified as exposed workers, and the following criteria for the exposure of members of the public are met in all feasible circumstances:

- For artificial radionuclides: the effective dose expected to be incurred by a member of the public due to the exempted practice is of the order of 10 μSv or less in a year.
- For naturally occurring radionuclides: the dose increment, allowing for the prevailing background radiation from natural radiation sources, liable to be incurred by an individual due to the exempted practice is of the order of 1 mSv or less in a year. The assessment of doses to members of the public shall take into account not only pathways of exposure through airborne or liquid effluent but also pathways resulting from the disposal or recycling of solid residues. The competent authority may specify dose criteria lower than 1 mSv per year for specific types of practices or specific pathways of exposure.
- For the purpose of exemption from authorization, less restrictive dose criteria may be applied.[1230]

1227. Annex III, Part I(3)(b) Law No. 164(I)/2018, which corresponds to Annex VII Part I(3)(b) Directive 2013/59/Euratom.

1228. Annex III, Part I(3)(c) Law No. 164(I)/2018, which corresponds to Annex VII Part I(3)(c) Directive 2013/59/Euratom.

1229. Annex III, Part I(3)(d) Law No. 164(I)/2018, which corresponds to Annex VII Part I(3)(d) Directive 2013/59/Euratom.

1230. Annex III, Part I(3)(e) Law No. 164(I)/2018, which corresponds to Annex VII Part I(3)(e) Directive 2013/59/Euratom.

Table 13 Activity Concentration Values for Exemption or Clearance of Materials Which Can Be Applied by Default to Any Amount and to Any Type of Solid Material: Artificial Radionuclides[1231]

Radionuclide	*Activity Concentration (kBq kg^{-1})*
H-3	100
Be-7	10
C-14	1
F-18	10
Na-22	0.1
Na-24	1
Si-31	1,000
P-32	1,000
P-33	1,000
S-35	100
Cl-36	1
Cl-38	10
K-42	100
K-43	10
Ca-45	100
Ca-47	10
Sc-46	0.1
Sc-47	100
Sc-48	1
V-48	1
Cr-51	100
Mn-51	10
Mn-52	1
Mn-52 m	10
Mn-53	100
Mn-54	0.1
Mn-56	10
Fe-52 ([1])	10
Fe-55	1,000

1231. Annex III, Part II(A) Law No. 164(I)/2018, which corresponds to Annex VII Table A Part 1 Directive 2013/59/Euratom.

Radionuclide	*Activity Concentration (kBq kg^{-1})*
Fe-59	1
Co-55	10
Co-56	0.1
Co-57	1
Co-58	1
Co-58 m	10,000
Co-60	0.1
Co-60 m	1,000
Co-61	100
Co-62 m	10
Ni-59	100
Ni-63	100
Ni-65	10
Cu-64	100
Zn-65	0.1
Zn-69	1,000
Zn-69 m ([1])	10
Ga-72	10
Ge-71	10,000
As-73	1,000
As-74	10
As-76	10
As-77	1,000
Se-75	1
Br-82	1
Rb-86	100
Sr-85	1
Sr-85 m	100
Sr-87 m	100
Sr-89	1,000
Sr-90 ([1])	1
Sr-91 ([1])	10
Sr-92	10
Y-90	1,000
Y-91	100

Radionuclide	*Activity Concentration (kBq kg^{-1})*
Y-91 m	100
Y-92	100
Y-93	100
Zr-93	10
Zr-95 ([1])	1
Zr-97 ([1])	10
Nb-93 m	10
Nb-94	0.1
Nb-95	1
Nb-97 ([1])	10
Nb-98	10
Mo-90	10
Mo-93	10
Mo-99 ([1])	10
Mo-101 ([1])	10
Tc-96	1
Tc-96 m	1,000
Tc-97	10
Tc-97 m	100
Tc-99	1
Tc-99 m	100
Ru-97	10
Ru-103 ([1])	1
Ru-105 ([1])	10
Ru-106 ([1])	0.1
Rh-103 m	10,000
Rh-105	100
Pd-103 ([1])	1,000
Pd-109 ([1])	100
Ag-105	1
Ag-110 m ([1])	0.1
Ag-111	100
Cd-109 ([1])	1
Cd-115 ([1])	10
Cd-115 m ([1])	100

Radionuclide	*Activity Concentration (kBq kg^{-1})*
In-111	10
In-113 m	100
In-114 m ([1])	10
In-115 m	100
Sn-113 ([1])	1
Sn-125	10
Sb-122	10
Sb-124	1
Sb-125 ([1])	0.1
Te-123 m	1
Te-125 m	1,000
Te-127	1,000
Te-127 m ([1])	10
Te-129	100
Te-129 m ([1])	10
Te-131	100
Te-131 m ([1])	10
Te-132 ([1])	1
Te-133	10
Te-133 m	10
Te-134	10
I-123	100
I-125	100
I-126	10
I-129	0.01
I-130	10
I-131	10
I-132	10
I-133	10
I-134	10
I-135	10
Cs-129	10
Cs-131	1,000
Cs-132	10
Cs-134	0.1

Radionuclide	*Activity Concentration (kBq kg^{-1})*
Cs-134 m	1,000
Cs-135	100
Cs-136	1
Cs-137 ([1])	0.1
Cs-138	10
Ba-131	10
Ba-140	1
La-140	1
Ce-139	1
Ce-141	100
Ce-143	10
Ce-144	10
Pr-142	100
Pr-143	1,000
Nd-147	100
Nd-149	100
Pm-147	1,000
Pm-149	1,000
Sm-151	1,000
Sm-153	100
Eu-152	0.1
Eu-152 m	100
Eu-154	0.1
Eu-155	1
Gd-153	10
Gd-159	100
Tb-160	1
Dy-165	1,000
Dy-166	100
Ho-166	100
Er-169	1,000
Er-171	100
Tm-170	100
Tm-171	1,000
Yb-175	100

Radionuclide	*Activity Concentration (kBq kg^{-1})*
Lu-177	100
Hf-181	1
Ta-182	0.1
W-181	10
W-185	1,000
W-187	10
Re-186	1,000
Re-188	100
Os-185	1
Os-191	100
Os-191 m	1,000
Os-193	100
Ir-190	1
Ir-192	1
Ir-194	100
Pt-191	10
Pt-193 m	1,000
Pt-197	1,000
Pt-197 m	100
Au-198	10
Au-199	100
Hg-197	100
Hg-197 m	100
Hg-203	10
Tl-200	10
Tl-201	100
Tl-202	10
Tl-204	1
Pb-203	10
Bi-206	1
Bi-207	0.1
Po-203	10
Po-205	10
Po-207	10
At-211	1,000

Radionuclide	*Activity Concentration (kBq kg⁻¹)*
Ra-225	10
Ra-227	100
Th-226	1,000
Th-229	0.1
Pa-230	10
Pa-233	10
U-230	10
U-231 ([1])	100
U-232 ([1])	0.1
U-233	1
U-236	10
U-237	100
U-239	100
U-240 ([1])	100
Np-237 ([1])	1
Np-239	100
Np-240	10
Pu-234	100
Pu-235	100
Pu-236	1
Pu-237	100
Pu-238	0.1
Pu-239	0.1
Pu-240	0.1
Pu-241	10
Pu-242	0.1
Pu-243	1,000
Pu-244 ([1])	0.1
Am-241	0.1
Am-242	1,000
Am-242 m ([1])	0.1
Am-243 ([1])	0.1
Cm-242	10
Cm-243	1
Cm-244	1

Radionuclide	*Activity Concentration (kBq kg⁻¹)*
Cm-245	0.1
Cm-246	0.1
Cm-247 ([1])	0.1
Cm-248	0.1
Bk-249	100
Cf-246	1,000
Cf-248	1
Cf-249	0.1
Cf-250	1
Cf-251	0.1
Cf-252	1
Cf-253	100
Cf-254	1
Es-253	100
Es-254 ([1])	0.1
Es-254 m ([1])	10
Fm-254	10,000
Fm-255	100

(1) Parent radionuclides, and their progeny whose dose contributions are taken into account in the dose calculation (thus requiring only the exemption level of the parent radionuclide to be considered), are listed in Table 14.

Table 14 Parent Radionuclides and Their Progeny[1232]

Parent Radionuclide	*Progeny*
Fe-52	Mn-52 m
Zn-69 m	Zn-69
Sr-90	Y-90
Sr-91	Y-91 m
Zr-95	Nb-95
Zr-97	Nb-97 m, Nb-97
Nb-97	Nb-97 m
Mo-99	Tc-99 m
Mo-101	Tc-101

1232. *Ibid.*

Parent Radionuclide	*Progeny*
Ru-103	Rh-103 m
Ru-105	Rh-105 m
Ru-106	Rh-106
Pd-103	Rh-103 m
Pd-109	Ag-109 m
Ag-110 m	Ag-110
Cd-109	Ag-109 m
Cd-115	In-115 m
Cd-115 m	In-115 m
In-114 m	In-114
Sn-113	In-113 m
Sb-125	Te-125 m
Te-127 m	Te-127
Te-129 m	Te-129
Te-131 m	Te-131
Te132	I-132
Cs-137	Ba-137 m
Ce-144	Pr-144, Pr-144 m
U-232	Th-228, Ra-224, Rn-220, Po-216, Pb-212, Bi-212, Tl-208
U-240	Np-240 m, Np-240
Np237	Pa-233
Pu-244	U-240, Np-240 m, Np-240
Am-242 m	Np-238
Am-243	Np-239
Cm-247	Pu-243
Es-254	Bk-250
Es-254 m	Fm-254

279. For radionuclides not listed in Table 13, the Radiation Control and Inspection Service shall assign appropriate values for the quantities and concentrations of activity per unit mass where the need arises. Values thus assigned shall be complementary to those in Table 13.

280. Values for exemption or clearance for naturally occurring radionuclides in solid materials in secular equilibrium with their progeny are the ones listed in Table 15.

Table 15 Naturally Occurring Radionuclides [1233]

Natural radionuclides from the U-238 series	1 kBq kg^{-1}
Natural radionuclides from the Th-232 series	1 kBq kg^{-1}
K-40	10 kBq kg^{-1}

281. The total activity values for exemption and the exemption values for the activity concentration in moderate amounts of any type of material are the ones set out in Table 16.

Table 16 Total Activity Values for Exemption (Column 3) and Exemption Values for the Activity Concentration in Moderate Amounts of Any Type of Material (Column 2)[1234]

Radionuclide	*Activity Concentration (kBq kg^{-1})*	*Activity (Bq)*
H-3	1×10^6	1×10^9
Be-7	1×10^3	1×10^7
C-14	1×10^4	1×10^7
O-15	1×10^2	1×10^9
F-18	1×10^1	1×10^6
Na-22	1×10^1	1×10^6
Na-24	1×10^1	1×10^5
Si-31	1×10^3	1×10^6
P-32	1×10^3	1×10^5
P-33	1×10^5	1×10^8
S-35	1×10^5	1×10^8
Cl-36	1×10^4	1×10^6
Cl-38	1×10^1	1×10^5
Ar-37	1×10^6	1×10^8
Ar-41	1×10^2	1×10^9
K-40(1)	1×10^2	1×10^6
K-42	1×10^2	1×10^6
K-43	1×10^1	1×10^6
Ca-45	1×10^4	1×10^7

1233. Annex III, Part II(B) Law No. 164(I)/2018, which corresponds to Annex VII Table A Part 2 Directive 2013/59/Euratom.

1234. Annex III, Part III Law No. 164(I)/2018, which corresponds to Annex VII Table B Directive 2013/59/Euratom.

Radionuclide	*Activity Concentration (kBq kg⁻¹)*	*Activity (Bq)*
Ca-47	1×10^1	1×10^6
Sc-46	1×10^1	1×10^6
Sc-47	1×10^2	1×10^6
Sc-48	1×10^1	1×10^5
V-48	1×10^1	1×10^5
Cr-51	1×10^3	1×10^7
Mn-51	1×10^1	1×10^5
Mn-52	1×10^1	1×10^5
Mn-52 m	1×10^1	1×10^5
Mn-53	1×10^4	1×10^9
Mn-54	1×10^1	1×10^6
Mn-56	1×10^1	1×10^5
Fe-52	1×10^1	1×10^6
Fe-55	1×10^4	1×10^6
Fe-59	1×10^1	1×10^6
Co-55	1×10^1	1×10^6
Co-56	1×10^1	1×10^5
Co-57	1×10^2	1×10^6
Co-58	1×10^1	1×10^6
Co-58 m	1×10^4	1×10^7
Co-60	1×10^1	1×10^5
Co-60 m	1×10^3	1×10^6
Co-61	1×10^2	1×10^6
Co-62 m	1×10^1	1×10^5
Ni-59	1×10^4	1×10^8
Ni-63	1×10^5	1×10^8
Ni-65	1×10^1	1×10^6
Cu-64	1×10^2	1×10^6
Zn-65	1×10^1	1×10^6
Zn-69	1×10^4	1×10^6
Zn-69 m	1×10^2	1×10^6
Ga-72	1×10^1	1×10^5
Ge-71	1×10^4	1×10^8
As-73	1×10^3	1×10^7

Radionuclide	*Activity Concentration* *($kBq\ kg^{-1}$)*	*Activity* *(Bq)*
As-74	1×10^{1}	1×10^{6}
As-76	1×10^{2}	1×10^{5}
As-77	1×10^{3}	1×10^{6}
Se-75	1×10^{2}	1×10^{6}
Br-82	1×10^{1}	1×10^{6}
Kr-74	1×10^{2}	1×10^{9}
Kr-76	1×10^{2}	1×10^{9}
Kr-77	1×10^{2}	1×10^{9}
Kr-79	1×10^{3}	1×10^{5}
Kr-81	1×10^{4}	1×10^{7}
Kr-83 m	1×10^{5}	1×10^{12}
Kr-85	1×10^{5}	1×10^{4}
Kr-85 m	1×10^{3}	1×10^{10}
Kr-87	1×10^{2}	1×10^{9}
Kr-88	1×10^{2}	1×10^{9}
Rb-86	1×10^{2}	1×10^{5}
Sr-85	1×10^{2}	1×10^{6}
Sr-85 m	1×10^{2}	1×10^{7}
Sr-87 m	1×10^{2}	1×10^{6}
Sr-89	1×10^{3}	1×10^{6}
Sr-90 ([2])	1×10^{2}	1×10^{4}
Sr-91	1×10^{1}	1×10^{5}
Sr-92	1×10^{1}	1×10^{6}
Y-90	1×10^{3}	1×10^{5}
Y-91	1×10^{3}	1×10^{6}
Y-91 m	1×10^{2}	1×10^{6}
Y-92	1×10^{2}	1×10^{5}
Y-93	1×10^{2}	1×10^{5}
Zr-93 ([2])	1×10^{3}	1×10^{7}
Zr-95	1×10^{1}	1×10^{6}
Zr-97 ([2])	1×10^{1}	1×10^{5}
Nb-93 m	1×10^{4}	1×10^{7}
Nb-94	1×10^{1}	1×10^{6}
Nb-95	1×10^{1}	1×10^{6}

Radionuclide	*Activity Concentration (kBq kg⁻¹)*	*Activity (Bq)*
Nb-97	1×10^{1}	1×10^{6}
Nb-98	1×10^{1}	1×10^{5}
Mo-90	1×10^{1}	1×10^{6}
Mo-93	1×10^{3}	1×10^{8}
Mo-99	1×10^{2}	1×10^{6}
Mo-101	1×10^{1}	1×10^{6}
Tc-96	1×10^{1}	1×10^{6}
Tc-96 m	1×10^{3}	1×10^{7}
Tc-97	1×10^{3}	1×10^{8}
Tc-97 m	1×10^{3}	1×10^{7}
Tc-99	1×10^{4}	1×10^{7}
Tc-99 m	1×10^{2}	1×10^{7}
Ru-97	1×10^{2}	1×10^{7}
Ru-103	1×10^{2}	1×10^{6}
Ru-105	1×10^{1}	1×10^{6}
Ru-106 ([2])	1×10^{2}	1×10^{5}
Rh-103 m	1×10^{4}	1×10^{8}
Rh-105	1×10^{2}	1×10^{7}
Pd-103	1×10^{3}	1×10^{8}
Pd-109	1×10^{3}	1×10^{6}
Ag-105	1×10^{2}	1×10^{6}
Ag-108 m	1×10^{1}	1×10^{6}
Ag-110 m	1×10^{1}	1×10^{6}
Ag-111	1×10^{3}	1×10^{6}
Cd-109	1×10^{4}	1×10^{6}
Cd-115	1×10^{2}	1×10^{6}
Cd-115 m	1×10^{3}	1×10^{6}
In-111	1×10^{2}	1×10^{6}
In-113 m	1×10^{2}	1×10^{6}
In-114 m	1×10^{2}	1×10^{6}
In-115 m	1×10^{2}	1×10^{6}
Sn-113	1×10^{3}	1×10^{7}
Sn-125	1×10^{2}	1×10^{5}
Sb-122	1×10^{2}	1×10^{4}

Radionuclide	*Activity Concentration (kBq kg⁻¹)*	*Activity (Bq)*
Sb-124	1×10^1	1×10^6
Sb-125	1×10^2	1×10^6
Te-123 m	1×10^2	1×10^7
Te-125 m	1×10^3	1×10^7
Te-127	1×10^3	1×10^6
Te-127 m	1×10^3	1×10^7
Te-129	1×10^2	1×10^6
Te-129 m	1×10^3	1×10^6
Te-131	1×10^2	1×10^5
Te-131 m	1×10^1	1×10^6
Te-132	1×10^2	1×10^7
Te-133	1×10^1	1×10^5
Te-133 m	1×10^1	1×10^5
Te-134	1×10^1	1×10^6
I-123	1×10^2	1×10^7
I-125	1×10^3	1×10^6
I-126	1×10^2	1×10^6
I-129	1×10^2	1×10^5
I-130	1×10^1	1×10^6
I-131	1×10^2	1×10^6
I-132	1×10^1	1×10^5
I-133	1×10^1	1×10^6
I-134	1×10^1	1×10^5
I-135	1×10^1	1×10^6
Xe-131 m	1×10^4	1×10^4
Xe-133	1×10^3	1×10^4
Xe-135	1×10^3	1×10^{10}
Cs-129	1×10^2	1×10^5
Cs-131	1×10^3	1×10^6
Cs-132	1×10^1	1×10^5
Cs-134 m	1×10^3	1×10^5
Cs-134	1×10^1	1×10^4
Cs-135	1×10^4	1×10^7
Cs-136	1×10^1	1×10^5

Radionuclide	*Activity Concentration (kBq kg⁻¹)*	*Activity (Bq)*
Cs-137 (2)	1×10^1	1×10^4
Cs-138	1×10^1	1×10^4
Ba-131	1×10^2	1×10^6
Ba-140 (2)	1×10^1	1×10^5
La-140	1×10^1	1×10^5
Ce-139	1×10^2	1×10^6
Ce-141	1×10^2	1×10^7
Ce-143	1×10^2	1×10^6
Ce-144 (2)	1×10^2	1×10^5
Pr-142	1×10^2	1×10^5
Pr-143	1×10^4	1×10^6
Nd-147	1×10^2	1×10^6
Nd-149	1×10^2	1×10^6
Pm-147	1×10^4	1×10^7
Pm-149	1×10^3	1×10^6
Sm-151	1×10^4	1×10^8
Sm-153	1×10^2	1×10^6
Eu-152	1×10^1	1×10^6
Eu-152 m	1×10^2	1×10^6
Eu-154	1×10^1	1×10^6
Eu-155	1×10^2	1×10^7
Gd-153	1×10^2	1×10^7
Gd-159	1×10^3	1×10^6
Tb-160	1×10^1	1×10^6
Dy-165	1×10^3	1×10^6
Dy-166	1×10^3	1×10^6
Ho-166	1×10^3	1×10^5
Er-169	1×10^4	1×10^7
Er-171	1×10^2	1×10^6
Tm-170	1×10^3	1×10^6
Tm-171	1×10^4	1×10^8
Yb-175	1×10^3	1×10^7
Lu-177	1×10^3	1×10^7
Hf-181	1×10^1	1×10^6

Radionuclide	*Activity Concentration (kBq kg⁻¹)*	*Activity (Bq)*
Ta-182	1×10^1	1×10^4
W-181	1×10^3	1×10^7
W-185	1×10^4	1×10^7
W-187	1×10^2	1×10^6
Re-186	1×10^3	1×10^6
Re-188	1×10^2	1×10^5
Os-185	1×10^1	1×10^6
Os-191	1×10^2	1×10^7
Os-191 m	1×10^3	1×10^7
Os-193	1×10^2	1×10^6
Ir-190	1×10^1	1×10^6
Ir-192	1×10^1	1×10^4
Ir-194	1×10^2	1×10^5
Pt-191	1×10^2	1×10^6
Pt-193 m	1×10^3	1×10^7
Pt-197	1×10^3	1×10^6
Pt-197 m	1×10^2	1×10^6
Au-198	1×10^2	1×10^6
Au-199	1×10^2	1×10^6
Hg-197	1×10^2	1×10^7
Hg-197 m	1×10^2	1×10^6
Hg-203	1×10^2	1×10^5
Tl-200	1×10^1	1×10^6
Tl-201	1×10^2	1×10^6
Tl-202	1×10^2	1×10^6
Tl-204	1×10^4	1×10^4
Pb-203	1×10^2	1×10^6
Pb-210 ([2])	1×10^1	1×10^4
Pb-212 ([2])	1×10^1	1×10^5
Bi-206	1×10^1	1×10^5
Bi-207	1×10^1	1×10^6
Bi-210	1×10^3	1×10^6
Bi-212 ([2])	1×10^1	1×10^5
Po-203	1×10^1	1×10^6

Radionuclide	*Activity Concentration (kBq kg⁻¹)*	*Activity (Bq)*
Po-205	1×10^1	1×10^6
Po-207	1×10^1	1×10^6
Po-210	1×10^1	1×10^4
At-211	1×10^3	1×10^7
Rn-220 (^{2})	1×10^4	1×10^7
Rn-222 (^{2})	1×10^1	1×10^8
Ra-223 (^{2})	1×10^2	1×10^5
Ra-224 (^{2})	1×10^1	1×10^5
Ra-225	1×10^2	1×10^5
Ra-226 (^{2})	1×10^1	1×10^4
Ra-227	1×10^2	1×10^6
Ra-228 (^{2})	1×10^1	1×10^5
Ac-228	1×10^1	1×10^6
Th-226 (^{2})	1×10^3	1×10^7
Th-227	1×10^1	1×10^4
Th-228 (^{2})	1×10^0	1×10^4
Th-229 (^{2})	1×10^0	1×10^3
Th-230	1×10^0	1×10^4
Th-231	1×10^3	1×10^7
Th-234 (^{2})	1×10^3	1×10^5
Pa-230	1×10^1	1×10^6
Pa-231	1×10^0	1×10^3
Pa-233	1×10^2	1×10^7
U-230	1×10^1	1×10^5
U-231	1×10^2	1×10^7
U-232 (^{2})	1×10^0	1×10^3
U-233	1×10^1	1×10^4
U-234	1×10^1	1×10^4
U-235 (^{2})	1×10^1	1×10^4
U-236	1×10^1	1×10^4
U-237	1×10^2	1×10^6
U-238 (^{2})	1×10^1	1×10^4
U-239	1×10^2	1×10^6
U-240	1×10^3	1×10^7

Radionuclide	*Activity Concentration (kBq kg⁻¹)*	*Activity (Bq)*
U-240 ([2])	1×10^1	1×10^6
Np-237 ([2])	1×10^0	1×10^3
Np-239	1×10^2	1×10^7
Np-240	1×10^1	1×10^6
Pu-234	1×10^2	1×10^7
Pu-235	1×10^2	1×10^7
Pu-236	1×10^1	1×10^4
Pu-237	1×10^3	1×10^7
Pu-238	1×10^0	1×10^4
Pu-239	1×10^0	1×10^4
Pu-240	1×10^0	1×10^3
Pu-241	1×10^2	1×10^5
Pu-242	1×10^0	1×10^4
Pu-243	1×10^3	1×10^7
Pu-244	1×10^0	1×10^4
Am-241	1×10^0	1×10^4
Am-242	1×10^3	1×10^6
Am-242 m ([2])	1×10^0	1×10^4
Am-243 ([2])	1×10^0	1×10^3
Cm-242	1×10^2	1×10^5
Cm-243	1×10^0	1×10^4
Cm-244	1×10^1	1×10^4
Cm-245	1×10^0	1×10^3
Cm-246	1×10^0	1×10^3
Cm-247	1×10^0	1×10^4
Cm-248	1×10^0	1×10^3
Bk-249	1×10^3	1×10^6
Cf-246	1×10^3	1×10^6
Cf-248	1×10^1	1×10^4
Cf-249	1×10^0	1×10^3
Cf-250	1×10^1	1×10^4
Cf-251	1×10^0	1×10^3
Cf-252	1×10^1	1×10^4
Cf-253	1×10^2	1×10^5

Radionuclide	*Activity Concentration (kBq kg^{-1})*	*Activity (Bq)*
Cf-254	1×10^0	1×10^3
Es-253	1×10^2	1×10^5
Es-254	1×10^1	1×10^4
Es-254 m	1×10^2	1×10^6
Fm-254	1×10^4	1×10^7
Fm-255	1×10^3	1×10^6

(1) Potassium salts in quantities less than 1,000 kg are exempted.

(2) Parent radionuclides, and their progeny whose dose contributions are taken into account in the dose calculation (thus requiring only the exemption level of the parent radionuclide to be considered), are listed in Table 17.

Table 17 Parent Radionuclides and Their Progeny

Parent Radionuclides	*Progeny*
Sr-90	Y-90
Zr-93	Nb-93 m
Zr-97	Nb-97
Ru-106	Rh-106
Ag-108 m	Ag-108
Cs-137	Ba-137 m
Ba-140	La-140
Ce-144	Pr-144
Pb-210	Bi-210, Po-210
Pb-212	Bi-212, Tl-208 (0.36), Po-212 (0.64)
Bi-212	Tl-208 (0.36), Po-212 (0.64)
Rn-220	Po-216
Rn-222	Po-218, Pb-214, Bi-214, Po-214
Ra-223	Rn-219, Po-215, Pb-211, Bi-211, Tl-207
Ra-224	Rn-220, Po-216, Pb-212, Bi-212, Tl-208 (0.36), Po-212 (0.64)
Ra-226	Rn-222, Po-218, Pb-214, Bi-214, Po-214, Pb-210, Bi-210, Po-210
Ra-228	Ac-228
Th-226	Ra-222, Rn-218, Po-214

Parent Radionuclides	*Progeny*
Th-228	Ra-224, Rn-220, Po-216, Pb-212, Bi-212, Tl-208 (0.36), Po-212 (0.64)
Th-229	Ra-225, Ac-225, Fr-221, At-217, Bi-213, Po-213, Pb-209
Th-234	Pa-234 m
U-230	Th-226, Ra-222, Rn-218, Po-214
U-232	Th-228, Ra-224, Rn-220, Po-216, Pb-212, Bi-212, Tl-208 (0.36), Po-212 (0.64)
U-235	Th-231
U-238	Th-234, Pa-234 m
U-240	Np-240 m
Np237	Pa-233
Am-242 m	Am-242
Am-243	Np-239

282. In addition to the general exemption criteria stated above, justified practices involving the following do not need to be notified: (a) radioactive materials where the quantities of the activity involved do not exceed in total the exemption values set out in Table 16, column 3, or higher values that, for specific applications, are approved by the competent authority and satisfy the general exemption and clearance criteria set out in paragraphs 267–274 above; (b) radioactive materials where the activity concentrations do not exceed the exemption values set out in Tables 13 and 15, or higher values that, for specific applications, are approved by the competent authority and satisfy the general exemption and clearance criteria set out in paragraphs 267–274 above; (c) apparatus containing a sealed source, provided that: (i) the apparatus is of a type approved by the Radiation Control and Inspection Service; (ii) the apparatus does not cause, in normal operating conditions, a dose rate exceeding 1μSv h^{-1} at a distance of 0.1 m from any accessible surface; and (iii) conditions for recycling or disposal have been specified by the Radiation Control and Inspection Service; or (d) any electrical apparatus provided that: (i) it is a cathode ray tube intended for the display of visual images, or other electrical apparatus operating at a potential difference not exceeding 30 kV, or it is of a type approved by the competent authority; and (ii) it does not cause, in normal operating conditions, a dose rate exceeding 1μSv h^{-1}at a distance of 0.1 m from any accessible surface.[1235] The Radiation Control and Inspection Service may exempt specific types of practices from the notification requirement subject to compliance with the general exemption criteria explained in paragraphs 267–274 above, on the basis of an assessment showing that exemption is the best option.[1236]

1235. Section 16(1)(a), (b), (c) and (d) Law No. 164(I)/2018, which corresponds to Art. 26(1)(a), (b), (c) and (d) Directive 2013/59/Euratom.

1236. Section 16(2) Law No. 164(I)/2018, which corresponds to Art. 26(2) Directive 2013/59/Euratom.

283. Having explained the general exemption criteria (*see* paragraphs 267–274 above) and the specific exemptions (*see* paragraph 275 above), notification is required for all justified practices to the Radiation Control and Inspection Service. In particular for workplaces where the radon concentration (as an annual average) continues to exceed the national reference level, which is specified in regulations, a notification is required. The same applies to existing exposure situations that are managed as a planned exposure situation.[1237] Moreover, the Radiation Control and Inspection Service may require notification of a practice, where, despite the exemption criteria set out in paragraph 275 above, there is concern that a practice identified in accordance with section 19, that being a practice including natural nuclear material, may lead to the presence of naturally occurring radionuclides in water liable to affect the quality of drinking water supplies or affect any other exposure pathways, so as to be of concern from a radiation protection point of view.[1238]

284. The notification shall be made prior to the practice commencing or, for existing practices, as soon as possible once this requirement is applicable. For practices subject to notification, the Radiation Control and Inspection Service shall specify the information to be provided in conjunction with the notification. Where an application for authorization is submitted, no separate notification is needed.[1239]

285. Notified practices which are not exempted from authorization shall be subject to regulatory control through registration or licensing.[1240]

II. Registration or Authorization

286. The practices, among others, of using in any way, operating, possessing, producing, storing, transferring, enabling transfer, supplying, importing, exporting, shipping, recycling, re-using, disposing or discharging radiation generators or accelerators or radioactive sources or materials for medical exposures or for non-medical imaging purposes are subject to registration or authorization. The same applies to radiation generators or accelerators, except electron microscopes, or radioactive sources for purposes not covered by the aforementioned. The Radiation Control and Inspection Service regulates the relevant procedure and requirements,[1241] whereas it may require approval through registration or authorization for other practices.[1242] It further decides on the form of approval and the information to be submitted with the application for approval.[1243] The regulatory decision to submit types of practices to either registration or licensing is based on regulatory experience, taking into account the magnitude of expected or potential doses, as well as the complexity of

1237. Section 13(6) Law No. 164(I)/2018, which corresponds to Art. 25(2) Directive 2013/57/Euratom.
1238. Section 13(7) Law No. 164(I)/2018, which corresponds to Art. 25(3) Directive 2013/57/Euratom.
1239. Section 13(1), (2), (3) and (4) Law No. 164(I)/2018, which corresponds to Art. 25(1) Directive 2013/57/Euratom.
1240. Section 12(3) Law No. 164(I)/2018, which corresponds to Art. 24(3) Directive 2013/57/Euratom.
1241. Section 14(1) Law No. 164(I)/2018, which corresponds to Art. 27(1) Directive 2013/57/Euratom.
1242. Section 14(4) Law No. 164(I)/2018, which corresponds to Art. 27(2) Directive 2013/57/Euratom.
1243. Section 14(3)(a) Law No. 164(I)/2018.

the practice.[1244] In addition, the Radiation Control and Inspection Service has the power to issue an approval on a temporary basis and for a limited time.[1245]

287. The disposal, recycling or reuse of radioactive materials arising from any authorized practice is subject to approval by the Radiation Control and Inspection Service.[1246] Materials for disposal, recycling or reuse may be released from regulatory control provided that the activity concentrations: (a) for solid material do not exceed the clearance levels set out in Tables 13 and 15; or (b) comply with specific clearance levels and associated requirements for specific materials or for materials originating from specific types of practices; these specific clearance levels shall be established by the Radiation Control and Inspection Service following the general exemption and clearance criteria set out in paragraphs 267–274 above, and taking into account technical guidance provided by the Community.[1247] For the clearance of materials containing naturally occurring radionuclides, where these result from authorized practices in which natural radionuclides are processed for their radioactive, fissile or fertile properties, the clearance levels comply with the dose criteria for clearance of materials containing artificial radionuclides.[1248] Deliberate dilution of radioactive materials for the purpose of them being released from regulatory control is prohibited. Mixing of materials that takes place in normal operations where radioactivity is not a consideration is not subject to this prohibition. The Radiation Control and Inspection Service may authorize, in specific circumstances, the mixing of radioactive and non-radioactive materials for the purposes of reuse or recycling.[1249]

288. Any approval may at any time be revoked by the Radiation Control and Inspection Service or be returned to the Radiation Control and Inspection Service by its holder.[1250] In such a case and at any time, during which the holder continues to bear liability, the Radiation Control and Inspection Service may give written instructions to the holder that are deemed necessary to avoid damage from ionizing radiation or from any other situation that has taken or is taking place at the specific building or facility.[1251] The Radiation Control and Inspection Service may ask the undertaking to surrender or transfer its liability for the facility to another undertaking specified by the service.[1252]

289. In such an event of revocation, the state shall pay compensation, which shall cover the value of any facility or equipment installed and the value of any building built according to the approval that may not be used anymore due to the revocation of the approval. This value is estimated at the time of revocation and any

1244. Section 14(5) *ibid*, which corresponds to Art. 27(3) Directive 2013/57/Euratom.
1245. Section 14(3)(b) Law No. 164(I)/2018.
1246. Section 18(1) *ibid.*, which corresponds to Art. 30(1) Directive 2013/57/Euratom.
1247. Section 18(2) Law No. 164(I)/2018, which corresponds to Art. 30(2) Directive 2013/59/Euratom.
1248. Section 18(3) Law No. 164(I)/2018, which corresponds to Art. 30(3) Directive 2013/59/Euratom.
1249. Section 18(4) Law No. 164(I)/2018, which corresponds to Art. 30(4) Directive 2013/59/Euratom.
1250. Section 24 Law No. 164(I)/2018.
1251. Section 26(1) *ibid.*
1252. Section 26(2) *ibid.*

value from selling the building, facility or equipment shall be reduced. Under national law, no further damage shall be compensated.[1253] However, no compensation shall be paid under national law, when the revocation in question: (a) was made with the consent of the undertaking; (b) was proved to be necessary for the protection of public health and the safety of any person, the protection of the environment, flora and fauna or the protection of property, as a consequence of the change of conditions, including safety conditions or political or geopolitical conditions, that could not have been reasonably foreseen at the time that approval was issued or following new scientific knowledge; or (c) was due to amending the approved practice.[1254] Still, denial of prompt, adequate and effective compensation on such grounds is not particularly convincing under International Investment Law.

290. Any undertaking affected by the revocation may submit an objection ('ένσταση') to the Minister within twenty-eight days. The Minister reviews the objection and the submitted reasons, along with any other information that he has at his disposal. He has the power to verify, annul or alter the decision of the Radiation Control and Inspection Service or alternatively, substitute such with any other decision that, in his opinion, had to have been initially issued.[1255]

III. Authorization

291. Authorization is required for the following practices:

(a) the deliberate administration of radioactive substances to persons and, in so far as the radiation protection of human beings is concerned, animals for the purpose of medical or veterinary diagnosis, treatment or research;
(b) the operation and decommissioning of any nuclear facility and the exploitation and closure of uranium mines;
(c) the deliberate addition of radioactive substances in the production or manufacture of consumer products or other products, including medicinal products, and the import of such products;
(d) any practice involving a high-activity sealed source;
(e) the operation, decommissioning and closure of any facility for the long-term storage or disposal of radioactive waste, including facilities managing radioactive waste for this purpose;
(f) practices discharging significant amounts of radioactive material with airborne or liquid effluent into the environment.[1256]

1253. Section 27(1)(a) *ibid.*
1254. Section 27(2) *ibid.*
1255. Section 29(1)(a) and (3) *ibid.*
1256. Section 15(a), (b), (c), (d), (e) and (f) *ibid.*, which corresponds to Art. 28 Directive 2013/59/Euratom.

A. Application for Authorization

292. The undertaking applying for approval via authorization has to demonstrate and establish sufficiently that it ensures compliance with sufficient nuclear or radiological safety, security and radiation protection at its facility.[1257] The extent of information that needs to be submitted for proving such level of safety is commensurate with the nature of the practice and the radiological risks involved.[1258] Such information that must be submitted together with the application for authorization is at least the following:[1259]

(a) responsibilities and *organizational* arrangements for protection and safety;
(b) staff competence, including information and training;
(c) design and planning features of the facility and of radiation sources;
(d) anticipated occupational and public exposures in normal operation;
(e) safety assessment of the activities, the practices and the facility in order to: (i) identify ways in which potential exposures or accidental and unintended medical exposures could occur; (ii) estimate, to the extent practicable, the probabilities and magnitude of potential exposures; (iii) assess the quality and extent of protection and safety provisions, including engineering features, as well as administrative procedures; (iv) define the operational limits and conditions of operation;
(f) emergency procedures;
(g) maintaining, testing, inspecting and servicing so as to ensure that the radiation source and the facility continue to meet the design requirements, operational limits and conditions of operation throughout their lifetime;
(h) management of radioactive waste and arrangements for the disposal of such waste, in accordance with the applicable regulatory requirements;
(i) management of disused sources;
(j) quality assurance;[1260]
(k) general information regarding the undertaking, such as its name as registered with the Official Receiver, address *and* particulars of the undertaking.[1261]

Should the Radiation Control and Inspection Service decide that the submitted information does not suffice for a decision to be reached, it may request further information. Any time limits established by the Radiation Control and Inspection Service for completion of the evaluation of the application commence from the date upon which all necessary information has been submitted.[1262]

1257. Section 17(3) Law No. 164(I)/2018.
1258. Section 17(4) *ibid.*, which corresponds to Art. 29(1) Directive 2013/59/Euratom.
1259. Section 17(5)(a) Law No. 164(I)/2018, which corresponds to Art. 29(2) Directive 2013/59/Euratom.
1260. Annex IV (a)-(j) Law No. 164(I)/2018, which corresponds to Annex IX(a)-(j) Directive 2013/59/Euratom.
1261. Annex IV(k) Law No. 164(I)/2018.
1262. Section 17(5)(b) *ibid.*

B. Evaluation of the Application for Authorization

293. The Radiation Control and Inspection Service reviews and assesses the information submitted regarding safety, security and protection from ionizing radiation in order to establish whether the facilities, practices and activities performed to comply with the regulatory provisions.[1263] This review and assessment are proportional to the radiological risks involved with the facility, the practice or the activity following the grated approach.[1264] In the process of its review and assessment of the facility, practice or activity, the Radiation Control and Inspection Service takes into account such considerations and factors as:

(a) the regulatory requirements;
(b) liability and organizational regulations for safety, security and protection from ionizing radiation;
(c) the nature and categorization of the associated hazards;
(d) the site conditions and the operating environment;
(e) the basic design of the facility or the conduct of the activity as relevant to safety;
(f) the records provided by the authorized party or its suppliers;
(g) best practices;
(h) the applicable management system;
(i) the competence and skills necessary for operating the facility or conducting the activity;
(j) arrangements for protection of workers, the public, patients and the environment;
(k) arrangements for preparedness for, and response to, emergencies;
(l) arrangements for nuclear or radiological security;
(m) the system of accounting for, and control of, nuclear material;
(n) the relevance of applying the concept of defence in depth to take into account inherent uncertainties, such as in the long term for the disposal of nuclear waste;
(o) arrangements for the management of radioactive sources, radioactive waste and spent fuel;
(p) relevant research and development plans or programmes relating to the demonstration of safety;
(q) feedback of operating experience, nationally and internationally, and especially of relevant operating experience from similar facilities and activities;
(r) information compiled during inspections of the Radiation Control and Inspection Service;
(s) information from research findings; and
(t) arrangements for the termination of operations.[1265]

1263. Section 33(1) *ibid.*
1264. Section 33(3) *ibid.*
1265. Annex VI Law No. 164(I)/2018, which, but for point (b), corresponds to point 4.45 IAEA GSR Part 1 Rev. 1.

The Radiation Control and Inspection Service, in order to reach a decision, reviews, assesses and takes into account any other risks emanating from the operation of the facility or the performance of the practice or activity of the undertaking that are not related to radiation and that must be included in the risk assessment ('έκθεση ασφαλείας') (*see* in this regard paragraphs 302 et seq. below).[1266] Equally important, it takes into account the opinion of the Technical Committee for Authorizations, save for the approval of transfer, import, export, shipment or supply of sources or radiation generators or accelerators. However, said opinion is not binding upon the Radiation Control and Inspection Service.[1267] The results of reviews and assessments are used as feedback for the regulatory process.[1268]

294. The Radiation Control and Inspection Service has the power to make such reviews and assessments both upon submission of an application for approval and during the operational lifetime of the facility or the performance of the practice or activity, whereas the source of information can be the applicant or any other party.[1269]

C. Granting an Authorization

295. An authorization may include specific terms and conditions that the Radiation Control and Inspection Service may impose upon granting the authorization or at a later point in time, as well as reference to the requirements of this law so as to ensure that the elements of the authorization are legally enforceable, and impose appropriate restrictions on the operational limits and conditions of operation. Terms and conditions also require, when appropriate, the formal and documented implementation of the principle of optimization.[1270] Without prejudice to the generality of this, terms and conditions may refer to the following, among others:

(a) obligations of the authorization holder;
(b) the minimum required characteristics of the authorization holder regarding skills and abilities;
(c) criteria of design and efficiency and demands of preserving radiation sources, apparatus, equipment and other systems;
(d) assessment of risks associated with the practice;
(e) control of radioactive material, including management from the perspective of safety and security of disused radioactive sources;

1266. Sections 33(5) and 45 Law No. 164(I)/2018, which partially corresponds to point 4.47 IAEA GSR Part 1 Rev. 1.
1267. Annex II Part 2(2) and (3) Law No. 164(I)/2018.
1268. Section 33(6) *ibid.*, which partially corresponds to point 4.48 IAEA GSR Part 1 Rev. 1.
1269. Section 33(1) and (2) Law No. 164(I)/2018.
1270. Section 20(1)(a) Law No. 164(I)/2018, which corresponds to Art. 29(3) Directive 2013/59/Euratom.

(f) implementing and maintaining effective systems for establishing, measuring and recording the presence and intensity of any form of ionizing radiation emitted from anything within the building or the facility or anything being transferred, removed or discharged there;
(g) design, planning, manufacture, installing, operating, amending, maintaining, terminating the operation or shutting down any building, facility or equipment that contains radioactive material or any radiation generator or accelerator or any nuclear facility;
(h) preparations for response and the measures that need to be taken in the event of an accident related to ionizing radiation;
(i) handling, treatment, transport, storage, discharge, disposal, recycling or reuse, whatever the case may be, of radioactive material and generators of radiation or accelerators;
(j) discharge of waste containing radioactive substances according to the relevant regulations aiming to control of releasing of waste containing radioactive substances to the environment; and
(k) management and transmission of information, including transmission of information from and to the Radiation Control and Inspection Service and the level of confidentiality of this information regarding, among others, the protection of radiation sources.[1271]

While deciding on the terms and conditions to be imposed on a given authorization, the Radiation Control and Inspection Service acts in consultation with the Technical Committee for Authorizations.[1272]

296. The aforementioned aside, the Radiation Control and Inspection Service has the power to issue authorizations on the base of general terms and conditions for which it has already consulted the Technical Committee for Authorizations. It may further publish a catalogue of the authorizations issued in such a manner along with the terms and conditions.[1273]

297. For existing practices, the Radiation Control and Inspection Service may impose, as the case may be, terms and conditions for discharge, disposal, recycle or reuse existing sources of radiation generators or accelerators or other electrical equipment according to standards set out in this or other law.[1274]

D. Rejection of Application for Authorization

298. Any undertaking affected by the rejection of application for approval via authorization may submit an objection ('ένσταση') to the Minister within twenty-eight days. The Minister reviews the objection and the submitted reasons, along

1271. Section 20(4)(a)–(k) Law No. 164(I)/2018.
1272. Section 20(5) *ibid.*
1273. Section 20(6) *ibid.*
1274. Section 20(1)(b) *ibid.*, which partially corresponds to Art. 29(4) Directive 2013/59/Euratom.

with any other information that he has at his disposal. He has the power to verify, annul or alter the decision of the Radiation Control and Inspection Service or alternatively, substitute such with any other decision that, in his opinion, had to have been initially issued.[1275]

299. Self-evidently, the applicant may also file an appeal ('προσφυγή') with the Supreme Court of Cyprus according to Article 146 of the Constitution.

E. Changes, Amendments and Revocation of Authorization

300. The terms and conditions of an authorization may be amended and an authorization itself may be revoked or annulled. The Radiation Control and Inspection Service defines the relevant purpose, criteria and conditions.[1276] Equally, a request for modifying the terms and conditions, which are attached to authorizations, may be filed by authorization holders at any time.[1277]In addition, should the authorization holder wishes to make any changes to a practice or facility, he bears specific statutory obligations, as explained below (*see* in this regard paragraph 299 below).

301. In an event of revocation, the state shall pay compensation, which shall cover the value of any facility or equipment installed and the value of any building built according to the approval that may not be used anymore due to the revocation of the approval. This value is estimated at the time of revocation and any value from selling the building, facility or equipment shall be reduced. Under national law no further damage shall be compensated.[1278] In an event of modifying the terms and conditions of an authorization, the compensation shall cover the value of any equipment installed to the satisfaction of the terms and conditions of the authorization, which may not be used any more due to said amendment and no further damage shall be compensated under national law. Still, no compensation shall be paid, when the revocation in question: (a) was made with the consent of the undertaking; (b) was proved to be necessary for the protection of public health and the safety of any person, the protection of the environment, flora and fauna or the protection of property, as a consequence of the change of conditions, including safety conditions or political or geopolitical conditions, that could not have been reasonably foreseen at the time that approval was issued or following new scientific knowledge; or (c) was due to amending the approved practice.[1279] As already argued (*see* paragraph 282 above), denial of prompt, adequate and effective compensation due to such statutory provision is implausible under International Investment Law.

1275. Section 29(1)(a) and (3) Law No. 164(I)/2018.
1276. Section 25(1) and (2) *ibid.*
1277. Section 25(3) *ibid.*
1278. Section 27(1)(a) *ibid.*
1279. Section 27(2) *ibid.*

§7. STATUTORY OBLIGATIONS

302. This law sets out statutory obligations for undertakings ('επιχείρηση') and employers ('εργοδότης'), following the approach of IAEA that refers to responsibilities of 'the person or organization responsible for facilities and activities that give rise to radiation risk'[1280] rather than of the EU, which provides for obligations of 'licence holders'[1281]. National law specifies these terms as follows: *undertaking* is 'any natural or legal person that bears a legal responsibility due to national legislation for an installation, for the performance of a practice or a source of radiation, including the cases where the owner or possessor of a radiation source does not perform relevant human activities'; and *employer* is 'any person that bears responsibility for a place of employment, building, undertaking and/or facility, where a worker works or has worked, including persons that employ no workers, but perform a financial activity or manage their undertaking with a non-profit aim or not'.[1282]

303. Having said that, undertakings and employers responsible for a facility or practice have certain statutory obligations related to responsibility, necessary measures, prior approval of amendments, risk assessment and emergency plans, which are described henceforth.

304. Importantly, they always have main responsibility for the safety and security of a facility and the radiation sources and safety from ionizing radiation.[1283] This responsibility includes applying the general principles of radiation protection (*see* in this regard paragraphs 260 et seq. above) and complying with the laws and regulations, the approval and any other regulatory provisions that have been set or approved by the competent authority[1284] during the lifetime of the facilities and the full duration of the activities, including management of radioactive waste, remediation of contaminated areas and transportation of radioactive materials.[1285] Such compliance does not release the undertaking or the employer from said responsibility.[1286] The undertaking or employer may not transfer same responsibility, unless a relevant notification has been made to the Radiation Control and Inspection Service and this service approves it.[1287]

305. Further, undertakings and employers responsible for a facility or practice have to take all necessary technical, organizational and administrative measures, in connection with a permit issued under this law, for ensuring safety and security of

1280. Points 2.39 et seq. IAEA GRS Part 3.
1281. Article 6 Directive 2009/71/Euratom.
1282. Section 2 Law No. 164(I)/2018.
1283. Section 44(1) *ibid*, which corresponds to Art. 6(1) Directive 2009/71/Euratom and Requirement 4 IAEA GRS Part 3.
1284. Section 44(2)(a) Law No. 164(I)/2018.
1285. Section 44(5) *ibid.*
1286. Section 44(2)(b) *ibid.*
1287. Section 44(3) *ibid.*

facilities and radiation sources, safety and protection of health of any person, as well as protection of use of property of any person and the environment.[1288]

306. In the event that the undertaking or the employer wishes to amend any practice or facility, they must inform the Radiation Control and Inspection Service providing it with the necessary information of the nature and other qualities of the amendment. Should the intended amendment have or may have an important effect on issues of nuclear or radiological security and safety and protection from ionizing radiation, protection of the use of property of any person or protection of the environment, as per the estimation of the Radiation Control and Inspection Service, then the undertaking or the employer must acquire a new approval prior to performing any amendment.[1289]

307. Turning to the actual operation, undertakings and employers are obliged to create and follow a management system, comply with general prevention principles, make a written risk assessment and draft an emergency plan. The appropriate management plan shall depend on the size of the undertaking, installation or practice for which a permit has been issued and shall include at a minimum the following: (a) the availability of policy and procedures demonstrating that safety, protection and protection from the risks of using ionizing radiation are its priorities; (b) risks emanating from ionizing radiation for the health and protection of humans, use of property and the environment, are promptly identified and corrective measures are taken, depending on the level of risk; (c) the responsibilities of each person as well as its powers for taking decisions regarding issues of safety, protection, health and protection of the public or protection of the environment are clearly specified and these persons are properly trained and have the necessary background; (d) information and guidelines on issues of safety, protection and protection from ionizing radiation are constantly available at all operational levels of the undertaking; (e) where it is practically feasible, radiation sources under the responsibility of the undertaking or the employer are identifiable, or, where this is not practically feasible, alternative procedures for identifying of these sources are in place; (f) where radiation sources are stored for an extended time period following authorization from the competent authority, the storage facility is appropriate to this end; and (g) appropriate and updated archives on the sources and activities are kept and are made available to the Radiation Control and Inspection Service.[1290]

308. Aside from the aforementioned management plan, undertakings and employers are obliged to comply with this law and the regulations issued under the same, while following general prevention principles. These principles read: (a) prevention of risks; (b) evaluation of risks that may not be prevented; (c) fighting risks at their source; (d) adjusting work to humans, especially regarding shaping places of work, as well as work equipment and work methods; (e) following the development of technology; (f) replacing dangerous with non-dangerous or less dangerous;

1288. Section 45(1) *ibid.*
1289. Section 45(3) *ibid.*
1290. Section 45(8)(a), (b), (c), (d), (e), (f), (g) *ibid.*

(g) developing a single and holistic prevention policy that may cover technology, work organization, working conditions, relations between stakeholders and the effect of factors related to working environment; (h) give priority to taking measures for group protection, without undermining the application of measures for the protection of specified persons; and (i) providing appropriate directives to persons at work.[1291]

309. Further, undertakings and employers have an obligation to make a written risk assessment ('έκθεση ασφαλείας'), which indicates that all risks that may lead to an accident have been identified and that the nature and the magnitude of any effects on workers or other persons, the facilities, the radiation sources, property and the environment have been specified.[1292] This risk assessment includes information such as:

(a) the name and address of the applicant, the undertaking or the person conducting the transport;
(b) the address of the buildings or facilities, where the relevant activities are carried out or of the undertaking conducting the transport;
(c) date of commencing the activities;
(d) general description of the buildings or facilities, including geographical location, meteorological, geological and hydrographical conditions, and in the event of transport: (i) the departure and arrival spot as well as the intermediate spots of transmission; or (ii) the criteria according to which the transport route is chosen;
(e) description of the radioactive substances and their amount;
(f) plans of the buildings or facilities;
(g) diagram and description of every equipment containing radioactive substances and description of the package or container of the radioactive substance, as well as the vehicle and the means containing the substance on or in the vehicle;
(h) description of all factors which may lead to constant leak of radioactive substances in the environment and the measures for avoiding or containing such;
(i) information on the management programme of the undertaking and the personnel;
(j) information on the population around the buildings or facilities;
(k) assessment of the area which may be affected by the release of radioactive substances and the time of duration of such release;
(l) assessment of the radiation doses to which any person or group of persons may be exposed; and
(m) assessment of whether an emergency plan is necessary.[1293]

1291. Section 45(9) *ibid.*
1292. Section 45(4)(a)(i) *ibid.*
1293. Section 45(4)(a)(iii) and Annex VII Part I *ibid.*

The Radiation Control and Inspection Service has the power, if it deems it proper, to ask the undertaking or the employer to make a more specific risk assessment, taking into consideration the following factors:

(a) analysis for the assessment of consequences of any risk, including the doses to which the population may be exposed, as well as the relevant odds;
(b) the number of persons, who might be affected;
(c) the management programme and the personnel, which applies or shall apply the safety measures for the identified risks;
(d) the safety systems, the methods and the systems for surveillance and registration for the control of risks;
(e) qualifications, experience and expertise of the personnel;
(f) planning, construction, operation and maintenance of the equipment used for interventions or risk control;
(g) the manuals of planning and operation;
(h) the plans and the operation of the containment and venting systems;
(i) the safety measures for any person in case the containment measures prove to be insufficient; and
(j) the procedure of communication of emergency from radiation and the process for drawing conclusions and lessons learned.[1294]

Every time there is significant change in the practices or the available knowledge or experience, this risk estimation must be reviewed.[1295]

310. Should the risk assessment indicate that there is a risk for the health of workers or other persons, the facilities, the radiation sources, property or the environment from an accident, which is likely to occur, the undertaking or the employer, as the case may be, have the duty to prevent such an accident, as well as to contain and mitigate the consequences of any accidents that do occur.[1296]

311. Risk assessment and efficiency control of safety measures in relation to ionizing radiation, which are applied by undertakings or employers, must be performed at different phases, including the decision on location, planning, building, construction, start of operation, maintenance and dismantling or demolition, as the case may be. The objectives for this gradual assessment are: determination of the manner in which persons are exposed or may be exposed to ionizing radiation;[1297] determination of the manner in which security and safety of the facilities or sources of radiation are or may be affected;[1298] determination of the manner in which loss of use of property or negative effect of environment occurs or is likely to occur;[1299]

1294. Section 45(4)(c) and Annex VII Part II *ibid.*
1295. Section 45(4)(a)(ii) *ibid.*
1296. Section 45(4)(b)(i) and (ii) *ibid.*
1297. Section 45(4)(d)(i) *ibid.*
1298. Section 45(4)(d)(ii) ibid.
1299. Section 45(4)(d)(iv) *ibid.*

specification of the level of any usual exposure ('συνήθης έκθεση');[1300] specification of the risk of any possible exposure and the level thereof;[1301] and assessment of the quality and effectiveness of security measures and safe operation of sources and other relevant electronic equipment.[1302]

312. When the risk assessment indicates the possibility of an emergency from radiation, the undertaking or employer are obliged to prepare a written emergency plan, which aims to constrain exposure to radiation of any person and the protection of the environment.[1303] Such a plan, which is defined as an internal emergency plan ('εσωτερικό σχέδιο έκτακτης ανάγκης'), is prepared taking into account two principles. According to the first one intervention shall be undertaken, unless minimizing the catastrophic effects due to an emergency from radiation is of such value that justifies damages and costs caused by the intervention, including social cost. The second principle prescribes that the type, extent and duration of the intervention must be such to ensure that exposure to radiation is preserved at the lowest possible level, generating benefit from reducing health damage, but for the damage that might be caused by intervention to maximize.[1304] Turning to the minimum elements of an emergency plan, these are the following: (a) the names and the positions of persons authorized to sign the alarm and put in place the internal emergency plan, and of the person that shall be responsible for coordinating actions for dealing with the effects in the buildings or facilities; (b) the name and the position of the person who shall liaise with the Radiation and Inspection Control Service, the local authorities and other services involved; (c) situations or events that may lead to emergency from radiation and description of actions that must be done and the measures that must be taken for constraining the consequences, including information for available safety equipment and the other available means and personnel; (d) arrangements for constraining risks for the persons within the building or the facility, including the manner of warning and alarm, and the actions that these persons are expected to take; (e) arrangements for prompt warning of the services that have the responsibility to implement the national emergency response plans, the information that the initial notification must include, and the arrangements for providing additional information, when newer information is available; (f) arrangements for providing help outside the buildings or facilities; and (g) arrangements for emergency exposure, as well as the levels of doses that have been determined as appropriate for the purpose of starting to apply the internal emergency plan.[1305] Said plan must be re-examined and reviewed, when necessary. In addition, it must be tested periodically at appropriate times taking into consideration any changes to practices performed, available knowledge and experience and the evaluation of risks, on which their preparation has been based. Finally, it shall be submitted to the Radiation Control and Inspection Service for evaluation.[1306]

1300. Section 45(4)(d)(v) *ibid.*
1301. Section 45(4)(d)(vi) *ibid.*
1302. Section 45(4)(d)(vii) *ibid.*
1303. Section 45(5)(b) *ibid.*
1304. Annex VII Part 3(a) and (b) *ibid.*
1305. Section 45(5)(b) and Annex VII Part 4(A)(a), (b), (c), (d), (e), (f) and (g) *ibid.*
1306. Section 45(5)(d)(i), (ii) and (iii) *ibid.*

313. In particular with regard to the transfer of radioactive substances or materials, the plan is entitled internal emergency plan for transfer ('εσωτερικό σχέδιο έκτακτης ανάγκης για μεταφορά') and it is prepared according to the same principles. Its minimum elements are: (a) the names and the positions of persons authorized to sign the alarm and put in place the internal emergency plan for transfer, and of the person that shall be responsible for coordinating actions for dealing with the effects; (b) situations or events that may lead to emergency from radiation and description of actions that must be done and the measures that must be taken for constraining the consequences, including information for available safety equipment and the other available means and personnel; (c) arrangements for prompt warning of the event, the information that the initial notification must include, and the arrangements for providing additional information, when newer information is available; and (d) arrangements for emergency reports, as well as the levels of doses that have been set as appropriate for the purpose of initiating the implementation of the internal emergency plan for transfer.[1307] The aforementioned re-examination, review, periodical testing and evaluation of the Radiation Control and Inspection Service of internal emergency plans equally apply here.[1308]

314. In addition to the obligation to prepare an emergency plan, the undertaking or employer makes arrangements for preparedness and response in emergency exposure situations. These arrangements include in particular: (a) procedures, directives and arrangements that respond to accidents that may occur during all phases of operation, termination of operation and transitionary phases, ensuring consistency among all these procedures and regulations and ensuring that these are tested, reviewed and updated; (b) efficient number of workers that are properly educated as well as appropriate and sufficient equipment and other necessary resources; (c) organizational structure with clear allocation of responsibility, as well as coordination between the same undertaking and the organizations responding to emergencies; (d) clear allocation of responsibility for prompt notification of emergency to the Radiation Control and Inspection Service and the organizations responding to emergencies; and (e) arrangements for external assistance.[1309]

315. Further, necessary equipment, safety systems and procedures must be applied. These minimize, as far as possible, the possibility of human error, which may lead to exposure of any person, loss of use of property or radioactive contamination of the environment.[1310] They further trace and timely correct human errors[1311] and ease access in case of accident.[1312] The employees of the authorized undertaking having responsibility for protection from ionizing radiation must be properly trained and qualified in order to comprehend their obligations and perform their duties according to specified procedures. Said training and qualification have

1307. Section 45(5)(c) and Annex VII Part 4(B)(a), (b), (c) and (d) *ibid.*
1308. Section 45(5)(d)(i), (ii) and (iii) *ibid.*
1309. Section 45(6)(a) and (b) *ibid.*
1310. Section 45(14)(a) *ibid.*
1311. Section 45(14)(b) *ibid.*
1312. Section 45(14)(c) *ibid.*

to be periodically repeated, depending on the case.[1313] Also, arrangements for education and training are to be made by all parties for their staff having responsibilities relating to the nuclear safety of nuclear installations so as to obtain, maintain and to further develop expertise and skills in nuclear safety and on-site emergency preparedness.[1314] During designing of equipment, work stations and operating procedures, the principle of ergonomics, which is, however, not defined in this law, is to be followed by undertakings or employers in cooperation with the suppliers, in order to ensure health and safety and environment protection as well as to eliminate the danger of accidents.[1315] Undertakings or employers also ensure that all necessary measures are taken so that equipment, appliances and tools, which are at the disposal of the workers, are appropriate for the work performed or appropriately adjusted to this end, in order to ensure safety and the protection of human health and of the environment during their use.[1316]

316. Moreover, undertakings and employers are to regularly assess, verify and continuously improve, as far as reasonably practicable, the nuclear safety of their nuclear installations in a systematic and verifiable manner under the surveillance of the Radiation Control and Inspection Service.[1317] That includes verification that measures are in place for the prevention of accidents and mitigation of the consequences of accidents, including the verification, natural protection barriers and technical security measurements as well as administrative procedures for protection of the authorization holder, whose failure may lead to important exposure ('σημαντική έκθεση') to ionizing radiation of the workers and of the population.[1318] They further establish and implement management systems which give due priority to nuclear and radiological safety and protection. To this purpose they must ensure, among others, the following: (a) minimize the impact of extreme external natural and unintended man-made hazards; (b) prevent abnormal operation and failures; (c) control abnormal operation and identify failures; (d) control accidents within the design basis ('σχεδιαστική βάση'), meaning the range of conditions and events taken explicitly into account in the design, including upgrades, of a nuclear installation, according to established criteria, so that the installation can withstand them without exceeding authorized limits by the planned operation of safety systems;[1319] (e) control severe conditions, including prevention of accidents progression and mitigation of the consequences of severe accidents; (f) operational infrastructure within the facility for emergency preparedness and response having clear allocation

1313. Section 45(12) *ibid.*
1314. Section 47(1) *ibid.*, which corresponds to Art. 7 Directive 2009/71/Euratom.
1315. Section 45(13)(a) Law No. 164(I)/2018.
1316. Section 45(13)(b) *ibid.*
1317. Section 45(16)(a) *ibid.*, which corresponds to Art. 6(c) Directive 2009/71/Euratom.
1318. Section 45(16)(b) Law No. 164(I)/2018, which partially corresponds to Art. 6(c) Directive 2009/71/Euratom.
1319. Section 2 Law No. 164(I)/2018, which corresponds to Art. 3(9) Directive 2009/71/EU.

of responsibilities and coordination between the competent authority and the organizations of emergency response taking into consideration all phases of an emergency are in place.[1320] They also provide for and maintain financial resources, including alternative methods of demonstrating their financial sufficiency, as well as human resources with appropriate qualifications and competences, and technical means necessary to fulfil their obligations with respect to the nuclear safety and protection of an installation, where practices with ionizing radiation are taking place, or the nuclear safety of a nuclear installation or the protection of sources of radiation, as these are defined in this law. Undertakings and employers also ensure that contractors and subcontractors under their responsibility and whose activities might affect the nuclear safety of a nuclear installation have the necessary human resources with appropriate qualifications and competences to fulfil their obligations.[1321] Undertakings and employers are finally obliged to comply with the Codes of Practice, the Standards and Requirements approved and issued by the Radiation Control and Inspection Service.[1322]

317. Necessary measurements and constant monitoring, measurements and registration of necessary parameters are ensured by all undertakings and employers to the purpose of complying with the provisions of this law.[1323] Any organs, methods and procedures for measurements, monitoring and registration used in this respect must be adequate as well as properly maintained and examined, and be calibrated periodically according to standards approved by the Radiation Control and Inspection Service.[1324] Measurement, monitoring and reporting results, including control data and calibration of measurement organs, are kept by undertakings and employers in a proper archive.[1325]

318. On matters of examination and testing of protective devices and measuring instruments all authorization holders consult qualified experts,[1326] who are persons having the knowledge and training needed to carry out physical, technical or radiochemical tests enabling doses to be assessed, and to give advice in order to ensure effective protection of individuals and the correct operation of protective equipment, whose capacity to act as a qualified expert is recognized by the Control Service. A qualified expert may be assigned the technical responsibility for the tasks of radiation protection of workers and members of the public.[1327] Said actions compose in particular prior critical examination of plans for installations from the point

1320. Section 45(16)(c)(i)–(vi) Law No. 164(I)/2018, which partially corresponds to Art. 8b(1)(a), (b), (c), (d), (e) and (f) Directive 2009/71/Euratom.
1321. Section 45(16)(d)(i) and (ii) Law No. 164(I)/2018, which partially corresponds to Art. 6(f) Directive 2009/71/Euratom.
1322. Sections 45(16)(e) and 63 Law No. 164(I)/2018.
1323. Section 46(1) *ibid.*
1324. Section 46(2) *ibid.*
1325. Section 46(3) *ibid.*
1326. Section 18(1) *ibid.*, which corresponds to Art. 23(1) Directive 96/29/Euratom.
1327. Section 2 Law No. 164(I)/2018, which corresponds to Art. 1 Directive 96/29/Euratom.

of view of radiation protection;[1328] the acceptance into service of new or modified sources or related equipment from the point of view of radiation protection;[1329] regular checking of the effectiveness of protective devices and techniques;[1330] regular calibration of measuring instruments and regular checking that they are serviceable and correctly used;[1331] and regular control of proper operation of equipment and performing any practice in a manner providing satisfactory ('ικανοποιητική') protection from ionizing radiation.[1332] Every authorization holder has to inform the Control Service for every arrangement done in relation to the aforementioned actions.[1333]

§8. Accidents and Emergencies

319. The set of facts triggering the application of the mechanisms described below are *accident* ('ατύχημα'), and *emergency* ('έκτακτη ανάγκη'). *Accident* is a notion deriving from European law ('accident' in French, 'Unfall' in German, 'ongeval' in Dutch) and means any unintended event, the consequences or potential consequences of which are significant from the point of view of radiation protection, safety, including nuclear safety or protection.[1334] The term 'emergency' equally derives from European law ('urgence' in French, 'Notfall' in German, 'noodsituatie' in Dutch). Its statutory definition reads 'a non-routine situation or event involving a radiation source that necessitates prompt action to mitigate serious adverse consequences for human health and safety, quality of life, property or the environment, or a hazard that could give rise to such serious adverse consequences'.[1335]

320. Any accident or catastrophic event ('καταστροφικό συμβάν'), a term undefined in this law, at any workplace or in relation to any source or practice may be investigated, if the competent authority deems this fit.[1336] The competent authority also defines the terms and conditions, under which these are investigated, as well as the properly qualified persons, who perform the investigation.[1337] Hence, the broad discretionary powers of the competent authority, that being the Minister of Labour and Social Security are pivotal in this regard, especially due to the value of protecting public health and the environment being neither explicitly mentioned in this particular context nor explicitly declared aim of this law.

1328. Section 18(1)(a) Law No. 164(I)/2018, which corresponds to Art. 23(2)(a) Directive 96/29/Euratom.
1329. Section 18(1)(b) Law No. 164(I)/2018, which corresponds to Art. 23(2)(b) Directive 96/29/Euratom.
1330. Section 18(1)(c) Law No. 164(I)/2018, which corresponds to Art. 23(2)(c) Directive 96/29/Euratom.
1331. Section 18(1)(d) Law No. 164(I)/2018, which corresponds to Art. 23(2)(d) Directive 96/29/Euratom.
1332. Section 18(1)(e) Law No. 164(I)/2018
1333. Section 18(2) *ibid.*
1334. Section 2 *ibid.*, which corresponds to Art. 3(6) Directive 2009/71/Euratom.
1335. Section 2 Law No. 164(I)/2018, which corresponds to Art. 4(26) Directive 2013/53/Euratom.
1336. Section 35(1) Law No. 164(I)/2018.
1337. Section 35(2) *ibid.*

321. Radiologic or nuclear accidents relating or affecting any practice, activity, facility or authorized nuclear plant must be communicated, without any delay, to Radiation Control and Inspection Service and any other persons stated in the authorization by the undertaking or employer. This notification obligation applies also to accidents during transportation of radioactive material.[1338] The Radiation Control and Inspection Service in such cases defines the area, in which the specified acceptable levels are exceeded, as well as the relevant time period for the protection of the public and the employees. It performs this in accordance with the national plan or plans of emergency response, or in every manner it considers proper, should such plans be absent.[1339] It also registers the names of all persons, who according to its information are within the specified area and other information related to investigating the accident with regard to each one of them.[1340]

322. In regard to the aforementioned national plan ('εθνικό σχέδιο') and emergency response plans ('σχέδιο αντιμετώπισης καταστάσεων έκτακτης ανάγκης') the following should be elaborated. The competent authority ensures that emergency response plans are established in advance for the various types of emergencies identified by an assessment of potential emergency exposure situations.[1341] The emergency response plans shall include the following elements, depending on whether they apply to emergency preparedness or emergency response.

323. For emergency preparedness they include: (a) reference levels for public exposure, taking into account the criteria laid down in regulations issued under this law,[1342] which nonetheless under EU law these criteria include at a minimum the reference levels for public exposure as referred to Articles 7 and 101 and Annex I Directive 2013/59/Euratom;[1343] (b) reference levels for emergency occupational exposure taking into account regulations on emergency occupational exposure issued under this law,[1344] which nonetheless under EU law have to be below the values of dose limits of 20 mSv in any single year, save for special circumstances or for certain exposure situations;[1345] (c) optimized protection strategies for members of the public who may be exposed, for different postulated events and related scenarios;[1346] (d) predefined generic criteria for particular protective measures;[1347] (e) default triggers or operational criteria such as observables and indicators of

1338. Section 56(1) *ibid.*
1339. Section 56(2) *ibid.*
1340. Section 56(3) *ibid.*
1341. Section 54(1) *ibid.*, which corresponds to Art. 98(1) Directive 2013/59/Euratom.
1342. Annex VIII Part II(a) Law No. 164(I)/2018, which corresponds to Annex XI Part B(1) Directive 2013/59/Euratom.
1343. Annex XI Part B(1) *ibid.*
1344. Annex VIII Part II(b) *ibid.*, which corresponds to Annex XI Part B(2) Directive 2013/59/Euratom.
1345. Annex XI Part B(2) and Articles 53 and 9 Law No. 164(I)/2018.
1346. Annex VIII Part II(c) *ibid.*, which corresponds to Annex XI Part B(3) Directive 2013/59/Euratom.
1347. Annex VIII Part II(d) Law No. 164(I)/2018, which corresponds to Annex XI Part B(4) Directive 2013/59/Euratom.

on-scene conditions;[1348] (f) arrangements for prompt coordination between organizations having a role in emergency preparedness and response and with all other Member States and with third countries which may be involved or are likely to be affected;[1349] and (g) arrangements for the emergency response plan to be reviewed and revised to take account of changes or lessons learned from exercises and events.[1350]

324. For emergency response, they include: (a) promptly implementing protective measures, if possible, before any exposure occurs;[1351] (b) assessing the effectiveness of strategies and implemented actions and adjusting them as appropriate to the prevailing situation;[1352] (c) comparing the doses against the applicable reference level, focusing on those groups whose doses exceed the reference level;[1353] and implementing further protection strategies, as necessary, based on prevailing conditions and available information.[1354]

325. Further, the emergency response plans include provision for the transition from an emergency exposure situation to an existing exposure situation.[1355] The competent authority equally ensures that emergency response plans are tested, reviewed and, as appropriate, revised at regular intervals, taking into account lessons learned from past emergency exposure situations and taking into account the results of the participation in emergency exercises at national and international level as well as the experience acquired from testing or materializing this plan or these plans.[1356] Where appropriate, they incorporate relevant elements of the emergency management system,[1357] as explained below.

326. The emergency management system is established by the competent authority that equally has the responsibility for providing adequate administrative provisions to maintain such a system.[1358] It is designed to be commensurate with the results of an assessment of potential emergency exposure situations and to be able to respond effectively to emergency exposure situations in connection with

1348. Annex VIII Part II(e) Law No. 164(I)/2018, which corresponds to Annex XI Part B(5) Directive 2013/59/Euratom.
1349. Annex VIII Part II(f) Law No. 164(I)/2018, which corresponds to Annex XI Part B(6) Directive 2013/59/Euratom.
1350. Annex VIII Part II(g) Law No. 164(I)/2018, which corresponds to Annex XI Part B(7) Directive 2013/59/Euratom.
1351. Annex VIII Part II(a) Law No. 164(I)/2018, which corresponds to Annex XI Part B(1) Directive 2013/59/Euratom.
1352. Annex VIII Part II(b) Law No. 164(I)/2018, which corresponds to Annex XI Part B(2) Directive 2013/59/Euratom.
1353. Annex VIII Part II(c) Law No. 164(I)/2018, which corresponds to Annex XI Part B(3) Directive 2013/59/Euratom.
1354. Annex VIII Part II(d) Law No. 164(I)/2018, which corresponds to Annex XI Part B(4) Directive 2013/59/Euratom.
1355. Section 54(3) Law No. 164(I)/2018, which corresponds to Art. 98(3) Directive 2013/58/Euratom.
1356. Section 54(4) Law No. 164(I)/2018, which corresponds to Art. 98(4) Directive 2013/58/Euratom.
1357. Section 54(5) Law No. 164(I)/2018, which corresponds to Art. 98(5) Directive 2013/58/Euratom.
1358. Section 53(1)(b) Law No. 164(I)/2018, which corresponds to Art. 97(1) Directive 2013/59/Euratom.

practices or unforeseen events.[1359] As a minimum, it includes: assessment of potential emergency exposure situations and associated public and emergency occupational exposures; clear allocation of the responsibilities of persons and organizations having a role in preparedness and response arrangements; establishment of emergency response plans at appropriate levels and related to a specific facility or human activity; reliable communications and efficient and effective arrangements for cooperation and coordination at the installation and at appropriate national and international levels; health protection of emergency workers; arrangements for the provision of prior information and training for emergency workers and all other persons with duties or responsibilities in emergency response, including regular exercises; arrangements for individual monitoring or assessment of individual doses of emergency workers and the recording of doses; public information arrangements; involvement of stakeholders; and transition from an emergency exposure situation to an existing exposure situation including recovery and remediation.[1360] The emergency management system shall provide for the establishment of emergency response plans with the objective of avoiding tissue reactions leading to severe deterministic effects in any individual from the affected population and reducing the risk of stochastic effects, taking account of the general principles of radiation protection and the reference levels specified in regulations.[1361]

327. In any event, the Minister of Labour and Social Security is competent for the final evaluation of potential emergency situations in Cyprus or abroad, as well as for evaluating emergency conditions and effects during an emergency and its evolution. Further, he is competent in evaluating exposure of the public, emergency workers and other groups of the public along with the application of appropriate safety measures.[1362] In addition, the following tasks fall under the competent authority's statutory obligations: (a) timely information to both public and workers of the risks and protective measures in cases of emergency;[1363] (b) availability of special teams for technical, medical and health intervention in such emergencies;[1364] (c) organizing interventions regarding the source, environment and humans and taking into consideration the particulars, assessment and recording of the effects of the situation as well as the effectiveness of the intervention;[1365] and (d) set doses functioning as reference levels in cases of intervention for dealing with emergencies, which may be exceeded exceptionally for the purpose of saving human life and

1359. Section 53(2)(a)(i) and (ii) Law No. 164(I)/2018, which corresponds to Art. 97(2) Directive 2013/59/Euratom.
1360. Annex VIII Part I(a)–(j) Law No. 164(I)/2018, which corresponds to Annex XI Part A(1)–(10) Directive 2013/59/Euratom.
1361. Section 53(3) Law No. 164(I)/2018, which corresponds to Art. 97(3) Directive 2013/59/Euratom.
1362. Section 53(2)(b) Law No. 164(I)/2018.
1363. Section 53(4)(a) *ibid.*
1364. Section 38(e) *ibid.*, which corresponds to Art. 50(3) Directive 96/29/Euratom.
1365. Section 53(4)(c) *ibid.*

only by volunteers who have been informed of the associated health risks.[1366] Procedures relevant to occupational emergency exposure and information of emergency workers and the public are regulated in regulations.[1367]

328. Turning to international cooperation, the competent authority in cooperation, where appropriate, with the Ministry of Foreign Affairs and the diplomatic missions abroad, ensures the cooperation of Cyprus with other Member States and with third countries in addressing possible emergencies on its territory which may affect other Member States or third countries, in order to facilitate the organization of radiological protection in those Member States or third countries.[1368] The competent authority shall, in the event of an emergency occurring on the territory of Cyprus or likely to have radiological consequences on its territory, promptly establish contact with all other Member States and with third countries which may be involved or are likely to be affected with a view to sharing the assessment of the exposure situation and coordinating protective measures and public information by using, as appropriate, bilateral or international information exchange and coordination systems. These coordination activities shall not prevent or delay any necessary actions to be taken on a national level.[1369] The competent authority, in cooperation with the Ministry of Foreign Affairs and the diplomatic missions abroad, shall ensure that Cyprus shares information and cooperates with other relevant Member States, third countries and international organizations regarding the loss, theft or discovery of high-activity sealed sources, other radioactive sources and radioactive material of concern and regarding related follow-up or investigations, without prejudice to relevant confidentiality requirements and relevant national legislation.[1370] Finally, the competent authority, once again in cooperation with the aforementioned bodies, ensures cooperation with other Member States and with third countries in the transition from an emergency exposure situation to an existing exposure situation.[1371]

§9. Existing Exposure Situations

329. The term 'existing exposure situation' ('κατάσταση υφιστάμενης έκθεσης')[1372] stands for an exposure situation that already exists when a decision on its control has to be taken and which does not call or no longer calls for urgent measures to be taken.[1373]

1366. Section 53(4)(d) *ibid. See* in this regard points 4.15 *et seq*. IAEA GRS Part 3 and Art. 52(1) of the repealed Directive 96/29/Euratom.
1367. Section 53(5) Law No. 164(I)/2018.
1368. Section 55(1) *ibid.*, which corresponds to Art. 99(1) Directive 2013/59/Euratom.
1369. Section 55(2) Law No. 164(I)/2018, which corresponds to Art. 99(2) Directive 2013/59/Euratom.
1370. Section 55(3) Law No. 164(I)/2018, which corresponds to Art. 99(3) Directive 2013/59/Euratom.
1371. Section 55(4) Law No. 164(I)/2018, which corresponds to Art. 99(4) Directive 2013/59/Euratom.
1372. The French term is 'situation d'exposition existante', the German one 'bestehende Expositionssituation' and the Dutch one 'bestaande blootstellingssituatie'.
1373. Section 2 Law No. 164(I)/2018, which corresponds to Art. 4(35) Directive 2013/59/Euratom.

330. Existing exposure situations are identified and evaluated upon indication or evidence of exposures that cannot be disregarded from a radiation point of view. The corresponding occupational and public exposures are also determined. The statutory obligation lays with the Radiation Control and Inspection Service.[1374] For said identification and evaluation, the following types of existing exposure situations are taken into consideration: (a) exposure due to contamination of areas by residual radioactive material from past activities that were never subject to regulatory control or were not regulated; an emergency, after the emergency exposure situation has been declared ended, as provided for in the emergency management system; and residues from past activities for which the undertaking is no longer legally accountable;[1375] (b) exposure to natural radiation sources, including: indoor exposure to radon and thoron, in workplaces, dwellings and other buildings; and indoor external exposure from building materials;[1376] and (c) exposure to commodities excluding food, animal feeding stuffs and drinking water incorporating radionuclides from contaminated areas specified in aforementioned point (a) or naturally occurring radionuclides.[1377] The Radiation Control and Inspection Service may decide, having regard to the general principle of justification, that an existing exposure situation warrants no consideration of protective or remedial measures.[1378] Existing exposure situations which are of concern from a radiation protection point of view and for which legal responsibility can be assigned shall be subject to the relevant requirements for planned exposure situations and accordingly such exposure situations are required to be notified to the Radiation Control and Inspection Service.[1379]

331. The competent authority arranges for the establishment of strategies to ensure the appropriate management of existing exposure situations commensurate with the risks and with the effectiveness of protective measures. Each such strategy contains the objectives pursued and the appropriate reference levels, which are set out in regulations.[1380] This strategy or strategies are implemented by the Radiation Control and Inspection Service that ensures appropriate coordination between relevant parties involved in the implementation of remedial and protective measures.

1374. Section 57(1) Law No. 164(I)/2018, which corresponds to Art. 100(1) Directive 2013/59/Euratom.
1375. Annex IX(a)(i)–(iii) Law No. 164(I)/2018, which corresponds to Annex XVII(a)(i)–(iii) Directive 2013/59/Euratom.
1376. Annex IX(b)(i)–(ii) Law No. 164(I)/2018, which corresponds to Annex XVII(b)(i)–(ii) Directive 2013/59/Euratom.
1377. Annex IX(c)(i)–(ii) Law No. 164(I)/2018, which corresponds to Annex XVII(c)(i)–(ii) Directive 2013/59/Euratom.
1378. Section 57(2) Law No. 164(I)/2018, which corresponds to Art. 100(2) Directive 2013/59/Euratom.
1379. Section 57(3) Law No. 164(I)/2018, which corresponds to Art. 100(3) Directive 2013/59/Euratom.
1380. Section 58(1) and (2) Law No. 164(I)/2018, which corresponds to Art. 101(1) and (2) Directive 2013/59/Euratom.

Stakeholders are involved in decisions regarding the development and implementation of strategies for managing exposure situations.[1381] The form, scale and duration of all protective measures considered for implementation of a strategy shall be optimized.[1382] The Radiation Control and Inspection Service is entrusted with assessing the distribution of doses that has resulted from the implementation of a strategy and examines the possibility of further actions with the aim of optimizing protection and reducing any exposures that are still above the reference level.[1383] It further ensures that those responsible for the implementation of a strategy under its supervision shall regularly: (a) evaluate the available remedial and protective measures for achieving the objectives and the efficiency of planned and implemented measures; (b) provide information to exposed populations on the potential health risks and on the available means for reducing their exposure; (c) provide guidance for the management of exposures at individual or local level; (d) with regard to activities that involve naturally occurring radioactive material and are not managed as planned exposure situations, provide information on appropriate means for monitoring concentrations and exposures and for taking protective measures;[1384] and (e) inform the Radiation Control and Inspection Service about the relevant results.[1385]

332. Radon ('ραδόνιο') meaning the radionuclide Rn-222 and its progeny, as appropriate,[1386] is regulated separately. In application of the aforementioned on existing exposure situations, the competent authority establishes a national action plan addressing long-term risks from radon exposures in dwellings, buildings with public access and workplaces for any source of radon ingress, whether from soil, building materials or water. The action plan, which has to be updated on a regular basis, shall take into account the following issues:[1387] (a) strategy for conducting surveys of indoor radon concentrations or soil gas concentrations for the purpose of estimating the distribution of indoor radon concentrations, for the management of measurement data and for the establishment of other relevant parameters (such as soil and rock types, permeability and radium-226 content of rock or soil); (b) approach, data and criteria used for the delineation of areas or for the definition of other parameters that can be used as specific indicators of situations with potentially high exposure to radon; (c) identification of types of workplaces and buildings with public access, such as schools, underground workplaces, and those in certain areas, where measurements are required, on the basis of a risk assessment,

1381. Section 59(1) Law No. 164(I)/2018, which corresponds to Art. 102(1) Directive 2013/59/Euratom.
1382. Section 59(2) Law No. 164(I)/2018, which corresponds to Art. 102(2) Directive 2013/59/Euratom.
1383. Section 59(3) Law No. 164(I)/2018, which corresponds to Art. 102(3) Directive 2013/59/Euratom.
1384. Section 59(4)(a)–(d) Law No. 164(I)/2018, which corresponds to Art. 102(4)(a)–(d) Directive 2013/59/Euratom.
1385. Section 59(4)(e) Law No. 164(I)/2018.
1386. Section 2 *ibid.*, which corresponds to Art. 4(82) Directive 2013/59/Euratom.
1387. Section 60(1) Law No. 164(I)/2018, which corresponds to Art. 103(1) Directive 2013/59/Euratom.

considering for instance occupancy hours; (d) the basis for the establishment of reference levels for dwellings and workplaces; if applicable, the basis for the establishment of different reference levels for different uses of buildings (dwellings, buildings with public access, workplaces) as well as for existing and for new buildings; (e) assignment of responsibilities (governmental and non-governmental), coordination mechanisms and available resources for implementation of the action plan; (f) strategy for reducing radon exposure in dwellings and for giving priority to addressing the situations identified under point (b) above; (g) strategies for facilitating post construction remedial action; (h) strategy, including methods and tools, for preventing radon ingress in new buildings, including identification of building materials with significant radon exhalation; (i) schedules for reviews of the action plan; (j) strategy for communication to increase public awareness and inform local decision makers, employers and employees of the risks of radon, including in relation to smoking; (k) guidance on methods and tools for measurements and remedial measures and criteria for the accreditation of measurement and remediation services shall also be considered; (l) where appropriate, provision of financial support for radon surveys and for remedial measures, in particular for private dwellings with very high radon concentrations; (m) long-term goals in terms of reducing lung cancer risk attributable to radon exposure (for smokers and non-smokers); and (n) where appropriate, consideration of other related issues and corresponding programmes such as programmes on energy saving and indoor air quality.[1388] This action plan also establishes the procedures for having appropriate measures to prevent radon ingress into new buildings. These measures may include specific requirements in national building codes. Said measures are communicated to all persons involved with the aim of harmonizing the action plans under their area of responsibility.[1389] Finally, the Radiation Control and Inspection Service identifies areas where the radon concentration (as an annual average) in a significant number of buildings is expected to exceed the relevant national reference level set out in regulations.[1390]

§10. Transparency and Protection of Information

333. Information in relation to justification of categories or types of practices, the regulation of issues on radiation sources and radioprotection are provided to undertakings, workers, the public as well as patients and other persons subjected to medical exposure. The Radiation Control and Inspection Service bears the responsibility for this.[1391] Necessary information in relation to the nuclear safety of nuclear installations and its regulation is made available to workers and the general public, with specific consideration to local authorities, population and stakeholders in the

---

1388. Annex X(a)–(n) Law No. 164(I)/2018, which corresponds to Annex XVIII(1)–(14) Directive 2013/59/Euratom.
1389. Section 60(2) Law No. 164(I)/2018, which partially corresponds to Art. 103(2) Directive 2013/59/Euratom.
1390. Section 60(3) Law No. 164(I)/2018, which partially corresponds to Art. 103(3) Directive 2013/59/Euratom.
1391. Section 49(1)(a) Law No. 164(I)/2018.

vicinity of a nuclear installation. That obligation includes ensuring that the competent authority and persons holding a permit, within their fields of responsibility, provide in the framework of their communication policy: (a) information on normal operating conditions of nuclear installations to workers and the general public; and (b) prompt information in case of incidents and accidents to workers and the general public and to the competent regulatory authorities of other Member States in the vicinity of a nuclear installation.[1392] Information shall be made available to the public in accordance with relevant legislation and international instruments, provided that this does not jeopardize other overriding interests, such as public security ('δημόσια ασφάλεια'), which are recognized in relevant legislation or international instruments.[1393] For the purpose of informing the public and ensuring speedy and effective sharing of information, the competent authority uses the most efficient in every case means, such as publications or announcements in newspapers or television and radio stations of Pancyprian or local range, putting up posters, e-mails, announcements in the website of the competent authority and making copies available at the offices of the affected local authorities.[1394] The competent authority further engages, as appropriate, in cooperation activities on the nuclear safety of nuclear installations with competent regulatory authorities of other Member States in the vicinity of a nuclear installation, *inter alia*, via the exchange and/or sharing of information.[1395] Finally, the general public is given the appropriate opportunities to participate effectively in the decision-making process relating to the authorization of nuclear installations, in accordance with relevant legislation and international instruments.[1396]

334. Trade, industrial and medical secrets are protected. The general rule is that no person having received knowledge of such secret during the exercise of his statutory duties may reveal it. However, this obligation ceases to exist in the following cases: (a) when the undertaking or the employer bearing the responsibility for the building, the equipment or the facility, where the information has been obtained from, consents; (b) when a form or an application for the purpose of application of this law contains a clause of non-confidentiality and applicant did not request specific protection of the supplied information; (c) for the purpose of application of any provisions of this law; (d) for the purpose of criminal procedure for a crime on the basis of this law; or (e) for the purpose of any research conducted by or on behalf of the competent authority, in relation to the application of any of the provisions, which it is obliged to apply.[1397] It is rather obvious that the generality of the exception clauses overturns the general rule transforming an anticipated rock-solid wall into a paper façade.

1392. Section 49(2) and (3) *ibid.*, which corresponds to Art. 8(1) Directive 2009/71/Euratom.
1393. Section 49(4)(a) Law No. 164(I)/2018, which corresponds to Art. 8(2) Directive 2009/71/Euratom.
1394. Section 49(4)(b) Law No. 164(I)/2018.
1395. Section 49(5) *ibid.*, which corresponds to Art. 8(3) Directive 2009/71/Euratom.
1396. Section 49(6) Law No. 164(I)/2018, which corresponds to Art. 8(4) Directive 2009/71/Euratom.
1397. Section 50(2)(a), (b), (c), (d) and (e) Law No. 164(I)/2018.

§11. Ensuring Compliance

I. Administrative Sanctions

335. Upon violation of any provision of this law or any Regulations, Code of Practice, Standards or Requirements, issued, the inspector may issue an improvement notification ('ειδοποίηση βελτίωσης'). This may also take place when any terms or conditions of approval are violated or the violation of a statutory provision takes place under circumstances that constitute possible it being repeated or continued. Said notification shall instruct the violator to remediate the violation, or the conditions causing it, as the case may be, within a time period of no less than fourteen days. However, in specific cases, this time period may be reduced to less than fourteen days, if the inspectors deem it fit.[1398] Said notification may be revoked by the inspector at any time, as long as no objection (*see* in this respect paragraphs 330 et seq. below) has been filed against it.[1399]

336. If danger of serious damage to human health or serious loss of use of property or serious environmental degradation from radiation may be caused by any building, facility, equipment, workplace or any practice or other activity performed in these areas, a notification of prohibition ('ειδοποίηση απαγόρευσης') may be issued by an inspector. This shall prohibit the use of these areas or the performance of such activities, until the danger is eliminated and has immediate effect.[1400] Also, said notification may be revoked by the inspector at any time.[1401]

337. An *objection* ('ένσταση') may be filed against the aforementioned notifications by any person, who considers to have suffered injustice.[1402] Hence, not just the addressee of the notifications is eligible to file this remedy. The objection may be filed to the Minister within fourteen days[1403] requesting revocation or modification of the notification. Filing an objection does not influence the legal effect unfolded by the notifications.[1404] The Minister is bound to decide on the submitted objection within fourteen days.[1405]

II. Penal Sanctions

338. Penal offences of this law relating to violation of its provisions, operating conditions and provisions on inspections. More specifically, any person bearing statutory obligations and failing to comply with those commits a penal offence. If found guilty by a court of law, he may be imprisoned for up to four years and/or

1398. Section 37(a), (b) and (c) *ibid.*
1399. Section 41(1) *ibid.*
1400. Section 38(1) and (2) *ibid.*
1401. Section 41(2) *ibid.*
1402. Section 42(1)(a) *ibid.*
1403. Section 42(2) *ibid.*
1404. Section 42(1)(b) *ibid.*
1405. Section 42(3) *ibid.*

convicted to a fine of up to EUR 80,000.[1406] These penalties may be imposed on any undertaking or employer not complying with operating conditions attached to its registration, authorization or other document issued under this law or with an improvement notification and notification of prohibition.[1407] Lastly, these penalties may be decided in case of any inspection's obstruction, which is described in much detail in this law. In particular, it is foreseen that any person doing any of the below is committing a penal offence:

- deliberately delays or obstructs an inspector from performing his powers or exercising his duties;[1408]
- obstructs or tries to obstruct any other person from presenting himself to the instructor or answer any question asked;[1409]
- knowingly or intentionally makes any false statement with the purpose of pretending compliance with statutory obligation to provide information;[1410]
- intentionally signs or makes false entries to any archive, books of notifications or other document that must be kept according to this law or uses such an entry with the intention to mislead;[1411]
- forges any certificate necessary according to this law;[1412]
- issues or signs such certificate in his knowledge that this is untrue, in relation to any material fact;[1413]
- presents or uses a certificate in relation to any material fact that in his knowledge is forged or is false;[1414]
- presents or uses a certificate in relation to the qualifications of any undertaking or person that in his knowledge does not relate to that person;[1415]
- pretends to be a person named in such a certificate;[1416]
- pretends to be an inspector;[1417]
- deliberately consents to the aforementioned forgery, signature, use, identity fraud or pretension;[1418]
- reveals any information in violation to the provisions on protection of information;[1419] and
- fails to submit an application for a notification, a registration or an authorization.[1420]

1406. Section 43(1) *ibid.*
1407. Section 43(2)(b) and (d) *ibid.*
1408. Section 43(3)(a) *ibid.*
1409. Section 43(3)(b) *ibid.*
1410. Section 43(3)(c) *ibid.*
1411. Section 43(3)(d) *ibid.*
1412. Section 43(3)(e) *ibid.*
1413. Section 43(3)(f) *ibid.*
1414. Section 43(3)(g) *ibid.*
1415. Section 43(3)(h) *ibid.*
1416. Section 43(3)(i) *ibid.*
1417. Section 43(3)(j) *ibid.*
1418. Section 43(3)(k) *ibid.*
1419. Sections 43(3)(l) and 50 *ibid.*
1420. Section 43(3)(m) *ibid.*

III. Other Sanctions

339. The court may in addition to the penal sanction imposed, as per the aforementioned, issue an order ('διάταγμα') instructing the accused to comply with this law within a certain time period. If he fails to do so, the court may further impose a penal fine of no more than EUR 2,000 and/or imprisonment of up to one month for each day of such failure.[1421] In addition, it is also foreseen that noncompliance with such order is a penal offence that may lead to imprisonment for up to four years and/or a fine of up to EUR 80,000.[1422]

§12. Archive

340. The Radiation Control and Inspection Service bears the responsibility of keeping an archive. This demonstrates the details of an installation, including nuclear facility, which were approved, as well as all actions, practices and sources related to a registration or authorization.[1423] The Radiation Control and Inspection Service ensures that copies of this archive are available for inspection by the public. However, it may classify as confidential and not publish any information that is deemed necessary to be kept as confidential.[1424] If it further deems that MIP risk to human health from ionizing radiation from anything that has been done or is currently being done which has taken place or is currently taking place at any place, building, installation or nuclear facility that does not bear any more a valid registration or authorization, is within acceptable levels for the protection of the public, it may delete the relevant information from copies of the archive available to the public.[1425]

1421. Section 43(4) *ibid.*
1422. Section 43(2)(a) *ibid.*
1423. Section 28(3) *ibid.*
1424. Section 28(4) *ibid.*
1425. Section 28(5) *ibid.*

Chapter 8. Industrial Emissions Control

341. Industrial Emissions are regulated by Law on Industrial Emissions[1426] (hereinafter 'Law No. 184(I)/2013'), which implements Directive 2010/75/EU.[1427]

§1. Objective

342. Scope of this law is integrated prevention and control of pollution arising from industrial activities set out in Parts III–VII through prevention or, where that is not practicable, reduction of emissions and prevention of generation of waste, in order to achieve a high level of protection of the environment taken as a whole.[1428]

§2. Area of Application

343. This law applies to certain plants and industrial activities that cause or are likely to cause pollution,[1429] that being direct or indirect introduction, as a result of human activity, of substances, vibrations, heat or noise into air, water or land which may be harmful to human health or the quality of the environment, result in damage to material property, or impair or interfere with amenities and other legitimate uses of the environment.[1430] These activities are the ones stated in Annex IV[1431] as well as combustion plants, the total rated thermal input of which is equal to or greater than 50 MW, irrespective of the type of fuel used,[1432] waste incineration plants and waste co-incineration plants which incinerate or co-incinerate solid or liquid waste, those being all incineration lines or co-incineration lines, waste reception, storage, on-site pre-treatment facilities, waste-, fuel- and air-supply systems, boilers, facilities for the treatment of waste gases, on-site facilities for treatment or storage of residues and wastewater, stacks, devices and systems for controlling incineration or co-incineration operations, recording and monitoring incineration or co-incineration conditions,[1433] with some exceptions.[1434] Said activities further include the ones

1426. Law on Industrial Emissions ('ο περί Βιομηχανικών Εκπομπών Νόμος') No. 184 of 2013, OGI(I) No. 4422 of 27 Dec. 2013, p. 1595.
1427. Directive 2010/75/EU of the European Parliament and of the Council on industrial emissions (integrated pollution prevention and control), OJ L 334, 17 Dec. 2010, p. 17.
1428. Section 3 Law No. 184(I)/2013, which corresponds to Art. 1 Directive 2010/75/EU.
1429. Section 4 Law No. 184(I)/2013, which corresponds to Art. 2(1) Directive 2010/75/EU.
1430. Section 2 Law No. 184(I)/2013, which corresponds to Art. 3(2) Directive 2010/75/EU.
1431. Annex IV Law No. 184(I)/2013, which corresponds to Annex I Directive 2010/75/EU.
1432. With reference to the excluded combustion plants *see* s. 45(2) Law No. 184(I)/2013, which corresponds to Art. 28 Directive 2010/75/EU.
1433. Sections 58(1) and 59(1) Law No. 184(I)/2013, which corresponds to Art. 42(1) Directive 2010/75/EU.
1434. With reference to the excluded plants *see* s. 59(2) Law No. 184(I)/2013, which corresponds to Art. 42(1) and (2) Directive 2010/75/EU.

listed in Part 1 of Annex V[1435] and, where applicable, reaching the consumption thresholds set out in Part 2 of same annex.[1436] Lastly, this law applies to plants producing titanium dioxide.[1437]

§3. Competent Authorities

344. The Minister of Agriculture, Rural Development and the Environment, the Council of Ministers, the Technical Committee on Protection of the Environment as well as the inspector-in-chief and inspectors have competence under this law.

I. The Minister of Agriculture, Rural Development and the Environment

345. The Minister of Agriculture, Rural Development and the Environment is the competent authority in relation to industrial emissions.[1438] In particular, this competence refers to the object of this law,[1439] approval and renewal of permits,[1440] operation conditions attached to permits,[1441] changes of operator, plant or permit,[1442] accidents,[1443] appointment, duties and powers of inspectors,[1444] ordering remediation of environmental damage,[1445] issuing decrees on regulation of matters of technical and administrative nature,[1446] determining the fees due upon submission of an application for a permit,[1447] keeping and updating an archive[1448] and forwarding a report to the Commission of the EU.[1449] The Minister is also the competent authority regarding the specific provisions on activities of Annex IV,[1450] malfunction or breakdown of the abatement equipment of combustion plants,[1451] waste incineration plants and waste co-incineration plants,[1452] and plants producing titanium dioxide.[1453] His competence further extends to provisions on greenhouse

1435. *See* in this respect Part 1 of Annex V Law No. 184(I)/2013, which corresponds to Part 1 Annex VII Directive 2010/75/EU.
1436. Section 72 Law No. 184(I)/2013, which corresponds to Art. 56 Directive 2010/75/EU.
1437. Section 81 Law No. 184(I)/2013, which corresponds to Art. 66 Directive 2010/75/EU.
1438. Annex I Law No. 184(I)/2013.
1439. Section 3 *ibid.*
1440. Sections 8, 9, 10, 11 and 14 *ibid.*
1441. Sections 12, 13 and 16 *ibid.*
1442. Sections 17, 18 and 19 *ibid.*
1443. Section 21 *ibid.*
1444. Sections 84 and 85 *ibid.*
1445. Section 91 *ibid.*
1446. Section 93(1) *ibid.*
1447. Section 94 *ibid.*
1448. Section 95 *ibid.*
1449. Section 97 *ibid.*
1450. Sections 23–44 *ibid.*
1451. Section 54 *ibid.*
1452. Sections 58–71 *ibid.*
1453. Sections 81 and 83 *ibid.*

gas emissions,[1454] geological storage of CO_2 [1455] and prohibition of discharging certain waste into any water body, sea or ocean.[1456]

346. Finally, the Minister may delegate any of his powers and competence regarding the proper application of this law and relevant decrees,[1457] in the fashion already discussed under Law No. 187(I)/2002 (*see* in this regard paragraph 31 above).

II. The Council of Ministers

347. The Council of Ministers has broad and nonrestrictive regulatory powers, as it is competent to issue regulations necessary for regulating any matter as well as for the best application of this law.[1458]

348. In particular, the Council of Ministers issues regulations for the best application of provisions on staying informed of developments in BAT and making that information available to the public concerned through publication in the Official Gazette.[1459] Such secondary legislation regulates further any matter relevant to determination, adoption and implementation of the best available practices taking into consideration the cost and profit derived from any measure, the criteria for determining BAT set out in Annex III[1460] and the *principles of care* ('αρχή της πρόνοιας') and *preventive action* ('αρχή προληπτικής δράσης').[1461] These principles are to be interpreted within the framework set out by European Environmental Law in view of the object of this law. Lastly, these regulations may impose specific measures for prevention, reduction or elimination of pollution from the operation of the plant and adherence to environmental quality standards.[1462]

1454. Section 22 *ibid.*
1455. Section 53 *ibid.* On geological storage of CO_2 in Cyprus *see* N. Charalampidou, ***Δίκαιο Περιβάλλοντος – Η Εναρμόνιση της Κυπριακής Νομοθεσίας με τις Οδηγίες της Ευρωπαϊκής Ενωσης***, 203 et seq. (Sakkoulas 2013).
1456. Section 82 Law No. 184(I)/2013.
1457. Section 5 *ibid.*
1458. Section 92(1) *ibid.*
1459. Sections 92(1) and 31 *ibid.* The latter corresponds to Art. 19 Directive 2010/75/EU.
1460. Criteria for determining best available techniques are the following: (1) the use of low-waste technology; (2) the use of less hazardous substances; (3) the furthering of recovery and recycling of substances generated and used in the process and of waste, where appropriate; (4) comparable processes, facilities or methods of operation which have been tried with success on an industrial scale; (5) technological advances and changes in scientific knowledge and understanding; (6) the nature, effects and volume of the emissions concerned; (7) the commissioning dates for new or existing installations; (8) the length of time needed to introduce the best available technique; (9) the consumption and nature of raw materials (including water) used in the process and energy efficiency; (10) the need to prevent or reduce to a minimum the overall impact of the emissions on the environment and the risks to it; (11) the need to prevent accidents and to minimize the consequences for the environment; (12) information published by public international organizations. Annex III Law No. 184(I)/2013, which corresponds to Annex III Directive 2010/75/EU.
1461. Section 92(1)(a) Law No. 184(I)/2013.
1462. Section 92(1)(b) *ibid.*

III. Technical Committee for the Protection of the Environment

349. A Technical Committee for the Protection of the Environment ('Τεχνική Επιτροπή για την Προστασία του Περιβάλλοντος') is being established via this law. In a manner similar to the Technical Committee for the Protection of Waters and Soil of Law No. 106(I)/2002 (*see* in this respect paragraphs 95 et seq. above), it is composed of representatives from same bodies.[1463] This committee advises the competent authority on determining environmental quality standards,[1464] on determining general operating conditions,[1465] on granting a permit[1466] as well as on termination, revocation or amendment of a permit or conditions attached to same.[1467] The particulars of the committee's ordinary and extraordinary meetings, agendas and information duties[1468] are similar to the ones stated under the Technical Committee for the Protection of Water and Soil of Law No. 106(I)/2002. Nonetheless, the chairman of the committee is a representative of the Ministry of Agriculture, Rural Development and the Environment.[1469]

IV. Inspector-in-Chief and Inspectors

350. The competent authority appoints public servants of both Ministries as inspectors and one of them as inspector-in-chief.[1470] It may also appoint any properly qualified private persons to exercise any of the inspectors' powers.[1471] The inspector's powers include the ones stated above for the inspectors of Law No. 187(I)/2002 (*see* in this respect paragraphs 34 et seq. above).[1472] In addition to those, inspectors may self-evidently bear any equipment or material necessary for performing their powers[1473] and perform any test or investigation, deemed necessary under the circumstances.[1474]

§4. Industrial Emissions Permit

351. The operation of any plant, combustion plant, waste incineration plant and waste co-incineration plant without an industrial emissions permit is prohibited.[1475] By way of derogation from the above, the competent authority may set a procedure

1463. Section 6(1)(a)–(h) *ibid.*
1464. Sections 7(1)(a) and 30 *ibid.*
1465. Sections 7(1)(b) and 12 *ibid.*
1466. Sections 7(1)(c) and 11 *ibid.*
1467. Sections 7(1)(d), 11, 13, 15 and 19 *ibid.*
1468. Section 6(5)–(9) *ibid.*
1469. Section 6(4) *ibid.*
1470. Section 84(1) and (2)(a) *ibid.*
1471. Section 84(3) *ibid.*
1472. Section 85(1)(a), (b), (d), (f)–(l) *ibid.*
1473. Section 85(2)(c) *ibid.*
1474. Section 85(2)(e) *ibid.*
1475. Section 8(1) *ibid.*, which corresponds to Art. 4(1) Directive 2010/75/EU.

for the registration of installations covered only by Part VI of this law.[1476] The procedure for registration is specified in a decree of the competent authority, which is published in the Official Gazette, and includes at least a notification to the competent authority by the operator of the intention to operate an installation.[1477]

352. Any plant, combustion plant, waste incineration plant and waste co-incineration plant having an air-waste permit and/or a waste disposal permit, is considered to have a temporary industrial emissions permit. Such temporary permit has the same validity period as the issued air-waste permit and/or waste disposal permit[1478] and is considered to be effective until its revocation or amendment.[1479]

I. Application for an Industrial Emissions Permit

353. The operator of any new plant must submit an application for an industrial emissions permit before initiating its operation.[1480] Same applies to any plant having a temporary industrial emissions permit at least six months prior to its expiration.[1481] The application for a permit includes a description of the following: the installation and its activities,[1482] the particulars of the operator,[1483] the conditions of the site of the plant,[1484] the products produced by the plant,[1485] the raw and auxiliary materials, other substances and the energy used in or generated by the plant,[1486] the sources of water used and/or consumed in the plant including the amount consumed and its qualitative characteristics,[1487] the sources of emissions from the plant,[1488] a baseline report of section 34(2),[1489] the nature and quantities of foreseeable emissions from the plant into air, water and soil as well as identification of significant effects of the emissions on the environment,[1490] the proposed technology and other techniques for preventing or, where this is not possible, reducing emissions from the plant,[1491] measures for the prevention, preparation for reuse, recycling and recovery of waste generated by the plant,[1492] measures planned to monitor emissions,[1493] the measures for utilization of air waste produced by the

1476. Section 8(2)(a) Law No. 184(I)/2013, which corresponds to Art. 4(1) Directive 2010/75/EU.
1477. Section 8(2)(b) Law No. 184(I)/2013.
1478. Section 8(5)(a) *ibid.*
1479. Section 8(5)(b) *ibid.*
1480. Section 9(1) *ibid.*
1481. Section 8(5)(c) *ibid.*
1482. Section 9(2)(a) *ibid.*, which corresponds to Art. 12(1)(a) Directive 2010/75/EU.
1483. Section 9(2)(b) Law No. 184(I)/2013.
1484. Section 9(2)(c) *ibid.*, which corresponds to Art. 12(1)(d) Directive 2010/75/EU.
1485. Section 9(2)(d) Law No. 184(I)/2013.
1486. Section 9(2)(e) *ibid.*, which corresponds to Art. 12(1)(b) Directive 2010/75/EU.
1487. Section 9(2)(f) Law No. 184(I)/2013.
1488. Section 9(2)(g) *ibid.*, which corresponds to Art. 12(1)(c) Directive 2010/75/EU.
1489. Section 9(2)(h) Law No. 184(I)/2013, which corresponds to Art. 12(1)(e) Directive 2010/75/EU.
1490. Section 9(2)(i) Law No. 184(I)/2013, which corresponds to Art. 12(1)(f) Directive 2010/75/EU.
1491. Section 9(2)(j) Law No. 184(I)/2013, which corresponds to Art. 12(1)(g) Directive 2010/75/EU.
1492. Section 9(2)(k) Law No. 184(I)/2013, which corresponds to Art. 12(1)(h) Directive 2010/75/EU.
1493. Section 9(2)(l) Law No. 184(I)/2013, which corresponds to Art. 12(1)(j) Directive 2010/75/EU.

plant, if necessary,[1494] the main alternatives to the proposed technology, techniques and measures studied by the applicant in outline,[1495] the suggested monitoring measures of air, water and soil quality of the site of the plant, if necessary,[1496] further measures planned to comply with the general principles of the basic obligations of the operator as provided for in sections 9 and 24 of this law[1497] and a non-technical summary of the details referred to above.[1498] The competent authority may request any additional information, data or study deemed necessary for the full examination of the submitted application, if this is justified by the category, nature, size or other characteristics of the plant.[1499]

II. Evaluation of an Application for an Industrial Emissions Permit

354. Upon beginning of the decision process, the competent authority posts a notification in the Official Gazette and in two newspapers and on the Internet informing the public of the following: the application for an industrial emissions permit,[1500] where applicable, the fact that a decision is subject to a national or transboundary EIA or to consultations between Member States,[1501] details of the competent authorities responsible for taking the decision, those from which relevant information can be obtained, those to which comments or questions can be submitted, and details of the time schedule for transmitting comments or questions,[1502] the nature of possible decisions or, where there is one, the draft decision,[1503] the fact that information relating to said application is available to the public during working days and hours at the office of the competent authority and the means through which it shall be available,[1504] the fact that any member of the public concerned[1505]

1494. Section 9(2)(m) Law No. 184(I)/2013.
1495. Section 9(2)(n) *ibid.*, which corresponds to Art. 12(1)(k) Directive 2010/75/EU.
1496. Section 9(2)(o) Law No. 184(I)/2013.
1497. Section 9(2)(p) *ibid.*, which corresponds to Art. 12(1)(i) Directive 2010/75/EU.
1498. Section 9(2)(q) Law No. 184(I)/2013, which corresponds to Art. 12(1) Directive 2010/75/EU.
1499. Section 9(3) Law No. 184(I)/2013.
1500. Section 37(1)(a) *ibid.*, which corresponds to Annex IV(1)(a) Directive 2010/75/EU.
1501. Section 37(1)(b) Law No. 184(I)/2013, which corresponds to Annex IV(1)(b) Directive 2010/75/EU.
1502. Section 37(1)(c) Law No. 184(I)/2013, which corresponds to Annex IV(1)(c) Directive 2010/75/EU.
1503. Section 37(1)(d) Law No. 184(I)/2013, which corresponds to Annex IV(1)(d) Directive 2010/75/EU.
1504. Section 37(1)(f) Law No. 184(I)/2013, which corresponds to Annex IV(1)(f) Directive 2010/75/EU. The same obligation to have the application available for inspection by the public is set out in s. 10(1)(b) Law No. 184(I)/2013.
1505. The *public concerned* ('public concerné' in French, 'betroffene Öffentlichkeit' in German, 'betrokken publiek' in Dutch) means the public affected or likely to be affected by, or having an interest in, the taking of a decision on the granting or the updating of a permit or of permit conditions, including non-governmental organizations promoting environmental protection. Section 2(1) Law No. 184(I)/2013, which corresponds to Art. 3(17) Directive 2010/75/EU.

may submit to the competent authority views or representations regarding the content of the application within thirty-five days from the notification date in the Official Gazette.[1506] Such views and representations submitted are being communicated to the public through an announcement on the internet.[1507] The person, who submitted those, is also informed in writing about the way that they have been considered.[1508]

355. The discretion of the competent authority to approve an application and grant an industrial emissions permit is limited by the following factors that must be met as per the explicit provisions of this. The competent authority must be satisfied that, in case of an existing plant, this has a valid urban planning permission ('πολεοδομική άδεια'), building permission ('άδεια οικοδομής') or certification of approval ('πιστοποιητικό έγκρισης'), as the case may be,[1509] or in the case of a new plant a certification of approval or a one-year permit, which may be renewed for four years as long as the plant operation did not alter,[1510] and that the operator has the machines and/or equipment needed for compliance to the demands of this law as well as to the conditions, which may be attached to the requested permit.[1511] Further, the competent authority must be certain that the operator shall be able to comply with emission limit values[1512] and/or environmental quality standards.[1513,1514] In addition to the aforementioned, the competent authority grants a permit, only if it is satisfied that: all appropriate measures for pollution prevention, including BAT not entailing excessive costs, have been taken;[1515] the operation of

---

1506. Section 37(1)(g) Law No. 184(I)/2013, which corresponds to Annex IV(1)(g) Directive 2010/75/EU. The same right of submitting views or recommendations is set out in s. 10(1)(c) Law No. 184(I)/2013.
1507. Section 37(2) *ibid.*
1508. Section 10(3) *ibid.*
1509. Section 11(1)(a)(i) and (4)(f)(i) *ibid.*
1510. Section 11(1)(a)(ii) and (4)(f)(ii) *ibid.*
1511. Section 11(1)(b) *ibid.* Especially for new plants, the competent authority may issue a permit even though such machines and equipment are not available. However, it shall set out a time period within which these must be installed and determine the time period, within which the operator is not expected to comply with certain operating conditions. Section 11(2)(a) and (b) *ibid.*
1512. *Emission limit value* ('valeur limite d'émission' in French, 'Emissionsgrenzwert' in German, 'emissiegrenswaarde' in Dutch) means the mass, expressed in terms of certain specific parameters, concentration and/or level of an emission, which may not be exceeded during one or more periods of time. Section 2(1) Law No. 184(I)/2013, which corresponds to Art. 3(5) Directive 2010/75/EU.
1513. *Environmental quality standard* ('norme de qualité environnementale' in French, 'Umweltqualitätsnorm' in German, 'milieukwaliteitsnorm' in Dutch) means the set of requirements which must be fulfilled at a given time by a given environment or particular part thereof, as set out in decree issued by the competent authority according to s. 30 of this law. Section 2(1) Law No. 184(I)/2013, which corresponds to Art. 3(6) Directive 2010/75/EU.
1514. Section 11(3) Law No. 184(I)/2013.
1515. Section 11(4)(a) *ibid.* The law however defined the term 'best available techniques' ('meilleures techniques disponibles' in French, 'beste verfügbare Techniken' in German, 'beste beschikbare technieken' in Dutch) that stands for the most effective and advanced stage in the development of activities and their methods of operation which indicates the practical suitability of particular techniques for providing the basis for emission limit values and other permit conditions designed to prevent and, where that is not practicable, to reduce emissions and the impact on the environment

the plant shall cause no pollution, especially through emitting certain polluting substances;[1516,1517] emission limit values shall not be exceeded;[1518] all limit values ('οριακές τιμές ποιότητας')[1519] and all environmental quality standards ('ποιοτικά πρότυπα περιβάλλοντος')[1520] shall be respected[1521] and the operator declares in writing that he is both able and committed to adhering to all operating conditions of the industrial emissions permit.[1522] If Law No. 127(I)/2018 (*see* in this respect paragraphs 647 et seq. below) is applicable on the plant, for which the application for a permit has been filled, the competent authority shall take into consideration all relevant information or conclusion available from the application of that law.[1523]

356. In ascertaining the operation conditions in the permit, the competent authority evaluates the circumstances which the undertaking operates under, and accommodates for prevention or remediation of all forms of pollution that the undertaking may cause, achieving a high standard of environmental protection in its entirety. It further ensures avoiding displacement or scattering of pollution from one environmental element to another. At the same time, the competent authority has to make sure that the operation conditions avoid reiteration and confusion, their application is effectively monitored, and finally their determination and monitoring are approached effectively and in a well-rounded manner.[1524]

357. The competent authority shall take into consideration the advice of the Technical Committee for the Protection of the Environment before issuing a permit. This permit may cover two or more plants or parts of plants operated by the same operator on the same site.[1525] Where a permit covers two or more plants, it shall

---

as a whole: (a) 'techniques' includes both the technology used and the way in which the installation is designed, built, maintained, operated and decommissioned; (b) 'available techniques' means those developed on a scale which allows implementation in the relevant industrial sector, under economically and technically viable conditions, taking into consideration the costs and advantages, whether or not the techniques are used or produced inside the Member State in question, as long as they are reasonably accessible to the operator; (c) 'best' means most effective in achieving a high general level of protection of the environment as a whole. Section 2(2) Law No. 184(I)/2013, which corresponds to Art. 3(10) Directive 2010/75/EU.

1516. *See* in this respect Annex VII Law No. 184(I)/2013, which corresponds to Annex II Directive 2010/75/EU.

1517. Section 11(4)(b) Law No. 184(I)/2013.

1518. Section 11(4)(c) *ibid.*

1519. *Limit value* ('οριακή τιμή' in Greek, 'valeur limite' in French, 'Grenzwert' in German, 'grenswaarde' in Dutch) means a level fixed on the basis of scientific knowledge, with the aim of avoiding, preventing or reducing harmful effects on human health and/or the environment as a whole, to be attained within a given period and not to be exceeded once attained. Section 2 Law No. 77(I)/2010, which corresponds to Art. 2(5) Directive 2008/50/EU. It must be assumed that this term is meant in Law No. 184(I)/2013 due to the explicit reference to Law No. 77(I)/2010, although the Greek term used is not identical.

1520. The environmental quality standards are set out according to Law No. 106(I)/2002.

1521. Section 11(4)(d) Law No. 184(I)/2013.

1522. Section 11(4)(e) *ibid.*

1523. Section 11(8) *ibid.*

1524. Section 11(7) *ibid.*

1525. Section 11(5)(a) *ibid.*, which corresponds to Art. 4(2) Directive 2010/75/EU.

contain conditions to ensure that each plant complies with the requirements of this law.[1526] The competent authority may also issue a permit covering several parts of a plant, which is operated by different operators. In such cases, the permit shall specify the obligations of each operator.[1527]

III. Granting an Industrial Emissions Permit

358. Upon granting an industrial emissions permit, the holder deposits to the competent authority sufficient guarantee for the expenses needed to deal with any pollution likely to be caused by the plant's operation. The particulars of the guarantee are regulated by notification of the competent authority, which is posted in the Official Gazette.[1528]

359. An industrial emissions permit that has been granted by the competent authority after consideration of the criteria stated above shall have operating conditions attached to it. These may be general operating conditions ('γενικοί όροι λειτουργίας') or operating conditions of a plant ('όροι λειτουργίας εγκατάστασης'). General operating conditions are applicable to certain categories of plants, combustion plants, waste incineration plants and waste co-incineration plants. They are specified in a decree published in the Official Gazette[1529] and are attached to a permit forming an indispensable part thereof.[1530] Lastly, granting permissions for all plants, on which general operating conditions are applicable, does not prerequisite the advice of the Technical Committee for the Protection of the Environment.[1531]

360. Operating conditions of a plant not falling under the aforementioned categories are specified by the competent authority and also form an indispensable part of the industrial emissions permit. They relate at least to the following matters: the nature, origin and composition of emissions;[1532] emission rate and total amount of substances that may be emitted within a specified time period;[1533] maximum emission limit values of any substances or group of substances;[1534] physical, chemical

1526. Section 11(5)(b) Law No. 184(I)/2013, which corresponds to Art. 4(2) Directive 2010/75/EU.
1527. Section 11(6) Law No. 184(I)/2013, which corresponds to Art. 4(3) Directive 2010/75/EU.
1528. Section 11(10)(a) and (b) Law No. 184(I)/2013.
1529. Section 12(1) *ibid.*
1530. Section 12(2) *ibid.* These correspond to the general binding rules ('prescriptions générales contraignantes' in French, 'allgemeine bindende Vorschriften' in German, 'algemene bindende voorschriften' in Dutch) stated to Art. 6 Directive 2010/75/EU and defined as emission limit values or other conditions, at least at sector level, that are adopted with the intention of being used directly to set permit conditions. Section 2(1) Law No. 184(I)/2013, which corresponds to Art. 3(8) Directive 2010/75/EU.
1531. Section 12(3) Law No. 184(I)/2013.
1532. Section 13(a) *ibid.* The power to impose a similar operating condition in a disposal permit is foreseen in s. 10(1)(d) Law No. 106(I)/2002.
1533. Section 13(b) Law No. 184(I)/2013.
1534. Section 13(c) *ibid.* The power to attach a similar operating condition to an air-waste permit is foreseen in s. 8(12)(b) Law No. 187(I)/2002.

and microbiological characteristics of any produced waste;[1535] quality standards of any material, including fuel used in the plant, as well as technical standards of any machine or equipment;[1536] planning and construction of any runoff pipes or waste exhaust ports for emitting liquid waste, as well as their precise location in water or soil;[1537] the technical standards, including height, regarding building a chimney through which emissions shall go into the air;[1538] the equipment that must be installed and used for prevention of emissions or for making them hazard-free for the environment;[1539] determining methods and procedures for process, storage, transportation and disposal of waste that result from the plant's operation with the aim of avoiding or reducing the effects on the environment;[1540] reasonably enabling the materialization of measurements and taking samples from any waste and substances used in the plant or are emitted by the same. Such enabling relates to manufacturing proper glory holes to chimneys as well as platforms, which secure free and safe access, and proper flow volumetric devices and sampler devices at points of liquid waste output;[1541] keeping records and data about composition, temperature, amount and rate of emissions and especially records about readings of measurement and other devices that the operator keeps according to its permit;[1542] installation of organs and following a schedule of emissions' monitoring, as well as to conditions of monitoring, which the operator must perform;[1543] organs, equipment or systems for storing measurements and teletransmission to the competent authority;[1544] drafting and complying with a programme monitoring the quality of water and soil at the plant site and points of waste discharge;[1545] technical reports that must be prepared by the operator regarding protection of the environment from emissions, including results from the application of the aforementioned schedule of emission's monitoring;[1546] the exact location, where operation of the plant is allowed;[1547] any additional demands that the competent authority deems necessary for the effective protection of the environment and public health;[1548] and measurement organs or other equipment that the operator has to install and bear the costs at spots that the Minister of Labour and Social Security approves for the purpose of measuring air quality.[1549]

1535. Section 13(d) Law No. 184(I)/2013.
1536. Section 13(e) *ibid.*
1537. Section 13(f) *ibid.*
1538. Section 13(g) *ibid.* Such standards may also be set in an air-waste permit according to s. 8(12)(g) Law No. 187(I)/2002.
1539. Section 13(h) Law No. 184(I)/2013. The power to attach a similar operating condition to an air-waste permit is foreseen in s. 8(12)(c) Law No. 187(I)/2002.
1540. Section 13(i) Law No. 184(I)/2013.
1541. Section 13(j) *ibid.*
1542. Section 13(k) *ibid.*
1543. Section 13(l) *ibid.*
1544. Section 13(m) *ibid.*
1545. Section 13(n) *ibid.* The power to impose a similar operating condition in a disposal permit is foreseen in s. 10(1)(k) Law No. 106(I)/2002.
1546. Section 13(o) Law No. 184(I)/2013.
1547. Section 13(p) *ibid.* The exact location may also be specified in additional operating conditions attached to an air-waste permit according to s. 8(12)(l) Law No. 187(I)/2002.
1548. Section 13(q) Law No. 184(I)/2013.
1549. Section 13(r) *ibid.*

361. Especially with reference to emissions of a greenhouse gas from a plant, which is stated in Annex I[1550] of the Law on Greenhouse Gas Emission Trading[1551] in relation to an activity carried out in that installation, it is set out that the permit shall not include an emission limit value for direct emissions of that gas, unless necessary to ensure that no significant local pollution is caused.[1552] For the aforementioned activities, the competent authority may choose not to impose requirements relating to energy efficiency in respect of combustion units or other units emitting carbon dioxide (CO_2) on the site.[1553] These provisions, however, do not apply to small installations which are temporarily excluded from the scheme for greenhouse gas emission allowance trading within the Union.[1554,1555]

362. In the event of violation of operating conditions, the operator must immediately inform the competent authority[1556] and take the measures necessary to ensure that compliance is restored within the shortest possible time.[1557] The competent authority has the authority to require the operator to take any appropriate complementary measures that the competent authority considers necessary to restore compliance.[1558] Should breaching the operating conditions pose an immediate danger to human health or threaten to cause an immediate significant adverse effect upon the environment, suspension of the plant's operation shall be imposed by the inspector through a notification of prohibition.[1559]

363. Time-related matters are also to be specified in the permit. Generally, all industrial emissions permits are valid for a specific time period specified therein that may not be longer than five years.[1560] Further, a time period, within which the permit shall not be revoked, is also to be set out in the permit.[1561] Additionally, a time period for every operating condition, within which this shall not be amended,[1562] and a time period, during which no new operating conditions shall be imposed are

1550. Annex I Law No. 110(I)/2011, which corresponds to Annex I Directive 2003/87/EC.
1551. Law on Establishing a Scheme for Greenhouse Gas Emission Trading ('ο περί της Θέσπισης Συστήματος Εμπορίας Δικαιωμάτων Εκπομπής Αερίων του Θερμοκηπίου Νόμος') No. 4290 of 2011, OG I(I) of 29 Jul. 2011, p. 2703, which implements Directive 2003/87/EC of the European Parliament and of the Council of 13 Oct. 2003 establishing a scheme for greenhouse gas emission allowance trading within the Community and amending Council Directive 96/61/EC, OL J 275, 25 Oct. 2003, p. 32, as amended. *See* in this respect N. Charalampidou (*supra* note 1414) 163 et seq.
1552. Section 22(1) Law No. 184(I)/2013, which corresponds to Art. 9(1) Directive 2010/75/EU.
1553. Section 22(2) Law No. 184(I)/2013, which corresponds to Art. 9(2) Directive 2010/75/EU.
1554. These installations are stated in s. 40 Law No. 110(I)/2011, which corresponds to Art. 27 Directive 2003/87/EC.
1555. Section 22(4) Law No. 184(I)/2013, which corresponds to Art. 9(4) Directive 2010/75/EU.
1556. Section 16(1)(a) Law No. 184(I)/2013, which corresponds to Art. 8(2)(a) Directive 2010/75/EU.
1557. Section 16(1)(b) Law No. 184(I)/2013, which corresponds to Art. 8(2)(b) Directive 2010/75/EU.
1558. Section 16(1)(c) Law No. 184(I)/2013, which corresponds to Art. 8(2)(c) Directive 2010/75/EU.
1559. Section 16(2) Law No. 184(I)/2013, which corresponds to Art. 8(2) Directive 2010/75/EU.
1560. Section 8(3)(a) Law No. 184(I)/2013.
1561. Section 14(a) *ibid.*
1562. Section 14(b) *ibid.*

stated in the permit. All mentioned time periods are valid save for reasons of protection of the environment, public health and/or public safety.[1563]

IV. Rejection of an Application for an Industrial Emissions Permit

364. In the event that an application for an industrial emissions permit is rejected, the applicant may file an appeal with the Cyprus Supreme Court according to Article 146 of the Constitution.

V. Amendments, Revocation and Renewal of an Industrial Emissions Permit

365. Amendments to an industrial emissions permit may be triggered by changes initiated by the operator or by the competent authority. In the first set of cases, when these are related to the identity of the operator of a plant, for which a permit has been issued, the following are foreseen. The new operator is obliged to notify immediately the competent authority[1564] and to comply with the operating conditions attached to the permit.[1565] He further bears all obligations and rights arising from this law, which were previously of the former operator.[1566] When changes are related to the plant, such as extension or amendment thereof, the operator must submit a new application for a permit before performing the intended changes, under the condition that additional significant negative effects[1567] may be effected to water, air and soil.[1568] However, such an application is not necessary,[1569] if a written confirmation is provided by the competent authority verifying such unnecessity.[1570]

366. Changes to the permit may be initiated by the competent authority. In particular, it may revoke a permit, amend any operating condition attached to such, add any new operating condition to such or shorten its validity period, if it considers this to be necessary for the protection of the environment, public health and/or public safety.[1571] Should the amendment of an operating condition or the imposition of a new one be decided during the time period, within which such could not take place according to the operating conditions, a compensation is being paid to the operator. However, this does not take place, if the decision results from change of conditions,

1563. Section 14(c) *ibid.*
1564. Section 17(1)(a) *ibid.*
1565. Section 17(1)(b) *ibid.*
1566. Section 17(2) *ibid.*
1567. Guidelines regarding the meaning of significant negative effects may be given by the competent authority through a decree published in the Official Gazette. Section 18(3) *ibid.*
1568. Section 18(1) *ibid.*, which corresponds to Art. 20(1) and (2) Directive 2010/75/EU.
1569. Section 18(2)(b) Law No. 184(I)/2013.
1570. Section 18(2)(a) *ibid.*
1571. Section 19(1)(a)–(d) *ibid.*

which could not have reasonably been foreseen at the time that the operating conditions had been initially decided.[1572] Change of information available to the competent authority is explicitly described in this law as such.[1573]

367. Operating conditions are periodically re-examined by the competent authority and may be updated.[1574] Re-examination is necessary in the following cases: when the pollution caused by the plant is of such significance that the existing emission limit values of the permit need to be revised or new such values need to be included in the permit;[1575] where developments in the BAT allow for the significant reduction of emissions;[1576] when the operator intends to extend, amend or otherwise change the plant;[1577] when the operational safety requires other techniques to be used;[1578] upon expiry of the time periods, during which amendments to operating conditions may not take place and new ones may not be added;[1579] and when this is foreseen in other legislation.[1580]

368. Renewal of an industrial emissions permit undergoes the above-described procedure as the application for one.[1581] The relevant application must be filed at least six months prior to expiration of the permit.[1582] However, if upon the expiration of a permit both the operation of the plant and the relevant environmental quality standards do not change, the competent authority may renew the permit for a period of two years.[1583]

§5. Ensuring Compliance

I. Administrative Sanctions

369. An improvement notification ('ειδοποίηση βελτίωσης') and a notification of prohibition ('απαγορευτική ειδοποίηση') may be issued by an inspector under the conditions and with the content and effect explained in Law No. 187(I)/2002 (*see* in this respect paragraphs 60 et seq. above).[1584]

370. Further, the competent authority may request a person to remediate or limit pollution to water or soil according to its instructions and within a reasonable time period, as long as this pollution has resulted from committing any of the criminal

1572. Section 19(2)(a) *ibid.*
1573. Section 19(2)(b) *ibid.*
1574. Section 15(1) *ibid.*
1575. Section 15(2)(a) *ibid.*, which corresponds to Art. 21(5)(a) Directive 2010/75/EU.
1576. Section 15(2)(b) Law No. 184(I)/2013, which corresponds to Art. 21(4) Directive 2010/75/EU.
1577. Section 15(2)(c) Law No. 184(I)/2013.
1578. Section 15(2)(d) *ibid.*, which corresponds to Art. 21(5)(b) Directive 2010/75/EU.
1579. Section 15(2)(e) Law No. 184(I)/2013.
1580. Section 15(2)(f) *ibid.*
1581. Sections 11, 7 and 8 *ibid.*
1582. Section 15(3) *ibid.*
1583. Section 15(4) *ibid.*
1584. Section 86(1), (2), (3), (4), (5), (6) and (7) *ibid.*

offences stated in this law.[1585] Should the person fail to comply with this request, said measures are taken by the competent authority and the relevant cost is restored from said person, as a civil debt to the state.[1586]

II. Criminal Sanctions

371. A series of criminal offences are set out in this law. Generally, any person performing an act or omitting such violation of this law, any regulations or decree issued in accordance with same, commits an offence. If found guilty, he might be sentenced to imprisonment of up to three years and/or a fine of up to EUR 500,000.[1587]

372. An operator or any other person operating, controlling or knowingly allows the operation of a plant not having an industrial emissions permit[1588] or in violation of the operating conditions attached to it commits a crime.[1589] If found guilty by a court of law, he may be imprisoned for up to three years and/or convicted to a fine of up to EUR 500,000.[1590] The accused may put forward action or omission of a third party as a defence only under certain conditions. These include giving information in writing, which shall assist in locating this other person, to the Attorney General at least seven days prior to hearing[1591] or having a court leave.[1592]

373. If the offence relates to violation of the operating conditions, the following defences may be put forward. The defendant may allege and prove that noncompliance was due to action or omission of a third party, accident or other cause beyond his control. At the same time, it is essential to prove that he took all reasonable precautions and showed all due care to avoid noncompliance and additionally, as soon as he realized it, he took all possible measures for remediation without undue delay.[1593] The defendant, who was employed in a plant, may also put forward the defence that he was instructed by the operator to act in such a way and that he had no reason to believe that complying with such instructions would lead to committing such a crime.[1594]

374. An operator operating or controlling a plant and performing any changes that may have additional significant negative effects on air, water and/or soil, prior

1585. Section 91(1) *ibid.*
1586. Section 91(2) *ibid.*
1587. Section 87(1) *ibid.*
1588. Section 20(1)(a) *ibid.*
1589. Section 20(1)(b) and (c) *ibid.*
1590. Sections 20(1) and 87(1) *ibid.*
1591. Section 20(3)(a)(i) *ibid.*
1592. Section 20(3)(a)(ii) *ibid.*
1593. Section 20(2) *ibid.*
1594. Section 20(4) *ibid.*

to obtaining a new permit or written notification commits an offence. If found guilty, he may be imprisoned for up to three years and/or fined for an amount of up to EUR 500,000.[1595]

375. Especially if a person obstructs an inspector from performing his duties and powers appointed to him by this law, he commits an offence. If found guilty, he faces imprisonment of up to six months and/or a fine of up to EUR 10,000.[1596] The same sentences are foreseen for obstruction of any police officer or other person escorting an inspector to enter a plant, failure to help an inspector,[1597] refusal to provide safe access to any part of a plant to an inspector or other person escorting him[1598] and denial or failure to comply with a request of an inspector.[1599]

III. Other Sanctions

376. During a court procedure for all aforementioned criminal offences, an interim order prohibiting the alleged illegal activity may be issued by the court,[1600] under the same circumstances and with the same effect as explained in Law No. 187(I)/2002 (*see* in this respect paragraphs 70 et seq. above).

377. Provisions on out-of-court settlement regarding the above-elaborated criminal offences are foreseen in this law. In particular, if the inspector has reasonable cause to believe that a criminal offence has been committed, he has the authority to serve to the alleged offender a notification stating the offence, the time that this was committed and the amount due, which may not be higher than EUR 4,000.[1601] The alleged offender has to cease the activity constituting the offence within forty-eight hours and pay the fine within fourteen days from the date the notification was served. If the said activity is not terminated within this time period, the inspector doubles the amount of the fine[1602] and every day that said activity is continued or repeated, it is considered a new offence that shall be prosecuted by the Attorney General.[1603] Timely payment of the imposed fine results in no prosecution of the offence[1604] and is not considered as conviction.[1605]

1595. Sections 18(4) and 87(1) *ibid.*
1596. Section 87(2)(a) *ibid.*
1597. Section 87(2)(b) *ibid.*
1598. Section 87(2)(c) *ibid.*
1599. Section 87(2)(d) *ibid.*
1600. Section 88 *ibid.*
1601. Section 90(1)(a) and (b), (2) *ibid.*
1602. Section 90(3) *ibid.*
1603. Section 90(4) *ibid.*
1604. Section 90(6) and (7) *ibid.*
1605. Section 90(8).

§6. Special Provisions on Activities Listed in Annex IV

378. Activities listed in Annex IV equally need to be authorized by an industrial emissions permit.

I. Application for an Industrial Emissions Permit for Activities Listed in Annex IV

379. The relevant application has to contain the above-stated information (section 9(2) of this law) as well as a study of EIA (*see* in this respect paragraphs 711 et seq. below) and available information on the grounds of legislation on control of major-accident hazards involving dangerous substance[1606] or other legislation.[1607] The general provisions on applying, granting an industrial emissions permit, general operating conditions and changes to plants (sections 7–11, 13–16 and 18 of this law) are applicable also to activities listed in Annex IV.[1608]

380. A baseline report[1609] must be submitted prior to imitating the plant's operation, where the activity involves the use, production or release of relevant hazardous substances and having regard to the possibility of soil and groundwater contamination at the site of the installation.[1610] The baseline report contains the information necessary to determine the state of soil and groundwater contamination so as to make a quantified comparison with the state upon definitive cessation of activities. It further contains at least the following: information on the present use and, where available, on past uses of the site; where available, existing information on soil and groundwater measurements that reflect the state at the time the report is drawn up or, alternatively, new soil and groundwater measurements having regard to the possibility of soil and groundwater contamination by those hazardous substances to be used, produced or released by the installation concerned. Where information produced pursuant to other laws fulfils the aforementioned requirements, that information may be included in, or attached to, the submitted baseline report.[1611]

1606. Regulations on Health and Safety at Work (Control of Major-Accident Hazards Involving Dangerous Substances) ('οι περί Ασφάλειας και Υγείας στην Εργασία (Αντιμετώπιση Κινδύνων Ατυχημάτων Μεγάλης Κλίμακας Σχετιζόμενων με Επικίνδυνες Ουσίες) Κανονισμοί') No. 347 of 2015, OGIII(I) 4900 of 23 Oct. 2015, p. 2109, as amended, which implement Directive 2012/18/EU of the European Parliament and of the Council of 4 Jul. 2012 on the control of major-accident hazards involving dangerous substances, OJ L 197, 24 Jul. 2012, p. 1.

1607. Section 25(2) and (3) Law No. 184(I)/2013.

1608. Section 25(1) *ibid.*

1609. *Baseline report* ('rapport de base' in French, 'Bericht über den Ausgangszustand' in German, 'situatierapport' in Dutch) means information on the state of soil and groundwater contamination by relevant hazardous substances. Section 2(1) Law No. 184(I)/2013, which corresponds to Art. 3(19) Directive 2010/75/EU.

1610. Section 34(2)(a) Law No. 184(I)/2013, which corresponds to Art. 22(2) Directive 2010/75/EU.

1611. Section 34(2)(b), (c) and (d) *ibid.*

II. Content of an Industrial Emissions Permit for Activities Listed in Annex IV

381. Additional operating conditions, apart from the ones explained above, may be attached to an industrial emissions permit. These may include at least the following: emission limit values for polluting substances listed in Annex VII, and for other polluting substances, which are likely to be emitted from the plant concerned in significant quantities, having regard to their nature and their potential to transfer pollution from one medium to another;[1612] appropriate requirements ensuring protection of the soil and groundwater and measures concerning the monitoring and management of waste generated by the plant;[1613] suitable emission monitoring requirements specifying measurement methodology, frequency and evaluation procedure and, where section 27(3)(b) is applied, that results of emission monitoring are available for the same periods of time and reference conditions as for the emission levels associated with the BAT;[1614] an obligation to supply the competent authority regularly, and at least annually, with information on the basis of results of emission monitoring referred to above and other required data that enables the competent authority to verify compliance with the permit conditions and where section 27(3)(b) is applied, a summary of the results of emission monitoring which allows a comparison with the emission levels associated with the BAT;[1615] appropriate requirements for the regular maintenance and surveillance of measures taken to prevent emissions to soil and groundwater as stated above and appropriate requirements concerning the periodic monitoring of soil and groundwater in relation to relevant hazardous substances likely to be found on site and having regard to the possibility of soil and groundwater contamination at the site of the installation;[1616] measures relating to conditions other than normal operating conditions such as start-up and shut-down operations, leaks, malfunctions, momentary stoppages and definitive cessation of operations;[1617] minimization of long-distance or transboundary pollution;[1618] assessing compliance with the emission limit values or a reference to

1612. Section 26(1)(a) *ibid.*, which corresponds to Art. 14(1)(a) Directive 2010/75/EU. Emission limit values may be supplemented or replaced by equivalent parameters or technical measures ensuring an equivalent level of environmental protection. Section 26(2) Law No. 184(I)/2013, which corresponds to Art. 14(2) Directive 2010/75/EU.
1613. Section 26(1)(b) Law No. 184(I)/2013, which corresponds to Art. 14(1)(b) Directive 2010/75/EU.
1614. Section 26(1)(c) Law No. 184(I)/2013, which corresponds to Art. 14(1)(c) Directive 2010/75/EU. Those monitoring requirements referred therein shall, where applicable, be based on the conclusions on monitoring as described in the BAT conclusions. Section 28(1) Law No. 184(I)/2013, which corresponds to Art. 16(1) Directive 2010/75/EU.
1615. Section 26(1)(d) Law No. 184(I)/2013, which corresponds to Art. 14(1)(d) Directive 2010/75/EU.
1616. Section 26(1)(e) Law No. 184(I)/2013, which corresponds to Art. 14(1)(e) Directive 2010/75/EU. The frequency of the periodic monitoring referred to there shall be determined by the competent authority in a permit for each individual installation or in general binding rules. Without prejudice to that, periodic monitoring shall be carried out at least once every five years for groundwater and ten years for soil, unless such monitoring is based on a systematic appraisal of the risk of contamination. Section 28(2) and (3) Law No. 184(I)/2013, which corresponds to Art. 16(2) Directive 2010/75/EU.
1617. Section 26(1)(f) Law No. 184(I)/2013, which corresponds to Art. 14(1)(f) Directive 2010/75/EU.
1618. Section 26(1)(g) Law No. 184(I)/2013, which corresponds to Art. 14(1)(g) Directive 2010/75/EU.

the applicable requirements specified elsewhere;[1619] and any other condition not stated above.[1620] Regardless of the nonexclusivity of the above matters and the general provision, this law further foresees that operating conditions may further regulate: the equipment or organs that must be installed at proper spots and used for measuring concentration, emission rate or total quantity of any substance emitted into the air, water and/or soil, during a certain time period, or any other parameter of function[1621] and schedule of measurements that the operator has to perform, the technical reports, including measurements' reports, as well as other relevant environmental data and the frequency of forwarding reports to competent authority.[1622]

382. BAT conclusions[1623] shall be the reference for setting the operating conditions of a permit.[1624] Without prejudice to section 30 of this law, the competent authority may set stricter permit conditions than those achievable by the use of the BAT as described in the BAT conclusions.[1625] Where the competent authority sets permit conditions on the basis of a best available technique not described in any of the relevant BAT conclusions, it shall ensure that that technique is determined by giving special consideration to the criteria listed in Annex III[1626] and the requirements of section 27 of this law are complied with.[1627] Where the BAT conclusions referred to above do not contain emission levels associated with the BAT, the competent authority shall ensure that the technique referred to above ensures a level of environmental protection equivalent to the BAT described in the BAT conclusions.[1628] Where an activity or a type of production process carried out within the plant is not covered by any of the BAT conclusions or where those conclusions do not address all the potential environmental effects of the activity or process, the competent authority shall, after prior consultations with the operator, set the permit conditions on the basis of the BAT that it has determined for the activities or processes concerned, by giving special consideration to the criteria listed in Annex III.[1629] Pending the adoption of a relevant decision by the Commission regarding BAT conclusions for a certain type of activity, the competent authority determines

---

1619. Section 26(1)(h) Law No. 184(I)/2013, which corresponds to Art. 14(1)(h) Directive 2010/75/EU.
1620. Section 26(1)(i) Law No. 184(I)/2013.
1621. Section 26(3)(a) *ibid.*
1622. Section 26(3)(d) *ibid.* Two further matters are mentioned in this law at s. 26(3)(b) and (c), but they were omitted, as they are also stated in s. 13(m) and (r) *ibid.*
1623. *BAT conditions* ('conclusions sur les MTD' in French, 'BVT-Schlussfolgerungen' in German, 'BBT-conclusies' in Dutch) means a document drafted according to Art. 13 Directive 2010/75/EU, which is a part of BAT reference document, and containing the parts of a BAT reference document laying down the conclusions on best available techniques, their description, information to assess their applicability, the emission levels associated with the best available techniques, associated monitoring, associated consumption levels and, where appropriate, relevant site remediation measures. Section 2(1) Law No. 184(I)/2013, which partly corresponds to Art. 3(12) Directive 2010/75/EU.
1624. Section 26(4)(a) Law No. 184(I)/2013, which corresponds to Art. 14(3) Directive 2010/75/EU.
1625. Section 26(4)(a) Law No. 184(I)/2013, which corresponds to Art. 14(4) Directive 2010/75/EU.
1626. Section 26(5)(a) Law No. 184(I)/2013, which corresponds to Art. 14(5)(a) Directive 2010/75/EU.
1627. Section 26(5)(b) Law No. 184(I)/2013, which corresponds to Art. 14(5)(b) Directive 2010/75/EU.
1628. Section 26(6) Law No. 184(I)/2013, which corresponds to Art. 14(5) Directive 2010/75/EU.
1629. Section 26(7) Law No. 184(I)/2013, which corresponds to Art. 14(6) Directive 2010/75/EU.

operating conditions on the basis of conclusions on BAT from BAT reference documents adopted by the Commission prior to 6 January 2011, with the exception of emission limit values.[1630] For plants of intensive rearing of poultry or pigs with more than 40,000 places for poultry, with more than 2,000 places for production pigs (over 30 kg), or with more than 750 places for sows,[1631] the above stated apply without prejudice to the legislation relating to animal welfare.[1632] The competent authority follows and is informed of developments in BAT and of the publication of any new or updated BAT conclusions and makes that information available to the public with a notification in the Official Gazette and online.[1633]

383. Environmental quality standards are determined by a decree of the competent authority published in the Official Gazette.[1634] Where an environmental quality standard requires stricter conditions than those achievable by the use of the BAT, additional measures shall be included in the permit, without prejudice to other measures which may be taken to comply with environmental quality standards.[1635]

384. General operating conditions can equally be set out for activities listed in Annex IV. When adopting general operating conditions, the competent authority ensures an integrated approach and a high level of environmental protection equivalent to that achievable with individual permit conditions.[1636] Those conditions are based on the BAT, without prescribing the use of any technique or specific technology in order to ensure compliance with the above stated on BAT.[1637] The competent authority also ensures that those conditions are updated to take into account developments in BAT.[1638] When a decree is being issued by the competent authority determining such general operating conditions, it must contain a reference to this law and Directive 2010/75/EU.[1639]

III. Emission Limit Values for Activities Listed in Annex IV

385. The emission limit values for polluting substances apply at the point where the emissions leave the installation, and any dilution prior to that point shall be disregarded when determining those values. With regard to indirect releases of polluting substances into water, the effect of a water treatment plant may be taken into account when determining the emission limit values of the installation concerned, provided that an equivalent level of protection of the environment as a whole is

1630. Section 26(8) Law No. 184(I)/2013, which corresponds to Art. 13(7) Directive 2010/75/EU.
1631. Annex IV 6.6 Law No. 184(I)/2013, which corresponds to Annex I 6.6. Directive 2010/75/EU.
1632. Section 26(9) Law No. 184(I)/2013, which corresponds to Art. 14(7) Directive 2010/75/EU.
1633. Section 31 Law No. 184(I)/2013, which corresponds to Art. 19 Directive 2010/75/EU.
1634. Section 30(1) Law No. 184(I)/2013.
1635. Section 30(2) *ibid.*, which corresponds to Art. 18 Directive 2010/75/EU.
1636. Section 29(1) Law No. 184(I)/2013, which corresponds to Art. 17(1) Directive 2010/75/EU.
1637. Section 29(2) Law No. 184(I)/2013, which corresponds to Art. 17(2) Directive 2010/75/EU.
1638. Section 29(3) Law No. 184(I)/2013, which corresponds to Art. 17(3) Directive 2010/75/EU.
1639. Section 29(4) Law No. 184(I)/2013, which partially corresponds to Art. 17(4) Directive 2010/75/EU.

guaranteed and provided this does not lead to higher levels of environmental pollution.[1640] The emission limit values and the equivalent parameters and technical measures referred to under additional operating conditions are based on the BAT, without prescribing the use of any technique or specific technology.[1641]

386. Emission limit values set by the competent authority ensure that under normal operating conditions, emissions do not exceed the emission levels associated with the BAT as laid down in the decisions on BAT conclusions referred to in Article 13(5) Directive 2010/75/EU through either of the following: setting emission limit values that do not exceed the emission levels associated with the BAT. Those emission limit values are expressed for the same or shorter periods of time and under the same reference conditions as those emission levels associated with the BAT,[1642] or setting different emission limit values than those referred to above in terms of values, periods of time and reference conditions. In such cases, the competent authority assesses, at least annually, the results of emission monitoring in order to ensure that emissions under normal operating conditions have not exceeded the emission levels associated with the BAT.[1643]

387. Derogation from the aforementioned is possible. The competent authority may, in specific cases, set less strict emission limit values. However, such derogation is only applicable, where an assessment shows that the achievement of emission levels associated with the BAT as described in BAT conclusions would lead to disproportionately higher costs compared to the environmental benefits due to: the geographical location or the local environmental conditions of the installation concerned; or the technical characteristics of the installation concerned.[1644] Temporary derogation is also possible, especially for the testing and use of emerging techniques for a total period of time not exceeding nine months, provided that after the period specified, either the technique is stopped or the activity achieves at least the emission levels associated with the BAT.[1645]

IV. Changes to Plants Involving Activities Listed in Annex IV

388. The operator is obliged to inform in writing the competent authority of any planned change in the nature or functioning, or an extension of the plant, which may have consequences for the environment. Where appropriate, the competent authority shall amend or revoke the permit.[1646] No substantial change[1647] planned by the

1640. Section 27(1)(a) and (b) Law No. 184(I)/2013, which corresponds to Art. 15(1) Directive 2010/75/EU.
1641. Section 27(2) Law No. 184(I)/2013, which corresponds to Art. 15(2) Directive 2010/75/EU.
1642. Section 27(3)(a) Law No. 184(I)/2013, which corresponds to Art. 15(3)(a) Directive 2010/75/EU.
1643. Section 27(3)(b) and (4) Law No. 184(I)/2013, which corresponds to Art. 15(3)(b) Directive 2010/75/EU.
1644. Section 27(5)(a) Law No. 184(I)/2013, which corresponds to Art. 15(4) Directive 2010/75/EU.
1645. Section 27(6) Law No. 184(I)/2013, which corresponds to Art. 15(5) Directive 2010/75/EU.
1646. Section 32(1)(a) and (b) Law No. 184(I)/2013, which corresponds to Art. 20(1) Directive 2010/75/EU.

operator may be made without a permit granted in accordance with this law.[1648] Therefore, the operator must submit an application to the competent authority, which is examined as if no application had been previously submitted by same person. Both applications for a permit and the decision by the competent authority cover those parts of the plant and those details listed in sections 9(1) and (2) and 25(2) and (3) of this law, which may be affected by the substantial change.[1649] In the event that Law No. 127(I)/2018 is applicable (*see* in this respect paragraphs 711 et seq. below), information available from the application of that law is taken into consideration by the competent authority.[1650]

389. The competent authority periodically reconsiders all permit operating conditions and, where it is deemed necessary to ensure compliance with this law, said conditions are updated.[1651] Reconsideration is performed in accordance with the following. At the request of the competent authority, the operator submits all the information necessary for the purpose of reconsidering the permit conditions, including, in particular, results of emission monitoring and other data, that enables a comparison of the operation of the installation with the BAT described in the applicable BAT conclusions and with the emission levels associated with the BAT. When reconsidering permit conditions, the competent authority uses any information resulting from monitoring or inspections.[1652] Within four years of publication of decisions on BAT conclusions relating to the main activity of a plant, the competent authority ensures that all the permit conditions for the installation concerned are reconsidered and, if necessary, updated to ensure compliance with this law, in particular, with section 27(3), (4) and (5), where applicable and the plant complies with those permit conditions.[1653] Where an installation is not covered by any of the BAT conclusions, the permit operating conditions are reconsidered and, if necessary, updated where developments in the BAT allow for the significant reduction of emissions.[1654] The permit conditions are reconsidered and, where necessary, updated at least in the following cases: the pollution caused by the installation is of such significance that the existing emission limit values of the permit need to be revised or new such values need to be included in the permit;[1655] the operational safety

---

1647. Any change in the nature or functioning or an extension of an installation shall be deemed to be *substantial* ('modification substantielle' in French, 'wesentliche Änderung' in German, 'belangrijke wijziging' in Dutch) if the change or extension in itself reaches the capacity thresholds set out in Annex IV. Section 32(5) Law No. 184(I)/2013, which corresponds to Art. 20(3) Directive 2010/75/EU.
1648. Section 32(2) Law No. 184(I)/2013, which corresponds to Art. 20(2) Directive 2010/75/EU.
1649. Section 32(3) Law No. 184(I)/2013.
1650. Section 32(4) *ibid.*
1651. Section 33(1) *ibid.*, which corresponds to Art. 21(1) Directive 2010/75/EU.
1652. Section 33(2)(a) and (b) Law No. 184(I)/2013, which corresponds to Art. 21(2) Directive 2010/75/EU.
1653. Section 33(3) Law No. 184(I)/2013, which corresponds to Art. 21(3) Directive 2010/75/EU.
1654. Section 33(4) Law No. 184(I)/2013, which corresponds to Art. 21(4) Directive 2010/75/EU.
1655. Section 33(5)(a) Law No. 184(I)/2013, which corresponds to Art. 21(5)(a) Directive 2010/75/EU.

requires other techniques to be used;[1656] where it is necessary to comply with a new or revised environmental quality standard in accordance with section 30;[1657] and when their time limit expires.[1658]

V. Environmental Inspections for Activities Listed in Annex IV

390. A system of environmental inspections of plants addressing the examination of the full range of relevant environmental effects from the plants concerned is set up by the competent authority.[1659] Each environmental inspection plan includes: a general assessment of relevant significant environmental issues; the geographical area covered by the inspection plan; a register of the installations covered by the plan; procedures for drawing up programmes for routine environmental inspections; procedures for non-routine environmental inspections; and where necessary, provisions on the cooperation between inspectors, where this is necessary.[1660]

391. Environmental inspections can be both routine and nonroutine. Programmes for routine environmental inspections include the frequency of site visits for different types of plants. The period between two site visits is based on a systematic appraisal of the environmental risks of the installations concerned and does not exceed one year for installations posing the highest risks and three years for installations posing the lowest risks. The systematic appraisal of the environmental risks are based on at least the following criteria: the potential and actual impacts of the installations concerned on human health and the environment taking into account the levels and types of emissions, the sensitivity of the local environment and the risk of accidents;[1661] the record of compliance with permit conditions;[1662] the participation of the operator in the Union EMAS, pursuant to Regulation (EC) No. 1221/2009[1663] and to Law on Voluntary Participation of Organisms to the Union EMAS.[1664,1665]

392. Non-routine environmental inspections are carried out to investigate serious environmental complaints, serious environmental accidents, incidents and

1656. Section 33(5)(b) Law No. 184(I)/2013, which corresponds to Art. 21(5)(b) Directive 2010/75/EU.
1657. Section 33(5)(c) Law No. 184(I)/2013, which corresponds to Art. 21(5)(c) Directive 2010/75/EU.
1658. Section 33(5)(d) Law No. 184(I)/2013.
1659. Section 35(1)(a) *ibid.*, which corresponds to Art. 23(1) Directive 2010/75/EU.
1660. Section 35(3) Law No. 184(I)/2013, which corresponds to Art. 23(3) Directive 2010/75/EU.
1661. Section 35(4)(a) Law No. 184(I)/2013, which corresponds to Art. 23(4)(a) Directive 2010/75/EU.
1662. Section 35(4)(b) Law No. 184(I)/2013, which corresponds to Art. 23(4)(b) Directive 2010/75/EU.
1663. Regulation (EC) No. 1221/2009 of the European Parliament and of the Council of 25 Nov. 2009 on the voluntary participation by organizations in a Community Eco-Management and Audit Scheme (EMAS), OJ L 342, 22 Dec. 2009, p. 1.
1664. Law on Voluntary Participation of Organisms to the Union Eco-management and Audit Scheme ('ο Περί της Εκούσιας Συμμετοχής Οργανισμών σε Κοινοτικό Σύστημα Οικολογικής Διαχείρισης και Οικολογικού Ελέγχου Νόμος') No. 10 of 2012, OGI(I) No. 4318 of 2 Mar. 2012, p. 100.
1665. Section 35(4)(c) Law No. 184(I)/2013, which corresponds to Art. 23(4)(c) Directive 2010/75/EU.

occurrences of noncompliance as soon as possible and, where appropriate, before the granting, reconsideration or update of a permit.[1666]

393. Following each site visit, the competent authority prepares a report describing the relevant findings regarding compliance of the plant with the permit conditions and conclusions on whether any further action is necessary. This report is notified to the operator concerned within two months of the site visit taking place and is made publicly available by the competent authority within four months of same point in time.[1667]

VI. Public Participation Regarding Activities Listed in Annex IV

394. It is ensured that the public concerned are given early and effective opportunities to participate in the following procedures: the granting of a permit for new installations;[1668] the granting of a permit for any substantial change;[1669] the granting or updating of a permit for an installation where the application of section 27(5) and (6) is proposed;[1670] and the amendment of a permit or permit conditions for an installation.[1671] The applicable procedure for such participation is set out in this law.[1672]

395. In particular with reference to public available information, when a decision on the above-mentioned has been taken, the competent authority makes available the following information: the content of the decision, including a copy of the permit and any subsequent updates;[1673] the reasons for which the decision is based;[1674] the results of the consultations held before the decision was taken and an explanation of how they were taken into account in that decision;[1675] the title of the BAT reference documents relevant to the installation or activity concerned;[1676] how the permit conditions referred to in section 14, including the emission limit values, have been determined in relation to the BAT and emission levels associated with the

1666. Section 34(5) Law No. 184(I)/2013, which corresponds to Art. 23(5) Directive 2010/75/EU.
1667. Section 34(6) Law No. 184(I)/2013, which corresponds to Art. 23(6) Directive 2010/75/EU.
1668. Section 36(1)(a) Law No. 184(I)/2013, which corresponds to Art. 24(1)(a) Directive 2010/75/EU.
1669. Section 36(1)(b) Law No. 184(I)/2013, which corresponds to Art. 24(1)(b) Directive 2010/75/EU.
1670. Section 36(1)(c) Law No. 184(I)/2013, which corresponds to Art. 24(1)(c) Directive 2010/75/EU.
1671. Section 36(1)(d) Law No. 184(I)/2013, which corresponds to Art. 24(1)(d) Directive 2010/75/EU.
1672. This is set out in ss 37, 38, 39, 40 and Annex VIII Law No. 184(I)/2013, which corresponds to Annex IV Directive 2010/75/EU.
1673. Section 36(3)(a)(i) Law No. 184(I)/2013, which corresponds to Art. 24(2)(a) Directive 2010/75/EU.
1674. Section 36(3)(a)(ii) Law No. 184(I)/2013, which corresponds to Art. 24(2)(b) Directive 2010/75/EU.
1675. Section 36(3)(a)(iii) Law No. 184(I)/2013, which corresponds to Art. 24(2)(c) Directive 2010/75/EU.
1676. Section 36(3)(a)(iv) Law No. 184(I)/2013, which corresponds to Art. 24(2)(d) Directive 2010/75/EU.

BAT;[1677] where a derogation is granted in accordance with section 27(5), the specific reasons for that derogation based on the criteria laid down in that paragraph and the conditions imposed;[1678] Further, the following information is made publicly available: relevant information on the measures taken by the operator upon definitive cessation of activities;[1679] and the results of emission monitoring as required under the permit conditions and held by the competent authority.[1680]

VII. Transboundary Effects of Activities Listed in Annex IV

396. The aforementioned information that was made publicly available is forwarded to a Member State, when the competent authority is aware that the operation of a plant is likely to have significant negative effects on the environment of such state, or where same state so requests. This information serves as a basis for any consultations necessary in the framework of the bilateral relations between the two Member States on a reciprocal and equivalent basis.[1681] Within the framework of their bilateral relations, Member States ensure that in such cases the applications are also made available for a period of time of no less than thirty-five days to the public of the Member State likely to be affected so that it will have the right to comment on them before the competent authority reaches its decision.[1682] The results of any consultations pursuant to the above are taken into consideration when the competent authority reaches a decision on the application.[1683] Lastly, the competent authority informs any Member State which has been consulted on the decision reached on the application and forwards to it the information available to the public upon granting a permit.[1684] The competent authority takes the measures necessary to ensure that that information is made available in an appropriate manner to the public concerned in its own territory.[1685]

VIII. Cessation of Activities Listed in Annex IV

397. Without prejudice to legislation on the protection of groundwater against pollution and deterioration and law on soil protection, the competent authority sets

1677. Section 36(3)(a)(v) Law No. 184(I)/2013, which corresponds to Art. 24(2)(e) Directive 2010/75/EU.
1678. Section 36(3)(a)(vi) Law No. 184(I)/2013, which corresponds to Art. 24(2)(f) Directive 2010/75/EU.
1679. Section 36(4)(a)(i) Law No. 184(I)/2013, which corresponds to Art. 24(3)(a) Directive 2010/75/EU.
1680. Section 36(4)(a)(ii) Law No. 184(I)/2013, which corresponds to Art. 24(3)(b) Directive 2010/75/EU.
1681. Section 43(1)(a) and (b) Law No. 184(I)/2013, which corresponds to Art. 26(1) Directive 2010/75/EU.
1682. Section 43(2) Law No. 184(I)/2013, which corresponds to Art. 26(2) Directive 2010/75/EU.
1683. Section 43(3) Law No. 184(I)/2013, which corresponds to Art. 26(3) Directive 2010/75/EU.
1684. Sections 43(4) and 36(3) Law No. 184(I)/2013, which corresponds to Art. 26(4) and 24(2) Directive 2010/75/EU.
1685. These are described in s. 43(5) Law No. 184(I)/2013.

permit conditions to ensure compliance with the below, upon definitive cessation of activities.[1686] When this is intended, the operator assesses the state of soil and groundwater contamination by relevant hazardous substances used, produced or released by the installation. Where the installation has caused significant pollution of soil or groundwater by relevant hazardous substances compared to the state established in the baseline report referred to above, the operator takes the necessary measures to address that pollution so as to return the site to that state. For that purpose, the technical feasibility of such measures may be taken into account.[1687] Without prejudice to the aforementioned, upon definitive cessation of the activities, and where the contamination of soil and groundwater at the site poses a significant risk to human health or the environment as a result of the permitted activities carried out by the operator before the permit for the plant is updated for the first time after 7 January 2013 and taking into account the conditions of the site of the installation established in accordance with section 9(2)(c) of this law, the operator takes the necessary actions aimed at the removal, control, containment or reduction of relevant hazardous substances, so that the site, taking into account its current or approved future use, ceases to pose such a risk.[1688]

398. In the event that the operator is not required to prepare a baseline, the operator shall, upon definitive cessation of the activities, take the necessary actions aimed at the removal, control, containment or reduction of relevant hazardous substances, so that the site, taking into account its current or approved future use, ceases to pose any significant risk to human health or the environment due to the contamination of soil and groundwater as a result of the permitted activities and taking into account the conditions of the site of the installation established in accordance with section 9(2)(c) of this law.[1689]

§7. Special Provisions for Combustion Plants

399. Generally, waste gases from combustion plants are to be discharged in a controlled way by means of a stack, containing one or more flues, the height of which is calculated in such a way as to safeguard human health and the environment.[1690]

I. Combustion Plants Authorized with an Air-Waste Permit

400. Combustion plants, which have been granted an air-waste permit pursuant to Law No. 187(I)/2002 before 7 January 2013 or which have submitted an application for such a permit prior to same date, must also comply with the provisions of

1686. Section 34(1) *ibid.*, which corresponds to Art. 22(1) Directive 2010/75/EU.
1687. Section 34(3)(a) and (b) Law No. 184(I)/2013, which corresponds to Art. 22(3) Directive 2010/75/EU.
1688. Section 34(3)(c) Law No. 184(I)/2013, which corresponds to Art. 22(3) Directive 2010/75/EU.
1689. Section 34(4) Law No. 184(I)/2013, which corresponds to Art. 22(4) Directive 2010/75/EU.
1690. Section 47(1) Law No. 184(I)/2013, which corresponds to Art. 30(1) Directive 2010/75/EU.

this law. In particular, operating conditions ensuring that emissions into air from these plants do not exceed the emission limit values set out in Part 1 of Annex VI are attached to the air-waste permit.[1691] Same applies to such plants that had been granted an exemption pursuant to Law No. 187(I)/2002 and were in operation after 1 January 2016,[1692] as well as for all plants having a permit not falling under the aforementioned.[1693]

II. Content of an Industrial Emissions Permit for Combustion Plants

401. Industrial emissions permits for combustion plants must entail, in addition to above-elaborated operating conditions, conditions relating to malfunction or breakdown of the abatement equipment.[1694]

III. Emission Limit Values for Combustion Plants

402. The emission limit values for air are regarded as being complied with if the conditions set out in Part 4 of Annex VI are fulfilled.[1695] The emissions of each common stack[1696] in relation to the total rated thermal input of the entire combustion plant underlie the emission limit values set out in Parts 1 and 2 of Annex VI as well as the minimum rates of desulphurization set out in Part 5 of that Annex.[1697] Where Annex VI provides that emission limit values may be applied for a part of a combustion plant with a limited number of operating hours, those limit values apply to the emissions of that part of the plant, but are set in relation to the total rated thermal input of the entire combustion plant.[1698]

403. Derogation from the obligation to comply with the emission limit values provided above is applicable in following cases. The competent authority may grant a derogation for a maximum of six months for sulphur dioxide in respect of a combustion plant which to this end normally uses low-sulphur fuel, in cases where the operator is unable to comply with those limit values because of an interruption in the supply of low-sulphur fuel resulting from a serious shortage. The EC is immediately informed of that by the competent authority.[1699] A derogation for a maximum of ten days from the obligation to comply with same emission limit values, may be granted in cases where a combustion plant using only gaseous fuel has to resort exceptionally to the use of other fuels because of a sudden interruption in the

1691. Section 47(2) Law No. 184(I)/2013, which corresponds to Art. 30(2) Directive 2010/75/EU.
1692. Section 47(3) Law No. 184(I)/2013, which corresponds to Art. 30(2) Directive 2010/75/EU.
1693. Section 47(4) Law No. 184(I)/2013, which corresponds to Art. 30(3) Directive 2010/75/EU.
1694. Section 54(1) Law No. 184(I)/2013, which corresponds to Art. 37(1) Directive 2010/75/EU.
1695. Section 56 Law No. 184(I)/2013, which corresponds to Art. 39 Directive 2010/75/EU.
1696. *See* in this respect s. 46(1), (2) and (3) Law No. 184(I)/2013, which corresponds to Art. 29(1), (2) and (3) Directive 2010/75/EU.
1697. Section 47(5)(a) Law No. 184(I)/2013, which corresponds to Art. 30(4) Directive 2010/75/EU.
1698. Section 47(5)(b) Law No. 184(I)/2013.
1699. Section 47(6) *ibid.*, which corresponds to Art. 30(5) Directive 2010/75/EU.

supply of gas and for this reason would need to be equipped with a waste gas purification facility. The operator immediately informs the competent authority of each such specific case. Again, the EC is immediately informed of that by the competent authority.[1700]

404. With reference to combustion plants firing indigenous solid fuel, which cannot comply with the emission limit values for sulphur dioxide referred to above due to the characteristics of this fuel, the competent authority may apply instead the minimum rates of desulphurization set out in Part 5 of Annex VI, in accordance with the compliance rules set out in Part 6 of that annex and with prior validation by the competent authority of the technical report referred to in section 97(3)(a) of this law.[1701] Further, with reference to combustion plants firing indigenous solid fuel, which co-incinerate waste, and which cannot comply with the Cproc values for sulphur dioxide set out in point 3.1 or 3.2 of Part 4 of Annex II due to the characteristics of the indigenous solid fuel, the competent authority may apply instead the minimum rates of desulphurization set out in Part 5 of Annex VI, in accordance with the compliance rules set out in Part 6 of that annex. In such cases, Cwaste as referred to in point 1 of Part 4 of Annex II shall be equal to 0 mg/nm^3.[1702]

405. Emission limit values for multi-fuel firing combustion plants are asset by the competent authority in accordance with specific and detailed steps set out in this law.[1703]

406. Lastly, said emission limit values do not apply to combustion plants burning diesel engines and recovery boilers within installations for the production of pulp.[1704]

IV. Transitional National Plan for Combustion Plants

407. During the period from 1 January 2016 to 30 June 2020, the competent authority may draw up and implement a transitional national plan covering combustion plants which were granted the first permit before 27 November 2002 or the operators which had submitted a complete application for a permit before that date, provided that the plant was put into operation no later than 27 November 2003. For each of the combustion plants covered by the plan, the plan shall cover emissions of one or more of the following pollutants: nitrogen oxides, sulphur dioxide and dust. For gas turbines, only nitrogen oxides emissions may be covered by the plan.[1705] The transitional national plan does not include any of the following combustion plants: combustion plants fulfilling the conditions set out in section 50(1) of

1700. Section 47(7) Law No. 184(I)/2013, which corresponds to Art. 30(6) Directive 2010/75/EU.
1701. Section 48(1) Law No. 184(I)/2013, which corresponds to Art. 31(1) Directive 2010/75/EU.
1702. Section 48(2) Law No. 184(I)/2013, which corresponds to Art. 31(2) Directive 2010/75/EU.
1703. Section 57(1), (2) and (3) Law No. 184(I)/2013, which corresponds to Art. 40(1), (2) and (3) Directive 2010/75/EU.
1704. Section 47(10) Law No. 184(I)/2013, which corresponds to Art. 30(8) Directive 2010/75/EU.
1705. Section 49(1) Law No. 184(I)/2013, which corresponds to Art. 32(1) Directive 2010/75/EU.

this law;[1706] those within refineries firing low calorific gases from the gasification of refinery residues or the distillation and conversion residues from the refining of crude oil for own consumption, alone or with other fuels;[1707] district heating plants fulfilling the conditions set out in section 52 of this law;[1708] and those which are granted an exemption pursuant to Law No. 187(I)/2002.[1709]

408. Exemptions from compliance with the emission limit values for the pollutants which are subject to the plan or, where applicable, with the rates of desulphurization referred to above may be granted for combustion plants covered by the plan. The emission limit values for sulphur dioxide, nitrogen oxides and dust set out in an air-waste permit for the combustion plant applicable on 31 December 2015, pursuant in particular to the requirements of Law No. 56(I)/2003[1710] and KDP 74/2003[1711] shall at least be maintained.[1712] Especially combustion plants with a total rated thermal input of more than 500 MW firing solid fuels have to comply with the emission limit values for nitrogen oxides set out in Part 1 of Annex VI, as long as they were granted the first permit after 1 July 1987.[1713]

409. The transitional national plan shall set a ceiling for each of the pollutants it covers, defining the maximum total annual emissions for all of the plants covered by the plan on the basis of each plant's total rated thermal input on 31 December 2010, its actual annual operating hours and its fuel use, averaged over the last ten years of operation up to and including 2010.[1714] Special provisions are foreseen for setting the ceiling for years 2016, 2017, 2018, 2019 and 2020 as well as for gas turbines.[1715] Where a plant included in the transitional national plan is closed or no longer falls within the scope of this monograph, this shall not result in an increase in total annual emissions from the remaining plants covered by the plan.[1716]

1706. Section 49(1)(a) Law No. 184(I)/2013, which corresponds to Art. 32(1)(a) Directive 2010/75/EU.
1707. Section 49(1)(b) Law No. 184(I)/2013, which corresponds to Art. 32(1)(b) Directive 2010/75/EU.
1708. Section 49(1)(c) Law No. 184(I)/2013, which corresponds to Art. 32(1)(c) Directive 2010/75/EU.
1709. Section 49(1)(d) Law No. 184(I)/2013, which corresponds to Art. 32(1)(d) Directive 2010/75/EU.
1710. Law on Integrated Pollution Prevention and Control ('ο περί της Ολοκληρωμένης Πρόληψης και Ελέγχου της Ρύπανσης Νόμος') No. 56 of 2003, OG I(I) No. 3724 of 13 Jun. 2003, which implemented Directive 96/61/EC. That law has been however upheld by Law No. 184(I)/2013.
1711. Regulations on Air Pollution Control (Limitation of Emissions of Certain Pollutants from Large Combustion Plants) ('οι περί Ελέγχου της Ρύπανσης της Ατμόσφαιρας (Περιορισμός των Εκπομπών στην Ατμόσφαιρα Ορισμένων Ρύπων από Μεγάλες Εγκαταστάσεις Καύσης) Κανονισμοί') No. 74 of 2003, OG III(I) No. 3679 of 31 Jan. 2003, p. 176. These regulations have been upheld by Regulations on Air Pollution Control (Limitation of Emissions of Certain Pollutants from Large Combustion Plants) (Upholding Application and Abolition) ('οι περί Ελέγχου της Ρύπανσης της Ατμόσφαιρας (Περιορισμός των Εκπομπών στην Ατμόσφαιρα Ορισμένων Ρύπων από Μεγάλες Εγκαταστάσεις Καύσης) (ρση Εφαρμογής και Κατάργηση) Κανονισμοί') No. 469 of 2013, OG III(I) 4743 of 27 Dec. 2013, p. 2854.
1712. Section 49(3)(a) and (b) Law No. 184(I)/2013, which corresponds to Art. 32(2) Directive 2010/75/EU.
1713. Section 49(3)(c) Law No. 184(I)/2013.
1714. Section 49(4)(a) *ibid.*, which corresponds to Art. 32(3) Directive 2010/75/EU.
1715. Section 49(4)(b), (c), (d) and (e) Law No. 184(I)/2013.
1716. Section 49(4)(f) *ibid.*

410. The competent authority communicates the transitional national plan as well as any changes of that to the EC,[1717] that evaluates the plan. It is considered to be accepted, where the EC has raised no objections within twelve months of receipt thereof. If such a plan is not in accordance with said rules, the competent authority is informed by the EC. The new version of the plan shall again be evaluated by the EC and considered to be accepted, where no objections within six months of receipt of that have been raised.[1718]

411. A temporary derogation (from 1 January 2016 to 31 December 2023) from emission limits values and aforementioned rates of desulphurization, where applicable, as well as from their inclusion in the transitional national plan could be granted to combustion plants from the competent authority[1719] under the following conditions. The operator of the combustion plant had to undertake, in a written declaration submitted by 1 January 2014 at the latest to the competent authority, not to operate the plant for more than 17,500 operating hours, starting from 1 January 2016 and ending no later than 31 December 2023.[1720] The operator was further required to submit each year to the competent authority a record of the number of operating hours since 1 January 2016.[1721] The emission limit values for sulphur dioxides, nitrogen oxides and dust set out in the permit for the combustion plant applicable on 31 December 2015, under Law No. 56(I)/2003 and KDP 74/2003, have at least to be maintained during the remaining operational life of the combustion plant.[1722] Combustion plants with a total rated thermal input of more than 500 MW firing solid fuels, which were granted the first permit after 1 July 1987, have to comply with the emission limit values for nitrogen oxides set out in Part 1 of Annex VI.[1723] Finally the combustion plant may not have been granted an exemption under Law No. 187(I)/2002.[1724]

1717. Section 49(6)(a) *ibid.*, which corresponds to Art. 32(5) and (6) Directive 2010/75/EU.
1718. Section 49(6)(b) and (c) Law No. 184(I)/2013, which corresponds to Art. 32(5) Directive 2010/75/EU.
1719. Section 50(1) Law No. 184(I)/2013, which corresponds to Art. 33(1) Directive 2010/75/EU.
1720. Section 50(1)(a) Law No. 184(I)/2013, which corresponds to Art. 33(1)(a) Directive 2010/75/EU. The number of operating hours are 18.000, starting from 1 Jan. 2020 and ending no later than 31 Dec. 2023, if a combustion plant is, on 6 Jan. 2011, part of a small isolated system and accounting at that date for at least 35% of the electricity supply within that system, which is unable, due to its technical characteristics, to comply with the emission limit values. Section 50(3) Law No. 184(I)/2013, which corresponds to Art. 33(3) Directive 2010/75/EU. The number of operating hours may be 32,000 in case of a combustion plant with a total rated thermal input of more than 1,500 MW which started operating before 31 Dec. 1986 and fires indigenous solid fuel with a net calorific value of less than 5,800 kJ/kg, a moisture content greater than 45% by weight, a combined moisture and ash content greater than 60% by weight and a calcium oxide content in ash greater than 10%. Section 50(4) Law No. 184(I)/2013, which corresponds to Art. 33(4) Directive 2010/75/EU.
1721. Section 50(1)(b) Law No. 184(I)/2013, which corresponds to Art. 33(1)(b) Directive 2010/75/EU. The date of this paragraph is 1 Jan. 2020 if a combustion plant is, on 6 Jan. 2011, part of a small isolated system and accounting at that date for at least 35% of the electricity supply within that system, which is unable, due to its technical characteristics, to comply with the emission limit values. Section 50(3) Law No. 184(I)/2013, which corresponds to Art. 33(3) Directive 2010/75/EU.
1722. Section 50(1)(c) Law No. 184(I)/2013, which corresponds to Art. 33(1)(c) Directive 2010/75/EU.
1723. Section 50(1)(d) Law No. 184(I)/2013.
1724. Section 50(1)(e) *ibid.*, which corresponds to Art. 33(1)(d) Directive 2010/75/EU.

412. The competent authority is obliged to have communicated at least by 1 January 2016 to the EC a list of any combustion plants that applied for a temporary derogation, including their total rated thermal input, the fuel types used and the applicable emission limit values for sulphur dioxide, nitrogen oxides and dust. The competent authority further communicates to the EC annually a record of the number of operating hours since 1 January 2016.[1725]

413. Similar temporary derogations are foreseen for small isolated systems[1726] and district heating plants[1727] under detailed strict provisions.

V. Changes to Combustion Plants

414. Where a combustion plant is extended, the emission limit values set out in Part 2 of Annex VI apply to the extended part of the plant affected by the change and are set in relation to the total rated thermal input of the entire combustion plant.[1728] In the case of a change to a combustion plant, which may have consequences for the environment and which affects a part of the plant with a rated thermal input of 50 MW or more, the emission limit values as set out in Part 2 of Annex VI apply to the part of the plant which has changed in relation to the total rated thermal input of the entire combustion plant.[1729]

VI. Monitoring of Emissions into Air from Combustion Plants

415. The competent authority ensures that the monitoring of air-polluting substances is carried out in accordance with Part 3 of Annex VI.[1730] Automated monitoring equipment is to be installed. Its installation and functioning are subject to control and annual surveillance tests as set out therein.[1731] Location of sampling or measurement points to be used for the monitoring of emissions is determined by the competent authority.[1732] All monitoring results are recorded, processed and presented in such a way as to enable the competent authority to verify compliance with the operating conditions and emission limit values which are included in the permit.[1733]

1725. Section 50(2) Law No. 184(I)/2013, which corresponds to Art. 33(2) Directive 2010/75/EU. This date is 1 Jan. 2020, if a combustion plant is, on 6 Jan. 2011, part of a small isolated system and accounting at that date for at least 35% of the electricity supply within that system, which is unable, due to its technical characteristics, to comply with the emission limit values. Section 50(3) Law No. 184(I)/2013, which corresponds to Art. 33(3) Directive 2010/75/EU.
1726. Section 51 Law No. 184(I)/2013, which corresponds to Art. 34 Directive 2010/75/EU.
1727. Section 52 Law No. 184(I)/2013, which corresponds to Art. 35 Directive 2010/75/EU.
1728. Section 47(8) Law No. 184(I)/2013, which corresponds to Art. 30(7) Directive 2010/75/EU.
1729. Section 47(9) Law No. 184(I)/2013.
1730. Section 55(1) *ibid.*, which corresponds to Art. 38(1) Directive 2010/75/EU.
1731. Section 55(2) Law No. 184(I)/2013, which corresponds to Art. 38(2) Directive 2010/75/EU.
1732. Section 55(3) Law No. 184(I)/2013, which corresponds to Art. 38(3) Directive 2010/75/EU.
1733. Section 55(4) Law No. 184(I)/2013, which corresponds to Art. 38(4) Directive 2010/75/EU.

VII. Malfunction or Breakdown of Combustion Plants' Abatement Equipment

416. In the event of malfunction or breakdown of the abatement equipment, the operator is obliged to notify the competent authority within forty-eight hours.[1734] In such cases, the competent authority may require the operator to reduce or close down operations if a return to normal operation is not achieved within twenty-four hours or to operate the plant using low-polluting fuels.[1735] The cumulative duration of unabated operation shall not exceed 120 hours in any twelve-month period.[1736] Derogation from said time limits may be granted when there is an overriding need to maintain energy supplies, or when the combustion plant with the breakdown would be replaced for a limited period by another plant which would cause an overall increase in emissions.[1737]

§8. Special Provisions for Waste Incineration Plants and Waste Co-incineration Plants

I. Application for an Industrial Emissions Permit of Waste Incineration Plants and Waste Co-incineration Plants

417. In addition to the aforementioned, a person submitting an application for an industrial emissions permit for a waste incineration plant or a waste co-incineration plant, must include a description of the measures which are envisaged to guarantee that the following requirements are met: the plant is designed, equipped, maintained and operated in such a manner that the explained requirements are met taking into account the categories of waste to be incinerated or co-incinerated;[1738] the heat generated during the incineration and co-incineration process is recovered as far as practicable through the generation of heat, steam or power;[1739] the residues are minimized in their amount and harmfulness and recycled where appropriate;[1740] and the disposal of the residues which cannot be prevented, reduced or recycled is carried out in conformity with Law No. 185(I)/2011 (*see* in this respect paragraphs 140 et seq. above).[1741]

1734. Section 54(2)(a) Law No. 184(I)/2013, which corresponds to Art. 37(2) Directive 2010/75/EU.
1735. Section 54(2)(b) Law No. 184(I)/2013.
1736. Section 54(2)(c) *ibid.*
1737. Section 54(3) *ibid.*
1738. Section 60(a) *ibid.*, which corresponds to Art. 44(a) Directive 2010/75/EU.
1739. Section 60(b) Law No. 184(I)/2013, which corresponds to Art. 44(b) Directive 2010/75/EU.
1740. Section 60(c) Law No. 184(I)/2013, which corresponds to Art. 44(c) Directive 2010/75/EU.
1741. Section 60(d) Law No. 184(I)/2013, which corresponds to Art. 44(d) Directive 2010/75/EU.

418. Equally the provisions on public participation are applicable to applications for an industrial emission permit for waste incineration plants and waste co-incineration plants (*see* in this regard paragraphs 392 et seq. above).[1742]

II. Content of an Industrial Emissions Permit of Waste Incineration Plants and Waste Co-incineration Plants

419. The competent authority ensures that waste incineration plants and waste co-incineration plants are operated and controlled by a natural person, who is competent in managing the plants.[1743] Industrial emissions permits for such plants include operating conditions according to the above stated. In addition to those and despite them being nonexclusive and general, operating conditions regarding the following may be attached thereto: a list of all types of waste which may be treated using at least the types of waste set out in Decree on Solid and Hazardous Waste (List of Wastes),[1744] if possible, and containing information on the quantity of each type of waste, where appropriate;[1745] total waste incinerating or co-incinerating capacity of the plant;[1746] limit values for emissions into air and water;[1747] requirements for the pH, temperature and flow of wastewater discharges;[1748] sampling and measurement procedures and frequencies to be used to comply with the conditions set for emission monitoring;[1749] maximum permissible period of any technically unavoidable stoppages, disturbances or failures of the purification devices or the measurement devices, during which the emissions into the air, water and/or soil water may exceed the prescribed emission limit values.[1750] In addition to those, the permit granted to a waste incineration plant or waste co-incineration plant using hazardous waste addresses the following: a list of the quantities of the different categories of hazardous waste which may be treated, as defined in the waste treatment permit ('άδεια διαχείρισης αποβλήτων') according to Law No. 185(I)/2011 (*see* in this respect paragraphs 157 et seq. above);[1751] and minimum and maximum mass flows of those hazardous wastes, their lowest and maximum calorific values

---

1742. Sections 71(1), 36, 37, 38, 39, 40, 41 and Annex VIII Law No. 184(I)/2013 that correspond to the obligation to enable public participation according to Art. 55(1) Directive 2010/75/EU.
1743. Section 66(7) Law No. 184(I)/2013, which corresponds to Art. 50(7) Directive 2010/75/EU.
1744. Decree on Solid and Hazardous Waste (List of Wastes) ('Περί Στερεών και Επικινδύνων Αποβλήτων (Κατάλογος Αποβλήτων) Διάταγμα') No. 157 of 2003, OG III(I) No. 3686 of 28 Feb. 2003, p. 581, which according to its preamble implemented Council Directive 75/442/EEC on waste, OJ L 194, 25 Jul. 1975, p. 39, Directive 91/156/EEC of 18 Mar. 1991 amending Directive 75/442/EEC on waste, OJ L 78, 26 Mar. 1991, p. 32, and 2000/532/EC: Commission Decision of 3 May 2000 replacing Decision 94/3/EC establishing a list of wastes pursuant to Art. 1(a) of Council Directive 75/442/EEC on waste and Council Decision 94/904/EC establishing a list of hazardous waste pursuant to Art. 1(4) of Council Directive 91/689/EEC on hazardous waste, OJ L 226, 6 Sep. 2000, p. 3.
1745. Section 61(1)(a) Law No. 184(I)/2013, which corresponds to Art. 45(1)(a) Directive 2010/75/EU.
1746. Section 61(1)(b) Law No. 184(I)/2013, which corresponds to Art. 45(1)(b) Directive 2010/75/EU.
1747. Section 61(1)(c) Law No. 184(I)/2013, which corresponds to Art. 45(1)(c) Directive 2010/75/EU.
1748. Section 61(1)(d) Law No. 184(I)/2013, which corresponds to Art. 45(1)(d) Directive 2010/75/EU.
1749. Section 61(1)(e) Law No. 184(I)/2013, which corresponds to Art. 45(1)(e) Directive 2010/75/EU.
1750. Section 61(1)(f) Law No. 184(I)/2013, which corresponds to Art. 45(1)(f) Directive 2010/75/EU.
1751. Section 61(2)(a) Law No. 184(I)/2013, which corresponds to Art. 45(2)(a) Directive 2010/75/EU.

and their maximum contents of polychlorinated biphenyls, pentachlorophenol, chlorine, fluorine, sulphur and heavy metals.[1752] A decree listing the categories of waste to be included in the permit which can be co-incinerated in certain categories of waste co-incineration plants may be issued by the competent authority.[1753]

III. Emission Limit Values for Waste Incineration Plants and Waste Co-incineration Plants

420. Generally, emissions into the air from waste incineration plants and waste co-incineration plants may not exceed the emission limit values set out in this law.[1754,1755] The emission limit values for air and water are regarded as being complied with, if the conditions described in this law[1756] are fulfilled.[1757] If more than 40% of the resulting heat release comes from hazardous waste in a waste co-incineration plant, or the plant co-incinerates untreated mixed municipal waste, specific emission limit values[1758] apply.[1759] Discharges to the aquatic environment of wastewater resulting from the cleaning of waste gases are limited as far as practicable and the concentrations of polluting substances do not exceed specific[1760] emission limit values.[1761]

421. Said emission limit values apply at the point where wastewaters from the cleaning of waste gases are discharged from the waste incineration plant or waste co-incineration plant.[1762] When wastewaters from the cleaning of waste gases are treated outside the waste incineration plant or waste co-incineration plant at a treatment plant intended only for the treatment of this sort of wastewater, the applicable emission limit values[1763] are applied at the point where the wastewaters leave the treatment plant.[1764] In cases that the wastewater from the cleaning of waste gases is treated collectively with other sources of same water, either on site or off site, the operator makes the appropriate mass balance calculations, using specific results of

---

1752. Section 61(2)(b) Law No. 184(I)/2013, which corresponds to Art. 45(2)(b) Directive 2010/75/EU.
1753. Section 61(3) Law No. 184(I)/2013, which corresponds to Art. 45(3) Directive 2010/75/EU.
1754. *See* analytically Annex II Parts 3, 4 and 2 Law No. 184(I)/2013, which corresponds to Annex VI Parts 3, 4 and 2 Directive 2010/75/EU.
1755. Section 62(2)(a) Law No. 184(I)/2013, which corresponds to Art. 46(2) Directive 2010/75/EU.
1756. These are set out in Annex II Part 8 Law No. 184(I)/2013, which corresponds to Annex VI Part 8 Directive 2010/75/EU.
1757. Section 65 Law No. 184(I)/2013, which corresponds to Art. 49 Directive 2010/75/EU.
1758. *See* analytically Annex II Part 3 Law No. 184(I)/2013, which corresponds to Annex VI Part 3 Directive 2010/75/EU.
1759. Section 62(2)(b) Law No. 184(I)/2013, which corresponds to Art. 46(2) Directive 2010/75/EU.
1760. *See* analytically Annex II Part 5 Law No. 184(I)/2013, which corresponds to Annex VI Part 5 Directive 2010/75/EU.
1761. Section 62(3) Law No. 184(I)/2013, which corresponds to Art. 46(3) Directive 2010/75/EU.
1762. Section 62(4)(a) Law No. 184(I)/2013, which corresponds to Art. 46(4) Directive 2010/75/EU.
1763. These are the ones set out in Annex II Part 5 Law No. 184(I)/2013, which corresponds to Annex VI Part 5 Directive 2010/75/EU.
1764. Section 62(4)(b) Law No. 184(I)/2013, which corresponds to Art. 46(4) Directive 2010/75/EU.

the measurements[1765] in order to determine the emission levels in the final wastewater discharge that can be attributed to the wastewater arising from the cleaning of waste gases.[1766] Under no circumstances shall dilution of wastewater take place for the purpose of complying with certain emission limit values.[1767,1768]

422. Where emission limit values are exceeded, the waste incineration plant or waste co-incineration plant or individual furnaces being part of a waste incineration plant or waste co-incineration plant may under no circumstances continue to incinerate waste for an uninterrupted period of more than four hours. The cumulative duration of operation in such conditions over one year may not exceed sixty hours. However, this time limit does not apply to those furnaces which are linked to one single waste gas cleaning device.[1769]

IV. Further Requirements on the Operation of Waste Incineration Plants and Waste Co-incineration Plants

423. This law sets out further requirements on waste incineration plants and waste co-incineration plants, with reference to their operation. These requirements further refer to their design, delivery and reception of waste and residues.

424. Both waste incineration plants and waste co-incineration plants discharge waste gases in a controlled way by means of a stack, the height of which is calculated in such a way as to safeguard human health and the environment.[1770] Further, the sites of such plants, including associated storage areas for waste, are designed and operated in such a way as to prevent the unauthorized and accidental release of any polluting substances into soil, surface water and groundwater. Also, storage capacity is provided for contaminated rainwater runoff from same sites or for contaminated water arising from spillage or firefighting operations. Said storage capacity is adequate to ensure that such waters can be tested and treated before discharge where necessary.[1771]

425. Waste incineration plants have to be operated in such a way as to achieve a level of incineration such that the total organic carbon content of slag and bottom ashes is less than 3% or their loss on ignition is less than 5% of the dry weight of

1765. These are the ones set out in Annex II Part 6 point 2 Law No. 184(I)/2013, which corresponds to Annex VI Part 6 point 2 Directive 2010/75/EU.
1766. Section 62(4)(c) Law No. 184(I)/2013, which corresponds to Art. 46(4) Directive 2010/75/EU.
1767. These are the ones set out in Annex II Part 5 Law No. 184(I)/2013, which corresponds to Annex VI Part 5 Directive 2010/75/EU.
1768. Section 62(4)(d) Law No. 184(I)/2013, which corresponds to Art. 46(4) Directive 2010/75/EU.
1769. Section 62(6)(a), (d) and (c) Law No. 184(I)/2013, which corresponds to Art. 46(6) Directive 2010/75/EU.
1770. Section 62(1) Law No. 184(I)/2013, which corresponds to Art. 46(1) Directive 2010/75/EU.
1771. Section 62(5) Law No. 184(I)/2013, which corresponds to Art. 46(5) Directive 2010/75/EU.

the material. If necessary, waste pre-treatment techniques are used.[1772] Same plants are designed, equipped, built and operated in such a way that the gas resulting from the incineration of waste is raised, after the last injection of combustion air, in a controlled and homogeneous fashion and even under the most unfavourable conditions, to a temperature of at least 850 °C for at least two seconds.[1773] Each combustion chamber of same plants is equipped with at least one auxiliary burner. This burner is switched on automatically when the temperature of the combustion gases after the last injection of combustion air falls below 850 °C or 1,100 °C, as the case may be.[1774] It shall also be used during plant start-up and shut-down operations in order to ensure that those temperatures are maintained at all times during these operations and as long as unburned waste is in the combustion chamber.[1775] Importantly, it is stated that the auxiliary burner may not be fed with fuels which can cause higher emissions than those resulting from the burning of liquefied gas, natural gas or diesel oil ('ακάθαρτο πετρέλαιο εσωτερικής καύσης (diesel oil)') as defined in Law on Specifications for Fuel Products and Fuel.[1776,1777] But, no such term is defined therein. The implemented directive provides a definition,[1778] which corresponds to the term 'gas oil' under Law on Specifications for Fuel Products and Fuel. In view of these, it must be assumed that instead of diesel oil, gas oil is meant in this law.

426. Conditions different than the above explained may be specified by the competent authority in an industrial emissions plant, provided the other requirements of this subchapter are met.[1779] Rules regulating such derogations are set out in a decree issued by the competent authority.[1780] For waste incineration plants, change in the operating conditions may not cause more residues or residues with a higher content

1772. Section 66(1)(a) and (b) Law No. 184(I)/2013, which corresponds to Art. 50(1) Directive 2010/75/EU.
1773. Section 66(2)(a) Law No. 184(I)/2013, which corresponds to Art. 50(2) Directive 2010/75/EU.
1774. Section 66(3)(a) Law No. 184(I)/2013, which corresponds to Art. 50(3) Directive 2010/75/EU.
1775. Section 66(3)(b) Law No. 184(I)/2013.
1776. Law on Specifications for Fuel Products and Fuel ('ο περί Προδιαγραφών Πετρελαιοειδών και Καυσίμων Νόμος') No. 148 of 2003, OG I(I) No. 3758 of 3 Oct. 2003. According to the preamble of this law, it implements Council Directive 1999/32/EC of 26 Apr. 1999 relating to a reduction in the sulphur content of certain liquid fuels and amending Directive 93/12/EEC, OJ L 121, 11 May 1999, p. 13, as amended.
1777. Section 66(3)(c) Law No. 184(I)/2013, which corresponds to Art. 50(3) Directive 2010/75/EU.
1778. *Gas oil* ('πετρέλαιο εσωτερικής καύσης (gas oil)' in Greek, 'gas-oil' in French, 'Gasöl' in German, 'gasolie' in Dutch) means any petroleum-derived liquid fuel, excluding marine fuel, falling within CN code 2710 19 25, 2710 19 29, 2710 19 47, 2710 19 48, 2710 20 17 or 2710 20 19, or any petroleum-derived liquid fuel, excluding marine fuel, of which less than 65% by volume (including losses) distils at 250 °C and of which at least 85% by volume (including losses) distils at 350 °C by the ASTM D86 method. Diesel fuels as defined in point 2 of Art. 2 of Directive 98/70/EC of the European Parliament and of the Council of 13 Oct. 1998 relating to the quality of petrol and diesel fuels are excluded from this definition. Fuels used in non-road mobile machinery and agricultural tractors are also excluded from this definition. Article 2(2) of Directive 1999/32/EC, Art. 50(3) Directive 2010/75/EU.
1779. Section 67(1)(a) Law No. 184(I)/2013, which corresponds to Art. 51(1) Directive 2010/75/EU.
1780. Section 67(1)(b) Law No. 184(I)/2013.

of organic polluting substances compared to those residues which could be expected under the conditions explained above.[1781]

427. Waste co-incineration plants are designed, equipped, built and operated in such a way that the gas resulting from the co-incineration of waste is raised in a controlled and homogeneous fashion and even under the most unfavourable conditions, to a temperature of at least 850 °C for at least two seconds.[1782] Operating conditions, different from the stated in the law regarding the total organic carbon content of slag and bottom ashes, the temperature of the gas resulting from the incineration of waste, the auxiliary burner and the automatic system for prevention of waste feed (section 66(1), (2), (3) and (4) of this law), may be decided by the competent authority and specified in an industrial emissions permit. However, total organic carbon and carbon monoxide emissions must comply with certain emission limit values set out in this law.[1783] Further, emissions of total organic carbon from bark boilers within the pulp and paper industry co-incinerating waste at the place of its production must comply with same emission limit values, as long as they were in operation, had a permit before 28 December 2002, if the competent authority authorizes operating conditions different than the ones stated in this law.[1784]

428. Further, an automatic system is necessary for both waste incineration plants and waste co-incineration plants. This system prevents waste feed in the following situations: at start-up, until the temperature of 850 °C or 1,100 °C, as the case may be or the temperature set out in section 67(1) of this law has been reached;[1785] whenever said temperatures are not maintained;[1786] and whenever the continuous measurements show that any emission limit value is exceeded due to disturbances or failures of the waste gas cleaning devices.[1787] Any heat generated by such plants are recovered as far as practicable.[1788]

429. Regarding delivery and reception of waste, operators of both plants take all necessary precautions in order to prevent or limit as far as practicable the pollution of air, soil, surface water and groundwater as well as other negative effects on the environment, odours and noise, and direct risks to human health.[1789] Prior to accepting waste, the operator of said plants determines the mass of each type of waste, if possible according to the Decree on Solid and Hazardous Waste (List of Wastes) (*see* in this respect paragraph 417 above).[1790] With reference to hazardous waste, if such with a content of more than 1% of halogenated organic substances, expressed

1781. Section 67(2) *ibid.*, which corresponds to Art. 51(2) Directive 2010/75/EU.
1782. Section 66(2)(b) Law No. 184(I)/2013, which corresponds to Art. 50(2) Directive 2010/75/EU.
1783. Annex II Part 3 Law No. 184(I)/2013, which corresponds to Art. Annex VI Part 3 Directive 2010/75/EU.
1784. Section 67(3) Law No. 184(I)/2013, which corresponds to Art. 51(3) Directive 2010/75/EU.
1785. Section 66(4)(a) Law No. 184(I)/2013, which corresponds to Art. 50(4)(a) Directive 2010/75/EU.
1786. Section 66(4)(b) Law No. 184(I)/2013, which corresponds to Art. 50(4)(b) Directive 2010/75/EU.
1787. Section 66(4)(c) Law No. 184(I)/2013, which corresponds to Art. 50(4)(c) Directive 2010/75/EU.
1788. Section 66(5) Law No. 184(I)/2013, which corresponds to Art. 50(5) Directive 2010/75/EU.
1789. Section 68(1) Law No. 184(I)/2013, which corresponds to Art. 52(1) Directive 2010/75/EU.
1790. Section 68(2) Law No. 184(I)/2013, which corresponds to Art. 52(2) Directive 2010/75/EU.

as chlorine, is incinerated or co-incinerated, the temperature required to comply with this shall be at least 1,100 °C.[1791] However, prior to accepting hazardous waste at said plants, the operator collects available information about the waste for the purpose of verifying compliance with the permit requirements specified in this law. That information covers the following: all administrative information on the generating process contained in documents required under Law No. 185(I)/2011, Regulation (EC) No. 1013/2006 and legislation on transport of dangerous goods;[1792] the physical, and as far as practicable, chemical composition of the waste and all other information necessary to evaluate its suitability for the intended incineration process;[1793] the hazardous characteristics of the waste, the substances with which it cannot be mixed, and the precautions to be taken in handling the waste.[1794] In addition to that information, the operator has to carry out the following procedures: checking of the documents required by Law No. 185(I)/2011 (*see* in this respect paragraphs 178 et seq. above), by Regulation (EC) No. 1013/2006, where applicable, and by legislation on transport of dangerous goods;[1795] and taking representative samples, unless inappropriate as far as possible before unloading, to verify conformity with the aforementioned information by carrying out controls and to enable the competent authorities to identify the nature of the wastes treated. These samples are kept for at least one month after the incineration or co-incineration of the waste concerned.[1796]

430. Exemptions from these obligations regarding delivery and reception of waste may be granted by the competent authority to plants which are a part of an activity listed in Annex IV and only incinerate or co-incinerate waste generated within that installation.[1797]

431. Residues must be minimized in their amount and harmfulness. They are also to be recycled, where appropriate, directly in the plant or outside,[1798] whereas transport and intermediate storage of dry residues in the form of dust takes place in such a way as to prevent dispersal of those residues in the environment.[1799] Prior to determining the routes for the disposal or recycling of the residues, appropriate tests are carried out to establish the physical and chemical characteristics and the polluting potential of the residues. Those tests concern the total soluble fraction and heavy metals soluble fraction.[1800]

1791. Section 66(2)(c) Law No. 184(I)/2013, which corresponds to Art. 50(2) Directive 2010/75/EU.
1792. Section 68(3)(b)(i) Law No. 184(I)/2013, which corresponds to Art. 52(3)(a) Directive 2010/75/EU.
1793. Section 68(3)(b)(ii) Law No. 184(I)/2013, which corresponds to Art. 52(3)(b) Directive 2010/75/EU.
1794. Section 68(3)(b)(iii) Law No. 184(I)/2013, which corresponds to Art. 52(3)(c) Directive 2010/75/EU.
1795. Section 68(4)(a) Law No. 184(I)/2013, which corresponds to Art. 52(4)(a) Directive 2010/75/EU.
1796. Section 68(4)(b) Law No. 184(I)/2013, which corresponds to Art. 52(4)(b) Directive 2010/75/EU.
1797. Section 68(5) Law No. 184(I)/2013, which corresponds to Art. 52(5) Directive 2010/75/EU.
1798. Section 69(a) Law No. 184(I)/2013, which corresponds to Art. 53(1) Directive 2010/75/EU.
1799. Section 69(b) Law No. 184(I)/2013, which corresponds to Art. 53(2) Directive 2010/75/EU.
1800. Section 69(c) Law No. 184(I)/2013, which corresponds to Art. 53(3) Directive 2010/75/EU.

V. Changes to Waste Incineration Plants and Waste Co-incineration Plants

432. Along with the general provisions on change of operation of plants, the competent authority periodically reconsiders and, where necessary, updates permit conditions.[1801] With reference to the term 'substantial change', it is being specified that a change of operation of a waste incineration plant or a waste co-incineration plant treating only non-hazardous waste in an installation listed in Annex IV, which involves the incineration or co-incineration of hazardous waste, is regarded as a substantial change.[1802]

VI. Breakdown of Waste Incineration Plants and Waste Co-incineration Plants

433. In the case of a breakdown, the operator of waste incineration plant and waste co-incineration plant reduces or closes down operations as soon as practicable until normal operations can be restored.[1803]

VII. Monitoring of Emissions of Waste Incineration Plants and Waste Co-incineration Plants

434. The competent authority ensures that the monitoring of emissions is carried out in accordance with this law[1804] by attaching the proper operating conditions to the industrial emissions permit.[1805] The location of the waste incineration plants and waste co-incineration plants as well as the functioning of the automated measuring systems are subject to control and to certain annual surveillance tests.[1806,1807] The location of the sampling or measurement points to be used for monitoring emissions is also determined by the competent authority in the industrial emissions permit.[1808] All monitoring results are recorded, processed and presented in such a way as to enable the competent authority to verify compliance with the operating conditions and emission limit values which are included in the permit.[1809] Continuous measurements of emissions into the air of heavy metals, dioxins and furans are to be carried out from the date set by the Commission.[1810]

1801. Section 61(4) Law No. 184(I)/2013, which corresponds to Art. 45(4) Directive 2010/75/EU.
1802. Section 70 Law No. 184(I)/2013, which corresponds to Art. 54 Directive 2010/75/EU.
1803. Section 63 Law No. 184(I)/2013, which corresponds to Art. 47 Directive 2010/75/EU.
1804. The procedure is elaborated in Annex II Part 6 and 7 Law No. 184(I)/2013, which corresponds to Annex VI Parts 6 and 7 Directive 2010/75/EU.
1805. Section 64(1) Law No. 184(I)/2013, which corresponds to Art. 48(1) Directive 2010/75/EU.
1806. These are set out in Annex II Part 6 (1) No. 184(I)/2013, which corresponds to Annex VI Part 6 (1) Directive 2010/75/EU.
1807. Section 64(2)(a) Law No. 184(I)/2013, which corresponds to Art. 48(2) Directive 2010/75/EU.
1808. Section 64(2)(b) Law No. 184(I)/2013, which corresponds to Art. 48(3) Directive 2010/75/EU.
1809. Section 64(3) Law No. 184(I)/2013, which corresponds to Art. 48(4) Directive 2010/75/EU.
1810. Section 64(4) Law No. 184(I)/2013, which corresponds to Art. 48(5) Directive 2010/75/EU.

VIII. Information to the EC

435. For waste incineration plants or waste co-incineration plants with a nominal capacity of two tonnes or more per hour, the report to be forwarded to the EC includes information on the functioning and monitoring of the plant and gives an account of the running of the incineration or co-incineration process and the level of emissions into air and water in comparison with the emission limit values.[1811]

IX. Public Information

436. The competent authority draws up and makes available to the public a list of waste incineration plants or waste co-incineration plants with a nominal capacity of less than two tonnes per hour. This is done in accordance with provisions on public information on activities of Annex IV.[1812] Further, the competent authority makes available to the public the report that forwards to the Commission in accordance with section 71(2) of this law.[1813]

§9. Special Provisions for Plants Producing Titanium Dioxide

I. Application for an Industrial Emissions Permit for Plants Producing Titanium Dioxide

437. The relevant application has to contain the above-stated information (section 9(2) and (3) of this law) as well as a study of EIA (*see* in this respect paragraphs 711 et seq. below).[1814]

II. Content of an Industrial Emissions Permit for Plants Producing Titanium Dioxide

438. The competent authority attaches to industrial emissions permits operating conditions, which ensure that emissions from plants into water do not exceed certain emission limit values[1815,1816] as well as emissions into air do not exceed other emission limit values[1817,1818] along with prevention of emission of acid droplets

1811. Section 71(2) Law No. 184(I)/2013, which corresponds to Art. 55(2) Directive 2010/75/EU.
1812. Sections 71(3) and 36(3) Law No. 184(I)/2013, which correspond to Art. 55(3) Directive 2010/75/EU.
1813. Section 71(2) Law No. 184(I)/2013, which corresponds to Art. 55(2) Directive 2010/75/EU.
1814. Section 83(1) Law No. 184(I)/2013.
1815. Annex IX Part 1 *ibid.*, which corresponds to Annex VIII Part 1 Directive 2010/75/EU.
1816. Section 83(2)(a) Law No. 184(I)/2013, which corresponds to Art. 68 Directive 2010/75/EU.
1817. Annex IX Part 2 Law No. 184(I)/2013, which corresponds to Annex VIII Part 2 Directive 2010/75/EU.
1818. Section 83(2)(b) Law No. 184(I)/2013, which corresponds to Art. 69(2) Directive 2010/75/EU.

from such plants.[1819] Imposed operating conditions further ensure that a systematic control and monitoring of emissions into water is performed for verifying compliance with operating conditions regarding emissions into air and prohibition of emission of acid droplets.[1820] Same applies to monitoring of soil, surface water and groundwater.[1821] Also, regularly and at least yearly, the results of this monitoring are submitted to the competent authority, along with further data deemed necessary for the effective control of plant's compliance with its operating conditions.[1822] For the purpose of monitoring, operating conditions may refer to exact points and methods of sampling,[1823] methods of measurement and analysis for every relevant parameter, in accordance with CEN standards or, if CEN standards are not available, International Organization for Standardization, national or other international standards which ensure the provision of data of an equivalent scientific quality,[1824] and the frequency of sampling, measurements and analysis.[1825]

III. Statutory Prohibitions for Plants Producing Titanium Dioxide

439. The disposal of certain waste into any water body, sea or ocean is prohibited. These are: solid waste;[1826] the mother liquors arising from the filtration phase following hydrolysis of the titanyl sulphate solution from installations applying the sulphate process; including the acid waste associated with such liquors, containing overall more than 0.5% free sulphuric acid and various heavy metals and including such mother liquors which have been diluted until they contain 0.5% or less free sulphuric acid;[1827] waste from installations applying the chloride process containing more than 0.5% free hydrochloric acid and various heavy metals, including such waste which has been diluted until it contains 0.5% or less free hydrochloric acid;[1828] filtration salts, sludges and liquid waste arising from the treatment (concentration or neutralization) of the waste mentioned above, except solid waste, and containing various heavy metals, but not including neutralized and filtered or decanted waste containing only traces of heavy metals and which, before any dilution, has a pH value above 5.5.[1829]

1819. Section 83(2)(c) Law No. 184(I)/2013, which corresponds to Art. 69(1) Directive 2010/75/EU.
1820. Section 83(3)(a) Law No. 184(I)/2013, which corresponds to Art. 70(2) Directive 2010/75/EU.
1821. Section 83(3)(b) Law No. 184(I)/2013, which partially corresponds to Art. 70(1) Directive 2010/75/EU.
1822. Section 83(3)(c) Law No. 184(I)/2013.
1823. Section 83(4)(a) *ibid.*
1824. Section 83(4)(b) *ibid.*, which corresponds to Art. 70(3) Directive 2010/75/EU.
1825. Section 83(4)(c) Law No. 184(I)/2013.
1826. Section 82(a) *ibid.*, which corresponds to Art. 67(a) Directive 2010/75/EU.
1827. Section 82(b) Law No. 184(I)/2013, which corresponds to Art. 67(b) Directive 2010/75/EU.
1828. Section 82(c) Law No. 184(I)/2013, which corresponds to Art. 67(c) Directive 2010/75/EU.
1829. Section 82(d) Law No. 184(I)/2013, which corresponds to Art. 67(d) Directive 2010/75/EU.

§10. Incidents and Accidents

440. Without prejudice to Law No. 189(I)/2007 (*see* in this respect paragraphs 749 et seq. below), in the event of any incident or accident significantly affecting the environment, the operator informs immediately and no longer than twenty-four hours to the competent authority.[1830] He further takes immediately all necessary measures to limit the environmental consequences and to prevent further possible incidents or accidents[1831] and all complementary measures that the competent authority considers necessary to limit the environmental consequences and to prevent further possible incidents or accidents.[1832]

§11. Archive

441. The competent authority keeps an archive, in which information on applications for granting or renewing permits and the relevant decisions are kept.[1833] It also contains information on amendments of permits or their operating conditions,[1834] revocations of permits,[1835] certain information on public participation in activities of Annex IV of this law,[1836] opinions and representations submitted by persons according to provisions on public participation in activities of same annex,[1837] any monitoring reports and results from measurements and analysis taking place according to operating conditions of an industrial permissions permit[1838] and all offences committed along with the imposed sentences.[1839] The archive is at the disposal of the public and may be reviewed at the office of the competent authority during working days and hours.[1840] Retrieving information from the archive is being regulated by Law No. 119(I)/2004 (*see* in this respect paragraphs 136 et seq. above).[1841] In addition to the above, the competent authority keeps online a catalogue containing information and data for all plants that a permit has been granted, including the name of the plant,[1842] nature and type of activity of the plant,[1843] location of same,[1844] date that the permit was issued[1845] and expiration date of same.[1846]

1830. Section 21(a) Law No. 184(I)/2013, which corresponds to Art. 7(a) Directive 2010/75/EU.
1831. Section 21(b) Law No. 184(I)/2013, which corresponds to Art. 7(b) Directive 2010/75/EU.
1832. Section 21(c) Law No. 184(I)/2013, which corresponds to Art. 7(c) Directive 2010/75/EU.
1833. Section 95(1)(a) Law No. 184(I)/2013.
1834. Section 95(1)(b) *ibid.*
1835. Section 95(1)(c) *ibid.*
1836. Sections 95(1)(d) and 36(3) *ibid.*
1837. Sections 95(1)(e) and 37(1)(g) *ibid.*
1838. Section 95(1)(f) *ibid.*
1839. Section 95(1)(g) *ibid.*
1840. Section 95(2) *ibid.*
1841. Section 95(3) *ibid.*
1842. Section 95(4)(a) *ibid.*
1843. Section 95(4)(b) *ibid.*
1844. Section 95(4)(c) *ibid.*
1845. Section 95(4)(d) *ibid.*
1846. Section 95(4)(e) *ibid.*

Part II. Nature Conservation and Management

442. An overview of matters examined under this part is set out in Table 18.

Table 18 Nature Conservation and Management: Overview

	Monuments Cap. 31	*Nature and Wildlife Law No. 153(I)/2003*	*Birds and Games Law No. 152(I)/2003*	*Agricultural*			*Forests Law No. 25(I)/2012*	*Fish Resources*		*Subsoil Cap. 270*
				Law No. 141(I)/2011	*Law No. 34(I)/2014*	*Law No. 32(I)/2006*		*Cap. 135*	*Law No. 117(I)/2000*	
Implemented EU directive (if any) according to the statutory preamble	N/A	92/43/EEC; 83/129/EEC	92/43/EEC; 79/409/EEC[1847];	N/A – but: Regulation (EU) No. 1107/2009	N/A – but: Regulation (EU) No. 528/2012	N/A – but: Regulation (EU) No. 2003/2003	N/A	N/A	N/A	N/A
Competent Ministry	Ministry of Communications and Works	Ministry of Agr., Nat. R. & Env.	Ministry of Interior	Ministry of Agr., Nat. R. & Env.	Ministry of Agr., Nat. R. & Env.	Ministry of Agr., Nat. R. & Env.	Ministry of Agr., Nat. R. & Env.	Ministry of Agr., Nat. R. & Env.	Ministry of Agr., Nat. R. & Env.	N/A – CoM decides
Conservation measures	Declaration as ancient monument (section 6(1)(a))/ decree on neighbourhood of ancient monument (section 11(1))/ protection zone of marine antiquities (section 18C(1))	Special areas of conservation (section 13(1))/ conservation of other habitats, species of local interest and priority (sections 11(8), 12(4), 13(6))/ prohibition re species of community and local interest (section 21)	Special areas of conservation (section 7(2), (3))/regulation of hunting (section 9)/ regulation of trade (section 10)	N/A	N/A	N/A	National forest policy (section 8)/forest management plan (section 18)	N/A	N/A	N/A

1847. This directive has been repealed by Directive 2009/147/EC of the European Parliament and of the Council of 30 Nov. 2009 on the conservation of wild birds, OJ L 20, 26 Jan. 2010, p. 7.

Public participation in these	N/A	opinion (section 15(2))	N/A	N/A	N/A	N/A	Comments (section 21(2))/ comments by local auth. and NGOs (section(5))	N/A	N/A	N/A
Legal remedy against these	Objection with CoM (section 6(2)) and adm. appeal with the CoM (section 8(3))/ adm. appeal with CoM (section 11(3))	N/A	N/A	N/A	N/A	N/A	N/A	N/A	N/A	N/A
Authorization (if any)	Excavations permit (section 14(1))/sea excavations permit (section 18D(1))	N/A	Hunting authorization (section 31)	Authorization of a plant protection product (section 7)	Authorization for biocidal products (section 7)	Authorization for fertilizers (section 7)	Permit for exercising any activity (section 22)	Fishing licence (section 3)	Permit for establishing and operating a fish farm (section 4)	Prospecting permit (section 13)/mining lease (section 23)/quarry permit (section 37)
Suspension or cancellation of this authorization	Upon breach of imposed terms (section 16(1)(g))	N/A	Following conviction for penal offence (section 90(1))	Approval criteria not fulfilled (section 19(2)) and temporary prohibition due to danger to human health, env. and animals (section 13)	Approval criteria not fulfilled (section 19(2)) and temporary prohibition due to danger to human health, env. and animals (section 13)	N/A – but: selling prohibition due to violation of this law or Regulation (section 16)	N/A	no compliance with conditions of the licence (section 3)	no compliance with conditions, fish disease, termination of operations, public policy (section 12)	Violation of this law (section 18)/ closure of mine or quarry due to danger to health and safety of employees (sections 31, 40)

	Monuments Cap. 31	*Nature and Wildlife Law No. 153(I)/2003*	*Birds and Games Law No. 152(I)/2003*	*Agricultural*			*Forests Law No. 25(I)/2012*	*Fish Resources*		*Subsoil Cap. 270*
				Law No. 141(I)/2011	*Law No. 34(I)/2014*	*Law No. 32(I)/2006*		*Cap. 135*	*Law No. 117(I)/2000*	
Sanctions	Penal (sections 26, 27, 4, 8, 10, 11, 11A, 14, 18, 18B–18D)	Penal (sections 39, 40)	Penal (sections 6, 8–11, 13, 77, 88), other (section 90)	Penal (section 20), adm. (section 19), other (section 20)	Penal (section 20), adm. (section 19), other (section 20).		Penal (sections 32–39, 41, 50, 51)), adm. (section 42), other (53, 42)	Penal (sections 3, 3A, 5, 7B, 9), adm. (sections 3, 8)	Penal (section 18), other (section 18, 18A)	Penal (sections 43, 13, 15, 16, 21–23, 33, 37), adm. (sections 28, 32, 40, 43A), other (section 43)
Archive	N/A	Yes (section 9)	N/A	Yes (section 11)	N/A	Yes (section 14)	Yes (sections 62, 63)	N/A	N/A	N/A
Reports	N/A	Every six years – published on OG and sent to Eur.Com. (section 27)	Every three years sent to Eur.Com. (section 14) and yearly on derogations (section 12(3))	N/A	N/A	N/A	N/A	N/A	N/A	N/A

Abbreviations:

adm. = appeal administrative appeal.
CoM = Council of Ministers.
env. = environment.
Eur.Com. = European Commission.
Ministry of Agr., Rur. Dev. & Env. = Ministry of Agriculture, Rural Development and Environment.
OG = Official Gazette.
re = regarding.

Chapter 1. Monuments and Landscapes

443. Monuments are protected in Cyprus via Antiquities Law[1848] (hereinafter 'Cap. 31'). This law repealed the Antiquities Law No. IV of 1905.[1849]

§1. Objective

444. This law does not explicitly state its objective.

§2. Area of Application

445. No provision of this law specifies its area of application. However, some notions are pivotal for the proper application thereof. More specifically, *ancient monument* ('αρχαίο μνημείο') means any object, building or site specified in the First or Second Schedule to this Law, as well as any other object, building or site in respect of which the Council of Ministers has made a decree under section 6 of this law. It shall also include any part of the adjoining land which may be required for the purpose of fencing, covering or otherwise preserving the monument from injury, as also the means of access to such monument. *Antiquity* ('αρχαιότητα') stands for any object, whether movable or immovable or a part of the soil, which has been constructed, shaped, inscribed, erected, excavated or otherwise produced or modified by human agency earlier than the last hundred years that was found, discovered or excavated in Cyprus, including the sea zones[1850] of Cyprus, together with any part thereof which has at a later date been added, reconstructed or restored. Especially for objects of ecclesiastical or popular art of great archaeological or cultural or historical importance, instead of the aforementioned hundred years threshold, the year 1940 shall be taken into consideration irrespective of their place of construction or origin.[1851] However, it is explicitly foreseen that no church, mosque or site used for religious observances, being the property of a religious community or the Evcaf Department,[1852] shall be inserted in the First Schedule or acquired under any provision of this law.[1853]

1848. A Law to Consolidate and Amend the Law Relating to Antiquities No. 41 of 1935, CG No. 2484 of 31 Dec. 1935, p. 979.

1849. A Law to Consolidate and amend the Law Relating to the Ancient Monuments and Antiquities of Cyprus and to provide Museum No. IV of 1905, CG No. 825 of 19 May 1905, pp. 5614, 5626. This law repealed the ottoman law of 20 Sefer 1291 and Law No. XIV of 1891.

1850. *Sea zones* ('θαλάσσιες ζώνες') means territorial sea, contiguous zone, exclusive economic zone and the continental self of Cyprus. Section 2 Cap. 31.

1851. Section 2 *ibid.*

1852. The Evcaf Department is the body supervising all vakfs, whose being religious trusts or pious foundations established for serving the common good and not unusually had the ownership of religious sites, buildings and places of warship. They are regulated by Cap. 337, although their administration is *temporarily* exercised by the Minister of Interior since 1991 under Law on Turkish-Cypriot Assets (Administration and Other Matters) (Temporary Provisions) of 1991.

1853. Section 24 Cap. 31.

§3. COMPETENT AUTHORITIES

I. The Minister of Communications and Works

446. The Minister of Communications and Works is a competent authority in this law. As it will be explained below, he is competent in defining the areas, where the use of organs for the purpose of discovering ancient monuments and antiquities is permitted.[1854]

II. The Council of Ministers

447. The Council of Ministers has wide powers in issuing regulations regarding a wide variety of matters. These may be any issue on discovering antiquities with the use of modern technology ('ανιχνευτών ή άλλων οργάνων'),[1855] particulars on granting permits,[1856] defining operating conditions that may be attached to a permit,[1857] operating conditions especially for permit for excavations,[1858] along with their validity period,[1859] and specifying the duties and obligations of permit holders.[1860] Regulations may further specify issuance of permits for using ancient monuments and museums for public performances, cultural events, expositions and ceremonies[1861] as well as production and commerce of photos, movies, copies and miniatures of ancient monuments and antiquities.[1862] They may further set out the opening hours and the entrance fees to museums.[1863] Regulations may also specify the establishment of a fund (to be called *The Antiquities Fund*) into which the moneys standing to the credit of the Cyprus Antiquities Fund established under the Antiquities Laws 1905–1928 and all legacies, donations and subscriptions shall be paid and prescribing the objects for which and the manner in which the moneys in such Fund may be expended.[1864] Interestingly, penal provisions that may lead to a monetary fine of up to EUR 15,000 and/or imprisonment of up to nine months may be set out in regulations.[1865] Lastly, these may refer generally to the better carrying out of the provisions of this law and marine archaeology.[1866]

1854. Section 10(4) *ibid.*
1855. Section 34B *ibid.*
1856. Section 35(a) *ibid.*
1857. Section 35(b) *ibid.*
1858. Section 35(h) *ibid.*
1859. Section 35(c) *ibid.*
1860. Section 35(d) *ibid.*
1861. Section 35(e) *ibid.*
1862. Section 35(f) *ibid.*
1863. Section 35(i) *ibid.*
1864. Section 35(j) *ibid.*
1865. Section 35(g) *ibid.*
1866. Section 35(k) and (l) *ibid.*

III. The Director of Antiquities

448. The Director of Antiquities ('Διευθυντής Αρχαιοτήτων') examines whether discovered antiquities are to be acquired for museums,[1867] supervises and studies antiquities in possession of third parties,[1868] advises the Council of Ministers in matters related to ancient monuments,[1869] authorizes modifications or any actions with reference to ancient monuments and provides subsidies to their conservation,[1870] advises on authorization of constructions, including placing of signs and cutting of trees in neighbourhoods of ancient monuments,[1871] performs excavations to the purpose of discovering antiquities[1872] and authorizes any such excavations by third parties,[1873] authorizes excavations within the exclusive economic zone and the continental shelf of Cyprus[1874] and controls the museums of Cyprus.[1875]

§4. Provisions on Finding Antiquities and Establishing Ancient Monuments

449. Generally, all antiquities lying undiscovered at the date of coming into operation of this law in or upon any land are state property.[1876] Equally state property are ancient monuments set out in the First Schedule[1877] of this law.[1878] Antiquities belonging to the state may be made loans to the governing bodies of museums or learned societies abroad by the Council of Ministers. Provided that the party to whom the loan is made shall at their own expense make adequate provision for the preservation, insurance and return of such antiquities.[1879]

450. Apart from that, antiquities may be accidentally discovered, ancient monuments may be declared as such and discovered while performing excavations. All of these are elaborated below.

1867. Section 5 *ibid.*
1868. Section 32 *ibid.*
1869. Section 6(1)(a) *ibid.*
1870. Section 8 *ibid.*
1871. Section 11(2) *ibid.*
1872. Section 13 *ibid.*
1873. Section 14(1) *ibid.*
1874. Section 18D(1) *ibid.*
1875. Section 21 *ibid.*
1876. Section 3 *ibid. See The Attorney-General of the Republic v. Mouzouris* (1996) 2 CLR 66.
1877. The First Schedule, as well as the Second Schedule, have not been translated in Greek as the translation was impossible ('εξ αντικειμένου αδύνατη') according to the note no. 2 of the Service of Revision and Consolidation of the Cyprus Legislation. The grounds for such difficulty are not clear. In any case, the original provisions of the Schedule as issued in 1935 provide with sufficient precision the ancient monuments in Nicosia District (under Part A), in Larnaca District (under Part B), in Limassol District and in Famagusta District (under Part C) in Paphos District (under Part D) and in Kyrenia District (under Part E).
1878. Section 7 Cap. 31.
1879. Section 30 *ibid.*

I. Accidental Discovery

451. Any person, who accidentally discovers an antiquity whether in or upon his own land or land being the property of another person or of the state without being in possession of a permit to excavate in accordance with this law, gives notice of this discovery. If same is portable, he shall deliver the antiquity to the local authorities, the police authorities, the closest archaeological museum or the archaeological museum of Cyprus and shall at the same time sufficiently indicate or describe the place where he found it.[1880] The authorized person, who takes delivery of the antiquity gives to the person, who delivers it a receipt containing a full description of such antiquity and shall send a duplicate of the receipt to the Director and shall, pending instructions from him, retain the antiquity in safe custody.[1881]

452. The Director upon receiving notice of the discovery of an antiquity considers whether such antiquity should be acquired for the Cyprus Museum or for any other archaeological museum. If it appears to him that the antiquity should be so acquired, he pays to the finder such sum as a complementary amount ('φιλοδώρημα') that appears to him to be reasonable under the circumstances.[1882]

II. Declaration as an Ancient Monument

453. Any object, building or site in any soil, which is considered to be of public interest by reason of the historic, architectural, traditional, artistic or archaeological interest attaching thereto, may be declared to be an ancient monument by a decree of the Council of Ministers following a recommendation of the Director. At the same time, it shall be declared whether such monument shall be added to the First or to the Second Schedule[1883] to this law, as the case may be.[1884] Necessary prerequisite for such declaration is for the Director to publish a notice in the Official Gazette of the proposed declaration not less than one month before the making of the decree. Any person, whose interests may be prejudicially affected by the proposed declaration may, within the period of one month aforesaid, lodge an objection for consideration by the Council of Ministers, whose decision thereon shall be final and conclusive.[1885] Lastly, any ancient monument specified in, or added to, either Schedule may also be transferred to the other Schedule to this law by a decree of the Council of Ministers.[1886]

1880. Section 4(1) *ibid.*
1881. Section 4(2) *ibid.*
1882. Section 5 *ibid.*
1883. The Second Schedule sets out in great detail ancient monuments in Nicosia District (under Part A), in Larnaca District (under Part B), in Limassol District (under Part C), in Famagusta District (under Part D), in Paphos District (under Part E) and in Kyrenia District (under Part F).
1884. Section 6(1)(a) Cap. 31. *See Antoniou v. The Republic* a.o. (1975) 3 CLR 169; *Allayioti Despina Georghiou v. The Republic* (1983) 3 CLR 251.
1885. Section 6(2) Cap. 31. *See Zevedeou* v. *The Republic* (1972) 3 CLR 236.
1886. Section 6(1)(b) Cap. 31. *See Mavronikola a.o. v. The Republic* (1994) 4 CLR 1238.

454. With reference to ancient monuments specified in the Second Schedule to this law, it is set out that no person beneficially interested therein, or in any other ancient monument as may from time to time be added thereto, make any alterations, additions or repairs affecting its architectural character to such ancient monument or fell any tree growing within the boundaries of the same save in accordance with the terms of a permit in writing from the Director previously obtained.[1887] Should any person be dissatisfied with any term imposed by the Director in such permit, this person may within one month from the date of notification of the decision of the Director, file an administrative appeal ('ιεραρχική προσφυγή') with the Council of Ministers.[1888] For the purpose of assisting any such person in the maintenance, preservation or restoration of such monument, the Director may, with the approval of the Minister, grant to same person such sum as to the Director may seem fit.[1889]

455. Where any object, building or site, which is privately owned, is declared to be an ancient monument and inserted in the First Schedule to this law, and hence becomes state property, compensation is payable to the owner thereof. Said compensation is payable in the like manner and in accordance with the provisions of the law for the time being in force relating to the compulsory acquisition of land for public purposes.[1890] Provided that in assessing any compensation payable for such monument, no regard shall be had to its historical, architectural, traditional, artistic or archaeological value, unless the owner can prove that he paid in good faith a higher price for the monument on account of such value.[1891]

456. Special provision ensures that buildings in the neighbourhood of an ancient monument as regards height and style of architecture are in keeping with the character and style of that monument and that the amenities thereof may be preserved. The Council of Ministers orders by a notice in the Official Gazette that, within such area as may be specified therein, no building shall be erected, reconstructed or repaired and no tree shall be felled save in accordance with the terms of a permit in writing from the Director of the Department of Urban Planning and Housing ('Τμήμα Πολεοδομίας και Οικήσεως'), the Urban Planning Authorities ('Πολεοδομικές Αρχές') and the District Officer ('Έπαρχος') previously

1887. Section 8(1) Cap. 31. *Michael v. The Improvement Board of Dhali Through Its Chairman the District Officer Nicosia a.a.* (1969) 3 CLR 112; *The Attorney-General v. Charalambous a.o.* (1983) 1 CLR 431; *S Raftis Co Ltd v. The Municipality of Paphos* (1985) 3 CLR 1664; *Ieros Naos Chryseleousis Strovolou v. The Republic* (1989) 3 CLR 3074; *The Attorney-General v. Argyrides a.o.* (1996) 1 CLR 1164.

1888. Section 8(3) Cap. 31.

1889. Section 8(2) *ibid.*

1890. This is being regulated by Law on Compulsory Acquisition for Public Purpose ('Νόμος Προνοών περί Αναγκαστικής Απαλλοτριώσεως Δια Δημόσιαν Ωφέλειαν') No. 15 of 1962, OG I(I) No. 133 of 1 Mar. 1962, p. 275, as amended. *See Kittou v. The Republic* (1971) 1 CLR 129; *Agroti v. EAC* (1981) 3 CLR 503; *Hadjioannou v. The Republic* (1983) 3 CLR 536; *Christophidou v. The Republic* (1986) 3 CLR 539; *Christophidou v. The Republic* (1988) 3 CLR 862; *Tsaggarides a.o. v. The Republic* (1990) 3 CLR 3392; *Stavrides v. The Republic* (1992) 3 CLR 303; *The Attorney-General v. Kouloumou a.o.* (1995) 1 CLR 728.

1891. Section 9 Cap. 31.

obtained.[1892] Before issuing such a permit, the District Officer requires the applicant to submit for the consideration of the District Officer and the Director such plans, sections and drawings as they may see fit. The District Officer consults the Director on this decision. In case of disagreement, the matter shall be referred to the Minister and the Minister of Interior for reaching a final decision. Lastly, terms may be attached to said permit with reference to preserving the character and style of the ancient monument, as these are specified in each permit.[1893] Any person, who is dissatisfied with any term imposed by the District Officer in said permit, may within one month from the date of notification of the decision of the District Officer, file an administrative appeal[1894] with the Council of Ministers.[1895] Should further the Council of Ministers be satisfied that in order to preserve the amenities of an ancient monument, it is desirable that no building should be erected upon any land in the proximity of such ancient monument, it may direct that such land be acquired on payment of such amount by way of compensation as may be agreed upon. In default of agreement the amount of compensation is determined in the like manner and in accordance with the Law on Compulsory Acquisition for Public Purpose.[1896] The same applies where he is satisfied that any building in the proximity of an ancient monument should be demolished. Provided that in assessing any compensation payable for such land or building no regard shall be had to any artificial rise in the value thereof due to any speculative dealings, which may have taken place in regard to such land or buildings after the commencement of this law.[1897]

III. Excavations

457. For the purpose of discovering antiquities, the Director may carry out excavations[1898] and in fact compulsory acquire land for this purpose.[1899] He may further authorize the performance of excavations. In particular, no person excavates or causes excavations to be made whether on his own land or elsewhere for the purpose of discovering antiquities without a permit in writing on that behalf first obtained from the Director.[1900] The prerequisites that must be fulfilled for such a permit to be granted are the following: competence by training and experience of the applicant to carry out excavations in accordance with the most recent scientific

---

1892. Section 11(1) *ibid*. *See Christophides v. The Republic* (1984) 1 CLR 796; *Galatiani Ltd v. The Republic* (1995) 4 CLR 917.
1893. Section 11(2) Cap. 31.
1894. In the original Greek text, mention to ***έφεση***, which means appeal, is being made. However, having in mind the fact that this may only be filed against a judgment of a First Instance Court with the Supreme Court of Cyprus as well as that it is not unusual for superior administrative bodies to review the decisions of the inferior ones with the remedy of ***ιεραρχική προσφυγή***, that being an administrative appeal, as per the provision of s. 8(3) Cap. 31, it may be safely assumed that the latter is meant.
1895. Section 11(3) Cap. 31.
1896. *See* in this respect footnote 1658 above.
1897. Section 12 Cap. 31.
1898. Section 13 *ibid*.
1899. Section 17 *ibid*.
1900. Section 14(1) *ibid*.

methods;[1901] recommendation of the applicant by an archaeological society or institution of repute;[1902] adequate provision has been made for the scientific publication of the results of any previous excavation on which the applicant has been engaged;[1903] the applicant or the person, society or institution on whose behalf he acts is prepared to expend on the proposed excavations a sum of money which in the opinion of the Director is sufficient to obtain satisfactory results;[1904] and the proposed excavations will not cause any damage or inconvenience to the inhabitants of the place, where it is proposed to excavate or to any place dedicated to religion or to any cemetery, school, watercourse, irrigation work or public road, or that if such damage is likely to be caused, adequate provision has been made for the payment of compensation therefor.[1905]

458. The content of a permit to excavate as well as relevant statutory obligations are set out in this law. In particular, every permit shall state the period, during which it shall remain in force, which period shall not exceed two years.[1906] Upon the expiration of the validity period of the permit, the Director may renew it for a further period not exceeding two years, either upon the same terms or upon such other terms as he may think fit.[1907] Every such permit shall be deemed to be subject to the following conditions: arranging the terms of entering upon the land with the owner of the land by the permit holder, if the land within which the permit is granted is private property;[1908] taking all reasonable measures for the preservation of the antiquities discovered by the permit holder as well as keeping detailed records and plans of the excavations along with photos thereof;[1909] all archaeological findings discovered shall be in possession ('περιέρχονται στην κατοχή') of the Cyprus Museum, along with the originals of the diaries, plans and negatives of photos without any payment;[1910] the licensee shall furnish plans and photographs of his excavations to the Director and shall, when requested by the Director, furnish him with lists of all the antiquities discovered and any additional information relating thereto which the Director may require;[1911] the holder of the licence shall supply the Director with two copies of any preliminary reports relating to the excavations;[1912] he shall further publish within a period of two years after the completion of the excavations, unless this period is extended by the Director, an adequate scientific report on the results thereof and shall supply the Director with two copies of this report and of any other publications relating thereto;[1913] and any other terms which the

1901. Section 15(1)(a) *ibid.*
1902. Section 15(1)(b) *ibid.*
1903. Section 15(1)(c) *ibid.*
1904. Section 15(1)(d) *ibid.*
1905. Section 15(1)(e) *ibid.*
1906. Section 16(1) *ibid.*
1907. Section 16(2) *ibid.*
1908. Section 16(1)(a) *ibid.*
1909. Section 16(1)(b) *ibid.*
1910. Section 16(1)(c) *ibid.*
1911. Section 16(1)(d) *ibid.*
1912. Section 16(1)(e) *ibid.*
1913. Section 16(1)(f) *ibid.*

Council of Ministers may by regulations from time to time prescribe.[1914] It is lastly foreseen that, save with the written permission of the Director, no person shall during any excavations destroy, damage, remove or conceal any antiquities or any human, animal or other remains discovered during such excavations.[1915]

459. In case of a breach of any of the terms upon which the permit is granted, the Director may suspend or cancel this permit. Where the permit is cancelled, the holder thereof shall forfeit his claim to any share of the antiquities excavated by him.[1916] Further, in the event of cancellation of the permit or upon failure of the holder of the licence to comply with the aforementioned obligation relating to publication, the Director is entitled to publish a report on the results of the excavations. For this purpose, he may make use of any preliminary reports supplied by said holder.[1917]

IV. Antiquities in the Sea

460. All antiquities lying within the exclusive economic zone and/or the continental shelf of Cyprus are state property, regardless of whether them being discovered or not at the time of issuing of this law.[1918] Prospecting for the discovery of antiquities or excavations within said zones may be performed if a written permit has been previously issued by the Director.[1919] The relevant application must be filed at least two months prior to the suggested date of initiating prospecting or excavations.[1920] The requirements that need to be considered by the competent authority prior to deciding on this application[1921] are the same as the ones explained for the permit for excavations (*see* in this respect paragraphs 455 et seq. above). Operating conditions may be attached to the permit. These may relate to: the duration of the permit;[1922] the persons authorized to perform prospecting or excavation;[1923] the geographical limits within which prospecting or excavations may be performed;[1924] the protection measures for the antiquities to be discovered; the keeping of records of the performed prospecting or excavations and the mandatory documentation via photographs or other similar images;[1925] the measures for avoiding or diminishing intervention with exploitation of natural resources, fishery or

1914. Section 16(1)(i) *ibid.*
1915. Section 18(1) *ibid.*
1916. Section 16(1)(g) *ibid.*
1917. Section 16(1)(h) *ibid.*
1918. Section 18A *ibid.*
1919. Section 18D(1) *ibid.*
1920. Section 18D(2) *ibid.*
1921. Section 18D(3)(a)–(e) *ibid.*
1922. Section 18D(4)(a) *ibid.*
1923. Section 18D(4)(b) *ibid.*
1924. Section 18D(4)(c) *ibid.*
1925. Section 18D(4)(d) *ibid.*

other marine activities;[1926] measures for prevention, reduction and control of environmental pollution;[1927] the publication of sufficient scientific report on the results of prospecting or excavations;[1928] and the operation of an AIS system or another one that transmits full and proper data of the ship performing prospecting or excavations for the purpose of monitoring by the authorities of Cyprus.[1929] The holder of the permit bears the statutory obligation to daily inform the competent authorities on the position of the ship performing the authorized activities and not to interfere with established shipping lanes.[1930] Especially removal of wrecks that are antiquities prerequisites for the granting of a special permit by the Director.[1931] Lastly, should any person discover antiquities within said marine areas and not hold this permit, he is obliged to immediately notify the Director regarding this discovery and provide all relevant information, including the geographical coordinates of their location.[1932]

461. Should antiquities lie within an area of the exclusive economic zone and/or the continental shelf of Cyprus that must be protected due to their historical, archaeological or cultural value, this area may be declared as a Protection Zone of Marine Antiquities ('Ζώνη Προστασίας Ενάλιων Αρχαιοτήτων') by the Council of Ministers and a previous recommendation of the Director.[1933] Within a Protection Zone of Marine Antiquities, the following activities are forbidden: to construct any installation, artificial island or other construction;[1934] to hold a vessel at anchor;[1935] to perform any fishing or diving activities that may cause damage or other intervention to antiquities;[1936] to drill, use explosives or introduce harmful substances into the marine environment;[1937] and to perform any action that may cause damage or other interference with antiquities.[1938]

§5. Ensuring Compliance

462. Compliance with the aforementioned statutory obligations is ensured through penal sanctions, which are elaborated below.

463. Trading of antiquities is a penal offence, which may impose imprisonment of maximum of five years or a monetary fine of up to EUR 45,000.[1939] Exporting

1926. Section 18D(4)(e) *ibid.*
1927. Section 18D(4)(f) *ibid.*
1928. Section 18D(4)(g) *ibid.*
1929. Section 18D(4)(h) *ibid.*
1930. Section 18D(8) and (9) *ibid.*
1931. Section 18D(6) *ibid.*
1932. Section 18B(1) *ibid.*
1933. Section 18C(1) *ibid.*
1934. Section 18C(2)(a) *ibid.*
1935. Section 18C(2)(b) *ibid.*
1936. Section 18C(2)(c) *ibid.*
1937. Section 18C(2)(d) *ibid.*
1938. Section 18C(2)(e) *ibid.*
1939. Section 26(2) *ibid.*

antiquities is also a penal offence. If the accused is found guilty by a court of law, the same penalties may be imposed.[1940] Any person excavating, ensuring the performance of excavations, sells or trades antiquities excavated in violation of this law, commits an offence. Conviction by a court of law may result into him being imprisoned for a period of up to five years and/or a monetary fine of up to EUR 45,000.[1941] Damage, transportation or concealing of any antiquities or any human, animal or other remains found during excavations may lead to imprisonment for up to three years and/or a monetary fine of up to EUR 30,000.[1942] Also, noncompliance with the obligations foreseen for any person, who is not a permit holder and accidentally discovers an antiquity, constitutes a penal offence that may lead to imprisonment for up to one year and/or a monetary fine of up to EUR 30,000.[1943] Especially with reference to antiquities in the sea, if their accidental discovery by a person not holding a permit is not notified to the Director, it may lead upon conviction to a monetary fine of up to EUR 100,000 and/or imprisonment for up to three years.[1944] The same penalties may lead any intervention or cause of damage to antiquities within the Protection Zone of Marine Antiquities[1945] or violation of the operating conditions of the granted permit for prospecting and excavations in the sea.[1946]

464. Penal sanctions also ensure compliance with the provisions on ancient monuments. More specifically, any person proceeding with amendment of ancient monuments in the absence of a written permit by the Director, commits an offence that may lead to a monetary fine of up to EUR 15,000 as well as bearing the financial burden of restoring its former condition, as decided by the Director.[1947] In these cases, the relevant works of amendment, addition, restoration, demolition, erection or building may be temporarily paused until the final judgment of the court, if an application for an interim order pursuant to the legislation on civil procedure is filed with the court and this deems it proper to grant it.[1948] Any person that destroys, causes damage or deterioration of any ancient monument or antiquity, or writes, sketches or engraves any writing, sketch or form on an ancient monument or antiquity commits a penal offence, that upon conviction may lead to imprisonment for up to three years and/or a monetary fine of up to EUR 45,000.[1949] If an animal enters an ancient monument of the First Schedule to this law, its owner and its possessor, if applicable, may be imprisoned for up to nine months and/or condemned to a financial penalty of up to EUR 4,500, as well as ordered to pay compensation

1940. Section 27(4) *ibid.*
1941. Section 14(2) *ibid. See The Attorney-General v. Sidki Mahmout* (1962) CLR 181; *Charalambous Petrou Patataris v. The Police* (1993) 2 CLR 58.
1942. Section 18(2) Cap. 31.
1943. Section 4(3) *ibid. See The Attorney-General v. Mouzouris* (1996) 2 CLR 66.
1944. Section 18B(2) Cap. 31.
1945. Section 18C(3) *ibid.*
1946. Section 18D(10) *ibid.*
1947. Section 8(4) *ibid.*
1948. Section 11A(1) and (2) *ibid.*
1949. Section 10(1) *ibid. See Polykarpou v. The Police* (1967) 2 CLR 152.

('αποζημιώσεις'), as the court may deem fit.[1950] The same penalties faces any person that litters an ancient monument listed in the First Schedule, and may be additionally ordered to remove at his own expenses the litter caused by such act or redress the costs of the Director for removing the same.[1951] Any person, who erects, builds, restores or demolishes a building in violation of the provisions of the neighbourhood of an ancient monument, commits a penal offence and may be convicted of a monetary fine of up to EUR 15,000 in addition to performing any necessary actions relevant to such building within a specific time frame, as these are defined in the court order. If the convicted person does not comply with the contents of the court order, further fine of up to EUR 750 may be imposed along with the District Officer carrying out the specified actions and claiming the expenses from the convicted person as a civil debt owed to the state. These penalties may also be imposed, if, during authorized erection, building, restoration or demolition of a building deviation from the permitted actions takes place.[1952] During this penal trial, an interim order under laws on civil procedure, suspending any alteration, restoration, construction or demolition until reaching a final decision may be granted.[1953]

1950. Section 10(2) Cap. 31.
1951. Section 10(3) *ibid.*
1952. Section 11(4)(a) and (b) *ibid.*
1953. Section 11A(1) and (2) *ibid.*

Chapter 2. Parks and Reserves

465. Thematic parks are regulated to the extent that a preliminary report on environmental impact is requested for their construction (*see* in this respect paragraphs 738 et seq. below). Reserves ('πόροι') are regulated in Law No. 25(I)/2012 (*see* in this respect paragraphs 561 et seq. below), whereas natural resources ('φυσικοί πόροι'), those being protected species and natural habitats, water and land,[1954] are protected under Law No. 189(I)/2007 (*see* in this respect paragraphs 749 et seq. below).

1954. Section 2 Law No. 189(I)/2007, which implements Art. 2(12) Directive 2004/35/EC. The French term is 'ressource naturelle', the German one 'natürliche Ressource' and the Dutch one 'natuurlijke rijkdommen'.

Chapter 3. Wildlife Protection

466. Wildlife is protected by Law on Protection and Management of Nature and Wildlife[1955] (hereinafter 'Law No. 153(I)/2003'), which implements certain directives of the EU,[1956] and Law on Protection and Management of Wild Birds and Games[1957] (hereinafter 'Law No. 152(I)/2003'), which also implements directives of the EU.[1958]

§1. Nature and Wildlife

I. Objective

467. The objective of this law is to ensure biodiversity through the conservation of natural habitats and of wild fauna and flora,[1959] maintaining or restoring, at favourable conservation status, natural habitats and species of wild fauna and flora of Community interest[1960] and prohibition of commercial import of leathers of certain seal pup and products therefrom.[1961]

II. Area of Application

468. No provision specifies the area of application of this law.

1955. Law on Protection and Management of Nature and Wildlife ('ο περί Προστασίας και Διαχείρισης της Φύσης και της 'Αγριας Ζωής Νόμος') No. 153 of 2003, OG I(I) No. 3758 of 3 Oct. 2003, p. 1149, as amended.
1956. Council Directive 92/43/EEC of 21 May 1992 on the conservation of natural habitats and of wild fauna and flora, OJ L 206, 22 Jul. 1992, p. 7, as amended; Council Directive 83/129/EEC of 28 Mar. 1983 concerning the importation into Member States of skins of certain seal pups and products derived therefrom, OJ L 91, 9 Apr. 1983, p. 30, as amended.
1957. Law on Protection and Management of Wild Birds and Games ('ο περί Προστασίας και Διαχείρισης 'Αγριων Πτηνών και Θηραμάτων Νόμος') No. 152 of 2003, OG I(I) No. 3758 of 3 Oct. 2003, p. 1030, as amended.
1958. Council Directive 92/43/EEC of 21 May 1992 on the conservation of natural habitats and of wild fauna and flora, OJ L 206, 22 Jul. 1992, p. 7, as amended; Council Directive 79/409/EEC of 2 Apr. 1979 on the conservation of wild birds, OJ L 103 of 25 Apr. 1979, p. 1, which has been however repealed by Directive 2009/147/EC of the European Parliament and of the Council of 30 Nov. 2009 on the conservation of wild birds, OJ L 20, 26 Jan. 2010, p. 7, as amended.
1959. Section 3(1)(a) Law No. 153(I)/2003, which corresponds to Art. 2(1) Directive 92/43/EEC.
1960. Section 3(1)(b) Law No. 153(I)/2003, which corresponds to Art. 2(2) Directive 92/43/EEC. *See* in this respect: Case C-441/03, *Commission of the European Communities v. Kingdom of the Netherlands*, [2005] ECR I-03043 [relevant review: M Gellermann, *Habitatschutz in der Perspektive des Europäischen Gerichtshofs*, 27 NuR 433 (2005); J.M. Verschuuren, *Hof van Justitie EG, 14-04-2005, C-441/03 (met noot)*, 1 M en R 443(2005)].
1961. Section 3(1)(c) Law No. 153(I)/2003, which corresponds to Art. 1(1) Directive 83/129/EEC.

III. Competent Authorities

A. The Minister of Agriculture, Rural Development and Environment

469. The Minister of Agriculture, Rural Development and Environment, when taking any measure under this law, takes account of economic, social and cultural requirements and regional and local characteristics.[1962]

B. The Council of Ministers

470. The Council of Ministers has the power to issue regulations for specifying any matter that needs to be specified, as well as for fully and effectively carrying out this law. In particular, and without prejudice to generally of the foregoing power, such regulations may provide for all or any of the following subjects: establishment of a system of licences for taking specimens or of quotas of fauna and flora of Community interest;[1963] and regulation of the purchase, sale, offering for sale, keeping for sale or transport for sale of specimens of fauna and flora of Community interest;[1964] and a system to monitor the incidental capture and killing of the animal species listed in Annex III Part A of this law, and defining any necessary additional research or conservation measures as required to ensure that incidental capture and killing does not have a significant negative impact on the species concerned.[1965]

1962. Section 3(2) Law No. 153(I)/2003, which corresponds to Art. 2(3) Directive 92/43/EEC. *See* in this respect: Case C-226/08, *Stadt Papenburg v. Bundesrepublik Deutschland*, [2010] ECR I-00131 [relevant review: B. Stüer, *Bestandskraft von Zulassungsentscheidungen wird durch FFH-Regime durchbrochen*, 125 DVBl 245 (2010); A. Cudennec, O. Curtil, C. De Cet-Bertin, G. Guéguen-Hallouët & V. Labrot, *Chronique Maritime – Environnement – Jurisprudence – Mise en oeuvre de la Directive 92/43/CEE (Directive Habitats)*, 542 RMC 605 (2010); S. Jolivet, *Directive Habitas*, 30 RJE 295 (2010); A. Glaser, *Mitgliedstaatliche Zustimmungsabsicht zu Gebietsschutz nach FFH-Richtlinie gegen Willen klagender Stadt*, 21 EuZW 225 (2010); K.F. Gärditz, *Kein Bestandsschutz für rechtmäßig genehmigte Vorhaben im europäischen Naturschutzrecht?*, 125 DVBl 247 (2010)]; Case C-2/10, *Azienda Agro-Zootecnica Franchini sarl and Eolica di Altamura Srl v. Regione Puglia*, ECJ [2011] I-06561 [relevant review: I. Koufaki, *Αιολική Ενέργεια και Περιβάλλον*, 59 NoB 1725 (2011); L. Squintani & H.H.B. Vedder, *Hof van Justitie EU, 25-07-2011, C-2/10*, 8 M en R 179 (2012)].
1963. Section 42(1) and (2)(a) Law No. 153(I)/2003. This measure has been stated in Art. 14(2) Directive 92/43/EEC. *See* in this respect Case C-6/04, *Commission of the European Communities v. United Kingdom of Great Britain and Northern Ireland*, [2005] ECR I-09017 [relevant review: M. Baum, *Der Gebiets- und der Artenschutz der FFH-Richtlinie im Lichte der Urteile des EuGH in den Vertragsverletzungsverfahren Rs. C-6/04 gegen das Vereinigte Königreich und Rs. C-98/03 gegen Deutschland*, 28 NuR 145 (2006); C.T. Reid & M. Woods, *Implementing EC Conservation Law*, 18 JEL 148 (2006)].
1964. Section 42(2)(b) Law No. 153(I)/2003. This measure has been stated in Art. 14(2) Directive 92/43/EEC.
1965. Section 42(2)(c) Law No. 153(I)/2003, which corresponds to Art. 12(4) Directive 92/43/EEC. *See* in this respect: Case C-308/08, *European Commission v. Kingdom of Spain*, ECR 2010 I-04281 [relevant review: A. Beier & A. Geiger, *Die Behandlung des artenschutzrechtlichen Tötungsverbots in der Planfeststellung bei Tierkollisionen*, 126 DVBl 399 (2011)].

C. The Scientific Committee

471. For the purpose of this law, the Scientific Committee ('Επιστημονική Επιτροπή') is established, that consists of the Director of the Department of Environment,[1966] an officer from the Hunting Service,[1967] the Director of the Department of Fisheries and Marine Research,[1968] the Director of the Department of Forests,[1969] the Director of the Institute for Agriculture Research,[1970] the Director of the Department of Urban Planning and Housing,[1971] a competent person suggested by the Union of Cyprus Municipalities,[1972] a competent person suggested by the Union of Cyprus Communities,[1973] a competent person suggested by the Cyprus Federation of Environmental and Ecological Organizations,[1974] a competent person suggested by the Cyprus Federation of Hunting and Preservation of Wildlife[1975] and two competent persons suggested by the Minister.[1976]

472. The Scientific Committee has the duty and the competence to advise and prepare opinions to the Minister and the Minister of Interior, on its own motion or following the request of any of them, on the following matters: encouraging research and any work required as a basis for the protection, management and use of the population of all wild fauna and wild birds;[1977] assessing the influence of methods of taking wild fauna and birds on population levels;[1978] developing or refining ecological methods for preventing the type of damage caused by wild fauna and wild birds;[1979] determining the role of certain species as indicators of pollution;[1980] studying the adverse effect of chemical pollution on population levels of wild fauna and wild bird species;[1981] encouraging the necessary research and scientific work having regard to the objectives set out in this law and the statutory obligation of monitoring;[1982] exchange information for the purposes of proper

1966. Section 4(a) Law No. 153(I)/2003.
1967. Section 4(b) *ibid.*
1968. Section 4(c) *ibid.*
1969. Section 4(d) *ibid.*
1970. Section 4(e) *ibid.*
1971. Section 4(f) *ibid.*
1972. Section 4(g) *ibid.*
1973. Section 4(h) *ibid.*
1974. Section 4(i) *ibid.*
1975. Section 4(j) *ibid.*
1976. Section 4(k) *ibid.*
1977. Section 7(1)(a) *ibid.*, which is similar to the wording of Art. 10 Directive 79/409/EEC. *See* in this respect: Case C-418/04, *Commission of the European Communities v. Ireland,* [2007] ECR I-10947 [relevant review: W. Vandenberghe, *Preserving Biodiversity in Europe: An Infringement-Led Approach*, 17 RECIEL 243 (2008)].
1978. Section 7(1)(b) Law No. 153(I)/2003, which is similar to the wording of Annex V(d) Directive 79/409/EEC.
1979. Section 7(1)(c) Law No. 153(I)/2003, which is similar to the wording of Annex V(e) Directive 79/409/EEC.
1980. Section 7(1)(d) Law No. 153(I)/2003, which is similar to the wording of Annex V(f) Directive 79/409/EEC.
1981. Section 7(1)(e) Law No. 153(I)/2003, which is similar to the wording of Annex V(g) Directive 79/409/EEC.
1982. Section 7(1)(f) Law No. 153(I)/2003, which corresponds to Art. 18(1) Directive 92/43/EEC.

coordination of research carried out for natural habitats and wild fauna;[1983] scientific work necessary for conservation of natural habitats and habitats of species;[1984] promoting education and general information on the need to protect species of wild fauna and flora and to conserve their habitats and natural habitats;[1985] and the areas determined as protected landscape and as coasts and areas of protection of nature in development plans according to Law No. 90/1972.[1986] The Committee may exercise any other duty appointed to it under this law.[1987] Importantly, it examines and takes into consideration the views of the local authorities that may be affected by any matter examined by itself aiming at the preservation of biodiversity.[1988]

D. The Director of the Department of Environment

473. The Director of the Department of Environment has the general responsibility for the administrative aspects of the Minister's decisions. He is competent for: preparing lists of species in danger of extinction or particularly endangered species, taking into account their geographical distribution;[1989] preparing the listing and ecological description of areas particularly important to migratory species on their migratory routes and as wintering and nesting grounds;[1990] representation of the state to the relevant organs of the EU and coordination of the contacts of various services with those;[1991] and generally performing the duties appointed to him under this law,[1992] such as proper keeping of archives.[1993]

E. Inspector-in-Chief and Inspectors

474. The Minister appoints an inspector-in-chief and inspectors for purposes of surveillance, inspection, control and application of this law.[1994] Their powers are similar to the ones set out for inspectors of Law No. 187(I)/2002 (*see* in this respect paragraphs 34 et seq. above).[1995] The inspector-in-chief further has the duty to compose every six months a report on the powers that were exercised in this period and the results of surveillance, inspections and controls. This report is to be forwarded to the Scientific Committee.[1996]

1983. Section 7(1)(g) Law No. 153(I)/2003.
1984. Section 7(1)(h) *ibid.*, which corresponds to Art. 18(2) Directive 92/43/EEC.
1985. Section 7(1)(i) *ibid.*
1986. Section 7(1)(j) *ibid.*
1987. Section 7(2) *ibid.*
1988. Section 8(4) *ibid.*
1989. Section 10(a) *ibid.*, which is similar to the wording of Annex V(a) Directive 79/409/EEC.
1990. Section 10(b) Law No. 153(I)/2003, which is similar to the wording of Annex V(a) Directive 79/409/EEC.
1991. Section 10(c) Law No. 153(I)/2003.
1992. Section 10(d) *ibid.*
1993. Section 9 *ibid.*
1994. Section 38(1) and (2) *ibid.*
1995. Section 39(1) *ibid.*
1996. Section 39(2) *ibid.*

IV. Conservation of Natural Habitats and Habitats of Species

A. *List of Sites of Environmental Importance*

475. The Minister prepares a list of sites of environmental importance ('περιοχές περιβαλλοντικής σημασίας') indicating which types of natural habitats of Community interest and priority natural habitat types[1997] and which local species of Community interest and local priority species[1998] that are native to its territory the site's host,[1999] as well as other important habitats and species.[2000] For animal species ranging over wide areas, these sites shall correspond to the places within the natural range of such species which present the physical or biological factors essential to their life and reproduction. For aquatic species which range over wide areas, such sites will be proposed only where there is a clearly identifiable area representing the physical and biological factors essential to their life and reproduction.[2001]

476. A necessary prerequisite for this list is the prior written opinion of the Scientific Committee, which assesses the importance of any site on the basis of certain criteria and scientific information. The site assessment criteria for a given natural habitat type of Annex I of this law are the following: degree of representativity of the natural habitat type on the site;[2002] area of the site covered by the natural habitat type in relation to the total area covered by that natural habitat type within national territory;[2003] degree of conservation of the structure and functions of the natural

1997. Natural habitat types of community interest whose conservation requires the designation of special areas of conservation are set out in Annex I Law No. 153(I)/2003, which corresponds to Annex I Directive 92/43/EEC. They include costal and halophytic habitats, coastal sand dunes and continental dunes, freshwater habitats, temperate health and scrub, sclerophyllous scrub, natural and semi-natural grassland formations, raised bogs and mires and fens, rocky habitats and caves and forests.
1998. Animal and plant species of community interest whose conservation requires the designation of special areas of conservation are set out in Annex II Law No. 153(I)/2003, which corresponds to Annex II Directive 92/43/EEC.
1999. Section 11(1)(a) and (b) Law No. 153(I)/2003, which corresponds to Art. 4(1) Directive 92/43/EEC. *See* in this respect: Case C-75/01, *Commission of the European Communities v. Grand Duchy of Luxemburg*, [2003] ECR I-01585; Case C-244/05, *Bund Naturschutz in Bayern eV and Others v. Freistaat Bayern*, [2006] ECR I-08445 [relevant review: D. Hönig, *Schutzstatus nicht gelisteter FFH-Gebiete*, 29 NuR 249 (2007); P. Schäfer, *Schutzregime vor Aufnahme eines Lebensraums in Liste der Gebiete von gemeinschaftlicher Bedeutung*, 18 EuZW 63 (2007); D. Winkler, *About the Protection of Potential FFH Areas According to ECJ, Case C-117/03 and Case C-244/05*, 4 JEEPL 314 (2007)]; judgment of 3 Apr. 2014 in Case C-301/12, *Cascina Tre Pini Ss v. Ministero dell'Ambiente e della Tutela del Territorio e del Mare a.o., digital* ECR [relevant review: E. Broussy, H. Cassagnabère & C. Gänser, *Chronique de jurisprudence de la CJUE. Droit institutionnel – Manquement sur manquement, L'actualité juridique*, 116 DA 1151 (2014)].
2000. Section 11(1)(c) Law No. 153(I)/2003.
2001. Section 11(2) and (3) *ibid.*, which corresponds to Art. 4(1) Directive 92/43/EEC.
2002. Section 12(2)(a)(i) Law No. 153(I)/2003, which corresponds to Annex III(A)(a) Directive 92/43/EEC.
2003. Section 12(2)(a)(ii) Law No. 153(I)/2003, which corresponds to Annex III(A)(b) Directive 92/43/EEC.

habitat type concerned and restoration possibilities;[2004] and global assessment of the value of the site for conservation of the natural habitat type concerned.[2005] In addition, one of the following has to be fulfilled: natural habitat types of Community interest are in danger of disappearance in their natural range;[2006] have a small natural range following their regression or by reason of their intrinsically restricted area;[2007] or present outstanding examples of typical characteristics of Mediterranean biogeographical regions.[2008] To put it more simply, the site has to be a natural habitat type of Community interest in the meaning of the implemented directive. The site assessment criteria for a given species in Annex II of this law are the following: size and density of the population of the species present on the site in relation to the populations present within national territory;[2009] degree of conservation of the features of the habitat which are important for the species concerned and restoration possibilities;[2010] degree of isolation of the population present on the site in relation to the natural range of the species;[2011] and global assessment of the value of the site for conservation of the species concerned.[2012] In addition, one of the following has to be fulfilled: species of Community interest are endangered, except those species whose natural range is marginal in national territory;[2013] vulnerable, i.e., believed likely to move into the endangered category in the near future if the causal factors continue operating;[2014] rare, i.e., with small populations that are not at present endangered or vulnerable, but are at risk, and the species are located within restricted geographical areas or are thinly scattered over a more extensive range;[2015] or endemic and requiring particular attention by reason of the specific nature of their habitat and/or the potential impact of their exploitation on their

2004. Section 12(2)(a)(iii) Law No. 153(I)/2003, which corresponds to Annex III(A)(c) Directive 92/43/EEC.
2005. Section 12(2)(a)(iv) Law No. 153(I)/2003, which corresponds to Annex III(A)(d) Directive 92/43/EEC.
2006. Section 12(2)(b)(i) Law No. 153(I)/2003, which corresponds to Art. 1(c)(i) Directive 92/43/EEC.
2007. Section 12(2)(b)(ii) Law No. 153(I)/2003, which corresponds to Art. 1(c)(ii) Directive 92/43/EEC.
2008. Section 12(2)(b)(iii) Law No. 153(I)/2003, which corresponds to Art. 1(c)(iii) Directive 92/43/EEC.
2009. Section 12(3)(a)(i) Law No. 153(I)/2003, which corresponds to Annex III(B)(a) Directive 92/43/EEC.
2010. Section 12(3)(a)(ii) Law No. 153(I)/2003, which corresponds to Annex III(B)(b) Directive 92/43/EEC.
2011. Section 12(3)(a)(iii) Law No. 153(I)/2003, which corresponds to Annex III(B)(c) Directive 92/43/EEC.
2012. Section 12(3)(a)(iv) Law No. 153(I)/2003, which corresponds to Annex III(B)(d) Directive 92/43/EEC.
2013. Section 12(3)(b)(i) Law No. 153(I)/2003, which corresponds to Art. 1(g)(i) Directive 92/43/EEC. *See* in this respect Case C-508/04, *Commission of the European Communities v. Republic of Austria*, [2007] ECR I-03787.
2014. Section 12(3)(b)(ii) Law No. 153(I)/2003, which corresponds to Art. 1(g)(ii) Directive 92/43/EEC.
2015. Section 12(3)(b)(iii) Law No. 153(I)/2003, which corresponds to Art. 1(g)(iii) Directive 92/43/EEC.

habitat and/or the potential impact of their exploitation on their conservation status.[2016] In other words, it has to comply with the term of species of Community interest, as set out in the implemented directive.

477. A notification of the list of sites of environmental importance is then published in the manner determined by the Minister in the Official Gazette and includes every site, the map, name, location, extent and data resulting from the written opinion of the Scientific Committee.[2017] Within thirty days following said notification, objections may be filed with the Director of the Department of Environment.[2018] Any such objections are examined by the Scientific Committee and it submits its opinion to the Minister, who after taking this into consideration finalizes the list of sites.[2019] The final list is submitted to the Council of Ministers for approval, published in the Official Gazette and forwarded to the EC.[2020]

B. Special Area of Conservation

478. Once a site of Community importance has been adopted by the EC,[2021] the Minister designates that site as a special area of conservation ('ειδική ζώνη διατήρησης') as soon as possible and within four years at most, through notification in the Official Gazette.[2022] Every special area of conservation is marked by notices, the content of which is specified by the Minister.[2023] Further, the Minister, on the basis of a written opinion of the Scientific Committee, establishes priorities in the light of the importance of the sites for the maintenance or restoration, at a favourable conservation status, of a natural habitat type in Annex I or a species in Annex II and for the coherence of Natura 2000, in the light of the threats of degradation or destruction to which those sites are exposed,[2024] and the obligation to prevent and

2016. Section 12(3)(b)(iv) Law No. 153(I)/2003, which corresponds to Art. 1(g)(iv) Directive 92/43/EEC.
2017. Section 11(4)(a), (b), (c), (d) and (e) Law No. 153(I)/2003.
2018. Section 11(5) *ibid.*
2019. Section 11(6) *ibid.*
2020. Section 11(7)(a) and (b) *ibid.*
2021. *See* in this respect Art. 4(2) Directive 92/43/EEC. *See* in respect of Art. 4: Case C-43/10, *Nomarchiaki Aftodioikisi Aitoloakarnanias and Others v. Ypourgos Perivallontos, Chorotaxias kai Dimosion ergon a.o., digital* ECR [B. Georgiou, ***Οι αποφάσεις του ΔΕΕ και του ΣτΕ για την εκτροπή του Αχελώου***, 60 NoB 2231 (2012); S. Roset, *Directive cadre sur l'eau et justification de la déviation du cours d'un fleuve*, Europe 44 (2012); A. Epiney, *Zur Reichweite der Ausnahme des Art. 4 Abs. 7 WRRL*, FS Koch 585 (2014)].
2022. Section 13(1) Law No. 153(I)/2003, which corresponds to Art. 4(4) Directive 92/43/EEC.
2023. Section 28 Law No. 153(I)/2003, which corresponds to Art. 17(3) Directive 92/43/EEC. However, the European provision foresees the marking of areas designated under that directive in general, as well as notices designed by a committee consisting of representatives of the Member States and chaired by a representative of the Commission.
2024. Section 13(2)(a) and (b) Law No. 153(I)/2003, which corresponds to Art. 4(4) Directive 92/43/EEC. *See* in this respect Case C-90/10, *European Commission v. Kingdom of Spain*, [2011] ECR I-00134; judgment of 21 Jun. 2012 in Case C-177/11, *Syllogos Ellinon Poleodomon kai Chorotakton v. Ypourgos Perivallontos, Chorotaxias & Dimosion Ergon a.o., digital* ECR; Case C-258/

avoid the deterioration of natural habitats and the habitats of species as well as disturbance of the species for which the areas have been designated, insofar as such disturbance could be significant in relation to the objectives of this law.[2025] The Scientific Committee, when preparing the written opinion on the priorities, assesses the conservative status of a natural habitat as favourable when: its natural range and areas it covers within that range are stable or increasing;[2026] the specific structure and functions which are necessary for its long-term maintenance exist and are likely to continue to exist for the foreseeable future;[2027] and the conservation status of its typical species is favourable.[2028] The latter is satisfied, when: population dynamics data on the species concerned indicate that it is maintaining itself on a long-term basis as a viable component of its natural habitats;[2029] the natural range of the species is neither being reduced nor is likely to be reduced for the foreseeable future;[2030] and there is, and will probably continue to be, a sufficiently large habitat to maintain its populations on a long-term basis.[2031]

479. The Minister issues a degree on conservation and protection of nature regarding a special area of conservation that may prohibit or order specific activity or operation and set out specific conservation measures.[2032] Prior to issuing such a degree, the Minister takes into consideration the written opinion of the Scientific Committee and the opinions submitted by the public. More specifically, the Scientific Committee in its written opinion: states the ecological requirements of the natural habitat types in Annex I of this law and the species in Annex II of this law that are present on the sites; defines every action, activity or operation, which degrade natural habitats and habitats of species in relation to conservation objectives and must be avoided; suggests proper conservation measures and management measures of such habitats and species; and defines whether its opinion relates to actions, activities and operations that also fall in the application area of any other legislation

11, *Peter Sweetman a.o. v. An Bord Pleanála, digital* ECR [*see* in this respect: A. Beier, *Die Beeinträchtigung eines FFH-Gebiets als solchem*, 128 DVBl. 1497 (2013)].

2025. Section 13(2)(c) Law No. 153(I)/2003, which corresponds to Art. 6(2) Directive 92/43/EEC. *See* in this respect: Case C-127/02 *Landelijke Vereniging tot Behoud van de Waddenzee v. Staatssecretaris van Landbouw, Natuurbeheer en Visserij*, [2004] ECR I-07405 [*see* in this respect: J.-M. Belorgey, S. Gervasoni & C. Lambert, *Le droit matériel. Natura 2000: Difficultés françaises et jurisprudence récente, L'actualité juridique*, 109 DA 309 (2005)]; Case C-293/07, *Commission of the European Communities v. Hellenic Republic*, [2008] ECR I-00182 [relevant review: I. Koufaki, *Επιτροπή Ευρωπαϊκών Κοινοτήτων κατά Ελλάδος, C-293/07, σχόλιο*, 57 NoB 187 (2009)]; Case C-535/07, *European Commission v. Republic of Austria*, [2010] ECR I-09483 [relevant review: C.J. Bastmeijer, *Hof van Justitie EU, 14-10-2010, C-535/07*, 7 M en R 30 (2011)]; Case C-241/08, *European Commission v. French Republic*, [2010] ECR I-01697 [relevant review: S. Jolivet, *Protection de la nature*, 35 RJE 704 (2010); J. Dupont-Lassalle, *Code de l'environnement français et directive 'habitats'*, Europe 33 (2010)].
2026. Section 13(3)(a) Law No. 153(I)/2003, which corresponds to Art. 1(e) Directive 92/43/EEC.
2027. Section 13(3)(b) Law No. 153(I)/2003.
2028. Section 13(3)(c) *ibid.*
2029. Section 13(4)(a) *ibid.*, which corresponds to Art. 1(i) Directive 92/43/EEC.
2030. Section 13(4)(b) Law No. 153(I)/2003.
2031. Section 13(4)(c) *ibid.*
2032. Section 15(1)(a), (b) and (c) *ibid.*, which corresponds to Art. 6(1) Directive 92/43/EEC.

and the extent to which opinions of competent authorities under such other legislation, if necessary under same legislation, were included in the present opinion.[2033] The Scientific Committee further publishes in the daily press a notification on the written opinion and invites any interested party to submit to the Director of the Department of Environment any opinion, observation or objection within thirty days.[2034] Any such views of the public are examined by the committee, which may accordingly change its opinion.[2035] The final written opinion is then submitted to the Minister stating the submitted views of the public and the manner in which these were handled.[2036]

C. Environmental Impact Assessment

480. Any plan or project that does not prerequisite an urban planning permission and is not directly connected with the management of the site, which falls within special area of conservation, but is likely to have a significant effect thereon, either individually or in combination with other plans or projects, is subject to environmental estimation ('περιβαλλοντική εκτίμηση'), if this is a plan, or to environmental approval ('περιβαλλοντική έγκριση'), if this is a project. The public is given the opportunity to express its opinion, according to a procedure set out in secondary legislation. The aim of this procedure is to appropriately assess its implications for the site in view of the site's conservation objectives and the relevant special area of conservation and the public opinion in such plan or project.[2037] An environmental estimation or environmental approval, as the case may be, is granted only after having ascertained that it will not adversely affect the integrity of the site concerned or cause alteration of its character. However, if no such estimation or approval may be granted due to adversely affecting the integrity of the site, the plan or project may nevertheless be carried out for imperative reasons of overriding public interest, including those of a social or economic nature. Where the site concerned hosts a priority natural habitat type and/or a priority species, the only consideration which may be raised are those relating to human health or public safety, beneficial consequences of primary importance for the environment or, further to an opinion from the EC, other imperative reasons of overriding public interest.[2038] Following granting such estimation or approval, specific measures are imposed as compensatory measures, which aim to eliminate or reduce the effects

2033. Section 15(2)(a), (b), (c), (d) and (e) Law No. 153(I)/2003.
2034. Section 15(3)(a) *ibid.*
2035. Section 15(3)(b) *ibid.*
2036. Section 15(3)(c) *ibid.*
2037. Section 16(1) *ibid.*, which corresponds to Art. 6(3) Directive 92/43/EEC.
2038. Section 16(2) Law No. 153(I)/2003, which corresponds to Art. 6(4) Directive 92/43/EEC. *See* in this respect: Case C-324/01, *Commission of the European Communities v. Kingdom of Belgium*, [2002] ECR I-11197 [relevant review: J.M. Verschuuren, *Nogmaals kokkels, hamsters en woelmuizen: recente ontwikkelingen rond de implementatie van de Vogel- en Habitatrichtlijn in Nederland*, NTER 34 (2003)].

that granting such estimation or approval may bring to the relevant special zone of conservation. The EC is informed of all compensatory measures taken.[2039]

481. Should a project prerequisite an urban planning permission, and be likely to have a significant effect on special area of conservation, as explained above, the aforementioned on granting an urban planning permission, public participation, imperative reasons of overriding public interest and compensatory measures, apply *mutatis mutandis*. These also apply to public projects or plans.[2040]

V. Conservation of Other Habitats, Species of Local Interest and Priority

482. The above-explained procedure for the conservation of natural habitats and habitats of species is also applied for creating a list of other habitats, species of local interest and priority.[2041]

VI. Protection of Species of Community and Local Interest

483. Species of community and local interest are protected through prohibition provisions that constitute a penal offence. In particular, for the protection of certain animal species[2042] in their natural range, the following actions are prohibited: all forms of deliberate capture or killing of specimens of these species in the wild;[2043] deliberate disturbance of these species, particularly during the period of breeding,

2039. Section 16(7) and (8) Law No. 153(I)/2003, which corresponds to Art. 6(4) Directive 92/43/EEC.

2040. Section 16(3), (4), (5), (6), (7) and (8) Law No. 153(I)/2003, which corresponds to Art. 6(3) and (4) Directive 92/43/EEC. *See* in this respect: Case C-143/02, *Commission of the European Communities v. Italian Republic*, [2003] ECR I-02877 [relevant review: M. Le Barbier-Le Bris, *Chronique de jurisprudence Communautaire (Année 2003)*, RDR 16 (2005)]; Case C-538/09, *European Commission v. Kingdom of Belgium*, [2011] ECR I-04687 [relevant review: A. Cudennec, *Chronique de jurisprudence 2011 de la Cour de justice de l'Union européenne*, RDR 14 (2012)]; Case C-182/10, *Marie-Noëlle Solvay a.o. v. Région wallonne*, *digital* ECR [relevant review: J. Bétaille, *Évaluation environnementale – Accès à la justice – Natura 2000*, 37 RJE 584 (2012)]; judgment of 15 May 2014 in Case C-521/12, *T. C. Briels and Others v. Minister van Infrastructuur en Milieu*, not reported in ECR [relevant review: K. Füßer & M. Lau, *Maßnahmenpools im europäischen Gebietsschutzrecht*, 36 NuR 453 (2014)].

2041. Sections 11(8), 12(4) and 13(6) Law No. 153(I)/2003.

2042. These are listed in Annex III Part A *ibid.*, which corresponds to Annex IV (a) Directive 92/43/EEC.

2043. Section 21(1) Law No. 153(I)/2003, which corresponds to Art. 12(1)(a) Directive 92/43/EEC. *See* in respect of Art. 12: Case C-103/00, *Commission of the European Communities v. Greece*, [2002] ECR I-01147; Case C-33/03, *Commission of the European Communities v.* United Kingdom, [2005] ECR I-01865; Case C-221/04, *Commission of the European Communities v. Spain*, [2006] ECR I-04515 [relevant review: A. Beier, *Neues aus Leipzig zum artenschutzrechtlichen Tötungsverbot*, 127 DVBl 149, 151 (2012)]; Case C-518/04, *Commission of the European Communities v. Greece*, [2006] ECR I-00042 [relevant review: C. Sobotta, *Artenschutz in der Rechtsprechung des Europäischen Gerichtshofs*, 29 NuR 642 (2007)]; Case C-342/05, *Commission of the European Communities v. Finland*, [2007] ECR I-04713; Case C-383/09, *European Commission v. France*, [2011] ECR I-04869 [relevant review: D. Simon, *Directive 'Habitats'. La France condamnée pour insuffisance de protection du 'grand hamster d'Alsace*, 11 Europe 43 (2011)].

rearing, hibernation and migration;[2044] deliberate destruction or taking of eggs from the wild;[2045] deterioration or destruction of breeding sites or resting places;[2046] and keeping, transport and sale or exchange, and offering for sale or exchange, of specimens taken from the wild.[2047] These prohibitions apply to all stages of life of these animal species.[2048] In addition, all these are applicable to species of local interest.[2049]

484. However, derogation from these prohibitions, may be granted by the Minister following a written opinion of the Scientific Committee, provided that there is no satisfactory alternative and the derogation is not detrimental to the maintenance of the populations of the species concerned at a favourable conservation status in their natural range.[2050] The grounds that may support such derogation are: interest in protecting wild fauna and flora and conserving natural habitats;[2051] prevention of serious damage, in particular to crops, livestock, forests, fisheries and water and movable or immovable property;[2052] public health and public safety, or other imperative reasons of overriding public interest, including those of a social or economic nature and beneficial consequences of primary importance for the environment;[2053] research and education;[2054] repopulating and reintroducing these species and for the breeding operations necessary for these purposes, including the artificial propagation of plants;[2055] and taking or keeping of certain specimens of these species in limited numbers, under strictly supervised conditions, on a selective basis and to a limited extent.[2056] The EC is informed every two years on derogations provided through a detailed report by the Director of the Department of Environment.[2057]

2044. Section 21(2) Law No. 153(I)/2003, which corresponds to Art. 12(1)(b) Directive 92/43/EEC. *See* in this respect: judgment of 15 Mar. 2012 in Case C-46/11, *European Commission v. Republic of Poland, digital* ECR [relevant review: S. Jolivet, *Conservation des habitats naturels, de la faune et de la flore sauvages*, 37 RJE 581 (2012)].
2045. Section 21(3) Law No. 153(I)/2003, which corresponds to Art. 12(1)(c) Directive 92/43/EEC.
2046. Section 21(4) Law No. 153(I)/2003, which corresponds to Art. 12(1)(d) Directive 92/43/EEC.
2047. Section 21(5) Law No. 153(I)/2003, which corresponds to Art. 12(2) Directive 92/43/EEC.
2048. Section 21(6) Law No. 153(I)/2003, which corresponds to Art. 12(3) Directive 92/43/EEC.
2049. Sections 21(7) and 11(8) Law No. 153(I)/2003.
2050. Section 26(1) and (2) *ibid.*, which corresponds to Art. 16(1) Directive 92/43/EEC. *See* in respect of Art. 16: Case C-98/03, *Commission of the European Communities v. Federal Republic of Germany*, [2006] ECR I-00053 [relevant review: W. Günther, *Die Auswirkungen des EuGH-Urteils C-98/03 zur mangelhaften Umsetzung der Fauna-Flora-Habitat-Richtlinie*, 4 EurUP 94 (2006); S. Lütkes, *Artenschutz in Genehmigung und Planfeststellung*, 27 NVwZ 598 (2008)]; Case C-183/05, *Commission of the European Communities v. Ireland*, [2007] ECR I-00137; judgment of 15 Mar. 2012 in Case C-46/11, *European Commission v. Republic of Poland, digital* ECR.
2051. Section 26(1)(a) Law No. 153(I)/2003, which corresponds to Art. 16(1)(b) Directive 92/43/EEC.
2052. Section 26(1)(b) Law No. 153(I)/2003, which corresponds to Art. 16(1)(a) Directive 92/43/EEC.
2053. Section 26(1)(c) Law No. 153(I)/2003, which corresponds to Art. 16(1)(c) Directive 92/43/EEC.
2054. Section 26(1)(d) Law No. 153(I)/2003, which corresponds to Art. 16(1)(d) Directive 92/43/EEC.
2055. Section 26(1)(e) Law No. 153(I)/2003, which corresponds to Art. 16(1)(d) Directive 92/43/EEC.
2056. Section 26(1)(f) Law No. 153(I)/2003, which corresponds to Art. 16(1)(e) Directive 92/43/EEC.
2057. Section 26(4) and (5) Law No. 153(I)/2003, which corresponds to Art. 16(2) and (3) Directive 92/43/EEC.

485. When said derogations are applied to the taking, capture or killing of said animal species, as well as of other species of wild fauna,[2058] it is prohibited to use all indiscriminate means capable of causing local disappearance of, or serious disturbance to, populations of such species, and in particular use of certain means of capture and killing, as well as any form of capture[2059] and killing from aircraft or moving motor vehicles.[2060]

486. A system to monitor the incidental capture and killing of certain animal species is established by the Minister following written opinion of the Scientific Committee.[2061] In light of the information gathered, the Council of Ministers may, following a written opinion of the Scientific Committee, define further research or conservation measures as required to ensure that incidental capture and killing do not have a significant negative impact on the species concerned.[2062]

487. Turning to protection of certain plant species[2063] and without prejudice to Law No. 25(I)/2012, the following actions are prohibited: the deliberate picking, collecting, cutting, uprooting or destruction of such plants in their natural range in the wild;[2064] and the keeping, transport and sale or exchange and offering for sale or exchange of specimens of such species taken in the wild.[2065] These prohibitions apply to all stages of the biological cycle of said plants.[2066]

488. In light of the surveillance performed by the inspectors[2067] (*see* in this respect paragraphs 34, 472 et seq. above) and following a written opinion to the Scientific Committee, measures may be ordered to ensure that the taking in the wild of

2058. These are listed in Annex IV Part A Law No. 153(I)/2003, which corresponds to Annex V (a) Directive 92/43/EEC.
2059. Regarding mammals these are: blind or mutilated animals used as live decoys; tape recorders; electrical and electronic devices capable of killing or stunning; artificial light sources; mirrors and other dazzling devices; devices for illuminating targets; sighting devices for night shooting comprising an electronic image magnifier or image converter; explosives; nets which are nonselective according to their principle or their conditions of use; traps which are nonselective according to their principle or their conditions of use; crossbows; poisons and poisoned or anaesthetic bait; gassing or smoking out; and semi-automatic or automatic weapons with a magazine capable of holding more than two rounds of ammunition. Regarding fish these are: poison and explosives. Section 25(3) and (4) Law No. 153(I)/2003, which corresponds to Annex VI(a) Directive 92/43/EEC.
2060. Section 25 Law No. 153(I)/2003, which corresponds to Art. 15 and Annex VI(b) Directive 92/43/EEC.
2061. These are listed in Annex III Part A Law No. 153(I)/2003, which corresponds to Annex IV (a) Directive 92/43/EEC, as well as in the list produced following the procedure of s. 11(8) Law No. 153(I)/2003.
2062. Section 22(1) and (2) *ibid.*, which corresponds to Art. 12(4) Directive 92/34/EEC.
2063. These are listed in Annex III Part B Law No. 153(I)/2003, which corresponds to Annex IV(b) Directive 92/43/EEC.
2064. Section 23(1) Law No. 153(I)/2003, which corresponds to Art. 13(1)(a) Directive 92/43/EEC. *See* in respect of Art. 13: Case C-98/03, *Commission of the European Communities v. Federal Republic of Germany*, [2006] ECR I-00053; Case C-508/04, *Commission of the European Communities v. Republic of Austria*, [2007] ECR I-03787.
2065. Section 23(2) Law No. 153(I)/2003, which corresponds to Art. 13(1)(b) Directive 92/43/EEC.
2066. Section 23(3) Law No. 153(I)/2003, which corresponds to Art. 13(2) Directive 92/43/EEC.
2067. Sections 19 and 39(1) Law No. 153(I)/2003.

specimens of certain species of wild fauna and flora[2068] as well as their exploitation is compatible with their being maintained at a favourable conservation status. Such measures, which include continuation of said surveillance, may also include in particular: regulations regarding access to private property; temporary or local prohibition of the taking of specimens in the wild and exploitation of certain populations; regulation of the periods and/or methods of taking specimens; application, when specimens are taken, of hunting and fishing rules of Law No. 152(I)/2003 and Cap. 153, which takes account of the conservation of such populations; regulation of breeding in captivity of animal species pursuant to Law on Protection and Wellbeing of Animals[2069] as well as artificial propagation of plant species, under strictly controlled conditions, with a view to reducing the taking of specimens of the wild. The effects of the adopted measures are to be assessed by the Scientific Committee on the basis of said surveillance.[2070]

VII. Reports and Research

489. Every six years, a report on the implementation of the measures taken under this law is drawn up, published in the Official Gazette and forwarded to the EC. It includes in particular information concerning the conservation measures,[2071] evaluation of the impact of those measures on the conservation status of natural habitats of Community interest and species of Community interest[2072] and the main results of the surveillance.[2073] The EC is also informed on compensatory measures, as stated above (*see* in this respect paragraphs 478 et seq. above).

490. The Scientific Committee studies the desirability of reintroducing certain species[2074] that are native to their territory where this might contribute to their conservation, provided that an investigation, also taking into account experience in other Member States or elsewhere, has established that such reintroduction contributes effectively to re-establishing these species at a favourable conservation status

2068. These are listed in Annex IV *ibid.*, which corresponds to Annex V Directive 92/43/EEC.
2069. Law on Protection and Wellbeing of Animals ('ο περί Προστασίας και Ευημερίας των Ζώων Νόμος') No. 46 of 1994, OG I(I) No. 2885 of 10 Jun. 1994, p. 685, as amended, which according to the preamble to the laws amending this, implemented: Council Directive 93/119/EC of 22 Dec. 1993 on the protection of animals at the time of slaughter or killing, OJ L 340 of 31 Dec. 1993, p. 21; Council Directive 2007/43/EC of 28 Jun. 2007 laying down minimum rules for the protection of chickens kept for meat production, OJ L 182 of 12 Jul. 2007, p. 19; Directive 2010/63/EU of the European Parliament and of the Council of 22 Sep. 2010 on the protection of animals used for scientific purposes, OJ L 276 of 20 Oct. 2010, p. 33.
2070. Section 24(2) and (3) Law No. 153(I)/2003, which corresponds to Art. 14(2) Directive 92/43/EEC.
2071. Section 27(a) Law No. 153(I)/2003, which corresponds to Art. 17(1) Directive 92/43/EEC.
2072. Section 27(b) and Annex I and II Law No. 153(I)/2003, which corresponds to Art. 17(1) Directive 92/43/EEC.
2073. Sections 27(c) and 19 Law No. 153(I)/2003, which corresponds to Art. 17(1) Directive 92/43/EEC.
2074. These are the ones listed in Annex III Law No. 153(I)/2003, which corresponds to Annex IV Directive 92/43/EEC.

and that it takes place only after proper consultation with every concerned person.[2075] The deliberate introduction into the wild of any species which is not native to Cyprus' territory is generally prohibited. This may be, however, permitted by the Minister under the conditions that he sets in secondary legislation according to his discretion.[2076] The relevant European provision does not provide such a wide discretion and prescribes that such deliberate introduction is regulated so as not to prejudice natural habitats within their natural range or the wild native fauna and flora.[2077]

491. Necessary scientific research on species of wild fauna that is regulated under this law, counting of stock thereof and relevant management measures are being performed by an authority or any third party, which is declared by the Minister following a written opinion of the Scientific Committee.[2078] This provision on research is narrower than the relevant European one, which encourages the necessary research and scientific work having regard to its objectives and the surveillance obligation and hence includes research on wild flora as well.[2079]

VIII. Ensuring Compliance

492. The following penal sanctions ensure compliance with the provisions of this law. No administrative sanctions are prescribed.

493. Any person, who in person, through his employee or other representative, commits an offence, when he acts or fails to act in violation of: priority measures;[2080] prohibition or mandatory provisions of a degree on conservation and protection of nature;[2081] compensatory measures;[2082] additional conservation measures;[2083] measures ensuring safe taking of specimens;[2084] derogation from prohibitions for the protection of species of community and local interest;[2085] provisions on protection of flora and fauna and using indiscriminate means for capture

2075. Section 29(a) and (b) Law No. 153(I)/2003, which corresponds to Art. 22(a) Directive 92/43/EEC. The European provision however provides for consultations with the *public concerned* (in Greek 'ενδιαφερόμενο κοινό', in French 'public concerné', in German 'betroffene Bevölkerungskreise' and in Dutch 'belanghebbende') and not any *interested person* ('ενδιαφερόμενο πρόσωπο'), as per the national provision, which due to implying persons having legal interest for participating in the consultations, inevitably narrows the applicability thereof.
2076. Section 30 Law No. 153(I)/2003.
2077. Article 22(b) Directive 92/43/EEC.
2078. Section 31(1) and (2) Law No. 153(I)/2003.
2079. Articles 18(1), 4 and 11 Directive 92/43/EEC.
2080. Sections 40(1)(a)(i) and 13(2) *ibid.*
2081. Sections 40(1)(a)(ii) and 15(1) *ibid.*
2082. Sections 40(1)(a)(iii) and 16(7) *ibid.*
2083. Sections 40(1)(a)(iv) and 22(2) *ibid.*
2084. Sections 40(1)(a)(v) and 24(1) *ibid.*
2085. Sections 40(1)(a)(vi) and 26 *ibid.*

and killing of species;[2086] lawful introduction of non-native species to natural environment;[2087] authorized scientific research;[2088] and certain regulations of the EU[2089] on hunting and import of wild flora and fauna.[2090] The penalties that may be imposed following conviction by a Court of Law are imprisonment of up to three years and/or a fine of up to EUR 17,100.[2091]

494. Should anyone obstruct an inspector from exercising his duties or interfere with the inspector's duties, he commits an offence, which may lead to imprisonment of up to six months and/or a fine of up to EUR 1,700.[2092]

IX. Archive

495. The Director of the Department of Environment keeps an archive, in which special zones of conservation,[2093] sites of Community importance,[2094] every site that includes natural habitat types or priority types regarding which consultations according to Article 5(1) Directive 92/43/EEC take place or a decision according to Article 5(3) Directive 92/43/EEC is expected,[2095] every special protection areas,[2096] every site that has been included in the catalogue prepared by the Minister and forwarded to the EC,[2097] and every special area of conservation, which is being de-characterized by the EC,[2098] are registered. This archive must be updated and available for a free inspection by the public during office hours.[2099] Lastly, every registration and amendment or removal therefrom must be notified to the owner or

2086. Sections 40(1)(b), 17(2), 21, 23 and 25 *ibid.*
2087. Sections 40(1)(c) and 30 *ibid.*
2088. Sections 40(1)(d) and 31 *ibid.*
2089. These are: Council Regulation (EEC) No. 3254/91 of 4 Nov. 1991 prohibiting the use of leghold traps in the Community and the introduction into the Community of pelts and manufactured goods of certain wild animal species originating in countries which catch them by means of leghold traps or trapping methods which do not meet international humane trapping standards, OJ L 308, 9 Nov. 1991, p. 1; Commission Regulation (EC) No. 35/97 of 10 Jan. 1997 laying down provisions on the certification of pelts and goods covered by Council Regulation (EEC) No. 3254/91, OJ L 8, 11 Jan. 1997, p. 2; Council Regulation (EEC) No. 348/81 of 20 Jan. 1981 on common rules for imports of whales or other cetacean products, OJ L 39, 12 Feb. 1981, p. 1; Commission Regulation (EC) No. 865/2006 of 4 May 2006 laying down detailed rules concerning the implementation of Council Regulation (EC) No. 338/97 on the protection of species of wild fauna and flora by regulating trade therein, OJ L 166, 19 Jun. 2006, p. 1; Council Regulation (EC) No. 338/97 of 9 Dec. 1996 on the protection of species of wild fauna and flora by regulating trade therein, OJ L 61, 3 Mar. 1997, p. 1; Regulation (EC) No. 1007/2009 of the European Parliament and of the Council of 16 Sep. 2009 on trade in seal products, OJ L 286, 31 Oct. 2009, p. 36.
2090. Section 40(1)(g), (h), (i), (j) and (k) Law No. 153(I)/2003.
2091. Section 40(2) *ibid.*
2092. Section 39(3) *ibid.*
2093. Section 9(1)(a) *ibid.*
2094. Section 9(1)(b) *ibid.*
2095. Section 9(1)(c) *ibid.*
2096. Section 9(1)(d) *ibid.* and s. 7 Law No. 152(I)/2003.
2097. Section 9(1)(e) Law No. 153(I)/2003.
2098. Section 9(1)(f) *ibid.* and Art. 9 Directive 92/43/EEC.
2099. Section 9(3) and (4) Law No. 153(I)/2003.

occupant of immovable property within that site, the competent land planning authority, the competent local authority and every other person according to the order of the Minister.[2100]

§2. WILD BIRDS

I. Objective

496. Generally, Law No. 152(I)/2003, apart from protecting wild fauna,[2101] aims to the protection, conservation, management and exploitation of all species of naturally occurring birds in the wild state,[2102] and the protection, maintenance of the population of said species at a level which corresponds in particular to ecological, scientific and cultural requirements, while taking account of economic and recreational requirements, or adaption of the population of these species to that level.[2103]

II. Area of Application

497. No general provision of this law specifies its area of application. However, it is set out that certain provisions apply to birds, their eggs and habitats.[2104]

III. Competent Authorities

A. The Minister of Interior

498. The Minister of Interior is the competent authority for the protection and management of wild fauna. For the objectives of this law as well as for preservation, maintenance or re-establishment of a sufficient diversity and area of habitats for all the species of birds, the Minister, following a written opinion of the Scientific Committee, has the power to issue decrees and notifications. Through those it

2100. Section 9(5)(a), (b), (c) and (d) *ibid.*
2101. Section 3(c) Law No. 152(I)/2003.
2102. Section 3(a) *ibid.*, which corresponds to Art. 1(1) Directive 2009/147/EC. *See* in this respect: judgment of 26 Jan. 2012 in Case C-192/11, *European Commission v. Republic of Poland, digital* ECR.
2103. Section 3(b) Law No. 152(I)/2003, which corresponds to Art. 2 Directive 2009/147/EC. *See* in this respect Case C-3/96, *Commission of the European Communities v. Kingdom of the Netherlands*, [1998] ECR I-03031 [relevant review: P.J. Leefmans, *Nederlandse vogels onvoldoende beschermd*, NTER 267 (1998); D. Gillies, *How Far Should You Go? The Obligation to Classify Special Protection Areas*, 1 EnvLRev 125 (1999); H.E. Woldendorp & H. Schoukens, *De Habitatrichtlijn als Doos va Pandora*, 11 M en R 1 (2015); G. Jazottes, M. Luby & S. Poillot-Peruzzetto, *Droit européen des affaires. Les politiques communes*, RTD Com. 249 (1999)]; Case C-159/99, *Commission of the European Communities v. Italian Republic*, [2001] ECR I-04007; Case C-259/08, *Commission of the European Communities v. Hellenic Republic*, [2009] ECR I-00002; Case C-573/08, *European Commission v. Italian Republic*, [2010] ECR I-00095.
2104. Section 5 Law No. 152(I)/2003, which corresponds to Art. 1(2) Directive 2009/147/EC.

is ordered to create protected areas,[2105] upkeep and manage them in accordance with the ecological needs of habitats inside and outside the protected zones,[2106] create biotopes[2107] and re-establish destroyed biotopes.[2108] Upkeeping and managing habitats may involve: restricting and/or controlling public's access at a particular area for a specific time period; restriction and/or regulation of various types of vehicles in a specific area for a specific time period; control and/or restriction of activities, including land reclamation and flattening with the use of machinery and making of roads; control and/or restriction of recreation activities; control and/or restriction of the use of plant protection products or other chemicals for a specific time period at a specific area; encouraging and/or fostering of the aforementioned targets through specific practices and/or activities related to agriculture and farming; and any other measures aiming to achieve same targets.[2109] Adopting other special measures of maintenance does not affect the obligation to create protected areas.

B. The Council of Ministers

499. The Council of Ministers has the power to issue regulations for specifying any matter that needs to be specified under this law and generally for the best application of the provisions of this law. In particular, and without prejudice to generally of the foregoing power, such regulations may provide for the prohibition of works or other activities that affect or may affect negatively or alter the quality of a biotope,[2110] any matter related to operation and use of public hunting areas[2111] and the establishment and operation of a School for GameKeepers, including the admission requirements, the modules to be taught and the requirements for graduation.[2112]

C. The Scientific Committee

500. The Scientific Committee established in Law No. 153(I)/2003 is a competent authority also under this law[2113] and prepares written opinions for advising the Minister, as elaborated below.[2114]

2105. Section 6(1)(a) Law No. 152(I)/2003, which corresponds to Art. 3(1) and (2)(a) Directive 2009/147/EC.
2106. Section 6(1)(b) Law No. 152(I)/2003, which corresponds to Art. 3(2)(b) Directive 2009/147/EC. *See* in this respect: Case C-259/08, *Commission of the European Communities v. Hellenic Republic*, [2009] ECR I-00002; Case C-573/08, *European Commission v. Italian Republic*, [2010] ECR I-00095.
2107. Section 6(1)(c) Law No. 152(I)/2003, which corresponds to Art. 3(2)(d) Directive 2009/147/EC.
2108. Section 6(1)(d) Law No. 152(I)/2003, which corresponds to Art. 3(2)(c) Directive 2009/147/EC.
2109. Section 6(1)(b)(i)–(vii) Law No. 152(I)/2003.
2110. Section 94(1) and (2)(e) *ibid.*
2111. Section 94(2)(f) *ibid.*
2112. Section 94(2)(g) *ibid.*
2113. Section 2 *ibid.*
2114. Sections 6(1), 7, 9(1), 10(4) and (5), 12, 13, 16 and 18 *ibid.*

D. The Hunting Service

501. Officers of the Hunting Service ('Υπηρεσία Ταμείου Θήρας') protect and conserve wild fauna and biotopes and ensure the application of this law in Cyprus including the exclusive economic zone.[2115] Generally, all officers perform the duties and powers appointed to them under this law.[2116] They collect information on offences of this law and protection of wild fauna and biotopes, prevent offences from being committed, bring offenders before justice and arrest any person, whom they may arrest under satisfactory conditions.[2117] Further, all officers of the Hunting Service or police officers may enter any area, with the exception of private residence, when they reasonably believe that an offence under this law is committed.[2118] Their powers regarding investigating any offences under this law are further described in detail in this law.[2119]

IV. Protection of Birds

A. General Frame

502. All requisite measures to establish a general system of protection for all species of birds are taken by the Minister. These measures prohibit in particular: deliberate killing or capture by any method;[2120] deliberate destruction of, or damage to, their nests and eggs or removal of their nests;[2121] taking their eggs in the wild and keeping these eggs even if empty;[2122] deliberate disturbance of these birds particularly during the period of breeding and rearing;[2123] and keeping birds of species the hunting and capture of which is prohibited.[2124] In addition, all necessary measures for the protection of local fauna and flora are taken for any introduction of species of bird which do not occur naturally in the wild state. The competent authority, prior to deciding on such measures, takes into consideration the opinion of the Scientific Committee and consults the EC.[2125]

2115. Section 73(1) *ibid.*
2116. Section 76(1) *ibid.*
2117. Section 76(2) *ibid.*
2118. Section 72(1) *ibid.*
2119. Section 77(1) and (2) *ibid.*
2120. Section 8(1) and (2)(a) *ibid.*, which corresponds to Art. 5(a) Directive 2009/147/EC. *See* in respect of Art. 5: Case 247/85, *Commission of the European Communities v. Kingdom of Belgium*, [1987] ECR 03029; Case 412/85, *Commission of the European Communities v. Federal Republic of Germany*, [1987] ECR 03503; Case C-339/87, *Commission of the European Communities v. Kingdom of the Netherlands*, [1990] ECR I-00851; Case C-288/88, *Commission of the European Communities v. Federal Republic of Germany*, [1990] ECR I-02721.
2121. Section 8(2)(b) Law No. 152(I)/2003, which corresponds to Art. 5(b) Directive 2009/147/EC. *See* in this respect: Case 252/85, *Commission of the European Communities v. French Republic*, [1988] ECR 02243.
2122. Section 8(2)(d) Law No. 152(I)/2003, which corresponds to Art. 5(c) Directive 2009/147/EC.
2123. Section 8(2)(c) Law No. 152(I)/2003, which corresponds to Art. 5(d) Directive 2009/147/EC.
2124. Section 8(2)(e) Law No. 152(I)/2003, which corresponds to Art. 5(e) Directive 2009/147/EC.
2125. Section 13(1) Law No. 152(I)/2003, which corresponds to Art. 11 Directive 2009/147/EC.

B. Protection of Wild Birds Through Special Protection Areas

503. For the conservation of certain wild birds,[2126] the most suitable territories in number and size are classified as *special protection areas* ('ζώνες ειδικής προστασίας') by the Minister following a written opinion of the Scientific Committee. This committee in order to ensure the birds' conservation, survival and reproduction in their area of distribution, takes into account the necessities for the conservation of these species in the geographical sea and land area as well as trends and variations in population levels. In the written opinion to the Minister, reference is being made to species in danger of extinction,[2127] species vulnerable to specific changes in their habitat,[2128] species considered rare because of small populations or restricted local distribution,[2129] and any other species requiring particular attention for reasons of the specific nature of their habitat.[2130] To the purpose of avoiding important pollution or deterioration of habitats or any disturbances affecting the birds, the provisions on special area of conservation and assessment of environmental impact of Law No. 153(I)/2003 are equally applicable.[2131]

C. Protection of Migratory Species

504. For the protection of regularly occurring migratory species, not falling under the aforementioned, special areas of conservation are similarly specified by the Minister. However, in this case the written opinion of the Scientific Committee includes their breeding, moulting and wintering areas, staging posts along their migration routes and wetlands, particularly the ones of international importance.[2132] The Minister establishes the protected areas bearing in mind their need for protection in the geographical sea and land area of the EU and ensures their survival and reproduction in their area of distribution. He further specifies measures for the upkeep and management in accordance with the ecological needs of habitats inside

2126. These are listed in Annex I Law No. 152(I)/2003, which corresponds to Annex I Directive 2009/147/EC.

2127. Section 7(2)(a) Law No. 152(I)/2003, which corresponds to Art. 4(1)(a) Directive 2009/147/EC. *See* in respect of Art. 4: Case C-355/90, *Commission v. Spain*, [1993] ECR I-04221 [relevant review: G. Winter, *Etappensieg für den Weissen Löffler*, 5 ZUR 308 (1994)]; Case C-44/95, *R v. Secretary of State for the Environment*, [1996] ECR I-03805 [relevant review: J.D.C. Harte, *Nature Conservation: The Rule of Law in European Community Environmental Protection*, 9 JEL 168 (1997)]; Case C-96/98, *v. France*, ECR 1999 I-08531 [relevant review: C. Pitaud & D. Rochard, *Actualité – Environnement et espace rural. Protection de la nature*, RDR 78 (2000)]; Case C-71/99, *Commission v. Germany*, [2001] ECR I-05811; Case C-220/99, *Commission v. France*, [2001] ECR I-05831; Case C-415/01, *Commission v. Belgium*, [2003] ECR I-02081 [relevant review: M. La Barbier-Le Bris, *Chronique de jurisprudence communautaire (année 2003)*, RDR 16 (2005)]; Case C-304/05, *Commission v. Italy*, [2007] ECR I-07495; Case C-535/07, *European Commission v. Austria*, [2010] ECR I-09483.

2128. Section 7(2)(b) Law No. 152(I)/2003, which corresponds to Art. 4(1)(b) Directive 2009/147/EC.

2129. Section 7(2)(c) Law No. 152(I)/2003, which corresponds to Art. 4(1)(c) Directive 2009/147/EC.

2130. Section 7(2)(d) Law No. 152(I)/2003, which corresponds to Art. 4(1)(d) Directive 2009/147/EC.

2131. Section 7(5) Law No. 152(I)/2003, which corresponds to Art. 4(4) Directive 2009/147/EC.

2132. Section 7(4) Law No. 152(I)/2003, which corresponds to Art. 4(2) Directive 2009/147/EC.

and outside said protected zones.[2133] Avoidance of pollution, deterioration of habitats and any disturbances inside and outside these special areas of protection is established in the same manner, as in the aforementioned.[2134]

D. Protection of Wild Birds Through Regulation of Hunting

505. Other wild birds[2135] may be hunted upon decision of the Minister following the recommendation of the director of the Hunting Service and the written opinion of the Scientific Committee.[2136] No specifications are provided about the written opinion of the Scientific Committee which is submitted to the director of the Hunting Service. The latter authority, however, while preparing its recommendation has to take into consideration the principles of wise use and ecologically balanced control of the species of birds concerned and the compatibility of this practice as regards the population of these species, in particular migratory species.[2137] In addition, it shall consider their population level, geographical distribution reproductive rate throughout the Union, while ensuring that the hunting of these species does not jeopardize conservation efforts in their distribution area.[2138] Especially during the rearing season or during the various stages of reproduction, these species are not hunted.[2139]

506. In respect of hunting, capturing or killing of wild birds, where this is permitted under this law, the use of all means, arrangements or methods used for the large-scale or nonselective capturing or killing of birds or capable of causing the local disappearance of a species is prohibited.[2140] Without prejudice to generally of the foregoing, specific measures of capture and killing are explicitly prohibited

2133. Section 7(3) *ibid.*
2134. Section 7(5) and (6) *ibid.*, which corresponds to Art. 4(4) Directive 2009/147/EC.
2135. These are: anser albifrons, anser, anser fabalis, anas penelope, anas strepera, anas crecca, anas platyrhynchus, anas acuta, anas querquedula, anas clypeata, aythya ferina, aythya fuligula, branta canadensis, lagopus scoticus et hibernicus, lagopus mutus, alectoris chukar, alectoris graeca, alectoris rufa, phasianus colchicus, coturnix, francolinus, perdix, fulica atra, lymnocryptes minimus, gallinago, scolopax rusticola, columba livia, columba palumbus, columba oenas, streptopelia turtur, streptopelia decaocto, alauda arvensis, turdus merula, turdus pilaris, turdus philomelos, turdus iliacus, turdus viscivorus, sturnus vulgaris, pica, corvus monedula and corvus corone. Annex II Law No. 152(I)/2003, which partially corresponds to Annex II A and B Directive 2009/147/EC.
2136. Section 9(1) Law No. 152(I)/2003.
2137. Section 9(2)(a) and (b) *ibid.*, which corresponds to Art. 7(4) Directive 2009/147/EC. *See* in this respect: Case C-157/89, *Commission of the European Communities v. Italian Republic*, [1991] ECR I-00057.
2138. Section 9(2)(c), (d) and (e) Law No. 152(I)/2003, which corresponds to Art. 7(1) Directive 2009/147/EC.
2139. Section 9(3) Law No. 152(I)/2003, which corresponds to Art. 7(4) Directive 2009/147/EC.
2140. Section 11(1) Law No. 152(I)/2003, which corresponds to Art. 8(1) Directive 2009/147/EC. *See* in this respect: Case C-72/02, *Commission of the European Communities v. Portuguese Republic*, [2003] ECR I-06597; Case C-79/03, *Commission of the European Communities v. Kingdom of Spain*, [2004] ECR I-11619.

under this law,[2141] as well as hunting from certain means of transport. However, for security reasons, the use of motorboats with a maximum speed of 18 km per hour may be permitted by the Minister.[2142]

E. Protection of Wild Birds Through Regulation of Trade

507. The sale, transport for sale, keeping for sale and offering for sale of live or dead birds and of any readily recognizable parts or derivatives of such birds is prohibited.[2143] However, these activities are not prohibited in respect of specific wild birds, those being Anas platyrhynchos, Lagopus scoticus et hibernicus, Alectoris rufa, Alectoris barbara, Perdix, Phasianus colchicus and Columba palumbus,[2144] provided that the birds have been legally killed or captured or otherwise legally acquired.[2145] In addition, any selling or other acquisition of any game may be performed only if a permit for trading games has been granted for such person.[2146] Same activities are further not prohibited for other wild birds, those being Anser albifrons albifrons, Anser anser, Anas penelope, Anas crecca, Anas acuta, Anas clypeata, Aytjua ferina, Aythya fuligula, Aythya marila, Somateria mollissima, Melanitta nigra, Lagopus mutus, Tetrao tetrix britannicus, Tetrao urogallus, Fulica atra, Pluvialis apricaria, Lymnocryptes minimus, Gallinago and Scolopax rusticola.[2147] Necessary prerequisites are that the birds have been legally killed or captured or otherwise legally acquired, as long as the EC that has previously been consulted, consider that no risk exists for their population levels, geographical distribution or reproductive rate thereof. Any additional restrictive measures may be imposed by the Minister.[2148] The Scientific Committee prepares a written opinion, taking into

---

2141. These are snares, limes, hooks, live birds which are blind or mutilated used as decoys, tape recorders, electrocuting devices, artificial light sources, mirrors, devices for illuminating targets, sighting devices for night shooting comprising an electronic image magnifier or image converter, explosives, nets, traps, poisoned or anaesthetic bait, semi-automatic or automatic weapons with a magazine capable of holding more than two rounds of ammunition. Section 11(2)(a), (b), (c), (d) and (e) Law No. 152(I)/2003, which corresponds to Annex IV(a) Directive 2009/147/EC. Further means that are prohibited are: plastic or other models of fauna or wild birds; sound-making devices; chemical substances for misleading of prey and wild birds; poisonous seeds or substances; device for tracing prey; feeding; and falconry. Section 11(2)(f), (g), (h), (i), (j), (k) and (l) Law No. 152(I)/2003.
2142. These means of transport are aircraft, motor vehicles and boats driven at a speed exceeding 5 km per hour. Section 8(2) *ibid.*, which corresponds to Art. 8(2) and Annex IV(b) Directive 2009/147/EC.
2143. Section 10(1) Law No. 152(I)/2003, which corresponds to Art. 6(1) Directive 2009/147/EC.
2144. Points 1–7 Annex III Law No. 152(I)/2003, which partially corresponds to Annex III Part A Directive 2009/147/EC.
2145. Section 10(2) Law No. 152(I)/2003, which corresponds to Art. 6(2) Directive 2009/147/EC. *See* in this respect Case C-535/07, *European Commission v. Republic of Austria*, ECR [2010] I-09483.
2146. *See* in this respect ss 54 and 55 Law No. 152(I)/2003.
2147. Points 8–26 Annex III *ibid.*, which corresponds to Annex III Part B Directive 2009/147/EC.
2148. Section 10(3) and (3A) Law No. 152(I)/2003, which corresponds to Art. 6(3) Directive 2009/147/EC. *See* in this respect Case C-226/08, *Stadt Papenburg v. Bundesrepublik Deutschland*, [2010] ECR I-00131; Case C-491/08, *Commission of the European Communities v. Italian Republic*, [2010] ECR I-00074.

consideration the results from surveillance, on whether these activities should continue to be permitted and submits it to the Minister, who reaches the relevant decision.[2149]

F. Derogations

508. Derogations from the statutory obligations of general protection of wild birds, protection through regulation of hunting and regulation of trade and prohibited means of capture and killing may be granted, where there is no other satisfactory solution. In particular, the Minister may, following a written opinion of the Scientific Committee, issue a relevant decree in the Official Gazette solely on the following grounds: in the interests of public health and safety; in the interests of air safety; to prevent serious damage to crops, livestock, forests, fisheries and water; for the protection of flora and fauna; for the purposes of research and teaching, of repopulation, of reintroduction and for the breeding necessary for these purposes; and to permit, under strictly supervised conditions and on a selective basis, the capture, keeping or other judicious use of certain birds in small numbers.[2150] The minimum content of this decree includes the species which are subject to the derogations,[2151] as well as their numbers,[2152] the means, arrangements or methods authorized for capture or killing,[2153] the conditions of risk and the circumstances of time and place under which such derogations may be granted,[2154] any other necessary restrictive means,[2155] any person, whom this derogation concerns,[2156] and any controls that must be carried out by the Hunting Service.[2157] A yearly report on any granted derogations is prepared by the Hunting Service and forwarded to the EC.[2158]

V. Ensuring Compliance

A. Penal Sanctions

509. Compliance is ensured by penalizing violation of most provisions of this law. In particular, the following are prescribed as offences: violating the provisions of a decree on upkeep and management of habitats and creation of biotopes;[2159] performing any development, work or intervention in a habitat without prior obtaining

2149. Section 10(4) and (5) Law No. 152(I)/2003.
2150. Section 12(1) *ibid.*, which corresponds to Art. 9(1) Directive 2009/147/EC.
2151. Section 12(2)(a) Law No. 152(I)/2003, which corresponds to Art. 9(2)(a) Directive 2009/147/EC.
2152. Section 12(2)(b) Law No. 152(I)/2003.
2153. Section 12(2)(c) *ibid.*, which corresponds to Art. 9(2)(b) Directive 2009/147/EC.
2154. Section 12(2)(d) Law No. 152(I)/2003, which corresponds to Art. 9(2)(c) Directive 2009/147/EC.
2155. Section 12(2)(e) Law No. 152(I)/2003.
2156. Section 12(2)(f) *ibid.*
2157. Section 12(2)(g) *ibid.*, which corresponds to Art. 9(2)(e) Directive 2009/149/EC.
2158. Section 12(3) Law No. 152(I)/2003, which corresponds to Art. 9(3) Directive 2009/147/EC.
2159. Section 6(2) and (1)(b) and (d) Law No. 152(I)/2003.

the relevant licence; violating terms and conditions of any licence and causing habitat degradation or destruction or wildlife nuisance;[2160] violating the general prohibitions for creating a general system of protection for all species of birds;[2161] hunting wild birds during the rearing season or during the various stages of reproduction;[2162] violating the provisions of trading of wild birds;[2163] violating the provisions on means of capture and killing;[2164] violating the provisions on any introduction of species of bird which do not occur naturally in the wild state;[2165] noncompliance with officers of the Hunting Service and preventing them from exercising their duties and powers or cursing and threatening them.[2166] These offences, may, after conviction by the Court of Law, lead to imprisonment of up to three years and/or a fine of up to EUR 20,000.[2167] Especially, if conviction for habitat degradation is ordered, the court may additionally impose a penal fine equal to the remediation cost.[2168] This is a straightforward demonstration of the polluter pays principle. Yet, explicitly characterizing cost recovery as a 'criminal fine' is not considered quite accurate.

B. Other Sanctions

510. In the event that a person is convicted for any of the aforementioned offences, the court may, in addition to any penal penalty imposed, prohibit him from carrying a hunting weapon for a period of up to ten years, confiscate any weapon, means of transportation or other object involved in the crime, as well as annul any permit issued under this law.[2169]

2160. Section 7A(1) *ibid.*
2161. Section 8(3) and (2) *ibid.*
2162. Section 9(4) and (3) *ibid.*
2163. Sections 10(6), (1) and (5) and 54(3) *ibid.*
2164. Section 11(5) *ibid.*
2165. Section 13(2) *ibid.*
2166. Section 77(3) *ibid.*
2167. Section 88 *ibid.*
2168. Section 7A(5) *ibid.*
2169. Sections 90(1), (2) and (3) and 7A(4) *ibid.*

Chapter 4. Agricultural Resources

511. Agricultural activity affects the environment in a variety of ways. Water is endangered through pollution caused by nitrates, that being caused by deposit, application or discharge of livestock effluents or by excessive use of fertilizers. The environment, as well as animals and humans, may suffer risks and hazards from plant production products that have not officially been tested and authorized as well as that have been incorrectly used.[2170] Biocidal products can pose risks to the environment, as well as to humans and animals, due to their intrinsic properties and associated use patterns.[2171] Lastly, fertilizers can be contaminated by substances that can potentially pose a risk to human and animal health and the environment.[2172] The relevant legislation follows this pattern and is focused on the regulation of water, plant protection products, biocidal products and fertilizers.

§1. Water

512. Prevention of water pollution caused by nitrates is being regulated by Law No. 106(I)/2002, as elaborated above (*see* in this respect paragraphs 86 et seq. above).

§2. Plant Protection Products

513. Plant protection products are regulated throughout the EU via Regulation (EU) No. 1107/2009.[2173] For the purpose of application of this regulation, Law on Plant Protection Products[2174] (hereinafter 'Law No. 141(I)/2011') has been issued.

I. Objective

514. The objective of this law is to provide the necessary complementary measures for the application of Regulation (EU) No. 1107/2009[2175] and set out general provisions and rules related to the procedure for issuing an authorization for plant

2170. Preamble no. 7 to Regulation (EU) No. 1107/2009 of the European Parliament and of the Council of 21 Oct. 2009 concerning the placing of plant protection products on the market and repealing Council Directives 79/117/EEC and 91/414/EEC, OJ L 309, 24 Nov. 2009, p. 1.
2171. Preamble no. 1 to Regulation (EU) No. 528/2012 of the European Parliament and of the Council of 22 May 2012 concerning the making available on the market and use of biocidal products, OJ L 167, 27 Jun. 2012, p. 1.
2172. Preamble no. 15 to Regulation (EC) No. 2003/2003 of the European Parliament and of the Council of 13 Oct. 2003 relating to fertilizers, OJ L 304, 21 Nov. 2003, p. 1.
2173. Article 1 Regulation (EU) No. 1107/2009.
2174. Law on Plant Protection Products ('ο περί Φυτοπροστατευτικών Προϊόντων Νόμος') No. 141 of 2011, OG I(I) No. 4300 of 27 Oct. 2011, p. 1256.
2175. Section 3(a) Law No. 141(I)/2011.

protection products,[2176] marketing and placing on the market,[2177] sustainable use of those,[2178] formal controls of those and their use,[2179] penalties imposed for violation of this law.[2180] Equally important is to set out the purpose of Regulation (EU) No. 1107/2009, which along with laying down rules for the authorization of plant production products and approval of active substances, safeners, synergists, adjuvants and co-formulants,[2181] is to ensure a high level of protection of both human and animal health and the environment. It further improves the functioning of the internal market through the harmonization of the rules on the placing on the market of plant protection products, while improving agricultural production.[2182] The provisions of this regulation are underpinned by the precautionary principle in order to ensure that active substances or products placed on the market do not adversely affect human or animal health or the environment.[2183]

II. Area of Application

515. This law is applicable to *plant protective products* (‘φυτοπροστατευτικά προϊόντα’),[2184] *active substances* (‘δραστικές ουσίες’),[2185] *safeners* (‘αντιφυτοτοξικά’),[2186] *synergists* (‘συνεργιστικά’),[2187] *co-formulants* (‘βοηθητικά’)[2188] and *adjuvants* (‘πρόσθετα’)[2189] as these are defined in Regulation (EU) No. 1107/2009.[2190]

2176. Section 3(b)(i) *ibid.*
2177. Section 3(b)(ii) *ibid.*
2178. Section 3(b)(iii) *ibid.*
2179. Section 3(b)(iv) *ibid.*
2180. Section 3(b)(v) *ibid.*
2181. Article 1(1) and (2) Regulation (EU) No. 1107/2009.
2182. Article 1(3) *ibid.*
2183. Article 1(4) *ibid.*
2184. It is specified that:

> [t]his Regulation shall apply to products, in the form in which they are supplied to the user, consisting of or containing active substances, safeners or synergists, and intended for one of the following uses: (a) protecting plants or plant products against all harmful organisms or preventing the action of such organisms, unless the main purpose of these products is considered to be for reasons of hygiene rather than for the protection of plants or plant products; (b) influencing the life processes of plants, such as substances influencing their growth, other than as a nutrient; (c) preserving plant products, in so far as such substances or products are not subject to special Community provisions on preservatives; (d) destroying undesired plants or parts of plants, except algae unless the products are applied on soil or water to protect plants; (e) checking or preventing undesired growth of plants, except algae unless the products are applied on soil or water to protect plants. These products are referred to as *plant protection products* (in French ‘produits phytopharmaceutiques’; in German ‘Pflanzenschutzmittel’, in Dutch ‘gewasbeschermingsmiddelen’). Article 2(1) *ibid.*

2185. *Active substances* (in French ‘substances actives’, in German ‘Wirkstoffe’, in Dutch ‘werkzame stoffen’) are substances, including microorganisms having general or specific action against harmful organisms or on plants, parts of plants or plant products. Article 2(2) *ibid.*
2186. *Safeners* (in French ‘phytoprotecteurs’, in German ‘Safener’, in Dutch ‘beschermstoffen’) are substances or preparations which are added to a plant protection product to eliminate or reduce phytotoxic effects of the plant protection product on certain plants. Article 2(3)(a) *ibid.*

III. Competent Authorities

A. The Minister of Agriculture, Rural Development and Environment

516. The Minister has the power to issue decrees for technical matters that need to be regulated according to this law or Regulation (EU) No. 1107/2009.[2191] This power is very wide, as the term 'technical matters' is neither defined nor definable.

B. The Council of Ministers

517. The Council of Ministers has the power to issue regulations for specifying any matter that needs to be specified, as well as for fully and effectively carrying out this law and Regulation (EU) No. 1107/2009.[2192] In particular, and without prejudice to generally of the foregoing power, such regulations may provide for all or any of the following subjects: data requirements and submission form of comprehensive and full file regarding active substances, synergists, safeners and plant protection products;[2193] methods for specifying the nature and amount of active substances, safeners and synergists and, depending on the case, impurity and co-formulants included in a plant protection product, if the latter are of toxicological, ecotoxicological and environmental relevance;[2194] requirements for issuing a parallel trade permit;[2195] requirements for issuing an authorization for use of adjuvants under Regulation (EU) No. 1107/2009;[2196] requirements for classification, packaging and labelling of plant protection product;[2197] inspections, especially regarding production, packaging, labelling, storage, transport, commerce, manufacture, parallel trade and use of plant production products;[2198] collection of information and submission of

2187. *Synergists* (in French 'synergistes', in German 'Synergisten', in Dutch 'synergisten') are substances or preparations which, while showing no or only weak activity as referred to in Art. 2(1) Regulation (EU) No. 1107/2009, can give enhanced activity to the active substance(s) in a plant protection product. Article 2(3)(b) *ibid.*

2188. *Co-formulants* (in French 'coformulants', in German 'Beistoffe', in Dutch 'formuleringshulpstoffen') are substances or preparations which are used or intended to be used in a plant protection product or adjuvant, but are neither active substances nor safeners or synergists. Article 2(3)(c) *ibid.*

2189. *Adjuvants* (in French 'adjuvants', in German 'Zusatzstoffe', in Dutch 'toevoegingsstoffen') are substances or preparations which consist of co-formulants or preparations containing one or more co-formulants, in the form in which they are supplied to the user and placed on the market to be mixed by the user with a plant protection product and which enhance its effectiveness or other pesticidal properties. Art. 2(3)(d) *ibid.*

2190. Section 3(2) Law No. 141(I)/2011.

2191. Section 23 *ibid.*

2192. Section 22(1) *ibid.*

2193. Section 22(2)(a) *ibid.*

2194. Section 22(2)(b) *ibid.*

2195. Section 22(2)(c) *ibid.*

2196. Section 22(2)(d) *ibid. See* in this respect also Art. 58 Regulation (EU) No. 1107/2009.

2197. Section 22(2)(e) Law No. 141(I)/2011.

2198. Section 22(2)(f) *ibid.*

reports on possible poisonings;[2199] the manner and procedure of sampling;[2200] specifying fees for evaluation of any application submitted under this law, granting any authorization issued or any registration performed under this law;[2201] sustainable use of plant protection products, reducing hazards and effects of using plant protection products on human health and the environment and promotion of using integrated plant protection and alternative approaches or techniques, such as non-chemical alternative solutions instead of plant protection products;[2202] import and production conditions for small amount of plant protection products that are not authorized for experiments and tests for the purpose of research and development;[2203] the qualifications, liabilities and obligations of sellers and professional users of plant protection products, including the obligation to be registered and have a relevant licence, along with the relevant fees;[2204] the criteria and specifications, which storage and shops of plant protection products must fulfil, the manner of storage and the species, which may be stored or sold within these;[2205] spraying means;[2206] and prohibition or restriction of advertising plant protection products in some communication means.[2207]

C. Council of Plant Protection Products and Biocidal Products

518. The Council of Plant Protection Products and Biocidal Products ('Συμβούλιο Φυτοπροστατευτικών Προϊόντων και Βιοκτόνων') is being established through this law. It consists of ten members, those being the General Director of the Ministry of Agriculture, Rural Development and Environment, four officers of the Department of Agriculture, two representatives of Ministry of Health, the Director of the Department of Labour Inspection of the Ministry of Labour and Social Security, a representative of the Agronomists' Council and the Director of the Department of Environment of the Ministry of Agriculture, Rural Development and Environment.[2208] The powers of this Council are not specified in this law. However, it is prescribed that under specific conditions elaborated in this law, the Council's (unspecified) powers may be delegated to any public officer.[2209]

2199. Section 22(2)(g) *ibid.*
2200. Section 22(2)(h) *ibid.*
2201. Section 22(2)(i) and (j) *ibid.*
2202. Section 22(2)(k) *ibid. Sustainable use of pesticides* ('utilisation des pesticides compatible avec le développement durable' in French, 'nachhaltige Verwendung von Pestiziden' in German, 'verwezenlijking van een duurzaam gebruik van pesticiden' in Dutch) is regulated by Regulations on sustainable use of pesticides ('οι περί Ορθολογικής Χρήσης Γεωργικών Φαρμάκων Κανονισμοί') No. 193 of 2012, OG I(I) No. 4572 of 1 Jun. 2012, p. 1287, which implements Directive 2009/128/EC of the European Parliament and of the Council of 21 Oct. 2009 establishing a framework for Community action to achieve the sustainable use of pesticides, OJ L 309, 24 Nov. 2009, p. 71.
2203. Section 22(2)(l) Law No. 141(I)/2011.
2204. Section 22(2)(m) and (o) *ibid.*
2205. Section 22(2)(n) *ibid.*
2206. Section 22(2)(p) *ibid.*
2207. Section 22(2)(q) *ibid.*
2208. Section 4(1)(a)–(f) *ibid.*
2209. Section 5(1), (2) and (3) *ibid.*

D. Department of Agriculture

519. The Department of Agriculture is the competent authority for receiving and assessing applications and data submitted under this law and submission of relevant report to the Council, as the case may be.[2210] It further performs inspections to ensure compliance with the provisions of this law and coordinates cooperation with the EC, the European Food Safety Authority, other Member States, applicants, producers and farmers.[2211]

E. Inspector-in-Chief and Inspectors

520. Inspector-in-chief and inspectors are appointed by the Minister for the purpose of application of this law.[2212] Their inspection powers are similar to the ones of inspectors under Law No. 187(I)/2002 (*see* in this respect paragraphs 34 et seq. above).[2213]

IV. Statutory Prohibitions

521. Any import, distribution, storage, possession, production for placement on the market, placement on the market, advertisement or use of any plant protection product is prohibited unless an authorization of Articles 28, 52 and 54 Regulation (EU) No. 1107/2009 has been granted and has not been revoked.[2214] Placement on the market of such products having a label in violation of its authorization's conditions is equally prohibited.[2215] The same applies to placing on the market of any such product that is not contained in proper packaging, according to Regulation (EU) No. 1107/2009;[2216] to usage of such product in violation of the instructions stated on its label or otherwise accompanying its packaging;[2217] to usage of such product in crop other than the ones stated on its label;[2218] to any in whole or in part manipulation, erasure, removal or destruction of any label under this law or removal or addition of any substance from or into any plant protection product in a way that it could circumvent the scope of this law;[2219] to repackaging of any such product without the prior consent of the competent authority;[2220] and to any advertisement

2210. Section 6(a) *ibid.*
2211. Section 6(b) and (c) *ibid.*
2212. Section 14(1), (2), (3) and (4) *ibid.*
2213. Section 15(1), (2) and (3) *ibid.*
2214. Section 12(1) *ibid.*
2215. Section 12(2) *ibid.*
2216. Section 12(3) *ibid.* For the packaging requirements *see* Arts 64 and 65 Regulation (EU) No. 1107/2009.
2217. Section 12(4) Law No. 141(I)/2011.
2218. Section 12(5) *ibid.*
2219. Section 12(6)(a) *ibid.*
2220. Section 12(6)(b) *ibid.*

of the quality control results without the prior consent of the competent authority.[2221] Further, when the competent authority has justified a reason to believe that a plant protection product or a substance poses an unacceptable risk to human or animal health or the environment, the use or selling thereof may be restricted or prohibited,[2222] and the EC along with the Member States are informed without any delay.[2223]

V. Authorization of a Plant Protection Product

522. A plant protection product may be placed on the market only if this has been authorized by the competent authority, that being the Council of Plant Protection Products and Biocidal Products, as provided for in Regulation (EU) No. 1107/2009.[2224] The application, technical data, studies and fees that need to be submitted in this regard are to be specified by the competent authority.[2225] The criteria according to which the application is evaluated are set out in the regulation.[2226]

523. The authorization holder bears liability for the correctness of data and information submitted to the competent authority while applying for the authorization as well as the obligation to ensure compliance of the plant protection product with this law. If the authorization holder does not reside in Cyprus, said liability and obligation are borne by the person responsible for placing this product on the market.[2227] Further, any person responsible for any activity related to plant protection products, active substances, safeners or synergists is obliged to provide all necessary means and information to the inspectors during the exercise of their duties.[2228] The granting of authorization and any other measures in conformity with this law and Regulation (EU) No. 1107/2009 is without prejudice to general civil and criminal liability of the producer, of the person responsible for placing the plant protection product on the market or using it.[2229]

524. The competent authority may revoke or suspend an authorization, if the conditions for approval were not or are not any more fulfilled.[2230]

2221. Section 12(8) *ibid.* With reference to further restrictions on advertising for the purpose of not misleading users of plant protection products or the public, *see* Art. 66 Regulation (EU) No. 1107/2009.
2222. Section 13(1) Law No. 141(I)/2011. The ground of unacceptable risk to human or animal health or the environment may lead to refusal of authorization according to Art. 38(3) Regulation (EU) No. 1107/2009, whereas the national provision is applicable both to authorized plant protection products and substances, as well as to those for which an application has been filed.
2223. Section 13(2) Law No. 141(I)/2011.
2224. Sections 7(1) and 2(1) *ibid.*
2225. Sections 8(a) and 10 *ibid.*
2226. Section 8(b) *ibid.* More specifically, the approval criteria are set out in Art. 4(1), (2) and (3) and Annex II Regulation (EU) No. 1107/2009.
2227. Section 9(1) and (2) Law No. 141(I)/2011.
2228. Section 16 *ibid.*
2229. Section 18 *ibid.* This is also prescribed in Art. 73 Regulation (EU) No. 1107/2009.
2230. Section 19(2)(d) Law No. 141(I)/2011.

VI. Archives

525. The Department of Agriculture keeps an archive of plant protection products, in which the authorized plant protection products are registered, along with an archive of the applications for such an authorization. The form of these archives lies at the discretion of the department.[2231]

VII. Ensuring Compliance

A. Administrative Sanctions

526. The competent authority, that being the Council of Plant Protection Products and Biocidal Products, performs inspections regarding any violations of this law and Regulation (EU) No. 1107/2009 either following a complaint or on its own motion.[2232] Should following such an inspection violation of any provision be established, the competent authority may order termination of that violation and prohibit repeating same in the future. In the event that the violation has already been terminated prior to such order, this compliance is being certified by the competent authority.[2233] The competent authority may also reserve for any period of time deemed necessary plant protection products and order that these remain or be transferred to a recommended place,[2234] be re-exported abroad, be shipped to the country of origin or be destroyed. The expenses are to be borne by the possessor of confiscated products or the person performing the violation, as the case may be.[2235] The competent authority may also impose an administrative penalty of up to EUR 10,000[2236] and prohibit, for as long as it deems necessary, harvesting corps for the purpose of making it commercially available. It has in addition the power to order the destruction of harvested corps; any related expenses are borne by the producer who may not claim any compensation.[2237]

527. Prior to imposing these administrative sanctions, the competent authority informs in writing the affected person of its intention along with the reasons for such an action and the right to submit any representations within fifteen days from the date that this information is served.[2238] Imposing these administrative sanctions has the form of a reasoned decision, which also informs about the right of the affected person to submit an administrative appeal to the Minister and is served to the affected person.[2239] The administrative appeal has to be filed within thirty days with the Minister, who may at his discretion give to the appellant the chance to further

2231. Section 11(1) and (2) *ibid.*
2232. Section 19(1) *ibid.*
2233. Section 19(2)(a) *ibid.*
2234. Section 19(2)(b) *ibid.*
2235. Section 19(2)(c) *ibid.*
2236. Section 19(2)(e) *ibid.*
2237. Section 19(2)(f) *ibid.*
2238. Section 19(3) *ibid.*
2239. Section 19(4)(a) and (b) *ibid.*

support the grounds of this appeal.[2240] The appealed decision may be confirmed, annulled, amended or replaced by a new one.[2241]

528. Should the affected person fail to pay the administrative fine, a lawsuit may be filed with the court requesting this to be paid as civil debt owed to the state.[2242] No provision is foreseen for the event of failure to comply with other administrative sanctions.

B. Penal Sanctions

529. The penalty of imprisonment of up to two years and/or a fine of up to EUR 40,000 may be imposed, following conviction for the offence of:

- violation of or failure to comply with this law or Regulation (EU) No. 1107/2009;[2243]
- presentation with untrue representations of a plant protection product in any advertisement;[2244]
- obstruction of inspectors or other competent authority from performing their duties;[2245]
- illegal use of an authorization number given under this law or using this number as if it was granted under this law;[2246]
- selling or exposing for selling or placing on the market a plant protection product, which following sampling and quality control it has been established that this does not comply with its composition as registered and approved by the competent authority during issuance of authorization;[2247]
- concealing, destroying or counterfeiting any document or other data;[2248]
- refusal or failure of compliance with any condition attached to an authorization issued under this law or Regulation (EU) No. 1107/2009;[2249]
- on purpose obstruction or misleading in any way an inspector during exercise of his duties or a person accompanying him;[2250]
- refusal to provide the inspector or any person accompanying him with safe access to any part of the establishment;[2251] and
- refusal or failure of compliance with any instruction or demands of the inspector.[2252]

2240. Section 21(1) and (2) *ibid.*
2241. Section 21(3)(a), (b), (c) and (d) *ibid.*
2242. Section 19(5) *ibid.*
2243. Section 20(1)(a) *ibid.*
2244. Section 20(1)(b) *ibid.*
2245. Section 20(1)(c) *ibid.*
2246. Section 20(1)(d) *ibid.*
2247. Section 20(1)(e) *ibid.*
2248. Section 20(1)(f) *ibid.*
2249. Section 20(1)(g) *ibid.*
2250. Section 20(1)(h) and (i) *ibid.*
2251. Section 20(1)(j) *ibid.*
2252. Section 20(1)(k) *ibid.*

C. Other Sanctions

530. With reference to the penal offences set out above and in addition to the aforementioned penalties, the court may order confiscation of plant protection products, which were involved in the offence, prohibition of selling same, their destruction or other treatment, as it deems fit.[2253]

§3. Biocidal Products

531. Biocidal products are regulated throughout the EU via Regulation (EU) No. 528/2012.[2254] For the purpose of application of this regulation, Law on Biocidal Products[2255] (hereinafter 'Law No. 34(I)/2014') has been issued.

I. Objective

532. The objective of this law is to provide the necessary complementary measures for the application of Regulation (EU) No. 528/2012[2256] and set out general provisions and rules related to the procedure for issuing an authorization for biocidal products,[2257] marketing and making available biocidal products to users,[2258] formal controls of placing same products on the market and using those[2259] as well as penalties imposed for violation of this law.[2260] Equally important is to state the purpose of Regulation (EU) No. 528/2012, which consists of improving the functioning of the internal market through the harmonization of the rules on making available on the market and use of biocidal products, while ensuring a high level of protection of both human and animal health and the environment. Also, the provisions of this regulation are underpinned by the precautionary principle, the aim of which is to safeguard the health of humans, the health of animals and the environment.[2261]

2253. Section 20(2) *ibid.*
2254. Regulation (EU) No. 528/2012 of the European Parliament and of the Council of 22 May 2012 concerning the making available on the market and use of biocidal products Text with EEA relevance, OJ L 167, 27 Jun. 2012, p. 1.
2255. Law on Biocidal Products ('ο περί Βιοκτόνων Νόμος') No. 34 of 2014, OG I(I) No. 4435 of 14 Mar. 2014, p. 169.
2256. Section 3(a) Law No. 34(I)/2014.
2257. Section 3(b)(i) *ibid.*
2258. Section 3(b)(ii) *ibid.*
2259. Section 3(b)(iii) *ibid.*
2260. Section 3(b)(iv) *ibid.*
2261. Article 1(1) Regulation (EU) No. 528/2012.

II. Area of Application

533. The provisions of this law apply to *biocidal products* ('βιοκτόνα')[2262] and *treated articles* ('κατεργασμένα αντικείμενα'),[2263] as specified in Regulation (EU) No. 528/2012.[2264]

III. Competent Authorities

A. The Minister of Agriculture, Rural Development and Environment

534. As under Law No. 141(I)/2011, the Minister of Agriculture, Rural Development and Environment has wide powers regarding issuing degrees on technical matters that need to be regulated under this law or Regulation (EU) No. 528/2012.[2265]

B. The Council of Ministers

535. The Council of Ministers has the power to issue regulations for specifying any matter that needs to be specified, as well as for fully and effectively carrying out this law and Regulation (EU) No. 528/2012.[2266] In particular, and without prejudice to generally of the foregoing power, such regulations may provide for all or any of the following subjects: specifying fees for evaluation of any application under this law;[2267] specifying fees for issuing any authorization or registration under this law;[2268] rational application ('ορθολογική χρήση') of biocidal products, minimizing dangers and effects of biocidal products' use to human health and the environment and application of integrated pest management principles with respect to

2262. *Biocidal product* ('produit biocid' in French, 'Biozidprodukt' in German, 'biociden' in Dutch) means any substance or mixture, in the form in which it is supplied to the user, consisting of, containing or generating one or more active substances, with the intention of destroying, deterring, rendering harmless, preventing the action of, or otherwise exerting a controlling effect on, any harmful organism by any means other than mere physical or mechanical action, any substance or mixture, generated from substances or mixtures which do not themselves fall under the first indent, to be used with the intention of destroying, deterring, rendering harmless, preventing the action of, or otherwise exerting a controlling effect on, any harmful organism by any means other than mere physical or mechanical action. A treated article that has a primary biocidal function shall be considered a biocidal product. Article 3(1)(a) Regulation (EU) No. 528/2012.

2263. *Treated article* ('article traité' in French, 'behandelte Waren' in German, 'behandeld voorwerp' in Dutch) means any substance, mixture or article which has been treated with, or intentionally incorporates, one or more biocidal products. Article 3(1)(l) *ibid.*

2264. Section 4 Law No. 34(I)/2014.

2265. Section 23 *ibid.*

2266. Section 22(1) *ibid.*

2267. Section 22(2)(a) *ibid.*

2268. Section 22(2)(b) *ibid.*

the use of biocidal products;[2269] the manner and procedure of sampling and performance of testing, analysis and measurements under this law;[2270] data requirements for placing on the market of treated articles;[2271] and the qualifications, liabilities and obligations of persons placing biocidal products on the market and professional users, including imposing the obligation for their registration and granting a permit for selling or professionally using biocidal products.[2272]

C. The Council of Plant Protection Products and Biocidal Products

536. The Council of Plant Protection Products and Biocidal Products ('Συμβούλιο Φυτοπροστατευτικών Προϊόντων και Βιοκτόνων') that has been established via Law No. 141(I)/2011 is a competent authority under this law as well.[2273] Its duties include: receiving and evaluating applications and data submitted under this law;[2274] granting authorizations;[2275] performing controls for ensuring compliance with the provisions of this law;[2276] keeping a record of biocidal products, in which authorized biocidal products as well as the submitted applications are registered;[2277] and receiving relevant information for formulating preventative and curative measures, in particular in the event of emergency health response, from importers and downstream users placing biocidal products on the market.[2278]

D. Inspector-in-Chief and Inspectors

537. Inspectors are appointed by the Minister for the purpose of application of this law. As powers of the inspectors appointed under Law No. 141(I)/2011, the powers of the inspectors are similar to the ones of inspectors under Law No. 187(I)/2002 (*see* in this respect paragraphs 34 et seq. above).[2279]

IV. Statutory Prohibitions

538. The statutory prohibitions regarding plant protection products explained above (*see* in this respect paragraphs 519 et seq. above) are equally applicable to

2269. Section 22(2)(c) *ibid.*
2270. Section 22(2)(d) *ibid.*
2271. Section 22(2)(e) *ibid.*
2272. Section 22(2)(f) and (g) *ibid.*
2273. Sections 6 and 2(1) *ibid.*
2274. Section 6(a) *ibid.*
2275. Section 6(b) *ibid.*
2276. Section 6(c) *ibid.*
2277. Section 6(d) *ibid.*
2278. Section 6(e) *ibid.*, Article 73 Regulation (EU) No. 528/2012 and Art. 45 Regulation (EC) No. 1272/2008 of the European Parliament and of the Council of 16 Dec. 2008 on classification, labelling and packaging of substances and mixtures, amending and repealing Directives 67/548/EEC and 1999/45/EC, and amending Regulation (EC) No. 1907/2006, OJ L 353, 31 Dec. 2008, p. 1.
2279. Section 15 Law No. 34(I)/2014.

biocidal products,[2280] with the exception of prohibition on using such product on other crops and publication of quality control results. Advertising is also regulated in a manner similar to plant protection products.[2281]

V. Authorization for Biocidal Products

539. Biocidal products are placed on the market and used in accordance with the provisions of Regulation (EU) No. 528/2012, only if an authorization has been issued by the competent authority or a Union authorization according to Article 42 Regulation (EU) No. 528/2012.[2282]

540. A person interested in being granted an authorization under this law, submits an application to the competent authority in a specified form, which is accompanied by a file including all technical elements and studies, as instructed by the competent authority.[2283] The criteria according to which the competent authority assesses applications are set out in Regulation (EU) No. 528/2012.[2284] When these are fulfilled, an authorization providing a unique number for every biocidal product is granted. Should the application be rejected, the relevant reasoned decision is being served to the applicant.[2285]

541. The authorization holder bears liability for the correctness of data and information submitted to the competent authority while applying for the authorization as well as the obligation of compliance of the biocidal product with this law.[2286] If the authorization holder does not reside in Cyprus, liability and obligation are borne by the person responsible for placing this product on the market.[2287] As under authorization for plant protection products, any person responsible for any activity related to biocidal products, active substance ('δραστική ουσία'),[2288] substance of concern ('ανησυχητική ουσία'),[2289] treated articles or nanomaterials

2280. Sections 12(1), (2), (3), (4), (5)(a) and (b) and 13(1) and (2) Law No. 34(I)/2014. *See also* the safeguard clause in Art. 88 Regulation (EU) No. 528/2012, which in any case has a provisional nature and may be revoked by the Commission.
2281. *See* in this respect Art. 72 Regulation (EU) No. 528/2012.
2282. Section 7(1) Law No. 34(I)/2014.
2283. Section 8 *ibid.*
2284. These are set out in Arts 4(1), 19(1)(b) and Annex VI Regulation (EU) No. 528/2012.
2285. Section 9 Law No. 34(I)/2014.
2286. Section 10(1) *ibid.*
2287. Section 10(2) *ibid.*
2288. *Active substance* ('substance active' in French, 'Wirkstoff' in German, 'werkzame stof' in Dutch) means a substance or a microorganism that has an action on or against harmful organisms. Article 3(1)(c) Regulation No. 528/2012.
2289. *Substance of concern* ('substance préoccupante' in French, 'bedenklicher Stoff' in German, 'tot bezorgdheid aanleiding gevende stof' in Dutch) means any substance, other than the active substance, which has an inherent capacity to cause an adverse effect, immediately or in the more distant future, on humans, in particular vulnerable groups, animals or the environment and is present or is produced in a biocidal product in sufficient concentration to present risks of such an effect. Article 3(1)(f) Regulation (EU) No. 528/2012.

('νανοϋλικό')[2290] provides all means and information to the inspectors during the exercise of their duties.[2291] The granting of authorization and any other measures in conformity with this law and Regulation (EU) No. 528/2012 is without prejudice to general civil and criminal liability of the producer, of the person responsible for placing the biocide product on the market or using it.[2292]

542. An authorization for biocidal products may be revoked or suspended when the approval criteria are not fulfilled.[2293]

VI. Ensuring Compliance

543. Administrative, penal and other sanctions are imposed upon violation of this law for the purpose of ensuring compliance with same,[2294] *mutatis mutandis,* the relevant provisions of Law No. 141(I)/2011 (*see* in this respect paragraphs 524 et seq. above). The provisions differentiate to the extent that they refer to biocidal products and the applicable administrative fine amounts up to EUR 5,000.[2295]

§4. Fertilizers

544. Fertilizers are regulated throughout the EU via Regulation (EC) No. 2003/2003.[2296] For the purpose of application of this regulation, Law on Fertilizers[2297] (hereinafter 'Law No. 32(I)/2006') has been issued.

2290. *Nanomaterial* ('nanomatériau' in French, 'Nanomaterial' in German, 'nanomateriaal' in Dutch) means a natural or manufactured active substance or non-active substance containing particles, in an unbound state or as an aggregate or as an agglomerate and where, for 50% or more of the particles in the number size distribution, one or more external dimensions is in the size range 1–100 nm. Fullerenes, graphene flakes and single-wall carbon nanotubes with one or more external dimensions below 1 nm shall be considered as nanomaterials. For the purposes of the definition of nanomaterial, *particle*, *agglomerate* and *aggregate* are defined as follows: *particle* means a minute piece of matter with defined physical boundaries; *agglomerate* means a collection of weakly bound particles or aggregates where the resulting external surface area is similar to the sum of the surface areas of the individual components; *aggregate* means a particle comprising strongly bound or fused particles. Article 3(1)(z) *ibid.*

2291. Section 16 Law No. 34(I)/2014.

2292. Section 18 *ibid.*

2293. Section 19(2)(d) *ibid.*

2294. Sections 19 and 20 *ibid.*

2295. Section 19(2)(e) *ibid.*

2296. Regulation (EC) No. 2003/2003 of the European Parliament and of the Council of 13 Oct. 2003 relating to fertilizers, OJ L 304 of 21 Nov. 2003, p. 1.

2297. Law on Fertilizers ('ο περί Λιπασμάτων Νόμος') No. 32 of 2006, OG I(I) No. 4076 of 17 Mar. 2006, p. 590.

I. Objective

545. The objective of this law is regulation of manufacturing, blending, packaging,[2298] composition and trade of fertilizers along with prescribing provisions for enabling the application of Regulation (EC) No. 2003/2003.[2299] Fertilizer ('λίπασμα') is defined as any substance or blending of substances that contain one or more nutrient elements and used in solid, liquid or air form, provides one or more nutrient elements, which are necessary for plant nutrition,[2300] and therefore differentiates from the one contained in Regulation (EC) No. 2003/2003.[2301]

II. Area of Application

546. No provision on specifying its area of application is contained in this law. However, the term 'fertilizer', as explained above, provides safe ground for setting its limits.

III. Competent Authorities

A. The Minister of Agriculture, Rural Development and Environment

547. The Minister of Agriculture, Rural Development and Environment may regulate any matters of technical nature related to fertilizers through decrees that are published in the Official Gazette.[2302] His power is wide, as in Law No. 141(I)/2011 and Law No. 34(I)/2014 (*see* in this respect paragraphs 514 and 532 respectively).

B. Council of Ministers

548. The Council of Ministers has the power to issue regulations for the best implementation of the provisions of this law.[2303] In particular, and without prejudice to the generality of the foregoing power, such regulations may provide for all

2298. Pursuant to Regulation (EC) No. 2003/2003, *package* ('emballage' in French, 'Verpackung' in German, 'verpakking' in Dutch) means a sealable receptacle used to hold, protect, handle, and distribute fertilizers and holding not more than 1000 kg. Article 2(u) Regulation (EC) No. 2003/2003.
2299. Section 3(a) and (b) Law No. 32(I)/2006.
2300. Section 2 *ibid.*
2301. According to that, *fertilizer* ('engrais' in French, 'Düngemittel' or 'Dügel' in German, 'meststof' in Dutch) means material, the main function of which is to provide nutrients for plants. Article 2(a) Regulation (EC) No. 2003/2003.
2302. Section 19 Law No. 32(I)/2006.
2303. Section 17(1) *ibid.* Up to now one Regulation has been issued: Regulations on Fertilizers ('οι περί Λιπασμάτων Κανονισμοί') No. 118 of 2006, OG III(I) No. 4089 of 22 Mar. 2006, p. 949. These provide for categories of fertilizers, minimum levels and properties of fertilizers, street

or any of the following subjects:[2304] any matter that under this law must or may be specified;[2305] classification of fertilizers in categories according to its nature or composition;[2306] process of granting an authorization for package, manufacture or composition of fertilizer, the authorization's type as well as the conditions that may be attached;[2307] the procedure for registration of fertilizer and specifying the fertilizer's type;[2308] the procedure that must be followed for registration and registration's renewal, revocation and suspension of imported, manufactured or composed fertilizer;[2309] fertilizer packaging and labelling, as approved by the Department of Agriculture;[2310] manner of sampling and particulars of analysis certificate;[2311] fees due for quality control, issuing authorization for manufacture or composition, registration, sampling, fertilizer analysis or any other matter under this law;[2312] and the way of disposing confiscated fertilizer.[2313]

C. *Council for Fertilizers' Control*

549. The Council for Fertilizers' Control ('Συμβούλιο Ελέγχου Λιπασμάτων') is being established for the objective of this law. It consists of the General Director of the Minister of Agriculture, Rural Development and Environment,[2314] the Director of the Department for Agriculture,[2315] an officer of the Department for Agriculture,[2316] the Director of the Lab for Chemical Analysis of the Department for Agriculture,[2317] an officer of the Institute of Agriculture Research,[2318] an officer suggested by the Minister of Energy, Commerce, Industry and Tourism[2319] and a representative of the Agronomists' Council.[2320] This council has the power to: advise the Minister and provide opinion on matters related to fertilizers;[2321] advises the Minister on the usefulness of experts participating in the council;[2322] ensures cooperation and inform the co-competent authorities of the Ministry of Agriculture,

sweepings, type of fertilizers, authorization for manufacture of fertilizers, authorization for package of fertilizers, registration of fertilizers, authorization of import of fertilizers, package of fertilizers, sampling for analysis of fertilizers and quality controls.

2304. Section 17(2) Law No. 32(I)/2006.
2305. Section 17(2)(a) *ibid.*
2306. Section 17(2)(b) *ibid.*
2307. Section 17(2)(c) *ibid.*
2308. Section 17(2)(d) *ibid.*
2309. Section 17(2)(e) *ibid.*
2310. Section 17(2)(f) *ibid.*
2311. Section 17(2)(g) *ibid.*
2312. Section 17(2)(h) *ibid.*
2313. Section 17(2)(i) *ibid.*
2314. Section 4(1)(a) *ibid.*
2315. Section 4(1)(b) *ibid.*
2316. Section 4(1)(c) *ibid.*
2317. Section 4(1)(d) *ibid.*
2318. Section 4(1)(e) *ibid.*
2319. Section 4(1)(f) *ibid.*
2320. Section 4(1)(g) *ibid.*
2321. Section 5(a) *ibid.*
2322. Section 5(b) *ibid.*

Rural Development and Environment, authorities of other Ministries, various organisms as well as other bodies involved in fertilizers;[2323] submits to Department of Agriculture suggestions for granting authorizations for production, package, import as well as registration of fertilizers;[2324] and ensures monitoring difficulties and problems from the implementation of this law and Regulation (EC) No. 2003/2003.[2325]

D. Department of Agriculture

550. The Department of Agriculture of the Ministry of Agriculture, Rural Development and Environment has the authority to take all necessary measures for ensuring the application of this law and Regulation (EC) No. 2003/2003.[2326] It further controls manufacturing, blending, packaging, composition and trade of fertilizers and complying with obligations of traders under this law and Regulation (EC) No. 2003/2003.[2327]

E. Inspectors

551. The Minister appoints inspectors to ensure the application of this law and Regulation (EC) No. 2003/2003.[2328] They may enter any premises, when they have reasonable suspicions or information that fertilizer is stored, packaged, composed or exposed for sale, for the purpose of verifying compliance with this law and Regulation (EC) No. 2003/2003.[2329] They further have the right to take a sample of fertilizers for quality control,[2330] inspect books, records and any other documents, when there is reasonable suspicion of being involved with the application of this law,[2331] confiscate any fertilizer that violates this law or Regulation (EC) No. 2003/2003[2332] and perform any other duties appointed to them,[2333] although it is not specified, who could appoint such to them. Lastly, inspectors advise the Department of Agriculture regarding applications for issuing authorizations for composition, manufacture, package and production as well as the applications for registration and import[2334] and prepare a written report to the Department of Agriculture for every violation of the provisions of this law and Regulation (EC) No. 2003/2003.[2335]

2323. Section 5(c) *ibid.* However, no further clarification is provided as to the grounds basing a co-competence or clarification as to the extent of the same.
2324. Section 5(d) *ibid.*
2325. Section 5(e) *ibid.*
2326. Section 6(2)(a) *ibid.*
2327. Section 6(2)(b) *ibid.*
2328. Section 11(1) *ibid.*
2329. Section 11(2) *ibid.*
2330. Section 11(3) *ibid.*
2331. Section 11(4)(b) *ibid.*
2332. Section 11(4)(e) *ibid.*
2333. Section 11(4)(d) *ibid.*
2334. Section 11(4)(a) *ibid.*
2335. Section 11(4)(c) *ibid.*

IV. Registration of Fertilizers

552. Lawful selling of fertilizers, but for 'fertilizers EC', prerequisites their registration.[2336] To this purpose, every manufacturer, packer, importer or distributor of fertilizer file a specific form, along with the therein specified documentation and receipt of payment of the due fees,[2337] copy of the intended labelling of this fertilizer,[2338] certificate of the chemical and/or microbiological analysis of the fertilizer, as the case may be, certifying minimum guaranteed percentage analogy of every component, electron conductance, presence of heavy metals or other elements as well as levels of any pathogen strength, along with further information for certificates of chemical analysis.[2339] Should the applicant be a company, certain corporate documentation has to be filed.[2340] The Department of Agriculture may, at its discretion, require submission of further data or information.[2341] The application for registration is granted no later than three months, when the Department of Agriculture is satisfied that the fertilizer fulfils the demands of this law and Regulation 118/2006,[2342] the labelling complies with the statutory provisions along with not containing any untrue or misleading indication.[2343] This registration remains in force for an indefinite period of time, unless this is annulled or suspended.[2344] Inconsistently, it is further foreseen that the grounds supporting a revocation or suspension, and not an annulment or suspension, are: false statements, concealment of essential facts during application for registration and violation of this law and KDP 118/2006;[2345] use of registered fertilizer being of poor value or harmful to plants, animals, public health or environment;[2346] registered fertilizers being not or not any more in line with the registration or submitted data and information;[2347] and any further cause, according to the discretion of the Department of Agriculture.[2348]

553. No registration of fertilizers is necessary for importing a sample of fertilizer for testing purposes,[2349] for importing fertilizers for use as raw materials for the purpose of manufacture of fertilizers,[2350] for manufacture and selling of fertilizers for the purpose of export,[2351] as well as for selling or other disposal of livestock manure in its natural form, but not when this is enriched with nutrients.[2352]

2336. Section 9(1) *ibid.*
2337. Regulation 11(1)(a) KDP 118/2006.
2338. Regulation 11(1)(b) *ibid.*
2339. Regulation 11(1)(c) *ibid.*
2340. Regulation 11(1)(d) *ibid.*
2341. Regulation 11(4) *ibid.*
2342. Regulation 11(5)(a) *ibid.*
2343. Regulation 11(5)(b) *ibid.*
2344. Regulation 11(8) *ibid.*
2345. Regulation 12(1)(a) *ibid.*
2346. Regulation 12(1)(b) *ibid.*
2347. Regulation 12(1)(c) *ibid.*
2348. Regulation 12(1)(d) *ibid.*
2349. Section 9(2) Law No. 32(I)/2006.
2350. Section 9(3) *ibid.*
2351. Section 9(4) *ibid.*
2352. Section 9(5) *ibid.*

V. Authorization for Fertilizers

554. It is specified that no person may import, manufacture, or compose, in any manner, fertilizers without previously obtaining a written authorization from the Department of Agriculture and in accordance with the conditions that may be attached to such authorization. It is further clarified that blending two or more types of fertilizers for own use does not fall under the term 'manufacture' or 'composition'.[2353] This authorization is not required for fertilizers designated 'EC fertilizer'.[2354] More specifically, for an authorization for manufacture of fertilizers to be granted, an application in the designated form, along with the therein specified documentation,[2355] receipt of payment of fees due,[2356] corporate documentation of the applicant, if applicable,[2357] and certificate that the buildings and manufacture facilities of the applicant have been inspected and comply with the legislation on factories, employees' safety and health and air and water pollution control, must be filed.[2358] The Department of Agriculture, being the competent authority, may further request any additional data or information deemed necessary for reaching a decision on the submitted application.[2359] Issuing an authorization for package of fertilizers, for any person not manufacturing such, prerequisites an application in specific form along with the therein requested documentation, as well as a copy of fertilizer's registration,[2360] corporate documentation of the applicant, if applicable,[2361] certificate that the buildings and manufacture facilities of the applicant have been inspected and comply with the legislation on factories, employees' safety and health, and air and water pollution control,[2362] and receipt of payment of the fees due.[2363] The Department of Agriculture may additionally request any further information or data deemed necessary for evaluation of the submitted application.[2364] Authorization for fertilizers' import is granted, only if the relevant fertilizer is already registered, to the person, who performed the registration. Additionally, submission of the specific form along with the therein specified documentation and payment of the due fees are necessary.[2365]

555. Necessary requirement for granting an authorization for fertilizers is compliance of fertilizers' manufacture and composition with the provisions of this law

2353. Section 7(1) *ibid.*
2354. Section 7(2) *ibid.*
2355. Regulation 7(2)(a) KDP 118/2006.
2356. Regulation 7(2)(b)(i) *ibid.*
2357. Regulation 7(2)(b)(ii) *ibid.*
2358. Regulation 7(2)(b)(iii) *ibid.*
2359. Regulation 7(3) *ibid.*
2360. Regulation 8(1)(a) *ibid.*
2361. Regulation 8(1)(b) *ibid.*
2362. Regulations 8(1)(c) and 7(2)(b)(iii) *ibid.*
2363. Regulation 8(1)(d) *ibid.*
2364. Regulation 8(2) *ibid.*
2365. Regulation 13(1) and (2) *ibid.*

and Regulation (EC) No. 2003/2003 to the satisfaction of the Department of Agriculture.[2366] Especially for authorization of fertilizers' package, this is granted, when it is established that the applicant has the necessary equipment for sustainably packaging fertilizers.[2367]

VI. Packaging and Sampling

556. No person may sell fertilizer, unless fertilizer is packed in sacks bearing clearly such marks and in such order, as the Department of Agriculture may determine. However, the Department of Agriculture may at its discretion allow in writing and under certain conditions, if any, wholesale or retail sale of any fertilizer, despite of this not being packed in sacks.[2368] Specific characteristics of the sacks and containers that may be used for packaging are set out in secondary legislation. These aim to safely and securely transfer their content, as well as accurate and true labelling.[2369]

557. Following sampling performed by inspectors and its analysis by the competent authority, the relevant analysis certificate, which states whether quality of the fertilizer complies with the one registered, is forwarded to the Department of Agriculture and the owner of the analysed fertilizer.[2370] Should the importer, manufacturer, packer or vendor of fertilizer wish to dispute the analysis certificate, he has the right to demand the inspector to forward the relevant sample to the State General Laboratory for analysis. Following this, the State General Laboratory forwards the analysis' results to the individual, who requested it, and to the Department of Agriculture.[2371] Every buyer of fertilizer may also request an analysis of any purchased fertilizer by the competent authorities and receive a certificate stating the results of the performed analysis.[2372]

VII. Register

558. The Department of Agriculture keeps a record of fertilizers, in which all fertilizers but 'fertilizers EC' are registered, and a record of arrived fertilizers, in which all fertilizers labelled 'fertilizer EC' are registered.[2373]

2366. Section 8 Law No. 32(I)/2006 and Regulation 7(4) KDP 118/2006.
2367. Regulation 8(3) *ibid.*
2368. Section 10 Law No. 32(I)/2006.
2369. Regulations 14 and 15 KDP 118/2006.
2370. Section 12(1) Law No. 32(I)/2006.
2371. Section 12(2) *ibid.*
2372. Section 13 *ibid.*
2373. Section 14(a) and (b) *ibid.*

VIII. Ensuring Compliance

A. Penal Sanctions

559. Imprisonment of up to one year and/or a fine of up to EUR 3,420 may be imposed upon conviction by a court of law for the following offences, whereas second conviction for the same offence may lead to imprisonment for up to one year and/or a fine of up to EUR 6,840:

– importing, packaging, manufacturing or composing fertilizer without an authorization or in violation of the conditions attached to such;
– selling fertilizer in violation of the provisions on packaging and registration;[2374]
– selling fertilizer that does not correspond to data stated on relevant sacks or containers;[2375]
– in any manner preventing or obstructing the inspector or any other authorized officer during exercise of their duties;[2376]
– enabling a third party to commit an offence under this law;[2377]
– hiding, destroying, manipulating or refusing to provide any book, document, fertilizer or raw material for inspection;[2378]
– violation of prohibition imposed following written notification;[2379]
– violation or failure to comply with any of the conditions attached to an authorization;[2380]
– violation of any provision of regulations issued under this law;[2381]
– violation of Articles 4–14, 17–19, 21, 23, 24, 26(1), 26(3), 27, 28 and 34 Regulation (EC) No. 2003/2003.[2382]

B. Administrative Sanctions

560. In the event that an inspector establishes that fertilizer is being sold, exposed, offered or possessed for the purpose of selling in violation of this law or Regulation (EC) No. 2003/2003, he may serve a written notification ('ειδοποίηση') of this event to the manufacturer, importer, distributor, vendor or possessor. During a period of fifteen days following service of this notification, the addressees thereof are prohibited from selling, disposing, using, transferring, exporting or destroying this fertilizer.[2383] A penal procedure may follow.

2374. Sections 15(b), 9 and 10 *ibid.*
2375. Section 15(c) *ibid.*
2376. Section 15(d) *ibid.*
2377. Section 15(e) *ibid.*
2378. Section 15(f) *ibid.*
2379. Sections 15(g) and 16(1) *ibid.*
2380. Section 15(h) *ibid.*
2381. Section 15(i) *ibid.*
2382. Section 15(j) *ibid.*
2383. Section 16(1) *ibid.*

C. Other Sanctions

561. During the penal procedure for the above-stated penal offences, an inspector may file an ex parte application to the court requesting a freezing order prohibiting selling, disposing, using, transferring, exporting or destroying fertilizer involved in the penal procedure until the final judgment of the court. Issuing such an order, as well as attaching conditions to it, if any, lies at the discretion of the court.[2384]

562. In addition to the aforementioned penalties for the penal offences, the court may order confiscation or prohibition of selling of any fertilizer involved in the established penal offence.[2385]

2384. Section 16(2) *ibid.*
2385. Section 15 *ibid.*

Chapter 5. Forests

563. The Law on Forests[2386] (hereinafter 'Law No. 25(I)/2012') regulates matters relevant to forests. It has abolished Law on Forests of 1967.[2387]

§1. Objective

564. This law aims to preserve, protect, sustainably manage and develop forests and forest areas,[2388] enforce the national forest policy[2389] and create a regulation frame for forest and forest areas management.[2390] Forest ('δάσος') means land spanning more than 0.3 ha with trees higher than 5 m and a canopy cover of more than 10% or trees able to reach these thresholds at maturity and includes forest road, fire belts and other small open space within, reforested land as well as burned forest land or areas that temporarily have low vegetation due to human intervention or natural causes and their rise is expected, but does not include city parks and gardens.[2391] This term is close to the one used by Food and Agricultural Organisation of the UN (FAO) in 2010.[2392] The specific deviation shall be evident following the lawful use of forest in Cyprus.

§2. Area of Application

565. This law does not contain a specific provision stating its area of application.

§3. Competent Authorities

I. The Minister of Agriculture, Rural Development and Environment

566. The Minister of Agriculture, Rural Development and Environment has the power to declare any part of state forest as forest monument or natural

2386. Law on Forests ('ο περί Δασών Νόμος') No. 25 of 2012, OG I(I) No. 4325 of 30 Mar 2012, p. 232.
2387. Law on Forests ('ο περί Δασών Νόμος') No. 14 of 1967, OG I No. 569 of 20 Apr. 1967, p. 431.
2388. Section 3(a) Law No. 25(I)/2012.
2389. Section 3(b) *ibid.*
2390. Section 3(c) *ibid.*
2391. Section 2 *ibid.*
2392. *Land spanning more than 0.5 hectares with trees higher than 5 meters and a canopy cover of more than 10 percent, or trees able to reach these thresholds in situ. It does not include land that is predominantly under agricultural or urban land use. Food and Agriculture Organization of the United Nations*, Global Forest Resources Assessment, Main Report, Rome 2010, p. 209, available at: http://www.fao.org/docrep/013/i1757e/i1757e.pdf.

micro-reserve,[2393] gives effect to Forest Management Plans,[2394] is involved in the public participation procedure,[2395] hears administrative appeals[2396] and controls entering into state forests.[2397]

II. The Council of Ministers

567. The Council of Ministers has the power to issue regulations for specifying any matter that needs to be specified, as well as for fully and effectively carrying out this law.[2398] In particular, and without prejudice to generally of the foregoing power, such regulations may provide for all or any of the following subjects: regulating logging, collection, receiving, exportation, processing and transport of any forest product or any specifically defined item of forest product from state forest;[2399] regulating, through issuing of permit or otherwise, the transport of tree, bush, round timber or other forest product that has been cut, received or collected;[2400] regulating, through issuing of permit or otherwise, grazing of animals within state forests;[2401] defining the due fees for issuance of any permit;[2402] the obligation of permit holders to keep records or books and make them available for inspection;[2403] termination, revocation, suspension and confiscation of permits;[2404] prohibition or regulation of possession, selling or export of forest products or specifically specified forest product, through issuing a permit or otherwise;[2405] the manner of disposing objects being confiscated under this law;[2406] prohibition or regulation of labelling trees, bushes and round timber and the construction, use and possession of labelling organs;[2407] prohibition or regulation of erection, use or operation of sawmills, wood processing industry, oven, furnace for the production of coal or other product or the operation of any other undertaking using wood as raw material or combustible material;[2408] prohibition of any activity that may cause damage to forest product in state forest;[2409] specifying the documentation used for the purposes of this law;[2410] erecting and maintenance of the necessary for the

2393. Section 16(a) and (b) Law No. 25(I)/2012.
2394. Section 18(3) *ibid.*
2395. Section 21(5) and (6) *ibid.*
2396. Section 25(1), (2) and (3) *ibid.*
2397. Section 44 *ibid.*
2398. Section 65(1) *ibid.*
2399. Section 65(2)(a) *ibid.*
2400. Section 65(2)(b) *ibid.*
2401. Section 65(2)(c) *ibid.*
2402. Section 65(2)(d) *ibid.*
2403. Section 65(2)(e) *ibid.*
2404. Section 65(2)(f) *ibid.*
2405. Section 65(2)(g) *ibid.*
2406. Section 65(2)(h) *ibid.*
2407. Section 65(2)(i) *ibid.*
2408. Section 65(2)(j) *ibid.*
2409. Section 65(2)(k) *ibid.*
2410. Section 65(2)(l) *ibid.*

proper settlement of any state forest or any part thereof;[2411] confiscation of wandering animals in state forests;[2412] prohibition or regulation of using forest roads;[2413] concession, exchange, rent or disposal of land, trees or immovable property in state forest;[2414] prohibition or regulation of trade or conduction of commercial activity within any state forest;[2415] prohibition or regulation of activities in natural reserves, national forest parks, protected forests, forest parks, forest monuments, natural micro-reserves and forest recreational areas;[2416] prohibition or regulation of erection, possession or parking of camping caravan, tent or other temporary construction within any state forest;[2417] keeping records and collection of data;[2418] adoption of measures for the implementation of EU law;[2419] import of timber and wood products from third countries;[2420] and recognition of owners of private forests.[2421] Regulations may set out penal offences and penalties of imprisonment of up to twelve months and/or a fine of up to EUR 5,000.[2422]

III. The Director of the Forest Department of the Ministry of Agriculture, Rural Development and Environment

568. The Director of the Forest Department of the Ministry of Agriculture, Rural Development and Environment is competent for the implementation of this law and regulations issued under the same. More specifically, he: ensures the preservation, protection, sustainable management and development of state forests;[2423] promotes the preservation, protection, sustainable management and development of private forests;[2424] ensures that national forest policy and national forest programme have been adopted and are being applied;[2425] prepares forest management plans and applies the adopted ones;[2426] proposes the declaration of state forests, natural reserves, national forest parks, protective parks, forest park, forest monuments, natural minor-reserves and community forests, where he deems necessary;[2427] issues permits according to this law and regulations published under the same;[2428]

2411. Section 65(2)(m) *ibid.*
2412. Section 65(2)(n) *ibid.*
2413. Section 65(2)(o) *ibid.*
2414. Section 65(2)(p) *ibid.*
2415. Section 65(2)(q) *ibid.*
2416. Section 65(2)(r) *ibid.*
2417. Section 65(2)(s) *ibid.*
2418. Section 65(2)(t) *ibid.*
2419. Section 65(2)(w) *ibid.*
2420. Section 65(2)(x) *ibid.*
2421. Section 65(2)(y) *ibid.*
2422. Section 65(3) *ibid.*
2423. Section 4(a) *ibid.*
2424. Section 4(b) *ibid.*
2425. Section 4(c) *ibid.*
2426. Section 4(d) *ibid.*
2427. Section 4(e) *ibid.*
2428. Section 4(f) *ibid.*

ensures the proper application of *acquis communautaire* in relation to forest and forestry;[2429] takes care of lifting the results of offences according to this law;[2430] plans and applies all necessary measures for prevention and repression of forest fires;[2431] settles offences;[2432] performs inquiries, collects data, particulars and information, prepares programmes, reports and plans and creates and maintains data bases and geographic information systems;[2433] maintains a record of forest products, forest enterprises and owners of private forests;[2434] establishes any sampling surface or organ on any land;[2435] and exercises the right of entering to private land for the purpose of application of this law.[2436] The Director may further issue rules to the purpose of protection, preservation and proper management of any natural reserve, national forest park, protected forest, forest park, forest monument, natural micro-reserve and forest recreational area.[2437] These rules may set out penal offences and penalties of imprisonment of up to three months and/or a fine of up to EUR 1,500.[2438]

IV. Forest Advisory Board

569. A Forest Advisory Board ('Δασικό Συμβουλευτικό Σώμα') is being established via this law. Its composition and operation are prescribed in the same.[2439] Its duty is to advise the Council of Ministers, the Minister, the Director or the Commission on Forest Expansion, as the case may be, on forest matters, including matters related to: declaring state forests;[2440] declaration as natural reserves, national forest parks, protective forests and forest parks according to this law;[2441] declaration as forest monuments and natural micro-reserves;[2442] declaration as community forests;[2443] declaration of part of state forest as public road;[2444] adoption and amendment of national forest policy and national forest programme;[2445] and any

2429. Section 4(g) *ibid.*
2430. Sections 4(h) and 42 *ibid.*
2431. Section 4(i) *ibid.*
2432. Sections 4(j) and 55 *ibid.*
2433. Section 4(k) *ibid.*
2434. Section 4(l) *ibid.*
2435. Section 4(m) *ibid.* Should this be private, land compensation is being paid to its owner, if a relevant agreement is reached between the owner and the Director. Should this fail, that land is compulsory acquired according to Law on Compulsory Acquisition for Public Purpose. Section 60 Law No. 25(I)/2012.
2436. Section 4(n) *ibid.*
2437. Section 66(1) *ibid.*
2438. Section 66(3) *ibid.*
2439. Sections 6 and 7 *ibid.*
2440. Section 5(a) *ibid.*
2441. Sections 5(b) and 15 *ibid.*
2442. Sections 5(c) and 16 *ibid.*
2443. Sections 5(d) and 26 *ibid.*
2444. Sections 5(e) and 17 *ibid.*
2445. Section 5(f) *ibid.*

other matters that may be forwarded to this body by the Minister and the Director or may be decided on said body's own motion.[2446]

V. Forest Officers and Police Officers

570. Specific duties are entrusted to forest officers and police officers for the purpose of implementing this law. In particular, they may: enter freely and without previous warning any immovable property within a private forest and any private property within which an activity that prerequisites a permit under this law, takes place or when he reasonably suspects that an offence under this law has been committed;[2447] stop and inspect any vehicle, when he has reasonable suspicions that a forest product is being transported in violation of this law;[2448] take photos and measurements for the purpose of inquiry and inspection;[2449] hold and confiscate any forest product, when he has reasonable suspicion that this is being received, sold or possessed in violation of this law, as well as any tool, organ, pipe, vehicle, machine or animal that was possibly used for committing any offence under this law or that may contribute to proving this;[2450] interrogate any person, who is reasonably believed to have violated this law;[2451] demand from any person, who is reasonably believed to have violated this law, to accompany him to the nearest forest or police station;[2452]

§4. National Forest Policy and National Forest Programme

571. The Director ensures the preparation, adoption and implementation of national forest policy ('Εθνική Δασική Πολιτική') regarding preservation, protection, sustainable management and development of forests and forestry.[2453] The same applies to national forest programme ('Εθνικό Δασικό Πρόγραμμα'), which is the implementation means of the national forest policy.[2454]

572. Prior to adoption of said policy and programme, the following public participation procedure is carried out. The Director publishes a relevant notification in the Official Gazette and in at least two daily newspapers, as well as in any other information source he deems necessary.[2455] This notification includes the draft of such policy or programme and invites all interested parties to submit in writing comments within a period of no less than two months since the publication in the

2446. Section 5(g) *ibid.*
2447. Section 50(1)(a) *ibid.*
2448. Section 50(1)(b) *ibid.*
2449. Section 50(1)(c) *ibid.*
2450. Section 50(1)(d) and (g) *ibid.*
2451. Section 50(1)(e) *ibid.*
2452. Section 50(1)(f) *ibid.*
2453. Section 8(1) *ibid.*
2454. Section 8(2) *ibid.*
2455. Section 21(1)(a) *ibid.*

Official Gazette.[2456] In addition to that, the Director sends one copy of said drafts to all concerned governmental departments, services and local authorities for their views[2457] and to the members of the Forest Advisory Board calling for a meeting giving at least a thirty days' notice.[2458] He further organizes at least one public meeting for discussing said drafts providing a thirty days' notice.[2459] The Director also ensures that copies of said drafts are available at forest stations and the offices of the Forests' Department for any interested person.[2460] The comments and views submitted in any form and from any source during the aforementioned procedures are taken into consideration by the Director and communicate to the Forest Advisory Board.[2461] Following consideration of such comments and any comments of the Forest Advisory Board, changes may be performed to said drafts by the Director. These drafts are then submitted to the Minister.[2462] The Minister, after evaluating the draft of the Director, may amend this as he deems fit and then submits a proposal to the Council of Ministers.[2463]

573. National forest policy and national forest programme are adopted with a decree of the Council of Ministers, which is published in the Official Gazette.[2464] They are reviewed at any time that this is deemed necessary by the Council of Ministers.[2465] Especially the national forest programme is reviewed prior to completing ten years since the last review.[2466]

§5. State Forests

I. Establishment of State Forests

574. Any forest, forested area or other area may be declared as state forest via a decree of the Council of Ministers, which is published in the Official Gazette. If private property is declared as state forest, the aforementioned public participation procedure is followed.[2467] This procedure is also applicable, when such a declaration has significant effect ('σημαντική επίδραση') on the living conditions of affected persons, significantly affects biodiversity or natural environment in general or covers areas larger than 100 ha.[2468]

2456. Section 21(2)(a) *ibid.*
2457. Section 21(3)(a) *ibid.*
2458. Section 21(3)(b) *ibid.*
2459. Section 21(3)(c) *ibid.*
2460. Section 21(3)(d) *ibid.*
2461. Section 21(4) *ibid.*
2462. Section 21(5) *ibid.*
2463. Section 21(6) *ibid.*
2464. Section 9(1) *ibid.*
2465. Section 9(2) *ibid.*
2466. Section 9(3) *ibid.*
2467. Section 10(1) *ibid.*
2468. Section 10(2)(a), (b) and (c) *ibid.*

575. All state forests are state property. They are being sustainably managed for multiple forest purposes.[2469] The Council of Ministers is authorized to assign, exchange, rent and dispose any land, trees or other immovable property on any state forest in exceptional cases that are justified under public interest ('δημόσιο συμφέρον') and according to terms, restrictions and criteria set out in regulations issued under this law.[2470]

II. Declarations of State Forests

576. The Council of Ministers has the power to declare any part of state forest as natural reserve, national forest park, protected forest and forest park as well as forest monument, public road and community forest, following the aforementioned public participation procedure, when specific requirements are met.

A. Declaration as Natural Reserve, National Forest Park, Protected Forest and Forest Park

577. Any state forest may be declared as natural reserve ('φυσικό απόθεμα'), when such forest: includes one or more representative or important ecosystems, plant and animal community or other natural elements;[2471] is being managed for the purpose of scientific research, monitoring and is being treated as scientific reference;[2472] and human presence and activity is being restricted to a minimum in order to ensure the free operation of plant processes.[2473] State forest may further be declared as national forest park ('εθνικό δασικό πάρκο'), when: it includes important elements of biodiversity, genetic resources and landscapes to an important decree;[2474] it is being managed for the purpose of protection and preservation of ecological procedures and includes remarkable natural elements;[2475] and gives the opportunity for environmentally and culturally compatible scientific, educational or recreational activities.[2476] When a forest due to its position, geological characteristics and soil steepness gains particular importance for the protection of water sources, the soil or properties and human settlement located at a lower altitude, may be declared to be a protected forest ('προστατευτικό δάσος').[2477] Lastly, a state forest may be declared as forest park ('δασικό πάρκο'), when it gains exceptional importance on the grounds of health, environmental education, aesthetics and recreation due to its position in relation to urban centres.[2478]

2469. Section 12 *ibid.*
2470. Section 14(1) *ibid.*
2471. Section 15(a)(i) *ibid.*
2472. Section 15(a)(ii) *ibid.*
2473. Section 15(a)(iii) *ibid.*
2474. Section 15(b)(i) *ibid.*
2475. Section 15(b)(ii) *ibid.*
2476. Section 15(b)(iii) *ibid.*
2477. Section 15(c) *ibid.*
2478. Section 15(d) *ibid.*

B. Declaration as Forest Monument

578. In addition, the Minister may declare any state forest as forest monument ('δασικό μνημείο'), when the area contains one or more specific natural, cultural or geomorphic elements of exceptional or unique value due to their monumental character, excellent aesthetics or cultural elements.[2479] He may also declare state forest as natural micro-reserve ('φυσικό μικρο-απόθεμα'), when the area contains one or more rare species of flora and fauna or other natural element of national, regional or global interest.[2480]

C. Declaration as Public Road

579. In exceptional cases and for the purpose of public interest ('δημόσιο συμφέρον'), the Council of Ministers may declare any part of state forest as public road. It is essential that it takes into consideration the opinion of the Forest Advisory Board and the opinion of the Director of the Department of Urban Planning and Housing ('Τμήμα Πολεοδομίας και Οικήσεως'). The effect of this declaration is that this public road shall be subject to the provisions of Cap. 96 and the Public Roads Law.[2481,2482]

D. Declaration as Community Forests

580. The Council of Ministers may declare any area of state forest as community forest ('κοινοτικό δάσος') for the purpose of management or development of affected forest area to the benefit of areas' residents that may include one or more communities.[2483] An agreement on management of a community forest is being reached between the Director and the relevant community council(s). The necessary technical support that may be requested by the community council(s) for reaching such an agreement is to be provided by the Director.[2484] This agreement specifies: its validity period;[2485] the rights and duties of the Director and the community council(s) regarding allocation of any financial or other benefits that may result from the management of a community forest and the effects in the event of violation of this agreement by any party;[2486] and the management plan of the

2479. Section 16(a) *ibid.*
2480. Section 16(b) *ibid.*
2481. A Road to Amend and Consolidate the Laws Relating to the Protection and Preservation of Public Roads No. 11 of 1948 ('Cap. 83'), CG No. 3362 of 18 Mar. 1948, p. 171.
2482. Section 17 Law No. 25(I)/2012.
2483. Section 26 *ibid.*
2484. Section 27(3) *ibid.*
2485. Section 27(2)(a) *ibid.*
2486. Section 27(2)(b) *ibid.*

affected area.[2487] Controls on ensuring the proper implementation of the agreements reached are being performed by the Director.[2488]

581. Community council(s) that have signed an agreement on management of a community forest may issue regulations on permits for cutting, collecting or transporting any forest product from such a forest, along with conditions for issuing such a permit and the fees due, as well as on any other purpose for the protection, sustainable management and development of community forests. The prior consent of the Director on such regulations is statutory prerequisite for their effect.[2489]

582. All proceeds obtained from an agreement on management of a community forest, as well as from regulations issued by community council(s), are deposited to the funds of the relevant community council(s).[2490]

III. Measures for Better Protection and Management of State Forests

583. For the purpose of better protection and management of any state forest as well as for the protection of forest flora and forest ecosystems of exceptional importance or rarity on any land within the state, the Council of Ministers may decide to acquire any land. This shall be done either in agreement with the land's owner or compulsorily for the purpose of public interest ('δημόσιο συμφέρον') according to the provisions of Law on Compulsory Acquisition.[2491]

IV. Permits for State Forests

584. It is foreseen that no right may be exercised or acquired in or on any state forest, unless a permit has been issued by the competent authority, that being the Director, and according to the provisions of this law and terms and conditions that the Director deems necessary to attach.[2492] In particular, no construction may be established or used for commercial purposes or other corporate transactions, unless a relevant permit is issued.[2493] The Director further grants such permits at his discretion.[2494] No further information on the application contents, application evaluation or permit holder's duties and rights is foreseen in this law.

585. Should the application be rejected or the attached terms and conditions be too strict, the applicant may file an administrative appeal ('ιεραρχική προσφυγή')

2487. Section 27(2)(c) *ibid.*
2488. Section 27(4) *ibid.*
2489. Section 28(1)(a) and (b) *ibid.*
2490. Section 29 *ibid.*
2491. Section 13 *ibid.*
2492. Section 22(1) and (2) *ibid.*
2493. Section 45 *ibid.*
2494. Section 22(3)(a) *ibid.*

within fifteen days since the notification of the Director's decision with the Minister.[2495] A relevant report of a competent public servant is submitted in this respect to the Minister, who may confirm or annul the relevant decision but not amend it. The Minister's decision on the administrative appeal is to be issued within thirty days.[2496]

V. Statutory Duties Related to State Forests

586. On the grounds of danger to a state forest's preservation or biodiversity, entrance to a specific area of state forest may be regulated or even prohibited at the Minister's discretion. Entrance to sampling areas established for experimental purposes at any area may also be regulated or even prohibited, if the Minister deems this necessary. Relevant notifications are to be published in the Official Gazette specifying the relevant time period as well as at least one access road to villages if necessary.[2497]

587. Measures deemed necessary for the prevention of forest fires are to be planned and implemented by the Director. Possible effect of forest functions and especially of the biodiversity and the forest area are to be considered. The Director is also the competent authority for curative measures, that being firefighting.[2498] He further has the competence to fight a fire on private property without previously informing the owners, if this is necessary for the protection of state forest.[2499] Any soil dangers and damages are to be dealt with under Law No. 106(I)/2002 and Law No. 189(I)/2007.

§6. Logging Off State Forests

588. Uprooting, logging and cutting the crown of specific trees and bushes growing on any land outside of state forests is a prerequisite to the granting of a relevant permit from the Director. Such trees and bushes include: certain species[2500] when their diameter with bark at the height of 130 cm above ground is larger than 15 cm;[2501] certain species[2502] when their diameter with bark at the height of 130 cm above ground is larger than 40 cm;[2503] Christmas trees, those being cupressus spp., pinus spp., cedrus spp., abies spp., sequoia spp. and sequoiadendron spp., when

2495. Section 25(1) *ibid.*
2496. Section 25(2) and (3) *ibid.*
2497. Section 44(1)(a) and (b) and (2) *ibid.*
2498. Section 46(a) and (b) *ibid.*
2499. Sections 47 and 49 *ibid.*
2500. These are: acer obtusifolium, alnus orientalis, arbutus spp., casuarina spp., cedrus spp., celtis spp., ceratonia siliqua, cupressus spp., crataegus spp., eucalyptus spp.,juniperus spp., laurus nobilis, morus spp., myrtus communis, pinus spp., pistacia atlantica, pistacia lentiscus, pistacia terebinthus, platanus orientalis, populus nigra var. thevestina, quercus alnifolia, quercus coccifera, quercus infectoria, salix alba, sorbus aria, styrax officinalis, tamarix spp., ulmus canescens and zizyphus lotus. Annex I Table 1 *ibid.*
2501. Section 23(1)(a) *ibid.*

logged and transferred in November and December;[2504] olea europaea, when their diameter with bark at the height of 130 cm above ground is larger than 50 cm and phoenix dactylifera L and washingtonia filifera when their diameter with bark at the height of 130 cm above ground is larger than 40 cm.[2505] Further permit is necessary for cutting a branch of aforementioned trees and bushes, when this branch grows at the height of more than 2 m from the ground and its diameter is more than 15 cm,[2506] as well as for digging a furrow deeper than 30 cm at a distance of less than 150 cm from these trees.[2507] Said permits are also necessary for transporting round timber of aforementioned trees and Christmas trees.[2508]

589. Against rejection of an application for said permits or alleged strictness of attached terms and conditions, an administrative appeal may be filed with the Minister[2509] according to the aforementioned under permits for state forests (*see* in this respect paragraph 577 above).

§7. Forest Management Plans

590. Forest Management Plans ('Δασικά Διαχειριστικά Σχέδια') on every natural reserve, national forest park, protected park and all other state forests are being prepared, adopted and implemented by the Director.[2510] Every Forest Management Plan may include one or more state forests or areas, as per the Director's discretion.[2511] It is based on data collected via mapping, stocktaking and other available data related to forest resources, whereas it has to be compatible with the content of national forest policy and national forest programme.[2512]

591. Specific provisions related to public participation are applicable in the event that such plan: refers to natural reserve, national forest park, protected forest or forest park;[2513] is expected to have an important effect ('σημαντική

2502. These are: abies spp., albizzia spp., araucaria spp., bauhinia spp., brachychiton diversiifolius, callistemon spp., castanea sativa, cercis siliquastrum, delonix regia, eleagnus angustifolia, ficus sycomorus, grevillea robusta, jacaranda mimosifolia, liquidambar styraciflua, populus spp., quercus spp., robinia pseudoacacia, salix spp., schinus spp., sequoia sempervirens, sequoiadendron giganteum, sephora japonica, tipuana tipu and ulmus spp. Annex I Table 2 *ibid.*
2503. Section 23(1)(b) *ibid.*
2504. Sections 23(1)(c) and 2 *ibid.*
2505. Section 23(1)(d) *ibid.*
2506. From this restriction pruning and cutting of the crown of olea europaea, ceratonia silique, robinia pseudoacacia, eucalyptus spp. and morus spp. are excluded, when they are performed for the purpose of care of such trees. Further exception applies to pruning of trees obstructing visibility of signs and traffic lights as well as to the purpose of free movement of vehicles and pedestrians. Section 23(2)(a) *ibid.*
2507. Section 23(2)(b) *ibid.*
2508. Section 23(3) *ibid.*
2509. Section 25(1), (2) and (3) *ibid.*
2510. Section 18(1)(a) and (b) *ibid.*
2511. Section 18(2) *ibid.*
2512. Section 19(1) *ibid.*
2513. Section 18(4)(a) *ibid.*

επίδραση') to living conditions of affected persons;[2514] has an important effect on biodiversity or generally the environment;[2515] or covers an area of more than 100 ha.[2516] More specifically, the Director has to send a copy of the draft of the forest management plan to all concerned governmental departments and services and requests their opinion that is to be submitted within one month.[2517] He further organizes at least one public presentation of said draft, to which affected local authorities and non-governmental organizations are invited.[2518] Such expressed views are taken into consideration prior to deciding on a Forest Management Plan.[2519]

592. Without prejudice to Law No. 152(I)/2003, Law No. 153(I)/2003 and Cap. 135, the Director has the power to manage state forest that is within an area of a Natura 2000 network.[2520] In such cases, the following are applicable. When a management plan according to Law No. 153(I)/2003 has been prepared and adopted for an area being a state forest according to this law, the management directions and other suggested measures included therein are incorporated in the forest management plan of such affected forest.[2521] When no such plan has been adopted, the forest management plan according to sections 18 and 19 of this law has to include terms implementing Law No. 152(I)/2003 and Law No. 153(I)/2003 which is to be submitted to the Scientific Committee established by Law No. 153(I)/2003.[2522]

593. The decision on the Forest Management Plan is reached by the Minister. Said plan is put in force via notification of the Minister, which is published in the Official Gazette.[2523]

§8. Private Forests

594. Any group or union of owners of private forests may be recognized as an organization of owners of private forests ('οργάνωση ιδιοκτητών ιδιωτικών δασών'). A relevant application must be filed with the competent authority, that being the Director, according to the specifics laid down in regulations under this law.[2524] The requirements that need to be fulfilled by the applicants for such a recognition to take place are the applicants' aim for sustainable management of the forests belonging to them[2525] and the support of such sustainable management by a relevant management plan.[2526]

2514. Section 18(4)(b) *ibid.*
2515. Section 18(4)(c) *ibid.*
2516. Section 18(4)(d) *ibid.*
2517. Section 18(5)(a) *ibid.*
2518. Section 18(5)(b) *ibid.*
2519. Section 19(1) *ibid.*
2520. Section 20(1) *ibid.*
2521. Section 20(2)(a) *ibid.*
2522. Section 20(2)(b) *ibid.*
2523. Section 18(3) *ibid.*
2524. Section 30(1) *ibid.*
2525. Section 30(2)(a) *ibid.*
2526. Section 30(2)(b) *ibid.*

595. Such organization as well as owners of private forests may agree with the Director to place under the latter's control the protection, management and development of such forests.[2527] This agreement includes a management plan of the area,[2528] the duration of the agreement,[2529] the rights and duties of both parties and the consequences of breaching this agreement.[2530] The Director is obliged to provide the organization or the owners with technical support for reaching such agreement, if this is requested by them.[2531]

§9. Records

596. Without prejudice to the provisions of Law on Protection of Personal Data, the Director keeps a Record of Forest Undertakings and Merchants of Forest Products ('Μητρώο Δασικών Επιχειρήσεων και Εμπόρων Δασικών Προϊόντων').[2532] The Director also keeps a Record on Owners of Private Forests ('Μητρώο Ιδιοκτητών Ιδιωτικών Δασών').[2533] No further duties and rights on these records or clarification, as to the information that they must contain, are foreseen under this law.

597. Forest undertakings and merchants of forest products registered in the aforementioned register must themselves keep a record of all purchasing and selling of forest products for a period of two years following every commercial transaction.[2534] The same obligation applies to owners of private forests.[2535] The Director may request from forest undertakings, merchants of forest products and owners of private forests information or data contained in said records and these have a statutory obligation to provide such to him.[2536]

§10. Ensuring Compliance

I. Penal Offences

598. A number of penal offences are related to prohibition of unauthorized kindling of fire in a state forest. In particular, no one may kindle a fire, leave unextinguished a kindled fire, dispose a lightened cigarette, match or other object that may cause fire or cause fire due to unreasonable or careless failure or omission of

2527. Section 31(1) *ibid.*
2528. Section 31(2)(a) *ibid.* The option to place a private forest under governmental control dates back from the date that Cyprus was a Colony according to s. 12 Cap. 60.
2529. Section 31(2)(b) Law No. 25(I)/2012.
2530. Section 31(2)(c) *ibid.*
2531. Section 31(3) *ibid.*
2532. Section 62 *ibid.*
2533. Section 63 *ibid.*
2534. Section 64(1) *ibid.*
2535. Section 64(2) *ibid.*
2536. Section 64(3) *ibid.*

taking all necessary precautions in a state forest or within a distance of 2 km from the edge thereof. Should this take place, this person is guilty of an offence that may lead to imprisonment for up to ten years and/or a fine of up to EUR 50,000.[2537] However, no offence is committed, when the written consent of a forest officer is obtained,[2538] when such an action was performed by a traveller exclusively for the purpose of preparing food within specially arranged areas[2539] and when this is performed by an occupier of a residence located in such an area exclusively to the purpose of preparing food.[2540]

599. Another set of penal offences is related to fighting illegal logging. In particular, unless a relevant permit was issued by the Director, any person logging or in any other way destroying or causing damage to tree, bush or timber,[2541] collecting any flora species or degrading their natural habitat,[2542] carrying away any other forest product,[2543] grafting any tree of bush[2544] and transporting Christmas trees or any round timber that were taken from state forest[2545] is guilty of an offence. This applies also for capturing and killing any animal species as well as degrading their biotope and destroying their nests and eggs and for releasing non-native flora and fauna species in state forests, without prejudice to Law No. 152(I)/2003 and Law No. 153(I)/2003.[2546] These offences are punishable with imprisonment of up to one year and/or a fine of no more than EUR 5,000.[2547] The penalties may also be imposed on anyone performing any activity for which a permit for logging outside of state forests is requested, and not holds this permit,[2548] anyone in possession of a forest product that has been cut, logged, taken or carried out in violation of this law,[2549] anyone who sells or exports overseas any same forest product[2550] and anyone allowing for unauthorized entrance of animals to state forests.[2551]

600. Any interference with a state forest, constitutes also a penal offence. In particular, any person cultivating, planting or digging land, placing or disposing any

---

2537. Section 32(1)(a), (b), (c) and (d) *ibid.*
2538. Section 32(2)(a) *ibid.*
2539. Section 32(2)(b) *ibid.*
2540. Section 32(2)(c) *ibid.*
2541. Section 33(1)(a) *ibid.* On illegal logging, *see Forest Department v. Michael Papa a.a.* (V12) 1 CLR 38, although it construes Law 22 of 1879.
2542. Section 33(1)(b) Law No. 25(I)/2012.
2543. Section 33(1)(c) *ibid.* This provision is not applicable to mushrooms under the condition that no instrument for digging soil has been used. However, the Director has the power to prohibit mushroom collection or regulate this is specific areas for the purpose of protecting biodiversity and the ecosystem.
2544. Section 33(1)(f) *ibid.*
2545. Section 33(1)(g) *ibid.*
2546. Section 33(1)(d) and (e) *ibid.*
2547. Section 33(1) *ibid.*
2548. Section 33(2)(a), (b), (c) and (d) *ibid.*
2549. Section 34 *ibid.*
2550. Section 35 *ibid.*
2551. Section 36 *ibid.* On forest trespass *see Rex v. Christos Vasili* (V13) 1 CLR 36, although in this the Delimitation Law No. 8 of 1881 is applied.

matter for any purpose,[2552] erecting any building, shed, fence, sign, advertisement or any other temporary or permanent construction,[2553] drilling, digging wells, laying pipes, constructing sluices, water tanks or using water in any other way,[2554] possessing or using any purpose land or forest building in a forest park,[2555] causing damage in any manner to forest buildings,[2556] forest phones,[2557] or forest roads as well as obstructing operation of such roads,[2558] disposing any garbage, waste, sewage waters or any other dangerous toxic fluid or substance,[2559] driving any motor vehicle off forest road and causing damage to forest flora and soil,[2560] and causing with any means and actions damage or degradation of any part, function or value of state forest is guilty of an offence.[2561] These offences may lead to imprisonment for up to one year and/or a fine of up to EUR 5,000.[2562] Further, leaving a vehicle or machine in state forest for a period of more than ten days is an offence punishable with imprisonment for up to six months and/or a fine of up to EUR 2,500.[2563]

601. Other offences are related to sampling and measuring. More specifically, any person interfering, disclosing, destroying or in any other way causing damage to any sampling surface or data,[2564] interfering, causing damage or affecting any measurement organ,[2565] interfering, causing damage to data or buildings used for sampling,[2566] in his knowledge providing false information to forest officer[2567] or entering an area, where entrance is prohibited[2568] commits an offence. Conviction by a court of law may lead to imprisonment for up to one year and/or a fine of up to EUR 5,000.[2569]

602. Forgery and alteration are also punishable. In particular, any person removing, altering or damaging any surveying mark situated by the Director or under his instructions,[2570] forging on any tree, bush, round timber or other forest product a label used by forest officers to prove that such object is state property or may be cut or transported legally or has been classified by forest officer,[2571] forging or issuing

2552. Section 37(a) Law No. 25(I)/2012.
2553. Section 37(b) *ibid.*
2554. Section 37(c) *ibid.*
2555. Section 37(d) *ibid.*
2556. Section 37(e) *ibid.*
2557. Section 37(f) *ibid.*
2558. Section 37(g) *ibid.*
2559. Section 37(h) *ibid.*
2560. Section 37(i) *ibid.*
2561. Section 37(j) *ibid.*
2562. Section 37 *ibid.*
2563. Section 38 *ibid.*
2564. Section 39(a) *ibid.*
2565. Section 39(b) *ibid.*
2566. Section 39(c) *ibid.*
2567. Section 39(d) *ibid.*
2568. Section 39(e) *ibid.* This provision is not applicable to police officers or officers of the Hunting Service ('Ταμείο Θήρας'), who reasonably suspect that a penal offence is committed therein.
2569. Section 39 *ibid.*
2570. Section 41(a) *ibid.*
2571. Section 41(b) *ibid.*

without authorization any permit under this law[2572] and altering, removing or counterfeiting any seal, label or permit used or issued by the Director under this law[2573] is guilty of an offence. These are punishable with imprisonment of up to one year and/or a fine of up to EUR 5,000.[2574]

603. Any person failing or refusing to comply with the suggestions of a forest officer, who acts within his statutory powers, commits a crime that may lead to a fine of up to EUR 1,000.[2575] If any person attacks a police or forest officer, while exercising their duties under this law, or obstructs them, he commits a crime and after conviction he may be imprisoned for a period of up to two years and/or ordered to pay a fine of up to EUR 10,000.[2576]

II. Administrative Offences

604. In the event of penal offences related to any interference with state forest, a written notice is served to the convicted person ('παραβάτη') ordering removal, demolition or dismantling of any construction, removal of any vehicle or machine or any object used for committing those offences within reasonable time by the Director.[2577] If compliance with this notice fails, the Director may proceed with materializing these orders and file a lawsuit against the convicted person requesting payment of all necessary expenses that resulted from such activity.[2578]

III. Other Sanctions

605. In addition to any penalty for committing any penal offence under this law, the court may order the convicted person to pay to the Director compensation for damages caused to any state forest during that established offence.[2579] In addition, the court may order the confiscation of any forest product obtained in violation of this law or any tool, organ, pipeline, vehicle, machine or animal used for committing such.[2580]

606. Penal offences related to interference with state forests may lead to further sanctions, besides a penal penalty imposed by the court and the aforementioned notice of the Director. The court may, at the end of the criminal procedure, order the destruction of any plantation or planting related to the established offence and

2572. Section 41(c) *ibid.*
2573. Section 41(d) *ibid.*
2574. Section 41 *ibid.*
2575. Section 50(3) *ibid.*
2576. Section 51 *ibid.*
2577. Section 42(1)(a) *ibid.*
2578. Section 42(1)(b) *ibid.*
2579. Section 53(1) *ibid.*
2580. Section 53(2) *ibid.*

cessation of the illegal intervention within a specific time period.[2581] The Court may also give instructions for the demolition of any shed or construction related to the established offence, removal of any pipes or material, filling any drilling or well and termination of established illegal activity.[2582] If compliance with those fails, the Director may proceed with materializing these orders, whereas the relevant expenses are to be paid by the convicted person as a penalty as per the provisions of Law on Criminal Procedure.[2583]

2581. Section 42(2)(a) *ibid.*
2582. Section 42(2)(b) *ibid.*
2583. Section 42(3) *ibid.*

Chapter 6. Fish Resources

607. Fish resources are being regulated by the Fisheries Law,[2584] commonly referred to as *Cap. 135*, which repealed Fisheries (Dynamite) Law of 1886.[2585] Cap. 135 used to regulate also aquaculture, which since 2000 is being exercised within the legal frame of Law No. 117(I)/2000.[2586] It should also be noted that Regulation on the Union Fishing Fleet Register[2587] and Regulation on the Common Fisheries Policy,[2588] which are applicable all over the EU, are equally applicable in Cyprus, but shall not be analysed here, as they form a part of the European legislation on Environment and not the national one.

§1. Fisheries

I. Objective

608. This law does not foresee any explicit provision on its objective. It has been ruled, however, that it aims to regulate fishing in the sea of Cyprus and necessities issuance of a fishing licence for fishing vessels.[2589]

II. Area of Application

609. This law does not foresee any explicit provision in its area of application. However, the terms 'fish', 'vessel' and 'fishing vessel' play an important role in its application. Fish ('ιχθύς') means any aquatic animal and includes shellfish, but does not include sponges, corals, mammals and protected species. Vessel ('σκάφος') includes ship, boat, lighter and craft of every kind and includes a Cypriot vessel, that being ship registered in the Shipping Register of Cypriot Ships ('Νηολόγιο Κυπριακών Πλοίων') and bears a Cypriot flag according to sections 6, 23C, 23D and 53 Law on Merchant Shipping,[2590] and vessel registered in the Small Fishing Vessels Register ('Νηολόγιο Μικρών Αλιευτικών Σκαφών')

2584. A Law to Regulate Fishing in the Waters of the Colony No. 3 of 1931, CG 2134 of 15 May 1931, p. 359, last amended by Law on Fisheries (Amendment) ('ο περί Αλιείας (Τροποποιητικός) Νόμος') No. 170 of 2019, OG I(I) No. 4738 of 19 Dec. 2019, p. 1633.
2585. Fisheries (Dynamite) Law No. II of 1886, CG No. 198 of 8 May 1886, p. 791.
2586. Law on Aquaculture ('ο περί Υδατοκαλλιέργειας Νόμος') No. 117 of 2000, OG I(I) No. 3419 of 14 Jul. 2000.
2587. Commission Regulation (EC) No. 26/2004 of 30 Dec. 2003 on the Community fishing fleet register, OJ L 5, 9 Jan. 2004, p. 25, as amended.
2588. Regulation (EU) No. 1380/2013 of the European Parliament and of the Council of 11 Dec. 2013 on the Common Fisheries Policy, amending Council Regulations (EC) No. 1954/2003 and (EC) No. 1224/2009 and repealing Council Regulations (EC) No. 2371/2002 and (EC) No. 639/2004 and Council Decision 2004/585/EC, OJ L 354, 28 Dec 2013, p. 22.
2589. *Partastampo Shipping and Fishing Ltd v. The Republic a.o.* (2011) 3 CLR 370.
2590. Law on Merchant Shipping (Register, Sale and Mortgage of Ships) ('ο περί Εμπορικής Ναυτιλίας (Νηολόγησις, Πώλησις και Υποθήκευσις Πλοίων) Νόμος') No. 45 of 1963, OG I(I) No. 259 of 25 Jun. 1963, p. 421, as amended.

according to section 6 Law on Fishing Vessels.[2591] Fishing vessel ('αλιευτικό σκάφος') means any properly equipped vessel, but for cargo ships, which is or may be used for commercial exploitation of fish, including fishing, storage, transport, transfer or process of fish and any other relevant activity and which is registered with the Register of Fishing Vessels kept by the Director of the Department of Fishing and Marine Research.[2592]

III. Competent Authorities

A. *The Minister of Agriculture, Rural Development and Environment*

610. The Minister of Agriculture, Rural Development and Environment is a competent authority in this law, as he may issue a decree prohibiting fishing on the grounds of public policy.[2593]

B. *The Council of Ministers*

611. The Council of Ministers may make regulations to be published in the Official Gazette for carrying out the purposes of this law.[2594] In particular and without prejudice to the generality of the foregoing power, such regulations may prescribe the areas and seasons within which the taking of fish is prohibited or restricted;[2595] restrict the size of fish which may be taken, landed or sold;[2596] prohibit or regulate any practices or methods or the employment of equipment, instrument or any other device or material for taking fish;[2597] prescribe the size of nets or of the mesh of nets which may be used for taking fish in Cyprus or any specified part thereof;[2598] regulate the licensing of, and the conditions to be observed by, vessels licensed under the provisions of this law;[2599] provide for the limitation by the Director of the number of licences to be issued in any year and the selection of applicants to whom such licences may be issued where the number of applications exceed the limited number of the licences and prescribe the conditions to be attached to such licences;[2600] without prejudice to Law No. 153(I)/2003 (*see* in this respect paragraphs 464 et seq. above), regulate conservation, protection and maintenance of any

2591. Law on Fishing Vessels (Register, Sale, Conveyance and Mortgage) ('ο περί Αλιευτικών Σκαφών (Νηολόγησις, Πώλησις, Μεταβίβασις και Υποθήκευσις) Νόμος') No. 77 of 1971, OG I(I) No. 913 of 30 Dec. 1971, p. 729.
2592. Section 2 Cap. 135.
2593. Section 5A *ibid.*
2594. Section 6(1) *ibid.* On the question of Regulations being ultra vires *see Menikos a.o. v. The Republic* (1983) 3 CLR 1130; *Vasilleiades v. Leitourgou Alieias* (1993) 4 CLR 655; *Partastampo Shipping and Fishing Ltd v. The Republic* (2008) 4 CLR 265.
2595. Section 6(2)(a) Cap. 135.
2596. Section 6(2)(b) *ibid.*
2597. Section 6(2)(c) *ibid.*
2598. Section 6(2)(d) *ibid.*
2599. Section 6(2)(e) *ibid.*
2600. Section 6(2)(f) *ibid.*

stock of fish, which in this respect means any aquatic organism;[2601] provide for imposing fees for issuing any licence under such regulations;[2602] provide for appointing advisory committees by the Minister that shall advise the Director on any matter within his competence;[2603] provide for administrative appeal ('ιεραρχική προσφυγή') with the Minister on any decision of the Comptroller;[2604] provide for a monitor and control system of fishing activities of vessels, on which this law is applicable, within and outside of the territorial waters of Cyprus;[2605] provide for inspection and control of vessels and their equipment, as well as the time, place, manner and rights of inspection and control;[2606] regulate matters related to the Register of Fishing Vessels of this law;[2607] demand a fishing licence also for floating constructions or other navigation means that are no vessels;[2608] and specify the cases and the procedure for imposing administrative fines by the controller.[2609]

C. The Director of the Department of Fishing and Marine Research

612. The Director of the Department of Fishing and Marine Research is a competent authority in this law, as he has the authority to issue,[2610] renew[2611] and annul fishing licences.[2612] His consent is necessary for the lawful construction, import of a fishing vessel, conversion of any vessel into a fishing vessel, or the registration of a vessel in the Register of Fishing Vessels,[2613] which is being kept by himself.[2614]

D. Public Officers

613. Any peace officer, officer of the Department of Fishing and Marine Research and officer of the Department of Merchant Shipping may, where he has reasonable grounds to suspect that an offence has been or is likely to be committed under the provisions of this law or any regulation made thereunder, without warrant perform the following acts:

– enter any premises, but not a residence, at any time, stop any vehicle, board any vessel and search such premises, vehicle or vessel, and examine any catch,

---

2601. Section 6(2)(g) *ibid.*
2602. Section 6(2)(h) *ibid.*
2603. Section 6(2)(k) *ibid.*
2604. Section 6(2)(l) *ibid.*
2605. Section 6(2)(m) *ibid.*
2606. Section 6(2)(n) *ibid.*
2607. Section 6(2)(o) *ibid.*
2608. Section 6(2)(p) *ibid.*
2609. Section 6(2)(q) *ibid.*
2610. Sections 3(2), 4(1) and 13(1)(a) *ibid.*
2611. Sections 4(2) and 13(1)(a) *ibid.*
2612. Section 3(3) *ibid.*
2613. Section 3A(1) *ibid.*
2614. Section 7A(1) *ibid.*

equipment, instrument or other device or material which may be used for taking fish and measure any fishing net therein; and
- seize and detain, pending a decision thereon, any vessel, catch, equipment, instrument or other device or material, which is or may be used in contravention of this law or any regulations made thereunder.

614. It should be noted that the catch may be sold and the proceeds thereof be detained pending the decision.[2615]

IV. Fishing Licence

615. No vessel may be used for the purpose of taking fish, unless a licence has been issued in respect thereof under the provisions of this law.[2616] This law prescribes nothing specific as to the content of an application for such a licence.

A. Evaluation of an Application for a Fishing Licence

616. Statutory prerequisites for a fishing licence to be granted, apart from the obvious one of paying the necessary fees,[2617] are the following. The relevant vessel must be registered in the Shipping Register of Cypriot Ships according to sections 6 and 53 Law on Merchant Ships or in the Small Fishing Vessels Register according to section 6 Law on Fishing Vessels. In addition to that, the majority of its shares must be beneficially held by a Cypriot citizen, a national of the EU or a company registered in Cyprus or another Member State of the EU. In the latter case, the majority of its shares must be also beneficially held by Cypriot citizens or nationals of the EU and half of its directors must be Cypriot citizens or nationals of the EU.[2618] Alternatively, the relevant vessel must be registered in the Shipping Register of Cypriot Ships according to section 23C and 23D Law on Merchant Ships and its charterer have the aforementioned nationalities. Should the vessel be older than twenty years old, said majorities are not sufficient as shares and number of directors rise to 75%.[2619] Further, the management and activities of the vessel, which also needs to be registered in the Register of Fishing Vessels of this law, are to be directed and controlled from Cyprus.[2620]

617. The Register of Fishing Vessels ('Μητρώο Αλιευτικών Σκαφών') is kept by the Director. All Cypriot fishing vessels are registered therein, but no registration is performed, when this would result in exceeding the 'fishing capacity of the shipping fleet of Cyprus as this is defined within the Common Fisheries Policy of the

2615. Section 7(a) and (b) *ibid.*
2616. Section 3(1) *ibid.*
2617. Section 4(1) *ibid. Koma tou Yialou Fishing Co. Ltd v. The Republic* (1993) 4 CLR 2196.
2618. Section 3(2)(a)(i) and (ii) Cap. 135. Judgment of 20 Feb. 2008 in appeal no. 985/2007, *Antonakis Gregoriou v. The Republic*, not published in CLR.
2619. Section 3(2)(b)(i) and (ii) Cap. 135.
2620. Section 3(2)(c) and (d) *ibid.*

EU.[2621] The data that are kept for each vessel in relation to their characteristics and fishing capacity are specified in Regulation No. 26/2004, Regulation No. 1380/2013, as well as in regulations issued under this law.[2622] All vessels registered therein constitute the fishing fleet of Cyprus.[2623] Registration of a vessel in said register bears two further effects. On the one hand, no change that may affect in any way the fishing capacity of the vessel may be performed without the prior written consent of the Director.[2624] On the other hand, no transfer of ownership of such vessel may take place, unless the Director has been informed and his approval has been obtained.[2625]

618. The owner or the operator of a vessel, as the case may be, who holds a special fishing licence ('ειδική αλιευτική άδεια'), that being a licence issued by a foreign country or international organization regarding a Cypriot vessel and allows for taking fish within the territorial waters, continental shelf, fishing zone or exclusive economic zone of this country or the area controlled by such organization is obliged to inform accordingly the Director within thirty days of granting such licence. This must be performed in writing and a copy of such licence needs to be forwarded to said authority.[2626] Failure to comply with this obligation, results in possible nonrenewal of a fishing permit of the relevant vessel.[2627]

B. Granting a Fishing Licence

619. The validity period of a fishing licence, which is specified therein, lies at the discretion power of the competent authority, but may not be longer than five years.[2628] A fishing permit also includes the terms under which this is being granted,[2629] as well as the specific fishery, which is authorized to be taken.[2630]

620. It is a statutory duty of the holder of a fishing licence to comply with the terms attached thereto[2631] at all times until the expiration of said licence. Should the holder not comply with any term for any reason, the Director must be informed

---

2621. Section 7A(1) *ibid.*
2622. Section 7A(3) *ibid.* The provision refers to Regulation No. 2090/98 and Regulation No. 2371/2002, which have been repealed by the aforementioned ones.
2623. Section 7A(2) Cap. 135.
2624. Section 10(1) *ibid.*
2625. Section 10(2) *ibid.*
2626. Section 4A(1) *ibid.*
2627. Section 4A(2) *ibid.*
2628. Section 4(2) *ibid.* On refusal to grand a fishing licence *see*: judgment of 5 Jul. 2002 in appeal 1505/00, *Markitsis v. The Republic*, not published in CLR; *Kouselinis v. The Republic* (2001) 4 CLR 1; judgment of 5 Jul. 2010 in appeal no. 1341/2008, *Stylianou v. The Republic*, not reported in CLR; judgment of 28 Apr. 2009 in appeal no. 425/2007, *Ttofinis v. The Republic*, not reported in CLR.
2629. Section 13(1)(b) Cap. 135.
2630. Section 13(2) *ibid.*
2631. Section 13(1)(b) *ibid.*

within fifteen days.[2632] Also, at least once annually said vessels need to approach a port of Cyprus for general inspection according to this law as well as for health inspection.[2633]

C. Renewal of a Fishing Licence

621. A fishing licence may be renewed for a period not exceeding five years.[2634]

V. Recreational Fishing Licence

622. No person may be engaged in recreational fishing, either in person or collectively, in the sea, lakes, rivers or sluice without previously obtaining a recreational fishing licence ('άδεια ερασιτεχνικής αλιείας') according to regulations issued under this law.[2635] Matters related to issuing such licence along with the terms and conditions that may be imposed are set out in said regulations.[2636]

VI. Statutory Duties

623. The use of explosives or poisons is prohibited. In particular no person may take, stupefy, kill or attempt to take, stupefy or kill any fish by the use of dynamite or other explosive substance or by the use of any noxious or poisonous matter. Also, in some circumstances, the possession of dynamite or other explosive substance or noxious or poisonous matter is prohibited, along with selling, exposing for sale or hawking, knowingly possessing or transporting fish which has been taken by the use of dynamite or any other explosive substance or by the use of any noxious or poisonous matter. Equally prohibited is taking, stupefying or killing any fish with the use of rifle-harpoon in combination with a breathing apparatus.[2637]

624. Fishing in any manner and crossing of ships may be prohibited by the Minister through a decree on the grounds of state safety, public policy or public interest, including the protection of fishing resources and aquatic organisms defined therein. He may also put into place a Management Plan for such sea areas that includes its scope and the relevant measures, prohibitions and special provisions in relation to specific activities, operational rules and entrance fees.[2638]

2632. Section 3(3) *ibid.*
2633. Section 7B(1) *ibid.* Judgment of 7 Oct. 2005 in appeal no. 876/2004, *Sea Dove Shipping Company Ltd v. The Republic*, not published in CLR; *Kenora Shipping Company Ltd v. The Republic* (2004) 4 CLR 1039.
2634. Section 4(2) Cap. 135. On refusal to renew a fishing licence *see*: judgment of 27 Dec. 2001 in appeal no. 6/99, *Lapertas Fisheries Ltd a.a. v. The Republic*, not published in CLR.
2635. Section 3B(1) Cap. 135.
2636. Section 6(2)(j) *ibid.*
2637. Section 5(a), (b), (c) and (d) *ibid.*
2638. Section 5A *ibid.*

VII. Ensuring Compliance

A. *Penal Sanctions*

625. Anyone using a vessel in violation of the statutory duty of holding a fishing licence, informing on the existence of a special fishing licence and complying with its terms at all times, as well as the owner or charterer of such vessel are guilty of an offence. They may face imprisonment for a period of up to three years and/or a fine of up to EUR 17,100.[2639] In this context, the presence of fishing equipment on or in a vessel is an arguable legal presumption that this vessel is used for the purpose of fishing.[2640] Further, any construction, import of a fishing vessel, the conversion of any vessel into a fishing vessel or the registration of a vessel into the Registry of Fishing Vessels without the consent of the Director is a penal offence, punishable with imprisonment of up to two years and/or a fine of up to EUR 3,420.[2641]

626. Violation of the statutory duties relating to the use of explosives and poisons is a penal offence, which may lead to conviction of up to two years and/or a fine of up to EUR 8,550.[2642] Noncompliance with the obligation of annual approaching to a port of Cyprus is a penal offence performed by the owner or the charterer thereof, as the case may be, punishable with imprisonment for up to three years and/or a fine of up to EUR 17,100.[2643]

627. Apart from the penal prosecution before a court of the aforementioned penal offences, the Director has certain powers on out-of-court settlement. In particular, when the Director reasonably believes that any person has committed a penal offence in contravention of this law, he may reach an out-of-court settlement by accepting the payment of an amount specified in his discretion, which, however, does not exceed the amount of the fine set out in this law or the amount of EUR 17,100, whichever is less.[2644] Such amount is considered to be a monetary fine imposed for conviction of the relevant offence.[2645] After payment of such amount and issue of the relevant receipt, no further procedure may be initiated for the same offence.[2646]

B. *Administrative Sanctions*

628. Upon failure of compliance with any term of a fishing licence and the relevant notification of the Director by the holder thereof, the Director may terminate

2639. Section 3(5) *ibid.*
2640. Section 3(6) *ibid.*
2641. Section 3A(2) *ibid.*
2642. Section 5(a), (b) and (c) *ibid.*
2643. Section 7B(2) *ibid.*
2644. Section 9(1) *ibid.*
2645. Section 9(2) *ibid.*
2646. Section 9(3) and (4) *ibid.*

such licence, according to his discretion. If the Director is not informed of said failure, same licence is considered to be suspended.[2647]

629. In addition to or in substitution for any punishment for a contravention of this law or any regulations made thereunder, upon conviction of the offender, the following may be ordered. Any vessel, equipment, instrument or any other device or material, which in the opinion of the court was used or intended to be used by him for taking, stupefying, killing or poisoning fish, shall, when the person concerned has been convicted of the offence of use of explosives or poisons, and may in any other case be adjudged by the court to be forfeited.[2648] Further, any fish in his possession seized under the provisions of this law, which in the opinion of the court was taken, stupefied, killed or poisoned, or the proceeds of the sale thereof, shall be adjudged by the court to be forfeited.[2649] Lastly, any licence issued to him under the provisions of this law may be cancelled by the issuing authority.[2650]

§2. AQUACULTURE

I. Objective

630. Law No. 117(I)/2000 does not include an explicit provision on its objective.

II. Area of Application

631. This law does not include an explicit provision on its area of application. The term 'aquaculture' is, however, of high importance for this. *Aquaculture* ('υδατοκαλλιέργεια') stands for rearing or reproduction of aquatic species for the purpose of commercial exploitation.[2651] Also in force is the definition of *aquaculture* ('aquaculture' in French, 'Aquakultur' in German, 'aquacultuur' in Dutch) as the rearing or cultivation of aquatic organisms using techniques designed to increase the production of the organisms in question beyond the natural capacity of the environment; the organisms remain the property of a natural or legal person throughout the rearing or culture stage, up to and including harvesting.[2652] However, this latter definition applies within the scope of establishing the European Fisheries Fund and defining the framework for Union support for the sustainable development of the fisheries sector, fisheries areas and inland fishing.[2653]

2647. Section 3(3) *ibid.*
2648. Sections 8(a) and 5 *ibid.*
2649. Section 8(b) *ibid.*
2650. Section 8(c) *ibid.*
2651. Section 2 Law No. 117(I)/2000.
2652. Article 3(d) Regulation No. 1198/2006.
2653. Article 1 *ibid.*

III. Competent Authorities

A. *The Minister of Agriculture, Rural Development and Environment*

632. The Minister of Agriculture, Rural Development and Environment is a competent authority for this law. His duties and powers are limited and include hearing an administrative appeal.[2654]

B. *The Council of Ministers*

633. The Council of Ministers may make regulations for carrying out the purposes of this law and to regulate any matter related to aquaculture falling under this law.[2655] In particular and without prejudice to the generality of the foregoing power, such regulations may prescribe: the procedure of issuing a permit, the form of the necessary application and necessary fees;[2656] the validity period of the permit, which depends on the type or size of the fish farm and its location;[2657] the prohibition of fishing near fish farms operating in the sea along with the respective penalties that may be imprisonment of up to six months and a fine of up to EUR 8,550[2658] details regarding equipment, construction and machines of fish farms and the operation of relevant facilities;[2659] control of fish farm waste;[2660] collection of any information and data on aquaculture by the Director;[2661] establishment of safety zones and positioning of proper signals for navigation safety in marine areas where fish farms are located;[2662] areas within which fish farms and relevant facilities may be established;[2663] means and manners of control systems for feed quality and quantity that is used in fish farming, along with imposing fees and charges when using any specific feed;[2664] handling of fish farming products;[2665] control of any hazards in wild life related to aquaculture;[2666] quality control of aquaculture products;[2667] the prerequisites of granting a permit for using a marine area for aquaculture as well as the procedure of submitting and evaluating the relevant application;[2668] preparation and implementation of operational control programmes by the owners of fish farms;[2669] providing instructions by the Director on order and demarcation of fish

---

2654. Section 14 Law No. 117(I)/2000.
2655. Section 23(1) *ibid.*
2656. Section 23(2)(a) *ibid.*
2657. Section 23(2)(b) *ibid.*
2658. Section 23(2)(c) *ibid.*
2659. Section 23(2)(d) *ibid.*
2660. Section 23(2)(e) *ibid.*
2661. Section 23(2)(f) *ibid.*
2662. Section 23(2)(g) *ibid.*
2663. Section 23(2)(h) *ibid.*
2664. Section 23(2)(i) *ibid.*
2665. Section 23(2)(j) *ibid.*
2666. Section 23(2)(k) *ibid.*
2667. Section 23(2)(l) *ibid.*
2668. Section 23(2)(m) *ibid.*
2669. Section 23(2)(n) *ibid.*

farms' facilities operating in the sea;[2670] any measures for environmental protection from activities relating to aquaculture, including payment of any expenses for environmental control;[2671] and the procedure of issuing a permit for expanding production.[2672]

C. The Director of the Department of Fisheries and Marine Research

634. The Director of the Department of Fisheries and Marine Research ('Διευθυντής Τμήματος Αλιείας και Θαλάσσιων Ερευνών') is the competent authority for issuing, renewing and revoking permits for establishing and operating a fish farm. He also has extensive authority related to inspection of facilities, confiscation of goods and cessation of activities. More specifically, he may: enter any area, but for residence, used for aquaculture and perform control of its facilities and products;[2673] stop, enter and inspect any means of transport, when he reasonably suspects that aquaculture products, which have been made illegally, are being transferred;[2674] confiscate any aquaculture products, when he reasonably suspects that these have been made illegally or prohibit their transfer from the fish farm;[2675] confiscate any means of transport, other object or means, when he reasonably suspects that this has been used for any action, which is a penal offence under this law;[2676] participate in implementation of any measures deemed necessary by the Director of Veterinary Services regarding confiscation and destruction of aquaculture products to the purpose of prevention of spreading of any fish disease or control thereof;[2677] and order cessation of any aquaculture activity, when he reasonably suspects that this is performed in violation of this law.[2678]

D. Advisory Committee on Aquaculture

635. An Advisory Committee on Aquaculture ('Συμβουλευτική Επιτροπή Υδατοκαλλιέργειας') is being established via this law, for the purpose of advising the Director on matters of aquaculture policy.[2679] This committee comprises the Director, a representative from the Directorate General for European Programmes, Coordination and Development, a representative from the Ministry of Commerce, Energy, Industry and Tourism, a representative from the Department of Veterinary

2670. Section 23(2)(o) *ibid.*
2671. Section 23(2)(p) *ibid.*
2672. Section 23(2)(q) *ibid.*
2673. Section 16(a) *ibid.*
2674. Section 16(b) *ibid.*
2675. Section 16(c) *ibid.*
2676. Section 16(d) *ibid.*
2677. Section 16(e) *ibid.*
2678. Section 16(f) *ibid.*
2679. Section 3(1) *ibid.*

Service, four representatives of agricultural organizations and a representative of the Cyprus Association of Professional Fishermen, appointed by the Minister.[2680]

IV. Permit for Establishing and Operating a Fish Farm

636. Without prejudice to the provisions of any other law or regulation, no fish farm ('ιχθυοτροφείο') may be established or operated without a permit issued by the Director in accordance with this law.[2681]

A. Application for a Permit for Establishing and Operating a Fish Farm

637. The exact application procedure for such a permit is being specified in Regulations of the Council of Ministers.[2682] Especially for fish farming in the sea, a specific notification requirement is foreseen in this law. The Director, who intends to grant a specific number of permits for establishing and operating such a farm, takes into consideration the opinion of the Minister of Interior. If the Minister of Agriculture, Rural Development and Environment agrees with the intention of the Director, a relevant notification is being published in the Official Gazette and in two daily newspapers inviting interested parties to submit a relevant application.[2683] In this notification, any information deemed necessary for the applicants and the public, including areas or locations of suggested fish farms and operating terms, might be attached.[2684]

B. Evaluating an Application for a Permit for Establishing and Operating a Fish Farm

638. Statutory requirements for granting a permit for establishing and operating a fish farm are: furnishing the Director with all data and documents requested either before or after submission of the application;[2685] obtaining all permits for the construction of the fish farm required under any law or regulation, including approvals related to use of space and water;[2686] and no conflict of the construction works and facilities of the fish farm with any provision of any other law.[2687] The Director must also take into consideration and apply any law, regulation or decision of the Council of Ministers regarding environmental impact from the construction or operation

2680. Section 3(2)(a)–(f) *ibid.*
2681. Section 4(1) *ibid.*
2682. Section 4(2) *ibid.*
2683. Section 5(1) *ibid.*
2684. Section 5(2) *ibid.*
2685. Section 6(1)(a) *ibid.*
2686. Section 6(1)(b) *ibid.*
2687. Section 6(1)(c) *ibid.*

of any works.[2688] He shall also ask for the opinion of the Director of Veterinary Services on matters of prevention and control of fish diseases.[2689]

C. Granting a Permit for Establishing and Operating a Fish Farm

639. The form of a permit for establishing and operating a fish farm, the necessary fees,[2690] its validity period[2691] are set out in regulations. Operating conditions may be attached to the permit, if these are considered necessary by the Director.[2692] These conditions relate to: disposition of the fish farm area;[2693] facilities, equipment machines and their maintenance;[2694] the time frame within which the operation of the fish farm must start its operation;[2695] the aquatic animals and the amount of those that may be imported in the fish farm for rearing;[2696] the composition, quality and quantity of feed used in the fish farm;[2697] use and control of any pharmaceutical compound or drug or prohibition of such, following the opinion of the Director of Veterinary Services;[2698] the obligation of the applicant, his representatives or employees to inform the Director of Veterinary Services of any symptoms of any fish disease that may occur in the facilities of the fish farm;[2699] the destruction or disposal of dead fish or any useless material deriving from the operation of the fish farm;[2700] the transfer of any fish to or from the fish farm;[2701] quality control of the water used in the fish farm;[2702] insurance cover of third parties for the facilities of the fish farm;[2703] keeping a record of the content of the fish farm as well as its operations;[2704] and providing any information and statistical data on the activities of the applicant regarding aquaculture.[2705]

640. The holder of a permit for establishing and operating a fish farm bears the obligation to provide the Director with any information regarding his fish farm or the production of any products in writing, should this be requested by said authority.[2706]

2688. Section 8(2) *ibid.*
2689. Section 8(3) *ibid.*
2690. Section 6(2) *ibid.*
2691. Section 7 *ibid.*
2692. Section 8(1) *ibid.*
2693. Section 8(1)(a) *ibid.*
2694. Section 8(1)(b) *ibid.*
2695. Section 8(1)(c) *ibid.*
2696. Section 8(1)(d) *ibid.*
2697. Section 8(1)(e) *ibid.*
2698. Section 8(1)(f) *ibid.*
2699. Section 8(1)(g) *ibid.*
2700. Section 8(1)(h) *ibid.*
2701. Section 8(1)(i) *ibid.*
2702. Section 8(1)(j) *ibid.*
2703. Section 8(1)(k) *ibid.*
2704. Section 8(1)(l) *ibid.*
2705. Section 8(1)(m) *ibid.*
2706. Section 9 *ibid.*

D. Rejection of an Application for a Permit for Establishing and Operating a Fish Farm

641. The Director may reject an application for a permit for establishing and operating a fish farm on the grounds that aquaculture activities: may lead to contagion of any disease to any fish;[2707] may create an *increased danger* ('αυξημένο κίνδυνο') of environment pollution or deterioration thereof;[2708] do not comply with any actions for the protection of preservation of the environment or the character of the area;[2709] may negatively affect transport or construction of any development works;[2710] and are contrary to public policy ('δημόσιο συμφέρον').[2711]

642. Against a rejection of an application for said permit, along with any decision of the Director, an administrative appeal ('ιεραρχική προσφυγή') may be filed within thirty days since the notification thereof with the Minister of Agriculture, Rural Development and Environment.[2712] The Minister, who reaches a decision without undue delay, is obliged to give the opportunity to the applicant to argue his case and may ask for opinions on specific matters from public servants of this Ministry.[2713] Also, rejection of an application for such a permit, or the decision of the Minister following the administrative appeal, may be challenged with an appeal before the Supreme Court of Cyprus according to Article 146 of the Constitution.

E. Changes, Amendments and Revocation of a Permit for Establishing and Operating a Fish Farm

643. A permit for establishing and operating a fish farm may not be transferred to another person, unless the written consent of the Director is being provided[2714] and the fees due are paid.[2715] The Director may amend any of the operating conditions in view of the permit's transfer to the new holder.[2716]

644. Any changes of the disposition of the fish farm area, its facilities, its machinery or the maintenance thereof on the initiative of the permit holder are prohibited, unless these are performed according to the operating conditions of the relevant permit or the consent of the Director.[2717] However, without prejudice to Law No. 127(I)/2018 (*see* in this respect paragraphs 711 et seq. below), the Director may order the transfer of the fish farm, when he deems this necessary due to violation of

2707. Section 11(1)(a) *ibid.*
2708. Section 11(1)(b) *ibid.*
2709. Section 11(1)(c) *ibid.*
2710. Section 11(1)(d) *ibid.*
2711. Section 11(1)(f) *ibid.*
2712. Section 14(1) *ibid.*
2713. Section 14(2) and (3) *ibid.*
2714. Section 15(1) *ibid.*
2715. Section 15(3) *ibid.*
2716. Section 15(2) *ibid.*
2717. Section 10 *ibid.*

any operating condition attached to the permit, public policy ('δημόσιο συμφέρον'), protection of rights and liberties of others and promotion or use of any property or space to the purpose of promoting public benefit ('δημόσια ωφέλεια').[2718] The costs of this transfer are borne by the permit holder, when the relevant ground is violation of operating condition. In all other cases, the costs are borne by the state or any authority requesting such transfer.[2719]

645. A permit for establishing and operating a fish farm may not be renewed on the same grounds, as an application for such a permit may be rejected.[2720] In addition to those, an application for renewal may be dismissed, if aquaculture activities of the applicant are contrary or do not comply with any operating condition attached to the expired permit.[2721] However, when the Director establishes that some of these grounds[2722] exist, he may, instead of rejecting the application for renewal, proceed with renewal and attach any new operating conditions deemed necessary under the circumstances.[2723]

646. Revocation of such a permit may be ordered upon failure to transfer the fish farm, which was ordered by the Director, according to the aforementioned (*see* in this respect paragraph 644 above).[2724] In addition, permit revocation or attachment of new operating conditions, as per the discretion of the Director,[2725] is possible on the specific grounds that are set out in this law. Fish disease or serious danger of contagious fish disease at the facilities of the authorized fish farm according to the opinion of the Director of Veterinary Services may lead to revocation of this permit.[2726] This is also applicable upon failure of compliance with any operating conditions of the permit[2727] or termination of aquaculture operations.[2728] Further, the permit may be revoked, if six months after the issuance of the permit, the authorized fish farm does not fully operate, or the amount of production does not comply with the relevant operating condition.[2729] Lastly, revocation of the permit may be founded on the grounds of public policy ('δημόσιο συμφέρον').[2730]

V. Permit for Use of Marine Space

647. Notwithstanding the provisions of any other law, the Council of Ministers has the authority to issue a *permit for use of marine space* ('άδεια χρήσης

2718. Section 13(1) *ibid.*
2719. Section 13(3) *ibid.*
2720. Section 11(1)(a), (b), (c), (d) and (f) *ibid.*
2721. Section 11(1)(e) *ibid.*
2722. These are the ones stated in s. 11(1)(c), (d) and (e) *ibid.*
2723. Section 11(2) *ibid.*
2724. Section 13(2) *ibid.*
2725. Section 12(2) *ibid.*
2726. Section 12(1)(a) *ibid.*
2727. Section 12(1)(b) *ibid.*
2728. Section 12(1)(c) *ibid.*
2729. Section 12(1)(d) *ibid.*
2730. Section 12(1)(e) *ibid.*

θαλάσσιου χώρου') within the territorial waters for the purpose of aquaculture.[2731] The application requirements, procedure and fees are set out in regulations.[2732]

VI. Statutory Duties

648. It is explicitly stated that no provision of this law gives the right or authorization to any person to fish within or under any fish farm in a manner contrary to this law or Cap. 135.[2733]

649. The Director may act on any matter related to animal disease or use of pharmaceutical preparation or drug in the fish farm, only following the opinion of the Director of Veterinary Services.[2734] Further, the Director and any officer of the Fisheries Department, who learn any commercial or financial information on a fish farm during the exercise of their duties under this law, are obliged not to reveal it, as this has confidential nature. This may only be exceptionally revealed, when a written consent of the holder of the permit for establishing and operating a fish farm is given,[2735] when this is deemed necessary for the purpose of implementing a governmental programme relevant to environmental protection or prevention and control of animal disease in the fish farm area,[2736] or for furnishing proof in a criminal case before the court.[2737]

VII. Ensuring Compliance

A. *Penal Sanctions*

650. Violation of any provision of this law or regulations issued under this is an offence punishable with imprisonment for up to three months and/or a fine of up to EUR 3,420.[2738] Any person operating a fish farm without holding a permit for establishing and operating a fish farm is guilty of an offence, which may lead to imprisonment for a period of up to one year and/or a fine of up to EUR 8,550.[2739] Noncompliance with the operating conditions of a permit is also an offence punishable with imprisonment for up to two months and/or a fine of up to EUR 3,420.[2740]

2731. Section 21(1) *ibid.*
2732. Section 21(2) *ibid.*
2733. Section 19 *ibid.*
2734. Section 20 *ibid.*
2735. Section 22(a) *ibid.*
2736. Section 22(c) *ibid.*
2737. Section 22(b) *ibid.*
2738. Section 18(8) *ibid.*
2739. Section 18(1) *ibid.*
2740. Section 18(2) *ibid.*

Unauthorized entrance to fish farm's facilities is an offence that may lead to imprisonment of up to one month and/or a fine of up to EUR 855.[2741] Unauthorized interference with operation or control of fish farm's facilities is an offence. If found guilty by a court of law, the accused may be imprisoned for up to six months and/or ordered to pay a fine of up to EUR 5,130.[2742] These penalties may further be imposed on any person releasing fish farms' products in the sea, lake or river, without the authorization of the Director[2743] and on any person obstructing the Director or any authorized officer from performing his duties or exercising his powers, or anyone refusing or failing to comply with any instructions, directions and prohibitions of the Director.[2744]

B. Other Sanctions

651. During a court procedure for the aforementioned penal offences of fish farm's operation without a permit or violation of any operating conditions of a permit, an order for cessation of fish farm's activities and selling or otherwise disposing these facilities may be issued.[2745]

652. An out-of-court settlement may be reached for the penal offences of violating operating conditions and unauthorized release of fish farm's products. This includes payment of an amount, which is to be determined by the Director but may not exceed the relevant fine set out in this law[2746] and issuing a relevant receipt with specific contents by the Director.[2747] Contradicting provisions are included in this law regarding the effect of such settlement. It is stated that this payment is considered a fine imposed due to conviction for such offence[2748] and that the out-of-court settlement and payment of relevant amount of money is not considered to be a conviction.[2749] This contradiction might be enlightened, when further effects of an out-of-court settlement are examined. First, should a court procedure be initiated for the facts surrounding a settled case, production of the aforementioned receipt leads to acquittal of the accused.[2750] Second, in the event of conviction for another similar offence, the court may take into consideration the facts surrounding the out-of-court settlement to the purpose of computation of punishment.[2751] Hence, said settlement prevents further conviction for the same facts, whereas these are taken into consideration according to the court's discretion for computation of punishment of a latter conviction.

2741. Section 18(3) *ibid.*
2742. Section 18(4) *ibid.*
2743. Section 18(5) *ibid.*
2744. Section 18(6) *ibid.*
2745. Section 18(7) *ibid.*
2746. Section 18A(1) *ibid.*
2747. Section 18A(4) *ibid.*
2748. Section 18A(3) *ibid.*
2749. Section 18A(6) *ibid.*
2750. Section 18A(5) *ibid.*
2751. Section 18A(6) *ibid.*

Chapter 7. Subsoil and Minerals

653. Mines and quarries are regulated by Law on Mines and Quarries[2752] (hereinafter 'Cap. 270'). This law repealed the Ottoman Mines Regulations of 1868, which were inspired by the French Mining Law of 1810[2753] and were the legal ground for granting the mining lease of ninety-nine years regarding asbestos.[2754]

§1. Objective

654. This law does not explicitly state its objective. Nevertheless, it is obvious that it regulates prospecting, mines and quarries. It is specified that the term 'mine' ('μεταλλείο') means an excavation or system of excavations made for the purpose of, or in connection with, the getting, wholly or substantially by means involving the employment of persons below ground, of minerals (whether in their natural state or in solution or suspension) or products of minerals.[2755] The term 'minerals' includes all materials of economic value forming part of, or derived naturally from, the crust of the earth including mineral oil, but not minerals while in solution or peat, trees, timber and similar kinds of forest produce or any quarry materials.[2756] Further, *quarry* ('λατομείο') means an excavation or system of excavations made for the purpose of, or in connection with, the getting of quarry materials (whether in their natural state or in solution or suspension) or products of quarry materials, being neither a mine nor merely a well or bore-hole or a well and bore-hole combined.[2757] Sand, stone, slate, granite or other rocks, chalk, clay, flint, gravel, gypsum, limestone, marble, marl and quartz are *quarry materials* ('λατομικά υλικά').[2758]

§2. Area of Application

655. The area of application of this law is merely specified by a negative provision stating that nothing in this law contained may be constructed so as to confer any right to prospect for, or to mine, any mineral oil,[2759] that being pitch, asphalt and natural gas.[2760]

2752. Law to Consolidate and Amend the Law Relating to Mines and Quarries No. 14 of 1953, CG No. 3697 of 4 Jun. 1953, p. 247, as amended.
2753. A. Tok, *The Ottoman Mining Sector in the Age of Capitalism: an Analysis of State-Capital Relations*, 33 (Boğaziçi University 2010); S.J. Shaw, *The Nineteenth-Century Ottoman Tax Reforms and Revenue System*, 6 Int. J. Middle East Stud., 434 (1975).
2754. *The Attorney-General v. The Asbestos Mines Ltd* (V20) 1 CLR 4.
2755. Section 3(1) Cap. 270.
2756. Section 2 *ibid.*
2757. Section 3(2) *ibid.*
2758. Section 2 *ibid.*
2759. Section 6 *ibid.*
2760. Section 2 *ibid.*

§3. COMPETENT AUTHORITIES

I. The Council of Ministers

656. The Council of Ministers is the main competent authority in this law, as it has various powers related to evaluating applications for prospecting permits, mining leases and quarry permits and deciding on whether these shall be granted, as it will be elaborated below. Apart from that, it has the power to make regulations for fully and effectively carrying out and giving effect to, all or any of the purposes, provisions and powers in this law contained.[2761] In particular, and without prejudice to the generality of the foregoing power, such regulations may provide for all or any of the following subjects: all matters which by this law are required or permitted to be prescribed;[2762] the manner in which application for prospecting permits, mining leases and quarry permits are made and the form to be used;[2763] the information to be supplied by the applicant or the person performing prospecting, mining or quarrying and the notifications that need to be published in the Official Gazette;[2764] the fees, duties and rentals to be paid for prospecting permits, mining leases and quarry permits;[2765] the size and shape of the areas over which prospecting permits, mining leases and quarry permits may be granted;[2766] the manner in which areas and boundaries are surveyed and marked, and the fees payable therefor;[2767] the working conditions to be applied to mining leases and quarry permits;[2768] the construction and use of roads, tramways and railways;[2769] the construction and erection of houses, pits, shafts, machinery and other works to be used for mining or quarrying purposes;[2770] the grazing of animals and the cutting down of timber for the purpose of carrying out prospecting, mining or quarrying;[2771] the registration in the office of the Inspector of Mines of prospecting permits, mining leases and quarry permits and the instruments under which any right or interest thereunder is transferred or surrendered and the fees payable therefor;[2772] the returns to be rendered and the accounts, registers, books and plans to be kept by the holder of prospecting permits, mining leases and quarry permits, as well as the manner in which the holder of a prospecting permit after successful research, may ensure the prospecting area for making efforts to obtain the necessary mining lease or quarry permit;[2773] the disposal of any poisonous or noxious products ('προϊόν') resulting from prospecting, mining or quarrying operations,[2774] although Law No. 82(I)/2009 that implemented

2761. Section 47(1) *ibid.*
2762. Section 47(2)(a) *ibid.*
2763. Section 47(2)(b) *ibid.*
2764. Section 47(2)(c) *ibid.*
2765. Section 47(2)(d) *ibid.*
2766. Section 47(2)(e) *ibid.*
2767. Section 47(2)(f) *ibid.*
2768. Section 47(2)(g) *ibid.*
2769. Section 47(2)(h) *ibid.*
2770. Section 47(2)(i) *ibid.*
2771. Section 47(2)(j) *ibid.*
2772. Section 47(2)(k) *ibid.*
2773. Section 47(2)(l) *ibid.*
2774. Section 47(2)(m) *ibid.*

Directive 2006/21/EC leaves little room for deviation therefrom; the amount of royalty payable to the state for minerals and quarry materials or their products and the form and manner in which these are paid and collected;[2775] securing safety and health of employees in or about mines or quarries, and carrying out mining and quarrying in a safe, proper and effectual manner;[2776] the reporting to the Inspector of Mines by the holder of a prospecting permit or a quarry permit of the lessee of a mining lease or by the manager or person in charge of any mine or quarry of any loss of life or serious personal injury to life or serious personal injury to any employee in or about a mine or quarry by reason of any accident or mishap at such mine or quarry;[2777] the holding of an inquiry, where evidence may be taken upon oath into any accident occurring in any mine or in connection with mining or prospecting operations conducted under a mining lease, mining right, temporary title or exclusive prospecting licence involving loss of life or serious injury to any person, the summoning and expenses of witnesses;[2778] the forfeiture of any mineral or quarry material illegally won, processed, sold, purchased or possessed as well as all machines, engines and tools used;[2779] the fees to be paid in respect of any matter or thing done under this law; the imposition of a penalty of two years imprisonment or EUR 20,000 fine or both such imprisonment and fine for any offence against the regulations;[2780] and the procedure regarding administrative appeal to the Council of Ministers under this law.[2781]

II. Inspector of Mines

657. Inspectors of Mines are appointed by the Council of Ministers.[2782] Their statutory duties include ensuring the proper application of this law via inspections and imposition of administrative sanctions, among others. More specifically, they inspect prospecting operations and make copies of any records and books in possession of the holder of prospecting permit,[2783] specify the necessary measures for the safety of a mining area,[2784] inspect books of a mining lessee,[2785] enter upon any land on which mining is being carried out or which is the subject of any mining lease, and inspect such mining or works in connection therewith,[2786] inspect and take copies of any registers, books, documents and plans connected with such mining[2787] and take samples, make surveys and perform any operation that they may

2775. Section 47(2)(n) *ibid.*
2776. Section 47(2)(o) *ibid.*
2777. Section 47(2)(p) *ibid.*
2778. Section 47(2)(q) *ibid.*
2779. Section 47(2)(s) *ibid.*
2780. Section 47(2)(t) *ibid.*
2781. Section 47(2)(u) *ibid.*
2782. Section 42(1) *ibid.*
2783. Section 15(1)(c) *ibid.*
2784. Section 23(4) *ibid.*
2785. Section 25(1)(h) *ibid.*
2786. Section 30(a) *ibid.*
2787. Section 30(b) *ibid.*

deem necessary for the purpose of making a report to the Council of Ministers.[2788] Further, they have the power to enter any quarry, inspect it, its quarrying operations and works in connection therewith[2789] and demand the production of any quarry permit by the holder thereof.[2790]

§4. General Provisions

658. The ownership in, and control of, all minerals and quarry materials in Cyprus shall vest in the state.[2791] Parallel to that, the ownership of minerals and quarry materials in, upon or under any land, which lies within the areas specified on the survey map signed by the director and deposited in the District Lands Office in accordance with the proviso to section 4(1) of the Immovable Property (Tenure, Registration and Valuation) Law, shall vest in the owner of the land.[2792]

659. Further, no person may carry out any prospecting, mining or quarrying on any land of Cyprus, except as in this law provided.[2793] Hence, the provisions on prospecting, mining and quarrying, which are elaborated below, are mandatory for any lawful operation. It should be noted, that in the event of a mine or a quarry be situated in a state forest, as defined above (*see* in this respect paragraphs 572 et seq. above), the views of the Director of Forest Department of the Ministry of Agriculture, Rural Development and Environment must be taken into consideration before issuing a permit or lease under this law.[2794]

I. Prospecting

660. Prospecting is lawful under a *prospecting permit* ('άδεια επισκόπησης') issued by the Council of Ministers. It should be, however, noted that the Council of Ministers has the power to prohibit inspecting for any specified mineral or quarry material by a notice in the Official Gazette. In such case, a prospecting permit, whether granted before or after such a notice, shall not authorize the holder thereof to prospect for such mineral or quarry material, unless the contrary is expressly provided in the permit.[2795] In addition, any area may be declared to be closed to prospecting by notice of the Council of Ministers in the Official Gazette either generally or for any specified mineral or quarry material for such period as may be specified in such notice or without period assigned.[2796] However, the Council of Ministers

---

2788. Section 30(c) *ibid.*
2789. Section 40(1)(a) *ibid.*
2790. Section 40(1)(b) *ibid.*
2791. Section 4(1) *ibid.*
2792. Section 4(2) *ibid.*
2793. Section 5 *ibid.*
2794. Section 24 Law No. 25(I)/2012.
2795. Section 12 Cap. 270.
2796. Section 21(1) *ibid.*

may grant authority on such terms as it may think fit to any person to prospect on any land which has been declared to be closed to prospecting.[2797]

661. A prospecting permit may be granted to any person applying therefor in the prescribed manner and on payment of the prescribed fees by the Council of Ministers.[2798] However, no prospecting permit shall be granted to any person in respect of an area for which a prospecting permit is already in subsistence, unless the later prospecting permit relates to a mineral or quarry material other than that for which the subsisting permit was granted and this does not prejudicially affect the rights or interests of the holder of the former such permit.[2799] Further specific parameters and conditions that need to be considered by the competent authority prior to deciding on this application are not set out in this law. A prospecting permit is granted in the prescribed form, subject to such terms and conditions as the Council of Ministers may determine[2800] and is valid for one year unless renewed by the competent authority.[2801] It is not transferable and any right or interest conferred thereby is not assignable, except with the previous consent of the Council of Ministers.[2802]

662. A holder of prospecting permit enjoys certain rights. In particular, he may enter upon and inspect any state land and the private land specified in his permit.[2803] Entering such private land is lawful, only following the previous consent of the owner or occupier of that private land, who may request the deposit of security for any disturbance of surface rights and any damage to the land or anything built, planted, grown or standing thereon.[2804] If such consent is not provided, the Law on Requisition of Property[2805] may be applied under the condition that the permit holder submits full details on the land, its owner or occupier, the nature of minerals and quarry materials to be prospected and furnishes an undertaking that he shall be liable to pay compensation to the owner or occupier of such land for any damage or loss, which may be caused to such owner or occupier by the prospecting thereon.[2806] It should be noted that Law on Requisition of Property prescribes that any property may be obtained only for the purpose of *public benefit* ('δημόσιας ωφέλειας').[2807] Although, this purpose is being defined in this law, not much

2797. Section 21(3) *ibid.*
2798. Section 13(1) *ibid. See* on the discretion of granting a prospecting permit: *Droushiotis v. The Republic* (1966) 3 CLR 722.
2799. Section 19 Cap. 270. *See Yiangou a.o. v. The Republic* (1975) 3 CLR 228; *Yiangou a.a. v. The Republic* (1976) 3 CLR 101.
2800. Section 13(2) Cap. 270.
2801. Section 13(4) *ibid. See Cytechno Ltd v. The Republic* (1976) 3 CLR 407; *Cytechno Ltd v. The Republic* (1979) 3 CLR 513.
2802. Section 13(3) Cap. 270.
2803. Section 14(1) *ibid.*
2804. Section 14(2) *ibid.*
2805. Law on Requisition of Property ('ο Περί Επιτάξεως Ιδιοκτησίας Νόμος') No. 21 of 1962, OG I(I) No. 138 of 22 Mar. 1962, p. 297.
2806. Section 14(3) Cap. 270.
2807. Section 3(1) Law No. 21/1962. *See* on the notion of public benefit for requisition of property: *Kouppas v. The Republic* (1966) 3 CLR 765; *Hadjiioannou a.a. v. The Republic* (1983) 3 CLR 536; *Demetriou a.o. v. The Republic* (1986) 3 CLR 664; *Christodoulidou a.a. v. The Republic* (1990) 3 CLR 2766; *Iosifides v. Attorney-General* (1990) 3 CLR 4599; *Kallimahou a.a. v. The*

certainty is being ensured, as its definition includes public safety, public policy, public health and morality ('δημόσια ασφάλεια, δημόσια τάξη, δημόσια υγεία ή δημόσια ήθη').[2808]

663. Further, the holder of a prospecting permit has certain statutory duties, those being: carrying on all prospecting on the lands comprised in his permit in a safe and workmanlike manner in accordance with any regulations made under this law;[2809] keeping such registers and books and make such returns as may be prescribed;[2810] permitting at all reasonable times the Inspector or Mines or any other person authorized in that behalf by the Council of Ministers to inspect any prospecting and to inspect and take copies of any register and book of account in the possession or under the control of the holder and kept in connection with the prospecting;[2811] not diverting water from any public river, stream, spring, well or watercourse without the previous consent in writing of the Inspector of Mines or any water privately owned without the previous consent in writing of the owner thereof;[2812] and at all times having a responsible agent supervising the prospecting of not personally residing on the lands comprised in his permit or sufficiently near to as to give continuous supervision to the prospecting of an offence.[2813] Such holder also makes payments to owner or occupier of any private land as a fair and reasonable compensation for any disturbance of surface rights or any damage to such land or anything built, planted, grown or standing thereon as a result of any prospecting on demand being made by said owner or occupier.[2814] In case of disagreement as to the compensation per se or its amount, this matter is being referred to the Director, who is authorized to decide on this.[2815] Against this, an appeal may be lodged with the Council of Ministers within fifteen days whose decision thereon is final and conclusive.[2816] Despite the clear text stating the finality of this decision, it may not be presumed that the parties are deprived of their constitutional right to

---

Republic (1991) 4 CLR 3803; *Charalambous a.o. v. The Republic* (1991) 4 CLR 22; *Markoullidou a.o. v. The Republic* (1991) 4 CLR 1384; *The Attorney-General v. Papantoniou* (1992) 2 CLR 403; *Venizelou v. The Republic* (1992) 4 CLR 2159; *Scordi & Vrahimi Investments Ltd a.a. v. The Republic* (1992) 4 CLR 2882; *The Republic v. Pandelides a.o.* (1993) 3 CLR 456; *Orphanou v. The Republic* (1993) 4 CLR 508; *Nikos Hadjigeorgiou Ltd v. The Republic* (1994) 4 CLR 1670; *Dikigoropoulos a.a. v. The Republic* (1994) 4 CLR 1847; *Ioannou a.o. v. The Republic* (1995) 4 CLR 1556; *Constantinou v. The Republic* (1995) 4 CLR 2192; *Loukaidou v. The Republic* (1996) 4 CLR 821.

2808. Section 3(2)(b) Law No. 21/1962.
2809. Section 15(1)(a) Cap. 270.
2810. Section 15(1)(b) *ibid.*
2811. Section 15(1)(c) *ibid.*
2812. Section 15(1)(d) *ibid.*
2813. Section 15(1)(e) *ibid.*
2814. Section 17(1) *ibid.*
2815. Section 17(2) *ibid.*
2816. Section 17(3) *ibid.* The Greek text, which is a translation of the English original text, makes mention of 'έφεση'. However, this must be attributed to a translation error, as the nature of this legal remedy is that of a higher administrative body (the Council of Ministers) reviewing an administrative act of a lower administrative body (the Director). Therefore, the legal remedy in question is an *administrative appeal* ('ιεραρχική προσφυγή') and not an *appeal* ('έφεση'), which is filed against a – civil or penal – court decision with the Supreme Court of Cyprus.

file an appeal ('προσφυγή') with the Supreme Court of Cyprus according to Article 146 of the Constitution as such construction would be contrary to Article 6 ECHR and Article 47 of the Charter of Fundamental Rights of the EU.

664. Minerals or quarry materials raised or obtained in the course of prospecting under the aforementioned permit are state property. They may not be removed from the land or disposed of by the holder of such permit or by any other person except with the consent in writing of the Inspector of Mines. However, this should not be construed in a manner prohibiting any such holder from removing from time to time samples of such minerals or quarry materials sufficient in quantity for tests, analyses or experiments for ascertaining the contents and the commercial value thereof.[2817] The Inspector of Mines has the power to authorize the removal of minerals or quarry materials from the land from which they have been raised or obtained to any place approved by him for safe custody, subject to such conditions as he may impose.[2818] Further, if the holder of a prospecting permit desires to retain or dispose of such material, he applies to the Inspector of Mines in the prescribed manner. The inspector may authorize the applicant to retain and dispose of the minerals or quarry materials in respect of which application is made on payment of the prescribed royalty, only if he is satisfied that such holder has been conducting such operations only as reasonably necessary for enabling testing the mining or quarrying potentialities of the land.[2819]

665. Any prospecting permit may be cancelled by the Council of Ministers, if in its opinion, the holder of such fails to comply with or observe any of the provisions of this law or any regulations made thereunder or any term or condition of such permit.[2820] Protection of the environment and prospective touristic exploitation of the relevant area constitute grounds of public interest that justify revocation of a prospecting permit,[2821] but not cancellation of the same.[2822]

II. Mining

666. Mining is lawful under a mining lease granted by the Council of Ministers. Provided that the Council of Ministers may, pending the grant of a mining lease, grant permission to the applicant for such lease to carry out mining operations on the area applied for on such terms and conditions and subject to such restrictions as it may think fit. Provided further that any such permission may, at any time, be cancelled by the Council of Ministers.[2823]

2817. Section 16(1) *ibid.*
2818. Section 16(2) *ibid.*
2819. Section 16(3) *ibid.*
2820. Section 18 *ibid.*
2821. *The Republic v. Saranti* (1979) 3 CLR 139.
2822. *Saranti v. The Republic* (1974) 3 CLR 338.
2823. Section 22(1) Cap. 270.

667. A mining lease shall be granted by the Council of Ministers if this is satisfied that the mineral-bearing qualities and quantities of the land in the area applied for are such as to justify the grant of such lease and that the applicant possesses or commands sufficient working capital and technical knowledge or assistance to ensure the proper development and exploitation of the area applied for. Where there is more than one applicant for a mining lease, the person who carried on adequate prospecting operations in the area under a prospecting permit shall be preferred. If such person is unable to obtain a mining lease on the ground that he does not command sufficient working capital and technical knowledge or assistance to ensure the proper development and exploitation of the area shall compensate such person in such an amount as shall be determined by the Council of Ministers.[2824]

668. A mining lease is granted in the prescribed form, specifies the area and the minerals in respect of which it is granted and is subject to the payment of such rentals, fees, royalties and other payments and to such covenants and conditions as the Council of Ministers may therein provide.[2825] It is further granted for such a term not being more than fifty years as the Council of Ministers may decide.[2826] In every such lease, in the absence of any express condition to the contrary, the following covenants and conditions on the part of the lessee are implied: that the lessee shall duly pay the rent and any royalty that may become due to the Council of Ministers at such time and in such manner as may, from time to time, be prescribed and to such persons as may, from time to time, be authorized to receive the same;[2827] that the lessee shall duly maintain all beacons in good condition and repair and shall keep a clear line of sight between any two beacons marking a boundary line;[2828] that, subject to the provisions of this law, the lessee shall commence mining operations in the area of the mining lease within a period of six months from the date of the lease, and shall thereafter, during the continuance of the lease, unless prevented by circumstances beyond his control or authorized in writing by the Council of Ministers, continuously, vigorously and effectively, carry on mining operations in such area;[2829] that the lessee shall fulfil the working obligations prescribed by the regulations;[2830] that the lessee shall carry on all his mining in a safe and workmanlike manner and shall not cause danger or damage to the occupiers, if any, of the lands within the area of the lease and shall observe and perform all regulations and decrees made, and directions given, in accordance with the provisions of this law;[2831] that the lessee shall not use any portion of the area included in his lease for any purpose other than mining or purposes ancillary thereto;[2832] that any person duly authorized by the Council of Ministers in this respect shall, at all reasonable

2824. Section 23(1) *ibid.*
2825. Section 23(2) *ibid.*
2826. Section 24(1) *ibid.*
2827. Section 25(1)(a) *ibid.*
2828. Section 25(1)(b) *ibid.*
2829. Section 25(1)(c) *ibid.*
2830. Section 25(1)(d) *ibid.*
2831. Section 25(1)(e) *ibid.*
2832. Section 25(1)(f) *ibid.*

times, have free access to the area of the lease and to all the workings therein;[2833] that the lessee shall keep, or cause to be kept, plans and true and sufficient books of account of the mining carried on within the area of the lease, and of the disposal of the minerals won, and shall, if so required, produce or cause to be produced such plans and books for the inspection of an inspector or of any person duly authorized by him in that behalf;[2834] and that the lessee shall take all due and proper precautions and shall comply with all requirements of mines officers as to the safety of all persons employed by him in mining operations.[2835] The Council of Ministers has further the power to set out in the mining lease explicit conditions that ensure, according to the dominant social, financial, technical or other circumstances, the satisfaction of demand of minerals or their products in the market, environmental protection, safety of the employees and generally the public, the quality of minerals or their products as well as the fulfilment of any obligations of the lessee to the state under this or any other law.[2836] Notwithstanding any statutory provision of this law or any term and condition of a permit, licence or lease given or granted under the provisions of this law, the Council of Ministers may issue a decree requiring the holder or grantee of any such permit, licence or lease to take such action as may reasonably be necessary to make the area safe to the satisfaction of the Inspector of Mines.[2837]

669. Apart from the aforementioned, certain statutory provisions relate strongly to environmental protection, from mining. In particular, in granting a mining lease, the Council of Ministers may require the reasonable restoration of any area used for mining operations by the replacement of the surface soil, the filling in of worked areas, the removal of any tailing or other dumps or heaps caused by mining operations and such other methods as may reasonably be required.[2838] Also, no mining lease may be construed as authorizing the lessee thereof: to divert the waters of any public river, stream, spring, well or watercourse, without the consent in writing from the Inspector of Mines first obtained;[2839] to divert any water privately owned, without the consent in writing of the owner thereof first obtained;[2840] or to pollute or permit to become polluted any water or in any way to render such water unfit for the purpose for which it is being used.[2841] Any person, who uses water in connection with mining operations, whether for the generation of power or for the removal of mineral substances or for concentrating, milling or otherwise has to make such provisions as will ensure that all water so used shall not contain an injurious substance in quantities likely to prove detrimental to human, animal or vegetable life, when it leaves the mining area in which it has been so used.[2842]

2833. Section 25(1)(g) *ibid.*
2834. Section 25(1)(h) *ibid.*
2835. Section 25(1)(i) *ibid.*
2836. Section 25(2) *ibid.*
2837. Section 23(4) *ibid.*
2838. Section 23(3) *ibid.*
2839. Section 28(1)(a) *ibid.*
2840. Section 28(1)(b) *ibid.*
2841. Section 28(1)(c) *ibid.*
2842. Section 29 *ibid.*

670. A mining lease confers on the lessee thereof the right to carry out mining operations of any description below the surface of the ground within the area for which such lease has been granted. Though this does not confer the right to carry out any mining on the surface of the ground except on such state land as is included within the said area.[2843] Surface mining operations in any private land within said area may be carried out only upon consent of the owner of such private land.[2844] Should such consent not be obtained, the Law on Compulsory Acquisition[2845] is applicable, under the condition that the lessee submits to the competent authority full details of the land, its owner or occupier and he also furnishes an undertaking that he shall be liable to prepay any compensation and files a relevant bank guarantee. The compensation payable to any person affected by the compulsory acquisition amounts to double the value thereof as assessed by the Director. The lessee is then also freed from any obligation to pay any contractual or statutory rent for this land.[2846] Said procedure for entering a private land is also applied in cases where minerals have prospected but mining was not yet initiated due to pending application for mining lease or when the specific area is necessary for accessing the area of proposed mining, for processing and disposition of the minerals and their products or for disposing mining waste.[2847] Further statutory right of the lessee is to remove all or any of his plant, buildings or other property within six months after the expiration or other determination of his lease, or within such further time, if any, as the Council of Ministers may allow, under the condition that he has paid all rents, royalties and other payments to be made by him under this law or under the terms of his lease.[2848] Should this right not be exercised, all the plant, buildings and property of the lessee on the land becomes state property and may be dealt with and disposed of in such manner as the Council of Ministers may direct.[2849]

671. The lessee of a mining lease may not transfer or assign his mining lease or any of the rights or privileges conferred thereby without the consent in writing of the Council of Ministers first obtained and signified by endorsement thereon.[2850]

672. A mining lease may be renewed under the following conditions. At the expiration of the term originally granted, the lessee has to carry on work in a normal and business-like manner, the mining lease should not be liable to be forfeited under any of the provisions of this law and the lessee must have given to the Council of Ministers six months' notice in writing to the purpose of renewing it. Upon payment of the prescribed fee, the lessee obtains a renewal of the lease for such term as may be approved, not exceeding fifty years, upon the conditions applicable to new leases and subject to all covenants and conditions which may be imposed under

2843. Section 26(1) *ibid.*
2844. Section 26(2) *ibid.*
2845. Law on Compulsory Acquisition for Public Purpose. *See* in this respect footnote 1944 above.
2846. Section 26(3) Cap. 270.
2847. Section 26(4)(a) and (b) *ibid.*
2848. Section 34(1) *ibid.*
2849. Section 34(2) *ibid.*
2850. Section 27 *ibid.*

the provisions of this law.[2851] In particular, any part of the area covered by such lease, which have been worked out or is no longer reasonably required for mining, may be ordered to be surrendered within a reasonable time. A mining lease may not be renewed until said surrender has been effected. Further, the lessee loses the right to renew, as described above, if reasonable time for said surrender lapses.[2852] Also, any defects existing in the plan of the area of the said lease may be corrected on renewal of said lease by the Council of Ministers, if this is considered desirable. This corrected plan is deemed to be the plan of such area, when endorsed on or attached to the lease.[2853]

673. A mining lease may further be surrendered in whole or in part, with the consent of the Council of Ministers, by the lessee. For this to be affected, he must give a six months' notice in writing to the Council of Ministers, forward the original lease, pay all sums due in respect thereof and pay all fees and charges prescribed for such surrender. Lastly, he has to carry out all obligations in respect of such lease. Also, prior to making an application to surrender the lease in the prescribed form, the applicant has to obtain the consent of any parties who may have an interest in such mining lease.[2854]

674. A mine may also be abandoned or closed down. The lessee of the relevant mining lease has to give notice to the Inspector of Mines not less than thirty-one days before such mine is abandoned or closed down. Within thirty-one days of the date of such abandonment or closing down, he has to lodge with the Inspector of Mines plans showing details of all works done on the mine, together with such further particulars as the Inspector of Mines may require.[2855]

III. Quarrying

675. The control of all quarries in Cyprus is vested in the Council of Ministers.[2856] It is lawful for a person to carry out quarrying operations on any land under a quarry permit ('προνομίου λατομείου') in the prescribed form from the Council of Ministers.[2857]

676. Granting a quarry permit lies at the discretion of the competent authority, which has to be exercised properly in the public interest.[2858] It has been ruled that implications on water resources forms a solid ground for refusing to grant such a

2851. Section 24(2) *ibid.*
2852. Section 24(3) *ibid.*
2853. Section 24(4) *ibid.*
2854. Section 24(5), (6) and (7) *ibid.*
2855. Section 33(1)(a) and (b) *ibid.*
2856. Section 36 *ibid.*
2857. Section 37(1) *ibid.*
2858. *Orictaco Co. Ltd v. The Republic* (1985) 3 CLR 1327.

permit.[2859] Quarry permits are granted subject to such covenants, terms and conditions and in respect of such areas and subject to the payment of such rentals and fees as may, from time to time, be determined by the Council of Ministers.[2860] Quarry permits are granted for such period, not exceeding twenty-five years and may be renewed for a further period or periods not exceeding twenty-five years at one time. In cases, where considerable capital expenditure or processing plant at or near the site is necessitated, the Council of Ministers may at its discretion grant a quarrying permit for a period not exceeding fifty years renewable for a further period not exceeding fifty years in accordance with any mining or quarrying regulations then in force.[2861]

677. The aforementioned undermining on permit's renewal, surrender, transfer and assignment, on rights of the lessee and on protection of water apply *mutatis mutandis* to quarry permits.[2862]

§5. Minerals and Quarry Materials in the Sea

678. Especially for minerals and quarry materials in the subsoil of territorial waters, continental shelf and exclusive economic zone of Cyprus, it is specified that their ownership and control are vested in the state.[2863] Necessary prerequisite for a prospecting permit, mining lease or quarry permit for such materials is to publish a notification in the Official Gazette. This notification specifies the form of the application, the time period for submitting an application, the area and minerals and quarry materials for which an application may be submitted, the necessary data that must be submitted, the terms and conditions under which a permit or lease may be granted and any other information under this law.[2864] Equally necessary prerequisite is the prior positive opinion ('θετική γνωμοδότηση') of the Environmental Authority according to section 20 Law No. 127(I)/2018 (*see* in this respect paragraphs 745 et seq. below).[2865]

2859. *Vassiliou v. The Republic* (1982) 3 CLR 220.
2860. Section 39(1) Cap. 270. *See* on conditions imposed on an applicant before favourably examining his application: *Leonida v. The Attorney-General* (1978) 3 CLR 247. *See* on conditions attached to quarry permit: *Protoyeros v. The Republic* (1987) 3 CLR 2025.
2861. Section 39(2) Cap. 270. In respect of renewal of a quarry permit *see*: *Oryctako Ltd v. The Republic* (1981) 3 CLR 174.
2862. Sections 39(3), 22(1), 24(3), (4), (5), (6) and (7), 25, 26, 27, 28, 29, 31 and 34 Cap. 270.
2863. Section 4(1) *ibid.*
2864. Section 4(4) and (5) *ibid.*
2865. Section 4(6) *ibid.*

§6. ENSURING COMPLIANCE

I. Administrative Sanctions

679. If quarry operations are carried out without quarry lease or mining operations are performed without a mining permit, the Inspector of Mines has the power to impose an administrative fine of up to EUR 10,000, depending on the nature, gravity and duration of the violation.[2866]

680. In the case of a continued breach on the part of the lessee of a mining lease of any of the covenants, terms or conditions therein implied or contained and if such lessee does not make good such breach within such period not being less than thirty days as the Council of Ministers may decide from the date of receiving notice in writing from said authority to do so, then the mining lease may be determined by the Council of Ministers, without prejudice to any claim against the lessee thereof, which shall already have accrued. Such determination of the mining lease is sufficiently notified to the lessee thereof by its publication in the Official Gazette. This determination is also applicable, if such lessee wholly discontinues mining during a continuous period of six months, unless prevented by circumstances beyond his control or authorized in writing by the Council of Ministers. It should be noted that the Council of Ministers further has the power, in lieu of determining the mining lease, to order the holder thereof to pay, in addition to the ordinary rent, an additional rent of such amount not exceeding three times the amount of the ordinary rent payable under such mining lease as the Council of Ministers may determine from the date on which the breach commenced until the same is made good.[2867] In particular, with reference to violation of the statutory provisions on prohibition of diversion and pollution of water the lessee may be ordered by a decree of the Council of Ministers to take such measures, as it thinks proper, in order to avoid such violation from repeating or continuing, within a specific time period. Failure to comply with such decree leads to suspension of the mining lease by the Council of Ministers, which is in force until compliance with said decree.[2868]

681. If upon inspection of a quarry, the Inspector of Mines considers that the quarry or any part thereof is in such condition as to render quarrying operations dangerous to the safety or health of employees in or about such quarry, he may order that such quarry or any part thereof is closed. He may also order that such works are executed as will enable quarrying operations to be carried out with due regard to the safety or health of persons employed in or about this quarry.[2869] The expenses of said works are to be undertaken by the holder of a quarry permit or out of moneys allotted to the Inspector of Mines from public funds for this purpose.[2870]

2866. Section 43A *ibid.*
2867. Section 32 *ibid.*
2868. Section 28(2) and (3) *ibid.*
2869. Section 40(2)(a) *ibid.*
2870. Section 40(3) *ibid.*

II. Penal Sanctions

682. Various penal sanctions foreseen in this law ensure compliance with the statutory obligations. According to the main penal provision, a person is guilty of an offence, if he: interferes with any prospecting, mining or quarrying authorized under this law;[2871] obstructs any person in the exercise of any right conferred by or under this law;[2872] interferes with any machinery, plant, works or property established on, in, under or over any land in exercise of a right conferred by or under this law;[2873] pollutes or permits to become polluted any water or in any way to be rendered unfit for the purpose for which it is being used. This person is liable to a term of imprisonment not exceeding two years and/or to a fine not exceeding EUR 50,000.[2874] These penalties apply also to the following offences:

- any person prospecting without a prospecting permit or any holder of a prospecting permit who fails to comply with or contravenes any of the terms and conditions of his prospecting permit;[2875]
- any prospecting permit holder not complying with his statutory duties;[2876]
- any person, who removes or disposes of any minerals or quarry materials raised or obtained in the course of prospecting in contravention of the provisions of section 16(1);[2877]
- any person who prospects within an area which is closed to prospecting;[2878]
- a lessee who fails to comply with or contravenes any covenant, term or condition of his mining lease is guilty of an offence;[2879]

683. – a lessee of any mining lease who fails to furnish such notice or to lodge such plans, or wilfully refuses to produce such plans or to allow them to be examined or copied by the Inspector of Mines or any other officer duly authorized thereto by the Council of Ministers, or conceals any part of the workings of the mine; and knowingly produces or transmits an imperfect or inaccurate plan.[2880] Furthermore, quarrying without a quarry permit and failure to comply with terms and conditions of an issued quarry permit, constitutes an offence punished with imprisonment of up to two years and/or fine of up to EUR 100,000. Similarly, mining without any mining lease or pending the grant thereof without permission from the Council of Ministers is an offence that may lead to imprisonment for a period of up to two years and/or a monetary fine of up to EUR 40,000.[2881]

2871. Section 43(1)(a) *ibid.*
2872. Section 43(1)(b) *ibid.*
2873. Section 43(1)(c) *ibid.*
2874. Section 43(1)(d) *ibid.*
2875. Section 13(5) *ibid.*
2876. Section 15(2) *ibid.*
2877. Section 16(1) *ibid.*
2878. Section 21(2) *ibid.*
2879. Section 23(5) *ibid.*
2880. Section 33(2)(a), (b), (c) and (d) *ibid.*
2881. Section 22(2) Cap. 270.

684. In addition to a penalty being imposed for the aforementioned penal offences, the court has the authority to further order a monetary fine equal to the value of minerals or quarry materials used, sold or disposed in violation of this law[2882] and/or to the specified royalties and charges[2883] and/or to the amount estimated by the Inspector of Mines that is necessary to the purpose of restoring safety in the area, where the illegal act was committed and in the case of state land, to the amount needed for environmental restoration.[2884] This fine may also include any expenses of the Inspector of Mines related to taking measures against said illegal act.[2885]

III. Other Sanctions

685. When mining or quarrying operations are being carried out without mining lease or quarry permit, the Inspector of Mines files an application according to the laws on civil procedure with the court requesting an order of immediate cessation of any activity in violation of this law and of immediate removal of all means used in said activities. He may also file an application for an interim order. The court has further the power to issue an order empowering the Inspector of Mines to freeze and seal tools, machines and installations that may be used for such illegal actions until the final judgment.[2886]

2882. Section 43(2)(a) *ibid.*
2883. Section 43(2)(b) *ibid.*
2884. Section 43(2)(c) *ibid.*
2885. Section 43(2)(d) *ibid.*
2886. Section 43(3)(a), (b) and (c) *ibid.*

Chapter 8. Other Sectors

686. No other sectors regarding nature conservation and management are foreseen.

Part III. Zoning and Land-Use Planning

Chapter 1. Assessment of the Effects of Certain Plans and Programmes on the Environment

687. Assessment of the Effects of Certain Plans and Programmes on the Environment is regulated by Law on Assessment of the Effects of Certain Plans and Programmes[2887] (hereinafter 'Law No. 102(I)/2005'), which implements Directive 2001/42/EC.[2888]

§1. Objective

688. The objective of this law is to provide a high level of protection of the environment and to contribute to the integration of environmental considerations into the preparation and adoption of plans and programmes with a view to promoting sustainable development, by ensuring that, in accordance with this law, an environmental assessment is carried out of certain plans and programmes which are likely to have significant effects on the environment.[2889] Pivotal to the understanding of this objective, is the notion of terms and programmes ('σχέδια και/ ή προγράμματα'), which stands for plans and programmes, including those co-financed by the EU, as well as any modifications to them, which are subject to preparation and/or adoption by an authority at national, regional or local level or which are prepared by an authority for adoption, through a legislative procedure by Parliament or Government, and which are required by legislative, regulatory or administrative provisions.[2890] Equally important is the definition of environmental impact ('επιπτώσεις

2887. Law on Assessment of the Effects of Certain Plans and/or Programmes ('ο περί της Εκτίμησης των Επιπτώσεων στο Περιβάλλον από Ορισμένα Σχέδια και/ ή Προγράμματα Νόμος') No. 102 of 2005, OG I(I) No. 4019 of 29 Jul. 2005, p. 646.

2888. Directive 2001/42/EC of the European Parliament and of the Council of 27 Jun. 2001 on the assessment of the effects of certain plans and programmes on the environment, OJ L 197 of 21 Jul. 2001, p. 30.

2889. Section 3 Law No. 102(I)/2005, which corresponds to Art. 1 Directive 2001/42/EC.

2890. Section 2 Law No. 102(I)/2005, which corresponds to Art. 2(a) Directive 2001/42/EC. The French term is 'plans et programmes', the German one 'Pläne und Programme' and the Dutch one 'plannen en programma's'. *See* in respect of Art. 2 the following judgments of CJEU: Joined Cases C-105/09 and C-110/09, *Terre wallonne ASBL (C-105/09) and Inter-Environnement Wallonie ASBL (C-110/09) v. Région wallonne*, [2010] ECR I-05611 [relevant review: T. Bunge, *Zum Anwendungsbereich der strategischen Umweltprüfung*, 34 NuR 593 (2012)]; Case C-567/10, *Inter-Environnement Bruxelles ASBL v. Government of the Brussels-Capital Region, digital* ECR

στο περιβάλλον') that includes positive or negative, direct or indirect, permanent or temporary, cumulative, secondary or synergistic, biophysical, social and other impact on human beings, human health or natural person, flora, fauna, biodiversity, natural, historical and traditional human landscape, soil, water, air and climate, any material goods and cultural heritage, including archaeological and architectural culture.[2891]

§2. Area of Application

689. An environmental assessment is carried out for the following plans and programmes, which are likely to have significant environmental effects.[2892] These are the ones, which are prepared for agriculture, forestry, fisheries, energy, industry, transport, waste management, water management, telecommunications, tourism, town and country planning or land-use and which set the framework for future development consent of projects according to Law No. 127(I)/2018,[2893] as well as the ones, which in view of the likely effect on sites, have been determined to require an assessment pursuant to section 16 Law No. 153(I)/2003 and section 7(5) Law No. 152(I)/2003 (*see* in this respect paragraphs 479 and 501 respectively).[2894]

690. When such plans and programmes determine the use of small areas at local level and minor modifications thereto, an environmental assessment is required only where the Environmental Authority decides that they are likely to have significant environmental effects.[2895] This is decided within a time period of no more than thirty days from receiving all necessary information, either through case-by-case examination or by specifying types of plans and programmes or by combining both approaches and on the basis of specific criteria,[2896] in order to ensure that plans and programmes with likely significant effects on the environment are covered by this law.[2897] Consultations with all interested public undertakings, local authorities and

---

[relevant review: D. Simon, *Directive 'évaluation stratégique des incidences sur l'environnement (ESIE)'*, Europe 222 (2012); J. Bétaille, *Évaluation environnementale*, RJE 583 (2012)]; judgment of 9 Apr. 2014 in Case C-225/13, *Ville d'Ottignies-Louvain-la-Neuve a.o. v. Région wallonne*, *digital* ECR; judgment of 10 Sep. 2015 in Case C-473/14, *Dimos Kropias Attikis v. Ypourgos Perivallontos*, *digital* ECR.

2891. Section 2 Law No. 102(I)/2005, which partially corresponds to Annex I(f) Directive 2001/42/EC and Art. 3 Directive 85/337/EEC.

2892. Section 4(1) Law No. 102(I)/2005, which corresponds to Art. 3(1) Directive 2001/42/EC.

2893. Section 4(1)(a) Law No. 102(I)/2005, which corresponds to Art. 3(2)(a) Directive 2001/42/EC. *See* in respect of Art. 3(2): Joined Cases C-105/09 and C-110/09, *Terre wallonne ASBL (C-105/09) and Inter-Environnement Wallonie ASBL (C-110/09) v. Région wallonne*, [2010] ECR I-05611; judgment of 11 Sep. 2012 in Case C-43/10, *Nomarchiaki Aftodioikisi Aitoloakarnanias a.o. v. Ypourgos Perivallontos, a.o.*, *digital* ECR.

2894. Section 4(1)(b) Law No. 102(I)/2005, which corresponds to Art. 3(2)(b) Directive 2001/42/EC.

2895. Section 4(3)(a) Law No. 102(I)/2005, which corresponds to Art. 3(3) Directive 2001/42/EC.

2896. The criteria for determining the likely significance of effects are set out in Annex II Law No. 102(I)/2005, which corresponds to Annex II Directive 2001/42/EC.

2897. Section 5(1) and (2) Law No. 102(I)/2005, which corresponds to Art. 3(5) Directive 2001/42/EC. *See* in this respect: Case C-295/10, *Genovaitė Valčiukienė a.o. v. Pakruojo rajono savivaldybė a.o.*, [2011] ECR I-08819 [relevant review: A. Langlais, *Chronique de jurisprudence 2011 de la*

governmental departments, but for the public affected and non-governmental organizations, also take place.[2898] Should the Environmental Authority estimate that no environmental assessment is required, it requests the views of the Committee of Environmental Impact Assessment for Plans and Programmes (EIAPP) and considers them before reaching the final decision. A note on this decision is published in the Official Gazette and two daily newspapers and on the Internet, along with information on that same decision is available in the archive.[2899]

691. Plans and programmes the sole purpose of which is to serve national defence or civil emergency and financial or budget plans and programmes do not fall in the area of application of this law.[2900] However, in the event of plans and programmes serving national defence or civil emergency that may have significant environmental effects due to affecting natural areas, landscapes of significant importance and protected species of flora or fauna, or may result in a significant waste of any form of energy or management of natural sources, a cooperation between the competent authorities of the Ministry of Defence and the Environmental Agency is prescribed. This cooperation focuses on examining any alternative solutions, arrangements or measures, which may be adopted for the purpose of minimizing or eliminating significant effects.[2901]

692. Lastly, it is explicitly stated that environmental assessment conducted under this law does not affect the application of Law on Assessment of the Effects of Certain Works on the Environment or other national or EU legislation.[2902]

§3. Competent Authorities

I. The Council of Ministers

693. The Council of Ministers may issue regulations for fully and effectively carrying out and giving effect to, all or any of the purposes, provisions and powers in this law contained. In particular, and without prejudice to the generality of the

---

Cour de justice de l'Union européenne. Plan règlementant la construction d'un complexe immobilier destiné à acceuillir un élevage intensif, RDR 27 (2012)]; judgment of 18 Apr. 2013 in Case C-463/11, *L v. M*, *digital* ECR [relevant review: B. Stüer & B. Garbrock, *Bebauungsplan der Innenentwicklung nach § 13a BauGB (nur) bei Wahrung der UVP-Pflichten europarechtskonform*, 128 DVBl. 778 (2013); S. Roset, *Directive évaluation stratégique des incidences sur l'environnement*, Europe 282 (2013)].

2898. Sections 5(3) and 14(1) Law No. 102(I)/2005.

2899. Section 4(3)(b) and (c) *ibid.*

2900. Section 4(5)(a) and (b) *ibid.*, which corresponds to Art. 3(8) Directive 2001/42/EC.

2901. Sections 4(5)(a) and 5(4) Law No. 102(I)/2005. The publicity obligation is set out in Art. 3(7) Directive 2001/42/EC.

2902. Section 28 Law No. 102(I)/2005. The relevant European provision reads [a]*n environmental assessment carried out under this Directive shall be without prejudice to any requirements under Directive 85/337/EEC and to any other Community law requirements.* Article 11(1) Directive 2001/42/EC.

foregoing power, such regulations may provide for all or any of the following subjects: specifying the plans and programme that fall within the area of application of this law;[2903] setting out measures for controlling and monitoring significant environmental effects of plans and programmes;[2904] prescribing coordinated and common procedures that comply with environmental legislation, in order to avoid duplication of environmental assessment procedures in the event that environmental assessment is prescribed in other legislation as well;[2905] defining detailed procedures for informing and carrying out consultations with authorities and the public, including public hearings;[2906] specifying the content of environmental report on certain categories of plans and programmes;[2907] and the qualifications of persons that may conduct an environmental report.[2908]

II. The Environmental Authority

694. The Environmental Authority ('Περιβαλλοντική Αρχή') is the Environmental Service of the Ministry of Agriculture, Rural Development and Environment.[2909] It plays an important role in this law, as it is the competent authority for scoping, receiving, evaluating and assessing the environmental report and publication requirements, as elaborated below.

III. The Committee of Environmental Impact Assessment for Plans and Programmes

695. A Committee of EIA for Plans and Programmes ('Επιτροπή Αξιολόγησης Επιπτώσεων στο Περιβάλλον από Σχέδια και/ ή Προγράμματα' – hereinafter 'Committee of EIAPP') is established under this law. It comprises the General Director of the Ministry of Agriculture, Rural Development and Environment, the General Director of the Ministry of Energy, Commerce, Industry and Tourism, the General Director of the Directorate General for European Programmes, Coordination and Development, the General Director of the Ministry of Communication and Works, the General Director of the Ministry of Interior, a representative of the Technical Chamber of Cyprus, a representative of the Cyprus Federation of Environmental and Ecological Organizations, a representative of the University of Cyprus and a representative of the Technical University of Cyprus.[2910] This committee has the duty to study the content of each environmental report and advise the Environmental Authority regarding environmental impact of

2903. Section 22(1) and (2)(a) Law No. 102(I)/2005.
2904. Section 22(2)(b) *ibid.*
2905. Section 22(2)(c) *ibid.*
2906. Section 22(2)(d) *ibid.*
2907. Section 22(2)(e) *ibid.*
2908. Section 22(2)(f) *ibid.*
2909. Section 2 *ibid.*
2910. Section 7(1) *ibid.*

plans and programmes. It also advises the Environmental Authority on any matter falling within its competence under this law.[2911]

§4. The Environmental Report

696. The environmental assessment, when necessary, is carried out during the preparation of a plan or programme and before its adoption an environmental report ('περιβαλλοντική μελέτη') is submitted by the authority preparing such plan or programme to the Environmental Authority.[2912] Where plans and programmes form part of a hierarchy, the Environmental Authority with a view to avoiding duplication of the assessment, take into account the fact that the assessment is carried out, at different levels of the hierarchy.[2913]

I. Determining the Necessity and the Content of an Environmental Report (Scoping)

697. In the event that an authority preparing a plan or a programme has doubts as to the necessity of an environmental report, it requests the opinion of the Environmental Authority while beginning the preparation of the relevant plan or programme.[2914] The Environmental Authority opines on the basis of certain criteria,[2915] whereas it asks for the views of the Committee of EIAPP, according to its discretion.[2916] Said discretion turns into obligation, when during the preliminary examination of a plan or programme it is estimated that no environmental report shall be necessary,[2917] as well as when the authority preparing the relevant plan or programme objects to the decision of the Environmental Authority.[2918] The final decision of the Environmental Authority is communicated to the EC before the relevant plan or programme is approved or materialized.[2919] Especially, when it is decided that no environmental report is necessary, a notification thereof is published in the Official Gazette, in two daily newspapers and on the Internet informing that this decision is available in the archive.[2920]

698. The authority preparing a plan or programme may further request in writing from the Environmental Authority to determine the exact form of the environmental report and the precise information that this must contain. Every such request is accompanied by a description of the nature of the relevant plan or programme,

2911. Section 7(2)(a) and (b) *ibid.*
2912. Section 6(1) *ibid.*, which corresponds to Art. 4(1) Directive 2001/42/EC.
2913. Section 6(5) Law No. 102(I)/2005, which corresponds to Art. 4(3) Directive 2001/42/EC.
2914. Section 11(1) Law No. 102(I)/2005.
2915. *See* in this respect footnote 2655 above.
2916. Section 11(2) *ibid.*
2917. Section 11(3) *ibid.*
2918. Section 11(4) *ibid.*
2919. Section 11(6) *ibid.*
2920. Section 11(5) *ibid.*

the purpose thereof, a surveying plan indicating the immovable property or the area that shall be affected, if this is relevant and practical, and any further information deemed useful or necessary regarding any possible environmental effects.[2921] The Environmental Authority may request, after the submission of such request, any additional information deemed necessary, as per its discretion.[2922]

II. Submission of an Environmental Report

699. Submission of an environmental report involves guidelines about its content, publicity requirements and certain consultations. An environmental report, once considered necessary, is prepared and contains description and evaluation of information on the relevant plan or programme. More specifically, the information to be provided is the following, to such extent and detail so that the assessment of environmental effects is reasonably possible and detailed reference to reasonable alternatives taking into account the objectives and the geographical scope of the plan or programme:[2923]

- an outline of the contents, main objectives of the plan or programme and relationship with other relevant plans and programmes of another sector, which have been approved or are submitted for approval in the wider area;[2924]
- an outline of the current state of the environment and the environmental characteristics of any area likely to be significantly affected by the materialization of the relevant plan or programme, as well as reference to the relevant aspects of the current state of the environment and the likely evolution thereof without implementation of the plan or programme;[2925]
- any existing environmental problems which exist in the area, where the materialization of the plan or programme is scheduled, and reference to whether the

2921. Section 12(1) and (2) *ibid.*

2922. Section 12(3) *ibid.*

2923. Section 15(1)(a) *ibid.*, which partially corresponds to Art. 5(1) Directive 2001/42/EC. *See* in respect of Arts 5, 6 and 9: Case C-474/10, *Department of the Environment for Northern Ireland v. Seaport (NI) Ltd a.o.*, [2011] I-10227 [relevant review: S. Turner, *The Strategic Environmental Assessment Directive: A Potential Lever for Independent Environmental Regulation in Northern Ireland?*, 24 JEL 357 (2012); O. Vidal, *Commentaire de l'arrêt de la CJUE du 20 octobre 2011, affaire C-474/10, Department of the Environment for Northern Ireland c/ Seaport (NI) LTD et autres*, 37 RJE 283 (2012); M. Aubert, E. Broussy & F. Donnat, *Chronique de jurisprudence de la CJUE. Environnement – Evaluation des plans ou programmes, L'actualité juridique*, 113 DA 2339 (2011)].

2924. Annex I(1) Law No. 102(I)/2005. The relevant European provision reads:

> an outline of the contents, main objectives of the plan or programme and relationship with other relevant plans and programmes. Annex I(a) Directive 2001/42/EC.

2925. Annex I(2) Law No. 102(I)/2005, which corresponds to Annex I(b) and (c) Directive 2001/42/EC.

eventual materialization of same shall improve or deteriorate this situation. Special reference is made to areas of special environmental importance that are protected under environmental legislation, such as special areas of conservation and special protection areas;[2926]

- analysis of the environmental protection objectives, established at international, Union or Member States level, or in Cyprus, which are relevant to the plan or programme and the way those objectives and any environmental considerations have been taken into account during its preparation;[2927]
- likely significant effects on the environment;[2928]
- the measures envisaged to prevent, reduce and as fully as possible offset any significant negative effects on the environment of implementing the plan or programme;[2929]
- an outline of the alternatives examined and the reasons for selecting the alternatives included in the plan or programme;[2930]
- a description of how the assessment was undertaken including any difficulties that came up due to technical or technological deficiencies or gaps encountered in compiling and analysis the required information;[2931]
- an analytical plan of monitoring the environment that must include monitoring measures and that are taken for the effective monitoring and timely facing the

---

2926. Annex I(3) Law No. 102(I)/2005. The relevant European provision reads:

> any existing environmental problems which are relevant to the plan or programme including, in particular, those relating to any areas of a particular environmental importance, such as areas designated pursuant to Directives 79/409/EEC and 92/43/EEC. Annex I(d) Directive 2001/42/EC.

2927. Annex I(4) Law No. 102(I)/2005. The relevant European provision reads:

> the environmental protection objectives, established at international, Community or Member State level, which are relevant to the plan or programme and the way those objectives and any environmental considerations have been taken into account during its preparation. Annex I(e) Directive 2001/42/EC.

2928. Annex I(5) Law No. 102(I)/2005. The relevant European provision reads:

> the likely significant effects on the environment, including on issues such as biodiversity, population, human health, fauna, flora, soil, water, air, climatic factors, material assets, cultural heritage including architectural and archaeological heritage, landscape and the interrelationship between the above factors. Annex I(f) Directive 2001/42/EC.

2929. Annex I(6) Law No. 102(I)/2005, which corresponds to Annex I(g) Directive 2001/42/EC.
2930. Annex I(7) Law No. 102(I)/2005, which partially corresponds to Annex I(h) Directive 2001/42/EC.
2931. Annex I(8) Law No. 102(I)/2005. The relevant European provision reads:

> a description of how the assessment was undertaken including any difficulties (such as technical deficiencies or lack of know-how) encountered in compiling the required information. Annex I(h) Directive 2001/42/EC.

effects that might come up from applying for the plan or programme, according to monitoring provisions of this law;[2932] and
- a non-technical summary of the information included in the report in a separate chapter of the same.[2933]

700. For providing the above information, relevant information already available and obtained at other levels of decision-making or through other environmental legislation may be used.[2934] In addition, the environmental report includes the information that may reasonably be required taking into account current knowledge and methods of assessment, the contents and level of detail in the plan or programme, its stage in the decision-making process and the extent to which certain matters are more appropriately assessed at different levels in that process in order to avoid duplication of the assessment.[2935] Lastly, a simple and without technical terms summary of the aforementioned information is included. This must be understood by persons not having special knowledge of the technical matters examined in that report.[2936]

701. The authority intending to implement the plan or programme consults public undertakings, local authorities and governmental departments that are likely to be concerned by environmental effects thereof, and the public that is affected or is likely to be affected by same, including non-governmental organizations.[2937] As it is paramount that these are given an early and effective opportunity within appropriate time frames to express their opinion on the draft plan or programme and the accompanying environmental report before the adoption of the plan or programme or its submission to the legislative procedure,[2938] the following publication requirements are set out. Upon submitting the preliminary plan or programme and the environmental report, the authority preparing those forwards them to said public authorities. It further publishes in the Official Gazette, in two daily newspapers and on the Internet a note informing the date of such report's submission along with the relevant authority, the nature of the suggested plan or programme and the concerned area, the possibility of reviewing those at the office of that authority and the Environmental Authority and the option of submitting views or representations regarding the content of that report or the environmental effects within thirty-five days.[2939] When estimating the extent and details of the information to be included

2932. Annex I(9) and s. 24 Law No. 102(I)/2005, which correspond to Annex I(i) and Art. 10 Directive 2001/42/EC.
2933. Annex I(10) Law No. 102(I)/2005, which corresponds to Annex I(j) Directive 2001/42/EC.
2934. Section 15(1)(c) Law No. 102(I)/2005, which corresponds to Art. 5(3) Directive 2001/42/EC.
2935. Section 15(1)(b) Law No. 102(I)/2005, which corresponds to Art. 5(2) Directive 2001/42/EC.
2936. Section 15(1)(d) Law No. 102(I)/2005.
2937. Section 14(1) and (2) *ibid.*, which corresponds to Art. 6(3) and (4) Directive 2001/42/EC. *See* in this respect: Case C-474/10, *Department of the Environment for Northern Ireland v. Seaport (NI) Ltd a.o.*, [2011] ECR I-10227.
2938. Article 6(2) *ibid.*
2939. Section 13(a), (b), (c) and (d) Law No. 102(I)/2005.

in the environmental report, the Environmental Authority and said public authorities consult further.[2940] In addition, the Environmental Authority may request any information deemed relevant or necessary for the purpose of preparing or evaluating the environmental report from said public authorities according to the provisions of Law No. 119(I)/2004, save for these considered of confidential nature under any law.[2941]

III. Evaluation of an Environmental Report

702. Within fifteen days of receiving the environmental report, the Environmental Authority sends a copy thereof to members of the Committee of EIAPP. Thereafter it examines, whether the information contained is sufficient.[2942] Should this not be the case, any additional information may be requested to be provided within a reasonable time period, which may not be longer than sixty days, from the authority that submitted said report.[2943] When it is established that the information provided is sufficient, a meeting of the Committee of EIAPP is convened for the evaluation of said report.[2944]

703. The Environmental Authority may submit a reasoned proposal to the Council of Ministers suggesting a public hearing on environmental reports of important plans or programmes before the evaluation by the committee is concluded. The scope and procedure of that hearing, the concerned public and any other matters are prescribed in regulations issued by the Council of Ministers.[2945] Further consultation takes place, where the Environmental Authority considers that the implementation of a plan or programme being prepared is likely to have significant effects on the environment in another Member State, or where a Member State is likely to be significantly affected so requests. In such cases, the Environmental Authority forwards a copy of the draft plan or programme, the relevant environmental report and sufficient information regarding the procedure of EIA under this law to the other Member State.[2946] Should that other Member State indicate that it wishes to enter into consultations on the specific plan or programme, consultations concerning the likely transboundary environmental effects of implementing the plan or programme and the measures envisaged to reduce or eliminate such effects take place. The Environmental Authority ensures that information and data are made available to both the authorities of the other Member State and its concerned public and that these are enabled to submit their opinion within reasonable time. An agreement is reached to this end between the Member States.[2947]

2940. Sections 15(2) and 14(1) *ibid.*, which corresponds to Arts 5(4) and 6(3) Directive 2001/42/EC.
2941. Section 16(1) Law No. 102(I)/2005.
2942. Section 17(1) and (2) *ibid.*
2943. Section 17(3) *ibid.*
2944. Section 17(4) *ibid.*
2945. Section 18(1) and (2) *ibid.*
2946. Section 19(1)(a) and (b) *ibid.*, which partially corresponds to Art. 7(1) Directive 2001/42/EC.
2947. Section 19(4) and (5) Law No. 102(I)/2005, which corresponds to Art. 7(2) Directive 2001/42/EC.

704. Any views and opinions submitted by the public or by a Member State are taken into consideration and reasoned recommendations on said report are provided by the committee to the Environmental Authority. Then the latter takes regard of these recommendations and issues an opinion, which may include the incorporation of certain environmental parameters in the plan or programme, specific amendments to the plan or programme aiming at the protection of the environment and reasonable management of natural resources and specifying the means of monitoring and controlling any environmental effects from the plan or programme. This opinion, which forms an integral part of the plan or programme, is forwarded to the authority intending to implement the plan or programme.[2948]

705. The opinion of the Environmental Authority is equally sent to any Member State that participated in the procedure in the event of transboundary effects. It is also filed in the archive and the public is informed thereof via a note in the Official Gazette, in two daily newspapers and on the Internet.[2949]

§5. Decision-Making

706. The environmental report, the opinions and views expressed by the public and public authorities, the opinion of the Environmental Authority, and the results of any public hearing or transboundary consultations are taken into account during the preparation of the plan or programme and before its adoption.[2950] The authority preparing the relevant plan or programme, when deciding on its implementation, takes into account environmental protection and financial growth in the frame of public interest.[2951] If said authority disagrees with any substantial conditions or measures contained in the opinion of the Environmental Authority, it informs the latter and forwards the matter to the Council of Ministers, who reaches a final and conclusive decision.[2952]

707. Should the authority decide to approve the plan or programme, it informs the Environmental Authority on the content of its decision and any attached conditions, the plan or programme, as approved along with description of the incorporation of conditions and measures contained in the opinion of the Environmental Authority, the grounds and estimation, on which the decision was based, and the other reasonable alternatives that were examined.[2953] It is then the Environmental Authority's duty to inform public enterprises, local authorities, governmental services, the public and any Member State that was consulted. It further publishes a note in the Official Gazette, in two daily newspapers and on the Internet informing that specific information, such as description of the approved plan or programme,

2948. Section 17(5), (6) and (7) Law No. 102(I)/2005.
2949. Section 17(9) and (10) *ibid.*
2950. Sections 20(1) and 15, 13, 14, 17(6), 18 and 19 *ibid.*
2951. Section 20(2) *ibid.*
2952. Section 21(1) and (2) *ibid.*
2953. Section 22(1) *ibid.*

description of the main negative effects that are expected to follow the implementation of the plan or programme and description of the monitoring measures and measures controlling any negative environmental effects from the implementation thereof, is available.[2954]

§6. Monitoring Obligations

708. The authority that implemented the plan and programme bears the duty to monitor any significant negative environmental effects of that implementation in order, *inter alia*, to identify those at an early stage and to be able to undertake any appropriate remedial action.[2955] In order to comply with that obligation, existing monitoring arrangements may be used, if appropriate, with a view to avoiding duplication of monitoring.[2956] The Environmental Authority has also the competence to monitor any condition or measure and informs accordingly said authority.[2957]

709. The authority that implemented the plan and programme prepares in addition a report on monitoring and submits this to the Environmental Authority. The latter may call a meeting of the Committee of EIAPP for the purpose of examining additional corrective or preventive measures for environmental protection to be taken by the authority that implemented the plan and programme.[2958]

§7. Archive

710. The Environmental Authority keeps an archive, where the following are filed: decisions and conclusions of the Environmental Authority;[2959] all studies submitted under this law;[2960] views and representations of any person submitted to the Environmental Authority;[2961] the opinions of the Environmental Authority;[2962] every document submitted within a public hearing;[2963] every document submitted by another Member State during transboundary consultations;[2964] information available to the public following the adoption of the plan and programme;[2965] and the

2954. Section 22(2) *ibid.*, which corresponds to Art. 9(1) Directive 2001/42/EC.
2955. Section 24(1) Law No. 102(I)/2005, which partially corresponds to Art. 10(1) Directive 2001/42/EC, as the European provision prescribes an obligation to monitor all significant environmental effects and not just the negative ones and aims to identifying unforeseen effects, whereas the national provision is silent on that.
2956. Section 24(2) Law No. 102(I)/2005, which corresponds to Art. 10(2) Directive 2001/42/EC.
2957. Section 24(3) Law No. 102(I)/2005.
2958. Section 25(1) and (2) *ibid.*
2959. Sections 23(1)(a) and 4(3), 23(1)(b) and 5(4), 23(1)(c) and 6(7), 23(1)(d) and 11(5) *ibid.*
2960. Section 23(1)(e) *ibid.*
2961. Sections 23(1)(f) and 13(d) *ibid.*
2962. Sections 23(1)(g) and 17 *ibid.*
2963. Sections 23(1)(h) and 18 *ibid.*
2964. Sections 23(1)(i) and 19 *ibid.*
2965. Sections 23(1)(j) and 22 *ibid.*

results of monitoring the environmental effects of the approved plan and programme.[2966] The public may visit the archive during working days and hours.[2967]

2966. Sections 23(1)(k) and 24 *ibid.*
2967. Section 23(2) *ibid.*

Chapter 2. Assessment of the Effects of Certain Projects on the Environment

711. Assessment of environmental effects of certain projects is regulated by Law on Assessment of the Effects of Certain Projects on the Environment[2968] (hereinafter 'Law No. 127(I)/2018'), which implements Directive 2011/92/EU.[2969] This law has repealed Law on Assessment of the Effects of Certain Projects on the Environment of 2005.[2970]

§1. Objective

712. The objective of this law is to materially contribute to ensuring a high-level protection of the environment, public health and quality of life, preserving the integrity of the areas of the Natura 2000 network and efficient use of resources through assessing the environmental impact of private and public works that may have significant effects on the environment prior to their licence or approval.[2971]

§2. Area of Application

713. This law is applied to every project falling under the categories of works listed in Annexes I and II of this law, including public projects and projects, which do not prerequisite an urban planning permission or other permit or approval under any law.[2972]

714. More specifically, the works listed in Annex I of this law are:

- Crude-oil refineries (excluding undertakings manufacturing only lubricants from crude oil) and installations for the gasification and liquefaction of 500 tonnes or more of coal or bituminous shale.[2973]
- Thermal power stations and other combustion installations with a heat output of 50 MW or more.[2974]

2968. Law on Assessment of the Effects of Certain Works on the Environment ('ο περί της Εκτίμησης των Επιπτώσεων στο Περιβάλλον από Ορισμένα 'Εργα Νόμος') No. 127 of 2018, OG I(I) No. 4670 of 31 Jul. 2018, p. 851.
2969. Directive 2011/92/EU of the European Parliament and of the Council of 13 Dec. 2011 on the assessment of the effects of certain public and private projects on the environment, OJ L 26, 28 Jan. 2012, p. 1, as amended.
2970. Law on Assessment of the Effects of Certain Projects on the Environment ('ο περί Εκτίμησης των Επιπτώσεων στο Περιβάλλον από Ορισμένα 'Εργα Νόμος') No. 140 of 2005, OG I(I) No. 4055 of 2 Dec. 2005, p. 1090.
2971. Section 3 Law No. 127(I)/2018.
2972. Section 4(1) *ibid.*
2973. Annex I(1) *ibid.*, which corresponds to Annex I(1) Directive 2011/92/EU.
2974. Annex I(2)(a) Law No. 127(I)/2018, which corresponds to Annex I(2)(a) Directive 2011/92/EU.

- Nuclear power stations and other nuclear reactors including the dismantling or decommissioning of such power stations or reactors (except research installations for the production and conversion of fissionable and fertile materials, whose maximum power does not exceed 1 kW continuous thermal load).[2975]
- Installations for the reprocessing of irradiated nuclear fuel.[2976]
- Installations designed: (i) for the production or enrichment of nuclear fuel; (ii) for the processing of irradiated nuclear fuel or high-level radioactive waste; (iii) for the final disposal of irradiated nuclear fuel; (iv) solely for the final disposal of radioactive waste; (v) solely for the storage (planned for more than ten years) of irradiated nuclear fuels or radioactive waste in a different site than the production site.[2977]
- petrol stations in areas or landscapes that have been declared and/or characterized protected under any laws, or forest areas, areas of the Natura 2000 network, coastal water and rivers.[2978]
- Integrated works for the initial smelting of cast iron and steel.[2979]
- Installations for the production of nonferrous crude metals from ore, concentrates or secondary raw materials by metallurgical, chemical or electrolytic processes.[2980]
- Installations for the extraction and storage of asbestos and for the processing and transformation of asbestos and products containing asbestos: for asbestos-cement products, with an annual production of more than 20,000 tonnes of finished products, for friction material, with an annual production of more than 50 tonnes of finished products, and for other uses of asbestos, utilization of more than 200 tonnes per year.[2981]
- Integrated chemical installations, i.e., those installations for the manufacture on an industrial scale of substances using chemical conversion processes, in which several units are juxtaposed and are functionally linked to one another and which are: (i) for the production of basic organic chemicals; (ii) for the production of basic inorganic chemicals; (iii) for the production of phosphorous-, nitrogen- or potassium-based fertilizers (simple or compound fertilizers); (iv) for the production of basic plant health products and of biocides; (v) for the production of basic pharmaceutical products using a chemical or biological process; (vi) for the production of explosives.[2982]
- Construction of lines for long-distance railway traffic and of airports with a basic runway length of 2,100 m or more.[2983]
- Construction of motorways and express roads.[2984]

2975. Annex I(2)(b) Law No. 127(I)/2018, which corresponds to Annex I(2)(b) Directive 2011/92/EU.
2976. Annex I(3)(a) Law No. 127(I)/2018, which corresponds to Annex I(3)(a) Directive 2011/92/EU.
2977. Annex I(3)(b) Law No. 127(I)/2018, which corresponds to Annex I(3)(b) Directive 2011/92/EU.
2978. Annex I(3)(c) Law No. 127(I)/2018.
2979. Annex I(4)(a) *ibid.*, which corresponds to Annex I(4)(a) Directive 2011/92/EU.
2980. Annex I(4)(b) Law No. 127(I)/2018, which corresponds to Annex I(4)(b) Directive 2011/92/EU.
2981. Annex I(5)(a)–(d) Law No. 127(I)/2018, which to a great extend corresponds to Annex I(5) Directive 2011/92/EU.
2982. Annex I(6) Law No. 127(I)/2018, which corresponds to Annex I(6) Directive 2011/92/EU.
2983. Annex I(7)(a) Law No. 127(I)/2018, which corresponds to Annex I(7)(a) Directive 2011/92/EU.
2984. Annex I(7)(b) Law No. 127(I)/2018, which corresponds to Annex I(7)(b) Directive 2011/92/EU.

- Construction of a new road of four or more lanes, or realignment and/or widening of an existing road of two lanes or less so as to provide four or more lanes, where such new road or realigned and/or widened section of road would be 10 km or more in a continuous length.[2985]
- Inland waterways and ports for inland-waterway traffic which permit the passage of vessels of over 1,350 tonnes.[2986]
- Trading ports, piers for loading and unloading connected to land and outside ports (excluding ferry piers) which can take vessels of over 1,350 tonnes.[2987]
- Waste disposal installations for the incineration, chemical treatment as defined in Annex II (D9) to Law No. 185(I)/2011, or landfill of hazardous waste, as defined in section 2 of same law.[2988]
- Waste disposal installations for the incineration or chemical treatment of non-hazardous waste as defined in Annex II (D9) to Law No. 185(I)/2011, with a capacity exceeding 100 tonnes per day.[2989]
- Groundwater abstraction or artificial groundwater recharge schemes where the annual volume of water abstracted or recharged is equivalent to or exceeds 250,000 m^3.[2990]
- Works for the transfer of water resources between river basins where that transfer aims at preventing possible shortages of water and where the amount of water transferred exceeds 500,000 m^3/year.[2991]
- In all other cases of transfer of water resources, works for the transfer of water resources between river basins where the multi-annual average flow of the basin of abstraction exceeds 10,000,000 m^3/year and where the amount of water transferred exceeds 5% of that flow.[2992]
- Wastewater treatment plants with a capacity exceeding 15,000 population equivalent.[2993]
- Extraction of petroleum and natural gas for commercial purposes and land supportives for extraction of hard coal, oil, natural gas and ores and rocks, as well as bituminous shale occupying a total area of more than 2,000 m^2.[2994]
- Exploration drilling (in original *ανόρυξη γεώτρησης εξερεύνησης*) by a non-production installation.[2995]

2985. Annex I(7)(c) Law No. 127(I)/2018, which corresponds to Annex I(7)(c) Directive 2011/92/EU.
2986. Annex I(8)(a) Law No. 127(I)/2018, which corresponds to Annex I(8)(a) Directive 2011/92/EU.
2987. Annex I(8)(b) Law No. 127(I)/2018, which corresponds to Annex I(8)(b) Directive 2011/92/EU.
2988. Annex I(9) Law No. 127(I)/2018, which corresponds to Annex I(9) Directive 2011/92/EU.
2989. Annex I(10) Law No. 127(I)/2018, which corresponds to Annex I(10) Directive 2011/92/EU.
2990. Annex I(11) Law No. 127(I)/2018, which corresponds to Annex I(11) Directive 2011/92/EU.
2991. Annex I(12)(a) Law No. 127(I)/2018, which greatly corresponds to Annex I(12)(a) Directive 2011/92/EU.
2992. Annex I(12)(b) Law No. 127(I)/2018, which greatly corresponds to Annex I(12)(b) Directive 2011/92/EU.
2993. Annex I(13) Law No. 127(I)/2018, which greatly corresponds to Annex I(13) Directive 2011/92/EU.
2994. Annex I(14)(a), (b) and (c) Law No. 127(I)/2018, which partly corresponds to Annex I(14) Directive 2011/92/EU.
2995. Annex I(15) Law No. 127(I)/2018. *Exploration* ('exploration' in French, 'Exploration' in German, 'exploratie' in Dutch) means drilling into a prospect and all related offshore oil and gas operations necessary prior to production-related operations under Regulation 2(1) of the Regulations on Safety and Health at Work (Safety of Offshore Oil and Gas Operations) ('οι περί

- Dams and other installations designed for the holding back or permanent storage of water, where a new or additional amount of water held back or stored exceeds 5,000,000 m3.[2996]
- Pipelines with a diameter of more than 800 mm and a length of more than 10 km: (a) for the transport of gas, oil, chemicals; (b) for the transport of carbon dioxide (CO2) streams for the purposes of geological storage, including associated booster stations.[2997]
- Subsea pipelines and relevant installations installed in the territorial waters, in the exclusive economic zone and/or the continental shelf of Cyprus, through which any liquid, solid and/or gas material is transferred, as well as the relevant on shore installations.[2998]
- Installations for the intensive rearing of poultry or pigs with more than: (a) 85,000 places for broilers or 60,000 places for hens; (b) 3,000 places for production pigs (over 30 kg); (c) 900 places for sows;[2999] or (d) 200 places for lactating cows.[3000]
- Industrial plants for the production of pulp from timber or similar fibrous materials and paper and board with a production capacity exceeding 200 tonnes per day.[3001]
- Quarries and open-cast mining where the surface of the site exceeds 25 ha, or peat extraction, where the surface of the site exceeds 150 ha.[3002]
- Construction of overhead electrical power lines with a voltage of 132 kV or more and a length of more than 15 km.[3003]
- Installations for storage of petroleum, petrochemical, or chemical products with a capacity of 200,000 tonnes or more.[3004]
- Renewable energy works, those being: (i) wind-turbines with an output of 10 MW or more; (ii) solar photovoltaic systems to be laid on land with an output of 1 MW or more; (iii) solar photovoltaic systems to be laid on land with an output of 500 kW and more but less than 1 MW within protected zones and areas as well as within agricultural zones; (iv) solar thermal parks with an output of 10 MW or more; other renewable energy works with an output of 1 MW or more; (v) works for the production of biofuel or bioliquids with a capacity of 20 m3 or more per

---

Ασφάλειας και Υγείας στην Εργασία (Ασφάλεια των Υπεράκτιων Εργασιών Πετρελαίου και Φυσικού Αερίου) Κανονισμοί') No. 424 of 2015 (OG III(I) No. 4911 of 11 Dec. 2015, p. 2511), which corresponds to Art. 2(15) Directive 2013/30/EU.

2996. Annex I(16) Law No. 127(I)/2018, which greatly corresponds to Annex I(15) Directive 2011/92/EU.
2997. Annex I(17) Law No. 127(I)/2018, which greatly corresponds to Annex I(16) Directive 2011/92/EU.
2998. Annex I(18) Law No. 127(I)/2018.
2999. Annex I(19)(a), (b) and (c) *ibid.*, which corresponds to Annex I(17)(a), (b) and (c) Directive 2011/92/EU.
3000. Annex I(19)(d) Law No. 127(I)/2018.
3001. Annex I(20)(a) and (b) *ibid.*, which corresponds to Annex I(18)(a) and (b) Directive 2011/92/EU.
3002. Annex I(21) Law No. 127(I)/2018, which corresponds to Annex I(19) Directive 2011/92/EU.
3003. Annex I(22) Law No. 127(I)/2018, which greatly corresponds to Annex I(20) Directive 2011/92/EU.
3004. Annex I(23) Law No. 127(I)/2018, which greatly corresponds to Annex I(21) Directive 2011/92/EU.

day; (vi) production of hydrogen intended for fuel; (vii) offshore installations for renewable energy, such as wind parks and wave energy works.[3005]

- Jetties and breakwaters.[3006]
- Marinas and fishing harbours.[3007]
- Golf courses and accompanying works and development, including works that serve directly or indirectly the function of said work, with the exception of mini-golfs.[3008]
- Storage sites pursuant to the Law on Geological Storage of Carbon Dioxide.[3009,3010]
- Installations for the capture of CO2 streams for the purposes of geological storage pursuant to Law on Geological Storage of Carbon Dioxide from installations covered by this paragraph, that being Annex I Law No. 127(I)/2018, or where the total yearly capture of CO2 is 1.5 megatonnes or more.[3011]
- Unified development of large and complex usage and buildings with floors more than two of the maximum number prescribed by the local plant and/or policy declaration under the applicable laws.[3012]
- Installations and industrial activities related to the energy sector, production and process of metals, the mining industry, the chemical industry, waste management, incineration plants, waste incineration and co-incineration, installations and activities using organic solvents and installations producing titanium dioxide.[3013]
- Any change to or extension of projects listed in this paragraph, that being Annex I Law No. 127(I)/2018, where such a change or extension in itself meets the thresholds, if any, set out therein.[3014]

715. The works listed in Annex II of this law are:

- Related to agriculture, silviculture and aquaculture: projects for the restructuring of rural land holdings; projects for the use of uncultivated land or semi-natural areas for intensive agricultural purposes; water management projects for agriculture, including irrigation and land drainage projects; initial afforestation and deforestation for the purposes of conversion to another type of land use; intensive

3005. Annex I(24) Law No. 127(I)/2018.
3006. Annex I(25) *ibid.*
3007. Annex I(26) *ibid.*
3008. Annex I(27) *ibid.*
3009. Law on Geological Storage of Carbon Dioxide ('ο περί της Αποθήκευσης Διοξειδίου του 'Ανθρακα σε Γεωλογικούς Σχηματισμούς Νόμος') No. 71 of 2012, OG I(I) No. 4338 of 8 Jun. 2012, p. 789, which implements Directive 2009/31/EC of the European Parliament and of the Council of 23 Apr. 2009 on the geological storage of carbon dioxide, OJ L 140 of 5 Jun. 2009, p. 114.
3010. Annex I(28) Law No. 127(I)/2018, which corresponds to Annex I(22) Directive 2011/92/EU.
3011. Annex I(29) Law No. 127(I)/2018, which corresponds to Annex I(23) Directive 2011/92/EU.
3012. Annex I(30) Law No. 127(I)/2018.
3013. Annex I(31) *ibid.* and ss 23–83 and Annex IV Law No. 184(I)/2013.
3014. Annex I(32) Law No. 127(I)/2018, which corresponds to Annex I(24) Directive 2011/92/EU.

livestock installations (projects not included in the above paragraph, that being Annex I Law No. 127(I)/2018); and intensive fish farming; and reclamation of land from the sea.[3015]

- Related to the extractive industry: quarries, open-cast mining and peat extraction (projects not included in the above paragraph, that being Annex I Law No. 127(I)/2018); underground mining; extraction of minerals by marine or fluvial dredging; deep drillings, in particular: (i) geothermal drilling; (ii) drilling for the storage of nuclear waste material; (iii) drilling for water supplies, with the exception of drillings for investigating the stability of the soil;[3016] and (iv) deep drilling for foundation of buildings;[3017] surface industrial installations for the extraction of coal, petroleum, natural gas and ores, as well as bituminous shale;[3018] land supportives for extraction of hard coal, oil, natural gas and ores and rocks, as well as bituminous shale occupying a total area of less than 2,000 m2.[3019]
- Related to the energy industry, as long as they are not included in the paragraph above, that being Annex I Law No. 127(I)/2018: industrial installations for the production of electricity, steam and hot water; industrial installations for carrying gas, steam and hot water; transmission of electrical energy by overhead cables; surface storage of natural gas; underground storage of combustible gases; surface storage of fossil fuels; industrial briquetting of coal and lignite; installations for the processing and storage of radioactive waste; installations for hydroelectric energy production; wind-turbines; installations for the capture of CO2 streams for the purposes of geological storage pursuant to the Law on Geological Storage of Carbon Dioxide;[3020] solar photovoltaic systems to be laid on land with an output of no more than 500 kW within protected zones and areas, including the Natura 2000 network, as well as agricultural zones; solar thermal parks and other renewable energy works with an output of no more than 10 MW; within protected zones and areas, including the Natura 2000 network, as well as agricultural zones; and works for the production of biofuel or bioliquids with a capacity of no more than 20 m3 per day.[3021]
- Related to the production and processing of metals: installations for the production of pig iron or steel (primary or secondary fusion) including continuous casting; installations for the processing of ferrous metals: (i) hot-rolling mills; (ii) smitheries with hammers; (iii) application of protective fused metal coats; ferrous metal foundries; installations for the smelting, including the alloyage, of nonferrous metals, excluding precious metals, including recovered products (refining, foundry casting, etc.); installations for surface treatment of metals and plastic materials using an electrolytic or chemical process;[3022] manufacture of

3015. Annex II(1)(a)–(g) Law No. 127(I)/2018, which correspond to Annex II(1)(a)–(g) Directive 2011/92/EU.
3016. Annex II(2)(a)–(d)(iii) Law No. 127(I)/2018, which correspond to Annex II(2)(a)–(d)(iii) Directive 2011/92/EU.
3017. Annex II(2)(d)(iv) Law No. 127(I)/2018.
3018. Annex II(2)(e) *ibid.*, which corresponds to Annex II(2)(e) Directive 2011/92/EU.
3019. Annex II(2)(f) Law No. 127(I)/2018.
3020. Annex II(3)(a)–(j) *ibid.*, which corresponds to Annex II(3)(a) – (j) Directive 2011/92/EU.
3021. Annex II(3)(k)–(m) Law No. 127(I)/2018.
3022. Annex II(4)(a)–(e) *ibid.*, which corresponds to Annex II(4)(a)–(e) Directive 2011/92/EU.

railway equipment;[3023] swaging by explosives;[3024] installations for the roasting and sintering of metallic ores;[3025] manufacture and assembly of motor vehicles and manufacture of motor-vehicle engines; shipyards; and installations for the construction and repair of aircraft.[3026]

– Related to the mineral industry: coke ovens (dry coal distillation); installations for the manufacture of cement; installations for the production of asbestos and the manufacture of asbestos products (projects not included in the paragraph above, that being Annex I Law No. 127(I)/2018); installations for the manufacture of glass including glass fibre; installations for smelting mineral substances including the production of mineral fibres; and manufacture of ceramic products by burning, in particular roofing tiles, bricks, refractory bricks, tiles, stoneware or porcelain.[3027]
– Related to the chemical industry: treatment of intermediate products and production of chemicals; production of pesticides and pharmaceutical products, paint and varnishes, elastomers and peroxides; storage facilities for petroleum, petrochemical and chemical products;[3028] and facilities for blending, packaging, repackaging and/or processing chemical substances.[3029]
– Related to the food industry: manufacture of vegetable and animal oils and fats; packing and canning of animal and vegetable products; manufacture of dairy products; brewing and malting; confectionery and syrup manufacture; installations for the slaughter of animals; industrial starch manufacturing installations; fish-meal and fish-oil factories; sugar factories;[3030] wineries and distilleries; sausage manufactories; bottling holls; and oil mills.[3031]
– Related to textile, leather, wood and paper industries: industrial plants for the production of paper and board; plants for the pre-treatment (operations such as washing, bleaching, mercerization) or dyeing of fibres or textiles; plants for the tanning of hides and skins; and cellulose-processing and production installations.[3032]
– Related to the rubber industry and in particular manufacture and treatment of elastomer-based products.[3033]
– Related to infrastructure projects, as long as they are not included in Annex I Law No. 127(I)/2018: industrial estate development projects;[3034] urban development

3023. Annex II(4)(f) Law No. 127(I)/2018, which corresponds to Annex II(4)(i) Directive 2011/92/EU.
3024. Annex II(4)(g) Law No. 127(I)/2018, which corresponds to Annex II(4)(j) Directive 2011/92/EU.
3025. Annex II(4)(h) Law No. 127(I)/2018, which corresponds to Annex II(4)(k) Directive 2011/92/EU.
3026. Annex II(4)(i) – (k) Law No. 127(I)/2018, which corresponds to Annex II(4)(f)–(h) Directive 2011/92/EU.
3027. Annex II(5)(a) – (f) Law No. 127(I)/2018, which corresponds to Annex II(5)(a)–(f) Directive 2011/92/EU.
3028. Annex II(6)(a) – (c) Law No. 127(I)/2018, which corresponds to Annex II(6)(a)–(c) Directive 2011/92/EU.
3029. Annex II(6)(d) Law No. 127(I)/2018.
3030. Annex II(7)(a)–(i) *ibid.*, which corresponds to Annex II(7)(a)–(i) Directive 2011/92/EU.
3031. Annex II(7)(j)–(m) Law No. 127(I)/2018.
3032. Annex II(8)(a)–(d) *ibid.*
3033. Annex II(9) *ibid.*, which corresponds to Annex II(9) Directive 2011/92/EU.
3034. Annex II(10)(a) Law No. 127(I)/2018, which corresponds to Annex II(10)(a) Directive 2011/92/EU.

projects, including the construction of shopping centres, supermarkets, complex commercial and entertainment development, buildings for cultural activities; cinema complex; higher education schools; university campuses; churches and other buildings for religious assemblies; athletic centres; research centres and/or centres for applied innovation, where applied research is conducted; car parks; football fields and stadiums; hospitals, treatment and recovery centres and special types of clinics, such as disintoxication units, mental health centres and centres for the treatment of infectious and transmissible disease;[3035] construction of railways, intermodal transhipment facilities and intermodal terminals; construction of airfields; construction of roads, harbours and port installations, including fishing harbours (projects not included in paragraph 707 above); inland-waterway construction, canalization and flood-relief works;[3036] construction of roads, including widening and in general upgrading of roads in mountain areas, in protected areas or zones or that affect, among others, river beds, river mouths or the natural coastline;[3037] enrichment dykes constructed at rivers aiming to enrich groundwater in mountain or forest areas; works for differentiation of river or torrent beds;[3038] tramways, elevated and underground railways, suspended lines or similar lines of a particular type, used exclusively or mainly for passenger transport;[3039] Coastal work to combat erosion and maritime works capable of altering the coast through the construction, for example, of dykes, moles, jetties and other sea defence works, excluding the maintenance and reconstruction of such works;[3040] groundwater abstraction and artificial groundwater recharge schemes; works for the transfer of water resources between river basins;[3041] installations for desalination of sea and brackish water;[3042] dams and other installations designed to hold water or store it on a long-term basis;[3043] installation of land pipelines for the transmission of liquid waste or chemical substances,[3044] long-distance aqueducts and oil and gas pipeline installations and pipelines for the transport of CO2 streams for the purposes of geological storage;[3045] and subsea cables and relevant installations in the territorial waters, in the exclusive economic zone and/or the continental shelf, and relevant installations on the coastal zone.[3046]

3035. Annex II(10)(b)(i)–(x) Law No. 127(I)/2018, which is much more detailed and descriptive than Annex II(10)(b) Directive 2011/92/EU.
3036. Annex II(10)(c)–(f) and (l)(ii) Law No. 127(I)/2018, which correspond to Annex II(10)(c)–(f) Directive 2011/92/EU.
3037. Annex II(10)(g) and (h) Law No. 127(I)/2018, which are much more detailed and descriptive than Annex II(10)(e) Directive 2011/92/EU.
3038. Annex II(10)(i) and (j) Law No. 127(I)/2018.
3039. Annex II(10)(k) *ibid.*
3040. Annex II(10)(l)(i) *ibid.*, which corresponds to Annex II(10)(k) Directive 2011/92/EU.
3041. Annex II(10)(m) and (n) Law No. 127(I)/2018, which correspond to Annex II(10)(l) and (m) Directive 2011/92/EU.
3042. Annex II(10)(o) Law No. 127(I)/2018.
3043. Annex II(10)(p) *ibid.*, which corresponds to Annex II(10)(g) Directive 2011/92/EU.
3044. Annex II(10)(q)(i) Law No. 127(I)/2018.
3045. Annex II(10)(q)(ii) and (iii) *ibid.*, which correspond to Annex II(10)(j) and (i) Directive 2011/92/EU.
3046. Annex II(10)(r) Law No. 127(I)/2018.

- Related to tourism and leisure: ski runs, ski lifts and cable cars and associated developments; holiday villages and hotel complexes outside urban areas and associated developments; permanent campsites and caravan sites; sea and land theme parks;[3047] and integrated casino-resorts and associated works and developments.[3048]
- Related to other projects: permanent racing and test tracks for motorized vehicles; installations for the disposal of waste; wastewater treatment plants; sludge-deposition sites; storage of scrap iron, including scrap vehicles; test benches for engines, turbines or reactors; installations for the manufacture of artificial mineral fibres; installations for the recovery or destruction of explosive substances; knackers' yards;[3049] antennas for mobile telephony in protected and/or forest areas; animal conservatory; separation of more than fifty plots; cemeteries; in situ works for soil remediation and/or remediation of water; facilities for treatment and/or final disposal of animal waste; scrapping of factories or warehouses that process or contain hazardous chemical substances and/or hazardous waste; ground satellite parks, including constructions of satellite radio communication stations that are situated within said parks; shooting ranges; and biotechnology projects.[3050]
- Any change or expansion of the projects stated in the aforementioned or this paragraph that have already been approved, executed or in the process of being executed, which may have significant adverse effects on the environment; and projects of the aforementioned paragraph undertaken exclusively or mainly for the development and use of new methods or products and not used for a period longer than two years.[3051]

716. A special provision regulates significant amendments to projects of Annex II. In particular, amendments to said projects that could have significant negative impact on the environment ('σημαντικές αρνητικές επιπτώσεις στο περιβάλλον'), such as when a project is going to develop significantly increased capacity and range, or when parameters, such as geographical expansion, technology, management practices or use, are going to significantly change, lead to reclassification of the project into an Annex I project. The relevant decision underlies the discretionary power of the Director of the Department of Environment of the Ministry of Agriculture, Rural Development and the Environment (hereinafter 'the Director'), whereas he has in particular to consider, whether the particular environmental conditions create the danger of causing significant negative environmental impact, as well as whether any other project together with the project in question may cause any accumulative impact.[3052]

3047. Annex II(11)(a)–(d) *ibid.*, which corresponds to Annex II(12)(a), (c), (d) and (e) Directive 2011/92/EU.
3048. Annex II(11)(e) Law No. 127(I)/2018.
3049. Annex II(12)(a)–(i) *ibid.*, which correspond to Annex II(11)(a)–(i) Directive 2011/92/EU.
3050. Annex II(12)(j)–(s) Law No. 127(I)/2018.
3051. Annex II(13)(a) and (b) *ibid.*, which partially correspond to Annex II(13)(a) and (b) Directive 2011/92/EU.
3052. Section 5(4) Law No. 127(I)/2018.

717. In case of lack of certainty, whether a work that may have significant adverse effects on the environment falls under Annex I or Annex II of this law, the Director has the authority to decide that the specific work is included in the closest or most related category of works and therefore falls under the relevant annex. To this purpose, the Director may, if he deems it appropriate, ask for the opinion of the concerned authorities, non-governmental organizations and the concerned public.[3053] It is statutory set out that concerned public ('ενδιαφερόμενο κοινό') means the public that is affected or may be affected or whose interests may be affected by the various decision-making processes regarding environmental impact according to this law. Non-governmental organizations setting out in their memorandum or articles of association as their main purpose the promotion of the protection of the environment are deemed to have interests that are affected. Similarly, concerned authorities ('ενδιαφερόμενες αρχές') are authorities that may be concerned by a project or have reasonable interest in any environmental effects of a project or have specialized know-how due to their special competence on environmental issues or due to their local authority. They include the local authorities, whereas depending on the nature of the project, they may include the General Chemical State Laboratory, the Authority for Game and Fauna, the Department for Fishing and Marine Research, the Department for Water Development, the Archaeological Department, the Geological Department, the Forest Department, the State Secretary for Maritime Affairs, the Department of Labour Inspection, the Department of Medical Services and Public Health, the Department of Meteorology, the Rural Development and Housing Department, the Department for Public Health, the Energy Service and the Hydrocarbons Service.[3054]

718. National defence purposes of a project, together with estimated negative effects on the objective of that project by the application of this law, may lead to the exclusion of such project from the area of application of this law, despite of it being listed in Annex I or II. This is decided by the Council of Ministers following a relevant request of the Minister of Defence, under the condition that the views of the Director are taken into account.[3055] Exclusion of such a project, however, does not necessitate disregard of environmental impact. To the contrary, a special committee examines any possible environmental effects and opines on taking appropriate measures for the elimination or reduction of such effects, especially if these affect habitat of protected flora and fauna, coastal areas of high environmental value, protected natural areas and landscapes of historical, cultural, architectural or archaeological importance.[3056]

719. Further, under the condition that the scope of this law is ensured, the Minister of Agriculture, Rural Development and Environment and the Minister of Interior may decide that a project or part of a project is wholly or partially excluded from the application of this law. Still, the sole purpose of such exclusion is to

3053. Section 5(1)(a) and (b) *ibid.*
3054. Section 2 and Annex III *ibid.*
3055. Section 4(2)(a) *ibid.*, which corresponds to Art. 1(3) Directive 2011/92/EU.
3056. Section 4(4)(a), (b), (c) and (d) Law No. 127(I)/2018.

respond to civil emergencies that call for taking special temporary measures and demand the materialization of a project without delay to protect humans, prevent damage to properties or to the environment or to the protection of public health or safety, if they are convinced that otherwise the project's purposes would be adversely affected.[3057] Following the construction of such project, the Director may, in cooperation with other governmental authorities and/or other agents, establish any significant effects on the environment that resulted from the measures taken and determine measures for their treatment as well as for restoration of the environment, to the extent that this is necessary and feasible. The Director is entrusted with supervising their implementation.[3058]

720. In exceptional circumstances and as long as the application of the provisions of this law would affect negatively the aim of a public work, the Council of Ministers may decide that said work falls outside the scope of application of this law, under the condition that the scope of this law is ensured. The latter is safeguarded through an environmental assessment performed by the Environmental Authority on the basis of information about the characteristics of the public work, its location and the particulars of any impact. The Environmental Authority is further authorized to determine measures for the treatment of any impact as well as to authorize the public regarding the outcome of the performed assessment. The Council of Ministers may reach such a decision under the following two statutory conditions: first, the construction and operation of the work are to be performed according to the measures specified by the Environmental Authority following the environmental impact assessment; in addition, the information obtained during said assessment along with the information related to granting an exception is to be made available to the public.[3059] In any event, the decision to exclude a public work may only be reached, if the Council of Ministers deems that the construction and/or the operation of the work shall not cause significant adverse effects on the environment of another state. This decision, along with its reasoning, is publicly available through the Official Gazette and the website of the Department of Environment of the Ministry of Agriculture, Rural Development and the Environment (hereinafter 'the Department'), whereas the EC is informed in this regard before that specific work is initiated.[3060]

721. All works that are excluded from the scope of application of this law, still underlie the obligation to undertake Special Ecological Evaluation (*see* in this respect paragraphs 768 et seq. below).[3061]

3057. Section 4(3) *ibid.* On the exception for civil emergencies *see* Art. 1(3) Directive 2011/92/EU.
3058. Section 4(5) Law No. 127(I)/2018.
3059. Sections 4(7)(a) and 4(8) and Annex IV *ibid.*
3060. Section 4(7)(c) and (d) *ibid.*
3061. Section 4(9)(b) *ibid.*, s. 16 Law No. 153(I)/2003 and s. 7(5) Law No. 152(I)/2003.

§3. COMPETENT AUTHORITIES

I. The Minister of Agriculture, Rural Development and Environment

722. The Minister of Agriculture, Rural Development and Environment, (hereinafter 'the Minister') has both regulatory and informative duties. With reference to the first, he has the power to amend the annexes of this law for the purpose of adjusting them to the scientific and technological progress.[3062] Notwithstanding the additional powers set out in other provisions of this law, the Minister may regulate: additional procedures regarding preparation and submission of studies of EIA or information and the submission of amendments or additions to those; regulating matters regarding notifications that must be published; determining the specifics and the operation of the archive; and specifies the minimum composition of the group of observers ('Μελετητής') in relation to a particular project.[3063] The Minister also has the power to determine the duties that he deems sufficient to cover the real expenses of examining the applications to issue instructions ('οδηγία'), of evaluating information or EIA submitted for projects of Annex I or II and granting of an Environmental Approval ('Περιβαλλοντική' Εγκριση'), Reasoned Finding ('Αιτιολογημένη Διαπίστωση') or Opinion ('Γνωμοδότηση'), of performing a public hearing and of an external controller. These duties are paid by the developer of the relevant project.[3064]

723. Turning to his informative duties, every six years since the enactment of this law, the Minister informs the EC, where such data are available, of: the number of projects referred to in Annexes I and II made subject to an EIA;[3065] the breakdown of EIAs according to the project categories set out in Annexes I and II;[3066] the number of projects referred to in Annex II for which the necessity of submitting a study of EIA or providing the specific information stated in section 23 was estimated;[3067] the average duration of the EIA process;[3068] and general estimates on the average direct costs of EIAs, including the impact from the application of this law to small and medium enterprises.[3069]

II. The Council of Ministers

724. The Council of Ministers has the power to issue regulations for fully and effectively carrying out and giving effect to, all or any of the purposes, provisions

3062. Section 51 Law No. 127(I)/2018.
3063. Section 50(a)–(d) *ibid.*
3064. Section 47(1)(a)–(d) *ibid.*
3065. Sections 52(a) and 10, 15, 21, 25–43 *ibid.*, which correspond to Arts. 12(2)(a) and 5–10 Directive 2011/92/EU.
3066. Section 52(b) Law No. 127(I)/2018, which corresponds to Art. 12(2)(b) Directive 2011/92/EU.
3067. Sections 52(c) and 22, 23 Law No. 127(I)/2018, which correspond to Arts. 12(2)(c) and 4(2) Directive 2011/92/EU.
3068. Section 52(d) Law No. 127(I)/2018, which corresponds to Art. 12(2)(d) Directive 2011/92/EU.
3069. Section 52(e) Law No. 127(I)/2018, which corresponds to Art. 12(2)(e) Directive 2011/92/EU.

and powers in this law contained and generally for the best application of this law.[3070]

III. The Committee of EIA

725. A Committee of EIA ('Επιτροπή Εκτίμησης Επιπτώσεων στο Περιβάλλον') is established by this law. It comprises the Director, who acts as the committee's chairman, the Director of the Department of Urban Planning and Housing or a representative, the Director of the Department of Employment or a representative, the Director of the Forest Department or a representative, the Director of the Water Development Department or a representative, the Chairman of the Department of Game and Fauna or a representative, the Chairman of the Technical Chamber of Cyprus or a representative, the Chairman of the Cyprus Federation of Environmental and Ecological Organizations, or a representative, and a representative of a non-governmental organization that is not represented by the Cyprus Federation of Environmental and Ecological Organizations.[3071] Self-evidently, any of said departments may not participate in the Committee of EIA, when their projects are being examined,[3072] and the particular persons participating in the Committee of EIA may not have any personal or financial gain either from the examined project or from the developer of same project. Impartiality is ensured through the statutory obligation to the committee's members to declare their personal and financial interests and to take an oath to perform conscientiously and impartially their tasks, upon accepting the office. Should in the course of the office, such an interest arise, regardless of it being direct or indirect, a member is obliged to declare it to the Secretary of the Committee of EIA.[3073] Depending on the features of a particular project, the characteristics of the environment that may be affected and the anticipated impact, the Director may invite experts, representatives of departments having specialized know-how, as well as representatives of specialized non-governmental or other institutions or organizations with expertise on the project and the nature of its impact.[3074] The same power is equally entrusted with the Committee of EIA, under the condition that the opinion or expertise in a particular subject matter may be deemed useful or necessary for its work.[3075] Notwithstanding the aforementioned, the Director may in exceptional circumstances delegate to a team of experts the evaluation of a Study of EIA, in whole or in part. Said team of experts, after the evaluation of the particular Study of EIA, submit a recommendation to the Environmental Authority.[3076] The duties of the Committee of EIA involve examining the impact that the performance and/or the operation of the project may have on the environment and the measures for minimizing or treating said impact.[3077]

3070. Section 49 Law No. 127(I)/2018.
3071. Section 10(1)(a) *ibid.*
3072. Section 10(1)(b) *ibid.*
3073. Section 15(1) and (2) *ibid.*
3074. Section 10(2) *ibid.*
3075. Section 11(2) *ibid.*
3076. Section 14(1) and (2) *ibid.*
3077. Section 11(1) *ibid.*

IV. The Authorized Observers

726. This law sets out the establishment of the Registry of Authorized Observers ('Μητρώο Εγγεγραμμένων Μελετητών Μελετών Εκτίμησης Επιπτώσεων στο Περιβάλλον'), along with regulating the particulars for registration in the registry and its operation.[3078] Six months after the enactment of this law, that being 31 December 2018, the Director announces an invitation to submit applications for registration in said registry as well as the relevant procedure.[3079] Thereafter, applications may be submitted at any time and are examined biannually.[3080] In line with the European principles of the free movement of workers and services, any observers registered in the corresponding registers of the EU, the EEA or third countries do not have an obligation to submit an application for registration with the registry.[3081] Any other matters related to its operation, fees for enrolment and certification fees are specified in a Ministerial Decree issued by the Minister.[3082] The Registry of Authorized Observers is annually published in the Official Gazette of Cyprus.[3083]

727. After the Registry of Authorized Observers is established and published, a Study of EIA is prepared exclusively by a group of Observers registered therein. Moreover, the Minister, depending on the particulars of projects, determines the minimum composition of the group of Observers via a Ministerial Decree.[3084] On a case-by-case basis, the developer of a project for which a Study of EIA is necessary, communicates to the Director the individuals participating in the group of Observers, and the Director has the authority to indicate any expertise missing from the particular group.[3085]

V. Inspectors

728. For the purpose of effective application of the provisions of this law and the decrees, approvals or directives issued upon its statutory authorization, the Minister appoints Inspectors. These Inspectors are public officers serving at the Ministry of Agriculture, Rural Development and Environment, or, if deemed necessary, public servants from other ministries, under the condition that their supervising Minister agrees thereto. Public servants of local authorities may also serve as Inspectors, as long as this is deemed necessary by the Minister and the relevant local authority has submitted a relevant request.[3086] Inspectors appointed by the apposite provisions of Law No. 184(I)/2013, Law No. 185(I)/2011 and Law No. 106(I)/2002

3078. Section 35(1) and Annex VIII *ibid.*
3079. Annex VIII(5)(b) *ibid.*
3080. Annex VIII(5)(c) *ibid.*
3081. Annex VIII(5)(f) *ibid.*
3082. Section 35(3) *ibid.*
3083. Section 35(4) *ibid.*
3084. Section 36(1) and (2) *ibid.*
3085. Section 36(4) and (5) *ibid.*
3086. Section 44(2)(a), (b) and (c) *ibid.*

may also perform duties of Inspectors under this law.[3087] Finally, any persons not serving as public servants may be appointed as Inspectors by the Minister, carrying out specific tasks, as the Minister thinks fit, under the conditions that they are fully qualified for such tasks and that they have no financial or other interest affecting their impartiality.[3088]

Generally, Inspectors conduct regular and extraordinary inspections of projects approved or authorized under the provisions of this law, for the purpose of establishing whether construction and/or operation is performed according to the environmental conditions that the Environmental Authority has set in the Environmental Approval ('Περιβαλλοντική 'Εγκριση'), that the Urban Planning Authority ('Πολεοδομική Αρχή') has set in an urban planning permission ('πολεοδομική άδεια'), that were undertaken by the Council of Ministers or by a public authority after a Reasoned Finding ('Αιτιολογημένη Διαπίστωση') or an Opinion ('Γνωμοδότηση').[3089] During these inspections, the Inspector may:

- enter any space, construction site or building in which any work or activity related to the project is performed;
- control the conditions set in an Environmental Approval ('Περιβαλλοντική 'Εγκριση'), Reasoned Finding ('Αιτιολογημένη Διαπίστωση'), Opinion ('Γνωμοδότηση') and relevant permissions through video recordings, photographs, measurements or sampling, if he deems it necessary; and
- ask to be provided with all relevant permits and inspect any entries, archives, registers, books or documents that contain information useful to the purpose of controlling any condition set regarding the inspected project.[3090]

§4. Environmental Impact Assessment

729. Without prejudice to Law No. 90/1972 or any other law or administrative practice, granting an urban planning permission or approval or authorization of a public project concerning a project of Annex I or II of this law, prerequisites taking into account as a substantial factor ('ουσιώδης παράγοντας'), the Reasoned Finding ('Αιτιολογημένη Διαπίστωση') and the Opinion ('Γνωμοδότηση') of the Environmental Authority as well as the representations and views of any Member State or the public that were expressed under this law.[3091] Hence, should said opinion, representations and views not be considered, the relevant urban planning permission or approval is illegal (section 13(1) and (2) Law No. 158(I)/1999)[3092] and may be annulled by an appeal ('προσφυγή') before the Supreme Court of Cyprus according to Article 146 of the Constitution.

3087. Section 44(3) *ibid.*
3088. Section 44(4)(a) and (b) *ibid.*
3089. Section 45(1) *ibid.*
3090. Section 45(2)(a), (b) and (c) *ibid.*
3091. Section 17(1) *ibid.*
3092. *Epiphaniou a.o. v. The Republic* (1983) 3 CLR 311.

730. Depending on the nature of the project, its location as well as the necessity of an urban planning permission, approval or authorization for the lawful construction thereof, a Study of EIA, Information of section 23, an Environmental Approval or a Special Ecological Evaluation is required under this law.

I. Scoping

A. Determining the Necessity of a Study of EIA and Information of Section 23

731. Every person intending to submit an application for an urban planning permission for a private project listed in Annex I or II of this law may apply to the Director for instructions regarding the necessity of preparing a Study of EIA or submission of the information foreseen in section 23 of this law (*see* in this respect paragraphs 753 et seq. below), as the case may be. The same applies to any project not requiring an urban planning permission.[3093] Every such application is accompanied by a map indicating the plot, where the project is intended to be executed, a summary description of the nature, size and volume of the project, as well as its objective, and any further information deemed useful or necessary regarding the environmental impact of the project. Additional information on the project itself or the environmental impact thereof may be requested by the Director and the application is not processed unless this is provided by the developer.[3094] The Environmental Authority examines the application according to the criteria set out in this law taking into consideration the submitted information, any relevant opinions submitted by specialized authorities and/or opinions of authorities that were submitted following a relevant request, along with any findings of its own research.[3095] It is noteworthy that according to section 2 of this law the Environmental Authority is the Director and the Director is the Environmental Authority. The reasons that triggered the legislator to use two legal terms for the same authority are unascertained, whereas ambivalence and hesitancy while applying this law are ineluctable.

732. Instructions may also be requested by a state authority intending to construct a public project listed in Annex I or II of this law. The aforementioned instructions regarding private projects apply *mutatis mutandis*.[3096]

B. Determining the Content of a Study of EIA

733. Any person or state authority that has to submit a Study of EIA may request a written opinion on the information, which must be submitted with said study, from the Director. The aforementioned information that must be provided, when requesting an opinion on the necessity of same study, must equally be submitted in the

3093. Sections 22(1) and 20 Law No. 127(I)/2018, which correspond to Art. 5(2) Directive 2011/92/EU.
3094. Section 22(2) and (3) Law No. 127(I)/2018. *See* in this respect Art. 5(2) Directive 2011/92/EU.
3095. Section 22(4) and Annex IV Law No. 127(I)/2018.
3096. Section 22(1) *ibid.*

present request.[3097] The Environmental Authority takes into consideration the information submitted by the developer of the project, while having the discretion to consider the proposals of the concerned authorities and the concerned public.[3098]

Notwithstanding the above, the Director may prepare general instructions for the content of Studies of EIA or even issue specialized relevant instructions for specific categories of projects. These are made public by the Minister in the form of a Ministerial Decree published in the Official Gazette.[3099]

II. Study of EIA

734. A Study of EIA ('Μελέτη Εκτίμησης Επιπτώσεων στο Περιβάλλον') is required for the construction of any private or public project falling under Annex I of this law that prerequisites an urban planning permission for private projects or an approval ('έγκριση') or authorization ('εξουσιοδότηση') for public ones. The Study of EIA is submitted as an integral part of the application for said permissions to the Urban Planning Authority, or in the case of approvals and authorizations to the Council of Ministers or other competent state authority.[3100]

A. *Content of a Study of EIA*

735. A Study of EIA includes at least the following:

- a description of the project comprising information on the site, design, size and other relevant features of the project;[3101]
- a description and analysis of the likely significant effects of the project on the environment;[3102]
- a description of the features of the project and/or measures envisaged in order to avoid, prevent or reduce and, if possible, offset likely significant adverse effects on the environment;[3103]
- a description of the reasonable alternatives studied by the developer, which are relevant to the project and its specific characteristics, and an indication of the main reasons for the option chosen, taking into account the effects of the project on the environment;[3104]

3097. Section 25(1), (2) and (3) *ibid.*
3098. Section 25(5) and Annex V *ibid.*
3099. Section 25(6) *ibid.*
3100. Sections 18(1)(a), 19(a) and 2(2)(b)(i) *ibid.*, which correspond to Art. 4(1) Directive 2011/92/EU. *See* in respect of the necessity thereof for public projects: judgment of 5 Nov. 2010 in Joined Cases Nos 885/2009, 1537/2009 and 229/2010, *Eustathiou v. The Republic, Tsiola v. The Republic, Ormidia Farming Co Ltd*, not published in CLR.
3101. Section 26(1) Law No. 127(I)/2018, which corresponds to Art. 5(1)(a) Directive 2011/92/EU.
3102. Section 26(1)(b) Law No. 127(I)/2018, which corresponds to Art. 5(1)(b) Directive 2011/92/EU.
3103. Section 26(1)(c) Law No. 127(I)/2018, which corresponds to Art. 5(1)(c) Directive 2011/92/EU.
3104. Section 26(1)(d) Law No. 127(I)/2018, which corresponds to Art. 5(1)(d) Directive 2011/92/EU.

- a non-technical summary of the information stated in aforementioned points along with description, analysis, evaluation and recommendations to the extent that they allow persons not having special technical knowledge of the matters examined in the Study of EIA to comprehend the text and understand the project, its impact and the study's proposals, correctly;[3105] and
- any additional information relevant to the specific characteristics of a particular project or type of project and to the environmental features likely to be affected.[3106]

Said additional information is statutorily defined and includes:

- a description of the project, including in particular: description of the location of the project;[3107] a description of the physical characteristics of the whole project and, if necessary, the necessary demolition works and the land-use requirements during the construction and operational phases;[3108] a description of the main characteristics of the production processes (especially the method of construction), for instance, energy demand and the energy to be used, the nature and quantity of the materials, energy and natural resources used (including waters, land, soil and biodiversity);[3109] an estimation, by type and quantity, of expected residues and emissions (such as water, air and soil pollution, noise, vibration, light, heat and radiation) and amount and streams of waste resulting from the construction and operation of the proposed project;[3110] and a digital archive of the geographical data of the project's area;[3111]
- an outline of the main alternatives studied by the developer that relate to the particular project, along with its special features and an indication of the main reasons for this choice, taking into account the environmental effects;[3112]
- a description of the current situation of the environment (basic scenario) and an outline of the potential development, if the project is not put into effect to the extent that, with reasonable effort, it is possible to assess the natural changes in the basic scenario, on the basis of the availability of environmental information and scientific knowledge;[3113]
- a description of the factors that are likely to be significantly affected by the proposed project, those being population, human health, biodiversity, such as fauna and flora, land, such as occupation of areas, soil, such as organic matters, erosion, compression and sealing, water, such as groundwater changes, amount and quality, air, climate, such as greenhouse gas emissions, any impact relevant to

---

3105. Section 26(1)(e) Law No. 127(I)/2018, which is much more detailed and descriptive than Art. 5(1)(e) Directive 2011/92/EU.
3106. Section 26(1)(f) Law No. 127(I)/2018, which corresponds to Art. 5(1)(f) Directive 2011/92/EU.
3107. Annex V(1)(a) Law No. 127(I)/2018.
3108. Annex V(1)(b) *ibid.*, which corresponds to Annex IV(1)(a) Directive 2011/92/EU.
3109. Annex V(1)(c) Law No. 127(I)/2018, which corresponds to Annex IV(1)(b) Directive 2011/92/EU.
3110. Annex V(1)(d) Law No. 127(I)/2018, which corresponds to Annex IV(1)(c) Directive 2011/92/EU.
3111. Annex V(1)(e) Law No. 127(I)/2018.
3112. Annex V(2) *ibid.*, which corresponds to Annex IV(2) Directive 2011/92/EU.
3113. Annex V(3) Law No. 127(I)/2018.

adoption to climate change, material assets, cultural heritage, including the architectural and archaeological heritage, and landscape;[3114]

- a description, covering the direct effects and any indirect, secondary, cumulative, transboundary, short, medium and long-term, permanent and temporary, positive and negative effects of the project, while taking into consideration other existing or approved projects, of the likely significant effects of the proposed project on the environment resulting, among others, from: the construction and the existence of the project, including, as the case may be, demolition works;[3115] the use of natural resources, especially land, soil, waters and biodiversity, taking into consideration sustainable development;[3116] the emission of pollutants, the creation of nuisances and the disposal and recovery of waste;[3117] the dangers for human health, cultural inheritance or the environment (e.g., due to accidents or disasters); the accumulative impact with other existing and/or approved projects, taking into consideration any problems of environmental nature that relate to areas with special environmental importance that may be affected or the use of natural resources; the impact of the project on the climate as well as the project's susceptibility to climate change ('ευπάθεια του έργου στην κλιματική αλλαγή'); and the technology and material to be used;[3118]
- a description of the methods for the prevention or the data used for the determination and assessment of significant environmental impact, including detailed data regarding the difficulties, such as technical weaknesses or lack of know-how, encountered in compiling the necessary information, as well as presentation of the main uncertainties;[3119]
- a description of the measures envisaged to prevent, reduce and where possible offset any significant adverse effects on the environment and, as the case may be, of any suggested monitor measures, during construction, operation and any abandonment and/or demolition of the project;[3120]
- a description of the anticipated significant adverse effects of the project on the environment deriving from project's susceptibility to serious accidents and/or disasters, while taking full advantage of information available on the basis of KDP 347/2015 (*see* in this respect footnote 1661 above) and the Nuclear Legislation (*see* in this respect paragraphs 230 et seq. above);[3121]
- a non-technical summary of the aforementioned information;[3122]

3114. Annex V(4) *ibid.*, which corresponds to Annex IV(3) Directive 2011/92/EU. The national much detailed provision does not foresee the interrelationship between the described factors.
3115. Annex V(5)(a) Law No. 127(I)/2018, which corresponds to Annex IV(4)(a) Directive 2011/92/EU.
3116. Annex V(5)(b) Law No. 127(I)/2018, which corresponds to Annex IV(4)(b) Directive 2011/92/EU.
3117. Annex V(5)(c) Law No. 127(I)/2018, which corresponds to Annex IV(4)(c) Directive 2011/92/EU.
3118. Annex V(5)(d), (e), (f) and (g) Law No. 127(I)/2018.
3119. Annex V(6) *ibid.*, which partially corresponds to Annex IV(8) Directive 2011/92/EU.
3120. Annex V(7) Law No. 127(I)/2018, which partially corresponds to Annex IV(6) Directive 2011/92/EU.
3121. Annex V(8) Law No. 127(I)/2018.
3122. Annex V(9) *ibid.*, which corresponds to Annex IV(7) Directive 2011/92/EU.

- a catalogue of the sources used for the descriptions and assessments included in the Study of EIA; and
- particulars for the group that wrote the Study of EIA.[3123]

Notwithstanding the above, a Study of EIA describes and properly evaluates in the light of each individual case the direct and indirect significant impact that a project may have on the environment, and in particular on the population and human health, biodiversity and especially the protected species according to Law No. 153(I)/2003 and 152(I)/2003, landscape, groundwater, surface water, air, soil, sea and climate, tangible goods, cultural inheritance, including antiquities, geological inheritance and the interactions between these factors.[3124] In said cases, impact includes any anticipated impact deriving from the sensibility of the project to dangers of serious accidents and/or disasters relevant to same project.[3125] During the preparation of the Study of EIA, any available results from other specialized evaluations and procedures are taken into consideration.[3126] Where it is possible for a project to have significant adverse effects on the environment of another Member State, the developer of the project asks from the competent authority of that state within the apposite procedure (*see* in this respect paragraph 744 below), a summary of the Study of EIA in the official language of same state.[3127]

Importantly, before the Study of EIA is submitted, the developer of the project is obliged to conduct a public consultation ('δημόσια διαβούλευση') and at least a public presentation ('δημόσια παρουσίαση') prior to finalizing its content. The aim of these publicity obligations is to give the opportunity to the concerned local authority and the public to submit comments and suggestions for the project's environmental impact. Particulars, as to bringing these publicity obligations into effect, are not set out in this law. Nonetheless, the submitted comments are quoted in the Study of the EIA, along with clarifications about the extent to which they were considered. Projects related to essential state interests, such as hydrocarbons within the exclusive economic zone, fall outside the scope of said publicity obligations.[3128] Equally outside the scope of said publicity obligations falls commercial and industrial confidentiality, under the condition that the Director thinks it fit. More specifically, if a Study of EIA contains such confidential information, including intellectual property, the law reads, the Director may, following a relevant request of the project's developer, approve the publication of a redacted version of the Study of EIA.[3129] Finally, in the event that a Study of EIA contains confidential information related to public interest ('δημόσιο συμφέρον'), the developer of the project bears the statutory duty to publish a redacted text and inform the Director in this

3123. Annex V(10) and (11) Law No. 127(I)/2018.
3124. Sections 26(3) and 2(2)(a) *ibid.*, which correspond to Art. 3 Directive 2011/92/EU.
3125. Section 26(4) Law No. 127(I)/2018.
3126. Section 26(5) *ibid.*
3127. Sections 26(6) and 21 *ibid.*
3128. Section 26(7) *ibid.* The obligation to offer early and effective opportunity to the public concerned to participate in the decision-making process is set out in Art. 6(4) Directive 2011/92/EU. The European provision does not provide for any exceptions.
3129. Section 37(1)(a) Law No. 127(I)/2018, which corresponds to Art. 10 Directive 2011/92/EU. Albeit the European provision does not provide for any discretion regarding protecting confidentiality.

regard.[3130] Notwithstanding other laws, no legal action may be taken against the Director or the Republic for bona fides publication of any document, in full or in part, or for any consequences resulting from such publication.[3131]

The detailed arrangements of a public hearing, which are foreseen in this law, do not share the mandatory nature of the aforementioned publicity obligations, as they entrust them to the discretionary powers of the Director. In particular, regarding projects of Annex I that require a Study of EIA, the Director has the authority to decide, whether performing a public hearing ('δημόσια ακρόαση') would be useful or appropriate, taking into consideration the characteristics of the project, whether such a project of the particular scale has never been performed before, the public interest for the project, as well as the urban planning and environmental impact and scale. The scope of said hearing is threefold: inform the public; provide thorough information to the Environmental Authority; and record the opinions of the public.[3132] Should the Director decide to perform a public hearing, he is responsible for organizing this, including specifying the dates, finding premises and clarifying issues considered essential for the appraised project and requiring opinions to be expressed. The Director performs the apposite publications and notifications at least fifteen days before the hearing, while making a copy of the Study of EIA together with its non-technical summary available for inspection by the public.[3133] During the day of the hearing, the Director, or its representative, chairs the hearing and manages the process while having the duty, to the extent possible, to give the opportunity to every person being present to express his opinion, questions and suggestions regarding the content of the Study of EIA and the environmental effects of the suggested development, including any omissions of the Study of EIA.[3134] Written reasoned representations may be submitted up until seven days after the conclusion of the public hearing.[3135] The expressed opinions and the submitted representations are noted by the Director, who within fifteen days after the conclusion of the public hearing prepares a summary of the opinions of essence that were expressed and makes them public on the Department's website, while forwarding them to the developer of the project.[3136]

736. The Environmental Authority offers to concerned authorities the opportunity to express their views on the Study of EIA that is submitted. To this end, it forwards to them the submitted Study of EIA and relevant information along with a note encouraging the submission of their established views and opinions within twenty days or more depending on the complexity of the issue at hand, or during

3130. Section 37(1)(b) Law No. 127(I)/2018. Special mention to safeguarding public interest is provided in Art. 10 Directive 2011/92/EU, as it was already provided in the proposal for a Council Directive concerning the assessment of the environmental effects of certain public and private projects of 16 Jun. 1980, which resulted in Directive 85/337/EEC. Thus, it is safe to assume that public interest is a European notion.
3131. Section 37(2) Law No. 127(I)/2018.
3132. Section 39(1)(a) and (b) *ibid.*
3133. Section 39(1)(c)(i) – (iii) *ibid.*
3134. Section 39(2) *ibid.*
3135. Section 39(3) *ibid.*
3136. Section 39(4) *ibid.*

meetings of the Committee of EIA or special groups or during meetings with experts according to section 10 or 14 of this law, as the case may be. The Environmental Authority may invite concerned authorities to meetings[3137] Should a state authority have information that could reasonably be deemed relevant or necessary for preparing or evaluating a Study of EIA, it bears the duty to provide this to the developer, when this is requested. The developer bears the relevant costs.[3138] In this regard, the Environmental Authority may – not shall – inform in writing any state authority, public organization or local authority of the usefulness and necessity of any studies or information that they may be holding to the purpose of preparing or evaluating the Study of EIA.[3139]

B. Evaluation of a Study of EIA

737. Upon submission of a Study of EIA, the developer of the project bears the duty of publishing a notification ('δημοσίευση γνωστοποίησης'). It is not clear whether the statutory terms *publishing a notification* and making a *public presentation* (*see* in this respect paragraph 738 above) address the same procedure, or, if this is not the case, where their differences lie. The temporal requirements attached to said terms strongly indicate that they do not stand for the same obligation. In any event, any person and every governmental authority that have to submit a Study of EIA under this law, bear the duty, upon submission of a Study of EIA, to publish a notification in two newspapers and on the website of the authority competent for granting the permit, approval or authorization of development, as the case may be. Said notification includes: (a) that an application for granting a permit, approval or authorization clearly stating the competent authority for the permit, approval or authorization, as the case may be, has been submitted; (b) the nature of the proposed project and the area in which this is intended to be constructed; (c) the necessity to assess the environmental impact and, as the case may be, transboundary environmental effects triggering the application of the relevant provisions (*see* in this respect paragraph 744 below); (d) the date on which the Study of EIA has been submitted and the identity of the submitter; (e) the nature of the possible decisions or, if existing, the decision draft; (f) the option to review the Study of EIA during working days and hours at the premises of the appropriate governmental authority; (g) the ability of any person to submit opinions or representations regarding the environmental impact of the project to the Director; and (h) the ability of any person to submit questions regarding the information announced and the proceedings conducted as explained in this paragraph to the Environmental Authority for the purpose of enabling the submission of opinions and representations. The Environmental Authority is under the statutory obligation to respond to the submitted questions within ten days.[3140] Notwithstanding the above, the Study of EIA is uploaded to the

3137. Section 8(1) and (2) *ibid.* The corresponding European provision regarding giving the opportunity to authorities to express their opinion is Art. 6(1) Directive 2011/92/EU.

3138. Section 9(1) Law No. 127(I)/2018.

3139. Section 9(2) *ibid. See* in this respect Art. 5(4) Directive 2011/92/EU.

3140. Sections 27(1)(a)–(g) and 21 Law No. 127(I)/2018.

website of the Department, is submitted to the archive for Studies of EIA and is forwarded to any person, who files a relevant request.[3141] The latest within thirty days since this publication, any person may submit to the Director opinions or representations regarding the content of the Study of EIA or regarding the impact that the construction or the operation of the project may have on the environment.[3142] Projects related to essential state interests, such as hydrocarbons within the exclusive economic zone, fall outside the scope of application of said publicity obligations.[3143]

738. Following receiving the Study of EIA, the Urban Planning Authority, or in the case of public projects, the Council of Ministers or the competent state authority, forwards copies thereof to the Director, along with the application and any additional information or data it has at its disposal, which it thinks to be useful or necessary to the purpose of evaluating the assessment that the construction and existence of the project shall have on the environment.[3144] Within twenty days following receipt of the Study of EIA, the Director examines its content, in order to establish whether the information contained therein is sufficient. In particular, he examines: whether the project and the environmental characteristics of the affected area are sufficiently described;[3145] whether all data, especially regarding all sources of potential pollution and/or degradation of the environment, is correct;[3146] and whether tools and methods of detection, analysis and prediction have been properly used.[3147] During this examination, the Director may, if he deems it appropriate, ask the opinions of concerned authorities and/or other authorities or organizations having specialized know-how for the particular project or its estimated environmental impact.[3148] Should the Director decide that the submitted information is not sufficient, he may require the developer to provide such additional information, or if he deems the Study of EIA to be inadequate, he shall return it to the developer providing reasoning for the lack of quality and the points causing uncertainty. In both cases, the process of evaluating the Study of EIA and issuing an Opinion ('γνωμοδότηση') is suspended.[3149]

739. An obscure detail that could cause vexation during the application of the law, deserves special mention. According to the statutory provision [t]*he Director is obliged to refuse the evaluation of a Study of EIA, if he establishes that a person*

3141. Sections 27(2) and 40 *ibid.*
3142. Section 27(4) *ibid.*
3143. Section 27(5) *ibid.*
3144. Sections 18(3) and 19(a) *ibid.*
3145. Section 28(1)(a) *ibid.*
3146. Section 28(1)(b) *ibid.*
3147. Section 28(1)(c) *ibid.*
3148. Section 28(2) *ibid.*
3149. Section 28(3)(a) and (b) *ibid.*

not registered in the Registry of Authorized Observers has participated in the preparation of that study as an Observer.[3150] This provision is abstruse on the following grounds. First, as already elaborated in the previous paragraphs, the Director at this early phase is authorized to examine the content of the Study of EIA, not to *evaluate* it. Further, the Director following this examination has the power to request further information or to return the Study of EIA to the developer, not to *refuse evaluation*. Second, the Committee of EIA is entrusted with the technical evaluation of the Study of EIA and has no authority to decline its evaluation, as explained in the paragraphs that follow. Third, equally as explained in the paragraphs that follow, the Environmental Authority issues an Opinion with a statutory-specified content, which does not include declining evaluation. In addition, it is not clear whether this refusal of evaluation satisfies the criteria of an administrative act and therefore allows for legal remedies to be filed against it. Having said that and in view of the newly constituted Registry of Authorized Observers, this provision could lead to considerable distress in the application of this law.

740. When the Director, now acting as the Environmental Authority, ensures the sufficiency of the content of the Study of EIA, he submits it to the Committee of EIA. At this stage, the Director has at his disposal, the Observers' views that prepared the particular Study of EIA, on the expressed comments by the public, as within fifteen days since summaries of public's opinions have been prepared and forwarded to the project's developer, the Observers' views are submitted to the Director.[3151] The Committee of EIA upon receiving a Study of EIA, proceeds with the technical evaluation. To this purpose, it takes into account opinions and representations of third parties submitted following public presentation ('δημόσια παρουσίαση'),[3152] along with the results of a public consultation ('δημόσια διαβούλευση'),[3153] and, where applicable, the outcome of the public hearing ('δημόσια ακρόαση').[3154] In the minutes kept, the opinions and suggestions of the members of the Committee of EIA are recorded, as this law provides.[3155]

C. *Transboundary Effects*

741. Where the Director is aware that a project is likely to have significant effects on the environment in another Member State or in the event such other state so requests, the Director forwards to this state a description of the project, together with any available information on its possible transboundary impact and information on the nature of the decision which may be taken. It further provides the state

3150. Section 39(6) *ibid*. The original text reads '[o] Διευθυντής υποχρεούται να αρνηθεί να αξιολογήσει μια Μελέτη εάν διαπιστώσει ότι πρόσωπο που δεν είναι εγγεγραμμένο στο Μητρώο έχει συμμετάσχει στην ετοιμασία της μελέτης ως μελετητής'.
3151. Section 39(5) *ibid*.
3152. Section 27 *ibid*. *See* in this respect paragraph 738 above.
3153. Section 26(7) *ibid*. *See* in this respect paragraph 738 above.
3154. Section 39 *ibid*. *See* in this respect paragraph 738 above.
3155. Sections 28(5), 10(1) and (2), 11(3) and 39(6) *ibid*.

a reasonable time in which to indicate whether it wishes to participate in the environmental decision-making procedures and forwards to it the same information on the procedure of EIA, a copy of the submitted study of EIA and the pieces of information that the developer is obliged to publish upon submission of that study.[3156] The Director further arranges that this information is made available within a reasonable time to the authorities of the state and the public thereof and that they are given the opportunity to forward their opinion within a reasonable time before the urban planning permission is granted or the competent authority proceeds with construction of the public project, as the case may be.[3157] Lastly, consultations take place between the Director and the other state regarding, *inter alia*, the potential transboundary effects of the project and the measures envisaged to reduce or eliminate such effects. They also agree on a reasonable time frame for the duration of the consultation period.[3158]

D. Opinion of the Environmental Authority

742. The Environmental Authority, to the purpose of preparing the Opinion ('Γνωμοδότηση'), has at its disposal the technical evaluation of the Committee of EIA, that being the minutes having recorded the opinions and suggestions of its members, as well as the relevant opinions or representations of any persons, committees, organizations, authorities or other states, which have been submitted to the same, in its capacity as the Director.[3159] For the purpose of avoiding aimless repeating of procedures and drafting similar studies or evaluations, along with proper consideration of their results at the application of this law, other studies, data, findings, conclusions and environmental terms prepared under other laws and related with the environmental impact of the specific project, are equally offered to the Environmental Authority.[3160] After taking into consideration said documents, it states the Opinion ('Γνωμοδότηση'). The Opinion may advise against the construction of the project due to significant adverse effects on the environment caused by the project's construction or operation that may not be reduced or eliminated through management measures and imposition of terms. It may further advise for the construction of the project with specific terms and management or other measures envisaged to reduce or eliminate the environmental impact, which are defined therein.[3161] Depending on the nature, location and size of the project, the Environmental

---

3156. Section 21(1) and (2) *ibid.*, which corresponds to Art. 7(1) and (2) Directive 2011/92/EU. The repealed Law No. 140(I)/2005 provided for such an option also to states that ratified the Convention on EIA in a Transboundary Context of 1991. Still, this was of low practical value as none of the neighbouring countries of Cyprus ratified said convention.
3157. Section 21(3) Law No. 127(I)/2018, which corresponds to Art. 7(3) Directive 2011/92/EU.
3158. Section 21(4) and (5) Law No. 127(I)/2018, which corresponds to Art. 7(4) Directive 2011/92/EU.
3159. Section 29(1) *ibid.*, which corresponds to Art. 8 Directive 2011/92/EC.
3160. Section 34(1) Law No. 127(I)/2018.
3161. Section 29(2)(a)(i) and (ii) *ibid.*

Authority may include environmental terms, monitoring conditions related to measures' implementation and the project's significant adverse effects on the environment (*see* in this respect paragraph 752 below) and define the parameters to be monitored, the duration and manner of monitoring and the preparation and submission of the relevant reports.[3162] Any measure or term contained in the Opinion may be specified as substantial ('ουσιώδης παράγοντας')[3163] Where necessary, the Director may impose additional terms to an Opinion already in force with the aim of treating any adverse effects on the environment from the construction and/or operation of the project.[3164] The Opinion is accompanied by a succinct note from the Environmental Authority regarding the manner and the extent to which the outcome of the public consultation and the information received following the public participation process were incorporated. Special mention is made to any observations received by an affected state, where section 21 of this law is applicable.[3165] The life of an Opinion prepared in the aforementioned manner is bound to the life of the urban planning permission or other permission, as long as during this time frame the conditions on which it was based do not change.[3166]

743. The Environmental Authority submits this Opinion to the Urban Planning Authority or, in the event of a public project to the state authority that shall conduct same project.[3167] At the same time, the Environmental Authority, acting as the Director, ensures the uploading of the Opinion on the Department's website and forwards a copy to authorities of another state, that participated in the decision-making process, as the case may be.[3168]

E. Decision on Urban Planning Permission or Construction of a Public Project

744. The Opinion of the Environmental Authority, along with the representations of another Member State and other representations submitted by persons or authorities under this law are substantial factors ('ουσιώδης παράγοντας') that need to be duly taken into consideration by the Urban Planning Authority, in the case of private projects, or by the Council of Ministers or other competent authority, in case of public projects, while reaching the decision about the requested urban planning permission, approval or authorization, as the case may be.[3169]

745. Within fifteen days since granting an urban planning permission, an approval or authorization, depending on the specific private or public project, the

3162. Section 29(4) *ibid.*
3163. Section 29(2)(b) *ibid.*
3164. Section 30(4) *ibid.*
3165. Section 29(3) *ibid.*
3166. Section 30(1) *ibid.*
3167. Section 29(1) *ibid.*
3168. Section 29(5) and (6) *ibid.*
3169. Section 17(1) *ibid.*

issuing authority provides the Environmental Authority with a copy thereof. Under this law, notwithstanding the provisions of other applicable laws, said administrative act includes at least the following:

- the Opinion of the Environmental Authority together with the imposed environmental conditions and a description of the project's characteristics and/or the measures for reducing or offsetting any significant adverse effects on the environment, along with monitoring measures, as suggested by the Environmental Authority in its Opinion;[3170]
- the main reasons and the grounds on which the decision of the competent authority was based;[3171]
- the manner in which the public's opinions were taken into consideration;[3172] and
- the basic reasons for denying the permission, approval or authorization, where applicable.[3173]

746. The terms imposed by the Environmental Authority in its Opinion are mandatory and binding to the project's developer.[3174]

747. Solely upon rejection of the application for issuing a permission, approval or authorization, as the case may be, the law reads, the Environmental Authority is entrusted with the following notification duties. It informs the concerned authorities that participated in the decision-making process, as well as any Member State with which consultation had been conducted. These actions must be performed within fifteen days of receiving the aforementioned information from the issuing authority.[3175] The Environmental Authority further notifies that a decision has been reached through an announcement on its website, while notifying that the following information is available in the Archive: (a) the content of the decision, as well as other documents that may accompany it, including the note on considering the public's opinions;[3176] (b) information on the procedure for enabling the public's participation, which was applied, including a summary of the outcome of the consultation and the information compiled during this procedure; (c) the manner and the degree to which information from the participation of the public and the consultation from interested authorities has been incorporated or not; and (d) any comments received from the affected Member State, with which consultation has been conducted.[3177]

F. Monitoring Duties

748. The Director ensures that a project's significant effects on the environment, as well as its imposed environmental terms, are monitored at an appropriate level

3170. Section 31(1)(a) *ibid.*
3171. Section 31(1)(b) *ibid.*
3172. Section 31(1)(c) *ibid.*
3173. Section 31(2) *ibid.*
3174. Section 41(1) *ibid.*
3175. Sections 32, 31(2), 8 and 21 *ibid.*
3176. Sections 32(a) and 29(3) *ibid.*
3177. Section 32(b) *ibid*, which partially corresponds to Art. 9 Directive 2011/92/EU.

and frequency. The manner of monitoring depends on the nature, location and size of the project, the gravity of environmental effects and the monitoring plan that is approved or is a part of the environmental terms imposed on the basis of the Opinion ('γνωμοδότηση'). Purpose of monitoring is to ensure that the project's developer applies the imposed measures for eliminating, reducing or setting-off significant effects on the environment and that the project's characteristics are maintained.[3178] Thus, the Director has the power to monitor every term imposed via the Opinion, whereas monitoring per se is performed by the Inspectors.[3179] Still, with the aim to avoid overlapping monitoring and to take full advantage of existing procedures, technology and know-how, the Director asks for and receives relevant data and findings from state authorities that already have monitoring procedures in place, those being Law No. 185(I)/2011, Law No. 106(I)/2002, Law No. 187(I)/2002, Law No. 184(I)/2013, Law No. 79(I)/2010, Law No. 13(I)/2004, KDP 347/2015, Regulations on Urban and Land Use Planning (Major-Accidents Involving Hazardous Substances),[3180] Law on Marine Strategy,[3181] and Law on Assessment and Management of Flood Risks,[3182] including repealed Law No. 102(I)/2005.[3183] The outcome of performed monitoring, regardless of the person having done that, i.e., Inspectors, other authorities or the developer, is made publicly available via electronic means, as per the Director's duty.[3184]

749. If it is so provided in the environmental terms imposed by an Opinion, the project's developer sees to preparing a report of environmental monitoring in a manner succinct and understandable by the public.[3185] Another environmental term that may be imposed through an Opinion, and in fact be characterized as a substantial one, is the obligation to engage an external environmental controller, who shall enter into a contract with the Director, but shall be remunerated by the project's operator. Such an engagement depends on the nature, duration and range of

---

3178. Section 41(1) Law No. 128(I)/2018.
3179. Sections 41(3) and 44 *ibid.*
3180. Regulations on Urban and Land Use Planning (Major-Accidents Involving Hazardous Substances) ('οι Περί Πολεοδομίας και Χωροταξίας (Ατυχήματα Μεγάλης Κλίμακας Σχετιζόμενα με Επικίνδυνες Ουσίες) Κανονισμοί'), No. 76 of 2017, OG III(I) No. 5002 of 10 Mar. 2017, p. 543, which implement Directive 2012/18/EU of the European Parliament and of the Council of 4 Jul. 2012 on the control of major-accident hazards involving dangerous substances, OJ L 197, 24 Jul. 2012, p. 1 (hereinafter 'KDP 76/2017').
3181. Law on Marine Strategy ('ο Περί της Θαλάσσιας Στρατηγικής Νόμος') No. 18 of 2011, OGI(I) 4271 of 25 Feb. 2011, p. 101, as amended, which implements Directive 2008/56/EC of the European Parliament and of the Council of 17 Jun. 2008 establishing a framework for community action in the field of marine environmental policy, OJ L 164, 25 Jun. 2008, p. 19 (hereinafter 'Law No. 18(I)/2011').
3182. Law on Assessment and Management of Flood Risks ('ο Περί Αξιολόγησης και Αντιμετώπισης Κινδύνων Πλημμύρας Νόμος') No. 70 of 2010, OGI(I) No. 4251 of 16 Jul. 2010, as amended, which implements Directive 2007/60/EC of the European Parliament and of the Council of 23 Oct. 2007 on the assessment and management of flood risks, OJ L 288, 6 Nov. 2007, p. 27, and Directive 2000/60/EC of the European Parliament and of the Council of 23 Oct. 2000 establishing a framework for Community action in the field of water policy, OJ L 327, 22 Dec. 2000, p. 1 (hereinafter 'Law No. 70(I)/2010').
3183. Sections 41(4) and 34(2) *ibid.*
3184. Section 41(6) *ibid.*
3185. Section 42 *ibid.*

expected effects, as well as on speciality, complexity and synthesis of environmental terms.[3186] The external environmental controller helps the project's developer to maintain proper and correct environmental data and archives, while providing an independent professional opinion on whether the drafted environmental reports present an adequate picture of the environmental management of the project and its functions. He also proves the sufficiency of the internal environmental management of the project and the practices and monitoring procedures and submits recommendations for their improvement.[3187] Finally, he prepares reports for the Director that are publicly available, as the latter files them in the Archive (*see* in this respect paragraph 771 below).[3188]

III. Information of Section 23

750. The submission of specific information ('Πληροφορίες άρθρου 23'), hereinafter 'Information of section 23', is required for the construction of any private or public project falling under Annex II of this law that prerequisites an urban planning permission for private projects or an approval ('έγκριση') or authorization ('εξουσιοδότηση') for public ones.[3189]

A. Specifics of Information of Section 23

751. A project's developer, for the purpose of examination of a project of Annex II, submits in a succinct manner the following information and data that relate to the characteristics of the project, the form, extent and duration of the impact that may be caused to the environment by the project's construction and/or operation and the measures envisaged to reduce or eliminate such effects:

- a description of the project, including in particular: (i) a description of the physical characteristics of the whole project and any demolition works; (ii) a description of the location of the project, with special emphasis on environmental sensitivity of geographical areas that might be affected; and (iii) a digital archive of the geographical data of the project's area;[3190]
- a description of the environmental elements that may be significantly affected by the project;[3191]
- a description, to the extent possible, of any significant effects that the project may cause on the environment through: (i) the expected residues, emissions and waste

3186. Section 43(1) *ibid.*
3187. Section 43(2)(a), (b) and (c) *ibid.*
3188. Section 43(3) *ibid.*
3189. Sections 9(1)(b) and 10(1)(b) *ibid.*
3190. Section 23(1)(a) *ibid.*
3191. Section 23(1)(b) *ibid.*

production, as the case may be; and (ii) the use of natural resources and especially land, soil, water and biodiversity;[3192] and

- a report and a description of any characteristics of the project and/or measures envisaged in order to avoid or reduce effects that in any other case would have been significant and adverse for the environment.[3193]

752. During the compilation of the aforementioned information, available results of any other studies, evaluations and findings of environmental impact, obtained especially under Law No. 185(I)/2011, Law No. 106(I)/2002, Law No. 187(I)/2002, Law No. 184(I)/2013, Law No. 79(I)/2010, Law No. 13(I)/2004, KDP 347/2015, KDP 76/2017, Law No. 18(I)/2011, Law No. 70(I)/2010, including repealed Law No. 102(I)/2005, are taken into account. In addition, the following criteria are considered, as the case may be:[3194]

- the characteristics of projects having regard, in particular, to: (a) the size and planning of the project, (b) the cumulation with other existing and/or approved projects, (c) the use of natural resources and especially land, soil, water and biodiversity, (d) the production of waste, (e) pollution and nuisances, (f) the risk of serious accidents and/or disasters related to that specific project, including dangers caused by climate change according to scientific knowledge, and (g) the dangers to human health, i.e., through water or air pollution);[3195]
- the environmental sensitivity of geographical areas likely to be affected by projects having regard, in particular, to: (a) the existing and approved land use, (b) the relative abundance, quality and regenerative capacity of natural resources in the area and its subsoil, (c) the absorption capacity of the natural environment, paying particular attention to the following areas: (i) wetlands, riparian and estuarine areas, (ii) coastal zones and marine environment, (iii) mountain and forest areas, (iv) nature reserves and parks, (v) areas classified or protected under Law No. 90/1972, Law No. 25(I)/2012, Law No. 153(I)/2003 and Law No. 152(I)/2003, (vi) areas in which it has already failed to keep the environmental quality standards laid down in Union legislation, (vii) densely populated areas, (viii) landscapes of historical, cultural or archaeological significance;[3196] and
- the potential significant effects of projects in relation to criteria explained above, and having regard in particular to: (a) the extent and spatial area of the impact (geographical area and size of the affected population), (b) the nature of the

---

3192. Section 23(1)(c) *ibid.*

3193. Section 23(1)(d) *ibid.*

3194. Section 23(2) *ibid.*, which corresponds to Art. 4(3) Directive 2011/92/EU. Still, the European provision sets out that these criteria are taken into consideration during a case-by-case examination, without providing for any discretionary power of the competent authorities, as the national provision reads.

3195. Annex IV(1) Law No. 127(I)/2018, which corresponds to Annex III(1) Directive 2011/92/EU. It is noteworthy that the European provision refers to *accidents*, and not to *serious accidents* as it was transposed into national law, resulting into distortion of the relevant criteria.

3196. Annex IV(2) Law No. 127(I)/2018, which corresponds to Annex III(2) Directive 2011/92/EU, but for point (c)(vi), in the sense that the national provision is divergent and utterly opposite from the European one, which provides for *exceeding* the European standards.

impact, (c) the transfrontier nature of the impact, (d) the magnitude and complexity of the impact, (e) the probability of the impact, (f) the anticipated initiation, duration, frequency and reversibility of the impact, (g) the accumulation of the impact with the impact of other existing and/or approved projects, and (h) the possibility of effective reduction of the impact.[3197]

B. Evaluation of Information of Section 23

753. When the Director receives the Information of section 23, he examines whether it is full and accurate on its face. To this end, he has the power to ask the opinion of concerned authorities and other authorities and/or institutions having expertise relevant to the particular project or its potential environmental effects.[3198] Should this not be the case, further information or clarifications may be requested.[3199]

754. When the Director, now acting as the Environmental Authority, is satisfied that all necessary information is available to it, it proceeds with its evaluation according to the criteria that the project's developer had taken into account upon compiling the information, as already explained in paragraphs 670 and 671 above.[3200]

C. Transboundary Effects

755. The aforementioned on transboundary effects (*see* in this respect paragraph 741 above) are equally applicable here.

D. Reasoned Finding of the Environmental Authority

756. Within thirty days since the submission of all information, including the one requested, the Environmental Authority prepares a Reasoned Finding ('Αιτιολογημένη Διαπίστωση'), which has the following – statutory prescribed – content:

– request the submission of a Study of EIA providing basic reasoning with reference to the criteria already explained above (*see* in this respect paragraph 734 above);[3201]

3197. Annex IV(3) Law No. 127(I)/2018, which is much more detailed than the corresponding Annex III(3) Directive 2011/92/EU.
3198. Section 24(1) *ibid.*
3199. Section 24(2) *ibid.*
3200. Section 24(3) *ibid.*
3201. Sections 24(4)(a) and 26 *ibid.*

- when the project in question requires an urban planning permission, instruct the competent Urban Planning Authority to submit specific terms in the relevant urban planning permission that shall avoid, reduce or offset the impact, while providing basic reasoning for deciding that a Study of EIA is not necessary and suggesting preventive measures;[3202]
- when the project in question is a public one, instruct the public authority to apply specific terms, when constructing the project in order to avoid, reduce or offset the environmental impact, while providing basic reasoning for deciding that a Study of EIA is not necessary and suggesting preventive measure;[3203] and
- when the project in question fulfils the criteria of a Special Ecologic Evaluation and may significantly affect an area of the Natura 2000 network, request the preparation of a Special Ecologic Evaluation,[3204] or if the integrity of the particular Natura 2000 area is possibly afflicted, reject the project.[3205]

757. Upon preparation of the Reasoned Finding, the Environmental Authority forwards this to the Urban Planning Authority, in case of a project requiring an urban planning permission, or to the state authority constructing the project, in case of a public project. If the project requires no urban planning permission, the Environmental Authority has additional powers, as explained below (*see* in this respect paragraphs 764–768 below). The Reasoned Finding is uploaded on the website of the Department.[3206]

758. Notwithstanding the above, the Director has the power to prepare General Directives ('Γενικές Οδηγίες'), after consultation with concerned authorities. General Directives shall provide for environmental terms, with which certain projects of Annex II shall have to comply, as minimum standards. Said General Directives may be enacted in a Ministerial Decree issued by the Minister and published in the Official Gazette. Publication of such on the website of the Department is optional.[3207]

E. Decision on Urban Planning Permission or Construction of a Public Project

759. The aforementioned (*see* in this respect paragraphs 747 et seq. above) apply to the Environmental Approval *mutatis mutandis*.

3202. Section 24(4)(b) and 24(5) *ibid.*
3203. Section 24(4)(c) and 24(5) *ibid.*
3204. Sections 24(4)(d) and 33 *ibid.*
3205. Section 24(4)(e) *ibid.*
3206. Section 24(6) *ibid*, which corresponds to Art. 4(4) Directive 2011/92/EU.
3207. Section 24(7)(a) and (b) Law No. 127(I)/2018.

F. Monitoring Duties

760. The aforementioned (*see* in this respect paragraphs 751 et seq. above) apply to the Environmental Approval *mutatis mutandis*.

IV. Environmental Approval

761. Environmental Approval ('Περιβαλλοντική Έγκριση') is necessary for projects that are listed in Annex I or II but do not require an urban planning permission.[3208] To this effect, an application is submitted to the Director, which is accompanied by a study of EIA when the project in question is listed under Annex I and by Information of section 23, in case of projects of Annex II.[3209]

762. The request submitted to the Director is decided by the Environmental Authority, which has the following powers. It may:

- deny the requested Environmental Approval on the ground that the construction and/or operation of the project shall cause significant adverse effects on the environment that may not be eliminated or reduced by any measures;
- issue the requested Environmental Approval without imposing any terms; and
- issue the requested Environmental Approval and impose specific terms regarding the construction of the project that aims to eliminate or reduce the effects that construction and/or operation of the project may impose on the environment.[3210]

763. The decision of the Environmental Authority, and where applicable, the Environmental Approval, are uploaded to the Department's website.[3211]

V. Special Provisions for Projects Affecting Special Protection Areas, Special Areas of Conservation and Sites of Community Importance

764. Specific provisions are set out for projects that require an EIA under this law, as well as a Special Ecological Evaluation ('Ειδική Οικολογική Αξιολόγηση') under Law No. 153(I)/2003 and Law No. 152(I)/2003,[3212] those being projects affecting a special protection area ('ζώνη ειδικής προστασίας')[3213] or

3208. Section 20(1) *ibid.*
3209. Section 20(2)(a)(i) and (ii) *ibid.*
3210. Sections 24(6) and 20(3) *ibid.*
3211. Section 20(4) *ibid.*
3212. Section 33(1) *ibid.*
3213. *See* in this respect s. 7 Law No. 152(I)/2003, which corresponds to Art. 4(1) Directive 2009/147/EC. The European provision uses the term 'zone de protection spéciale' in French, 'Schutzgebiet' in German and 'speciale beschermingszone' in Dutch.

special area of conservation ('ειδική ζώνη διατήρησης').[3214] On projects that are not included in Annexes I and II of this law, but may nevertheless affect a site of Community importance ('τόπος κοινοτικής προστασίας')[3215] or a special protection area or a special area of conservation, Law No. 153(I)/2003 and in particular section 16 thereof, is applied.[3216]

765. The Special Ecological Evaluation forms a part of the procedure of environmental impact protection, as defined in this law. More specifically, it establishes a binding, indispensable, but clearly distinct part of the procedure for issuing Environmental Approval ('Περιβαλλοντική Έγκριση'),[3217] a Reasoned Finding ('Αιτιολογημένη Διαπίστωση')[3218] or an Opinion ('Γνωμοδότηση').[3219] Generally, in order to draft a Special Ecological Evaluation, the developer conducts a study taking particular note of the purpose of preserving a site of Community importance, the relevant special area of conservation or special protection area. Exclusive aim is to ensure that the project shall not harm the integrity of said site or areas and shall not change their characteristics, while imposing terms to mitigate any effects.[3220]

766. With reference to projects of Annex I, the Special Ecological Evaluation is prepared under Law No. 153(I)/2003 and forms an integral part of the Study of EIA, allowing for possible effects to be evaluated during the evaluation of said study, which has already been analysed above (*see* in this respect paragraphs 740 et seq. above). In these cases, the Special Ecological Evaluation includes the following information to the extent that it is relevant to the project, the area and the possible effects:[3221]

– information about the project: (a) the project's characteristics that may affect the greater area; (b) the total area that the project shall occupy; (c) the size and other specifications of the project; (d) characteristics of existing, proposed or other approved projects, that might cause interactive or cumulative effects together with the project under evaluation and might affect the area; (e) scheduled or forecasted initiatives (measures or actions) on nature preservation that might affect the status of the area in the future; and (f) map illustration of the relationship between the proposed project and the Natura 2000 network area;[3222]

3214. *See* in this respect s. 16 Law No. 153(I)/2003, which correspond to Art. 4 Directive 92/43/EEC. The European provision uses the term 'zone spéciale de conservation' in French, 'besonderes Schutzgebiet' in German and 'speciale beschermingszone' in Dutch.
3215. *See* in this respect s. 2 Law No. 153(I)/2003, which corresponds to Art. 1(k) Directive 92/43/EEC. The European provision uses the term 'site d'importance communautaire' in French, 'Gebiet von gemeinschaftlicher Bedeutung' in German and 'gebied van communautair belang' in Dutch.
3216. Section 33(4) Law No. 127(I)/2018.
3217. Sections 33(2) and 20 *ibid.*
3218. Sections 33(2) and 24 *ibid.*
3219. Sections 33(2) and 29 *ibid.*
3220. Section 33(3) *ibid.*
3221. Section 33(7) *ibid.*
3222. Annex VI(1) *ibid.*

- information on the Natura 2000 network area: (a) grounds for classifying the area as a Natura 2000; (b) targets of preservation and protection of the area and parameters contributing to the value of its preservation; (c) existing status of the area; (d) existing situation of the area, such as habitat, species, landscape and tenacity of the area; (e) basic characteristics of the habitat under Law No. 153(I)/2003 and Law No. 152(I)/2003; (f) ecology of the species and habitat and generally of the ecosystem; (g) ecological demands and parts of the area deemed sensitive to change, especially to land use change; (h) man-made and seasonal effects, including both biotic and abiotic factors; (i) other issues of management, preservation and protection related to the area, including possible future natural changes, taking into account man-made factors;[3223]
- information related to the targets for preserving the protected area in relation to the project: (a) relationship of the project to the management of the area; (b) effects of the project's construction on the targets for preserving the protected area and the elements of the landscape; (c) the possibility of causing delays to achieving the target for preserving the area; (d) the possibility of affecting progress for achieving the target for preserving the area; (e) the possibility of distorting the abiotic and biotic factors that maintain the favourable situation of the area; (f) other targets, such as information in whether the project may affect factors that define the structure and function of the habitat, change the dynamics of relationships that define the structure and function of the habitat, interfere with natural changes of the area that had been ignored or are expected, diminish the habitat of the area and the connectivity of the Natura 2000 network areas, diminish the population of flora and fauna or change the balance of their species, diminish the area's biodiversity, cause disruptions that could affect the size of the population or the density or the balance between species and cause fragmentation of the habitat;[3224] and
- other information: (a) alternative solutions that have been examined; (b) whether supreme reasons of public interest ('επιτακτικοί λόγοι δημοσίου συμφέροντος') support the construction of the project; (c) proposed offset and diminishing measures; (d) information on the group that wrote the study.[3225]

767. With reference to projects of Annex II, Information of section 23 is submitted to the Environmental Authority, along with specific information including – at least – the following:

- succinct description of the area, including the main ecological characteristics, on the basis of cartographic, descriptive, statistic and other data available for areas of Natura 2000 network, the protection purpose and the provisions of the management plan;[3226]
- assessment of the possible effects on the area or the object of protection using data and information available, including the ones described above and other

3223. Annex VI(2) *ibid.*
3224. Annex VI(3) *ibid.*
3225. Annex VI(4) *ibid.*
3226. Section 33(5)(a) *ibid.*

available environmental information, which is supplemented, if necessary, by field information from the site and ecological research;[3227] and
- determination of whether the found effects may be significant, clarifying that, in the case of uncertainty, the effects have to be determined as significant.[3228]

The Special Ecological Evaluation is assessed by a group of experts, which are assigned by the Director on his own motion or after the suggestion of the Committee of EIA (*see* in this respect paragraph 728 above).[3229] The experts examine and assess the data deriving from the Special Ecological Assessment in order for the Environmental Authority to receive the necessary documentation that the project shall not harm the integrity of the special protection area, the special areas of conservation and the sites of Community importance, as the case may be, and shall not cause a change into their characteristics, while proposing relevant terms to diminish any other effects on said site or area, as the case may be.[3230] Thus, the Environmental Authority may issue a positive Opinion ('θετική Γνωμοδότηση').[3231] Nonetheless, the Opinion of the Environmental Authority is negative ('αρνητική Γνωμοδότηση'), when the result of the evaluation points to adverse and non-reversible environmental effects.[3232]

§5. Archive for EIA

768. The Director keeps an Archive for EIA ('Αρχείο Εκτίμησης Επιπτώσεων στο Περιβάλλον') that is available to the public both physically and electronically in a separate section of the Department's website.[3233] The physical archive is accessible to the public during working days and hours.[3234] The following data and information are registered in the Archive:

- studies of EIA and information submitted under this law; in the case of large and complicated Studies of EIA, a non-technical summary is uploaded along with information, as to the manner for inspecting copies;[3235]
- all plans of projects along with maps and photos of the area, where the project shall be situated and the area, which shall be affected by the project;[3236]
- every document submitted or sent by another Member State, in case of trans-boundary effects;[3237]

3227. Section 33(5)(b) *ibid.*
3228. Section 33(5)(c) *ibid.*
3229. Section 14(1) *ibid.*
3230. Section 33(8) *ibid.*
3231. Section 33(9)(b) *ibid.*
3232. Section 33(9)(a) *ibid.*
3233. Section 40(1) *ibid.* The Archive is retrievable here: http://www.moa.gov.cy/moa/environment/environmentnew.nsf/page49a_gr/page49a_gr?OpenDocument (accessed on 3 Dec. 2018).
3234. Section 40(3)(a) *ibid.*
3235. Section 40(2)(a) *ibid.*
3236. Section 40(2)(b) *ibid.*
3237. Section 40(2)(c) *ibid.*

- all invitations of the Director to the public for enabling public participation;[3238]
- the views, Reasoned Findings ('Δικαιολογημένες Διαπιστώσεις') and Opinions ('Γνωμοδοτήσεις') that the Environmental Authority submitted to the Urban Planning Authority or to the developer of a project or any state authority under this law;[3239]
- the views of any organization, authority or person regarding a Study of EIA that were submitted to the Director, or information submitted under this law;[3240]
- Environmental Approvals ('Περιβαλλοντική Έγκριση') that have been issued;[3241]
- decisions to issue permission taken by the Urban Planning Authority or the competent state authority following an Opinion ('Γνωμοδότηση');[3242]
- the minutes of the meetings of the Committee of EIA or the group of experts, as well as any submitted reports;[3243]
- copies of information provided for public presentation;[3244]
- copies of monitoring reports and reports of the Inspectors with reference to the compliance measures ('μέτρα επιβολής') that have been taken;[3245] and
- any other information that the Director deems to be relevant and useful.[3246]

769. The Director is entrusted with taking measures for safeguarding commercial and industrial secrets, as well as national security ('εθνική ασφάλεια') and public interest ('δημόσιο συμφέρον'), as long as he is notified that a document registered in the Archive for EIA contains such information.[3247] Still, projects related to substantial state interests ('ουσιώδη συμφέροντα του Κράτους'), such as activities connected to hydrocarbons within the exclusive economic zone, are not subjected to publicity requirements through the Archive for EIA.[3248]

§6. Ensuring Compliance

I. Penal Sanctions

770. Penal sanctions provide for compliance with this law. More specifically, any person that:

3238. Section 40(2)(d) *ibid.*
3239. Section 40(2)(e) *ibid.*
3240. Section 40(2)(f) *ibid.*
3241. Section 40(2)(g) *ibid.*
3242. Section 40(2)(h) *ibid.*
3243. Section 40(2)(i) *ibid.*
3244. Sections 40(2)(j) and 32 *ibid.*
3245. Section 40(2)(k) *ibid.*
3246. Section 40(2)(l) *ibid.*
3247. Section 40(3)(b) *ibid.*
3248. Section 40(5) *ibid.*

- violates any terms and/or conditions imposed by the Environmental Authority in an Environmental Approval ('Περιβαλλοντική 'Εγκριση'), Reasoned Finding ('Αιτιολογημένη Διαπίστωση') or Opinion ('Γνωμοδότηση');[3249]
- conducts any action or omission or refuses to comply with any provisions of this law or anything issued on the basis of same law;[3250]
- knowingly provides false or misleading statements;[3251]
- deliberately or neglectfully fails to act as foreseen in this law, or provides misleading information or inaccurate data or omits or hides data in relation to any matter within this law, including Studies of EIA and Information of section 23;[3252] and/or
- prevents an Inspector from performing his duties and exercising his powers given on the basis of this law, is guilty of a penal offence punished with a monetary fine of no more than EUR 5,000. In the case of a second or further conviction, same crimes are punished with imprisonment of no longer than six months and/ or monetary fines of no more than EUR 10,000.[3253] Further, failure to comply with a court's interim or final order (*see* in this respect paragraph 775 below) constitutes a penal offence, which is punished with imprisonment of no more than twelve months and/or a monetary fine of no more than EUR 50,000.[3254] In the event that said penal offences are committed by a legal person and members of the board of directors, the management board or the committee managing the affairs of such a legal person, or the general director, the director or the executive director have consented, co-acted or tolerated such offence, then the prosecution may turn against the legal person and all or any of these natural persons.[3255]

II. Administrative Sanctions

771. Administrative sanctions may be imposed by Inspectors. More specifically, when an Inspector finds a violation of any environmental term imposed by the Environmental Authority in an Environmental Approval, Reasoned Finding or Opinion, he may serve the project's developer with a compliance notice ('ειδοποίηση συμμόρφωσης'). Therein, mention shall be made to finding violation of an environmental term and to the specific term(s) that has been violated, while giving specific instructions for measures to be taken for the purpose of compliance with the relevant environmental term and specifying a time frame for compliance with this notice.[3256] Moreover, the Inspector has the power, instead of providing a time period for compliance with a compliance notice, to inform the competent authority that has issued the relevant permission, to terminate it.[3257]

3249. Section 46(1)(a) *ibid.*
3250. Section 46(1)(b) *ibid.*
3251. Section 46(1)(c) *ibid.*
3252. Section 46(1)(d) *ibid.*
3253. Section 46(1) *ibid.*
3254. Section 46(4) *ibid.*
3255. Section 46(6) *ibid.*
3256. Section 45(3)(a), (b), (d) and (e)(i) *ibid.*
3257. Section 45(3)(e)(ii) *ibid.*

An Inspector may further issue a compliance notice, when the danger of significant damage to the environment or to any person is caused by grave violation of an imposed term. In such an event, the content of the compliance notice shall mention, aside from the aforementioned information, the reasons that cause or may cause said danger.[3258] Still, the Inspector is ineffectual in the event of danger, despite compliance with imposed terms and conditions.

III. Other Sanctions

772. In the event that any of the aforementioned penal offences (*see* in this respect paragraph 709 above) is accompanied by the assertion that committing such causes or may cause environmental damage or danger to public health, an interim order may be issued following a request of the Attorney General. Such request may be submitted ex parte. This interim order may prohibit continuing or repeating the alleged illegal act or omission and, if granted, it expires upon the final decision on the initiated penal procedure.[3259] In the event that the addressee of the order fails to comply therewith, the measures may be taken by the Department, whereas the relevant expenses are retrieved by the addressee as a civil debt to the state.[3260]

In the final decision of court regarding the alleged crimes, the court is further given the power to order demolition, removal or proper adjustment of the project to the purpose of compliance with the terms set out in the Environmental Permission, Reasoned Finding or Opinion, as the case may be. Moreover, the court has the authority to order the restoration of the environment by the project's developer and, importantly, determine the time within which compliance has to be achieved.[3261] In the event that the developer fails to comply with such an order, the aforementioned (*see* in this respect paragraph 773 above) apply *mutatis mutandis*.[3262]

3258. Section 45(3)(c) *ibid.*
3259. Section 46(2)(a), (b), (c) and (d) *ibid.*
3260. Section 46(5) *ibid.*
3261. Section 46(3) *ibid.*
3262. Section 46(5) *ibid.*

Part IV. Liability Questions

Chapter 1. Environmental Liability

773. Environmental liability is regulated by Law on Environmental Liability[3263] (hereinafter 'Law No. 189(I)/2007'). Pursuant to its preamble, this law has been enacted for the purpose of implementing Directive 2004/35/EC.[3264]

§1. Objective

774. No provision specifies the objective of this law. However, in view of the implemented directive, it may safely be assumed that they share the same objective. Hence, the purpose of this law is to establish a framework of environmental liability based on the polluter pays principle, to prevent and remedy environmental damage.[3265] Environmental damage ('περιβαλλοντική ζημιά') stands for damage to protected species and natural habitats,[3266] which is any damage that has significant adverse effects on reaching or maintaining the favourable conservation status of such habitats or species. The significance of such effects is to be assessed with reference to the baseline condition, taking into account certain criteria.[3267] Environmental damage further includes water damage, which is any damage that significantly adversely affects the ecological, chemical or quantitative status or the

3263. Law on Environmental Liability with regard to Prevention and Remedying of Environmental Damage ('ο περί της Περιβαλλοντικής Ευθύνης όσον αφορά την Πρόληψη και την Αποκατάσταση Περιβαλλοντικής Ζημιάς Νόμος') No. 189 of 2007, OG I(I) No. 4154 of 31 Dec. 2007, p. 1849.

3264. Directive 2004/35/CE of the European Parliament and of the Council of 21 Apr. 2004 on environmental liability with regard to the prevention and remedying of environmental damage, OJ L 143, 30 Apr. 2004, p. 56.

3265. Article 1 Directive 2004/35/EC.

3266. Damage to protected species and natural habitats does not include previously identified adverse effects which result from an act by an operator which was expressly authorized by the relevant authorities in accordance with ss 16 and 26 Law No. 153(I)/2003 and s. 12 Law No. 152(I)/2003. Section 2 Law No. 189(I)/2007, which corresponds to Art. 2(1)(a) Directive 2004/35/EC.

3267. The significance of any damage that has adverse effects on reaching or maintaining the favourable conservation status of habitats or species has to be assessed by reference to the conservation status at the time of the damage, the services provided by the amenities they produce and their capacity for natural regeneration. Annex II Law No. 189(I)/2007, which corresponds to Annex I Directive 2004/35/EC.

ecological potential[3268] of the marine waters concerned, or the environmental status of the marine waters[3269] concerned and land damage, which is any land contamination that creates a significant risk of human health being adversely affected as a result of the direct or indirect introduction, in, on or under land, of substances, preparations, organisms or microorganisms.[3270]

§2. Area of Application

775. This law applies to environmental damage caused by occupational activities listed in Law No. 184(I)/2013, waste management activities requiring an authorization under Law No. 185(I)/2011, water-related activities needing a permission under Law No. 106(I)/2002, manufacture and use of dangerous substances, dangerous preparations, plant protection products and biocidal products, transportation activities, air-related activities pre-requesting a permission under Law No. 187(I)/2002, contained use and deliberate release of genetically modified organisms, transboundary shipment of waste, management of extractive waste and operation of storage sites of CO_2.[3271] It is also applicable to any imminent threat of such damage occurring by reason of any of those activities. Further, it applies to damage to protected species and natural habitats caused by any occupational activities other than those mentioned above, and to any imminent threat of such damage occurring by reason of any of those activities, whenever the operator has been at fault or negligent.[3272] Lastly, this law applies to environmental damage or to an imminent threat of such damage caused by pollution of a diffuse character, where it is possible to establish a causal link between the damage and the activities of individual operators.[3273]

776. However, this law does not cover environmental damage or an imminent threat of such damage caused by an act of armed conflict, hostilities, civil war or insurrection, a natural phenomenon of exceptional, inevitable and irresistible character[3274] and an incident in respect of which liability or compensation falls within

3268. As this is defined in Law on Protection and Management of Waters ('ο περί Προστασίας και Διαχείρισης των Υδάτων Νόμος') No. 13 of 2004, OG I(I) No. 3812 of 20 Feb. 2004, p. 85, which implements Directive 2000/60/EC of the European Parliament and of the Council of 23 Oct. 2000 establishing a framework for Community action in the field of water policy, OJ L 327, 22 Dec. 2000, p. 1.
3269. Marine waters are the ones defined in Law No. 18(I)/2011.
3270. Section 2 Law No. 189(I)/2007, which corresponds to Art. 2(1) Directive 2004/35/EC. The French term is 'dommage environnemental', the German one 'Umweltschaden' and the Dutch one 'milieuschade'.
3271. Annex III Law No. 189(I)/2007, which corresponds to Annex III Directive 2004/35/EC.
3272. Section 3(a) Law No. 189(I)/2007, which corresponds to Art. 3(1) Directive 2004/35/EC.
3273. Section 3(c) Law No. 189(I)/2007, which corresponds to Art. 4(5) Directive 2004/35/EC.
3274. Section 4(1)(a) and (b) Law No. 189(I)/2007, which corresponds to Art. 4(1) Directive 2004/35/EC.

the scope of certain International Conventions.[3275] In addition, it does not apply to activities the main purpose of which is to serve national defence or international security, nor to activities, the sole purpose of which is to protect from natural disasters,[3276] and to such nuclear risks or environmental damage or imminent threat of such damage as may be caused by the activities covered by the Treaty establishing the European Atomic Energy Community or caused by an incident or activity in respect of which liability or compensation falls within the scope of certain international instruments,[3277] including any future amendments thereof.[3278]

777. With reference to some time-related aspects of this law's application, the following need to be noted. It applies neither to damage caused by an emission, event or incident that took place before the date of its enactment nor to damage caused by an emission, event or incident which takes place subsequent to the date of its enactment, when this derives from a specific activity that took place and finished before the said date. Lastly, in any event, it does not apply to damage, if more than thirty years have passed since the emission, event or incident, resulting in the damage occurred.[3279]

§3. Competent Authorities

I. The Minister of Agriculture, Rural Development and Environment

778. The Minister of Agriculture, Rural Development and Environment takes measures to encourage the development of financial security instruments and markets by appropriate economic and financial operators, including financial mechanisms in case of insolvency, with the aim of enabling operators to use financial guarantees to cover their responsibilities under this law.[3280] He may further amend any of the annexes of this law that relate to the remediation of environmental damage, criteria for assessing damage, activities of plants falling within the area of

3275. These are the following: the International Convention of 27 Nov. 1992 on Civil Liability for Oil Pollution Damage; the International Convention of 27 Nov. 1992 on the Establishment of an International Fund for Compensation for Oil Pollution Damage; the International Convention of 23 Mar. 2001 on Civil Liability for Bunker Oil Pollution Damage; the International Convention of 3 May 1996 on Liability and Compensation for Damage in Connection with the Carriage of Hazardous and Noxious Substances by Sea; and the Convention of 10 Oct. 1989 on Civil Liability for Damage Caused during Carriage of Dangerous Goods by Road, Rail and Inland Navigation Vessels. Annex IV Law No. 189(I)/2007, which corresponds to Annex IV Directive 2004/35/EC.
3276. Section 4(3) Law No. 189(I)/2007, which corresponds to Art. 4(6) Directive 2004/35/EC.
3277. These are: the Paris Convention of 29 Jul. 1960 on Third Party Liability in the Field of Nuclear Energy and the Brussels Supplementary Convention of 31 Jan. 1963; the Vienna Convention of 21 May 1963 on Civil Liability for Nuclear Damage; the Convention of 12 Sep. 1997 on Supplementary Compensation for Nuclear Damage; the Joint Protocol of 21 Sep. 1988 relating to the Application of the Vienna Convention and the Paris Convention; and the Brussels Convention of 17 Dec. 1971 relating to Civil Liability in the Field of Maritime Carriage of Nuclear Material. Annex V Law No. 189(I)/2007, which corresponds to Annex V Directive 2004/35/EC.
3278. Section 4(4) Law No. 189(I)/2007, which corresponds to Art. 4(4) Directive 2004/35/EC.
3279. Section 26 Law No. 189(I)/2007, which corresponds to Art. 17 Directive 2004/35/EC.
3280. Section 15(1) Law No. 189(I)/2007, which corresponds to Art. 14(1) Directive 2004/35/EC.

application of this law, international conventions and instruments restricting its area of application, and information to be forwarded to the EC.[3281] He also appoints, at his discretion, a competent or co-competent authority, an authority other than the Department of Environment, according to the nature of the damage. A relevant decree is to be issued in the Official Gazette.[3282]

II. The Council of Ministers

779. The Council of Ministers generally has the authority to issue regulations for fully and effectively carrying out and giving effect to, all or any of the purposes, provisions and powers in this law contained.[3283] It may also issue regulations for any matter related to financial security instruments that are encouraged by the Minister.[3284]

III. The Department of Environment

780. The Department of Environment ('Υπηρεσία Περιβάλλοντος') of the Ministry of Agriculture, Rural Development and Environment is a competent authority under this law. Its duties include locating the operator causing damage or imminent threat thereof, assessing the significance of the damage and specifying the restoration measures.[3285] The competent authority may order the operator to carry out an assessment and provide all data and information necessary,[3286] to immediately cessate all activities, as well as prohibit reoperation and instruct taking necessary preventive and remedial measures,[3287] as well as a request from any third party to take same measures.[3288] When said measures are ordered, the relevant administrative decision must be due reasoned and communicated to the operator, who has to be informed about the legal remedies at his disposal and the applicable limitations.[3289]

§4. Preventive Action

781. Preventive measures ('προληπτικά μέτρα') are measures taken in response to an event, act or omission that has created an imminent threat of environmental damage, with a view to preventing or minimizing that damage.[3290]

3281. Section 25 Law No. 189(I)/2007.
3282. Section 23 *ibid.*
3283. Section 24 *ibid.*
3284. Section 14(2) *ibid.*
3285. Section 6(1) *ibid.*
3286. Section 6(2) *ibid.*
3287. Section 22(1) *ibid.*
3288. Section 6(3) *ibid.*
3289. Section 6(4) *ibid.*
3290. Section 2 *ibid.*, which corresponds to Art. 2(10) Directive 2004/35/EC. The French term is 'mesures préventives' or 'mesures de prévention', the German one 'Vermeidungsmaßnahmen' and the Dutch one 'preventieve maatregelen'.

I. Duties of Operators and the Department of Environment

782. Preventive action duties are imposed on both operators and the Department of Environment. The operator takes without delay the necessary preventive measures, where environmental damage has not yet occurred but there is an imminent threat of such damage[3291] occurring.[3292] Further, when the Department of Environment deems necessary and in any event, whenever the imminent threat of environmental damage is not dispelled despite the preventive measures taken by the operator, the latter is to inform the competent authority of all relevant aspects of the situation, as soon as possible.[3293] Most importantly, operators' duty is to take preventive measures and bear the financial cost thereof.[3294]

783. The Department of Environment may at any time and at its discretion require the operator to provide information on any imminent threat of environmental damage or in suspected cases of such an imminent threat,[3295] as well as to take the necessary preventive measures[3296] or give instructions to the operator to be followed on the necessary preventive measures to be taken.[3297] Lastly, the department may itself take the necessary preventive measures,[3298] especially when the operator does not comply with his statutory obligation of taking such measures.

II. Transboundary Preventive Action

784. Cooperation between Member States is prescribed, where environmental damage affects or is likely to affect several Member States, including through the appropriate exchange of information, with a view to ensuring that preventive action is taken in respect of any such environmental damage.[3299] Should damage be identified within Cyprus, which has not been caused within itself, the Department of Environment may report the issue to the EC and any other Member State concerned. It may further make recommendations for the adoption of preventive measures and it may seek to recover any incurred costs.[3300]

3291. *Imminent threat of damage* ('menace imminente de dommage' in French, 'unmittelbare Gefahr eines Schadens' in German and 'onmiddellijke dreiging van schade' in Dutch) means a sufficient likelihood that environmental damage will occur in the near future. Section 2 Law No. 189(I)/2007, which corresponds to Art. 2(9) Directive 2004/35/EC.
3292. Section 7(1) Law No. 189(I)/2007, which corresponds to Art. 5(1) Directive 2004/35/EC.
3293. Section 7(2) Law No. 189(I)/2007, which corresponds to Art. 5(2) Directive 2004/35/EC.
3294. Section 7(4) Law No. 189(I)/2007, which corresponds to Art. 5(4) Directive 2004/35/EC.
3295. Section 7(3)(a) Law No. 189(I)/2007, which corresponds to Art. 5(3)(a) Directive 2004/35/EC.
3296. Section 7(3)(b) Law No. 189(I)/2007, which corresponds to Art. 5(3)(b) Directive 2004/35/EC.
3297. Section 7(3)(c) Law No. 189(I)/2007, which corresponds to Art. 5(3)(c) Directive 2004/35/EC.
3298. Section 7(3)(d) Law No. 189(I)/2007, which corresponds to Art. 5(3)(d) Directive 2004/35/EC.
3299. Section 16(1) Law No. 189(I)/2007, which corresponds to Art. 15(1) Directive 2004/35/EC.
3300. Section 16(3) Law No. 189(I)/2007, which corresponds to Art. 15(3) Directive 2004/35/EC.

III. Costs of Preventive Action

785. As a rule, the costs of preventive action are to be borne by the operator, regardless of whether such action is performed by himself or not. In the event that the competent authority carried out such actions, the relevant costs are being recovered through a lawsuit requesting those as a civil debt owed to the state,[3301] or via security over property or other appropriate guarantees, as per the discretion of the Minister.[3302] Cost recovery proceedings against the operator or a third party, as the case may be, are to be initiated within five years from the date on which those measures have been completed or the liable operator, or third party, has been identified, whichever is the latter.[3303]

786. Exceptions are foreseen to this rule. In particular, the operator is not required to bear the cost of preventive action when he can prove that the environmental damage or imminent threat of such damage was caused by a third party and occurred despite the fact that appropriate safety measures were in place,[3304] or resulted from compliance with a compulsory order or instruction emanating from a public authority other than an order or instruction consequent upon an emission or incident caused by the operator's own activities.[3305] Should in such cases the costs incurred be already paid by the operator, the latter may furnish relevant evidence to the competent authority, requesting recovery of such costs.[3306] Moreover, the Department of Environment may decide not to recover the full costs where the expenditure required to do so would be greater than the recoverable sum or where the operator cannot be identified.[3307]

IV. Multiple-Party Causation

787. In the events of multiple-party causation, costs shall be allocated, especially between the producer and the user of a product.[3308] No provisions elaborating on the manner of allocation are prescribed.

§5. Remedial Action

788. *Remedial measures* ('μέτρα αποκατάστασης') are defined as any action, or combination of actions, including mitigating or interim measures to restore, rehabilitate or replace damaged natural resources and/or impaired services, or provide

3301. Section 7(4) Law No. 189(I)/2007. The power of the authority to take itself preventive measures is foreseen in Art. 5(4) Directive 2004/35/EC.
3302. Section 8(3) Law No. 189(I)/2007, which corresponds to Art. 8(2) Directive 2004/35/EC.
3303. Section 13 Law No. 189(I)/2007, which corresponds to Art. 10 Directive 2004/35/EC.
3304. Section 8(1)(a) Law No. 189(I)/2007, which corresponds to Art. 8(3)(a) Directive 2004/35/EC.
3305. Section 8(1)(b) Law No. 189(I)/2007, which corresponds to Art. 8(3)(b) Directive 2004/35/EC.
3306. Section 8(2) Law No. 189(I)/2007, which corresponds to Art. 8(3) Directive 2004/35/EC.
3307. Section 8(4) Law No. 189(I)/2007, which corresponds to Art. 8(2) Directive 2004/35/EC.
3308. Section 12 Law No. 189(I)/2007, which corresponds to Art. 9 Directive 2004/35/EC.

an equivalent alternative to those resources or services as foreseen in this law[3309] regarding remediation of damage to water or protected species or natural habitats and remediation of land damage.[3310]

I. Duties of Operators and the Department of Environment

789. Where environmental damage has occurred, the operator shall, without delay and regardless of fault, negligence or intent,[3311] inform the Department of Environment of all relevant aspects of the situation and take all practicable steps to immediately control, contain, remove or otherwise manage the relevant contaminants and/or any other damage factors in order to limit or to prevent further environmental damage and adverse effects on human health or further impairment of services[3312] and the necessary remedial measures.[3313] The remedial measures have been agreed beforehand between the operator and the Department of Environment. More specifically, within six months after the enactment of this law, operators have identified potential remedial measures and have submitted them to the department for approval, whereas the department has decided which remedial measures are to be implemented and with the cooperation of the relevant operator, as required.[3314]

3309. These are listed in detail in Annex I Law No. 189(I)/2007, which corresponds to Annex II Directive 2004/35/EC.

3310. Section 2 Law No. 189(I)/2007, which corresponds to Art. 2(11) Directive 2004/35/EC. The French term is 'mesures de réparation', the German one 'Sanierungsmaßnahmen' and the Dutch one 'herstelmaatregelen'.

3311. Case C-378/08, *Raffinerie Mediterranee (ERG) SpA, Polimeri Europa SpA and Syndial SpA v. Ministero dello Sviluppo economico a.o.*, [2010] ECR I-01919 [relevant review: M. Bary, *Chronique de jurisprudence 2010 de la Cour de justice de l'Union européenne (1ère partie). La responsabilité environnementale au sens de la directive 2004/35/CE du 21 avril 2004*, RDR 23 (2011); H. Hauenschild, *Sanierungsmaßnahmen nach der UmwelthaftungsRL 2004/35/EG*, Ecolex 423 (2010); P. Steichen, *Responsabilité environnementale*, 35 RJE 503 (2010); V. Michel, *Champ d'application et conditions de la responsabilité environnementale*, Europe 34 (2010); L. Bergkamp, *Comment on Case C-378/08, 9 March 2010*; Joined Cases C-379/08 and 380/08, *9 March 2010*; Joined Cases C-478/08 and C-479/08, *9 March 2010*, 7 JEEPL 355 (2010)].

3312. Section 9(1)(a) Law No. 189(I)/2007, which corresponds to Art. 6(1)(a) Directive 2004/35/EC.

3313. Section 9(1)(b) Law No. 189(I)/2007, which corresponds to Art. 6(1)(b) Directive 2004/35/EC.

3314. Section 10(1) and (2) Law No. 189(I)/2007, which corresponds to Art. 7(1) and (2) Directive 2004/35/EC. *See* in this respect: Joined Cases C-379/08 and C-380/08, *Raffinerie Mediterranee (ERG) SpA, Polimeri Europa SpA and Syndial SpA v. Ministero dello Sviluppo economico a.o. (C-379/08) and ENI SpA v. Ministero Ambiente e Tutela del Territorio e del Mare and Others (C-380/08)*, [2010] ECR I-02007 [relevant review: L. Bergkamp, *Comment on Case C-378/08, 9 March 2010;* Joined Cases C-379/08 and 380/08, *9 March 2010;* Joined Cases C-478/08 and C-479/08, *9 March 2010*, 7 JEEPL 355 (2010); V. Michel, *Champ d'application et conditions de la responsabilité environnementale*, Europe 34 (2010); M. Aubert, E. Broussy & F. Donnat, *Chronique de jurisprudence communautaire. Environnement – Principe du pollueur-payeur, L'actualité juridique*, DA 942 (2010); M. Bary, *Chronique de jurisprudence 2010 de la Cour de justice de l'Union européenne (1ère partie). La responsabilité environnementale au sens de la directive 2004/35/CE du 21 avril 2004*, RDR 23 (2011)]; Joined Cases C-478/08 and C-479/08, *Buzzi Unicem SpA and Others v. Ministero dello Sviluppo economico and Others (C-478/08) and Dow Italia Divisione Commerciale Srl v. Ministero Ambiente e Tutela del Territorio e del Mare and Others (C-479/08)*, [2010] ECR I-00031.

790. Turning to the duties of the Department of Environment, this may at any time require the operator to provide supplementary information on any damage that has occurred.[3315] Parallel to that, it may take, require the operator to take or give instructions to the operator concerning, all practicable steps to immediately control, contain, remove or otherwise manage the relevant contaminants and/or any other damage factors in order to limit or prevent further environmental damage and adverse effect on human health, or further impairment of services.[3316] Also, this department may require the operator to take the necessary remedial measures,[3317] give instructions to the operator to be followed on the necessary remedial measures to be taken,[3318] or itself take the necessary remedial measures.[3319] If the operator fails to take such measures, cannot be identified or is not required to bear the costs under this law, the competent authority may take these measures itself, as a means of last resort.[3320]

II. Transboundary Remedial Action

791. The aforementioned on transboundary preventive action apply here *mutatis mutandis*. It must be further noted that where environmental damage has occurred, the Department of Environment has to provide sufficient information to the potentially affected Member States.[3321]

III. Costs of Remedial Action

792. The aforementioned on costs of preventive action equally apply to costs of remedial action.[3322] In addition to those, the operator may be excluded from bearing the cost of remedial actions, where it is demonstrated that he was not at fault or negligent and that the environmental damage was caused by an emission or event expressly authorized by, and fully in accordance with the conditions of, an authorization conferred by or given under legislation regulating activities falling within the application area of this law, as applied at the date of the emission or event.[3323] Alternatively, it must be proved that such damage was caused by an emission or activity or any manner of using a product in the course of an activity which the operator demonstrates was not considered likely to cause environmental damage

3315. Section 9(2)(a) Law No. 189(I)/2007, which corresponds to Art. 6(2)(a) Directive 2004/35/EC.
3316. Section 9(2)(b) Law No. 189(I)/2007, which corresponds to Art. 6(2)(b) Directive 2004/35/EC.
3317. Section 9(2)(c) Law No. 189(I)/2007, which corresponds to Art. 6(2)(c) Directive 2004/35/EC.
3318. Section 9(2)(d) Law No. 189(I)/2007, which corresponds to Art. 6(2)(d) Directive 2004/35/EC.
3319. Section 9(2)(e) Law No. 189(I)/2007, which corresponds to Art. 6(2)(e) Directive 2004/35/EC.
3320. Section 9(3) Law No. 189(I)/2007, which corresponds to Art. 6(3) Directive 2004/35/EC.
3321. Section 16(2) Law No. 189(I)/2007, which corresponds to Art. 15(2) Directive 2004/35/EC.
3322. Section 11(1), (2), (3) and (4) Law No. 189(I)/2007, which corresponds to Art 8(1), (2) and (3) Directive 2004/35/EC. *See* in respect of Art. 8(3): Judgment of 4 Mar. 2015 in Case C-534/13, *Ministero dell'Ambiente e della Tutela del Territorio e del Mare a.o. v. Fipa Group Srl a.o.*, digital ECR.
3323. Section 8(4)(a) and Annex III Law No. 189(I)/2007, which corresponds to Art. 8(4)(a) and Annex III Directive 2004/35/EC.

according to the state of scientific and technical knowledge at the time when the emission was released or the activity took place.[3324]

IV. Multiple-Party Causation

793. The aforementioned on multiple-party causation also apply to remedial action.

§6. Ensuring Compliance

I. Penal Sanctions

794. Any person refusing or failing to take any preventive measures, remedial measures or any decision of the Department of Environment commits an offence, which may lead to imprisonment of up to three years and/or a fine of up to EUR 342,000.[3325]

II. Administrative Sanctions

795. The Department of Environment may impose an administrative penalty on any person violating any measures under this law or failing to comply with those. Before issuing such an administrative decision, the department has to communicate this intention to any concerned person and inform him of his right to submit its views within seven days.[3326] The administrative decision imposing a penalty, which may amount up to EUR 342,000, has to be duly reasoned and communicated in writing to the concerned person. In the event of repeated violation or failure, an additional penalty of up to EUR 342,000 may be imposed along with a daily penalty of up to EUR 8,550.[3327] In the event of noncompliance with these penalties, the Department of Environment may file a lawsuit requesting the amounts due as a civil debt owed to the state.[3328]

796. Against an imposed administrative fine, an addressee may file an administrative appeal ('ιεραρχική προσφυγή') within twenty-one days with the Minister. He examines without any delay such an appeal and, if he deems it necessary, he may give the opportunity to the addressee to express further the grounds supporting

3324. Section 8(4)(b) Law No. 189(I)/2007, which corresponds to Art. 8(4)(b) Directive 2004/35/EC.
3325. Section 20(a), (b) and (c) Law No. 189(I)/2007.
3326. Section 18(2) and (3) *ibid.*
3327. Section 18(1) and (4) *ibid.*
3328. Section 18(6) *ibid.*

such an appeal. The Minister's decision may affirm the appealed decision of the Department of Environment, annul or amend same, or issue a new decision replacing the appealed one.[3329]

III. Other Sanctions

797. Following a conviction for any penal offence under this law, the court may order the operator bear the financial cost of remedial action.[3330]

3329. Section 19(1), (2) and (3) *ibid.*
3330. Section 20 *ibid.*

Part V. Juridical Actions of Individuals

798. Individuals are informed of authorizations, studies and reports on the environment either through specific notification in the newspapers or on the Internet (*see* in this respect paragraphs 133, 139, 182, 289, 348, 683, 679, 690, 701, 705, 715, 737 above) or through the possibility of accessing the archives kept by the competent authorities under the environmental legislation. This is ensured by Law No. 119(I)/2004, provided that such disclosure does not adversely affect: the confidentiality of the proceedings of public authorities;[3331] international relations, public security or national defence;[3332] the course of justice, the ability of any person to receive a fair trial or the ability of a public authority to conduct an enquiry of a criminal or disciplinary nature;[3333] the confidentiality of commercial or industrial information;[3334] intellectual property rights;[3335] the confidentiality of personal data and/or files relating to a natural person where that person has not consented to the disclosure of the information to the public;[3336] the interests or protection of any person who supplied the information requested on a voluntary basis;[3337] and the protection of the environment.[3338] Nevertheless, these exceptions do not apply in their majority to information regarding emissions into the environment.[3339] Apart from being provided with the option to express their views and representations in the decision-making procedure, as explained above (*see* in this respect paragraphs 353, 470, 477, 570, 591, 679, 690, 701, 704, 719, 728), the public may under specific conditions request administrative and judicial remedies.

3331. Section 8(3)(a) Law No. 119(I)/2004, which corresponds to 4(2)(a) Directive 2003/4/EC.
3332. Section 8(3)(b) Law No. 119(I)/2004, which corresponds to 4(2)(b) Directive 2003/4/EC.
3333. Section 8(3)(c) Law No. 119(I)/2004, which corresponds to 4(2)(c) Directive 2003/4/EC.
3334. Section 8(3)(d) Law No. 119(I)/2004, which corresponds to 4(2)(d) Directive 2003/4/EC.
3335. Section 8(3)(e) Law No. 119(I)/2004, which corresponds to 4(2)(e) Directive 2003/4/EC.
3336. Section 8(3)(f) Law No. 119(I)/2004, which corresponds to 4(2)(f) Directive 2003/4/EC.
3337. Section 8(3)(g) Law No. 119(I)/2004, which corresponds to 4(2)(g) Directive 2003/4/EC.
3338. Section 8(3)(h) Law No. 119(I)/2004, which corresponds to 4(2)(h) Directive 2003/4/EC.
3339. Section 8(5) Law No. 119(I)/2004, which corresponds to 4(2) Directive 2003/4/EC.

Chapter 1. Administrative Remedies

799. In the event of environmental damage, as defined in Law No. 189(I)/2007, as well as in the event of imminent threat of damage,[3340] every natural or legal person, who is affected or likely to be affected by environmental damage or is having a sufficient interest in environmental decision-making relating to the damage or, alternatively, alleging the impairment of a right, is entitled to submit in writing to the competent authority any established observations relating to instances of environmental damage, of which she is aware, and to request the department to take action under this law.[3341] This request for action is to be accompanied by relevant information and data supporting the allegations regarding the environmental damage in question.[3342] Where the request for action and the accompanying observations show in a plausible manner that environmental damage exists, the department considers any such observations and requests for action. In such circumstances, it gives the relevant operator an opportunity to make his views known with respect to the request for action and the accompanying observations.[3343] The Department of Environment reaches a reasoned decision on the request for action as soon as possible and in any event not later than thirty days and informs the persons that filed this accordingly.[3344]

3340. Section 14(5) Law No. 189(I)/2007, which corresponds to Art. 12(5) Directive 2004/35/EC.
3341. Section 14(1) Law No. 189(I)/2007, which corresponds to Art. 12(1) Directive 2004/35/EC.
3342. Section 14(2) Law No. 189(I)/2007, which corresponds to Art. 12(2) Directive 2004/35/EC.
3343. Section 14(3) Law No. 189(I)/2007, which corresponds to Art. 12(3) Directive 2004/35/EC.
3344. Section 14(4) Law No. 189(I)/2007, which corresponds to Art. 12(4) Directive 2004/35/EC.

Chapter 2. Judicial Remedies

800. With reference to EIA, when an urban planning permission for a private project, an approval for a public project or an environmental approval affects the interests of any legal person, whose scope is environmental protection, such a person may file an appeal ('προσφυγή') requesting the review of this decision with the Supreme Court of Cyprus according to Article 146 of the Constitution.[3345]

801. Any decision concerning preventive and remedial measures for environmental damage, which is taken by the Department of the Environment under Law No. 189(I)/2007, may be challenged by persons affected or likely to be affected by environmental damage, or having a sufficient interest in environmental decision-making relating to the damage, as long as these persons have interests affected by such decision. To this purpose, an appeal ('προσφυγή') is filed with the Supreme Court of Cyprus according to Article 146 of the Constitution.[3346]

3345. Section 48(1) Law No. 127(I)/2018.
3346. Sections 17 and 14(1) Law No. 189(I)/2007.

Selected Bibliography

Aggelides, A. *ο περί Γενικών Αρχών του Διοικητικού Δικαίου Νόμος* (N. 158(I)/ 1999) *και η μεταγενέστερη νομολογία του Ανωτάτου Δικαστηρίου της Κυπριακής Δημοκρατίας* (in Greek). Research, Studies and Publications Service of the House of Representatives, 2008.

Bergkamp, L. *Liability and Environment.* Kluwer Law International, 2001.

Charalambous, N. *Η Δράση και ο 'Ελεγχος της Δημόσιας Διοίκησης* (in Greek). Nicosia, 2004.

Charalampidou, N. *Δίκαιο Περιβάλλοντος, η Εναρμόνιση της Κυπριακής Νομοθεσίας με τις Οδηγίες της Ευρωπαϊκής 'Ενωσης* (in Greek). Sakkoulas, 2013.

de Sadeler, N. *Environmental Principles*, S. Leubuscher (translation). OUP, 2005.

Epiney, A. *Umweltrecht in der EU.* Carl Heymanns, 2005.

Grabitz, E., M. Hilf & M. Nettesheim (eds). *Das Recht der EU – Kommentar.* C.H. Beck, 2011.

Jans, J.H. & H.H.B. Vedder. *European Environmental Law.* Europa Law Publishing, 2008.

Kloepfer, M. *Umweltrecht.* C.H. Beck, 2004.

Krämer, L. *EU Environmental Law.* Sweet & Maxwell, 2012.

Meßerschmidt, K. *Europäisches Umweltrecht.* C.H. Beck, 2011.

Schmidt, R. & W. Kahl. *Umweltrecht.* C.H. Beck, 2006.

Streinz, R. (ed.). *EUV/AEUV.* C.H. Beck, 2012.

Table of Cases

Index

The numbers here refer to paragraph numbers.

Index

Made in the USA
Monee, IL
18 October 2026

66041413R10254